ovolo

Housebuilder's
Bible 13

Housebuilder's Bible® 13

Ovolo Books

Thirteenth edition published August 2019

Content © Mark Brinkley
This edition © Ovolo Books 2019
Contact: markbrinkley@mac.com

Photography: Author and also Mathew Smith 07540 769814 who undertook te Case Study work

ISBN 978-1-9160168-0-4

CONTENTS

CONTENTS

INTRODUCTION

THE BUILDERS' DILEMMA

The triangle on the right represents the age-old conundrum for all builders. It is said that you can have any two of these points in a building job but only at the expense of the third. Thus you can have a good, cheap job but it won't be quick, or a cheap, quick job that won't be any good.

So when you hear claims – as you may – of people having built (or more likely 'put up') a house in just eight weeks you can reply,

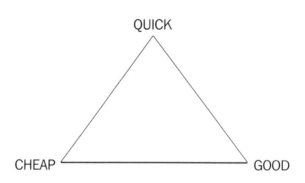

confidently, "Ah, but how much did it cost you?" And, similarly, if you meet someone who claims to have built a house for £45 per sq ft, you can look them in the eye and

exclaim "I bet it took you years" – and you'll be right. So before you set out to build a new house, first examine your motives and see where you fit into the triangle.

INTRODUCTION

THE CHEAP HOUSE

The average new house is constructed entirely by builders, takes about 6-8 months to complete and costs around £120/ft² (that's £1200ish/m²). It is built to standards that meet – and do not exceed – the current building regulations. If you want to maximise the financial return on your new house – in all but the most up-market areas – it pays to keep it dead simple. For a cost-effective house the following advice should be carried out to the letter.

Dispense with any notions of individual design. Aim for a four-square box drawn up by a technician or a surveyor or, better still, from a book of house plans. Avoid architects at all costs.

Avoid all of the following:
▪ layouts with more than four external corners
▪ anything round or curved
▪ anything poking out through the roof (dormers, chimneys)
▪ anything other than large format concrete tiles on the roof
▪ anything other than face brickwork on external walls
▪ anything other than straight stairs
▪ complicated sites (unless at a bargain price)
▪ fancy Continental plumbing systems
▪ trying to build an 'Eco' house
▪ big glazed features
▪ underfloor heating
▪ central vacuum cleaning systems
▪ kitchens that don't come from Ikea or B&Q
▪ bathrooms that don't come from B&Q or Bathstore

▪ anything but boring plastic windows
▪ home cinema rooms
▪ handmade anything at all (bricks, tiles, etc)
▪ Agas
▪ garages – especially with remote-controlled doors
▪ porches and entrance canopies
▪ conservatories
▪ built-in cupboards
▪ hardwood floors
▪ data cabling
▪ any lighting that doesn't hang from a pendant in the middle of each room
▪ almost everything second-hand – it's only been salvaged because it's worth more than new.

What you will end up with will have all the charm of a 1950s council house. But if space for bucks is your main motive in taking on a construction project, then you'll be very happy. Much of the book that

This 2012 selfbuild in Cambridgeshire was designed and built by architect Michael Goodhart. It cost £350,000 to build, around £1650/m². That's in the upper reaches of the selfbuild galaxy, but actually represents very good value for the quality achieved.

follows is concerned with the options that might turn a cheap house into a good house and therefore much of the book will be of little relevance to you. I have, however, always tried to indicate what the cheapest option is in each element of the house.

THE QUICK HOUSE

The quick house will almost certainly be a kit house, which is largely prefabricated in a workshop or factory. It will also, very likely, be a timber-framed house, or maybe a SIPs house, which is a variation on timber frame that is gaining in popularity.

But are they really quicker? What really takes up a builder's time is the finishing tasks and these are pretty much the same whatever your chosen building method.

THE GOOD HOUSE

Most would-be individual housebuilders are not hard up nor in a hurry – at least they're not when they're just planning it all; they might beg to differ when they're halfway through building. They can afford to browse and contemplate and research. They will look at many different options before embarking and will probably be keen that the finished product should somehow be an expression of their personality as well as a way of meeting their individual needs in a way that an off-the-peg house couldn't hope to.

Even if you are building for resale rather than personal occupation, you are more than likely to want to build an attractive house that passers-by will come to admire and occupants will love to call their home.

After all, the house is likely to be standing long after any transient profit is banked and spent, and may well still be there when they are burying your grandchildren. To build well, you have to know what's going on and not just rely on experts: the more you are involved in the design, the more you will appreciate the outcome, and the more you are involved in the building, the better that outcome will be.

IS THIS BOOK FOR YOU?

What follows is housebuilding's original bodice ripper, a warts-n-all rough guide. It is not a DIY manual (there are enough of those) and it is not a disguised advertisement (I'm not selling anything apart from this book). Although primarily concerned with new housebuilding, there is also much information specifically tailored for people converting or restoring existing properties.

Many of the tricks and tips described I have learnt the hard way since I started building in 1980. As the old saw goes: experience is the best education, but it is also the most expensive. My hope is that some of my 'experience' and research will help you avoid expensive pitfalls, many of which I've had the doubtful pleasure of falling victim to myself.

In short, the aim of this book is to enable you to build a good house cheaply and quickly. Now hang on a minute, I thought that wasn't possible.

HOUSEBUILDING IN THE UK

Housebuilding in this country has always been a boom or bust activity, and this has never been more clearly illustrated than in recent times. My experience of the property business began in the 1980s (in my late twenties) and it is worth recalling what went on then, for the benefit of younger readers. That period saw a surge in private housebuilding, caused partly by post-war baby-

boomers (like me) entering the housing market and partly by people choosing to live in smaller groups. This increased demand also led to a huge increase in house prices which, in turn, encouraged more people to jump onto the home ownership bandwagon, encouraged by the Thatcher government which made property-owning a key plank of its programme.

THE 1988 SLUMP

This particular bandwagon came juddering to a halt on August 1, 1988 when Nigel Lawson, then Chancellor of the Exchequer (but now better known for being Nigella's dad) stopped a tax perk known as double mortgage tax relief.

I remember the day well. I was property developing at the time, owed the bank about a quarter of a million and had just learned that I was to become a father for the first time. It was also the day my business partner and I completed on the purchase of a rather large barn for conversion in Comberton, a village near Cambridge. The timing was about as bad as it could be.

Double mortgage tax relief sounds like rather an obscure tax perk, as indeed it was; these days we have no tax relief of any description on mortgages but, back in 1988, both halves of an unmarried couple could claim tax relief on a mortgage, which was worth a few bob. It was an anomaly and Chancellor Lawson strove to eliminate anomalies.

The problem was that he announced his intention to do so in

How Brickie's Rates Track Average House Prices

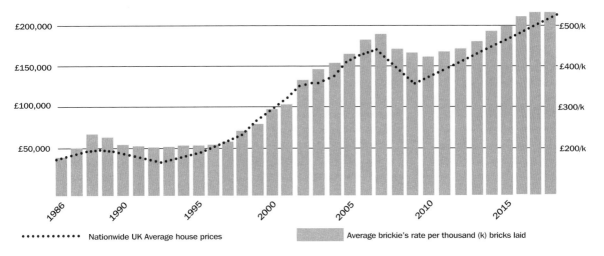

• • • • • • • • • • • Nationwide UK Average house prices ▢ Average brickie's rate per thousand (k) bricks laid

his budget speech in March, telling us all that the elimination of this particular anomaly would take place at midnight on the 31st of July. People who, in more normal times, would never have considered house purchase together were suddenly bounced into it by a fear that it was now or never for the housing ladder. The housing market, already toppy, duly went ballistic for four months in the rush to get sales completed before the Chancellor's cut off point.

In Cambridge, average house prices jumped by 25% overnight. Many of the 'Lawson couples' lived to regret the unwarranted emotional entanglement caused by this feverish speculation. All of them lived to regret the financial chaos brought on by the price bubble bursting on August 1st that year. For almost all of them, it would be ten years before the houses they bought at ridiculous

prices in 1988 would be worth the same again.

For us property developers, it was more painful still. But then, as a group, we have never elicited much sympathy. What happened on August 1st was distinctly eerie. The housing market just came to a standstill. Viewing stopped. Offers to buy were withdrawn. People just lost interest in buying homes altogether. The events of 2008, when the property market also stopped dead in its tracks, were eerily reminiscent, although there was no pivotal moment then, as happened in 1988.

Back then, prices didn't fall immediately. But, with hardly any house sales happening, it was hard to know what house prices were really doing. However, over the next year or two it became apparent that all the estate agents' talk of the market "just taking a breather" was bull and, as the

number of sales continued to decline, the rout set in. Things weren't helped at all by another of Nigel Lawson's foibles, the decision to peg the pound to the Deutschmark (remember that currency?) which led to interest rates going up and up – the base rate was 15% from October 1989 to October 1990. As you can imagine, housebuilders took a bath.

It wasn't until 1993 that house prices stopped falling. Even then, the recovery was painfully slow. Rather than being a return to the good old days before Lawson's bubble when house prices gently rose year-on-year (or so it seemed), everything remained resolutely frozen. Newspapers were full of stories of families stuck in 'negative equity' and of unhappy young homeowners just handing their keys back to the mortgage lenders and going back to live with Mum and Dad.

Chapter 1

NEW LABOUR

The climate all changed once again with the election of New Labour in 1997. Strange to think of a supposedly left-wing government riding to the rescue of the property-owning classes, but then life was ever full of such ironies.

The fact is that average house prices were back to roughly the same level in May 1997 as they had been on that fateful day nine years earlier when Nigel Lawson delivered his now infamous budget speech.

From 1997, house prices started rising once again, just as they did from the 1950s through till 1988. This situation continued for another ten years until it finally started unravelling in late 2007, brought on by the global credit crunch that made it much harder to borrow money.

We had had a ten-year Blair boom: now we were into a Brown bust. The slump that followed was rather different to the 1988 one. Price falls weren't so deep and transactions didn't stop as they had done in 1987. The housing market has been propped up by 0.5% interest rates, the lowest they have ever been.

BREXIT

The Coalition years saw the market come back to life, certainly in London and the South-East, and this trend continued after the Tories were returned on their own in 2015. Mortgage lending is once again in full spate although the number of new mortgages agreed is still well down on 2007 levels. The government has been propping up

the market with ultra-low interest rates and various schemes like Help-to-Buy which subsidise new home ownership.

But the buoyant market was not evenly spread across the country and in quieter areas prices remained little changed in a decade. This was perhaps reflected in the 2016 Brexit referendum which saw a groundswell of dissatisfaction overturning David Cameron's hopes of killing off UKIP once and for all. Now we face a very uncertain future with (at time of writing) negotiations getting underway to pave the way for a UK withdrawal from the EU. Whilst the UK seems to be split in two by the prospect of an independent future, it remains none too clear what effect this will have on the housing market.

HOW WE BUILD HOUSES

There are many unusual aspects to the British housebuilding scene besides the topsy-turvy nature of the housing market. Particularly pertinent to this book is the way we go about building homes – more particularly who builds them.

If you were to imagine a pie chart representing the total number of houses built each year in the UK there would be three slices in it marked:
▪ speculative housebuilders (the vast proportion);
▪ social housing (a small but reasonable slice); and
▪ others (another still reasonable slice – maybe 15%)

This type of arrangement has existed for decades. The big

housebuilders get hold of giant parcels of land to develop (or re-develop in the case of city centre regeneration), and they build identikit estates and sell their houses into the private market. The councils insist that they also build some social housing in return for granting them the right to build. Social housing has more or less taken over from the council housing schemes, which were such a feature of the middle years of the 20th century. It's an area alive with innovation and some fascinating schemes have been built in the past few years. Indeed standards for social housing have been consistently higher than those used in the private sector, because the government and councils have insisted on it.

And then there are 'the others.' This book is primarily intended for the builders down here at the bottom of the housebuilding heap. The small builders and the others. Particularly the others.

In many ways, this 'others' grouping is by far the most interesting. Although it may account for less than 15% or so of new homes, that still amounts to between 12,000 and 20,000 each year. And the great bulk of these are built by individuals for their own occupation – what the media and everyone else has learned to call 'selfbuild'.

Before getting stuck into the world of selfbuild, I think it's important to point out that there is a huge grey blanket of an area spread out between the sort of selfbuild featured in Channel 4's 'Grand Designs' and the output of a small spec builder who builds a house or two for sale every year and every so often builds a new one for himself – that way netting a nice little tax free earner. I have often heard builders referring to odd plots of land they own as 'their pension' and all good pensions should be tax free, shouldn't they?

Many good people, academics amongst them, have tried to assess the size of the UK selfbuild market and they get into all sorts of difficulties, because selfbuild is not a clearly defined entity. The first 10,000 selfbuilds are easy to spot – they show up on the VAT returns – but the next 10,000 get murkier and murkier the higher the total gets. Hence I quite like the term 'others'. It covers a lot of nefarious undertakings.

This Norfolk selfbuild has an internal floor area of 197m², pretty typical for a rural 4 or 5 bedroomed house

How Big Is That House?

	m²	ft²	Range of building costs
One-bedroom flat	40	430	£40,000-£80,000
Terraced two-bedroom house	60	650	£60,000-£125,000
Semi-detached, 3 bedrooms	90	970	£90,000-£200,000
Detached 3/4 bedrooms	130	1,400	£130,000-£350,000
Large detached 4/5 bedrooms	200	2,150	£200,000 upwards

SELFBUILD

Many years ago, back in the 1970s and 1980s, selfbuild had a decidedly alternative flavour to it. Selfbuild was usually group selfbuild. This typically involved a number of individuals or families pooling their labour to build homes for themselves in a little estate.

Group selfbuild enjoyed a boom in the 1980s but came horribly unstuck when the Lawson bubble burst in 1988. Groups were left with homes worth less than they had paid for them and some of these schemes were abandoned half-built. Private group selfbuild all but disappeared off the radar screens after this.

But group selfbuild also existed in another guise where the schemes were done for rent rather than ownership – it's now known as Community Selfbuild – and this small sector continues to flourish although it rarely accounts for more than a dozen schemes each year.

In order to form a Community Selfbuild group, you need to have identified a number of people living in the same area who are in genuine housing need. Whereas the country is stuffed full of people in genuine housing need, not many of them have the time or inclination to go about meeting it by building a house which they then have to rent. Co-housing is another form of this, but here the emphasis is on shared ownership.

Whilst this specialised niche is alive and thriving, it is dwarfed by the mainstream selfbuild market, which consists of people acting as what the Americans call *paper contractors* – do-it-yourself property developers.

This group tends to be fairly well-off and tends to build relatively high spec houses; some estimates reckon that over a third of all detached housing in the UK is now selfbuilt. For many of this new breed

In Berlin, there are large numbers of selfbuilt apartments known as baugruppen. This one houses three families on six floors and includes a communal area in the basement. These cohousing models are beginning to appear in the UK, but they can be slow and difficult to get off the ground

of selfbuilder there will be little or no physical involvement in the construction of their homes. They are instead providing the nous and the money to purchase a plot of land and build a new home on it.

Throughout the postwar years, this group was typically doing up old wrecks of houses, but as the wrecks with the most potential have mostly been snapped up now, their attention has moved on to building from scratch. In response, there is now a recognisable selfbuild industry that supports many specialist businesses, three national magazines

– 'Build It', 'Selfbuild & Design' and 'Homebuilding & Renovating' – and various exhibitions up and down the land. Not to mention, of course, its very own TV programme, 'Grand Designs', which more than anything has promoted the idea that selfbuild is a noble activity, or at least an aspirational one.

So why *do* people selfbuild? There are two distinct camps here. One is to work your way up the property ladder (aka making a bit of money): the other is to individuate – to get exactly what you want (aka spending a bit of money).

The recent governments have been hugely supportive of selfbuild and have instituted a number of measures to make life easier for selfbuilders. One is to make selfbuilders exempt from development taxes (Section 106 agreements and Community Infrastructure Levy). Another is to prompt councils to undertake studies to work out what the local demand for selfbuild is, and then to start putting forward land specifically for selfbuild.

The government has been particularly keen to promote custom build, which is a little different to individual selfbuild in that it requires a developer to subdivide larger parcels of land and sell serviced plots to selfbuilders, something that happens a lot in other countries but has been absent from the UK scene for decades.

LAND COSTS ARE THE KEY

The way in which prices for building plots are set is based on subtracting the building costs from the estimated value of the completed house. For example, if the estate agent or surveyor marketing a plot reckons that a nicely finished house might fetch £300,000 and that it might cost around £120,000 to build, then they will probably recommend that the plot be sold for around £130,000, maybe more, leaving a small element of profit for the builder. There is obviously a return here but the problem is that there are many more costs involved than just the plot price and the building costs.

If house prices increase by 15%

during the time it takes you to build, all appears well and good and you do appear to get a fantastic return on your efforts; but if house prices don't go up you'll have to throw an almighty number of hours at your building project if you are to keep costs down to a level at which you appear to make a profit of more than a few per cent.

The bulk of the profit in a greenfield housing site tends to go to the landowner who succeeded in gaining planning permission to turn whatever was there into building land.

In most parts of the UK, agricultural land is worth around £10,000 per acre. In contrast, in SE England at least, half-acre building plots are still fetching over a hundred times as much.

One effect of this relationship between land costs and finished housing costs is that building plots tend to go up in value faster than house prices when house prices are rising; conversely, plot prices fall further than house prices when house prices slump.

If you just add plot costs and building costs together you'd see a 20-30% profit, but a more thorough analysis reveals that the figure is nowhere near this amount. In particular, finance costs eat into the gross profit at an alarming rate and the effect of a) interest rates going up and b) failure to obtain a quick sale are disastrous.

Anyone who borrows to finance a project as large as a new house is extremely vulnerable to changes in interest rates.

When interest rates start to rise, professional developers get squeezed not just by the extra cost of this finance but also by the fact that the level of sales tend to decline, sometimes accompanied by the dreaded fall in house prices. Housebuilders are very vulnerable in these circumstances and what looks like a healthy profit on a house can evaporate within a matter of weeks.

A selfbuilder is in a subtly different situation to a speculative developer and this may mean that they are able to hang on to more of this gross profit margin. The selfbuilder doesn't need to find a buyer and therefore has no selling costs; also the selfbuilder can keep construction costs down by carrying out supervision and some construction work. Against this, however, it is unlikely that they can build as cheaply as a professional developer, whatever construction methods they use.

ARE THERE REAL SAVINGS?

The costs of the average residential building job are made up of around 50% on-site labour and 50% materials. In theory, you could therefore achieve savings of around 50% on construction costs if you carried out all the labour yourself – but here we have to look at some rather complex actuarial calculations about the value of your time and the cost of borrowed money. Only if you are both rich and unemployed can you afford to ignore these calculations.

Most DIY projects are of low value (say, less than £1,000) and

have little effect on house values. They are carried out because the occupants appreciate their amenity value. However, larger building projects – extensions, conversions, rehabilitations and especially new housebuilding – call for much closer assessment of your labour input.

By taking on even part of the work yourself, you are in effect becoming a speculative builder whose work will be rewarded by an increase in the value of your property. The more work you carry out yourself, the less you pay to others and the greater your eventual profit (in theory).

The problem with this sort of work is that your labours are far more likely to be rewarded in line with property price movements rather than with how hard or well you yourself work. In boom times your rate per hour may appear to be enormous (and you'd probably think yourself very clever for embarking on this nice little tax-free earner). However, building through a slump puts all that into a new perspective, and many DIY builders will have found that they have actually lost money – and the more masochistic will have converted that into a loss per hour which begins to make slavery look like an attractive option.

Most people would not consider carrying out all the work themselves. In fact, the vast majority of people would have no more wish to take on such a task than they would choose to educate their children at home; life simply isn't that long.

There are, however, many people who find their work is seasonal,

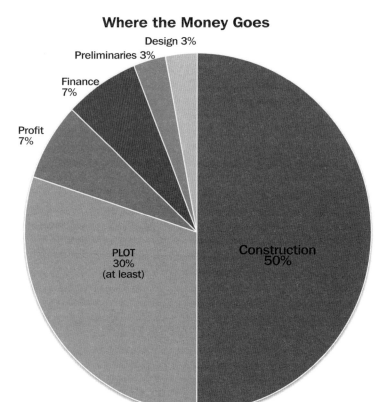

Where the Money Goes

Design 3%
Preliminaries 3%
Finance 7%
Profit 7%
PLOT 30% (at least)
Construction 50%

This pie chart shows the breakdown of costs on a typical small developer model. The 30% plot cost is variable in the extreme: it can be as much as 50% in the more expensive areas – but the final profit figure is still fairly realistic. The final profit level is very dependent on economic conditions, not in the control of the developer.

intermittent or out of normal working hours, to whom a high level of involvement in a building project makes good sense. They will tend to be practical and experienced in problem solving and those that are already running their own business will have much of the organisational backup in place already. The extra costs involved will not be enormous and even if their work only nets them £2.50 per hour, that's still more than they'd get doing nothing.

However, for many people selfbuilding may just prove to be a lousy option. They will be committing themselves to 2,000-3,000 hours work – often very hard and dirty work – putting up an overpriced structure to a design that isn't very good in the vague hope of making a 'dream home' and a 'fantastic windfall profit' to boot. Ask yourself two questions:

1. If it is that easy to make money, why don't more selfbuilders turn into professional property developers?

2. If builders' profits are so exorbitantly high, how come so many of them keep going bust?

I started as a selfbuilder (albeit with a renovation not a new build) and went on to become a 'professional' (in that other people paid me for my labours), often working alongside selfbuilders. It'll come as no surprise when I report that the hours are long, the work is backbreaking and the pay is often crap. The pay rates usually follow the economic cycle, so that in boom times the rates can go sky high, whereas in busts they fall back pretty quickly.

MANAGEMENT WITH A BROOM

For every seven or eight hours spent on construction, one hour has to be put into servicing the site. This can involve any and everything from sweeping up, filling skips and unloading lorries to meeting building inspectors and buying materials. Many selfbuilders take on this 'management with a broom' role thinking that they may not be able to plaster a wall or fit a staircase, but they had no trouble organising the school run, therefore...

Be warned. You'd be right to think that the organisational skills are not in themselves exceptional, but their efficient execution is very dependent on a reasonable working knowledge of the building trades and the local building practices and prices.

After three or four projects, you'll start to get halfway good; if it's your first time, most people find it an almighty struggle and you'll be unlikely to do it well. Your subcontractors will very quickly realise they are working for a novice and the less scrupulous ones may be tempted to take advantage of this and to cut corners or to bodge, particularly if you've negotiated 'keen' labour prices.

Whilst your building inspector should ensure that the structure is adequate, very little professional checking takes place above foundation level and, in any event, building regulations do not cover most of the finishing trades.

Furthermore, don't kid yourself that you're doing away with the overheads of employing a main contractor by managing the project yourself. Your phone bill will be up by £100-£200 a quarter; your mileage will increase two or three fold, even if you are living on site; you will need site insurance; you will suffer damage to materials which will have to be replaced at your own expense; you will end up with leftovers that you cannot easily get rid of; and at the end of the job, you'll have to chase yourself to get all those little snags finished.

More than half of a main contractor's mark-up goes on paying overheads that would be common to professionals and amateurs alike. And there is still the tricky little matter of finance. There are many other costs besides plot and building costs, and they all conspire to eat away your paper profit.

STILL WANT TO SELFBUILD?

Having got all that off my chest, I will also readily point out that I have met many selfbuilders who have made a tidy packet out of their dealings. Nevertheless, I would argue that the rewards of selfbuilding are not chiefly financial. What it really allows is the freedom to design and build a new house to your specifications, something that you will not be able to do by any other route.

For many people selfbuilding represents one of the great challenges in life. The more they are involved in the project, the more they get out of it and the whole attraction of selfbuild is the pure adventure of it all. If this is your motivation then more power to your elbow.

You may well end up just a little disappointed by the outcome and will perhaps be haunted by a whole host of 'what ifs' and 'if onlys.' Fear not, this is an experience common to all designers and builders. You'll just have to do it all again.

However, if your motivation is mainly financial then I warn you to look very carefully at the sums involved.

Yes, you can save money selfbuilding but it may not be as much as you might first expect.

Don't ignore the well-trodden route of hiring a designer (who in turn manages the job for you) just because you think it will be expensive.

Don't forget that property developing (for that's what you're doing) is a risky business.

Unlike many financial products that are now sold with warnings attached, building plots and the houses that go on them are sold on the understanding that the buyer knows the risks involved. You are assumed to be a sophisticated investor; make sure that you actually are.

MONEY MONEY MONEY

Be a little bit wary of the published costs you see. A selfbuilder has an emotional investment in their project and really wants to believe that all their work actually makes sense financially. Unlike the professional builder, who has good reason not to exaggerate the profitability of any scheme they undertake. To do so would be to hand money over to the taxman. Thus the professional builder will account for every cost they possibly can whereas the selfbuilder will be inclined to overlook many of the legitimate overheads in order to make the final sum look more pleasing.

Nowhere is this discrepancy greater than in the area of finance. To a developer, finance is just another job cost, essentially no different than the cost of the land or the building costs. When the house is sold on, they will total up all the loan interest they have paid and add it in as a legitimate business cost.

The selfbuilder is in a rather different position. They may – probably will – already have a mortgage before they even think of taking on a major project like a new house or a major renovation. By transferring this mortgage from an existing house to a building plot

Chapter 1

they are not necessarily altering their cashflow at all and do not have to add this cost into their calculations.

What they are doing is exchanging a year or two's hardship (such as living with the in-laws or in a caravan on site) for the opportunity to live in a bigger or better house than they could otherwise afford. Whilst a cost accountant would probably say that the selfbuilders are deceiving themselves, it seems to me to be a perfectly legitimate approach to things.

If there is a danger for the selfbuilder in all this, it is that they will tend to get greedy and to overreach themselves. It is notoriously difficult to predict building costs and the world is full of people with a vested interest in making building costs look less than they actually are. Getting prices out of builders and subcontractors is often much easier said than done and the chances are that most selfbuilders will have to commit themselves to a building project before they have a clear idea of the actual costs. Often people realise at a comparatively late stage that they can't afford the scheme they have embarked on and desperately look for ways of reducing the costs.

Many will complain bitterly just how expensive builders are when the root of the problem is that they always had inflated expectations of what they could achieve with the money at their disposal.

Many people are bounced into becoming project managers because they think it is bound to be cheaper to build directly with subcontractors. This is not the way to become a selfbuilder; it's the way to become a headless chicken. Even hard-bitten professionals have problems reconciling their dreams with their budgets and it is essentially in response to this problem that I wrote this book – to help put you, the person paying all the bills, back in control of the situation. "Taking back control" — isn't that the phrase of the moment?

Well maybe...

THE MODEL HOUSE

The early editions of the Housebuilder's Bible were based on the build of an actual house, one that had been constructed in the year or so prior to publication. It was always a four or five bedroomed detached house, built by either a selfbuilder or sometimes a small developer. The idea had been to extract the information from the project and to feed it into the new edition.

But this approach came with a problem attached. The houses were never the same and so comparing them with one another was a fraught task.

Since the 11th edition, I have been doing it differently. I've created a model house which will run through future editions. It's not a house that's ever been built: it's a virtual house aka a spreadsheet consisting of nothing more than a series of numbers, areas and volumes which reflect what goes on in a typical house.

It makes my job easier and it also reads better because it can be used to make useful comparisons over time. And given that no one sets out to build a second version of one of my exemplar homes, it's hardly a great loss to the Bible that the model house is simply a theoretical model.

THE NEW MODEL HOUSE
The model house has an internal floor area of 160m², divided between two floors. That's pretty much average for a UK selfbuild, and average for all the benchmark houses I have used in previous editions. They ranged in size from 110m² up to 220m².

The model house is rectangular, measuring 13m x 7.3m externally. As the walls are 375mm wide, the internal dimensions are 12.25m x 6.55m, or 80m² per floor. Double this and you get your 160m². There is a pitched roof with gable end walls at either end of the house.

A chimney? A good question. Every benchmark house I have used, until the 9th edition, had a fire or at least a wood stove and therefore a chimney. The 9th edition broke with this because it featured two homes which were specifically low energy – one being a Passivhaus – and neither of them had a conventional central heating system, nor a fire. So my model house, in the spirit of a brave new future, has no fire and no chimney either, but you can look elsewhere to find the cost of adding these.

In fact there are a lot of things like stoves that selfbuilders aspire to which can be taken out of a model house and it begins to look suspiciously cheap to build. But therein lies an important lesson. Much of the rising cost of building a house – and it has risen a lot in the 25 years I have been writing about it – is down to consumer preferences. Not just wood stoves, but fancy kitchens with quartz worktops, hardwood flooring, wet rooms, LED lighting schemes, glass balustrades, not to mention various forms of renewable heating.

The model house can take them all, but it chooses not to. It's a very basic, simple build. There isn't even a garage. That's probably a bit unlikely for a detached house these days but once again it's fairly easy to cost it as an extra.

What's interesting is that the cost of building this model house is around £230,000, or £1400/m². You can look up cost tables which suggest that you can build for a lot less than this, maybe even half as much, but my experience leads me to believe that a lot of these figures are fanciful. Persimmon, our largest housebuilder, maybe able to build at these costs but it very difficult for individuals to get close to these prices. Each individual row is discussed in detail in the relevant chapter and there are more detailed cost tables to be found there. The following spread (overleaf) shows the assumptions that went into creating the model house.

MODEL HOUSE: Summary of Building Costs

	Materials	Labour	Plant	Fees	Rounded Totals	Total
Professionals (Design, fees, Chapters 4 and 5)				£11,000		£11,000
Groundworks (Ch 6)						£35,000
Groundworks	£8,400	£6,900	£5,400		£21,000	
Drains + Services	£4,700	£2,900			£8,000	
Service Connections				£5,600	£6,000	
SuperStructure (Ch 7)						£64,000
Inner Skin	£2,600	£3,300			£6,000	
Steels and Lintels	£1,300	£200			£1,500	
External Cladding	£7,000	£7,000			£14,000	
Insulation	£3,900	£1,500			£5,000	
Joinery	£11,000	£2,000			£13,000	
Internal Floor	£3,900	£2,500			£6,000	
Internal Walls	£1,600	£1,800			£3,000	
Roof Carpentry	£2,500	£1,500			£4,000	
Roof Cover	£6,200	£3,200			£9,000	
Rainwater/Fascia	£1,000	£1,300			£2,000	
Plumbing & Heating (Ch 8	£4,300	£3,100				£7,000
Electrics (Ch 9)	£3,000	£6,000				£9,000
Finishes (Ch 10)						£58,000
Plastering/Screeding	£3,300	£10,300			£14,000	
Wall/Floor Finishes	£10,100	£5,400			£16,000	
2nd Fix Carpentry	£3,700	£5,700			£9,000	
Painting/Decorating	£700	£6,200			£7,000	
Externals	£6,000	£6,000			£12,000	
Room by Room (Ch 11)						£22,000
Kitchen	£11,000	£2,300			£13,000	
Bathrooms	£4,200	£4,400			£9,000	
Wardrobes/Storage						
Garage	not costed					
Prelims (Site costs, Ch 5)		£3,000	£10,000			£13,000
Project Management		£12,000				£12,000
Rounded Totals	**£100,000**	**£99,000**	**£15,000**	**£17,000**		**£230,000**
Floor Area	160 m²				Cost per m²	**£1,440**
	1,722 ft²				Cost per ft²	**£130**

Chapter 1

The costings in this edition are based around a Model House, a theoretical structure which has never been built but which encompasses everything average about an average house.

These tables show the assumptions that go into building such a house and they are used throughout the book to build up an overall cost. The summary cost table is on the previous page. Throughout the book there are tables with white text headings. These all refer to this model house and how much it would cost to build or heat.

MODEL HOUSE Vital Measurements

	UNIT	Ranges	Notes
BASICS			
External Dimensions	13.0 x 7.3m		
Internal Dimensions	12.25 x 6.55m		
Internal floor area (two floors)	160 m^2	110-200	Twice internal dimensions
House perimeter	40 m	33-60	
House Footprint	95 m^2	60-110	Area of external dimensions
Oversite area	140 m^2	120-240	50% larger than footprint
Oversite excavation volume	35 m^3	21-42	Depth dependent but usually around 0.25m
Heated volume	430 m^3	244-536	Int gr floor area x 5.4
SUPERSTRUCTURE			
Setting Out Foundations	120 m^2	95-200	Footprint plus 25%
Foundation length	70 lin m	45-100	
Excavating Foundations	40 m^3	22-55	Assume Length x 0.6 width x 1.0 deep
Readymix (600mm deep)	25 m^3	10-50	Dependent on depth
Footings (550 deep)	40 m^2	18-30	Dependent on depth of readymix
House Floor Slab Area	95 m^2	60-110	Same as Footprint
Screed	80 m^2	55-100	Int floor area, one floor
Foul Drains	40 m	15-50	Site specific
Rainwater Drains	60 m	25-75	Site specific
Service Trenching	15 m	15-25	Site specific
External Wall Area inc Openings (Gross)	235 m^2	150-250	House perimeter x 5.4, plus 2 gables
Combined Gable Area (35° pitch)	19 m^2		Worked with roof calcs, but used as part of ext wall calcs
Joinery Area	35 m^2	18-40	Often surprisingly close to 35m2
Ext Wall Area minus Openings (Net)	200 m^2	115-215	
Inner Skin (gross)	220 m^2	125-220	Note it's around 7% less than external measurements
Inner skin area (net)	185 m^2	110-200	
Ext Lintels	16 No		Typical for 35m^2 of Joinery
Possible Lintel Length	25 m		Typical for 35m^2 of Joinery
Windowboards	20 m		Typical for 35m^2 of Joinery
Chimney	Absent		The model house has no chimney!
First Floor Area	80 m^2		The stairwell will, in practice, reduce it by a little
INSULATION			
Insulation GF	80 m^2		Derived from Screed measuerments
Insulation Ext Walls	200 m^2		Derived from Ext Walls (Net) measurements
Insulation Ceiling	80 m^2		Derived from First Floor Area
Insulation Sound Floor	75 m^2		Derived from First Floor Area
Insulation Sound Walls	60 m^2		Derived from Int Walls (Studwork)

	UNIT		Ranges	Notes
INTERNALS				
Internal room-dividing wall area (net)	130	m²	86-185	Net means door openings have been deducted. Ext walls not included here
Internal Walls masonry	70	m²		Helpful to split internal walls by type
Internal walls studwork	60	m²		Helpful to split internal walls by type
Steel Beams	2	No.	0-5	Most houses of this size have a beam or two, but its not a prerequisite
Plastered area	490	m²	380-650	Sum of plastered walls and ceilings: if alternative mats used, then further breakdown required
Plastered walls net of openings	350	m²	280-420	Worked out on a room-by-room basis
Plastered Ceilings	140	m²	110-240	Worked out on a room-by-room basis; calcs are complex with sloping ceilings, but model house has none
Coving	150	m	115-175	Ceiling-wall junction measurement, worked out on a room-by-room basis
Architraves	130	m	110-200	Door openings have (conventionally) 5.1m of architrave each side
Skirtings	120	m	100-160	Wall-floor junction measurement, worked out on a room-by-room basis
Internal Doors	13	No.	12-14	Remarkable how small the range is. Maybe not.
Door Lining Lengths	65	m	60-75	Conventionally 5.1m per opening
Upstairs Floor Area	80	m²		
ROOF				
Roof Cover (in plan)	100	m²	70-150	Generally 10% more than footprint due to overhangs.
Roof Cover (actual 35° pitch, dual pitch)	122	m²	120-213	35° roof usually 20% larger than plan: 45° roof usually 40% larger
Chimney	Absent		0-2	There is no chimney on the model house
Eaves	26	m	20-35	Varies depending on roof shape: here it's combined front and back elevations
Ridge	13.2	m	4-15	Varies depending on roof shape: here it's half the eaves length
Hips	Absent		0-10	Model house does not have a hipped roof
Verges (Bargeboards)	18	m	0-20	The verge is the gable-roof junction. Model house has gables at both ends of roof.
Rainwater (Gutters and Downpipes)	48	m	36-95	Eaves gutter 13mx2; Downpipes 5.4mx4
Scaffold Run	40	m	33-60	Taken from house perimeter
FINISHES				
Rigid kitchen units	10	m³	4-13	Unusual way to estimate kitchen costs but can be quite helpful
Worktops	10	lin m	8-12	Even small houses seem to have long worktops these days
Kitchen sinks	2	No.		
Bathrooms	2.5	No.		2.5 means there are two bathrooms upstairs and a small WC downstairs: bog standard
Hardwood Flooring	60	m²	0-115	Flooring costs equate to int floor area but the split is elective
Floor Tiling	30	m²	0-65	Flooring costs equate to int floor area but the split is elective
Carpet	70	m²	0-95	Flooring costs equate to int floor area but the split is elective
Wall Tiling	40	m²	10-60	10 is a minimum: above this it's elective
EXTERNALS				
Base Preparation	160	m²	120-160	Surprisingly similar results from all manner of houses
Driveway	140	m²	100-160	
Block Paving	20	m²	0-160	
Paving slabs	15	m²	0-60	
Fencing	30	m	0-50	
Close boarded Fencing	15	m	0-25	
Turfing	140	m²	0-140	
Garage	Absent		0-1	Garage is excluded from model house. Cost £8k for single; £12k for double.

CASE STUDY

This edition's case study has to be my own build. As I write this, it's June 2019 and I've just completed a project that started nearly five years ago and it's been both an adventure and an education.

I last built a house in 1992. In the intervening years, I had only been indirectly involved in the building process, mostly via writing about it in this book and in magazines. I've met hundreds of selfbuilders, visited dozens of homes and interviewed countless individuals involved in the building process. But I hadn't built a house for 25 years.

Then in 2014, with cash in the bank from a previous house sale and a new partner in my life, I saw a derelict warehouse for sale on Rightmove, situated in the Victorian back streets of Cambridge. I already knew the site and also knew it would be snapped up at way over the asking price. I asked Mandy, my new partner, whether she fancied moving back into town with me, and without the blink of an eye she said yes. We actually shook hands on it on the pavement outside the warehouse, there and then. We had made a deal.

The site we acquired had once been used as a commercial warehouse, built in the 1940s, but had lain empty for 30 years. It had no architectural merit and wasn't worth saving but it sat in a Conservation Area and this meant that it couldn't be demolished until a full planning permission had been granted. As it stood, there was no planning permission for anything and, with no less than nine adjoining neighbours, there were bound to be plenty of issues to resolve.

"Never buy a Plot without Planning Permission." I must have given that advice hundreds of times to potential selfbuilders over the years. And here I was ignoring it.

However, it wasn't that reckless a thing to do. Knowing the area well, I was pretty confident we would get permission for a detached house, but I didn't think it would take a year and a half to get the planning sorted. It did. And then another nine months to demolish the warehouse, sort out the garden and work through the many planning conditions imposed by the planners. The house building didn't get underway until May 2017, two and a half years after we bought the site. In retrospect, the building seems like the easy part.

By and large, the neighbours welcomed the change we brought about. The site had been something of an eyesore for decades and several neighbouring gardens were being overrun by the all-too-lush vegetation. The derelict warehouse would not be missed, but we knew that there were many toes that we could inadvertently tread on, so we were careful.

We decided to hire Mole Architects to help bring our plans to fruition. I'd known Meredith Bowles, the man behind Mole, for some time and knew he would come up with a contemporary design which would tick all our boxes. We wanted to build something that would not only be great to live in, but would lift this shabby corner of the street, and raise the spirits of the passers-by. We went through a series of iterations of what we might do and having decided on a plan we liked, we had a model built which we then showed the neighbours at an open event.

The story in two pictures.

Above: As it looked in 2014 when it came onto the market. Contrasted with how it looks in 2019 (below).

All it took was about half a million quid and the best part of four years of my life. But I really enjoyed the challenge and love what we have created.

The application we submitted was welcomed by the planning committee who passed it unanimously.

Two years later, the same Cambridge planning team voted the house their best new small development in their annual awards.

HOW WE BUILT IT

Because of the sensitive nature of the site, there were no less than 18 planning conditions placed on the development and many of these had to be fulfilled before construction began. The neighbours proved to be

Above: The south wall trench. Before we could dig the foundations, we had to build the studio and stack the bricks in the garden. Below: the architect's model shows the tight constraints of this site.

incredibly helpful in this respect and enabled unfettered access down both flanks of the structure, even when it meant temporarily sacrificing their garden space.

Deliveries were also very challenging as the house sits on a narrow one-way street. Skip changeovers involved temporarily reversing the traffic flow. I decided that offsite construction was the way to go in order to reduce the amount of coming and going and we chose to work with Kingspan Potton, using their TEK structurally insulated panel system. The access issues held no fear for Potton and they drew up the details in conjunction with the architects.

I acted as project manager throughout the build, stopping all too briefly to get married to Mandy during a break in the groundworks in 2017.

The first phase of the work was done on fixed price contracts with minimal supervision, but the finish trades were hired on a day rate which is best for quality but requires a constant presence. We chose a lot of very fine finishes like a Douglas Fir ceiling in the living room and Portuguese limestone floor tiles throughout the downstairs. And there were numerous finish details, built on site, such as vanity units, wardrobes, under stair cupboards and a unique external bin store complete with its own green roof.

Externally, the house is clad in brick with louvred cedar boards used as a rainscreen on the unsupported walls, and highlighted with copper detailing. The zinc roof features seven photovoltaic panels as well as two Velux rooflights, providing daylight to the ensuite bathroom. Unusually for a new house in an urban setting, it has a 20 metre garden and the back of the house is designed to flow out into the garden via a set of sliding doors.

One of the main design issues was how to get light into the kitchen area at the back of the house. It was obvious that the light source would have to be overhead, as side windows were ruled out because they would have looked directly into the neighbours' back gardens. But there are a number of suppliers using a variety of methods and we visited many of them, including a trip to Scotland. We eventually chose to work with Cantifix, one of the original structural glazing companies, who came up with a bespoke design featuring a sliding rooflight. It is not only triple-glazed but it features

a low-g glass which reflects solar radiation away, thus reducing the "conservatory effect" of having an overheated kitchen.

We moved in in May 2018, just at the start of the summer heat wave, and to our surprise we found that, such was the effectiveness of the solar reflection, the kitchen was actually cooler at midday with the roof light closed. We waited until the evening before we opened it up and got the breeze blowing through.

COSTS

The whole project cost us £550,000, not including the cost of site acquisition (£320,000). That is about £100,000 more than I anticipated at the outset. The overrun was partly driven by higher building costs, and partly by us choosing to up the specification in certain areas.

What we have for this is a beautifully finished project, complete with a large open plan kitchen cum living room, opening up onto a paved garden with a studio at the far end.

Many of the costs were standard for contemporary selfbuilds but getting that modern look just right is fiddly, time consuming and expensive. Although the measured internal floor area is only 137m2, there isn't a square inch of the 6m x 40m site that isn't planned and detailed, from the dry garden above the bin store to the stainless steel clothes line poles alongside the raised lawn with rusting steel edges.

In fact, what I have learned is that there is a world of difference between a conventional rural

Above: The SIPs panel with the twin Velux rooflights is craned into place

Below: The same twin Veluxes sit central in the south facing roof, between solar PV panels.

selfbuild — the type I did 25 years ago — and a contemporary, architect-designed urban plot. Throw near Passivhaus-style energy efficiency into the equation, with its 200mm of insulation in walls, floors and roofs, and triple-glazed doors and windows, and you can see how our spend figure is way in excess of anything

you might look up in a table of conventional build costs.

The final build cost turned out to be £3,400/m², about 2.5 times as much as the model house featured in Chapter 1. Add in my time, and a few frills that turn a house into a home (bookshelves, mirrors, dining tables, chairs) and we are close to the Chapter 3 table entitled How to Treble Your Build Costs. If you only look at one table in this book, that's the one to check out.

PASSIVHAUS

Initially, I was keen to build a Passivhaus which is reckoned to be the international gold standard for energy efficient homes. But a decision was made early on in the design process to pull back from this exacting standard. There were two principal reasons.

Firstly, the site is only 6m wide and the house is built hard against the boundaries. This means that overall wall width is critical to internal room sizes and it was felt that a 400mm-wide wall was a sensible compromise between insulation value and footprint.

Secondly, the house is a very complex shape in order to avoid overlooking and loss of light issues. Passivhaus works best with simple, box-like formats, where the so-called form factor helps reduce heat loss.

Nevertheless, the Passivhaus construction principles were adhered to and close attention was paid to airtightness detailing (with a final score of 1.0) and triple glazing. The house features the very best mechanical ventilation with heat recovery system, the Paul Novus, supplied by the Green Building Store. Furthermore, there is no wood stove nor any other supplementary heating. It just has underfloor heating downstairs and radiators upstairs, heated by a small gas boiler.

The house retains its heat so well

that the thermostatically controlled underfloor heating system didn't cut in till mid-October and the first winter's space heating bill was just £140 (3500kWh @ 4p/kWh).

The overall energy load for the house including electricity and gas is just under 10,000kWh/annum which splits roughly a third space heating, a third hot water and a third (electricity only) for lighting and appliances. The lighting is all LED, designed by Nicky Burridge, and the appliances were chosen for their efficiency. We put a seven panel solar PV array on the roof at a cost of £5,000 and this produces around 1800kWh of electricity a year.

The PV system includes a Solar iBoost diverter which directs otherwise unused electricity into the immersion heater on the hot water tank and this reduces the gas demand by a further 500kWh/annum.

I remain an enthusiastic supporter of the Passivhaus standard and think it's the best way of getting a low-energy, comfortable home. But we had to make some compromises here and I feel that in the circumstances we've got a good solution. I'm also delighted that our first winter in residence has proved that the house works as designed.

Top: The footprint of the house is very simple. Two bedrooms upstairs, three rooms opening off the hallway below and a connecting staircase. The back half of the house is single storey and is one large kitchen cum living room, opening out onto the patio
Below: A cedar bin store with its own sedum roof. Lots of little details like this turn a house into a home.

CONTACTS

Architect	Mole
Structure	Kingspan Potton
Energy consultant	Enhabit
Lighting	Nicky Burridge nbll.co.uk
Groundworks	Mead Construction
Roofing	White Roofing
Triple Glazed Joinery	Livingwood
Sliding rooflight	Cantifix
Kitchen	Tomas Kitchens
Limestone Floor	Mandarin Stone
Cement Tiles	Mosaic del Sur
Garden Studio	My Space
Carpentry	Artisan Structures
Exterior Paving	Latham Builders
Landscaping	Cambridge Grandscapes
Plumbing & Heating	Huttie
Decorating/Carpentry	Matt Kear 07989 37990
Site Management	Ray Stillwell 07739 570224

The back of the house is open plan, single storey. Visitors refer to it as a Tardis.

Top: View into the garden from the open plan kitchen living room.

Middle: The Tomas Kitchen beneath the opening triple glazed rooflight

Bottom: Mark and Mandy take tea on the patio

PITFALLS

Before we get into the mechanics of design and construction, I want to take a chapter to look at the pitfalls and risks involved in selfbuild. It is not, repeat not, a walk in the park and there are numerous little traps for the unwary.

Everyone and their aunt has watched Grand Designs and week after week the story tends to follow a pattern. It was a huge struggle, it cost far more than they anticipated but…..(as Kevin McCloud does his famous piece to the camera at the end of each show)…it was all worthwhile in the end. Just bear in mind that the Grand Designs team weed out all the not-so-great selfbuilds or the ones that are still on site fifteen years after starting.

Most people do muddle through and most people do end up feeling glad they have done it. But there are risks and they tend to fall into certain well-worn categories.

Firstly, people cant find a building plot at a price they can afford, meaning their selfbuild dream is stillborn. This may cost you a lot of time, but it won't bankrupt you or cause you sleepless nights. But it gets worse.

No 2 is that they manage to get hold of a site but end up in a battle royal with planners and/or neighbours about what it is they can build there.

Then comes the issues with the site itself which often turns out to be far more expensive to develop than they had hoped.

Then the builders turn out to be too expensive and plans have to be amended.

Mistakes happen on site leading to large dollops of money having to be spent on repairs or finding replacement builders.

Money then gets tight and they can't see how to finish it.

Finally, the people doing the

SETTLEMENT BOUNDARIES

Development is controlled around every settlement in the country. The usual way of doing this is to draw dotted lines on a map, known as framework boundaries. Outside the lines, the land is deemed to be agricultural and changes hands at £10,000 an acre. Inside, the land costs over £1m an acre in southern England. This map was included in my 1st edition in 1994. It is the village in S Cambs I then lived in. In the intervening 25 years, the location of the boundaries hasn't changed an inch.

selfbuild fall out with one another and have to sell up in order to build new lives separately.

Now I can breezily write all this stuff down and somehow it only seems to add to the attraction of selfbuild. I get emails which say "Thanks for pointing this out Mark, but we are going ahead anyway." In fact, I don't think I've persuaded a single person to go and do something different. Selfbuild seems to be something that draws people to it, like a moth to a flame.

And to be fair, I and my new partner and wife-to-be Mandy took on a most reckless challenge in 2014 when we spent too much on a difficult plot in central Cambridge

with no planning permission. Just couldn't resist it. It took four years to turn it into a beautiful home but we got there. So who am I to persuade you not to go down this route? But you have been warned, and here follows a little bit more flesh on what these pitfalls actually consist of.

FINDING LAND

Every year in Britain there are between 10,000 and 15,000 selfbuilds undertaken, and probably as many major renovations and conversions. This number has held rather steady for many years, despite some people predicting that we would run out of

plots and that every tumbledown old wreck had already been tarted up. The ravages of the credit crunch only managed to dent the total a little. The overall number is down about 15% from the pre-crunch numbers, even though the total spend seems to be much the same. It seems there are fewer houses being built, but they each cost more than they used to. The opportunities are out there and the business is being done. So, the question is, why do people find it so hard to get started?

I fear that the answer can be summarised in one uncompromising phrase – unrealistic expectations. Or, to put it another way, the opportunities are rather more expensive than people can afford.

The property market is pretty ruthless in valuing opportunity and the idea that you can pick up a really nice building plot for next to nothing is fallacious. The selfbuild exhibitions are full of people who are 'seriously looking at building a house' who basically can't afford to, or at least can't afford it in the expensive areas they live in. They will make enquiries, log onto websites and register interest, and even buy books, without ever really realising that they haven't got the wherewithal to make it happen. It doesn't help matters that TV still has lots of programmes about doing up property and 'making it all happen': this just pulls even more people into the whirlpool. Without some serious financial assets and/ or income, it's not really going to fly. After two or three frustrating years, would-be builders withdraw, saying they wanted to do it but they couldn't find a plot. But there are plots, and some people do make it happen.

So what are the essential ingredients for people who do manage to get on and make it happen? I think they tend to fall into three camps. Either they are rich and can afford to pay the prices needed to secure prime building plots. Or they are lucky and happen to already own a piece of land which is developable. Or they are not too fussy about where they live and will buy anything that comes up, within reason. This last group are the really keen selfbuilders who tend to do it over and over again because they love the whole process of building houses.

There are always dozens of opportunities on offer in every county during the course of a year: if people are deadly serious, they will find something. If they are just sticking a toe in the water, they will always find a reason to not go for a property or they will never bid enough to get it. Or they will complain that they can't afford the prices being asked.

PROFESSIONAL PLOT FINDING

Plot finding is actually becoming more organised and more professional. There are plot finding websites out there that will allow you to zoom-in, in aerial photograph mode, and give you a pretty good idea of what the place is like before you visit.

You can subscribe to plot databases for individual counties and you can also check details of recent planning permissions granted in your district so you get advance warning of plots before they even come to market. Even so, tracking down opportunities is a time consuming process and it pays to be professional about it: always think like a developer, because that is what you are.

According to Buildstore, which runs the Plotsearch database, in 2019 you can find plots in Northern Ireland and some parts of Scotland for under £10,000 whereas in Hertfordshire, the cheapest plot they have on their books is over £300,000. Those are the two extremes. It follows directly from this that selfbuild in Hertfordshire is somewhat different to selfbuild as practised in rural Aberdeenshire. In the Home

Counties, selfbuilders tend to either be replacing their own dilapidated houses or building in their back garden whilst selling off their original house. In Scotland, there is a more conventional selfbuild market with plots being bought by 'ordinary folk'. It also means that selfbuild is far more common in the cheaper areas.

Of the 15,000 selfbuilds taking place each year in the UK, over half the total are in Wales, Scotland or Northern Ireland whose combined population is just 10 million, compared to 50 million people living in England.

Single plots in SE England are so expensive that they attract professional developers whereas in the rest of the country they tend to be sold to amateurs wishing to build for themselves.

So it pays to be realistic. If you live somewhere expensive, you need a plot or a wad of cash to make it happen; alternatively, you can move somewhere cheaper and upset the locals with all your flash, big city money. The opportunities are out there.

UNCONSENTED LAND

There are several companies selling 'land' for knock down prices, usually just a few thousand pounds. The adverts seem very enticing but, if you keep your wits about you, you will realise that this land has no planning permission and has very little chance of ever getting planning permission. It's on the wrong side of the planning boundaries and planning boundaries very rarely move, despite what the sales literature would have you believe. Usually the giveaway is that they advise you not to bother with a solicitor. Here's what Gladwish Land Sales suggests: 'No Solicitors necessary! Unlike buying a house, when buying land you do not need to ensure vacant possession (unless you want to scare birds away) nor do you have to ensure all the fixtures stay. Most land that we sell is cheaper than buying a car. Do you use a solicitor to buy a car? The car could be stolen and the log book a forgery! With land, nobody can steal the land you buy and the transfer document you get, once signed, is irrevocable.'

There is nothing illegal about all this. They don't make any false claims. They make it clear the plots don't have planning permission. They do, sort of, insinuate that they will get planning permission but are very careful with their choice of words here. 'We negotiate with local councils on your behalf so that you don't have to worry about getting planning permission.' That's good wording, isn't it? You 'don't have to worry about it' because nothing is ever going to happen on that front.

The moral? Don't buy land without planning permission from anybody unless you are certain what you are letting yourself in for. If you are tempted by any plot always talk to local planners who will be able to tell you about the history of any applications and the likelihood of getting planning consent. Just occasionally, some of this land may get zoned for building, especially true now that government policy is set to

If you can find a bungalow on a big plot and buy it at the right price it may be possible to get permission for a larger replacement home. It is a well-trodden route that can be cost-effective, but it is not a certainty, and there will be costs involved.

relax planning boundaries. But it's something to be very wary of.

IS IT A PLOT AT ALL?

Don't assume that any building that has once been occupied by humans will automatically qualify for residential planning permission. Councils take widely differing attitudes to what constitutes abandonment and the most telling factor in whether or not an old building can be converted into a new home is usually the quality of the building, not its previous usage. Always check on the status of a derelict property in the local plan to see whether redevelopment is likely to be controversial. Often the planners will allow the conversion of a particularly fine old barn

just to stop it from disintegrating and sometimes this permission is dependent on the structure being maintained, even when this is a costly and relatively dangerous course to take.

There have been cases of planning permission being withdrawn from barn conversions after the builder has undertaken demolition of a few select walls.

BUYING LAND

There are basically five methods by which property (including building plots) can change hands in these islands.

■ Public auction: The best thing about this is that it's open. It gives the seller (or vendor in these circles) a legally binding agreement. On the other hand the expensive pre-sale work has to be undertaken with no guarantee of success. Sometimes, in the excitement of an auction, it doesn't get done at all. A 10% deposit is usually taken at the auction so the buyer has to have funds to hand.

■ Formal tender: as practised in Scotland. Once a bid is accepted, the deal becomes legally binding. Otherwise similar to the auction in terms of pros and cons.

■ Informal tender: buyers are asked to send in sealed bids for the property by a fixed date, together with details of their own financial position. All the bids are opened at the same time and the sale is agreed, usually with the party considered to be in the best position to buy. Buyers are wary and object to the decision being made in private and with no opportunity to increase their bid. However it's probably less stressful than an auction and gives more flexibility to the vendor.

■ Informal telephone auction: the common method of property sales everywhere outside Scotland. It gives much more flexibility to both sides. This is both its strength and its weakness – you get flaky offers from purchasers and you get gazumping and other evils because the contracts are not binding until physically exchanged. Furthermore, when there are more than three buyers competing for one property, it can get very difficult to organise proceedings because someone is often away or can't make up their mind. In

these situations agents often decide to switch to informal tender (see previous point), to close the deal.

■ Private sales: often referred to as 'Sale by Private Treaty'. If a buyer and a seller can agree on a price, then there is no obligation for them to go through the more public channels indicated above. A lot of land changes hands this way. You'd be surprised. Or maybe you wouldn't.

The actual process of buying land (or derelict buildings) is similar to that involved in buying houses. You usually employ solicitors and surveyors to ensure that you are not buying a pig in a poke. Likewise with plots, you want to ensure that you can build what you want on it at a price you can afford. But, the whole process of buying plots (and, especially, renovation opportunities) is more complex because there are more things that can go wrong.

When buying an existing property at least you know that it is there, even if it might just fall down next week! With a building plot you are buying nothing more than a field that comes with a promise, a hope for the future. And unlike the conventional house market, the chances are that you will have to purchase your plot without knowing exactly what you can build.

LIMITS OF PROFESSIONAL HELP

You don't have to hire any help but it's usual to do so because the stakes are high and you don't want to make a silly mistake. If you hire the services of a solicitor or a licensed conveyancer, look for a property

specialist. If you are buying in an area new to you, you'd be well advised to look for a local rather than sticking with someone you've used before who might be 200 miles away. Now is the time you need as much information, official and unofficial, as you can get. A good solicitor will uncover more than just that which is revealed by undertaking searches and checking for legal complications and boundaries.

One common pitfall occurs when the planning permission only allows you to build on one part of the site – a frequent occurrence when close to village framework boundaries and the like. Some solicitors spot this, others don't. You should be able to check this yourself on the web: I was able to download my own parish development plan within three minutes of typing the name of my district council into Google (clue – look for the Local Plan maps). But even the best solicitor is not going to be able to advise you as to whether the plot is an A1 purchase because there are a number of other areas that are outside the remit of even the most scrupulous legal beaver.

PURCHASE TAXES

You pay exactly the same taxes on land purchase as you do on house purchase. It's called stamp duty. The government likes stamp duty: it's a stealth tax because, although people don't like it, it's not going to lose them the next election, and it's relatively easy to police. Only the buyer pays the stamp duty, which

STAMP DUTY 2019

Plot or Property Price	Duty
up to £125k	0%
Between £125k and £250k	2%
Between £250k and £925k	5%
Between £925k and £1.5m	10%
over £1.5m	12%
different bands in Scotland	

gives selfbuilders a small advantage because they are usually buying cheap (plots) and building expensive (houses).

Stamp duty rates were last changed in 2014 to general approval. The old system switched the rate entirely when the value crossed a given threshold so that you paid just 1% tax if the price was £249,000 but 3% tax if it cost £250,000. Now it's been tiered so that if your property costs £350,000, then you'd pay 2% on the bit between £125k and £250k (£2,500) plus 5% on the tranche between £250k and £350k (£5,000), making a total of £7,500.

The HMRC website is the place to go for the more detailed analysis. The rates apply all across the country but note that Scotland applies significantly lower thresholds. Plus there are now punitive rates for people buying-to-let.

Any other charges? There are fees payable to bodies like the Land Registry (between £200 and £500) and for council searches, maybe another £400, but they are not significant in the scheme of things. And of course your legal fees.

ASSESSING BUILDING SITES

One of the things that catches people out at this very early stage is that no two building plots are the same. Whilst they can be very simple to develop, they can often present a number of issues which aren't apparent at the initial stage of investigation. There may be legal constraints on what you can build. There may be difficulties over access arrangements. The site may itself need expensive remedial work, or it may prove to be impossibly expensive to get services to site. In summary, you need to be aware that there are plot development costs which are quite distinct from run-of-the-mill building costs. Let's look at some of the issues in more detail.

LEGAL COVENANTS

Building plots are often sold with legal constraints over what may and what may not be done to them. The most common form of constraint is the covenant whereby the vendor (i.e. the person selling the plot) requires that the purchaser should fulfil a number of conditions. Many of these might not cost a euro – i.e. no caravans to be stored in the back garden or no trees to be planted where they might block someone else's view – but others can involve substantial costs.

The commonest type of covenant deals with boundary fencing and would read something like this: 'The purchaser covenants to erect six foot high fencing to the southern and

eastern boundaries of the plot before any building work takes place.'

Sometimes the covenant will be very much more specific and ask for a brick wall nine inches thick or something like that. A condition such as this is expensive to meet and should really be reflected in a lower plot price.

It is also common now to find covenants preventing any further development. The point behind such conditions is not to preserve the unique beauty of your setting but to hold on to any uplift in value you may be clever enough to negotiate with the planners. Covenants have beneficiaries and you can usually remove covenants if you are prepared to throw money at the beneficiaries. The going-rate for buying off a no-development covenant is around 50% of the value created – an arm and a leg, in other words.

Sometimes there are some very old covenants lurking on the deeds and it's long since ceased to be clear who exactly the beneficiary is. Maybe they have died and their heirs are not very apparent: unfortunately, covenants don't disappear with the death of the beneficiary. In such cases, you can insure against anyone coming forward and laying claim to the uplift.

BOUNDARY DISPUTES

It is unfortunately very common to encounter problems with fuzzy boundaries. Just because someone offers a piece of land for sale, it doesn't follow that they own all of it – or even any of it sometimes. Plot boundaries are usually drawn in title deeds as relatively thick lines on OS maps and there is frequently lots of room for disagreement about where exactly these lines are on the ground.

In 2003 an amended Land Registration Act was passed, which established a framework for registering boundaries using satellite positioning technology. This should improve transactional disputes over time, but progress remains slow. There are still millions if unregistered properties all over the UK and it will be decades before we see an end to such disputes entirely.

RANSOM STRIPS

Another potential problem occurs when someone else owns part of the land needed to successfully develop a plot. Typically, this is land needed to access the plot. This is often referred to as a ransom strip. Ransom strips can usually be bought off although you may be staggered to find out that you will be required to pay over as much as half of the plot value – they are not called ransom strips for nothing.

RIGHTS OF WAY AND WAYLEAVES

There are any number of complications that should, repeat should, be uncovered by your solicitor's search: rights of way crossing the plot, existing wayleaves for services and cables to cross the plot, complex shared ownership of access roads, to name but three. Even if you can live with these arrangements, they may well affect resale values and make finance much

harder to get and insurance more expensive. Many of these problems can be sorted out by throwing money at them – but the canny buyer should ensure it's the vendor's money not theirs.

USING OPTIONS

If there are major problems to sort out (as discussed above) in order to turn the bit of land you want to build on into a legitimate building plot, you might consider taking out an option, rather than pressing ahead with a more straightforward purchase.

What is an option to buy? The bare bones of a contract might look like this: you agree a price on a plot of land (though even this doesn't have to be fixed in stone). This remains in place for, say, two or three years; the length of the option is entirely up to you. During that time the vendor is prohibited from selling to anyone else. Some contracts involve interest payments to the vendor: this acts as a spur to the purchaser to get on with it and protects the vendor from time-wasters. The big plus from the purchaser's point of view is that an option protects you from gazumping and other forms of treachery.

How much would you be expected to pay for an option? Well, that depends. If the planning angle is difficult and you are taking on the costs of obtaining planning permission (which could be several thousand), then there may well be no payment made to the vendor at all. They would be very happy for someone else to do all this work for

them. However if market conditions are buoyant, then you may have to part with up to 5% of the plot price just to tempt the vendor into an option. Also the buyer may want to make the plot price conditional on what you manage to squeeze out of planning so that the price is £120,000 if you get permission for one house but £200,000 if you get permission for two.

If there is a pitfall in all this, it is that you can spend a lot of money and get nowhere. But that's a pitfall that all property developers have to face.

ACCESS & SERVICES

When assessing a plot or a barn, you should take note of the distance you think you will have to take the services and the access you will have to build.

Many backland developments come onto the market these days – typically the rear of someone's garden – and the prices asked for these sites are often little different to the prices asked for somewhere with a road frontage. Yet the budget cost of laying private driveways, drains, water and electricity combined with providing fencing is upwards of £500/m; that means that a plot set 30m back from a road is going to cost at least £15,000 more to develop than one with a road frontage.

Whereas the layout of vehicle access arrangements are usually easy to work out, finding out about the services requires detective work.

DRIVEWAYS

The basic cost of laying a drive can be budgeted at around £80-£100 per linear metre, rather more if it is required to be fenced off as well. Often there is extra work involved in connecting to the public highway: typically you may have to construct a dropped kerb if you are crossing a raised pavement, at the very least you will have to provide a small apron of asphalt or tarmac so that there is no unsightly gap between your drive and the public highway. In some situations you may be required to create a visibility splay, which may involve removing existing obstructions and rebuilding them further back from the road.

On the other hand, you may have to construct a bridge over a ditch or even make an opening through an existing building. There are, in fact, so many potential access problems that it is almost pointless trying to summarise them – you will, in all probability, discover them when you first visit the site. Just be aware that whilst a straightforward highway junction will cost a couple of hundred quid, complicated access arrangements may well set you back several thousand pounds.

SERVICE CONNECTIONS

Gas, electricity, water, sewage, phones. Together, these constitute the services and you need to have them (or as many as you can get) to turn a building plot into a home. Just how much this will cost you will vary enormously, depending largely on your site layout. Generally speaking, the further the services have to run, the more expensive it will get.

You'd think that the utility businesses would be delighted to have new customers and would bend over backwards to help accommodate them and get them connected for next to nothing. The reality is usually very different: selfbuilders struggle with service connections. They are costly, lead times are unpredictable and there are often strange administrative hoops to be jumped through.

Utilities have been largely privatised for twenty or thirty years now, yet the new connection work tends to be carried out by the same old institutions that ran the publicly-owned boards, and there is very little evidence of competition having come into play. BT run the copper phone cables, although Virgin control a lot of the fibre-optic network. Water and sewage are the domain of your local water company and electricity rests with the same electricity outfit that's been in place since the year dot, although it's now referred to as your Local Electricity Distribution Company - there are eight in the UK as a whole. Gas infrastructure is now run by Cadent.

A selfbuilder's first port of call is to get in touch with these service providers and to ask for a quotation for a new supply. It's one area where Google is still pretty useless – search terms like selfbuild new supply turn up all manner of strange things, but not the New Homes Department of your local utilities. You have to persist! Eventually you will find the people you need.

Bear in mind that you don't have to own a plot of land to generate a quotation. Thus, getting new connection prices is often one of the first tasks to undertake when assessing the viability of a plot purchase. Sometimes, the resulting high connection fees can be enough to render a project unviable.

OVERHEAD CABLES

Power cables running across your plot are bad news. They may intersect with your proposed building, in which case they will have to be moved; even if they don't they will detract from the resale value of the property. Burying them is the obvious solution but it can be horribly expensive; even a low voltage cable can cost over £40 per m to bury, which can easily make a short diversion cost £5,000 or more. Again, the trick is to get quotations for this before entering into any contract to buy.

EXISTING DRAINS

This is one real nightmare for rookies and professionals alike: existing drains and water mains running across your proposed building. Do whatever you can to find out if they are present, but sometimes there are no records and no surface evidence. Drains vary in their importance; small runs connecting one or two households to a sewer may very easily be diverted – depending on the lie of the land – but sewers and pumped drains cannot readily be moved and discovering one of these in your footings is a Grade A disaster, though

When digging a trial hole, the convention is to go down somewhat deeper than the proposed (or existing) foundations. Normally, you dig two or three trial holes just outside the proposed footprint – not under it.

thankfully this doesn't happen too often. The situation with mains is very similar; you probably will not be able to build within 2 or 3m. Again the key is to find out as much as possible about the plot before you exchange contracts to purchase. If there is any doubt in your mind, then try and place a retention in the sale contract which is only payable should nothing untoward be found under the ground.

PLOT PROBLEMS

Next on the list of potential booby traps is the problem of difficult ground. There are three basic causes of alarming cost expansion:
■ slopes
■ bad ground
■ trees.

Straightforward excavation and foundation work can be relatively cheap. Typically, the groundworks make up 10% or less of the overall build cost on a new house. On a straightforward site, this is usually

around £200/m² of footprint (i.e. the area you are enclosing). However any of the above problems encountered on site could conspire to make things a lot more expensive and, if you have more than one of these problems, expect your foundation costs to treble.

For more detail on these problems and how they are overcome, read Chapter 6: Groundworks. Here I simply want to give a few pointers about what to look for in assessing plots.

VISUAL INSPECTION

The first step in assessing any building plot is to take a walk over the site and the surrounding area. Be on the look out for clues as to what may have gone on in the past. Some points to watch out for are:
■ foundations of former buildings on site
■ evidence of drains, old watercourses or wells
■ subsidence cracks in neighbouring buildings

■ overhead cables
■ springy ground – suggests high water table
■ slopes greater than 1:25
■ trees within 30m of your proposed foundations – species, size and girth should be noted
■ any evidence of ground having been disturbed or used as a dump

BACKGROUND DETECTION

Investigations with local council, service companies, etc., should reveal more historical and geographical data on which to assess likely problems. Talk to neighbours, local builders or building inspectors who may well know the lie of the land. Your legal searches should turn up useful information but you can't rely on them.

TRIAL PITS AND BORINGS

To dig or not to dig, that is the question. Whether it is better to leave everything to chance and let the building inspector decide how deep your foundations must go when the time comes, or investigate in detail beforehand and risk having to do more than you really need. Many cautious builders now tend to dig or bore trial holes as a matter of course, whatever the history or geology of the ground. The normal practice is for the pits to be dug to a depth of 3m (close to, but not under, the foundations) in the presence of a structural engineer who takes a long gander at the ground conditions before the digger fills the holes back in. The engineer then decides whether the house foundations can proceed as normal or whether a more complicated foundation solution is needed.

Expect to pay an engineer between £200 and £500 for this service, though their fees will be much higher if special foundation designs are needed; a JCB for an hour should cost an additional £50-£100 (depending on travel time). Augured boreholes are another alternative – likely to cost around £300 each (and you'll need two) but a good option when access to JCBs is not possible or you have other problems like high water tables.

But there is also a natural tendency for the experts, having been called in, to suggest very expensive, fee-swelling, solutions when they may not be necessary. Jeremy Bulbrook built three houses in the Cambridgeshire Fenland town of March during 2001 and he ended up feeling badly let down by his professional advice: 'I had a couple of boreholes drilled on my architect's suggestion. The soil report that came back from these recommended a piled foundation, on the basis that the first two metres or so could possibly be made-up ground, even though it was gravel/sand.

'My building inspector asked why I hadn't spoken to them first. He said that they would have been happy with strip footings, but as a recommendation for piles had been made, they had no choice but to force me down the piled route.

'Now whilst I don't want the houses to fall down,' he adds, 'I do wonder if some of the engineers that produce these reports are too scared

to say that strip footings would be OK, because if it goes wrong in the future, then they have to bear some responsibility. After all, it doesn't cost an engineer a penny more to say he would recommend piled foundations. In fact he may earn more, if he gets to design the footings as well.

'If I was starting again, I would definitely talk to the building inspectors first. There's always the risk that when you dig you find something unexpected, but that could still happen even if you have boreholes drilled,' he said.

CONTAMINATED LAND

Where the problems with the site are caused by the natural characteristics of the land, the solutions are usually fairly straightforward, if expensive. However, if you are recycling building land — taking on something like an old garage or workshop — you may find yourself up against ground with a whole cocktail of nasties such as heavy metals, chemicals or methane. Now local authorities up and down the land are currently preparing registers of contaminated land and they will be empowered to issue Remediation Notices, which will require the landowner to make the site safe, which usually means either excavating and burying the pollutants elsewhere (the Foot and Mouth option) or encasing them in concrete or clay (the Chernobyl option).

Sometimes the solution may be relatively cheap – for instance

specifying sulphur-resistant cement – but it will be some time before housebuilders are able to accurately budget for contamination problems.

As with other land issues, potentially contaminated land is going to require investigation which likely means drilling boreholes. On my recycled site in Cambridge in 2016, I was charged £750 +VAT for the initial desk study and a further £2670 + VAT for the investigation (which involved drilling four holes) and the report. Interestingly, the remediation work, which involved removing the top 150mm of soil from the garden area, cost rather less than the investigations.

PLANNING ISSUES

Since they introduced the concept of planning permission in 1947, it's got progressively harder to obtain. Every government makes noises about reforming the planning system but that has invariably been code for introducing yet more controls. The current (2018) government has produced a 76-page England-only document, the National Planning Policy Framework, or NPPF, which revises an earlier (and shorter) version which attempted to simplify the whole process. The 2012 version didn't really succeed in this ambition and I doubt the new version will fare any better.

What NPPF does include is help for selfbuilders, albeit hidden away as an afterthought in paragraph

Chapter 3

61. Coupled with Right To Build legislation, selfbuild is at last on the planners' radar but the signs are that the rate of increased uptake will be pretty glacial. Even if selfbuilders do get some support from central government, they still have to grapple with all the other aspects of the planning jungle.

What people shouldn't expect is to be able to put any piece of land they fancy forward for planning permission and get a positive result, at least not in the short term. Just because you own a paddock next to your house doesn't mean you can build on it. If only...

Perhaps the biggest fear for would-be selfbuilders here is being unable to get planning permission at all. I've touched on this already and the advice must always be to only purchase land which already has planning permission granted. This leads to another issue: what if you don't much like what they have in place and want to change it?

Hmm. Good luck. But you may have a right planning battle on your hands here and you may have just started a fight with your would-be neighbours, because they may not see things quite the way that you do. Bear in mind that as a selfbuilder, you will one day be living side-by-side with these neighbours and most people instinctively want to get on well with them. So if you battle too hard and upset the locals, you may live to regret it in years to come. In any event, you may not be able to get your revised plans through the planning process.

HOW PLANNING WORKS

There will be more detail on this in the following chapter, but I wish here to point out that planning is a political matter and in order to win planning permission you have to convince some of your neighbours, most of the planning committee and also to get some support from the professional planners who inhabit the council offices. Planning is dealt with at a local level although there are national policies in place which provide guidance across the countries that make up the UK. You need to first work out what you want to build: you can do this yourself though it is usual and probably sensible to hire a professional to help you through this bit. You then put an application in to the council and then it whirrs its way slowly through the several steps needed to win (or be refused). If you want to bone up on this, search on the Planning Portal which covers England & Wales

Your application is posted online and neighbours are encouraged to look your plans over and to comment on them. This is often a fraught process. Neighbour objections carry weight with the council, so it often helps to discuss your plans with your neighbours before you put the application in.

PLANNING CONCERNS

Even if the neighbours love your plans, the professional planners themselves may not much like what you propose.

The planners are concerned with far more than whether a particular

plot can be zoned for building. Some of the major areas they are likely to look at will be:

■ size of the house: is it 'too big for the plot?'
■ site of the house: don't assume you can build anywhere on the plot
■ neighbours' privacy and right to light
■ style of the house: design and materials 'must be in keeping', or at least architecturally stimulating
■ if the site is in a Conservation Area or in the curtilage of a listed building, there will be loads more hoops you will have to jump through. It won't stop you building but it will make it more expensive and longer to achieve planning permission.
■ there will probably be a whole raft of planning conditions placed upon your approval, and these will also take time to resolve and cost money. You may have to look for contaminated ground, you may have to protect newts or bats, look for archaeology, or go to great lengths to build in a certain (expensive) style
■ vehicular access and turning heads: a particular problem on narrow fronted plots, less than 12m wide. The highways department insists that not only will adequate visibility splays be provided, but that there must be adequate room on site for cars to turn around or, as they say in planning speak, 'enter and leave in a forward gear.'
■ trees and hedges: often have to be retained or replanted.

TACTICS

It takes several months to get from

planning proposals to winning permission. If you get turned down, you can appeal or you can start all over again. Tactics are involved here, and each case has to be judged on its merits. They chances are that (if the site is zoned for building) you will be able to build something, but it may not meet with your expectations or budget.

BUILDING COSTS

One of the biggest pitfalls that lays in wait for the unsuspecting selfbuilder is knowing just how much it will cost to build a house. There are cost tables you can refer to but often they only give you a glimpse at what the actual costs might be. There are often ancillary costs which fall out of the normal run of build costs . Some plots require a great deal of money just to turn them into building plots. They may have access down a lane, or through someone else's garden, or they may involve having to remove some existing structure. The ground may need work to bring it up to scratch. Or, having completed the build there may be many thousands still to be spent to turn the site into a habitable home.

In truth, there are always hidden costs involved, even when you are just moving house. It can sometimes take years to organise and pay for all this stuff, but it does tend to get finished eventually. Just bear in mind that when you read case studies in magazines of selfbuilders costs, they often have a desire to make it look

like they spent less than they actually did because they don't want to look stupid.

RENOVATE OR REBUILD?

As virgin, greenfield building sites become more and more difficult to obtain, people are looking to purchase dilapidated dwellings to demolish and to build afresh. These are basically recycled building sites, sometimes referred to as brownfield sites.

Planning permission is usually much easier to obtain on a site with established residential usage and there are also usually considerable savings to be made because the service connections are already in place. A few sites will have problems with contaminated ground, but the requirements of today's foundations to go much deeper than was previously thought necessary mean that any existing foundations will be excavated and disposed of. In addition to buying a serviced plot, you have an existing structure from which you may be able to salvage some useful materials.

So far so good. The decision to demolish, however, is often not as clear-cut as this. For a start, few people care to sell their existing properties at building plot prices. To do so is to admit that your home is worthless which can be a bitter pill to swallow, even if it's true. In any event it's usually the case that the house is not worthless, it's just old and dilapidated and with a little bit of tender loving care and a whole lot of money it could continue to make

a very serviceable home. So problem number one is the extra expense of buying such a site.

Then you are faced with a decision: whether to knock down and start again or whether to work with what is already there. Now here things start to get complicated because the chances are that it is not a clear-cut issue: most renovation opportunities fall somewhere between the two extremes. Added to which it is a fiendishly difficult exercise to compare costs between the two approaches because this major decision has to be made at a pre-plan stage and you will have to work with ballpark figures. Whether the building is worth saving at all is an issue that only you (and the planners) can decide – each case has to be argued on its merits and there is little point making any broad generalisations here.

As a rule, new builds tend to be cheaper than conversions on a £ per metre square basis, but such crude comparators don't always make much sense as often conversions involve building extensions and other quasi-new build bits.

One factor working in new builds favour is the VAT treatment. New builds don't have to pay (much) VAT, whereas on renovations, conversions and extensions VAT is payable on the bulk of the work. More on the ins and outs of VAT in Chapter 5.

EXPERIMENTAL METHODS

One of the things I learned in talking to hundreds of selfbuilders, is best expressed in a saying. "Never underestimate how little they know but never overestimate their intelligence." This manifests itself in a number of ways but chiefly the symptoms exhibit in men (almost exclusively) who latch onto some new method which they believe will revolutionize the staid-old building industry and will be the best thing since sliced bread.

Take containers. There are lots of people that think using containers to make houses is a really neat idea. There are millions of them out there, they are dirt cheap and they are sort of shed sized. Why not put a simple roof on, stick some windows in and a door and, voila, you've just got a house for a few hundred quid. "I want to build using disused containers". Sure it can be done, but it turns out that once you've done drainage connections, got the services in, insulated it properly, added an external skin, worked out how to waterproof the windows, and then joined two together because one on its own is a bit pokey, you are well on the way to doubling your build costs.

The moral is that experimental build methods are always interesting but never cheap. And if you want builders to work with you on such ventures, expect to have to pay a big risk premium as well.

DESIGN ISSUES

What is it exactly you would like to build? Having hopefully got to grips with the money side of things, you have to decide what you want

to make. Do you want to build something fairly conventional, that fits in with the neighbourhood, or do you want to make a statement and do something radically different? How big do you want it? How high? What will the neighbours think of your plans? How hard do you want to make it for yourself?

Some people have a pretty good idea of what they want to build, whilst others start with a clean slate and are open to all sorts of ideas. One or two salient points are worth making here. If you have no background in architecture and design, the chances are that your knowledge will be limited and that you will be drawn to what you know and have seen in magazines and TV, or seen in friend's homes or in hotels and the like. You could end up with a home with lots of features but poor overall style, or no style at all.

One frequent mistake that people make is to opt for masses and masses of glazing, thinking this is a great way to bring the outside in and to get daylight everywhere. Get this wrong, and you can feel like you are living in an airport departure lounge. You can actually have too much daylight and end up getting baked on any sunny day worth it's salt. Getting the joinery and glazing right is one of the keys of good design and that's not a skill easily learned.

NEIGHBOURS

Your new home or extension ideally wants to sit easily with the neighbours. It is worth cultivating the neighbours a little to let them

know what you are trying to do and to understand their concerns. If your plans manage to piss everybody off big time, then you are more likely to face extra hurdles when it comes to building, especially if you require access through their property, or are even building close to it. Neighbours have the power to be quite obstructive and to this end there exists (in England & Wales only) a Party Wall Act which gives guidance on how neighbour building issues should be resolved. It's not straightforward, it can be expensive to implement and it can also be very time consuming. More on this in Chapter 4.

Sometimes neighbours will be irrationally opposed to your plans and no amount of polite approaches will make a blind bit of difference. You may have to build (and live) against a background of hostility that is unlikely to go away until one of you moves (or dies). But that's not really a selfbuild problem – it can happen almost anywhere over almost anything. It's just that building work makes it somehow more visceral, as though you are gaining something at their expense. If it's a nice view you are blocking, or invading their privacy by overlooking them, they may just have a point.

SKIMPING ON DESIGN

How much money to spend on the design stage? A very good question indeed. I have met selfbuilders who've been happy buying the services of designers for less than a thousand pounds, getting the plans "knocked off" in a weekend. Whereas a top notch architect may well cost as much as £50,000 to bring forward cutting-edge designs and incredibly detailed working drawings. Clearly, the service offered is not the same thing, and it behoves you to understand exactly what the difference is. The next chapter covers this in more detail. But just be aware that if you skimp too much on design fees, there are invariably other costs which appear elsewhere, as builder have to scratch their heads to work out how to solve unforeseen problems. And the overall value of the build is likely to be less because the design isn't very imaginative.

UNDER ESTIMATING

Wouldn't it be great if you estimated a price for your project (on the back of an envelope, naturally) and then you put the job out to tender and it came in on budget. Oh, and the builders then went ahead and did everything really well, finished on time and didn't charge a penny in extras.

Yes, of course it would.

But do you really expect that to happen?

No, of course you don't.

Instead you mug up on build costs, looking at tables which suggest you can build a house for £2,000/m². You think that's a lot, even though you are not sure what "/m²" actually means, or how you measure it, let alone what it includes and doesn't include. You'll

HOW TO TREBLE YOUR COSTS			
	Basic	Tricky Site	Luxury
Professionals	£11,000	£25,000	£70,000
Prelims	£13,000	£26,000	£20,000
Project Management	£12,000	£30,000	£40,000
Groundworks, Drains, Services	£35,000	£50,000	£50,000
Internal Structure	£21,000	£25,000	£50,000
External Cladding	£14,000	£18,000	£40,000
Insulation	£5,000	£5,000	£20,000
Joinery	£13,000	£13,000	£50,000
Roof Cover, Rainwater	£11,000	£11,000	£30,000
Plumbing & Heating	£7,000	£7,000	£15,000
Electrics	£9,000	£9,000	£30,000
Finishes	£58,000	£58,000	£80,000
Kitchen	£13,000	£13,000	£40,000
Bathrooms	£9,000	£9,000	£20,000
Garage	£0	£0	£20,000
Garden/Landscaping	£0	£5,000	£40,000
Renewable Heat & PV	£0	£0	£20,000
Rounded Totals	**£230,000**	**£304,000**	**£635,000**
Internal Floor Area	160 m²		
Cost per m²	**£1,400**	**£1,900**	**£4,000**

The above table looks at three variations on the same house, our model house of four-bedrooms, 160m² floor area. The Basic column repeats the costs incurred in the Model House Costs table in Ch 1. You can, if your are lucky, build for less than this, but you can also build for much more. The middle column, Tricky Site, looks at what can go wrong with a development budget just through difficulties encountered on site. And the last column, Luxury, indicates the amount you could easily spend if you wanted to upscale. This would probably be a contemporary style, architect-designed home with lots of interesting materials and lots of glazing.

find examples of perfectly nice houses that appear to cost rather less than this, some even below £1,000/m², and you'll start wondering just what a variety of outcomes there are, as you will also note that some people build at over £5,000/m².

You can see where this is heading. Whilst the likes of Barratt and Persimmon manage to build their 120m² four bedroomed homes for £200,000, you visit one of their show homes and figure out that the fourth

bedroom is the size of a tea towel and that your cat would quickly die as she hit all four walls if you tried to swing her in it. And that anyway, you don't want a house that is the same as 60 others on the same estate.

Turns out most selfbuilders want 160m² (our model house) or very often 200m² (comfortable five bedroom jobbie). And if they want a half decent kitchen, underfloor heating, timber floors, glass balustrades and a big glass sliding door at the end of the living room, then lo and behold suddenly £2,500/m² begins to look light.

And then the tenders start coming in and, bugger me, if the builders don't want to make a profit as well. Whilst you want to hold them to a timetable and a guarantee that if anything goes wrong, they will stump up, the builders want to charge for the risk this involves.

All of a sudden, you are looking at quotes of £750,000 for this fancy new house.

And you'd thought that maybe £400,000 would have done it?

But you already have the plot. There is no escape. You have to rethink. Cut down the size of the house? Maybe, but you've already got planning. Cut back on the materials used? Possibly, but now you've set your heart on it, it could turn out to be a huge disappointment if you make just like a Persimmon. How about throw the builders by the wayside and take on the project management yourself? It should in theory save you money, but you are committing your self to maybe 1,000 hours work (which you may not have time to do) and you don't know shit from a tree when it comes to building, so you risk making some horrendous cock-ups or at least paying over the odds for tradesmen and materials.

Finally, get a caravan, live on site and undertake as much of the work as possible. Fine if you know your way around a building site and are very practical sort, plus you have a few years to complete this edifice.

But life in a caravan is no holiday, especially during the British winter where mud will be your constant companion. You might as well get a job as an extra in a remake of Blackadder Goes To War.

Any mitigation strategies? By all means read build cost tables, but treat them with a pinch of salt. Note what I've already said about the difference between build costs and development costs – there are lots of costs which are real enough but which aren't normally thought of as build costs.

Whilst not skimping on the basics, don't be obsessed with fitting all the latest gear. Don't be greedy about size – most selfbuilders build too much house for what they actually need, and often it gets wasted in needless circulation space. Which is a fancy way of saying don't skimp on good design. It may seem that design costs a lot, but if it gets you a better house for less footprint it's actually a bargain.

And don't go into this without a sizeable contingency. There are always unforeseen expenses.

LACK OF HELP

If you do decide to take on work, either management or hands on skills, get some guidance. Don't wallow about learning it all from You Tube. There are good architects and surveyors out there and some highly talented builders who you can lean on (OK pay) to keep you sane. It really helps to have a friend who knows the ins and outs of the trade.

CRAP BUILDERS

Another all too common problem is getting into bed with builders who are useless, or who try to rip you off. Or go bust. They are all mini-nightmares and such things are unfortunately all too common.

How do you guard against this? Whilst there are no 100% fool-proof ways, there are some well-worn routines for sorting the wheat from the chaff.

One is to employ an architect to oversee the whole process and to let the job to a builder with a watertight contract. Usually works, but it's expensive, although it is still significantly cheaper than hiring a complete bozo.

If you want to do it on a DIY project management basis, you must undertake the due diligence stage yourself and check out who can deliver and who can't.

But things happen to builders over time. The world doesn't neatly divide into good guys and cowboys. Sometimes builders get stressed by life events, they get ill or they get divorced. And sometimes good builders get brought to their knees by cowboy clients who won't pay on the slightest excuse. Or can't pay because they have underestimated just how expensive the whole job is.

Often there are two sides to these sorry stories and one thing you can do to minimise risk is to be a good client. More on this in Ch. 5.

COCK UPS

Every now and then, a builder makes an almighty cock-up and lots of work has to be redone. It's not always obvious that it's a cock-up until much later in the build programme, and that makes it even more expensive to rectify.

Examples? You might miss out a steel and the building starts to sag. Or maybe the drains didn't get tested on installation and you find they leak after completion. You might set the building out at the wrong level and the finished roof ends up being much higher than the planning permission demanded. A neighbour complains and you have a mighty battle on your hands.

What the hell do you do then? It rather depends on the nature of the building contract you have in place. If the builder is responsible, then the builder has to pay for the rectification. Only for many small builders, they simply don't have the wherewithal to rebuild half a house at nil cost, so they declare bankruptcy. Hmm.

If you are project managing your own build, there is no one to pin the blame on other than yourself. This sort of situation is perhaps the very worst thing that can happen on a selfbuild, short of maiming yourself in an accident.

These things do happen, and they are not an insurable risk, but they are fortunately rare. The best way of avoiding such events is to make sure you use professional help whenever you are working beyond your skill set. Anyone can set out a house, or an extension, but anyone can get in wrong as well. Make sure key stages like this are thoroughly checked before a tool is lifted in anger.

CLOSING THOUGHTS

Finally, let's touch on what you get out of all this. No one doubts that undertaking major building work is a huge hassle. Just how huge depends on how you do it and what you decide to do, but it's invariably going to take over a big part of your life.

The question is, is it worth it? There is no guarantee that the finished product will be worth more than what you have paid in cash. Let alone effort. There is no guarantee that you will actually like it as much as you had hoped. There is no guarantee that you will even feel a sense of achievement. You are just as likely to feel knackered and broke.

If your relationship was dodgy beforehand, it is likely to be well dodgy long before you finish, and indeed it may not even survive. Making tons of quick-fire decisions without either of your really knowing what it is you are deciding on is a sure-fire way to stir up trouble and to expose relationship cracks. Especially when there is loads of money riding on it. Remember you are not just making a house, you are hoping to turn it into a home and you also really want it to be a happy home. Throwing money at a building project won't save a troubled relationship, it will blow it apart.

So why do so many people undertake all these spectacular projects? Why don't we all just stay in bed and look at holiday deals on the internet?

The answer is of course that people love a challenge and making something hopefully beautiful AND valuable is probably one of the most exciting things we can do. In comparison, getting a promotion or going somewhere exotic for three weeks looks a little trifling. The fact that it's a bit risky just adds to the mystique of it all. We love beautiful houses and beautiful gardens – National Trust properties are seemingly always packed out, at least when I venture anywhere near them. Wouldn't it be great if we could add a little to the built environment in a positive way, and to build something that truly reflects our aspirations? Instead of moving into a second-hand home or a developer's idea of what we might want, here is our chance to make something that we do actually want, to make our mark on the sod, and to leave something behind more substantial than a gravestone. Perhaps our little bit of immortality.

DESIGN

HOUSE DESIGN is the trickiest issue faced by every potential builder. The central point that shouldn't be forgotten is that you want to build the best possible house for a price you can afford. Easily written, but how the hell do you do it? What is the 'best possible' house? And how do you go about designing it?

Questions abound. Is an architect necessarily an expensive option? What about using a designer who is not a qualified architect? Isn't it cheaper to use a package build design? Won't the planners force me to redesign the whole thing in any event? Where do you start?

PLANNING CONSULTANTS

One aspect to look at is deciding what you can actually get on the plot of land you are assessing. What exactly can the planning process deliver? It's not always easy to get to grips with this and knowing the ins and outs of the local planning scene can make a big difference. You might, for instance, be able to squeeze a second house on the plot? Or maybe get a bigger one than seems obvious. If there is a question mark over what you can or maybe want to build, then first consider hiring a planning consultant rather than an architect or designer.

They can come later.

Planning consultants make their living from maximising the gain from land and they tend to be better at it than those who make a living designing homes. The downside of using a planning consultant is that you can very easily get drawn into a prolonged planning battle which may stretch on for years. If you get too greedy, you are also almost inevitably going to piss off most of your neighbours and that may not be a price you want to pay, especially if you dream of living side by side with them in years to come. You will be viewed as a property developer (hiss, hiss) rather than a cuddly, heroic selfbuilder. Nevertheless, a professional planning consultant can sometimes be worth their weight in gold if they manage to unlock value in a parcel of land that wasn't obvious at the outset.

DESIGN PROCESS

It is conventional to subdivide the design process into a number of parts; some fixed points with known costs and others elastic in the extreme. Below is a list of the stages that you need to go through. You don't have to do it in this order (you could for instance apply for building regulations approval before you have planning permission) but it would be frankly very strange not to do it this way.

- site survey and feasibility study
- design process, leading to sketches of options
- commission drawings for planning permission
- submit plans for planning permission (fee)
- try and negotiate positive planning outcome
- do this over and over again till outcome *is* positive
- detailed designs and specifications
- submit detailed designs for building regulations approval (fee)

SITE SURVEY

Unless you are very confident of your surveying and drafting abilities, you should have a specialist (search Topographic Surveys) carry out an accurate site survey to measure and plot all the existing buildings, boundaries, levels, access arrangements, trees, drains, neighbouring buildings and any other information thought to be relevant. On simple sites this will cost around £500 + VAT, but expect to pay double this on large or complex sites. Bear in mind that there are sites where you have to undertake a fair amount of clearance work and/or demolition before you can even undertake a site survey. A site survey forms the basis for a set of accurate plans: without it, you risk building in the wrong place or at the wrong height.

FEASIBILITY STUDY/SKETCHES

Assuming you have a plot and a budget, the most important questions are: what can you build on it and how much will it cost? It may seem very early in the whole mysterious design process but you have already reached crunch point: this is the key moment when you start to commission the building and at this point your decisions will have costly implications down the line. I have distinguished between a stage called feasibility study and another called sketches of options. This is helpful in understanding how one grows out of the other but in reality there is no hard and fast dividing line between them and how you and your designer get from an empty page to a full planning application is a very individual thing.

Nevertheless, there tends to be a clear path, which leads from the site survey stage into a feasibility stage (which, if you like, is about

Architects often build models to help clients and planners visualise the house. This one is the Denby Dale Passivhaus, written up in the 9th edition of the Bible

eliminating impractical options) into outlining practical solutions and, from there, plumping for your best choice,

Can you do it yourself? I've met some plucky souls, without any training or experience, who've done just this, but it's hard to do it well first time and their resultant buildings are almost always very unimaginative. You can use books of house plans for inspiration (despite the fact that they're mostly anything but), but do not expect to fit an existing plan on to your plot; the chances of it working without amendment are small and amending existing plans can be as expensive as starting from scratch. My advice is to work with someone who knows what they are doing and has a track record of getting planning permissions for homes similar to what you would like to build.

A professional at £75 per hour upwards may seem a luxury, but they will (or at least should) understand the issues and concentrate your thinking on the relevant areas. There may or may not be any consultation with local planners at this stage, depending on how confident you or your agent feels. You may be able to get informal advice from the duty planning officer at your local council, but this is likely to be very basic. If you want a more considered response to your proposals without going through the trauma of a full planning application, then consider getting 'pre-application advice' where planning officers will spend some time considering your plans and charge for the process. Current fees

are £100 for written opinions or £200 if you want to have a face-to-face meeting.

The cost of this stage is naturally very open-ended. For many independent designers and architects, the early part of the process is the most challenging and the most interesting and they would anticipate spending around a third of their time on this stage. The biggest variable is you, the client. The more sussed out you are, the better your brief, and the shorter and cheaper this process will be.

Even if you are planning to build a kit house or use an off-the-shelf design, it is still worthwhile getting a professional designer to undertake some sort of study if only to sort out practicalities like drain runs, though note that many package suppliers have their own in house designers who will undertake this work, often included within the overall price.

PLANNING DRAWINGS

A good designer with a thorough working knowledge of local practices and trends will be able to help you marry your ideas with the views of the planners, hopefully pre-empting any potential areas of conflict. Planning departments are surprisingly diverse in their ideas, often reflecting the individual tastes of the chief planning officer, and knowing the whys and wherefores of local planning decisions is one way in which local knowledge scores heavily over nationwide services. Whoever you choose, they will have to produce a set of planning permission drawings

to present to the local planning department. Budget anything from £500 for pre-drawn plans through to £20,000 for architect one-offs. This may look like an extraordinary chasm cost-wise, but bear in mind it almost invariably reflects the amount of time taken. If your site is challenging, maybe with close neighbours to look out for, maybe in a Conservation Area, that sort of thing, and you want to look at a range of options, then the amount of time spent in the early stages will quickly escalate. If you want or need to hire someone for three months to look at many options, then expect it to cost tens of thousands.

For a detailed look at the mechanics of applying for planning permission, and the likely fees, search on Planning Permission adding the name of your local council, who oversee the process. There are a number of plans and drawings that the planners require and your chosen designer/agent should know this rigmarole backwards – indeed if they don't I would tend to be rather suspicious.

WORKING DETAILS

If designing from scratch, it is conventional not to decide on all the construction details until planning constraints are established. This is simply to avoid having to do things twice. However, construction details on conventional houses are remarkably similar and often the details can be lifted from previous jobs. On simple projects, the plans, construction details and specification (known as the spec with a hard or soft 'c' – the choice is yours) can all be contained on two sheets of A1 (840 x 592 mm) plans which would detail:

- floor plans
- foundation plan
- drainage plan
- first floor joist layout
- roof truss/rafter layout
- N,E,S and W elevations (or eye-level views)
- section or sections through the middle of the house, showing room heights, floor levels, wall constructions, joist depths, staircase dimensions
- window and door schedule (list of joinery manufacturers' codes)
- text explaining construction standards (lots of B.S. numbers here).

On more complicated jobs, there may be extra plans perhaps running to many pages, showing various complicated details like eaves or dormer windows. Up-market jobs tend to have the specification written separately from the drawings and a serious architectural practice may write a specification running to fifty pages or more. How much of this is necessary depends on a) the complexity of the work and b) the attitude of the client. Rookie builders would be well advised not to attempt anything too unusual first time around, in which case the standard two-sheet plans are probably adequate. Many experienced subcontractors never look at plans in any event – quite a few can't read – and complex plans could be wasted on many.

I know of a number of small builders who basically dispense with the working drawings stage. They work from little more than the planning drawings which can be littered with notes like 'To be confirmed on site' or 'To Building Inspector's Satisfaction'; they are on site every day and they prefer to work out these details as they go along. Once you've done it a few times, it works fine provided you stick to fairly standard solutions (they do). But if you are new to this game and/or you can't be there on site a good deal, then you would do well not to skimp on working drawings as these form, in effect, your detailed instructions to your builder.

Much of this detailed work and, in particular, the writing of the specification, forms the very heart of any forthcoming building contract. If you want an element of protection from the perils of badly executed building work, then a professionally written specification is worth far more than any off-the-peg contract you might be tempted to sign.

The cost of producing working drawings for a one-off design may be as little as a couple of thousand pounds if it all sticks to tried and tested solutions, However, this part of the design work can also cost ten times as much for unusual houses, as unusual features take time to design, not to mention build. Here you might expect workshop joinery, arched openings, fancy staircases, patterned brickwork. Generally expensive features are also expensive to design.

If you are building to a tight budget and are happy with conventional solutions, then make it clear that you do not want unusual detailing and, as a result, a) your working details should not cost too much, b) your house isn't likely to be expensive to build and c) it is less likely to run over budget but d) it won't win any awards.

The danger in trying to put a price to all this is that you may lose sight of the fact that, as with so many things in life, you get what you pay for; if someone knocks up a set of plans for you over a couple of weekends for a few hundred quid, the chances are that your finished house will reflect the fact. On the other hand, if you are interested in creating a wonderful one-off home, you'd be daft to skimp on the design stages.

If you want to save money, you'd probably do better to build a smaller house. There is a real conundrum in here. People don't want to be ripped off by some fancy-dan architect charging the earth. But bear in mind that the average architect earns less than the average plumber and that what you are hiring from them is their time. A good architect can often justify the fees because they actually add value to the finished product. If an architect or designer can do the business, then the thousands of pounds they charge is money well spent.

STRUCTURAL ENGINEER
Having been called in during the ground investigation stage, if the designs take on any non-standard features, the structural engineer may have to make another appearance. All

beams, lintels, roofs and foundations (the so-called structural elements) of a building require proof that they are sufficient to do the job asked of them. Standard solutions to standard problems are regarded as tried and tested, but anything out of the ordinary will require 'proving' to the satisfaction of the building inspector. A structural engineer will calculate the forces applied to beams or foundations and come up with adequate solutions. If the ground you plan to build on is at all dodgy, then an engineer will be required to prove your foundation design; also many very ordinary situations like using steel beams or opening up a loft space require structural proving.

Detailed drawings and structural calculations (if needed) are presented to the local council's building control department for examination.

SUB-DESIGNS

Design and specification of finishes is often left to the client or builder to sort out and this is more often than not passed down the line to the tradesmen involved on the job. Therefore, the plumber designs the central heating system, the electrician designs the lighting, a kitchen specialist will take over design of the kitchen. This sort of arrangement obviously works, as it is what happens in 90% of homes built, but arguably it could be much better co-ordinated by a single designer.

On large commercial contracts specialist professionals who draw up a specification and then arrange quotes from it deal with all these areas separately. One-off housing is really too small to justify the expense of all these extra professionals and much of the work, designed and installed by the various tradesmen, is consequently very unimaginative. The degree of competence varies enormously: many act as much as salesmen as designers and most make no charge provided you buy their product, which is all very well but it makes you very vulnerable to uncompetitive practices.

It's really a very difficult area to negotiate, even for hard-bitten professionals. Many architects are not qualified to give advice on, say, lighting design or interior decorating. If you are happy with tried and tested solutions to problems then you will be well advised to keep it simple and deal directly with your chosen contractor; if, however, you want to explore the many and varied options open to you, then you could do worse than read the rest of this book...

IN CONCLUSION

Design and professional expenses are the hardest areas to budget, because they are so variable. To a large extent they are dependent on the brief that you, as a client, present to the designers. An off-the-peg house plan can be purchased for a few hundred pounds but will very probably require a great deal of alteration to fit both the site and your ideas. In contrast, an architect will probably charge between 3% and 5% of the overall build costs just for the planning drawings for a house. It does not follow that the off-the-peg plans are necessarily better value.

PLANNING PERMISSION

Planning permission and building regulations are two big hurdles that every would-be housebuilder will have to jump. They are complex and not easily mastered, and many building professionals have bald patches on their heads where they have torn their hair out from negotiating paths through or around the maze of regulations and precedents that govern our construction activities. For a rookie builder this can all seem rather daunting, especially when you're not even clear what the difference is between planning permission and building regulations – or *regs* as they are known in the trade, as in 'God, there's been another bloody change in the regs.' The regs are dealt with later in this chapter – first planning permission.

WHAT EXACTLY IS IT?

Various Acts of Parliament (notably the Town and Country Planning Acts) require that local authorities should control what can be built where, and how buildings (and land) should or should not be used. Planning permission is not concerned with how you build – that's the building regs – nor with who owns the land on which you wish to build. There are many small construction projects that do not require planning permission but something of the size of a new house invariably does.

The power-that-bees in this respect is your local council. Not your County or Metropolitan Council, but your District or City council. In Scotland and N Ireland the system works slightly differently, as it does in National Parks, but then they wouldn't want to make it too straightforward, would they? It gets worse. Officially, the licence to build is granted by the elected councillors, but every council has a full-time planning department staffed by planning officers, and these are the people who actually deal with planning applications. Indeed, the chief planning officer has powers to make certain decisions off his or her own bat. Even when they choose not to exercise these powers they make 'recommendations' to the committee of councillors as to whether an application should be accepted or refused. The planning committee rarely goes against the recommendations of its planning officers.

FOREPLAY

You don't have to have any contact with the planners before submitting your application, but it is commonplace to do so. Tactics are involved here and there is no such thing as a correct way of going about it – every case stands on its own. On the one hand, you don't want to be faced with the expense of drawing up plans only for the planners to fall about laughing at the very thought that anyone could build on that piece of land; on the other hand, if you wander into the planning department with questions like 'What sort of house could I build on this spot?'

then you are inviting the planners to design the house for you. This they won't do, but what will happen is that they will get in their minds all kinds of constraints that will severely limit your options: 'You must do...' and 'You can't have...' Like our legal system and our parliament, our planning system is adversarial; you may not get exactly what you want out of it – most planning decisions are the result of compromise – but you stand a far better chance of getting more of what you want if you choose the battleground on which to fight; i.e. submit plans with minimal reference to the planners. Getting the planners too closely involved before submitting your application can be seen as ceding this battleground.

In the past few years, planning departments have been under cost constraints and are under pressure to maximise income. One clever ruse they have come up with is charging for pre-application advice, a service they were once happy to dispense for free. There is no compulsion to take such advice and it may be that your planning application is not terribly controversial and that the planners will be delighted with your ideas.

But there is every chance they won't be, and that pre-application advice is often worth paying for.

CONSERVATION OFFICERS

There is a whole extra raft of planning you may have to submit to if you are building in a conservation area, or close to a listed building. Here you will come under the auspices of the local council's

conservation department who are a law unto themselves as to what they like and dislike. You can usually guess at where they will be heading: they don't like plastic windows or satellite dishes or anything in fact which smacks of being common. They do like lots of natural materials and well designed finishes. Even if you have employed a very fancy architect, and are prepared to pay good money to sail through the conservation hoops, you can still expect to take about twice as long to get a planning permission because the conservation department is always overworked and way behind schedule. Be patient.

SUBMITTING AN APPLICATION

The mechanics of submitting an application are straightforward but time consuming. The application consists of a number of forms that you have to fill out, together with your plans and your payment. It is now routinely done online. You will require (for something as complex as a new house):
▪ location plan (taken off OS map at a scale of 1:1250)
▪ existing site plan (boundaries outlined in red) at 1:500
▪ proposed site plan – showing position of house, garage, driveway, access
▪ layout plans and elevations of any existing structures on site
▪ layout plans and elevations of proposed dwelling at 1:100 or 1:50
▪ details of materials to be used
▪ details of trees to be felled.
▪ Design & Access statement
In addition to these, it often helps

Chapter 4

Some Planning Terms Explained

1 OUTLINE

Often used by landowners who are trying to find out whether development would be acceptable in principle without going through the hassle of having detailed plans drawn up. Outline permission to build is what turns a garden or a field into a building plot; getting it makes you seriously rich but it doesn't, on its own, allow you to build. Outline permission lasts for five years, but a detailed application must be agreed within three years or else the permission lapses.

2 FULL APPLICATION

As its name suggests, a full planning application seeks to approve both the principle and the details of development. It lasts for three years. However, it usually comes with numerous conditions attached which each have to be agreed on before you can complete the building.

3 APPROVAL OF RESERVED MATTERS

This is used to convert outline permission to detailed. There are often matters which are flagged up with an outline permission which have to be dealt with when the full permission is granted.

4 RENEWAL

Planning permission can be renewed, but only if consent has not expired so this route is used to get an extension to an existing permission. If the permission has lapsed, then a new application has to be made.

5 RELAXATION

If you have one too many troublesome conditions, you can apply to have them removed at a later date. Don't hold out too much hope.

6 AMENDMENTS

If you purchase a plot with detailed permission for a house that you don't actually want to build, you may be able to amend the plans without submitting a whole new application. There is a small charge for amendments but if your changes are substantial the planners may not accept them and you'll be back to square one.

7 EXTENSIONS / CONVERSIONS

If your building project involves work to an existing structure, you may not need planning permission. Phone your local council's planning department and ask their advice. Or check the government website www.planningportal.gov.uk for planning in England & Wales. Scotland and N. Ireland have their own sites.

---

to have three-dimensional bird's-eye view drawings (isometric projections), which show how the house fits with its neighbours. Planning officers and committee members like a nice drawing, just like the rest of us, and apocryphal evidence suggests that they are likely to be better disposed towards a well presented application. Some people even go to the trouble of building scale models. This is probably over the top for routine applications but if there are close neighbours who will be affected by the new buildings, it does help to have a contextual drawing or two so they can see just how the development sits in relation to what is already there.

In England and Wales, the Planning Portal website is the place to go for the lowdown (search on Planning Portal). I don't know what happens in Scotland and N Ireland, but planning applications are seemingly headed into the online world.

OWNERSHIP CERTIFICATE

You also have to fill out a form stating ownership of the land in question. You don't actually have to own land in order to apply for planning permission over it but you are required to notify the owner of your intentions.

FEES

Outline fees in England in 2019 are £462 for each 0.1 hectare (or 1,000m² which is a small plot) of site area applied for. Detailed permission for one dwelling is also £462 and if you apply for outline and then move on to a detailed application it will cost you twice £462; interestingly, when I first published this book in 1995, the fee was £160, so it has nearly trebled in 24 years. The only way to avoid this double fee is to go straight for detailed permission, which involves more costly drawings: in some situations this is a risk worth taking but if the application is likely to be controversial, just go for the outline. The current fees are set nationally and can be viewed online at the Planning Portal.

CHANCES OF SUCCESS

After submitting your application, the planners then go to work on assessing it. These days they all seem to work in teams, and this makes it even harder to get any sense out of them as to how they think the application is progressing. They are meant to take eight weeks to reach a determination, but in practice it depends on how busy they are – it can all take much longer. This in turn has led to pressure from central government and targets have been set to turn round planning applications more quickly; all that has happened is that applications are more likely to be rejected. As recently as 2002, only one in five applications were rejected; today it appears to be around one in three. Which only makes your task ever more daunting. Don't despair.

Keep ringing them to find out what's happening to your application; sooner or later they will reach some sort of provisional verdict and this is the point at which negotiations start. If they are completely hostile, then you may do better to withdraw the application and start anew; if they express some reservations (they usually

do), then you must be prepared to compromise hard. Eventually, the planning officials will either grant planning permission (unlikely on a new house) or refer it to the planning committee of the local council who, typically, meet once a month. This referral will come with a recommendation either way, which the committee habitually accepts.

CONDITIONS

Planning permission is now usually granted with conditions attached; if you are Sainsburys wanting to build a supermarket, these conditions may be something big, but for a one-off housebuilder they are not likely to be terribly onerous though in some parts of England additional money is being asked for 'planning gain' – this can run to several thousand pounds.

At time of writing in 2019, central government has instructed local councils not to charge selfbuilders any planning gain fees but this has become a hotly disputed political topic and it could change during the next parliament.

However, the conditions they attach to a successful planning application seem to be growing ever more taxing and they now charge £34 to discharge each condition and they can take eight weeks or more to decide on whether your conditions pass muster. My latest build included conditions about garden fencing design and methods of securing bikes, not to mention the more usual bricks, joinery and roofing. Fortunately, I wasn't hit with any payments for planning gain.

REASONS FOR REFUSAL

There can be any number of reasons why planners take a negative view of your proposals. In rural districts the land is zoned (via the 'local plans', which you can inspect at your library or online), and if you are applying to build in a non-building zone then you've got your work cut out trying to get anywhere. Assuming they accept that the site is suitable for development, here are several reasons why they may still not play ball:
- lack of adequate parking
- can't turn a car around on the hard standing
- overlooking neighbours
- roof too high
- house too big for plot
- not enough garden
- development out of keeping with neighbourhood
- wrong position on the plot
- don't like your choice of materials or overall design.

I could go on. Suffice it to say that many of these reasons are perfectly justifiable and if you weren't so greedy and pig-headed you would be able to see the sense in them. But applicants are apt to feel aggrieved whenever the outcome goes against them.

LOBBYING

You don't have to take the views of the planning officials lying down. Many people have taken to lobbying their councillors to overrule the recommendation for refusal. This is real grass roots politics and in many parts of the world sums of money would change hands in order to get planning permissions through on the nod, but in Britain, of course, we don't do that. I don't wish to sound too sarcastic because, by and large, this is true – people tend not to go into local politics for money, but they do have a tendency towards self-importance and many are not averse to a little bit of flattery. This is the network at work: it all depends on personalities and who you do or do not know.

Even if you don't get very far with councillors, you should at least consider lobbying your neighbours. A couple of letters from neighbours saying positive things about your plans is worth a lot at a planning committee meeting. However, there is every chance that your neighbours may not feel as enthusiastic about your plans as you do and this tactic can backfire. In order to increase your chances with neighbour support, it does of course help to have made contact with the said neighbours and shown them your plans. I went so far as to hold an open day in the old warehouse I wanted to demolish to make way for our home, and had a model on display to show the neighbours what we intended to do, and why. It may have helped, although we still garnered objections.

APPEAL v NEW APPLICATION

If you shoot your bolt and, despite all your lobbying, your application is refused you are faced with three choices:
- give up
- submit a new application
- appeal.

The first is the cheapest but it doesn't get you very far. If you want to persist,

then there is no reason why you can't go to appeal on your first application whilst simultaneously submitting a new one. Surprisingly, there is no charge for making an appeal but it does take time, around six months, and many people can't wait that long, especially if there's borrowed money riding on it. Appeals are presided over by an independent inspector, often a QC, sometimes an architect, and on small projects like individual housebuilding the usual way of going about it is to produce written evidence. Basically, you must write your side of the story and explain to the inspector why you think you should have been granted planning permission in the first place. On the due date the inspector will visit the site and shortly afterwards they will make their ruling known. That's it. There are alternative methods of appeal, notably using the informal hearing method, which gathers all the interested parties together to discuss the issue at hand, but the written representation is the simplest and least time-consuming (as well as cheapest, if you are paying a professional to act for you).

Only one in three appeals succeed and from my limited experience it is difficult to predict the outcome in advance, so you are taking a big gamble in going to appeal. You can hire a professional to make the appeal for you, but this will be expensive and may not add to your chances. As there is no further drawing work to be undertaken – you can't amend your plans between first refusal and appeal – the appeal process can easily be

undertaken by any lay person capable of using pen and paper, although a thorough understanding of planning issues will obviously stand you in good stead.

For many people, it will be cheaper and much quicker to submit a new planning application. When an application is refused, the planners have to state grounds for refusal. In an ideal world these issues could have been sorted out before the application ever came before the committee, but sometimes it takes a refusal to actually bring the problems out into the open. Armed with refusal reasons, you can make suitable amendments in your next application and, provided you can genuinely sort out the issues, you should have a much better chance of gaining planning permission, although the outcome is likely to be some way from your original ideas.

Changes to the planning system are always being mooted but all that ever seems to happen on the ground is that the whole process becomes ever more troublesome and time consuming.

BUILDING REGULATIONS

As mentioned at the beginning of the previous section, the building regs are a different matter altogether from planning permission. As with planning permission, there are a number of small works that are exempted from having building regulations applied to them, but again a project as large as a house will invariably fall inside building control. Once again, the online Planning Portal is the place to go for up-to-date information about building control.

Each local council has a building control department that employs building inspectors, who both assess plans submitted to them and visit sites to ensure that the plans are actually put into practice. The plans submitted to building control are more detailed than those used for gaining planning permission and so this work is usually commissioned as an additional service after a successful planning application.

Alternatively, you are now able to use a private building inspector to oversee your job and to negotiate a fee directly with them

It is worth noting, however, that much of the detail needed to satisfy building regulations is to do with written specifications rather than drawings and that much of this is standard to all housing. Phrases peppered with BS numbers and sentences finishing with 'to the satisfaction of the building inspector' are commonly placed in specifications precisely to meet the regs. Furthermore, what is often the most important part of an inspector's job, checking that the foundations are adequate, can really only be done on site.

Getting approval for building regulations is not a political matter and there are no committees to go before or councillors to lobby. You just have to reach agreement with

your appointed building inspector – which, by and large, means doing as he (occasionally she) says. If you stick to conventional methods of construction this is generally not too difficult. However, expect problems if you are inclined to unusual techniques.

The building regulations actually consist of a number of separate booklets known as Approved Documents, generally referred to as Parts. Each part is given a letter and currently the English & Welsh versions of these run from Part A (which deals with Structure) to Part R (Broadband). You can also download all the parts for free from the Planning Portal website. Building regulations are a devolved matter, so Scotland, Wales and Northern Ireland have their own building regulations, which are very similar but employ different labelling systems.

The building regs are technical publications and most builders have never clapped eyes on them; instead they rely on their designer to have satisfied the regs in the drawings and their building inspector to put them straight if the situation on site requires it.

The building regs are always getting tightened and their scope is forever being increased. What started life as a motley collection of bye-laws, which attempted to eliminate jerry-building practices in Victorian times has grown into a sophisticated instrument of social engineering, most obviously in the introduction of disabled access regulations in 1999.

BUILDING CONTROL FEES

Local authority fees are no longer set nationally. However the fees for new houses tend to cluster around the £700 mark. My local authority charges £180 + VAT for plan approval and an additional £387 + VAT for site inspections on new houses up to 300m^2 internal floor area. With smaller works like extensions, the fees are correspondingly less. VAT is charged on building control fees for new dwellings (unlike planning application fees) and is generally not reclaimable.

Note that warranties for newbuild homes are also administered by building inspectors, but serve a rather different function. More on warranties in Ch. 5.

PARTY WALL ACT

There is more to the red tape than just planning permission and building regulations. If you are lucky these two will be the only bits you encounter but there are other things to consider as well. Close to a neighbour? Within six metres? You may have to treat with The Party Wall Act, which has been in effect in 1996 throughout England and Wales – prior to that it was restricted to London. The idea behind this piece of legislation is to protect the neighbouring properties from damage when your construction work is carried out. The Act is very specific about just where and when it comes into effect.

Chapter 4

If your foundations are to be deeper than your neighbour's, you must observe the Party Wall Act provisions if you are within three metres of those buildings – note not boundary, but buildings. In addition to this, there is a provision which states that if you are building much deeper than the neighbouring house's foundations, then you may still be affected by the provisions of the Act at a distance of six metres. You draw a line at 45° down from the bottom of your neighbour's foundations and if it strikes your projected foundation works within six metres, then Ka Boom – you are in the net. It's likely to be pointed out to you when you put a full planning application in.

If the Party Wall Act does come into effect – and in many urban areas it is likely to – you are obliged to notify your neighbour and to assuage their concerns that your building work may damage their property. Often this can be done with an informal exchange of letters but, if the neighbour is worried about what you are up to, then he or she is entitled to hire, at your expense, a qualified structural engineer or surveyor to verify your plans. A Party Wall Surveyor starts at around £500 and this figure will rise if the work gets very complicated.

You must state whether you propose to strengthen or safeguard the foundations of the building or structure belonging to the adjoining owner. Such aspects need to be considered at the design stage of the project to avoid unexpected costs arising. This can, naturally, become a

long and involved process, as the two surveyors have to reach agreement about just how the work should be undertaken. Your neighbour cannot prevent you undertaking this work but they can delay you. If the next door building is split into flats, then you have to entreat with each occupier individually. Doesn't that prospect fill you with joy? The Party Wall Act doesn't apply in Scotland or N Ireland. If you want to know more, then search on Party Wall Act and go to the Gov.uk site.

CHOOSING A DESIGNER

There are two distinct approaches to house design. One is to hire a designer (be they architect or not) and to let them get on with the task of melding your ideas with their expertise; the other is to approach a package build company who specialise in selling standard houses, which can be adapted to particular needs. In some ways the differences are not that great – after all both involve building houses – but conceptually it's the difference between painting from scratch and painting by numbers.

PACKAGE BUILD

Whilst the creative types would probably be appalled at the idea that you could buy an off-the-peg kit house, package-build does have one big advantage going for it and that is WYSIWYG. For those not up in computing circles, WYSIWYG

(pronounced Whizz-Ee-Wig) stands for What You See Is What You Get, and it describes perfectly the attraction of the package-build philosophy in that you know in advance what your home will look like. Furthermore, you know you'll have a conventional, re-saleable property because it wouldn't be on offer if it wasn't. This is a very comforting and reassuring selling factor for selfbuilders.

Package builds will almost certainly not be the cheapest route to a finished house: in fact, as reference to the next section of this chapter will show, they are often considerably more expensive than the route taken by volume developers. However, they do offer the novice housebuilder something that few architects ever do and that is a price in advance – though I should add that in reality they only offer a price for the parts of the house they actually supply and erect, which is often no more than a quarter or a third of the total building costs.

Take a hill-trekking holiday in the Himalayas as a comparison. Many people would want to go on such a holiday first time with a package deal, but having done it once, would realise that it was not so difficult to organise and that, if they ever went again, they would go on their own, have more independence and save money. Housebuilding is not so dissimilar; the comfort of having a professional organisation behind you in your first venture and a feeling that you know what the final bill will be is worth a lot more than the vague hope that you just might be saving money.

What buyers of package building services should realise is that they are not getting free design. Rather, the design work is being paid for within the package price. The package build companies all employ architects or designers and these people get paid just like their freelance cousins, and who do you think pays their salaries? Now the logic of using pre-drawn house plans is that the whole design process is reduced to a matter of a bit of photocopying which should be much cheaper for all concerned. However, British planning restrictions being what they are today, there are virtually no uncomplicated building plots on which you can plonk an off-the-peg house: the houses all require 'adaptation', which is tantamount to admitting that the brochure designs are just sales hooks to entice you, and that the actual house you have built will have had a fair amount of additional design work done to it in order to get it to fit both your ideas and the limitations of the plot. This extra work is invariably charged and you may well end up having a package build company designing your home from scratch.

Which begs the question 'Why start with an off-the-peg design at all?' In theory, a freelance architect or architectural designer should be able to provide a similar service to a package build designer and really shouldn't cost any more. But, for many people, the prospect of hiring a freelance is off-putting and not just because they think it will be expensive.

If you happen to know somebody in the trade, then there is every chance that you'll appoint them (however inappropriate) just because it takes away the difficult task of finding a compatible stranger. Many people without any contacts will, however, be lured into the package build option just because it's there. Eyeing up package build companies is like visiting Amsterdam's red light district: you can trawl up and down all night looking at the wares on offer but you don't have to consummate any deals if you don't like what's on offer. However, involving freelance architects and designers is more like Tinder: if you don't know them then it is akin to going on a blind date. You may or may not end up in bed together but you have to go through a courting stage just to find out where you want it to end up. It's a time-consuming and involved process and the outcome is just as likely to hinge on personal – not to say sexual – chemistry as it is on the designer's suitability and competence to carry out your brief.

Of course it doesn't have to be thus. If you're the professional, organised type, there is absolutely nothing to prevent you having a sort of beauty contest between three or four designers, in which you interview them and ask to see photographs of their previous work, ask for references and even ask them to prepare a quotation for design work, and possibly building work as well. The fact that architects hate this sort of thing is by-the-by: you'll be paying their bills and there is no reason at all

why you shouldn't organise a parade of talents so that you can make an informed judgement.

Red light districts, blind dates, and beauty contests – it's all getting a bit far away from building houses. So who are all these people?

ARCHITECT
Use of the very word architect is a touchy subject. The general public thinks an architect is someone who designs houses but the title *architect* is, in Britain at least, protected in law, just like the titles *doctor* and *lawyer*. To be qualified to call yourself an architect you must have completed seven years' training and passed all the relevant exams; an architect will regard him or herself as the natural choice for a commission such as designing an individual house and most architects love to take on such projects; trouble is, they may be rather high falutin' for your simple project and – worse fears – expensive. Just how expensive an architect is depends on how desperate they are for work but what can't be denied is that architects design only a small fraction of new homes in this country.

Traditionally, architects worked on a percentage fee basis; 3% of the contract value to prepare plans for planning permission, another 3% for working details and doing the tendering work and yet another 3% for administering the contract and (if you are lucky) certifying that the work has been done correctly – that's 9% in total for the full works. Some architects charge more than this. If they have a good reputation they can

Meredith Bowles, whose practice, Mole Architects worked our scheme through planning and detailed design. Pictured here inspecting our brick panel, which the planning conditions insisted on.

easily charge a total of 15% or more. But they don't have to work on a percentage basis.

A newly qualified rookie might cost less than a technician – say £300 per day – whereas a top-notch, in-demand architect could go out at that much per hour. One of our internationally renowned architects quotes £70,000 for designing and administering a one-off house – more than many humble abodes cost to build. That's exceptional – although the house probably would be as well. But fees of £30,000 plus for up-market projects costing a quarter of a million or more to build are now commonplace. But there are still loads of small architectural practices that work for rather less. Bear in mind that architects fees are nowhere near as high as equivalent professions like medicine, law or accountancy, and the typical architect earns no more than a good on site tradesman.

Qualified architects are required to register with the Architects Registration Board. There is a body called the Architects Registration Council, who you can call to check whether someone who is calling themselves an architect is fully qualified.

If they then choose to join the Royal Institute of British Architecture (RIBA) or its Celtic equivalents, they are able to call themselves Chartered Architects. The RIBA runs a nationwide Client's Advisory Service, which will supply a list of suitable local practices who are actively looking for your sort of business.

There is a collection of architects (known as the Association of SelfBuild Architects or ASBA) who got together to cater specifically for selfbuilders and although as a collection of individuals it can't guarantee excellence, it has done some innovative marketing – including quoting for architectural services on a unit area cost basis.

ARCHITECTURAL TECHNOLOGISTS
There is a second body, the Chartered Institute of Architectural Technologists, which issues a quite separate qualification (architects would say it is a lesser one), which is relevant in the field of house design. Traditionally this group was thought of as draughtsmen, beavering away in offices, turning architect's sketches into working drawings, but many of them work in practice independently. And some of them are very good. CIAT oversees and publishes a Directory of Practices and a regional list of self-employed members interested in taking on new work. Search on CIAT.

BUILDING SURVEYORS
Chartered building surveyors carry out lots of good design work. The problem is finding them. As a professional body, they are

administered by the Royal Institute of Chartered Surveyors (known as the RICS) but this amorphous group includes every flavour of surveyor including estate agents and building inspectors. The key is to find the right grouping – the Chartered Building Surveyors. If you ask for a list by post, you'll wait a long time but again you can search by region and area of expertise on the RICS website.

MANY OTHERS

There is in fact no requirement for anyone to have any qualifications to design houses. The country is stuffed full of unqualified but nevertheless competent designers. Some may have undertaken some architectural studies but never qualified, some may have qualifications in other related fields, notably structural engineers, quantity surveyors and building inspectors. And there are whole rafts of individuals who are 'qualified by experience' – often designer builders – who do perfectly good work, some of it every bit as good as professional architects turn out. Obviously these designers are not regulated in the way that architects and surveyors are and you should be aware that if you hire an unqualified designer they are unlikely to carry professional indemnity insurance; on the other hand, unqualified designers are likely to steer you down a route where insurance is handled by third parties, such as the NHBC, so this is not actually as big a risk as you might imagine. You pays your money, you takes your choice.

DESIGN AND BUILD

This is a method of building that straddles the traditional distinction between designers and builders. In some ways it is similar to package build in that you are faced with an all-in-one solution but, unlike package build, there are usually no pre-drawn plans on the table, so in other respects, design and build is more akin to hiring a freelance designer.

In fact many design and build businesses are based around the skills of a designer who also happens to run a construction business. It is hard to generalise because individual businesses will go about things in markedly different ways.

I worked in a design and build business for ten years from 1986 to 1996 and if anything characterised this particular business it was the wide variety of projects taken on; some clients used us just as designers, some just as builders, most as both. Some clients subjected us to beauty contests, some to competitive tendering, some to both of these and some to neither, preferring to work in an atmosphere of trust all the way from initial contact to completion of building work.

Unqualified designers will tend to be a little cheaper and will also tend to be a little less imaginative, which can be a good thing if you want to build cheaply. Engineers and surveyors in particular have a reputation for designing to a cost, something which has been known to elude more up-market architects.

CAD PACKAGES

Computer-aided design (CAD) has been around for decades but architects tend to look down their noses at it all: they continue to sketch stuff on paper in the time honoured fashion and then hire a 'CAD operator' to turn their works of art into engineered drawings.

Operating a full blown CAD package (the market leader is AutoCAD) is no mean feat but what has changed recently is that there are a number of really very cheap 3D software products around, which anyone can pick up and play around with on their home PC. An awful lot of architetcs now use SketchUp which is free in its simple version but costs when you want the bells and whistles.

DIY DESIGN

You can, of course, go the whole hog and design your own home. It's not as unusual as all that and it's not desperately difficult to undertake planning drawings. I once wrote an article for 'Homebuilding & Renovating' magazine about a 77-year old grandmother who did just that, having sacked her architect because he kept trying to 'improve' her plans. She knew what she wanted and successfully undertook all the negotiations with the planners.

However, there is a large chasm of knowledge between doing outline sketches and filling in all the construction details, a chasm which can only realistically be filled by training and/or experience (preferably both). Most DIY designers get an experienced professional on board at some stage if only to satisfy all the building regulations – as indeed did my intrepid lady.

The problem with DIY design is that it's difficult to get pleasing results if it's your first time. Design sense and spatial awareness are not skills that can be quickly or easily mastered and you have to be supremely confident in your own abilities to be entirely happy with your own work. Fine if what you were producing was just a set of drawings but, of course, it's not, it's a recipe for a real, live house.

People are naturally afraid that they will be building an ugly or impractical structure and so the vast majority are keen to get some professional opinion on board. Most architects expect to feed in ideas and improvements to your initial ideas and most people reckon that they are very good at this and welcome the added input. But not everyone.

There is in fact a groundswell of opinion that rates building professionals in general, and architects in particular, as nothing less than a cancer working to destroy an otherwise simple and healthy process called building. Here's building pundit Colin Harding quoted in 'Building Magazine' in 1999:

'Very few architects have the construction management skills to justify their claims to be team leaders. Most of the contracts we work on suffer to a varying degree as a direct result of the designer's failure to do their job properly and professionally. Typical lapses are:

■ specifying inappropriate materials and systems, then being incapable of devising professional solutions to overcome the technical problems created
■ lack of knowledge of basic construction techniques
■ no understanding of buildability
■ unwillingness to accept budget constraints
■ inability to manage the design process so that information is often late or inaccurate.

'What is so disappointing is that, in my opinion, the standard of professionalism among architects is still falling,' he wrote.

Harding's is not a lone voice. Here's selfbuilder Rick Hughes's assessment of the service he received on his project in Swansea: 'I would never use an architect again, this practice has proved difficult, frustrating, incredibly slow, and, although very good on conceptual items, struggle greatly once things leave the drawing board and enter the real world.'

Hmm. Doesn't look good, does it? But in defence of architects I hear of rather more successful relationships than failures. Indeed I have heard many selfbuilders go as far as to say that their project would have been hell without an architect on board and that using one had got them a far nicer house for much less money.

Try this one for a counter blast from home extender Marc Arnall: 'I decided to build an extension and, in order to save money, I wanted to use a technician to draw the plans as opposed to using an architect. Meanwhile I talked to an architect that I knew, after explaining to him that, unfortunately, I couldn't afford to make use of his services. He was most understanding and offered to check over my ideas and costings, with no charge to me.

'The end result? Richard (the architect) has designed a far better extension, organised and put in my planning application, organised a good discount with suppliers and has reduced my costings by some £8,000. He is going to supervise the work, thereby ensuring that I comply with all regulations and that any labour I hire fulfils his/her part of the deal. Thank goodness for architects!'

Well this game of architectural ping-pong could go on all night. It seems you either love 'em or hate 'em. What would be fair to say though is that there is a significant minority of architect/client relationships that are bedevilled with problems and that if you choose to work with an architect, choose very carefully.

In my own experience, I think much of the problems stem from getting architects to do the first bit and then either winging it from then on (in order to save money) or hiring someone cheaper to finish off the job. The result is a bodged project with workers on site spending far more time head scratching (which of course costs in other ways) and getting into long convoluted arguments about the final bill because the job was never properly designed in the first place. I reckon architects are usually worth every penny they charge.

THE SELECTION PROCEDURE

Building is one of the ultimate network businesses, there being very little formal long-term work around so it is not surprising that your designer should arrive on your (yet to be) doorstep by word of mouth. But bear in mind that all designers have tastes and quirks that are individual to them and even the simplest house commission is likely to receive radically different treatments. Make sure that you can at least live with your chosen designer's ideas by taking a look at their previous stuff. And you really should, if possible, talk to their previous clients. If you have very particular ideas yourself, then you would be well advised to seek out a like-minded soul.

One of the keys to hiring an architect or designer and not paying through the nose is to be very upfront about money from the first meeting. Conventionally, architects like to work on a percentage fee basis but there is no reason why you should: some argue it encourages architects to make you spend more than you want. You could, for instance, ask for an estimate to undertake the design of your house and specify that your project should cost no more than £XXX,000 and that it has to be designed to a budget. Some designers will flee a mile when faced by such demands but a surprising number will actually appreciate such specific requests from their clients – they get very tired of the polite to-ing and fro-ing that goes on around issues like this. The more specific your brief is, the better pleased you will be with the results.

OFFSITE CONSTRUCTION

When arranging the running order for the 'Housebuilder's Bible', I initially thought that I should put this section into the superstructure chapter, up there with walls and roofs. Because, if you buy a timber frame kit, then it's basically the superstructure you are buying. Logic would seem to dictate that that's where it should go, and indeed there is a piece on timber frame as an inner skin up there in Chapter 7. If you want to know what a timber frame wall is, or what a Structural Insulated Panel is, look in that Chapter. And there's a brief discussion of the merits of lightweight versus heavyweight building in the Green Chapter, as well.

But I believe that the main reason for choosing a timber frame package build (and the same goes for its close cousin, Structural Insulated Panels or SIPS) is not to do with the merits or otherwise of selecting timber or SIPS as your walling material, but rather to do with selecting a specialist custom home builder as your supplier. The fact that these custom home builders choose to build with timber is of secondary importance. And, as if to prove my point, there are one or two package home suppliers who don't build in timber frame. So it's the fact that it's package build, which makes it end up here in the design chapter.

In England, Wales and Ireland (though not Scotland), the building trade traditionally builds houses using masonry blockwork for the structural walls. In Scotland, they love timber frame and it accounts for the majority of new houses there. In the rest of Britain, builders are of course happy to use timber in the roof and usually for the floors above ground level so, in a sense, even these houses have some timber framing in them but masonry walls have been the preferred way of building homes since we ran out of forests around three hundred years ago.

Timber frame houses in Europe have developed down a very different path to North America. North Americans build their timber homes on site: we tend to make them in factories, far away from the building site, and consequently timber frame housebuilding is a very different process to 'normal' housebuilding.

It's harder for builders to 'add value' by using timber frame or SIPS. By taking much of the labour input off-site and putting it into a factory, builders are in effect doing themselves out of a job and there is little incentive for them to change their ways. Architects are similarly disadvantaged in that timber frame construction requires an extra stage of panel drawing and extra structural calculation, both of which are technical in nature and best dealt with by specialists. There is thus an unwritten understanding between design professionals and builders to leave things as they are.

ADVANTAGES

Selfbuilders, of course, don't have to run along with the crowd and selfbuilders throughout the UK have taken to timber frame in a big way for much the same reasons as

Britain's first selfbuild village, Graven Hill in Oxfordshire, has around 1900 selfbuild and custom build plots. And new homebuilding businesses are here offering bespoke one-off homes, built in factories and assembled on site. The old distinction between architect-designed and package build is starting to melt away.

Scotland as a whole has. Not only is a timber frame house potentially much quicker to build than a masonry one, but – because the frame itself is largely hollow – it is easy to insulate to a high standard and yet still maintain a clear cavity between the frame and the outside walling material. Timber frame houses are therefore inherently energy efficient and they are warm and comfortable to live in.

At least as important as any technical differences between the building systems is the question of procurement. I've touched on the fact that most architects and most builders like to use traditional masonry construction because it suits their own purposes. Because of this, there has grown up a quite distinct timber frame industry in the UK which has had to specialise in meeting all or most of the would-be housebuilder's needs. A timber frame company can't just build a factory, set up its jigs and wait for the orders to come rolling in. Rather they have to go out and grow the business by attracting the end users. As there are few independent architects prompting clients down the timber frame route, the companies themselves need to attract selfbuilders at the initial design stage and, by and large, they do this with attractive brochures of houses they have already built or a set of off-the-peg house types, which you can choose or adapt to your own requirements. In effect, most timber frame companies design your house as well as provide and erect the superstructure.

It follows therefore that the frame is only one part of the service provided by these businesses. What they are really about is what is known as design and build or what the Americans call custom home building where you can pitch up with a few ideas, maybe a few sketches, and they will transform these into a workable home, delivered and erected on your site.

The fact that your superstructure is made of timber is almost incidental to the procurement process – in order to sell you a frame kit, it is first necessary for them to capture your imagination and your confidence. Often they have a range of standard house types from which you can choose or adapt but most of them admit to rarely, if ever, building these standard houses.

These days, selfbuild clients are choosing to have a much greater say in how their houses should look and function and consequently most timber frame houses start life as a sketch done by the selfbuilder or a more detailed drawing carried out by their architect.

Even companies with an established reputation for standard house ranges find they are doing more and more 'one-offs'.

THE BUSINESSES

There are a surprising number of frame businesses throughout the country catering for the selfbuilder. By and large, they tend to offer a similar range of services. Almost all the businesses offer a design service to turn your preliminary drawings into a fully engineered structure. In this respect a timber frame house is quite different to a masonry brick and block house: the design for a timber frame structure needs to be proved so that the building inspector is satisfied that it won't collapse in a heap or that it won't take off in the wind. This work is normally carried out in-house, though you can commission a structural engineer to undertake it for you if you want. To do it on a one-off basis is a complex and time-consuming process and you also need to draw up technical drawings for the timber frame wall panels which, by hand, can take almost as long as it does to actually assemble them. This is all work that can be carried out easily on a computer and this is another contributory factor helping to develop the timber frame industry into a unique entity, quite distinct from the mainstream building industry.

Beyond the design and assembly of the timber frame, the businesses offer various levels of service from frame erection right through to a complete build, often known as a turnkey service. Many of the businesses tend to offer different levels of service depending on distance – for instance, they will be happy to quote for an entire build or a waterproof shell

Timber frame comes in many different guises. Above: A green oak house from TJ Crump Oakwrights mixing traditional idioms with masses of glass and open plan living. Oakwrights are one of several UK businesses producing bespoke oak homes for the selfbuild market Right: German factory housebuilder Baufritz have been supplying the UK for a number of years – they specialise in biologically healthy buildings.

within, say, a forty mile radius but beyond that feel that they are bound to be uncompetitive. Others have developed contacts all over the country and feel comfortable taking on entire builds far away from home – indeed some of the timber frame builders think nothing of going overseas. If anything characterises the industry it is the word flexibility. Having said that, it often pays dividends to work

with a local business – the level of service is usually better.

Some of the businesses are known for specific styles or designs. Market leader Kingspan Potton are still best known for their Heritage range, half-timbered Tudor cottages, though they have long since branched out into more modern designs. They have spawned several imitators. There are a clutch of Scandinavian or Scandinavian-inspired companies, a couple of American ones and an increasing number from Germany and places further east like Poland and Lithuania. There is also a small number specialising in SIPS, as opposed to timber frame. The selfbuild magazines are the best place to get information and contact details and the selfbuild exhibitions, particularly the annual jamboree at Birmingham's NEC in March, are where you can most easily make face-to-face contact.

The majority of frame companies offer to work with any and every style. In all there are around sixty businesses active in the field, although around half are based in Scotland, reflecting the popularity of timber frame there. There is a trade association, the Structural Timber Association, which is a good place to check out who does what. Oak framers are something of a race apart – they don't do trade associations! There are one or two offering to do very similar things with steel frames and Design & Materials is unique in working in a similar method to timber frame companies but actually supplying masonry materials to build houses in the traditional way.

Generally, the concept homes are expensive; for instance, a Potton Heritage home of equivalent size to a developer's house is going to cost about 15-20 % more to build. However, if you strip out the vernacular elements of the Potton Heritage style – notably the posts and beams – the cost differential all but vanishes. Typically the price of the

kit is between a third and a quarter of the overall build costs though the amount of goods supplied with the kit varies quite considerably.

When making comparisons you have to become adept at looking at the small print to see what's provided and what isn't. The Scandinavian kit home suppliers tend to provide the bulk of what you need but at a considerable price; they also have a nasty habit of listing their floor areas gross – that is including the external walls – which makes the homes appear to be 15% larger than the competition, which works with net floor areas. Watch out for this. In Scotland, the timber frame market is more mature than elsewhere and there tends to be a standard Scottish package (which includes the plasterboard), which makes cost comparisons more straightforward.

PREPAYMENT ISSUES

Because a large amount of work is being carried out off-site, most timber frame companies want some form of prepayment. The timing and amounts of deposit required vary enormously from some businesses that want 100% of the frame costs before delivery to others who expect payment after work has been carried out.

From a client's point of view, the nightmare lurking over the horizon is that the company they are dealing with may be about to go bust and that their cheque will be cashed before anything has arrived on site. Timber frame companies are no more secure than any other type of business

and one piece of advice frequently given to selfbuilders is 'never pay for anything upfront'. On the other hand, the suppliers have legitimate fears that the customer can't or won't pay and many have learned the hard way that a contract as large as a timber frame house, usually measured in tens of thousands of pounds, should not be undertaken without some form of deposit and some form of guarantee that the client is able to pay. Unlike other expensive items such as cars, timber frame kits are bespoke and can't just be sold on to another customer.

One way around this problem is to use a solicitor's stakeholder account where the majority of your payment is lodged, usually about a week before delivery of the main frame. This way the supplier can see that you have cleared funds in place, but they are not drawn down until the frame is on site. Another often acceptable solution, used widely for car purchases, is to get a bankers' draft or a building society cheque – i.e. the sort of cheque that won't bounce – made out to the supplier a week or so before delivery. This is then shown but not handed over until goods are on site.

However, this raises another problem for selfbuilders borrowing to fund their build. Many lenders will not release funds against goods still being fabricated in a factory and consequently many selfbuilders get caught in a Catch 22 situation where they are unable to proceed.

However, there are now mortgage products on the market, like

Buildstore's Accelerator Mortgage, which are designed to unlock funds before a critical stage is reached. Alternatively, many timber frame suppliers will accept undertakings from lenders to pay them directly on delivery.

The important thing to bear in mind is that you must plan ahead and discuss the matter with your chosen supplier and your lender.

SHAPE AND SIZE

Before you even approach a designer or a package company, you would do well to take on board a few home truths about the cost implications of your design decisions. If you are after cheap space, then you need to build your house in a simple shape, preferably a simple box with a simple roof. This doesn't have to look cheap – indeed it doesn't have to be cheap – but the point is that it is almost always going to be the simplest (and therefore cheapest) form of construction available to you. Many traditional houses take this form and they are not all peasants' cottages.

So why should a rectangular box shape be cheaper than say two rectangular box shapes stuck together? In a word: junctions. You are introducing junctions at every stage of the building process and junctions always involve head scratching and usually expensive detailing. Your brickwork will take just that little bit longer to build, your carpentry will become just that little bit more complicated, your roofing will become much more complicated.

However, it is important not to exaggerate the cost implications of building complex shapes: I estimate that every time you create a junction you add 1% to your build budget. Therefore if you were to build in an L-shape, for instance, you would scarcely notice the extra cost.

But wherever you interrupt the basic shell shape of a house you are adding junction costs and if you choose a complex form with extensions, dormers, porches and the like then you can take it that the overall cost will increase by much more than the unit cost per square metre at which you build the main shell.

CIRCULATION SPACE

There is another hidden cost brought about by using non-standard shapes in house design and this is to do with having adequate circulation space – i.e. hallways, stairwells and landings. This is virtually impossible to quantify because no two situations are the same, but the basic tenet holds that the more complex your form, the more difficult it becomes to provide adequate circulation space or, put another way, the more space you end up using just to get around from A to B. For instance, in our lean, box-design developer house, circulation space occupies just over 18m², which is 16% of the internal floor area. That's a pretty tight ratio.

Reconfigure the house in a 'T' shape and you'll probably be looking at circulation space taking up 25% or more of your internal floor area. Now you may not mind that, you might even want a minstrel's gallery set under a glass atrium in your entrance hallway, but do be aware of the constraints you put on your space by choosing more complex designs.

Bear in mind also that the current trend for heavily insulated walls comes at a cost of reducing internal floor area. A Passivhaus wall, with its 300 mm wide cavities, may eat up as much as an extra 5% of the internal floor area.

PROJECT MANAGEMENT

WHAT EXACTLY is project management? It's become a buzzword among builders who assume that it's the be-all and end-all of running a building site. There are now professional project managers who apparently keep building sites going armed only with a mobile phone and a fast car, the yuppies of the building trade. It's all about networking and contacts, being at the very centre of a huge web of information.

Well, yes, there is this aspect, but don't get carried away. Really, project management is nothing new; it's what contractors have always done, which is to organise building work. There is power here and if you've never employed anyone other than a baby-sitter that can be an attraction to many of us frustrated prefects. But, as the old saw goes, with that power comes a responsibility and, in the case of the contractor, that responsibility is considerable. Whilst you are hopefully making a bit on everybody's labour, you also have to pick up the tabs for everybody's cock-ups. You are where the buck stops.

So, project management goes on at every building site, even out-of-the-way ones where they've never even heard of it. It's really rather a holdall term that covers just about every non-manual aspect of running a building site. And there are no rules as to who can and who can't be a project manager; it could be the self building client, or their architect or quantity surveyor, or it could be the main contractor or their foreman. And of course it doesn't all have to be carried out by one individual – the various functions may be split between people, though when this happens you can expect even more cock-ups than usual.

RAISING FINANCE

The first step in the management of a project such as building a house is to have the finance organised to pay for it. For the majority of selfbuilders and small developers that translates as how much you are able to borrow. Well, how do you go about borrowing on a property that doesn't even exist? You will find it a lot easier to borrow money if you have a) substantial assets and b) substantial income, preferably both. If you don't fall into either of these categories then you are by no means ruled out of the game; you'll just have to work harder at impressing the mortgage lender.

There are currently around 20 institutions actively seeking selfbuild borrowers; some of these are prepared to lend up to 75% of the finished value of the property and several will potentially lend rather more than this – though most will expect you to come up with a hefty deposit for land purchase.

Since the credit crunch, several big names have dropped out of this specialised niche and almost all the running is now made by the old fashioned mutual building societies. The nearest thing to a broker is Buildstore who pioneered the Accelerator Mortgage, which enables you to borrow ahead of the prearranged stage payments.

As with conventional mortgages, the amount you can borrow is dependent on your income. The conservative approach is to restrict the borrowing levels to three times the main income or two and a half times the combined incomes. But the actual limits depend a lot on market conditions; when banks are keen to lend then the multiplier tends to stretch upwards. If you are self-employed or you actively want to sell on the finished property for a profit, then the regular avenues may well be closed to you but there are still a number of specialist brokers who it is worth approaching, many of whom advertise in the selfbuild magazines. Another very useful contact is the Ecology Building Society who are particularly helpful in lending to those undertaking unusual constructions and renovations which mainstream lenders shy away from. Professional developers have traditionally borrowed from the major clearing banks but there are a number of finance boutiques catering for them as well. A good place to check who is currently active in this field is the small ads in Housebuilder magazine, which can be accessed online.

YOUR PRESENTATION

Many lenders recommend that you contact them early, when you are still at the dreaming stage. If you have an existing mortgage, start by talking to this source and trying to gauge their attitude to your ideas. Talk in broad sweeps about what you are trying to achieve and try and winkle out of them how far they will be prepared to come along with you. Together you may be able to shape up a budget to work to.

If you feel they are being unduly negative, then start looking at other lenders. The lenders themselves are tending towards centralised decision making, which can make things more transparent but also rather less flexible.

When the time comes to act, you will in all probability have to act quickly and you will need whatever ammunition you can get hold of — agent's details of the proposed purchase, copy of planning permission, your salary details, a building budget. If you've no plans, then show them a copy of this book and say you've read it from cover to cover – that'll impress them. You shouldn't have to show any plans at this stage because it is ludicrous to expect there to be any yet but this is one area where the timber frame package companies tend to win out because you can actually present a budget AND a plan, even if the house you end up building is nothing like this.

SCHEDULING

Unlike conventional mortgage lending, development loans and selfbuild mortgages are released in stages as the work progresses. For someone new to this, it can be a daunting process, especially if they have to borrow to complete the plot purchase for a house that's not even designed, let alone built.

The key to doing this is to prepare a schedule of works, the sort of thing that is outlined in the diagram overleaf. This shows how a typical British house is built, taking around eight months to complete. The costings are for a total build of just under £180,000, enough to

Chapter 5

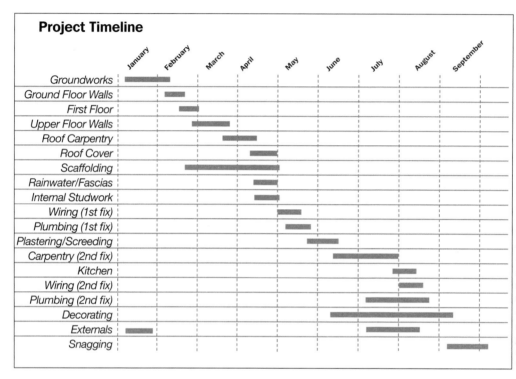

Project Timeline

	January	February	March	April	May	June	July	August	September
Groundworks	███								
Ground Floor Walls		██							
First Floor		█							
Upper Floor Walls			██						
Roof Carpentry				██					
Roof Cover					█				
Scaffolding			████████						
Rainwater/Fascias					█				
Internal Studwork					█				
Wiring (1st fix)					██				
Plumbing (1st fix)					██				
Plastering/Screeding						██			
Carpentry (2nd fix)							███		
Kitchen								█	
Wiring (2nd fix)								██	
Plumbing (2nd fix)							███		
Decorating							██████		
Externals	█						███		
Snagging									██

An idealised timeline for a project such as a large detached four-bedroomed house. Eight months is a typical time for a professional housebuilder to take, without exactly busting a gut. It's comfortable. It represents around 3,500 hours work, or three guys for 30 weeks. The rate of spending is pretty constant at around £7,500 a week.

construct a four-bedroomed house. It's interesting to note that the rate of spending is surprisingly constant throughout the job.

Eight months is generally a good time to set to build a simple house, unless you plan to take on a lot of the work yourself, in which case it is likely to take a whole lot longer. As you can see from the timeline, there are nearly twenty major tasks to accomplish, all needing co-ordinating and timetabling so that they occur in the right order at the right time. At this speed, you are actually paying the wages of three men to be on site continually and if that were how houses got built there really wouldn't

be any problems trying to schedule a workforce. But in reality each house is built by upwards of 30 people, each with different skills and each with their own schedules to work to; you can't expect everyone to turn up at the drop of a hat so you have to programme some slack into the schedule to allow for this.

SPEEDY BUILDS

Some houses do get built in much less time than eight months. If you want to build quickly, then either be prepared to spend good money on professional supervision of the whole construction process or to have a half-finished house with lots of snags,

which will probably never get sorted out.

It's quite feasible to build a house from scratch in just three months but in order to do so you have to concertina all the events. Realistically, this means planning the whole process months in advance so that everybody involved in the construction knows exactly what they are required to do and when they are required to do it, just the sort of intricate project planning for which British builders are famous! It also requires that the correct materials be delivered to site on the appropriate day (ditto British builder's merchants). Speedy builds?

It can be done, but... be prepared to spend the time you saved in the building process planning the whole thing instead.

STAGE PAYMENTS

What are the key stages or landmarks which trigger release of development funds? Each lender seems to use slightly different criteria to define when each stage is completed but a typical regime would involve four or five stage payments coinciding with:
- groundworks complete (say 15%)
- first floor joists (say 30%)
- structure roofed in and watertight (say 50%)
- plastered out (say 75%)
- finished.

Normally the lender will insist on a surveyor making a site visit to check that the work has progressed as far as you claim, although some of the more intrepid bank managers will do this checking themselves.

MANAGING CASHFLOW

One critical point to take note of is that the lenders only ever release payments after a stage is completed, so that you have to be able to float the works between the payments. This fact has undone many a small builder in the past and will doubtless continue to do so in future. Typically, the builder runs out of cash towards the end of the job and gets stuck in a Catch-22 where they can't get the final (largest) instalment of the loan because they haven't finished building and they can't finish building because they haven't got the final stage of the loan. A tricky little pitfall made

all the worse because builders (and surveyors) habitually underestimate the cost of finishing building works off and the time that the finishing soaks up.

One of the major advantages of building reasonably quickly is that the strain on cashflow is minimised because the subcontractors may well be happy for you to withhold payment for a couple of weeks until the next stage payment is authorised; if that couple of weeks becomes a few months, then this option is effectively removed. However, there are now mortgage products on the market, like Buildstore's Accelerator Mortgage, designed to unlock funds before a critical stage is reached.

There is another little pitfall here awaiting the slower-than-average selfbuilder: the VAT reclaim procedure. The what? Check out the VAT section of this chapter.

WHERE DO WE LIVE?

Selfbuilders are faced with the problem of finding somewhere to live during the construction of their new home. The lucky ones can stay on in their existing homes and, if the market is rising, enjoy a two-for-one tax-free punt on the property market whilst their build takes place. However, the majority are faced with having to sell up their existing home in order to raise enough money to buy the plot. In this situation you have to find somewhere short-term.

The two main options are a short-term rental or a caravan on site. The first is expensive, often costing rather more than servicing a mortgage,

and you can use this fact to try and persuade your mortgage lender not to have to make you sell up in the first place. The caravan is seen as the cheap and cheerful option but it's not without its hidden costs as well.

Usually people buy static caravans. Purchase costs vary from around £2,000 to £6,000 depending on size and quality. Add to this the costs of getting it to site and installing it once there, usually between £500-£1,000. Many firms supplying static caravans will buy them back from you although only expect to get between a half and two-thirds what you paid.

You need to have drainage, water and electricity supplies sorted before the installation which can make it hard to move into directly from selling an existing house. Also consider the cost of storing your possessions. Quotes to do this professionally usually come in at around £50 per month plus the added cost (say £500) of moving everything twice. Amateur storage is feasible but often results in damaged furniture – fabrics, bedding, books, pictures should not be stored in unheated sheds through a winter if you value them at all.

BUILDING'S 4 PRS

There are four cost centres in construction which are similar sounding — they all begin with Pr….. — but they differ in content and hence rather confusing for lay people. It's time to get to grips with them, however you plan to build.

What they have in common is that they are concerned with the supporting aspects of a building project that don't involve the actual materials to be used nor the fixing of them. Add them all together and they can account for up to a third of your overall expenditure…..

NO 1 PROFESSIONALS

Professional costs covers costs concerned with both design and getting the relevant permissions in place to undertake a building project. The major fee here is usually paid to the architect but there may also be fees paid to structural engineers, quantity surveyors and party wall advisors together with statutory fees for planning permissions and building regs approvals, plus insurance and warranties. There may also be fees for such items as energy assessments, airtightness testing and health and safety compliance.

Typical professional fees: £20,000 upwards. The most important component here is almost always the architects' costs. There is a huge gulf between what you would pay a competent but unambitious designer for a set of house plans (£3,000 is perhaps a minimum) and an architecture practice looking to produce something unusual and cutting edge (£50,000 and on upwards). Other professional costs tend to be more predictable: typically all in at around c £3,000 - £5,000. When looking at ballpark building costs per m^2, items marked as Professionals are usually excluded.

NO 2 PRELIMS

Prelims (short for preliminaries) is a blue-collar version of professionals and covers such items as setting up a site office and a site loo, providing scaffolding and site fencing, together with security and safety equipment and maybe a skip or seven. Another way of looking at prelim costs is to see them as temporary structures required to run the site which will be removed on or before completion. Sometimes, prelims include money set aside for a site manager's time, but this is more usually included as a Project management fee (see No 3).

Typical prelim totals for a new house: £10,000 to £25,000, depending on site complexity. Scaffolding in particular can balloon in price if complex features such as temporary roofing-over are involved — scaffolding costs in such instances can be as much as £20,000.

NO 3 PROJECT MANAGEMENT

The site management time is conventionally costed as **No 3** — **Project Management**. In order to get a building site to run smoothly, someone has to manage the processes. They have to ensure that the right people are hired in the right order and that the correct materials are on site as and when needed, as well as checking that the work is carried out properly and that the site is left clean and safe everyday. They have to keep things on the *critical path*. And they have to ensure everyone and everything gets paid correctly.

This sort of thing doesn't happen by magic: a neat ratio to bear in mind is that for every seven hours spent "on the tools", one hour needs to be set aside for managing the whole process in order to do it efficiently. A typical British selfbuild, using on-site construction methods, requires around 3,500 hours site work (costing around £75,000 at £20/hour) and this work will require an additional 500 project management hours (costing around £15,000 at £30/hr.) or between 10% and 12% of the overall project cost. Often this work is carried out by selfbuilders themselves and therefore gets lost in the overall cost analysis. It's rarely costed separately unless you specifically hire a project manager to run the site on your behalf, where additional fees would be charged for travel and office overheads.

NO 4 PROFIT

The final PR is **Profit**. Everybody has an idea what profit is and what it means but it's difficult to define precisely, partly because it's not easy to separate profit from regular costs. Everybody who supplies goods or services to a building project is hoping to realise some sort of profit on the transactions — simply covering costs is never enough to keep the wheels of commerce oiled.

But in this context, profit has a more specific meaning. A builder or main contractor quoting for a project such as a new house will allow for all the costs of building the house, the prelims and the project management fees (but not usually the professionals, which are charged separately). These are the costs which they need to recover in order not to make a loss. But over and above this they will add a profit margin in order to make the job worth doing.

You only normally come across the term Profit when you work with a Quantity Surveyor who adds a percentage over and above the job costs so that you can gauge what a builder's quote might be. Trying to figure out likely profit margins is something of a black art and it is notoriously difficult to predict builder's quotes in advance. Looked at from a builder's point of view, there are essentially two things to consider here.

Firstly, there is risk involved in taking on any job for a fixed price. There may well be a punitive contract in place which will cost the builder a great deal of money if things don't go as smoothly as hoped for. So the builder has to assess the risk and make an informed guess of how likely your job is to go well. The greater the risk, the more you will be charged a risk premium — i.e. a higher profit margin.

The second point to consider is just how much the builder wants your work. The busier they are, the more they are likely to add to their margin as it can be an almighty hassle to

---

Selfbuilder Stuart Meier's Guide to Project Management

Add up the appropriate factor from each box to give an overall multiplier for your eight months....

Experience

I've done numerous previous projects successfully:	*factor 0*
I've done quite a bit before, I'm tediously well organised:	*factor +50%*
I've never tried and my wife thinks I'll lose control:	*factor +300%*

Complexity

Everyone says it's a very boring design:	*factor 0*
It has a few unusual features:	*factor +50%*
Architect is really chuffed with it:	*factor +200%*

Site

Flat open site with loads of room:	*factor 0*
It's a bit tight around the edges, and slopes too:	*factor +50%*
On a clifftop with 4wd access only:	*factor +200%*

Publicity

"Good lord, no":	*factor 0*
Grand Designs want to film it:	*factor +50%*
Grand Designs are GOING to film it:	*factor +200%*

---

organise a large job and their costs tend to expand by more than they would like. Many builders work with the same team of people over many years and know their strengths and weaknesses and how best to manage them. Taking on extra staff to cope with a greater workload can lead to unforeseen problems and costs overruns. Once again, to counter this problem, the builder is likely to add a significant margin.

So how much profit will a builder add? It's often hard to say because the quotes aren't broken down. But as a rule, the builder is likely to add 15% to the raw build costs (Inc. prelims) in order to cover the project management element, plus whatever the market will bear over

and above this. It could be as low as 5% or as high as 50%. So expect a fixed price quotation to be anything from 25% to 75% more than the raw build costs. That's a lot of money and one principal reason why so many selfbuilders choose to become their own project managers.

If you want to have the comfort of a fixed price contract and, with it, professional management, and you don't want to pay through the nose for this service then

▪ build in a recession when times are hard for builders and they don't have too much work

▪ design something simple and easy for them to build - something in their comfort zone

▪ be as nice as pie when you come

to interview the builders and let them know that you are not forever teetering on the edge of bankruptcy. Some evidence of ability to pay is always welcome — many perfectly good builders go bust because their clients run out of money.

Note on VAT: New build is zero-rated for VAT purposes within the UK. This means that you either don't get charged or you can reclaim any VAT that you may be charged. However, the zero-rating doesn't extend to Professionals or Prelims, where you will be charged VAT at 20%. The only way of avoiding these VAT charges is to employ a single contractor to both design and build the whole project, so that you only pay one company throughout.

WORKING WITH BUILDERS

The question everybody wants answered is: 'How do I find a good builder?' I suspect that people have been asking the same question all over the world for several thousand years now and I've yet to come across a convincing answer. I'm not going to even try. Instead I think it's a good idea to look at the question from a number of different angles, to try and grasp just what it is that goes wrong with construction work that causes people to tear their hair out with exasperation. In an effort to close in on the main question, I'll take a look at several supplementary questions.

DO I NEED A BUILDER AT ALL?

The building trade is a free market but, all in all, it's not a very good advert for the free market. It is widely perceived as being expensive, inadequate and inefficient, certainly when it comes to domestic work. Indeed one of the main drivers behind selfbuilders' willingness to take on the project management role themselves is a widespread lack of trust with general builders.

When times are tough in the building trade, builders are falling over themselves to try and get work but an alarming number are simultaneously going bust. On the other hand, when times are good it can be extremely hard to even get builders to quote for work – some of the more reliable builders I know get booked up with work for over a year. The problem becomes one of finding a builder at any price rather than one at the right price. There is an added danger that less scrupulous builders will take your job on knowing full well they are inadequately resourced, hoping their contact book will see them through. Mistakes multiply when main contractors get stretched beyond their capabilities.

IS A GENERAL BUILDER, NECESSARY?

The main ingredient that a general builder brings to the party is this magic phrase 'project management'. Co-ordination of material deliveries, subcontractors, building inspectors, plant hire, office administration, you name it. Anyone who has ever

managed a business of whatever size will know that it's time consuming. Anyone who has ever managed a building business will know that it's almost impossible to get it just right. Rookie builders with experience in management can and frequently do take on the role (and risk) of a general builder, undertaking the hiring and firing of tradesmen together with all the other activities. However what should not be underestimated is the amount of time and energy this all takes up. Realistically, you need some sort of professional management help if you can't be on site every day (although not necessarily all day). For many people, hiring a general builder makes a lot of sense.

WHY AREN'T BUILDERS ANY GOOD?

However much sense it makes in theory, in practice many people end up feeling let down by their main contractor. More often than not, this is because contractors tend to be incredibly busy people and they are forever juggling timetables and deadlines.

Whilst the typical general contractor would make a good project manager on one particular job, the wheels start to fall off when the number of sites being supervised gets above three. Yet in order to make a decent living and to keep a run of work going for various tradesmen, most general contractors simply have to keep going at several jobs simultaneously.

I know from experience that it's incredibly demanding and stressful trying to co-ordinate building work going on across a wide area. As a builder you may start out with the best intentions in the world but you rapidly end up employing the same knee-jerk excuses used by everyone else in the trade (and despised by its clientele). Appointments start to get missed, calls start to go unanswered, promises start getting broken.

WHY CAN'T BUILDERS DELIVER?

I'm not sure there is an easy answer to this. The glib answer is 'You try doing it and see if you are any better'. But that's not terribly helpful. In truth, most general contractors do deliver eventually but often at a standard well below their customers' expectations. So perhaps the advice should be by all means use a main contractor but don't set your standards too high. Or perhaps we are not prepared to pay enough for the level of service we want.

WHAT SCARES BUILDERS?

Money for a start. It is an axiom often repeated that you should avoid paying a builder upfront for anything, wherever possible. However, there is another side of this coin – it is the builder who is consequently extending you credit, which immediately puts him at a disadvantage. And despite the so-called power of the consumer these days, the levels of unsecured credit you are likely to get from a builder are way beyond anything else you are going to be offered on the high street.

Try buying a new car by offering to pay in 30 days only if you are completely satisfied and then withholding 5% of the price for six months. Little wonder that so many builders experience cashflow problems. Sure, they are buying their materials on credit but this only lasts 30 to 60 days and subcontract labour want cash more quickly than that.

So one way you can smooth your relationship with your builder is to agree how payments will be met before the contract starts and then stick rigidly to those terms. If you are having to borrow large dollops of money to finance your building work and this money is only released in stages, then be open with your builder about this and make it clear just what he has to do to trigger the stage payments – at least he'll know that you are being realistic about money.

One of the bugbears of today's builder is to be told at the end of the job that although the client is perfectly happy with the finished result, the final £20,000 is going to have to wait a bit because they've overspent and run out of money: yet it happens all the time, builders getting used as sources of interest-free finance.

Another frequent scam foisted on builders is the excuse that the money is locked into a 30 or 60 day savings account and that payment is being withheld until the full withdrawal period is up. The builder is quite likely to be struggling with an overdraft as big as a mortgage. Yet such behaviour by clients is all too common and is verging on being really abusive but

when the builder is the creditor he can basically do very little about it.

As you can see, the builder is actually in a very vulnerable position. But clients play still worse tricks; some will withhold payment of many thousands of pounds on the flimsiest of excuses, such as resolving a few snags that might be worth just a few hundred pounds at most. Sometimes these machinations are born of frustration with the performance of the builder but sometimes the client uses these excuses to cover up for the fact that they never had enough money in the first place. Yes, these are the real cowboy clients.

My business was 'locked out' on a couple of occasions on the excuse that the standard of workmanship was not good enough when subsequently it emerged the real reason was that the client was in financial difficulties and simply had no way to settle the bill. Rather than admit to the humiliation of being unable to settle a debt, it is altogether easier and more convenient to tell everyone that the builder is an incompetent rogue from whom you have had to withhold money or, even more likely, submitted an extortionate bill for the extras.

Whilst the client is telling everyone who will listen just how awful the builders are and receiving a sympathetic ear, able to point to work which is half finished in evidence, the builder is often forced to bear such indignities in silence. Often the amounts at dispute are too large for the small claims court but not large enough to warrant risking a full-blown legal challenge and many

One way of spotting a good builder is to see how tidy they are. This ICF house, under construction in Perthshire in 2014, looks to have a well organised, efficient site. Just as well when you look at the scale of the retaining wall behind it.

thousands of pounds get written off this way. Clients withholding money for whatever reason is easily the commonest reason for builders going bust and it can happen to even the best builders.

DOES THE BUILDER CHOOSE THE CLIENT?

Small wonder then that builders are just as wary of potential customers as the customers are of them. The vetting process that goes on between contractors and clients is very much a two-way thing and part of the skill of being a good builder is one who knows which clients to work with and which to avoid. Your

builder chooses you as much as you choose your builder. It's back to that marriage thing again. More often than not, a builder who suspects that a job is a potential lemon will not even bother to quote for it or, if they do, they will add a very high percentage to the overall profit figure to cover their back should they win the contract.

WHAT'S WRONG WITH COMPETITIVE TENDERING?

One practice that is prevalent is for busy builders to get together and divide up the work in a way (and for a price) that suits them – it's called covering. It works like this. A job is put out to tender – typically by an architect – to four or five local builders. Some of them are so busy that they simply don't want to take on any more work. Architects tend to regard refusals to quote rather badly and the builders feel that, rather

than risking losing the possibility of quoting for future work, they would like to put in some price, any price. So the next step is to chat with the competition – it's not hard, it happens naturally anyway – and soon an informal cartel is in place.

Reg: 'Have you been asked to quote for the Old Rectory job at Chipping Butty?'

Charlie: 'Yes. I like the look of it.'

Reg: 'I really can't see any way we could do that one – could you do us a favour and cover us.'

Charlie: 'Sure – I've no doubt you'll be able to return the favour soon.'

So Charlie puts in his price and tells Reg to put in a price maybe £20,000 higher. Reg knows he won't get the job but he hasn't spent any time or money quoting for it, and he hasn't upset the architect so he'll stand a chance next time around when he does want the work.

Occasionally the builders know all the other tenderers on any given job – in matters like this the grapevine works extremely efficiently – so that there are cases where every builder on the tendering list has been in on the scam. They all know who is providing the lowest quote and, consequently, the lowest quote is in reality quite a high one. Such a complete stitch-up is perhaps rare but frequently two or three of the quotes will be for show purposes only.

Partly this problem stems from the way building work is procured in the first place. And in particular the practice of builders quoting for free causes a lot of problems. It sounds too good to be true and of course it is. It takes a good deal of time to generate an accurate quotation and most builders simply send tender documents off to a quantity surveyor who carries out the work for them (for a scaled fee, depending on the size of the job). Now builders often end up quoting for five or six jobs in order to win one, so the overheads of quoting for jobs they don't get becomes a significant business expense in itself. Anything that helps to ease the load of having to quote for jobs is manna from heaven for builders so you can see the attraction of any informal price fixing arrangements they might concoct.

OTHER OPTIONS?

What's advantageous to the builder is obviously less welcome news for the consumer. What ways are there for clients to avoid being on the wrong end of one of these cartels? The obvious one is to avoid using general contractors at all, as previously discussed.

You can elect to be your own main contractor and hire all the labour yourself but for many busy people this is an unrealistic option and in many parts of the country it is becoming harder and harder to track down good labour. Alternatively, you can hire a project manager who will do all this work for you for a fee. However, such people are thin on the ground and there are potential contractual problems when the job overruns or goes wrong in some way. There is also little guarantee that the project manager will succeed in hiring the best labour at the best

price unless you hold him to a fixed price for the whole job – in which case – hey presto! – he's just become a general builder.

A third approach is to select a builder first, preferably even before the design stage, and to work in a sort of loose partnership with them throughout the project. Design and build – it's a buzzword in big commercial construction at the moment (where, incidentally, the problems are remarkably similar if only on a different scale).

Rather than trying to tie builders down to the lowest possible price for a set of plans they have had no part in formulating, start by asking them what they think are the most cost effective ways of getting what you want and who is the best person to design such a house. This way you can work to the strengths of your builder and hopefully use these to drive down costs.

Some builders will respond very positively to such an approach – others will run a mile, much preferring to work in the traditional ways. And whilst a more open, trusting approach to building can reap dividends, it's also not without its share of problems.

Just because you start out talking partnering and understanding doesn't mean that you'll end up there – and untangling a messy design and build contract can be more work than sorting out the more traditional adversarial way of working. However, I do feel there is a lot to be said for it, particularly if you don't want to get keel-hauled by builders putting

huge risk margins on your job. If the builder is prepared to open his books for you to see his costs, then maybe a cost plus arrangement has a chance of working. You need to keep on top of the costs as they arise and monitor, monitor, monitor. But if the job runs to an agreed programme, then the cost overruns should be minimal. Tip here: a job that finishes on time never goes over budget (well hardly ever).

WHAT MAKES A GOOD BUILDER?

Hugely successful contractors (or project managers if you prefer) are a rare breed. Though they almost invariably have their roots in one of the building trades, the skills that are required for managing building work are quite different. Good, clear communication is perhaps the most important and, if you are weighing up potential contractors, it is probably the aspect to which you should give the most careful consideration. After all, if you can understand what they are on about then chances are that they will understand what you are on about too, and anyone working for them will also understand their instructions. Of the things that go wrong on building sites, 90% of the time it's because of misunderstandings or plain bad instructions.

In some ways this is good news, because if you meet someone face to face then you do at least get an immediate impression. It doesn't follow they will do a good job but there is a much higher chance that they'll do the job you want them to do rather than one they want to do. This calls into question your judgement of character: can you tell the difference between the hard-working, trustworthy, reliable characters and the shifty, slapdash and chaotic ones? It's terribly difficult, particularly as long exposure to the building game has a habit of turning the most upright people ever so slightly cynical and bitter. I suspect that the truth is it's always a bit of a gamble; there is no cast-iron way of making sure you are entering into a marriage made in heaven. This doesn't mean that it's not worth taking some elementary precautions.

SELECTING A BUILDER

1 Try and start with a sensible shortlist. Get one or two of the bigger local builders on board whom you suspect will do a good job even though you expect they might be expensive. Try and choose the smaller ones from recommendations rather than pins in the 'Yellow Pages'.

2 Don't waste everybody's time by selecting fifteen or twenty contractors. It's much better to have three of four who you contact (even visit) personally beforehand to see if they have the time or the inclination to do your job. If the response is lukewarm, don't bother to send documents for quotation, look elsewhere.

3 If you want to check on financial standing and/or membership of trade organisations now is the time to do it. Don't get someone to quote for your work if you are going to reject them later because they don't meet your standards.

4 The more detailed your plans, the more meaningful will be the quotations. Ideally, you should send drawings already approved by the building inspector. If you have a separate written specification, the process of quotation becomes much more straightforward (and therefore tends to increase accuracy).

5 Ask what the day-work rates are and what mark-ups will be applied to materials supplied, which were specifically excluded from the quotation – usually done to allow you to make up your mind nearer the time.

6 Be suspicious of very low quotations. Often you may find that most of the replies cluster around a figure (say £70,000) but one comes in way below (say £45,000). Without revealing your hand, try and elicit how this quotation was arrived at: what does this guy do that the others don't know about? Why is he so desperate for the work? It may just be the cheap one is the only one not in on the price fixing scam but, even so, be wary.

7 If there is no clear winner on price, then have a second informal round of interviews (probably by phone) to elicit more information. Are they busy? Are they very busy? If you haven't got a contract specifying a completion date, find out when could they start and how long would they take? Who would actually be running the job? Could you meet this person on their current site (good chance for a snoop)? Do they have a mobile number? Are they contactable out of hours?

8 If all still equal, then go for the best communicator. The one who you understand best, or just get on with best, will also be the one who will understand you best. It's that old chemistry at work again. If you've got to this stage and still haven't made up your mind, then trust your instinct.

Some of the very best of our small builders are extremely unambitious and don't go out chasing work. They keep a gang of three, four or five guys going and will turn work away rather than take on twice their normal workload. They don't advertise and you won't find them in the 'Yellow Pages'. Often they don't even do quotations. Clients willingly wait months, even years, to get hold of these builders and work is almost always carried out in a spirit of trust and co-operation, usually with very few subcontractors involved at all. If you value quality above price and informality above deadlines then this may be the route for you. If there are any of these mediaeval craft gangs in your neck of the woods, chances are your architect or building inspector will know of them.

WHAT MAKES A GOOD CLIENT?

Be straight about money. If money is tight then sit down at the beginning of the job and discuss how and when payments will be made. Don't leave it until the end.

Communicate well. Choose a builder you can talk to easily and one who you in turn understand. If you choose to use a main contractor, then work with him all the time.

Don't issue instructions to the subcontractors over the head of the main contractor. There is a chain of command and you should stick to it. It's sometimes very tempting to short-circuit it, but it very quickly gets messy. This dictum gets terribly hard to stick to when the main contractor has gone AWOL.

If you enter into a written contract, then understand what the basic terms are. This applies even if the arrangement is less formal.

Don't be afraid to ask questions. If the job starts taking off on a course you hadn't envisaged, then find out why at once.

Realise that part of the key to getting good building work done is to be a good client, which translates as being a good manager. Don't be a passive consumer. And avoid letting things decline into a 'them and us' situation.

Don't keep changing your mind. And don't abuse the 'free quotation' ethos that general contractors operate on. It's one thing to get a free quotation at the outset of the job, it's quite another to demand costed alternative quotes for every finish item in your house. Main contractors spend an inordinate amount of time generating quotations and the more they are asked to provide them, the less time they have to spend on managing their business.

If you want to withhold money because you feel something has not been done satisfactorily then be specific about exactly how much you are withholding and why. Explain what you want the builder to do in order for you to release the payment.

This still doesn't guarantee success. But if you as a client play your part to the full and don't mess your builder around, then you won't be doing your chances of success any harm. In my experience, a good client is the single most important element of a successful building project – indeed, good clients tend to get good building work done for them. And if there is a key to being a good client, it is to understand just what your role is and playing it to the full.

HIRING SUBBIES

If you've chosen to dispense with the main contractor then you'll almost certainly be in the business of hiring subcontractors. Project management – piece of piss, mate. Subcontractors – no problem – there are simple ground rules, aren't there! Well there are. They go something like this.

WHAT SHOULD HAPPEN IS:
- never hire anybody who hasn't been personally recommended to you
- always check on their previous work
- always get three quotations in writing
- never hire anybody on an hourly rate; get all work priced beforehand
- check to see if they are members of a reputable trade organisation
- check to see what guarantee they offer
- never pay up front
- always get 'extras' priced and put in writing before they are carried out

- impose a time schedule with penalties for late completion. All sounds good, sensible stuff.

WHAT ACTUALLY HAPPENS:
- never hire anyone who hasn't been personally recommended to you: You might have to wait a long time.
- always check on their previous work: Has anyone seriously got time to do this? Chasing up old working contacts for subcontractors who may only be on site for a day or two doesn't feature highly on most 'To Do' lists.
- always get three quotations in writing: You must be joking. You may have to approach about ten to get three to respond in writing and even then you may have to wait (and chase) for two months.
- never hire anybody on an hourly rate; get all work priced before hand: Fine for most trades, but sometimes this is totally impractical. You have to have a detailed specification ready and chances are, if you are trying to save money, you won't have.
- check to see if they are members of a reputable trade organisation: They'll probably be more expensive if they are.
- check to see what guarantee they offer: Worth checking on for kitchens and plumbing but a bit meaningless for most subbies. They've either done it right or they haven't and you'll have to check.
- never pay up front: Good advice for anybody anytime. Sometimes it's very hard to keep.
- always get 'extras' put in writing before they are carried out: Alright in

principle but, again, sometimes totally impractical if you are in a hurry (you will be). Get a site diary instead. If you want it to go down in writing be prepared to do the writing yourself.

■ impose a time schedule with penalties for late completion: Risk losing your subbies.

SUBCONTRACTORS

Legally a subcontractor (or subbie) is a worker who gets hired and paid by a main contractor. If a subcontractor works directly for you then they are, strictly speaking, not subcontractors at all but ordinary (or main) contractors.

The difference is crucial because if you become a main contractor you also become responsible for policing your subcontractors' tax affairs – lots of unpaid admin! However, if you are the client, this all flows over your head – i.e. you don't have to know anything about it. Even though your subbies won't be subbies at all when they are working for you, everybody still refers to them as subbies.

Generally speaking, when we say 'subbies' we are referring to tradesmen providing a specific skill, like a plumber or a brickie. Sometimes subbies will be one-man bands. Sometimes they will be small firms employing several people. The one-man bands will tend to work for a cheaper hourly rate but may well be just as expensive when it comes to quoted works.

ESSENTIAL SUBBIES

Generally, you will be able to build a house by hiring the following characters:

■ groundworkers. Someone with a JCB and access to a lorry

■ brickwork (brickies). Often overlaps with groundworkers – one of the two (or you) will have to lay the drains. Often work in gangs of three (two brickies/one labourer). Don't usually supply materials

■ carpenters (chippies, or joiners up north and in Scotland). Often work in twos (no labourer). Don't usually supply materials

■ roofers. Most often hired in small gangs who supply and fix, sometimes doing the scaffolding as well

■ plasterers/dry liners. Mixture of one-man bands and small firms

■ plumbers. Same mixture of one-man bands and small firms

■ electricians. Same mixture

■ decorators. Most selfbuilders do this themselves but there are plenty of 'professionals' around.

There are a number of other specialist subbies who you may want to use: glaziers, garage door fitters, kitchen specialists, pavers and drive layers, landscapers, scaffolders. Refer to Chapter 12 on 'Shopping' for more details.

CHOOSING A GOOD SUBBIE

I'd like to come up with an easy rule for picking good subbies but I don't know what it is. If you've found one perhaps you would let me know. Obviously, you can go to great lengths to see that you appoint a master, but this can be very time-consuming and

if the guy is only going to be on site for a few days it seems like a big case of overkill. Generally, contractors and subbies know the going rates for various trades and they can usually work out an amicable agreement over a cup of tea and a ten minute chat, and this is how 99% of subbies get hired. It's easy come, easy go and if someone is useless they usually get asked to move on. However, if you want to ensure high standards from the start then you have to do a great deal more work, taking up references and talking to other contacts.

NB: Don't forget the builders' dilemma explained in Chapter One. High standards don't tend to go with cheap prices. You gets one or you gets the other.

LABOUR-ONLY v SUPPLY & FIX

Subbies tend to come in two distinct flavours. The labour-only subbies are usually hired singly or in small informal gangs. They tend to be concentrated in the heavy building side (brickworkers, carpenters, plasterers). Many of the later trades – i.e. those concerned with finishes – are more often organised by small businesses, which prefer to sell a package whereby they supply the materials and the labour to fix the materials: typically, roofers, plumbers, electricians, glaziers and kitchen fitters. These supply and fix subbies will tend to be more organised – you'll be able to get quotes out of them – and possibly a little more expensive, particularly as they are in the business of marking-up materials they buy on your behalf. In effect, you are introducing an extra layer of management, which has to be paid for.

From a small builder's point of view, the big advantage of hiring small firms, rather than singletons, is that cost control becomes much clearer. If someone is quoting to supply and fit a kitchen into your new house for £15,000 then you know in advance what the damage is. However, if you rely on your own buying power plus Jim's joinery skills (paid for on an hourly rate) then you will just have to hope that it'll be less than £15,000; logic says it should be, but such finishing jobs have a habit of running over budget. You could ask Jim to quote to install your kitchen but Jim might well be reluctant to do so, especially if you are supplying the kitchen fittings. And what about co-ordinating with the plumber, the electrician and the tiler? Who will do this? If it's to be you and they end up keeping Jim waiting (they will) then it's you who is taking advantage of Jim's fixed price and he'd have every right to cry foul. This sort of finishing work involves so much intricate planning that it is unrealistic to expect every part of it to be quoted for separately, so it tends to be either subbed out in its entirety or done on a time and materials basis.

Not all these vans are white, but you get the picture. Subbies virtually live in vans and it's hard to see how you could build a house without some parking issues.

On urban sites, the problem is more acute and it calls for tact and diplomacy with neighbours. By and large, if you keep everyone informed as to what is happening, people are incredibly helpful.

DAYWORK v PRICED WORK

Daywork is the term commonly used to describe payments by the hour (or day) and it contrasts with priced work, where payments are related to specific works having been completed. For example, a brickie on daywork might hope to get paid, say, £150 per day: if he was on a price, he would hope to get paid something like £300 for every 1000 bricks laid. All things being equal, you would hope that he would lay about 500 bricks per day whichever system was being used to pay him, but human nature being what it is, it is widely assumed that the person paying the brickie will get better value from priced work. Many advisors say you should only ever hire builders on a price work basis but there are many situations where a daywork arrangement is both easier and more flexible.

If you are building to a tight budget, price work is almost certainly the route to take. For a rookie builder this is perhaps doubly important because you don't know what's in a day's work. Ask yourself how many doors a chippie should be able to hang in a day; if you haven't got a clue then you qualify as a rookie builder.

The main problem with always insisting on price work stems from the fact that it is, contractually, a much tighter type of agreement and that, for it to work, you need to be able to describe the work accurately before you can readily ask for it to be quoted. So really you need to have a professionally written specification for it all to make sense to subcontractors. It's not enough to say, 'Here is a set of plans. How much will you charge to put the brickwork and blockwork up?', because there are any number of little incidentals that increase the size of this work and make a mockery of your attempts to limit the damage.

MEASURED RATES

Another problem is that many subbies find plans about as easy to read as you do. This is less of a problem with the finishing trades where they can come and give the house a once over and don't have to resort to plans, but often the hardest parts of a job to quote are the first parts when no house shell yet exists. Here a common ruse is to agree a rate for each section of work (say £400 per 1000 bricks laid) and then to total up when the work is completed.

This is a perfectly sensible way of going about it and protects the subbie from any dispute about differences between what's on the plan and what actually got built: however, there is a great scope here for disagreements over the quantities actually built. Even qualified quantity surveyors will disagree by a few per cent and they work to an agreed set of measuring rules: a contractor and a subcontractor may end up 10% apart.

Note also that brickies like to 'measure through openings' for both brickwork and blockwork. Thus they don't deduct anything from the overall surface areas to account for windows and doors, which can account for as much as 25% of the area being built up. In return, they normally fit the joinery in as they go without any extra charge.

CASH PAYMENTS

One of the big advantages of organising your own building work is the ability to negotiate discounts with tradesmen in return for paying them in cash. This is, of course, illegal and any serious publication such as this cannot, naturally, condone such behaviour. But cash payments for casual work are not going to stop because I start being self-righteous.

The normal builder's scam is to take off VAT in exchange for payments in cash, but this does not make much sense in new housebuilding because almost all the work is zero-rated so you are not paying it in the first place. Unlike the professional contractor, a selfbuilder is not required to police subcontractors' tax arrangements and if you choose to pay them in cash then that is a matter between you and them – it is not illegal simply to pay cash. Should the subcontractor then fail to declare this income it is they who are committing an offence, though subsequent inquiries might get back to you to uncover these payments.

Cash payments actually do very little to benefit the new housebuilder unless they are used to negotiate lower prices from subcontractors, something most subbies are reluctant to do.

CONTRACTS

'DO I NEED ONE?'

You've already got one. It's a principle of contract law that every time you buy something or hire someone (or something) you enter into a contract. Any item you purchase should perform adequately, any person you hire should carry out the work described competently and you, in turn, should pay them the agreed amount. In essence, it's that simple and this basic principle holds whether you are hiring a baby-sitter or constructing the Channel Tunnel.

All building work is covered by these principles – it's why builders are referred to as contractors – and don't think that just because you haven't got a written contract then you have no redress should things go wrong. However, it is also true to say that if things do go wrong, the more written evidence you can produce to show how and why, the stronger your case will be.

If you can produce a written contract, signed by the builder, to say that he should have been finished by the end of August, and it's now November and you still haven't got any glazing in, then you've got a pretty good case for withholding payment. Without something written down, it's your word against his and – well there might just be two sides to the story: you're not in a completely hopeless position, but your case is much weaker.

'SO A WRITTEN CONTRACT IS ESSENTIAL?'

Not at all. It's actually one of the most overrated of safety features devised by professionals largely to justify their fat fees. Take the aforementioned Channel Tunnel, the largest construction project undertaken in these parts in my lifetime. Teams of lawyers were drafted in by both sides to negotiate contracts designed to be as watertight as they hope the tunnel will be. Did it get the tunnel built on time and to budget? Of course not. Re-enter those same teams of lawyers to argue about compensation, etc. Who benefits out of all this? The contractors, Eurotunnel and its shareholders – or the lawyers?

'IT'S ALL DOWN TO A HANDSHAKE?'

Not at all. That's throwing the baby out with the bath water. The basis of a building contract is that the client contracts to pay a specified sum in return for completion of a list of specified tasks. The more detailed this list, the stronger the contract becomes. If you have a professionally drawn up specification of works, then you already have about as good a contract as you can get. Signing a formal written contract for work that is only specified in the loosest terms is, in comparison, a complete waste of time and money.

'YOU THINK ACCEPTANCE OF A QUOTE IS ENOUGH?'

Yes. If a builder has seen whatever plans and specifications you have, by quoting for them he is committing himself to carry out the work competently. If there are further conditions you wish to set (such as time limits), then you should add these to your specifications. Should it later prove that your specifications are inadequate then so be it; the situation would be no better had you signed a written contract.

'IS THE SPEC WITH MY OFF-THE-PEG PLANS?'

You've missed the point. No contract is ever completely watertight. The more detail you put into a contract, the tighter it gets. There isn't a point at which it suddenly becomes OK; rather you get what you pay for. It's like asking how much life insurance is enough when you know that there's a 99% chance that you won't need any and a one per cent chance that twenty million would be very useful. Very detailed specifications are time-consuming to produce and are, therefore, expensive; only you can decide whether you need one.

'BUT I'M PLANNING TO ORGANISE THE WORK MYSELF?'

It's unusual to sign contracts with labour-only subcontractors or indeed to put anything down in writing. Normally, the work is described verbally or with reference to any plans and specifications to hand. However, the contractual principles involved in hiring subcontractors are no different and neither are your chances of redress, should things go wrong.

One of the penalties of building on the cheap is that you are more exposed to bad practice, but hopefully you can compensate to some extent by your frequent site presence. In the absence of any written undertakings, keep a site diary to record the comings and goings and at least you'll have some written evidence in case of trouble. Even to be able to say, 'Gary and Pete were there just two days in that week and no-one else turned up till the 27th,' puts you in a much stronger position than saying 'they were hardly ever there'.

'I SAY. I SAY, I SAY'

The above section appeared verbatim in the original edition of the 'Housebuilder's Bible' and its assertion that you don't need a contract has caused one or two people to hop up and down with indignation. Perhaps they have a point. The fact that I've never built with contracts doesn't necessarily prove that they are a waste of time.

Julian Owen, a well known selfbuild architect, pointed out that he was required professionally to work with a contract and that they didn't have to be expensive or difficult to understand. He particularly favours the simple 16-page JCT Minor Works Contract that is written in clear English and helps all sides to understand their responsibilities. I won't argue against this proposal but I stand by my original line that a contract is no substitute for a detailed written specification of work.

There's also the little point that a builder faced with a formal looking contract to sign will react by upping his quote. And if he sees penalty clauses, he will up his quote even more.

ANYTHING ELSE TO SORT OUT?

There are some things that you need to be clear about that are not to do with the technical specifics of building. The formal way of dealing with them would be to enclose the terms along with the plans and specs you send for quotation; by putting in a quotation, the contractor implicitly accepts your terms. However, you could choose to sort these terms out more informally after acceptance of quotation; if you are confident that the terms are not too onerous on the builder, he should be happy to accept and, if he isn't, then you've just been given the clearest indication you'll ever get that this marriage was not made in heaven. Reconsider. Sorting out these matters is in the interest of both parties and very often the first move will come from the builder.

INSURANCE

For terms and rates, see 'Insurance' section later in this chapter. Whoever is organising the building work should have cover. Make sure it's in place.

PAYMENTS

Agree payment terms. If a lender is advancing your money in stages, be open with the builder about when and what these stages are. Generally it's the builder who is advancing you credit and this makes him even more vulnerable than you are.

RETENTION

It is quite common to withhold a little money (between 2 and 5%) until snags are adequately sorted out. However, don't try and spring this on a builder halfway through a job as if it was a matter of course. It's not. Furthermore, it's always a delicate issue – it reeks of a lack of trust – and some perfectly good builders find it all rather insulting and choose to steer clear of such contracts. After all, how would you feel if 5% of your pay was withheld until such time as your employers saw fit. An awful lot of builders, when faced with a retention clause, just add the sum onto their initial quotation.

There is an additional problem with retentions. How do you define the end of the job? What is *practical completion*? People often take possession of their new home or extension long before the builder is really ready to hand over and what tends to happen is that a rolling snags list develops. Some items are clearly down to the builder to complete satisfactorily, some are extras, and many snags are rather indeterminate contractually. You could argue that the job is not completed until the snags list is finalled off, but if so, what is the retention money being held back for? Snagging the snags? If that's what you want, then really you are looking for a guarantee, which is a slightly different matter.

TIME PENALTIES

Usually, these take the form of damages, which are to be deducted from the overall contract value if the work is not completed to an agreed schedule. For some reason I've not been able to fathom, these are conventionally referred to as liquidated damages. Again, it's one to sort out right at the outset and it's a very adversarial condition to place on a builder.

Time penalties make sense when you will suffer financial hardship (such as paying extra rent). However, when a job overruns it is more often than not very hard to decide who is to blame. You have to be prepared to keep your side of the bargain, which means no delays in agreed payments along the route and no changes to the specification of works. This still leaves the messy grey area of unavoidable delays (weather, strikes, illness, disputes with architects) which could keep an impartial referee busy for weeks. You need a very tight specification to be able to argue your side effectively.

These added conditions are really nothing more than specialised forms of insurance and if you load a contract with retention clauses and time penalties you can expect to pay more overall for the works described.

EXTRAS

The biggest single contractual nightmare any builder faces is how to adequately negotiate what the trade calls variations but what everyone else refers to as extras. People call them extras because, like Topsy, they seem to grow and grow. Some do shrink (hence variations being a more accurate term) but for every one that shrinks or even disappears there must be a dozen that expand. It's a particularly critical problem with renovations and smaller works (where often 40% of the final bill is made up of items not originally quoted for) but the new housebuilder is not immune from catching these particular bugs.

If you've got plenty of time and money and like a nice loose specification where you can make up your mind as you go along then you'll be wondering what all the fuss is about, but if you belong to the 95% of builders who break out into a sweat every time a bank statement arrives you will want to know how to avoid these nightmares.

The good news is that you can inoculate yourself against most of them. The bad news is that immunisation is itself expensive and time-consuming. Many extras can be avoided by having a professionally written specification, but people wanting to save money will probably have avoided paying for one in the first place and are usually the same people who can least afford extras.

As if the fact that extras occur at all isn't bad enough, when they do occur, you, the client, are negotiating with a gun to your head; you can hardly hire another builder just to do the extras. If you've gone in a bit hard at the beginning, including onerous time penalties and retentions, you can be sure that the builders will have their revenge here. Not only can they

potentially stitch you up pricewise, but also they have a cast-iron excuse for blowing your time penalty clauses out of the water. Even if things haven't descended to this sabre rattling, adversarial level there is still ample scope to misunderstand and to misconstrue – 'Oh I didn't realise that meant the glass had to be toughened as well.' 'Well that's an extra £200.' If you are the kind of client who expects your builder to give you fully costed options for free throughout the job, as in 'How much extra would it be if we had a bidet in the kitchen?' you probably deserve to pay over the odds in any event.

Each little decision forms a mini-contract in itself and accounting for them can take up over half the total admin time spent on a job. The golden rules are:
▣ make it clear that extras need to be authorised by you before work starts on them
▣ always negotiate extras direct with the main contractor – that is the person with whom you placed the initial contract, not with anyone working for them
▣ write down what you've agreed – even if it's just in a site diary
▣ the reasons for extras are many and various. Sometimes it is down to unquantifiable works discovered after the building work has begun – in new buildings, this type of problem usually occurs underground. Most often it is down to the client adding to the original specification of works as the job progresses or, as it's known in the trade, 'changing their bloody minds again'.

There are two specialised forms of extras, or variables, which deserve closer attention.

PRIME COST SUMS

PC sums are not a new form of anti-sexist arithmetic but a good old builder's routine for dealing with loose specifications. PC sums are put into contracts to allow you, the client, the freedom to select a particular product at a later date. For instance, you might put a PC sum of £500 for a bathroom suite into a specification. The contractor will have included this amount in the quotation but the actual figure you pay will be down to which bathroom suite you choose.

There is a nasty little problem here because things like bathroom suites have list prices and they have trade prices – indeed the trade price is a matter for negotiation. Don't bulldoze in and buy the kit yourself, because the builder (or perhaps plumber in this case) is expecting to make a profit on this deal and they would have every right to expect you to reimburse them for their lost profit.

The normal arrangement is that the builder buys what you specify, and that you get to pay list price and the builder pockets the difference between list price and his trade price; but this can work out very expensive, particularly if you up the spec. There is no reason why you shouldn't negotiate a radically different deal whereby you pay trade prices, but make damn sure that you negotiate it beforehand – preferably right at the beginning. Again, the sure way to avoid these sorts of problems is to have a tight specification and that means one without PC sums. This requires decisions on things like kitchen and bathroom finishes before the job starts.

PROVISIONAL SUMS

Like their cousins, the PC sums, the provisional sums are placed in contracts where there is an element of doubt about the amount of work to be carried out. They are much more common in renovations than in new building but there are nevertheless areas – notably underground works – which most builders will only estimate rather than enter into a fixed price quotation. Understandably so. It's a buck-passing device, a way of saying that if there's more work to do than can reasonably be anticipated, then you, dear client, will be the one who has to pay. Well, you knew it was a risky game. Provisional sums are just one of the things that makes building work such a gamble. You can try to force contractors to take on the risk themselves but their understandable response is to hoick prices through the roof; more realistically you can establish guidelines for how provisional works will be charged: a labour rate, a mark-up applied to materials, that sort of thing.

MANAGING PRELIMS

Tool and equipment hire is a rather specialised area that deserves a mention. As with most things in the field of project management, a little planning beforehand will reap dividends along the way. What equipment you need to hire (or buy) depends very much on how you plan to manage your build. For instance, if you are entrusting the whole shooting match to a main contractor, then you really shouldn't need anything at all. But if you are acting as the main contractor and hiring subcontractors to complete the various trades, you will need to discuss each subcontractor's requirements beforehand.

It can be a confusing area. For instance, some subcontractors – notably plumbers, electricians and most carpenters – tend to come fully fitted out with toolkits and access equipment: others, typically bricklayers, expect you to provide everything other than their trowels and their levels. With groundworks, you tend to hire the kit and the labour together as a single unit – thus when a JCB is quoted at £400 a day you are getting both a JCB and a driver for that price.

TOOL HIRE SHOPS

If you want to stay ahead of the game, then make sure you have opened trading accounts with a couple of tool hire shops because you will save yourself an awful lot of faffing about. For many novice project managers, tool and plant hire is one of those things that you just stumble into once the project is up and running. But after you've been and hired three things and left £50 deposits which did or didn't get credited to your final bill and anyway you've gone and lost the paperwork which was in the front of the car but now you can't find it...you'll wish you had opened a trading account at the hire shop too. If you do, you will be able to take tools for as long as you want without having to pay any deposit. Deliveries and collections are also much easier to organise – most hire shops will deliver and pick-up for a small charge (around £5-£10).

Generally, the hire charges are structured so that you pay the highest rate over the first 24 hours, then the daily rate falls significantly if you hire for longer periods. After about ten weeks you will have paid as much in hire charges as it would cost you to buy, so hiring really only makes sense over shorter periods. The number of things you can hire never ceases to amaze me and rather than bore you with a long list, if you are interested get hold of a catalogue yourself – Hewdens is particularly good.

HIRING v BUYING

Which begs the questions: what should you hire and what should you buy? There are a few basic bits of kit that it would seem near essential to have with you permanently and therefore you should buy if you haven't already got them. I would include in this basic hand tools like a 5m tape measure, hammer, saw, screwdriver, 1.2m spirit level, the sort of thing you need to put up shelves or assemble flat-pack kitchen units. I would also place a cordless (£100+) power drill, a 30m cable reel extension lead (£30) and a 6m ladder (£120) on my list of essentials;

this equipment will be useful for on going maintenance, not just for housebuilding.

How much else it is worth buying is really only a question you can answer. It depends on how quickly you plan to build, how much direct involvement you will have in the building process and whether or not your selected subbies will have their own equipment. A brickie gang will, for instance, very often expect you not only to supply tea but also a cement mixer, and it may well make good sense to buy one that you can sell on at the job's end (though don't expect very much for a used mixer). If you work in the trade or have serious DIY pretensions, then you will probably have all of the above plus a lot more and you may view your project as a wonderful opportunity to expand your range of tools. But if you don't intend to carry on building after you've finished your house, then it is pointless to lay out thousands to buy tools which will only ever fill up your precious storage space and provide rich pickings for would-be thieves.

Whether you hire or buy, the proportion of your total bill going on either hiring or buying equipment is large (often around 2% of total build costs) and can be one major hidden cost to creep up on the unwary. Also note that selfbuilders are not able to reclaim VAT on tool purchases or tool and plant hire, including such items as scaffolding and fencing.

SCAFFOLDING
Scaffolding is normally undertaken by dedicated scaffolders or

Scaffolding is good indicator of the quality of the builder. Has it been erected properly? Is it clean? Is it all in place or have boards been borrowed for other tasks? Are the ladders secure? All tell-tale signs to look for.

occasionally roofing gangs. A standard scaffolding contract would specify an agreed price for a hire period of eight or, perhaps, ten weeks; if the hire continues beyond the agreed period, a surcharge is levied – typically 5% of the original price per week. The original price would include for three or sometimes four visits from the scaffolders to erect the different levels (known as lifts) needed for the other trades to put up the house.

Single-storey houses (and detached garages) will typically need only one lift but its level will have to be adjusted between brickwork and roofing; a two-storey house needs

two lifts, each being adjusted in level at some point. Guide prices for scaffolding are £50 per m run per storey and to calculate the relevant metre runs add 15% to the perimeter measurements of the buildings you wish to scaffold to get the scaffolder's lengths.

If you want to take control of the scaffolding process itself, there is a system called Kwikstage by Kwikform UK which just slots together, rather similar to erecting an aluminium tower scaffold, making it particularly suitable for those who are taking a more hands-on approach and want to have scaffolding erected for much longer than the normal time span.

Chapter 5

One of the skills of project management is working out what needs to be where and when. Our urban site had no rear or side access and heavyside materials like bricks and sand had to be placed in the garden area before the foundations were dug.

Kwikform provide some training for people who have never used scaffolding before or, alternatively, can provide an erection service. Rental prices for a four-bedroom house sized project work out at around £80 a week.

SKIPS

Part of your build plan should involve a close look at how you plan to dispose of waste; for many small builders a skip is a practical and economical solution. The basic cost of a builder's standard sized skip has more than doubled since the introduction of Landfill tax in 1996. By 2019, this tax had risen to £91 per tonne, and as most skips

hold a tonne or three, it has had a significant impact on prices. It's not all bad news: skip companies are able to recycle some of the typical skip waste, such as timber and metal, and this reduces the effects of the Landfill Tax.

Skips are usually charged at a flat rate which includes delivery, swapping over, final removal and waste disposal. You don't get charged for keeping a skip on site, unless you are paying the council for a road permit, which is added to the bill separately. If you plan to use skips, it is well worth setting up an account with your chosen supplier.

Skips come in three sizes:
- LARGE hold 6.2m³ (8 yards),

which is a maximum 7-8 tons and will cost £150-£200
- MEDIUM hold 3m³ (4 yards), equals around 5 tons and will cost £100-£120
- MINI-SKIPS hold 1.5m³ (2 yards), equals up to 2.5 tons at a cost of around £80-£100.

If you want a skip on the road, there is red tape and a permit involved, often around £70 for a fortnight. You can save a little money if you can guarantee that you will be filling a skip with inert waste, and even more money if you can fill it with usable hardcore. And you can also use skips to get sand and aggregates delivered to site, which saves on added transportation costs.

Given that all building sites produce copious quantities of rubbish, I think that having a skip on site (certainly during the latter stages of the build) is essential: if you disagree, then at least have some coherent alternative strategy worked out for waste disposal.

SITE FENCING

There are an increasing number of sites where some sort of perimeter fencing is advisable, if only to stop unwanted visitors clambering all over your building site and walking off with your toolkit.

The standard steel fences (often referred to as Heras fencing) hire come in 3.5m lengths and cost about £5/length/week. If you need security fencing for more than five months, it will probably pay you to buy it and resell when you have finished.

SECURITY TIPS

▓ Have valuable materials (joinery, sanitaryware, kitchen goods) on site for as short a time as possible before fixing

▓ If you have nowhere to lock up kit like cement mixers, barrows and hand tools then at least hide them so that the casual visitor does not see them from the road

▓ Take small tools (especially power tools) home with you

▓ Get the windows glazed and the external doors hung as soon as is practicably possible

▓ If your site is particularly vulnerable, consider building the detached garage first (if you have one) to use as a strong room. Alternatively, do what many of the professionals do and hire a container for the duration. An onsite CCTV camera will also help as a deterrent.

One way of keeping thieves off a site is to install CCTV. We did this on our site in Cambridge and, lo and behold, we caught a thief on film very early one May morning. Not that it made a lot of difference. The full story is to be found in Ch.15.

HEALTH & SAFETY

Building sites are by their very nature dangerous places. We demand finished buildings that are themselves structurally sound, weatherproof and safe to live-in but in order to create them we have to go through a series of steps, which are inherently unsafe. Anyone managing small building sites is legally required to be aware of these risks and to take measures to minimise their impact. New housebuilding is actually one of the safer sectors of the construction industry – a fact borne out by lower insurance premiums – but there are still a large number of potential hazards to be negotiated.

EXCAVATIONS

Trench work is usually fairly safe at levels down to about 1m (waist height), but thereafter the dangers of trench collapse become very much greater. There are well proven techniques for shoring up trenches and if you are not sure what you are doing then for God's sake get hold of someone who is.

Deep foundations are potentially very dangerous and you need to guard against not just trench collapse but also materials and people falling down into them. If you are working close to or underpinning an existing structure there is the additional problem that you could undermine it and cause a potentially catastrophic collapse.

Another problem to always be aware of is encountering buried cables and pipes, something that is common when you are opening roads to make service connections. You can reduce this risk by doing your homework and trying to establish just where cables are likely to be buried.

PLANT

Control machinery. Heavy plant can kill or maim if not properly controlled. If you get behind the wheel of a dumper truck don't play silly buggers, be very wary. They are not difficult to drive but they can be difficult to control, particularly if it's wet and muddy. They can easily end up crushing someone. Dumpers are often used to pour concrete into foundations and this frequently leads to accidents. Also, ensure cement mixers are properly seated before you start loading.

LADDERS

Don't be tempted to be macho – anchor the top end on to something secure. Don't make do with funky old ladders with broken rungs. And wonky step ladders are a nightmare you can live without.

SCAFFOLDING

Don't be afraid to spend money on extra scaffolding. If you are uneasy about doing some task off a ladder (or a scaffold tower) then get proper scaffolding erected. It's surprisingly cheap and you'll get the job done in half the time. Also be very wary about 'rearranging' scaffolding. Usually, this means nicking boards off the scaffolding to use elsewhere. Think who might be going to use the scaffolding in the near future and make sure they know what's been going on.

POWER TOOLS

If you don't already have a kit of power tools but are planning to buy some, then buy 110v ones rather than 240v. You'll need a transformer to get them to work but they are far safer. When you hire power tools you should be offered a choice of 110 or 240v. If you are committed to using 240v power tools then ensure that your temporary electricity supply is protected with RCDs (Residual Current Devices).

ELECTRIC CABLES

Long extension leads are a menace (though sometimes unavoidable). Try and avoid trailing them across site where vehicles may drive over them.

Get a cordless screwdriver – they are brilliant and you won't need all those extension leads.

Cables on building sites tend to get gashed and generally bashed about and it's not unusual for bare wires to get exposed.

Keep your eyes open for this sort of thing and if you come across badly frayed cable then replace it, don't bodge it with insulating tape.

STEEL TOE-CAPS

Bruised and broken toes are still one of the commonest of accidents. Yet you still see subbies wearing trainers on site. If you are buying purpose made shoes, get some with steel toe caps (from most builder's merchants from around £30). If you manage to acquire a pair with Doctor Martens written on them you'll have a valuable fashion accessory to boot. Most builder's merchants also do a line of steel toe-capped wellies.

HEAD INJURIES

Most 'serious' sites insist on hard hats being worn at all times, yet you won't even find a hard hat on most small sites – which is a shame because small sites are no less dangerous and, when people are working above you, a hard hat makes good sense. Yet, because they have an image of being 'for the big boys only,' the small builders and their subbies tend to shun them at all times. At least make an effort. Have a couple of hard hats on site and wear them when people are working on scaffolding above you.

SHARPS

Remove nails from loose timber lying around site. Common sense really but it usually gets overlooked. If you keep a clean and tidy site, this will be no

extra work. If you don't then chances are the only way you'll even know that nails are lying in wait is when you tread on them. Ouch.

LIFTING

Back injuries are by far the commonest cause of lost time for builders. They can usually be easily avoided by asking for some help when lifting heavy objects like bags of cement. Again, don't feel you have to be macho just because you're on a building site. Ask for help.

MINOR ACCIDENTS

Have a small first aid kit on site. Most injuries are minor and can readily be treated with TCP and a bandage.

CDM REGS

In April 2015, the CDM (Construction Design and Management) Regulations were expanded to include selfbuild for the first time. The CDM regs began life in 1995 and received a major upgrade in 2007. The earlier versions of CDM specifically excluded domestic clients but made substantial administrative demands on small builders running commercial sites. There was a key appointment of a CDM co-ordinator who had to take on responsibility for developing a Health and Safety file and ensuring that everybody involved on the job had some level of competence. The 2015 regs not only do away with this Co-ordinator role but make no mention at all of competence. Maybe competence was just too much to police. Maybe it was dropped because it was needlessly bureaucratic. But it's gone, and with it much of the purpose of CDM.

What's left? The Health and Safety file is still required but the guidance offered by the Health and Safety Executive (HSE) is to download an App called CDM Wizard (available only on Android and IoS, which shows just where this is being pitched). Fill it out — mostly a series of checkboxes, about 15 minutes work — and "This is the Construction Phase Plan of your job as required under CDM 2015." Sorted.

You also have to notify large jobs to the HSE before you start but many selfbuilds will not be classified as large. The threshold is that the job lasts longer than 30 working days and has more than 20 workers working simultaneously at any point in the project, or that the job as a whole exceeds 500 person days. Typical selfbuilds will come in somewhere around here, but few of them actually get as far as estimating this figure beforehand. If you have to comply, then look for form F10 which you can fill in online.

It is also noticeable that the 2007 CDM regs guidance was a much longer document and was frankly over-complicated. It didn't include any information about health and safety risks, merely their management. In contrast, nearly half of the 90-page CDM 2015 guidance concerns itself with managing specific risks you are likely to meet on site.

For instance, if you are involved in demolition, you are required to plan and carry it out in such a manner as to prevent danger or, where it is not practicable to prevent it, to reduce danger to as low a level as is reasonably practicable. It's hardly going to say anything else, is it? You are also required to have a written record of your plans before commencing, but if you have filled out the CDM Wizard, you will be there already.

So what exactly is required of today's selfbuilder, now that almost all building work comes under CDM? The guidance includes a flowchart (p86) which is about as clear as mud, as it bandies around terms like DIY and contractor without defining them. But if you work your way through this, you will find that you are more than likely deemed to be a domestic client and that you really don't have to do anything because the people working for you, be they designers, main contractors or individual tradesmen, become responsible for CDM by default, unless you want someone in particular to act as the CDM guy.

I don't happen to believe that CDM 2015 is particularly taxing on designers and contractors either. Designers are required to design in ways to minimise risk to workers and to follow-on maintenance, which isn't a bad idea and hardly needs a set of regulations to tell us as much. And contractors have to produce a health and safety file, which it appears can be done for free via the CDM Wizard. For large complex

jobs, CDM may come to have a significant role to play. But at the domestic client scale, it's now not far short of being a simple check-box exercise.

INSURANCE & WARRANTIES

There is a great deal of risk involved in building. One of the keys to successful building is to be able to manage this risk so that it doesn't overwhelm you, and one of the most useful tools, in this respect, is insurance.

Risk comes in two flavours, physical and financial. The physical risk on building sites is largely a health and safety matter and managing that risk is looked at in the previous section 'Site Safety'. But there is an overlap between the two types of risk because an injured subbie or passer-by may well choose to sue you for negligence and so the first (and arguably most important) layer of insurance rears up at you. In fact, you need two separate policies in place to cover this risk because the risk to the general public is dealt with quite differently to the risk to people working for you.

EMPLOYER'S LIABILITY

If you employ any subcontractors – and if you undertake your own project management you are deemed to be an employer, at least from an insurance angle – and any one of these subcontractors then has an accident, which might be construed to be your fault, then they can sue you. If this is a serious accident the sums of money at stake will be large.

Most policies now cover you for £10 million. A general builder is required by law to have an Employer's Liability policy in place and if you, as a client, are using a general contractor then you don't need your own policy in place as well. But you should check to see if your chosen contractor's policy is in place.

PUBLIC LIABILITY

This covers people (or objects) who you are not employing but might, nevertheless, still have cause to regret your building site ever existed. Maybe the mud from your site led to an accident, maybe your scaffolding fell down on someone's car, or maybe some kids were playing in your foundation trenches when... This is 'what if' insurance with a vengeance, but although the chances of a claim are small, any such claim could be extraordinarily large. Most standard policies cover you for £2 million worth of damage.

CONTRACT WORKS INSURANCE

Financial risk can never be entirely covered – for instance no one is going to insure you against your finished house being worth less than it cost to build. But there are various catastrophes that you can, to a certain extent, guard yourself from. The basic level of insurance here is covered by the Contract Works or All Risks policy, used to cover theft of plant and materials from site

(usually with a hefty excess) together with fire or structural damage to any structures that you may be working on. Your lender will probably insist that you have all risks cover just as a conventional mortgage lender will insist that buildings insurance is in place on any property they mortgage.

If you are employing a builder to erect your house, again you shouldn't need to take out your own policy as well but again you must check to see that they have current all risks insurance in place and that it's large enough to cover the value of your completed house – very often the policies stipulate a maximum contract value above which they won't pay out.

One important point to note is that contract works insurance does not cover any existing structure you may be altering, converting or extending. You would be expected to have this covered by a regular buildings insurance policy.

There is another particular problem, which occurs with unconverted barns with valuable planning permission riding on the back of them. The nominal value of the structure may be very low indeed – in fact it may well be a liability rather than an asset – but the planning permission depends on the building continuing to exist. Were it to burn down before conversion work is started, you could theoretically have the planning permission revoked, which would be far more expensive than replacing the original fabric. So the risk you are insuring in these cases is not the value of the building but the value of the

planning permission. Make sure that your insurance company understands the difference.

Contracts Works or All Risks policies are not mandatory and they usually come with dozens of options for you to pick and choose just which risks you want to cover. These go from the catastrophic (such as the building being destroyed) down to the inconvenient (such as some kid nicking your power tools). Just where you draw the line and just what excess you choose to bear yourself has an enormous impact on the cost of the policy.

There are only a handful of insurance companies active in the construction market and most of them are open to the needs of selfbuilders as well as the professionals. The names with the track records currently are Selfbuildzone, Self-builder.com and Buildstore via their Buildcare package.

Expect to pay around 0.5% of the total project value to get most of the cover you really need to build with a safety net. That translates at around £800 for a typical, four-bedroom detached house. Small builders pay much the same rate on their overall turnover. This would cover you for all the main areas that professional builders are supposed to cover, being employer's liability, public liability and all risks insurance, all summarised above.

If you are selfbuilding, then these policies cease to have any validity once you have completed and so then you need to transfer to regular building and contents policies.

WARRANTIES

A specialised area of insurance, the structural warranty only applies to new build homes. It's a one-off payment, usually costing around £2,000, which covers structural failures in homes for the first ten years. It apes what happens in the developer market where the NHBC (the National Housebuilding Council) rules the roost.

The NHBC were active in the selfbuild arena till recently but have now left the field open to a number of smaller, more nimble operators, principally Selfbuildzone, Premier Guarantee and LABC (Local Authority Building Control).

Why have a 10-year warranty at all? A little back story.

If you buy a car or a computer, it is usual for it to come with a one-year or two-year guarantee, provided free of charge by the manufacturer. The new homes market once operated in exactly the same way – i.e. the builder supplied their own guarantee – but back in the 1930s depression, there was such a huge number of housebuilders going bust that the house-buying public lost all confidence in the guarantees being offered by individual builders. Those housebuilders who remained in business decided to pool together the risk and that's how the NHBC was born.

The original NHBC warranty was therefore created to assure people buying off-plan that their new home would be finished, even if the builder they were dealing with went under.

Over the years, the remit of the NHBC changed so that it started to cover defects which might appear in the structure after completion. Things like damp walls, roof failures, subsidence. Gradually, it became standard for the mortgage lenders to require sight of an NHBC warranty to ensure that the property they were lending against was covered if there were latent defects. And then this requirement for a mortgage started to spread to selfbuild, where the risks were very different.

Thus selfbuilders found themselves needing a warranty (or something similar) in order to qualify for a mortgage. It is this requirement which drives the warranty market.

How do warranties work? Initially, you submit your plans, which are scrutinized and sometimes returned for one or two amendments. The warranty providers then carry out onsite inspections to see if you are building what your plans suggest you should be building.

Unlike traditional building inspections, which take place at pre-arranged landmarks, the warranty inspectors habitually turn up randomly, although you usually get warned of their visit beforehand. Having satisfied themselves that you have carried out the building work correctly, you then get a completion certificate.

The crucial difference between ordinary building control and a warranty scheme is that the latter is turned into an insurance policy, which allows you to make a claim against the builder (or its insurance company) in the event of defects arising in the future.

But, of course, you have to pay for this policy and, for selfbuilders, it's an expensive exercise. There is no requirement to take out a warranty, but if you want to borrow money, you will be well advised to have one in place.

In contrast, your standard building control doesn't come with any guarantee.

Regular building inspectors have the power to act as construction policemen, making you redo bits of your work so as to satisfy the building regs. And they are able to issue (or withhold) a completion certificate for your works, which is a mighty handy thing to have when you come to sell your house. But you have no redress against them if their inspections should prove to be negligent. That is where warranties come into their own.

By and large, warranty inspections and building inspections are carried out by different people, despite the work being almost identical. Whether this arrangement is sensible is open to question, but this is how it works in practice. Most selfbuilders work with one insurance company from the outset and get them to cover site insurance and warranties.

If you work with your local authority building inspection team (the traditional route), they may steer you towards an LABC warranty. As LABC stands for Local Authority Building Control you might surmise that this warranty is organised by your local building inspectors. But they are in fact administered from the same office in Birkenhead that an apparent rival in this market, Premier Guarantee, hails form. Interesting market, warranties.

ARCHITECT'S CERTIFICATES

There is an alternative to buying warranties. If an architect (or in some cases a surveyor or a chartered builder) is supervising your job, you can elect to have them issue progress (and completion) certificates throughout the job which say that the work has been done to their satisfaction.

Most lenders are more than happy to take the word of a suitably qualified (and insured) professional instead of a latent defects warranty. However, your professional is unlikely to provide such a service for free and the overall cost may well end up being very similar to third party insurance.

There is a pitfall here too for the unwary. Your architect is not an insurance company and making a claim against an architect is no easy matter. If your double glazing (say) was to fail after five years you would have difficulty establishing whether this failure was down to poor design or to manufacturing defect. If you think the blame lies with your architect's design or supervision, you would then have to pursue the architect for compensation.

Now it is part of a properly qualified architect's job to have

Professional Indemnity (PI) insurance in place for just such eventualities so they can't just roll over and play dead the moment you get heavy, but what isn't often understood is that their insurance policy will cover their costs but not yours. And unless you have all costs awarded to you (which is extremely rare) then you are likely to end up with huge legal bills.

So, another financial risk looms and, lo and behold, there is yet another policy available to cover this particular risk, although I only know of one such policy, the Selfbuild Legal Protection scheme. It will pay reasonable legal expenses for actions you might wish to take against a whole raft of characters over and beyond your architect: your main contractor, your subbies, your materials suppliers, even your solicitor. It costs about £125 and is valid for up to two years after you move in.

What if you are using a designer who doesn't carry PI insurance? Many very good house designers are not formally qualified and would find it very difficult to get PI cover.

In these instances, your protection would have to lie with a the third-party warranty provider. Once your plans are accepted by your chosen warranty provider, then they are taking on responsibility for their outcome, though you need to read the small print to get a handle on what is covered and what isn't. Straightforward it is not.

BOOK-KEEPING

SITE DIARY

Even if you loathe the thought of record keeping, do try and keep a site diary and write down a summary of every day's action:
- weather
- what work was done
- who was on site and how many hours they worked
- quotations, orders, deliveries, shopping trips
- payments made
- contacts made, phone numbers
- site visits by building inspectors, architects, surveyors, etc.
- comments, feedback from casual visitors, neighbours
- accidents (however small), breakages, theft

This not only provides a fascinating historical record, but a site diary has a more immediate benefit if a dispute arises; you have a written record of transactions as they occur. Whether you choose to work with or without a formal contract, a site diary will provide you with loads of unexpected ammunition should things ever turn nasty.

BASIC ACCOUNTS

What level of accounts you keep on a project like a selfbuilt house is very much up to you. Because you are able to reclaim VAT on most purchases going into a newly built house, it is a must to keep every VAT receipt that comes your way (I recommend a lever-arch file and a hole puncher for filing). When the time comes to make your claim, you will have to total all the figures, but whether it's worth keeping a running total of costs going whilst the job is in progress is doubtful.

Running trading accounts with builder's merchants and plant hire shops can be a big help; not only is buying more convenient (and often cheaper) but just the fact that tax invoices get sent by post to your home address makes it much easier to keep tabs on paperwork. Trading accounts is a subject dealt with in greater length in Chapter 13 'Shopping'.

MANAGEMENT ACCOUNTS

If money is tight then you should consider putting a lot more effort into job accounting. You need an early warning system in place to warn you when costs start to overshoot. The key to doing this is to split your whole project down into a number of little joblets such as groundworks, external masonry, roofing, etc. Prepare a detailed budget for your house showing how much you expect to spend on each joblet and prepare a job schedule sheet showing how long each stage of the job should take. Analyse costs as they occur and use your site diary to estimate how much of each stage is completed each week.

You don't go into a project like building a new home without some sort of a budget. Sticking to the budget is obviously crucial to the success of the project, but in my experience you are more likely to come adrift through making an unrealistic budget in the first place rather than overspending on budgeted items. The other great

budget breaker is the unavoidable extras (often to do with extra foundations or drains). There is only one safe way around this and that is to make a largish – say 5% – contingency sum available for such eventualities. If your budget doesn't stretch to this, then how about building a smaller house? The more loosely organised your management of the job is, the higher the chance there is of encountering unavoidable extras. No amount of clever management accounting will make up for an incomplete specification.

CORRESPONDENCE

Keep handy copies of all correspondence to do with your house from plot purchase to suppliers' terms. Some of this now happens using email, but an awful lot still gets done on paper. Even if it's email, it's still not a bad idea to print it out and keep a hard copy. A lever-arch file with about ten sub-dividers should be sufficient. Don't forget that correspondence means keeping copies of your letters as well as ones received, so work out some system of making and keeping copies of your side.

When you express any kind of an interest in building, you soon find yourself getting snowed under with mailshots for this, that or the other. Some of this is junk, some of it is incredibly useful, but you will need to be on the ball about organising it or you'll never be able to retrieve the useful bits when you need them. Again, a subdivided lever-arch file is a real winner here, though you may need to invest in a heavy-duty hole

puncher (c. £25) to pierce the thicker tomes. In addition, get a pack of cardboard magazine files, which you can use to hold really thick literature like you get from kit home suppliers and certain kitchen manufacturers.

VAT

VAT rates can change. Indeed they may well do during the lifespan of this edition. It only takes a single announcement in the House of Commons. This edition is based on the situation that applied in early 2019, whist the whole country is watching out for the outcome of Brexit. It assumes that nothing much major happens in the following months or years, but in reality it could all change very quickly. All prices mentioned in this book are VAT-free (unless otherwise stated). The peculiar situation that selfbuild finds itself in is about to be described in some detail but it's worth noting here that you can download the selfbuild VAT reclaim form from the Revenue & Customs website on www.hmrc.gov.uk. Hint — look for Notice 431NB (for newbuild) or 431C (for conversions) in the VAT section.

New housebuilding (and conversions of non-domestic property into homes) enjoy a privileged position in the UK VAT world. They are mostly zero-rated. This means, in layman's terms, that you can reclaim almost all the VAT charged to you in the course of creating your new house. This is something of

VAT refunds for DIY housebuilders
Claim form for new houses

HM Revenue & Customs

Official use only
Claim reference number

To claim back the VAT you have paid on building materials used to construct your new house, answer the questions on this claim form. The information you give at part B will show us whether you are eligible to claim back the VAT. Refer to the notes that came with this claim form. If you are not sure how to answer a question, phone the Helpline on **0300 200 3700**.

A Personal details
Answer all the questions in this part. If you leave any answer blank we may reject your claim

1 Your full name, including your title Mr, Mrs, Miss, etc. If a charity, name of charity for whom the building has been constructed

2 If more than one claimant, title and full name of other claimant(s)

B Are you eligible to claim?
Refer to the guidance notes

9 Is the property that you have built a new build? By new build we mean a building that has been constructed from scratch which does not incorporate any part of an existing building

No ☐ Yes ☐

10 Is your claim for the fit out and finish of a building shell?

No ☐ Yes ☐

This is VAT form 431NB (stands for new build). The form for conversions is 431C.

RECLAIMING VAT

So much for politics. Here follows an explanation of the VAT position in Great Britain as of 2019. The position varies depending on how you organise your construction. If you are a professional builder undertaking a spec build for the first time, it could hardly be simpler; you just reclaim the VAT inputs each quarter when you do your VAT returns. The only complexities come with certain costs where VAT is not reclaimable. More on these in a minute. For selfbuilders, HMRC runs a special scheme called VAT refunds for DIY builders and converters. Really, this claim pack is a must-have item unless, of course, you think the government deserves the money more than you do. You can use the DIY reclaim scheme even if you have very little input into a new house: if a builder undertakes a turnkey project for you, you can still reclaim VAT on items like fencing and paint that you might put in yourself.

How you run a job has a bearing on the VAT situation. Design fees and professional services and preliminary costs are not normally eligible for VAT refunds but if you start by appointing a builder who provides design as part of the overall package (as you might with many timber frame companies), then it's all considered one design and build contract and you can reclaim all fees (provided the invoicing doesn't separate out the fees from the construction). It's called creative invoicing.

an anomaly. Since the introduction of VAT in 1983, almost all other building work has been standard-rated, which means that you cannot reclaim the VAT.

The reason new housebuilding survives VAT-free is that VAT cannot be levied on second-hand house sales since such sales are private, and so it would be regarded as inequitable for new housebuilders to have to charge VAT on their product when 90% of all house sales escape it. Nevertheless, the imposition of VAT on new housebuilding is a possibility that all new housebuilders must face and it has occasionally come to the fore in the political debate about the future of housing.

Having warned you of that, the changes in VAT rules for homebuilders recently have actually been pretty helpful. The definition

of a non-domestic property was widened in 2001 to include anything that hadn't been lived in for ten years so conversions of all kinds of buildings into homes was brought into the zero-VAT net – prior to that they had to have been unoccupied since 1973.

Gordon Brown, as Chancellor, also introduced a 5% VAT band, which applies to work on properties empty for more than two years, and also to changing the number of living units in a building. This latter was presumably brought in to encourage builders to convert large houses into flats but it seems to equally well apply to people who want to turn a block of flats into a large house.

What Brexit may or may not bring is a matter of utter speculation and this is as true of VAT on housebuilding as it is on everything else.

If you are taking on the project management yourself, there are quite a few ground rules you need to be aware of.

You can't reclaim VAT from subcontractors for their labour, or on supply and fix contracts. If it's a regular new build, then make sure they don't charge VAT in the first place. Just to make things complicated, if the project you are undertaking is classed as a conversion, not a new build, then you are able to reclaim VAT on labour, even though VAT on the labour should be being charged at the reduced rate of 5% – you have to ensure that it is.

You can only make one claim and this must be within three months of completion. Completion is not the same thing as occupation: they expect you may well occupy before technical completion but if the delay between the two is longer than six months then they become suspicious and will demand explanation. Tread cautiously here.

Valid VAT receipts, made out to you, must support all purchases you wish to reclaim the VAT on. A VAT receipt is one that includes the supplier's VAT No (but doesn't necessarily separate out the VAT). Credit card slips, cheque stubs, delivery notes are not VAT receipts. Note also that if some of your material supplies are purchased through a subcontractor who is not VAT registered, you will not be able to reclaim VAT – the original invoice must be made out to you.

WHAT IS ZERO-RATED?

As discussed already, recent changes in VAT rules have somewhat simplified the rules and made definitions of what can and cannot be zero-rated much easier to grasp. There are two areas to consider. Firstly, how does the job as a whole stack up in the VAT reclaim stakes? And secondly, which costs incurred can you reclaim?

The first area has always been looked on as a minefield. If you are in doubt, you can get hold of the rules on the web at www.hmrc. gov.uk where you want to get hold of two documents, VAT notice 708 (Buildings and Construction) and VAT information sheet 0501 There are of course still grey areas – for instance what happens when you convert a pub that has a self-contained flat – but it's still simpler than it was. A bit. And no, building new holiday lets doesn't qualify for zero-rating. What's in and what isn't is all determined with reference to these lengthy documents.

Provided you can establish that your project is a new build, almost all the construction costs are eligible for zero-rating of VAT. That is to say, those suppliers who are knowingly supplying a zero-rated project should not add VAT to their invoices and if VAT is applied (currently at 20%) you should be able to reclaim it. The situation with conversions is subtly different. Here you are expected to pay VAT on all supplies, including labour, albeit at the reduced rate of 5%. You can still reclaim using the DIY builders VAT refund system.

As your house nears completion, you will find a number of items that HMRC, in their wisdom, regard as fittings that lie outside the zero-rating net. If there is any ground rule at all it is that if the items are fixed into the building then they are zero-rated but if they are removable then you must pay the VAT.

However, there are many exceptions to this rule and the rules are often subject to review. I present the following list for general guidance only; the VAT office may view things differently. Please don't jump down my throat if you find you are unable to reclaim VAT on something I've said you can. It's the VAT office you should be arguing with and, if you're canny, you will do this before you start construction. VAT Notice 431 includes a similar list, which you should refer to for the latest views from the VAT office.

Having tried to get myself off this particular hook, let's look at the current state of play. Personally, I find this catalogue of what's in and what's out ridiculous, and I'd be tempted to laugh at it if there wasn't so much damn money riding on it. Don't keep telling your VAT official that 'This is crazy!'; they know it and they've heard it a thousand times before.

▪ Kitchens: Fitted kitchens are zero-rated but white goods (cookers, washing machines, dishwashers, etc.) are not. There is no distinction made between integrated and freestanding equipment – you must pay VAT on them – so things like waste disposal units and water softeners are standard-rated. However there are some zero-rated appliances, most notably cooker hoods and built-in vacuum cleaners.

▮ Agas: Standard-rated except when they have an integral boiler; then they are regarded as part of the heating system and VAT can be reclaimed.

▮ Fitted cupboards: At present the ruling seems to be this – if you build the cupboards (i.e. fitting doors across alcoves formed in the walls) then it seems that you can reclaim the VAT on all the materials, but if you buy in fitted cupboards then you can't. If that's not clear then ask your VAT office.

▮ Flooring: All forms of carpeting are standard-rated. Everything else is zero-rated.

▮ Heating/plumbing/sanitaryware: All zero-rated except water treatment units. Fireplaces are also zero-rated. Solar panels, heat recovery systems and air conditioning also qualify for zero-rating.

▮ Electrics: All zero-rated. Light fittings should be OK provided they are fitted, but a zealous inspector may disagree.

▮ Alarms: Both smoke alarms and burglar alarms are zero-rated. Also fire safety equipment is now zero-rated.

▮ Furnishings: Movable furniture is invariably standard-rated. The status of fitted shelves is unclear. Curtains and blinds are standard-rated but you can reclaim VAT on curtain rails.

▮ Decorating: Paint is zero-rated and you shouldn't have any problem with wallpaper. Also, if you want to have decorative finishes (like pine match boarding) you should be able

to reclaim the VAT.

▮ Garages and driveways: Zero-rated, but note that other outbuildings are standard rated.

▮ Landscaping: They will generally accept a limited amount of turning and paving as zero-rated. The rule seems to be that if the landscaping is included as part of the planning permission, then it's zero-rated. Otherwise it's standard rated.

▮ Swimming pools: Standard-rated unless it's inside a building, which is at least attached to the main house.

▮ Outbuildings/conservatories: Detached outbuildings (except garages) are standard-rated. However, attached extensions like conservatories are zero-rated. The rule seems to be if it's attached, it's zero-rated: if it's detached, you have to pay the VAT. The only exception is the detached garage (see above).

▮ Plant hire, scaffolding: These are standard-rated items, which you cannot reclaim, although note that scaffolding erection and dismantling is technically zero-rated whilst the hire is not. Therefore, you can save money by getting your scaffolder to invoice separately for the two services.

▮ Professional fees: Standard-rated.

END OF THE PARTY

A selfbuilder can only make one reclaim from the VAT office and so when it's done, it's done. This presents a major cashflow problem to many as there is usually several thousand pounds waiting to be reclaimed, several thousand pounds which most selfbuilders could well use to finish off their project; many end up forgoing

further VAT reclaims in order to get their hands on this money before the house is complete. If you employ a VAT registered builder to construct your house this reclaim problem does not occur as the builder's invoices are zero-rated for all but the exempt items though note that you can still use the DIY reclaim scheme if you buy just the odd can of paint and a few curtain rails on your own account.

LISTED BUILDINGS

Listed buildings used to enjoy a semi-privileged VAT position in that whilst repairs were standard rated, improvements were zero-rated. Lots of fun was had by designers and builders, trying to show that a repair was actually an improvement, but this game was stopped in its tracks by then-Chancellor George Osborne who made all listed building work standard rated (i.e. 20% VAT) in 2012.

VAT IN THE EU

The VAT regimes for new housebuilding vary substantially around the EU. There is no such thing as zero-rating anywhere else (as far as I can establish). In the Republic of Ireland, VAT is collected at over 20% on all building materials though there is a tax break if you employ a registered builder on a new house – you pay VAT at 12.5% instead.

But one piece of good news is that if you are undertaking zero-rated building in the UK you can reclaim VAT on materials purchased anywhere in the EU. Of course Brexit may well change all that, but at time of writing (2019) the EU directives still apply.

OTHER TAXES

Whereas professionals and selfbuilders are on a level playing field when it comes to VAT, selfbuild really comes into its own when you start to look at other taxes. If you are building your one and only house, then you really don't have to pay any taxes at all on the profits you make. The two taxes that you might expect to get clobbered by are income tax and capital gains tax (CGT). If you are a professional, you will get caught by one of these two. Typically, income tax is levied on you if your livelihood involves building homes for sale, and CGT cuts in if you buy and sell second homes or houses to let out. Here you would be expected to pay income tax on any rental income, and CGT on any gains you make when you come to sell the house. However, neither income tax nor CGT have ever been levied on 'your principal private residence' so any profits you make on your private homebuilding are consequently tax-free. Even if you sell off part of your garden for someone else to build a house, you don't pay any tax on the proceeds, although you can trip into the tax net if the garden area exceeds 0.5 hectares.

Now the selfbuilders' tax exempt status raises a few interesting possibilities. What if you move into a house you have built, make it your 'principal private residence', and then sell it shortly afterwards? What if you step from one selfbuild house to another to another? Welcome to the world of the serial selfbuilder. It's actually a long established practice in the UK. I remember a builder doing exactly this in the Cambridgeshire village I grew up in. My parents bought a house from him in 1950. By the time we left the village when I was 13, he'd moved house about five times and was at work on another, all in the same village.

Many small builders live a semi-nomadic, selfbuild lifestyle like this, interspersing regular work with the odd homebuilding or renovating project. As long as you establish each house as your 'principal private residence', you should be in the clear tax-wise, although there are signs that the Revenue is beginning to take an interest in this area. There is no published guidance on how long you have to stay in a house before it is accepted as your 'principal private residence' that would distinguish you from a commercial developer but 12 months is often quoted as a broadly acceptable period. The key point to establish isn't how long you live in a house but that the project wasn't undertaken with profit in mind. 'Private residence relief is not intended to relieve speculative gains,' reads the Inland Revenue Help Sheet 283. 'Relief is not therefore available where you acquire or spend money on your dwelling-house wholly or partly to realise a gain on its disposal.' Ominous wording, especially as it could be applied to just about anyone who ever bought a house in Britain. It's worth bearing in mind. Although the number of people pursued for tax on their 'speculative' profits on selfbuild is tiny, it would be as well not to make too much of a song and dance about how much money you may have made.

In reality, not that many people will keep on moving house and building and moving and building indefinitely. Whilst it's a great way to build up equity and reduce mortgages, it doesn't actually bring in any extra cash unless you start trading down. It's also pretty exhausting and doesn't fit easily into the requirements of family life. But it probably beats babysitting as a way of eking out a little bit extra. Until such time as the property market decides to take another tumble…

GROUNDWORKS

Groundworks is the term used to describe all the things that builders do beneath ground level. It's actually a hotch potch of different activities – excavation, drainage, service connections, concreting and some brickwork.

The advent of JCBs, readymix concrete and plastic drainware has taken a lot of the graft out of this part of building, but it still remains an exacting and potentially hazardous task. It is also incredibly messy, especially when there's rain about. Whilst neighbours will look on in horror as you recreate the battlefield of the Somme, you must

shrug your shoulders and utter asinine comments like 'You can't make an omelette without breaking eggs'.

Groundworks is really a question of getting from A to B as cheaply and easily as possible. There are many reasons for using something other than the standard solutions for your underground work, but all of them involve sorting out or avoiding problems, not increasing amenity value. This is not to say that the housebuilder does not face choices of how best to get the groundworks completed, but these choices are for the most

part to do with ease, speed and cost of installation. This chapter concentrates on these issues as well as taking a closer look at how some of the problems, outlined in Chapter 3 'Pitfalls', are solved.

Given a straightforward site and a straightforward house design, the groundworks can progress with remarkable speed at a comparatively low cost. However, a problem site can easily double the base costs, so I cannot emphasise enough how important it is to analyse thoroughly the costs involved in just getting your house out of the ground.

Groundworks is also one of the

MODEL HOUSE: Groundworks Cost Summary

	Quantity	Rate	Materials	Labour	Plant	Totals
EXCAVATION						£ 6,000
Clearing Oversite/Site Strip	35 m³	£ 46 per m³			£ 1,610	
Setting Out & Preparation	120 m²	£ 10 per m²		£ 1,200		
Excavating and Muck Away	50 m³	£ 46 per m³			£ 2,300	
Dumper Hire	5 days	£ 160 per day			£ 800	
FOUNDATIONS						£ 8,000
Foundation labour	50 m³	£ 50 per m³		£ 2,500		
Readymix in Trenches	25 m³	£ 80 per m³	£ 2,000		£ 350	
Blockwork Footings	40 m²	£ 50 per m²	£ 1,240	£ 760		
Face Brick Footings	12 m²	£ 83 per m²	£ 580	£ 420		
GROUND FLOOR	95 m²					£ 7,000
Beam and Block floor	95 m²	£ 38 per m²	£ 2,380	£ 1,220	£ 350	
125mm Celotex Insulation	80 m²	£ 29 per m²	£ 1,800	£ 300		
DPM	80 m²	£ 2 per m²	£ 50	£ 140		
50mm Leanmix concrete	80 m²	£ 8 per m²	£ 320	£ 320		
Totals			£ 8,400	£ 6,900	£ 5,400	£ 21,000
Overall Footprint	95 m²		Internal Floor Area		160 m²	
Cost per m² Footprint	£221 m²		Cost per m² Floor Area		131 m²	

£6,000 is at the low end of excavation costs. If there is any slope on the site that needs excavating, or if deeper trenches are required, the costs will multiply. See section on Slopes, Bad Ground and Trees.

Similarly, foundation costs can also escalate. On many sites now, engineered foundations are required, so that overall costs can stretch to as much as £50,000 in some situations.

areas of housebuilding most prone to mistakes being made. The setting out of foundations and levels and the correct siting of drain terminals is not a job to be undertaken lightly; add a slope into the equation and you have a job to tax the most skilled surveyor. Yet the supervision of groundworking is often left to harassed digger drivers who 'want to get on with it' and often barely refer to any plans that may have been drawn up. The horror stories that you occasionally hear of completed houses having to be taken down because they were put up in the wrong place are a testament to the consequences of rushed excavations.

THE NEED FOR ACCURACY

If you've never been involved in setting out foundations, you can sit back and laugh at the incompetence; not until it's just you and a stroppy JCB driver do you begin to realise just how difficult it is and how easy it is for it to go badly wrong. Of all the areas of housebuilding, groundworks is the one that needs the most management and the best management. If you are a DIY project manager, this is the big one. Crack this and you will have no problems down the line.

Most builders choose to subcontract all the groundworks but, whilst this makes it very much easier to navigate this stage, it is still vital to check that you are getting exactly what you asked for. You must check that the foundations are in the right place, are square, and are at the right height (this last can be difficult to measure). You must check that the access arrangements have been properly constructed, with falls going the right way and that the drains and the services have been installed correctly. Your building inspector will provide some guidance and should be able to pinpoint errors and bad practice but is not paid to be a surveyor and will have no idea if your trenches are off-square or in the wrong position. It is much harder to ferret out mistakes on groundworking than on later parts of the build and usually much more expensive to rectify at a later date.

On traditional masonry work, accuracy is not so important because the bricklayers can correct errors in setting out and levels – to a certain extent – as they go about their work. But most of the so-called modern methods of construction – timber or steel frame, SIPs, ICFs or thin-joint masonry – have little room for error and the tolerance standards are much more exacting, so getting groundworks accurate at this stage is vital. TRADA, the timber people, suggest the following standards for foundations under a timber frame house:

- Wall lengths should be within ± 10mm of plans
- Diagonals: ±5mm up to 10m, or ± 10mm over 10m
- Floor slabs level to ±5mm

Sounds easy. Good luck.

EXCAVATIONS

A flat site is a cheap site; clearing debris off the oversite will not take long and digging normal depth foundations for a four-bedroom house will take a JCB no more than a day. Note, however, that the crucial task of setting out the foundations on the ground has to be carried out after the undergrowth is stripped away. It's not a job to rush, especially if you are new to the game, and so you ideally want to leave a couple of days between site clearance and the start of excavation. The key to getting this done accurately is to have an accurate site survey to hand, complete with datum heights, and an accurate set of plans drawn up based on the survey. A good groundworker will set out all the key points, and check they are square by measuring the diagonals. Heights will be checked with lasers. They will also want to know trench widths and depths, though this may vary according to ground conditions. The key datum point is conventionally Finished Floor Level (FFL) and everything is expressed

in millimetres above or below FFL. Lasers make this all much easier than in the past, but mistakes still get made.

Unless you are working in a confined area where mechanical plant cannot reach, then you will want to get hold of a JCB or some similar digger. Some builders have diggers and digger drivers in their armoury, but most just have contacts with guys who are self-employed and own their own machine. They tend to charge for travelling time so it's worth getting someone local and – depending on how busy they are – they often charge for a minimum of half a day even when they're only around for a couple of hours. But at around £300 per day for driver plus JCB, they can do the work of around ten to twenty men and therefore represent a bargain not to be sniffed at. They can also do a lot of damage.

The one-man-band digger drivers tend to be the most helpful, but they do like to get on with it. If you're not 100% on top of what's to be done then the chances are that you'll get rushed into mistakes. Trench excavations happen remarkably quickly: expect around 50m per day, enough for a small house.

DEMOLITION MAN?

If you've an existing structure to demolish, then you'll have a choice of taking it down slowly and salvaging materials, or getting a machine to demolish it, which is not very green but far more exciting. I'd suggest that it is almost entirely dependent on the value of the salvaged materials.

There are also health considerations, whichever method you employ: watch out for asbestos, which was very common in much of the 20th century housing now being demolished. In fact you are unlikely to demolish anything substantial without encountering asbestos. You will need to ensure that your demolition contractor is licensed to undertake this sort of work and has in place a risk assessment and management plan to dispose of hazardous waste. All this is likely to be covered by planning conditions, in any event.

MUCK AWAY

Charming expression for getting rid of the spoil. The topsoil is stripped off and stored on site for later use, but the subsoil is usually dumped somewhere else. Many digger drivers operate in tandem with a 15 or 20 tonne lorry and will have local dumping contacts. Alternatively, it is worth chasing up local landowners to see if they have any holes to fill.

Subsoil taken out of the ground 'bulks-up' at least 30% when piled in a heap (or on a lorry). This means that just under 12m³ dug out of the ground will fill the 15m³ space on a 20-tonne lorry: those sorts of calculations are typical when doing muck away sums – a cubic metre in the ground tends to weigh between 1.5 and two tonnes. Some ground conditions, notably clay, bulk-up at much more than 30%: a 50% or even 60% bulk-up rate can

GROUNDWORKS

be expected. Make sure if you get a quote per cubic metre whether you are dealing with muck in the ground or bulked-up on the lorry.

LANDFILL TAX

Landfill tax was introduced in 1996 and it's one of those taxes that gets subjected to an escalator. This means it keeps going up, rather like the taxes on petrol, cigarettes and alcohol. Unlike these, you don't really notice landfill tax, until you come to start to clear building sites.

There is an important distinction between inert waste and man-made stuff. Inert is a term used to cover ground you might dig out in the course of excavations. It still gets taxed but at a much lower rate, currently £2.90 per tonne. In contrast, the man-made waste gets really clobbered, and the current rate is £91 per tonne. That adds around 30% to the cost of muck away lorries and skips, so it's important to make sure everyone knows just what is being excavated.

SUMMARY

On many sites you will be unable to get heavy plant like JCBs to the back of the house once you have completed the trench excavations. If you have plans for landscaping or drainage or even plan to build a swimming pool or a summer house at a later date, this may be your only opportunity to get the groundwork done quickly and cheaply and a change of plan or an oversight can have costly ramifications later.

Another area to sort out on day

one is the site access; it pays to get your drive levelled and hardcored as early as possible.

To work out your likely excavation and muck away costs, first work out the volume you need to remove. If it's fairly easy digging, it's likely to cost around £12 per m³ to dig out of the ground and an additional £30 - £35 per m³ to remove it to a licensed tip (of which £5 will be tax). If the digging is hard (rock, for instance) the excavation costs can double or even treble but the muck away costs should be unaffected.

FOUNDATIONS

If you ever get involved in working around the foundations of some pre-20th century buildings, as you might if you were building an extension on to a Victorian house, you will be amazed at how shallow and how basic the existing foundations appear to be compared with what we build off now. 'How come this house is still standing?' will be your first thought. Followed by 'If these foundations have supported this house for so long, what am I doing messing around a metre further down below ground?' Both good questions. Neither has a simple answer.

The history of foundations is vaguely interesting and a little instructive. The current idea of building up off slabs of concrete at depths of a metre or more below ground level is relatively new, very much a 20th century innovation. The Victorians used to step the walls out at the base, pyramid style, over

a depth of just three or four brick courses, that way spreading the load of the house across a wider area. These below-ground courses were known as footings and the footings were effectively the foundations. Today we still refer to footings but we put concrete foundations under them. 21st century footings are simply the brick or blockwork sandwiched between the concrete foundations and the damp proof course that is usually installed at 150mm above ground level.

GROUNDWORK KEY PRICES		
Groundworker	£ 22	per hr
JCB Hire with driver	£ 60	per hr
JCB digs in easy ground	5 m³	per hr
JCB digs in hard ground	2 m³	per hr
20 tonne lorry	£ 350	per load
20 tonne lorry holds	12 m³	spoil
Landfill tax (inert)	£ 3	tonne
Readymix Concrete	£ 80	per m³
Concrete Pump Hire	£ 350	per day
Dumper Hire	£ 160	day
Setting Out Foundations	£ 10	min per m²
Foundation Work	£ 50	min per m²

EXCAVATION COMPOSITE RATES		
EASY DIG		
Excavation with JCB	£ 12	m³
Muck away in lorry rate	£ 29	m³
Plus Landfill tax	£ 5	m³
Total	£ 46	m³
HARD GROUND DIG		
Excavation with JCB	£ 30	m³
Muck away in lorry rate	£ 29	m³
Plus Landfill tax	£ 5	m³
Total	£ 64	m³

The reality of foundations for many people. You dig 'em – they fill up with water before you can order the readymix

When concrete foundations were first adopted widely, in the 1920s, they were sold to builders as being a cheaper and quicker method of building-in adequate load bearing. In fact, the load imposed by a typical house (which maybe weighs around 100 tonnes in total) really isn't that great – it's similar (on a weight per area basis) to that imposed on the ground by your feet when you stand up. The problems arise from the fact that the ground has a nasty habit of shifting about, which itself has a nasty habit of causing all manner of disruption on the very rigid structures placed on it. Building foundations out of concrete may sound very

hard and solid but when the ground starts moving then they look as feeble and spindly as you could want. Consequently, foundations have been getting deeper and deeper over the years in an attempt to get down below the trouble zone.

The Building Research Establishment investigated the phenomenon of ground movement in the 1990s and found a particular site that regularly heaved up and down by 50mm over the course of a year, not to mention a 60mm sideways movement as well. Mostly it's sites with large trees and clay soils but it's also rather unpredictable, so consequently the momentum

is towards deeper and deeper foundations, which means more and more concrete. This usually works but we still have a large number of new houses that subsequently suffer from foundation failure.

The best advice is to follow the advice you are given as closely as you can – don't cut corners. Readymix concrete and excavations are moderately expensive but nothing like as expensive as having to fix later failures.

As foundation requirements have grown deeper over the years, two options have evolved about how to construct them – at least on largely problem-free sites. One is to pour the minimum amount of concrete possible into the foundation trenches and then build upwards in brick or blockwork – these are known as strip foundations. The other system reverses this logic altogether and pours as much concrete as possible into the trench before starting on the bricklaying – this is usually called trenchfill. Both methods have pros and cons.

With strip foundations, laying footings below ground level, is cheap on materials but heavy on labour; it is also slower. In contrast, trenchfill is much quicker but, of course, uses more concrete. When pouring concrete into clay soils, you will probably have to use the trenchfill method.

An important consideration when designing foundations is to set the level of the concrete so that it 'works blocks'. Blocks are laid either flat in courses of 110mm or in vertical

FOOTINGS: Key Rates				
7N Concrete Blocks	£11.00 m²			
Trenchblock 300mm	£30 m²			
Celcon Blocks	£12 m²			
Regrade Bricks	£10 m²			
Face bricks	£48 m²			
Blockwork mortar	£1.00 m²			
Brickwork mortar	£3.60 m²			
DPC	£1.00 m			
Readymix Concrete	£ 80 m³			
M² RATES FOR FOOTINGS		**Materials**	**Labour**	**Combined**
Lay Footings (100mm blocks, vertical)		£ 13	£ 15	**£ 28**
Lay face bricks		£ 52	£ 35	**£ 87**
Lay 300mm Trenchblocks		£ 30	£ 19	**£ 49**
Alternative to Footings				
Readymix Trenchfill	600w	£ 48	£ 5	**£ 53**
	450w	£ 36	£ 6	**£ 42**

courses of 225mm (ish). If you have surveyed the site accurately, your datum measurements will show exactly where the damp proof course will be so you can ensure that you stop the concrete at 225, 450 or 675mm below that point. That ensures that you keep the fiddling about and cutting to a minimum – provided, of course, that you pour your foundations level! If you have a detailed foundation plan in place, your designer should have worked this all out in advance and you simply have to follow the instructions.

The depth and length of the trenches are not in your control, but the trench width is largely down to which bucket the JCB uses to dig with (the general choices being 450 and 600mm wide). Using a 450mm wide bucket is going to reduce the amount of readymix used by a quarter (as well as reducing excavation costs) but it is not to be recommended to rookie builders. Cavity walls – generally now 350mm wide and set to get wider still as cavity widths get increased to cope with ever more insulation – sit uncomfortably on such a narrow trench; internal load bearing wall foundations are obviously less of a problem, but the key factor in all this is accurate setting out of trenches.

Unless you are an experienced surveyor, you really want to play safe and set trenches at 600mm wide.

GROUND FLOORS

The 'industry standard' is to build a concrete or masonry ground floor and a timber first floor. This is how 90% of single homes are built in the UK. Only in Scotland does the practice change – there they still love timber

Traditional Strip Footings

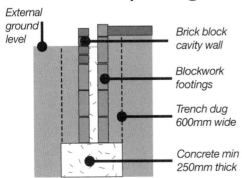

External ground level

Brick block cavity wall

Blockwork footings

Trench dug 600mm wide

Concrete min 250mm thick

Trenchfill

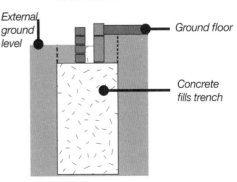

External ground level

Ground floor

Concrete fills trench

GROUND FLOORS: Key rates

	Materials		Labour	Combined
	Unit Cost	m² rates	m² rates	m² rates
Beam and Block Floor (inc blocks)		£25	£13	**£38**
Hanson Jet Floor (insulation, no concrete)		£26	£13	**£39**
Hollow core floor		£40	£13	**£53**
Telescopic Vents	£ 5.00 ea	£ 1.30	£ 1.80	**£3**
Airbricks	£ 3.50 ea	£1	na	**£1**
100m2 DPM	£ 50.00 roll	£ 0.60	£ 1.80	**£2**
125mm Celotex Insulation		£20	£4	**£24**
150mm Celotex Insulation		£25	£4	**£29**
175mm Exp Polystyrene Insulation		£14	£4	**£18**
Crane Hire	£350 day			
65mm Readymixed Screed		£8	£7	**£15**
50mm Gypsum Screed		£20	S&F only	**£20**
100mm Concrete	£80 m³	£8	£9	**£17**
50mm Leanmix slurry concrete	£80 m³	£4	£4	**£8**
Reinforcing Mesh		£4	£4	**£8**
150mm Hardcore	£56 m³	£8	£8	**£16**
Sand Blinding over hardcore	£56 m³	£3	£2	**£5**
50x200mm Joists	£4 m	£14	£17	**£31**
50x200mm I beams	£10 m	£25	£11	**£36**
22mm Chipboard	£13 sheet	£11	£6	**£17**

GROUND FLOOR OPTIONS: All-in Rates per m²

Concrete Slab (Un-reinforced)	£ 76 inc 100mm Jablite and 65mm screed finish
Concrete Slab (Reinforced)	£ 83 inc 100mm Jablite and 65mm screed finish
Beam and block floor	£ 77 inc 100mm Jablite and 65mm screed finish
Hollow core floor	£ 90 inc 100mm Jablite and 65mm screed finish
Hansons Jet Floor	£ 77 inc 65mm Screed Finish (insulation built-in)
Insulated Timber joist ground floor	£ 89 inc base concrete and chipboard floor cover
Insulated I-beam ground floor	£ 94 inc base concrete and chipboard floor cover

your knees in floor. Add in a little re-inforcement in the concrete (not uncommon), maybe some underfloor heating pipes laid on some sort of backing board in the screed, and another plastic DPM layer above the concrete (sometimes specified) and you have a very complex as well as a very thick construction.

The problem from a costing point of view is that the floor finishes are usually considered separately. On top of that, it's also common practice to consider the intermediate layers such as the underfloor heating and the screed in yet another compartment. Yet they are also all related. Ideally, you need to start with your floor finish and work downwards to get your most cost effective floor. Again a thorough design will itemise all these different layers and make construction relatively simple

SOLID SLABS

A solid concrete slab is usually laid 100mm thick over a layer of compacted hardcore. This is the most labour intensive system and, conversely, the cheapest on materials, which makes it suitable for DIY builders with access to cheap or free labour.

You have a choice of placing the insulation layer – you have to have an insulation layer – either above or below the concrete.

It's sort of conventional to finish a concrete slab floor off with a cement screed on top, laid at a later stage of the build. But there is no requirement to do so and some builders dispense with the screed layer, choosing to

ground floors. First floors, known as intermediate floors, are in a section all of their own in the next chapter. Here, I just look at ground floors.

Comparing floor costs is a bit of a nightmare. The problem is to know where to begin and end. I was struck by this when visiting the National Selfbuild and Renovation Centre in Swindon. There they have a small display showing the main floor types,

being timber, solid slab and pre-cast concrete suspended floors.

On the solid slab exhibit I counted seven different layers in the sandwich: from the bottom, hardcore, sand, damp proof membrane (DPM), concrete, insulation, screed, floor cover. In total, nearly 500mm in depth. That's just phenomenal. If it were all, miraculously, to turn to jelly, you would be wading about up to get a smooth finish on the concrete using a power floater. There is no reason why you couldn't place your insulation beneath your slab, and sink your underfloor heating pipes (if you want them) into the concrete: it's just that not many people think this far ahead. The trend for polished concrete finished floors also plays into this. But more on this later.

SUSPENDED FLOORS

Pre-cast concrete floors are a factory-produced alternative to ground-bearing slabs. Because of the added transport costs, they are rarely economic over small areas, say below 50m², so you don't see them used for house extensions but they become an increasingly cost-effective solution as the floor area increases. The increasing popularity of pre-cast floors has been driven by a number of factors:

■ floors can be laid in a day and worked on the next day
■ no wet trades involved - no readymix lorries required
■ have to be used on sites where there would otherwise be excessive backfill under the ground-bearing slab
■ they can be used on intermediate floors as well as ground floors

Perhaps the main downside to using pre-cast floors is that each one needs to be manufactured to order and you may well find that you have to wait six to eight weeks for them to be delivered. If you plan on using a pre-cast floor, then you must plan well ahead. The other issue that needs attention is the requirement

The concept behind the beam and block floor is dead simple. The concrete beams form an upturned 'T' section, enabling the blocks to sit loosely between the beams. This technique was introduced in the 1970s and has been widely taken up across the country. Builders like them because they are quick, dry and relatively easy to use, but they are expensive on smaller footprints, below 100m²

for ventilation in the void under the floor: this is achieved with airbricks built into the external wall, usually with offset ducts placed within the cavity.

BEAM AND BLOCK

Beam and block is the cheapest and commonest form of precast floor: it consists of number of evenly spaced concrete beams, similar to timber joists, infilled with normal building blocks. It has been gaining in popularity with developers since it first appeared in the 1970s, largely because it's fast and largely dry.

As with all pre-cast options, beam and block floors are provided by specialists who work from drawings

supplied. A number of businesses cater for this market and many have links with builders merchants who act as middlemen. The floors are designed to work with standard concrete blocks (i.e. 100 x 225 x 440mm) as used in wall construction. There is often more than one way to run the beams and you may be able to take advantage of 225mm beams that can span up to 8m and can sometimes enable you to do away with sleeper walls within the main floor area.

Another thing to watch out for is the 1:300 camber on these pre-stressed beams. It's surprisingly large: as much as 13mm on a 4m long beam. If you lay a screed over the

Chapter 6

floor you can of course get a level finish and if you want a dry finish or a floating floor, you need the floor to be level.

INSULATED BEAM FLOORS

A variation on the standard beam and block floor uses polystyrene infill blocks to fill the voids between the beams. They have become increasingly popular as a ground floor option since changes to the building regs in 2002 brought in a requirement for floor insulation, previously a green option only. It's a little more expensive than a block infill floor but it does away with an added layer – you can, and indeed must, just place a structural screed on top of it before you have a working platform. This can make it difficult to work with underfloor heating unless you add another screed layer above.

The best-known insulated floor beam system is Forterra's Jet Floor. Whilst these flooring systems undoubtedly work well and have been tried and tested over many years, they do suffer from cold bridging at the edges where the heat is able to divert away from the beams into the walls. If you want cold bridge free foundations, you need to look at using an insulated polystyrene raft, where the walls themselves are built up off the insulated base.

HOLLOW CORE

Hollow core planks are another form of craned-in precast floor though this time more commonly used as an intermediate floor. Instead of concrete beams being laid and infilled with blocks, the whole floor is laid in a series of wide concrete planks - hollowed out to reduce the weight, hence the name. Hollowcore is the most expensive of the pre-cast options but leaves you maximum flexibility: you don't have to align your internal walls above load-bearing walls or supporting beams – you can build anything anywhere. However, the internal walls where the planks meet end-to-end have to be double thickness in order to have adequate bearing. Hollowcore floors are prized for their soundproofing qualities and are thus commonly used in apartments.

HYBRIDS

Most pre-cast floors are topped off with a cement screed, if only to get a smooth surface on which to lay a floor cover. But there are a number of options that require a structural screed or concrete slab in order to gain sufficient strength. The insulated beam floor is one example but there are others, used widely in Continental Europe, sometimes known as lattice girder plate floors.

The advantage of using such a system is that you can get greater spans per floor depth. Indeed, you can get a span of over 9m on just a 250mm depth floor.

TIMBER

Suspended timber ground floors could potentially be very cheap and simple to build. They were commonly installed by the Victorians but have gone out of fashion for two reasons. Firstly, a requirement, which has come into the building regs, to cover the ground beneath a timber ground floor with a concrete capping capable of withstanding the passage of moisture, which adds at least £5/m² to costs; secondly by the added complexity of fixing underfloor insulation between the joists. Upstairs, of course, no such extra work applies and here timber joisting is easily the cheapest option.

On the ground floor, timber still makes a lot of sense if you want a timber floor cover because you can have an entirely dry construction. Around half the cost of a timber ground floor goes into the sheeting (usually chipboard or plywood) that is laid over the joists and where a plank floor finish is desired this sheeting can be dispensed with. The problem with doing this is that either the planking will be exposed for the duration of construction, which will almost certainly lead to damage, or some form of temporary sheeting will have to be installed which will cancel out most of the perceived cost advantages. However, the technique works well with reclaimed boards that need to be sanded and sealed and can serve as both temporary and finished floor covering.

INSULATION

Underfloor insulation on the ground floor is not quite mandatory but recent changes to the building regs make it expensive to avoid. There are several methods of insulation available. The cheapest and most readily understood is to lay flooring grade expanded polystyrene at 200mm thickness over the sub-floor and under the screed or chipboard. Or you can use a thinner layer (around 125mm) of one of the more efficient insulation boards such as Polyfoam, Kingspan or Celotex.

These techniques of underfloor insulation are relatively new and there are possibly problems building up in the future should the insulation not prove to be as rigid as expected: ensure that the insulation you specify is flooring-grade. More cautious builders will continue to use some form of reinforcement in their screeds to counteract any such failures.

Aficionados of underfloor heating will wonder what all the fuss is about. Such systems only work well with very high levels of underfloor insulation – otherwise much of the heat would be lost – and, whatever problems there may have been with underfloor heating systems, laying insulation under heavy cement screeds does not appear to be one of them.

FLOOR SCREEDS

Traditionally, the floor screeding is undertaken by plasterers, and it happens much later in the build process than the groundworks. But it's also pretty much a first fix process because it gets covered over by floor finishes (unless of course you go for a polished concrete floor finish).

Although it looks simple, it's one of the hardest and most skilful aspects of housebuilding and, as such, is ripe for a little techno-fix. Which is precisely what has been happening in the world of screeding.

Traditional, 20th century-style screeding, involves a two-and-one gang, mixing up a very dry, comparatively strong, 1:3 cement:sand mix and laying it by hand, 65mm or 75mm deep. The screeding gang work on their hands and knees, smoothing out the screed mix, trowelling off the surface, and keeping a very close eye on the levels across the floor. It's very easy to get it horribly wrong and end up with a sloping floor or one with hills and valleys in it, which clients tend not to appreciate very much. In my costing tables, I have 65mm screeding down at being around 25 mins/m². Most experienced screeding gangs work at something nearly twice this rate, enabling them to do over 100m² per day. But their art/skill is so highly regarded that they can charge two or three times as much as ordinary tradesmen and the only way I can make sense of their charging rates is by making it appear to take longer than it actually does.

Anyway, the screed business is slowly changing. Site mixed screeding, as I have just described, is dying out and it now accounts for less than a third of the overall screed market. The bulk of screeds are now delivered readymixed, which is good for quality and does away with a third of the two-and-one gang. But the real growth market is in gypsum-based screeds, which are sprayed out of a nozzle and are self-placing. They have been available in the UK since the 1990s and have captured something like 20% of the market. The cost is about £180/m³ as opposed to £100/m³ for readymixed screed, but these screeds can be laid at half the depth (i.e. 35mm - except where you have underfloor heating; then its 50mm as opposed to 65mm.) It's particularly suitable for underfloor heating as it doesn't require wheelbarrows with the potential to damage the pipes. Look out for Gyvlon, Cemex Supaflo or Tarmac Truflow. Also check out Screedflo, an interesting independent business in this arena that is making a name for itself and has a natty specification called Screedflo dB which is designed to be poured onto intermediate timber floors to aid sound proofing and provide a medium for underfloor heating.

It's still the province of specialist contractors, which makes it rather more expensive than traditional screeds, but not by very much. It also dries a little more quickly. Talking of drying....

DRYING TIMES

Screeds, whether cement or gypsum based, take time to dry and it's important that they are thoroughly dried out, especially if there is a timber floor being laid on top of them. I have seen beautiful oak floor boards buckle and warp because moisture from the screed below was still evaporating. Seventy days is reckoned to be time enough for most screeds: in the summer months it will be a little less. If you have underfloor

Screedflo being poured over underfloor heating. The process is quick and it uses far less materials than conventional screed.

heating fitted, you can speed the process but only gently: cement screeds must be left for 28 days before any heating is applied at all, and even then it has to be turned on slowly, a few degrees higher each day.

WHY SCREED AT ALL?

You often don't have to. If you are finishing your floor in timber, you may not need to lay an intermediate floor, but if you are laying tiles and/or carpet, you will need a smooth surface to work off and it's hard (though not impossible) to get a concrete slab smooth enough for this. Underfloor heating is

another complication: it can be laid in concrete early on in the build process, but it's not without its issues. I have come across a case where the pipes were tested in the autumn and left full of water over the winter whilst the rest of the house was built. Frost got to them and caused the pipes to split and this wasn't discovered until the house was finished. Ouch.

POLISHED CONCRETE

Polished concrete, as it is known, is uber-cool, the kind of thing you find in art galleries. It's laid instead of a screed, usually at the groundworks stage in the proceeding. It goes well with underfloor heating too. Although it's not cheap, when it is placed against the cost of the alternatives it isn't really a budget

buster either. You will find more about this flooring method in Chapter 10, where I discuss floor finishes.

SLOPES, BAD GROUND & TREES

If you have worked through the book to this point from 'Pitfalls' you will have twigged that, although groundworks can work out to be relatively cheap, they can also turn into a budget-crippling nightmare.

There are three basic causes of alarming cost expansion:
- slopes
- bad ground
- trees.

SLOPES

Obviously, it all depends on how much it slopes, but even quite gentle slopes can create havoc with a tight budget. Brinkley's Slope Law states that, no matter how you deal with it, each one degree of slope will add £1,500 to your development costs. Obviously this represents an enormous over-simplification of different situations but you will be disappointed to discover that it rarely works out less than this and sometimes it can be a whole lot more, especially if you are constructing a mansion larger than 200m^2. The fact is, you just can't get away with building a sloping house and so adjustments have to be made between the lie of the land

and the lie of your house and these adjustments are expensive. It's not just excavating out the ground so you can build on the level; if the slope is greater than five degrees, there are complications with access roads and pavings, drains, and landscaping. Steeper still and you are likely to require retaining walls and possibly even safety railing. Aficionados of Grand Designs may remember a couple in Bath, filmed in 2007, who managed to spend £300,000 taking out a slope before they even got to dig their foundations. According to my law, they must have had a 200°slope, which is going it some, so be warned it's not really a law at all. I expect you already realised that.

Faced with a sloping site, there are basically three options for the new housebuilder.

EXCAVATE AND CART AWAY

Here you dig a large, house-sized hole out of your slope, dispose of all the excavations and fit the house into the hole. This is perhaps the simplest and the one that the planners are likely to prefer, as it will keep your roofline low. There will be the cost of excavation and carting away which, depending on the lie of the ground, could easily cost £5,000-£10,000. Add to this the cost of any retaining walls that might have to be built: budget £100/lin m for a one metre high retaining wall, and bear in mind that retaining walls get wider as they get higher, so tall ones are exponentially more expensive

BUILD OUT FROM HIGH POINT

Here you substitute the cost of excavating with the cost of building supporting walls. There may not be much to choose between the two in

cost terms, but this method is likely to leave you with expensive steps to build up to the back/front of the house. The overall structure is also likely to be far more imposing and, consequently, much less likely to pass muster with the planners.

FIT HOUSE TO SLOPE

Arrange the house as a series of steps, running up the slope. Building basements and/or mezzanine split-levels may well be architecturally the most pleasing but it is also the most expensive. Split-levels have cost implications at almost every stage of the building works: stepped foundations, shuttering for floor slabs, special stair joinery, complex service routes, and complex roof details. Split-level building adds between 10 and 20% to your overall building costs.

Brinkley's Slope Law

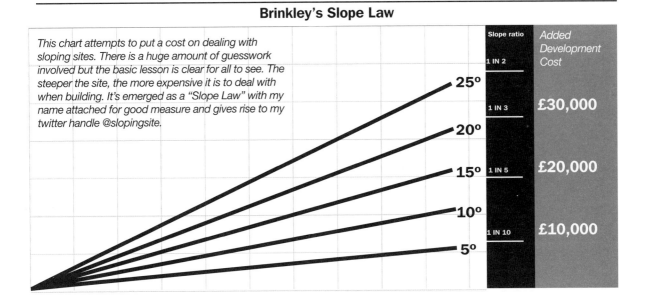

This chart attempts to put a cost on dealing with sloping sites. There is a huge amount of guesswork involved but the basic lesson is clear for all to see. The steeper the site, the more expensive it is to deal with when building. It's emerged as a "Slope Law" with my name attached for good measure and gives rise to my twitter handle @slopingsite.

Raft v Pile

Two competing foundation systems often specified by engineers when ground conditions are not straightforward. The concrete raft extends under the entire building, acting as both wall foundation and floor slab. Concrete piles are sunk deep into the ground and support a horizontal beam which acts as the wall foundation.

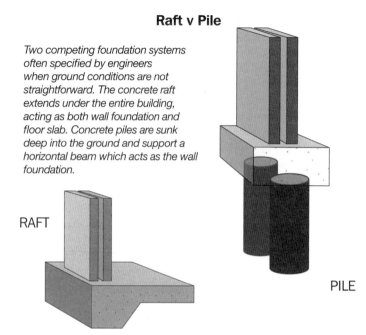

RAFT

PILE

Whichever method you choose to overcome the problems set by a sloping site, you will be faced with extra landscaping expenses – steps, turfed banks, rockeries. Although these costs can generally be deferred over a number of years, they will add significantly to the overall development.

BAD GROUND

A variety of problems are dealt with under the category of bad ground. The commonest are clay soils and the presence of tree roots, but also you must be prepared for bog conditions, mining subsidence, wells, water courses, old factory workings, disused refuse tips, even problems when ancient remains are discovered. It's

worth carrying out any amount of detective work to ascertain exactly what has happened on your site because the ramifications can be expensive.

A site appraisal is likely (but not definitely) going to uncover the problems you will meet below ground and your foundation design is almost definitely going to be in the hands of an engineer.

The key to understanding the cost implications of these alternative foundation solutions is to hang on to the ballpark figure that applies to normal groundworks. This is currently around £200/m² of footprint covered. This includes the cost of providing foundations, below ground walling and a ground floor to the externally

measured areas of house and any outbuildings such as garages.

There are three likely solutions to bad ground:
■ deeper foundations (usually reinforced with steel)
■ raft foundations
■ piling.

DEEPER FOUNDATIONS

You will have to excavate to good bearing ground (if it's there). If it's just a question of going down to 2.5m, you may get away with the regular trenchfill foundation. But this will be expensive; it will add around £10/m² to the ballpark footprint figure (remember base equals £200/m²) for every 100mm deeper you have to dig.

Deeper than 2m, it starts to look like other engineered systems will save you money – see following items. Trouble is, if you are discovering how bad it all is as you dig, then it's realistically too late to switch to one of the alternative foundations systems.

One technique commonly used in clay areas is to fit a collapsible board against the side of the trench, rather like lining paper on the side of a cake tin. The idea is that clayboard is flexible enough to allow the clay to heave without moving the enclosed concrete foundations. There are a number of dedicated products available for this application; the two best known are Claymaster which is made of polystyrene and Clayboard which uses a honeycomb filler very similar to that used in moulded doors.

RAFTS

On a problem-free site, the floor slab is laid a couple of stages further on than the foundations. However, with rafts, you pour the foundation concrete together with the floor slab concrete in one operation. With various cambered design profiles and a whole mass of steel reinforcement, you create a concrete raft, which will move as one. If subsidence occurs, the raft will absorb the changes without imposing extra strains on the superstructure above.

A raft foundation uses vast amounts of concrete and steel and is unlikely to cost less than £200/m² footprint. There have been a few high profile problems with raft foundations where the raft as a whole starts shifting; leaving the house above perched at a precarious angle. They are not a solution for every site.

PILING

Increasingly specified as the engineering solution of choice for difficult sites, piling is also reckoned to be cost effective in situations where foundations would otherwise have to be deeper than 2m. The number of piles and the depth of each pile can only be determined by drilling trial holes. A typical installation would place piles 2.5m apart under every load-bearing wall (including detached garages) and each pile would go down until solid ground was reached. All the holes are then filled with concrete (either poured wet or precast) and tied together with a concrete ground beam, which would be all that you would eventually see of the operation, and would look much like a regular trenchfill concrete foundation. Budget prices are £40 per m depth for individual piles (depth anywhere from 3-10m) and £80/lin m for ground beams.

There are various other techniques that can be used as an alternative to concrete piling or reinforced rafts but these are really the province of the specialist engineer. One interesting option is Abbey Pynford's Housedeck, which is designed to be cost effective for single house developments; it's actually a floating or suspended raft, which gives you a well-insulated slab. Housedeck will typically cost upwards of £25,000 for a 150m² footprint. Abbey Pynford's Phil Jones commented to me: 'Our unit area rate gets lower as the footprint increases, up to about 250m². We are never going to be competitive with simple strip foundations but we find that Housedeck starts to make sense if you have to dig down more than 1.5 metres'.

TREES

There are two different ways in which trees may affect your development costs. One is visual; planners and neighbours may view the importance of your trees quite differently from you. The other is to do with the effect of tree roots on your foundations. A site with mature trees will tend to look immediately attractive but you should pay close attention to just where these trees are located in relation to your proposed foundations.

TREE ROOTS

Tree root systems can spread a very long way from the trunks and they can suck water from even greater distances causing movement and shrinkage in soils, which is bad news for house foundations. The solution to this problem is not to cut down the offending trees – this can actually make the situation worse for up to ten years afterwards – but to have deeper foundations, or specialist ones. The NHBC publishes tables showing the foundation depth needed for different tree species at varying distances but this is too technical in scope for this humble work: the summary table is designed to let you roughly gauge the effect on construction costs. There are four variables that determine the foundation depth when tree roots are present; these are:

■ shrinkability of the soil – clay soils are the usual issue
■ water demand from tree species: some species such as poplar, willow and elm, are very thirsty whereas others, such as beech and birch, have much less impact on your foundations
■ mature height of tree species
■ distance of tree from foundations

The worst-case scenario would be to have a tall and thirsty tree, located 7m (or less) from your foundations,

Distance at which roots cease to have any effect on foundations

Distance within which specialist foundations will be required

TREE TABLE			
Very Thirsty	**Mature Height**	**Safe Distance**	**Call the Engineer**
Elm	24m	30m	within 12m
Oak	20m	25m	within 10m
Poplar	25m	30m	within 12m
Willow	16-24m	20-25m	within 2m
Hawthorn	10m	12m	within 4m
Cypress	20m	15m	within 5m
Moderately Thirsty			
Chestnut	20m	15m	*not required*
Lime	22m	16m	*not required*
Beech	20m	15m	*not required*
Ash	23m	18m	*not required*
Plane	26m	20m	*not required*
Sycamore	22m	16m	*not required*
Apple	10m	8m	*not required*
Most conifers	20m	8m	*not required*
Not v Thirsty			
Birch	14m	7m	*not required*
Elder	10m	5m	*not required*
Hornbeam	17m	8m	*not required*
Hazel	8m	4m	*not required*

which are in clay. God help you! The NHBC would want you to dig foundations over 3m deep or use piles or rafts. And, of course, it would cost.

ACTION

If your plot has any of these problems it will pay dividends to seek advice at the survey stage. The person who would normally deal with such matters is a structural engineer, but if you are employing a designer to solve your problems, it would be as well not to engage another professional off your own bat; let the designer choose how (and who) best to overcome the difficulties. A possible source of free and impartial advice is your local building inspector.

If there is good news in here it is that there is now effectively some sort of cap on the amount your foundation costs may grow. The new techniques coming on stream – especially piling and ground beams – are slowly but surely getting cheaper. If you have bad ground, your total groundworks costs (including laying of the ground floor) may well double from a base of around £200/m² footprint, but they are unlikely to treble. If you are excavating blind – i.e. without a clue what lies beneath – then a contingency fund of around £80/m² of footprint would be a good idea.

SERVICES

What exactly do we mean by running services? It's an easy phrase that drops off the tongue, like going for a gentle jog around the local park. But it's often more like a marathon, and it can easily end up driving selfbuilders to distraction. The services are what connects your to-be-house with the rest of the world, the very things that turn a 16th century hovel into a 21st century palace. Electricity (vital), water (even more vital), gas (useful) and telecoms/broadband (what, no Instagram?) all need to be fitted into place and all come with a cost attached. Technically, it is possible to live entirely off the grid, but it's not straightforward and it too comes with a bag of attendant costs, so it's easier to imagine you are building a normal house in a normal place and you want the normal 21st century stuff.

It's a difficult area to estimate because every site is different and the costs involved are highly variable. Electricity supplies are usually seen as the most important because there are often ways around the others. Gas can be supplied in its bottled or LPG format, or oil can be used as an alternative. Water can sometimes be taken from under the ground via a borehole and broadband and telecoms are frequently available by means other than a direct cable connection. These are the sorts of things you have to look at when assessing the viability of a plot in the first place.

But electricity? So much of modern life hinges on our use of electricity that not to have a supply would be very difficult indeed. And the cost of that supply depends to a large extent on how far away the street mains are, as a big part of the cost is in excavating the trenches to site and the reinstatement afterwards. High connection charges can render a site undevelopable. First things first, get a quote to find out how much the electric is going to be.

This work isn't carried out by the regular utility companies like nPower and EDF. For electricity, you have to go to a Distribution Network Operator (DNO) and there are nine of them in the UK. A web search will show you who carries work out in your area. The gas grid runs on similar lines. A good source of information on this is the Energy Networks site. Back in the day, when I first started writing about selfbuild, this was all pretty difficult to work out, but the services offered are a lot more transparent now and the providers I recently used, UK Power Networks for electricity and Cadent for gas, have good websites which explain the likely range of costs you will be faced with.

Both the gas and electric services run on similar lines. The suppliers are responsible for getting the service to your meter box and you are responsible for the meter box itself and the works on the house side of the meter box. Where the meter box is placed is open to a little negotiation with the surveyor who comes to site. And also if you want a temporary site

Tip: Decide where the services will come into the house (i.e. in the utility room) and lay ducting under the house floor between the external meters and this point. Each supply needs its own duct - don't be tempted to double up. It may also make sense to lay further ducts under the ground floor to get services from inside the house out into the garden for electrics, water and even gas for BBQs.

supply, you can arrange that for an additional cost.

The actual meter is the responsibility of your chosen supplier with whom you will be expected to take out a contract. The small independent power suppliers don't get a look in here — you have to work with one of the big six. And it sort of makes sense to go for a dual fuel option here if you are fitting gas as well. They will in all likelihood supply you with an internal smart meter which, depending on the model, makes it very hard to change suppliers. If you want to know more, search on smart meters and find out what a mess the government

sponsored roll out has been. The first generation of Smart Meters, the SMETS1, effectively tie you into the supplier who fits them so you lose the ability to switch suppliers easily. So see if you can get a SMETS2 fitted on your new home. On the other hand your new home will be so energy efficient (won't it?) that you won't need to worry about fuel bills in future.

Water isn't so very different either. There will be one supplier in your area and you have to get through to their new supplies department and take it from there. They will want to fit a water meter somewhere in the ground probably close to your

Chapter 6

site boundary and leave everything beyond that point up to you. Worth noting that water pipes are required to be buried 750mm below ground level (to prevent freezing), whereas gas and electricity cables go down 450mm.

Telecoms and broadband supply needs to be considered as well. In fact they have a brand new building regulation (Part R in England) requiring all new homes to be broadband ready. The route into the house depends on what is available on your boundary. It may be an overhead connection. Unlike the other services, broadband/telecom connections are usually put in free in exchange for signing up to a contract.

By way of example, on my recent self build I paid £1,080 for the water supply, £447 for the gas and £1694 for electricity. They are fairly typical of the lower end of costs — one of the few advantages of building in the middle of town where supplies are in the street outside. Virgin broadband was installed for free.

If you find the prospect of dealing with all these service providers too daunting, there are businesses out there, such as Gas and Electricity Connections, who will for a fee, undertake water, electricity and gas supplies to new homes up to the meter boxes.

The services works extend on your side the meter box. You have to run cables and pipes to your consumer unit, your gas and your water tap, and to your telecoms outlet. The chances are that you want to bring them into

the house somewhere like the utility room which may not be next to the external meter boxes. Electricity will use armoured cable, gas will use TracPipe and water will be run in 25mm MDPE pipe which must be insulated if it runs under a suspended floor as it runs a freezing risk if not. You can run these service cables and pipes at any reasonable depth in the floor so they don't have to be done before the floor base or the beam and block floor is laid, but they do have to be considered before the floors are finished.

Another thing to consider at this stage is the supply of these same services to the external areas of the house. You may well plan for water, gas, electricity and broadband in your garden. Think garden lighting, summerhouses or studios, gas BBQs, hot tubs and fountains. These are best laid downstream from your consumer units and gas and water stop taps, so a second set of routes should be planned as well.

One way around this conundrum of what to lay when is to run twin wall cable ducting through the foundations. If you are blessed with huge amounts of foresight, you will even leave drawstrings inside the ducting so that when the time comes you can simply pull the cable or gas pipe through the duct, although in reality most services can be pushed through almost as easily, provided there are no sharp bends to negotiate. Don't be spare with it and don't be tempted to double up by putting two services through one duct. Water pipes shouldn't be left exposed in

areas that might freeze so need to be wrapped in pipe lagging. If you can't be doing with all this hassle, there are businesses out there that will take all the hassle of your hands and arrange for quotes, and installations of electricity, gas and water. Check out Gas and Electricity Connections.

DRAINAGE

First things first: it is important to understand the difference between foulwater and rainwater.

■ Foulwater is the waste generated by normal household usage - flushing loos, emptying baths and sinks, washing machines, dishwashers etc. Foulwater is sometimes subdivided as black water (toilets) and grey water (most other outlets).

■ Rainwater, as its name suggests, is what falls out of the sky and flows down the gutters and downpipes from the roof, not to mention the hardstanding areas as well.

Generally our sewage systems are working at near capacity levels and therefore it is a standard requirement that rainwater is not added to the load. Hence it is normal to lay two separate drain systems to dispose of their respective wastes in different ways. In certain locations it may be possible to run rainwater into the main sewerage system (refer to your water company) but it would be unwise to assume that this is the case. You will need to prove that there is no alternative.

FOUL WATER

In assessing the likely costs of any individual scheme there is one overriding question that must be answered at the outset. That is, 'Where the hell am I going to dump all this crap?' There are other questions as well, notably: 'How do I get it there?' but 'Where to?' is the 'big one'. So, although it may seem illogical to start at the end, we'll look at the drainage options this way around.

RUNNING INTO THE MAIN DRAINS

Even a relatively simple mains drainage connection can be an expensive business. Locating main drains can be a problem; the water companies hold what records exist and, whilst access is open to all, accuracy is not guaranteed.

The amount of work in excavating and connecting to the main drain (usually referred to as 'doing a road opening') can vary enormously depending on the depth of the drain, whether there are vacant junctions (known as laterals) already present to connect on to, the presence/absence of other utilities and the attitudes and charges of local authorities and water companies.

To open a public highway you must contact the council highways department in order to purchase a road-opening permit, now generally known as a Street Works Licence (prices very variable but probably going to set you back as much as £300 in total). Inspections of the opening and connection need to be carried out by a) your water company, b) your own building inspector and c) the council highways department who inspect no less than five times to ensure the surface reinstatement is in order. A busy road may require traffic lights and if your main drain runs under the other side of the road, the whole process becomes very much more complicated.

The water company is going to insist that you employ a competent groundworker to make the connection and therefore it is a sensible idea to get some quotes for this work before proceeding.

BACKDROP MANHOLES

It is much cheaper, easier and safer to lay house drains at depths of between 600 and 1200mm below ground level. Normally, drains are best laid at gentle falls (around 1:80) and sharp inclines are discouraged. If your main drain level is way beneath your optimum house drain level, you will probably find it easiest to construct a backdrop manhole near your boundary line. A backdrop manhole works a bit like a waterfall: it's a sudden drop from one level to another and it requires special construction methods and access arrangements.

PUMPS

If your outlet drain is higher than your house drains you have the option of pumping the waste up hill. This is often done by building in a tank of some description, similar to a small septic tank (say, 2m deep and 1m in diameter) into which the house

DRAINS: Key rates

Plastic pipe & fittings	£16	m run
Pea Shingle	£56	m^3
Excavation	£46	m^3
Road Openings	£500-£8,000	
Soakaway	£ 1,000	
Storm Drain Connection	£ 1,000	
Main Drain Interceptor	£ 500	

	Kit	Installation	Drainage Fields	Total
Septic Tanks	£ 600	£ 700	£ 3,500	£ 4,800
Mini Treatment Works	£ 3,000	£ 2,500	£ 2,000	£ 7,500
Cesspool	£ 2,500	£ 2,500		£ 5,000
Reed Beds	£ 6,500	£ 3,500		£ 10,000

DRAIN COSTS per LINEAR METRE

	Materials	Time in mins	Lab @ £20/hr	Combined
Foul Drain Runs	£ 34	80	£ 29	**£ 63**
Rainwater Drain Runs	£ 34	60	£ 22	**£ 56**
Service Trenching	£18	40	£ 15	**£ 33**

MODEL HOUSE: Drainage and Services Costs				
DRAINS		Rate per m run	Materials	Labour	Cost
Foul Drains	40 m	£ 63	£ 1,360	£ 1,170	£ 2,530
Rainwater Drains	60 m	£ 56	£ 2,040	£ 1,320	£ 3,360
Service Trenching	15 m	£ 33	£ 270	£ 220	£ 490
Soakaway ea			£ 1,000	£ 200	£ 1,200
		Total	**£ 4,700**	**£ 2,900**	**£ 7,600**
SERVICE CONNECTIONS					
Electrics					£ 2,500
Mains Gas					£ 500
Water					£ 1,800
Road Connection for Drains					£ 750
				Total	**£ 5,600**

drains run, and fitting either a solid handling pump or a macerator or grinder pump. The macerator pump is the more expensive but allows the waste to be expelled in a 32 or 50mm pipe, which makes it a better bet for long distances. A control panel is placed somewhere indoors or in a weatherproof casing.

Expensive though a pump is, it can be cost effective to install one when the main drain connection is further than 300m away, even if it is downhill. This is because it can pump out into a small bore pipe that can be laid in a flat trench, much reducing excavation costs. On the other hand, any system that works by gravity alone is ultimately preferable because it isn't going to break down.

Budget between £2,000 and £4,000 for making a road opening and maybe a further £3,000 if you need a pumping station. Occasionally road openings can be done for less but don't count on it. Recently the tendency is upwards, not down, and some selfbuilders are being quoted

ridiculous amounts, like £8,000, for a simple T-off a main drain just 3m away. And another instance of £10,000 for a double sewer and storm drain connection across a very quiet road. When costs start getting silly like this, it might be time to look at the alternative, an off-mains solution.

OFF-MAINS DRAINAGE
The simplest and the cheapest off-mains solution is usually to install a septic tank. It's a tried and tested method and there are millions of them in operation, dotted around the countryside – it's a very rural thing. A septic tank is one of the simpler concepts to understand in the field of sewage treatment: it is an underground chamber (traditionally constructed of brick, more recently from concrete or GRP), into which your foul waste system empties. There is no power needed, there are no moving parts and, as long as the solids at the bottom of the tank are regularly pumped out (or desludged),

then the septic tank should give decades of trouble-free service.

The cost of the tanks varies depending on the volumes they are designed to deal with but single household units are often priced between £400 and £600. Added to this is the cost of the groundworkers installing the tanks (often around £1,500) and the cost of excavating and installing a herringbone soakaway system - again depending on the volumes to be dealt with and also ground porosity. It would be wise to budget £4,000 to £5,000 for a new septic tank system.

However, simple septic tanks won't work in every location. The Environment Agency will be taking a look at your site and may well come to the conclusion that your ground conditions require something else, typically a sewage treatment plant, which is like a septic tank on steroids. Well, it has a power source to speed up the digestion process.

The simpler plants use a little power to drive an air pump whilst the unique Klargester Biodisc is designed around a series of rotating metal discs. And there is one, the Bio Bubble, which acts like a super-super-charged septic tank and eats the solids as well as the liquor and therefore doesn't need any desludging.

DISCHARGE CONSENT
In England and Wales, sewage disposal comes under the aegis of the

Environment Agency and they have a say in what you can and can't do. They used to operate a permit system called A Consent to Discharge but this has been replaced (in 2010) by a Water Discharge Consent, known as EPP2, which makes the process much easier if you are using conventional solutions, but much more expensive if you plan anything unusual.

If you use a EPP2 registered supplier, such as Klargester, then provided you follow the instructions and take out a service contract, your site is deemed to qualify. If you choose something or someone who hasn't registered, then you have to convince the Agency that what you are doing is adequate and you also have to buy a permit (around £900).

The situation in Scotland and N.Ireland is different but they too seem to be in the business of introducing something like EPP2 in the near future.

The advent of plastic pipes has made laying drains easier. Pre-formed inspection pits have a number of outlets. These drains are benched on concrete to get the falls right and will shortly be supported with pea shingle elsewhere. Building inspectors will usually want to have sight at this stage, but failing that, be sure to photograph this stage.

ALTERNATIVE OPTIONS

There is a growing interest in alternative forms of sewage disposal. Some of these are seen as being greener than the conventional methods but it's a tag that many of the alternative practitioners themselves are reluctant to emphasise: most readily admit that there is a time and place for almost all the sewage systems on the market and it is often stretching things a bit far to make out a case that any one system is greener than another.

The best known of the alternative disposal systems is the use of reed beds (aka Constructed Wetland Sewage Systems). A reed bed system can be used to upgrade the effluent coming out of a tank so that it meets the same discharge standards as a package treatment plant and can, therefore, be discharged into a watercourse. Although it sounds very organic and natural, successful reed bed drainage involves a surprising amount of construction and no way is this a cheap option – installation costs are similar to a package treatment plant and you require an area the size of half a tennis court. And like a septic tank or package treatment plant, you still have to pump out the solids, which are collected in a primary settlement tank. Reed beds also require some weekly maintenance so they tend to attract enthusiasts rather than the fit-and-forget brigade.

Reed bed treatment is well accepted as a sewage treatment method and is now being specified on a large scale by some of our water companies. There are however other options, including the use of dry composting toilets. Increasingly, selfbuilders are turning their attention to the whole picture of water and waste management and seeking to combine aspects such as rainwater harvesting and grey water recycling with efficient treatment of sewage waste.

Normally it is a principle of all foulwater drainage systems that rainwater should be disposed of separately: the problem being that whereas most sewage digestion systems need a steady supply of blackwater to keep working smoothly, rainfall has a habit of arriving in large quantities which can disrupt the workings of the sewage systems. However, if rainwater is being collected separately, it is usually used to flush toilets and this way the two systems can be effectively combined at one stage removed.

SITING OF TANKS

Any off-mains drainage system that uses a tank which needs desludging (and that includes most of the options) has to consider tanker access – 30m is reckoned to be the limit that a tanker's hose can extend to. In Scotland, tanks must be a minimum of 15m from the house. No minimum exists in England and Wales but if you have a sensitive nose you would do well to stick to the Scottish standards.

RAINWATER DISPOSAL
SOAKAWAYS

The traditional destination of rainwater is a soakaway in the garden that is nothing more than a hole dug into the ground, traditionally filled with free draining hardcore or brick rubble. Whereas soakaways used to be afterthoughts, completed with the

garden works as and when, these days building inspectors want to see calculations on the porosity of the subsoil and estimates of how the drains will cope in 1 in 100 year events (i.e. freak thunderstorms).

Consequently, soakaway construction has become far more elaborate and it is not unusual to have to excavate a very large hole of 3m^3 and to fill it will plastic crates rather than brick rubble. Coupled with the tendency for people to want sliding folding doors with flat levels between internal floors and patios, which requires close attention to rainwater drainage, rainwater disposal is an area which has become much more expensive in my lifetime in building.

SUDS

The idea of SUDS (Sustainable Urban Drainage Systems) is to stop flash flooding caused by rainwater cascading off hard surfaces like roofs and roadways, and to store rainwater somewhere where it won't cause flooding. It could result in a more complex soakaway design (see above) but it could also be a pond or a swale. It could even be a blue roof: that is one that is designed not just to be home to vegetation (that's a green roof) but to also store significant amounts of stormwater for slow release into the drainage system. If you think green roofs are expensive (they are), you will blanche when you find how much a blue roof costs, as you are basically placing a reservoir on your flat roof and you need some very beefy

joists to support it, not to mention some extremely expensive waterproof detailing to ensure it doesn't leak. SUDS also addresses hard paving areas and look to use not only permeable paving but to have deep pockets of hardcore installed underneath, again with the idea of absorbing large quantities of stormwater.

It is something of a hot issue because we seem to be suffering from frequent flash flooding events, probably as a result of climate change. Whereas SUDS designs can make a significant impact on large developments, on single sites, their impact will only ever be limited. It is perhaps worth considering installing some SUDS features on your selfbuild, especially if you are concerned about flood risk.

STORM DRAINS

Common in urban areas, rare in the country, they are actually designed to stop the roads flooding, but can sometimes be used for house rainwater. Budget £1,000 to make a connection to a storm drain. Storm drains are often over 100 years old and in a poor state of repair, and locating them can be a hit and miss affair. Typically, these are managed by the highways department of the local council (rather than the local water company) and they often flatly refuse to accept any additional rainwater discharge, even when it is obviously the best option. If you have well-honed negotiating skills, here's a good place to use them.

RAINWATER INTO MAIN DRAINS

Attitudes to this vary from area to area, but nowhere is it encouraged. But when soakaways and storm drains are impracticable, this course will often be accepted as a last resort. There must be an interceptor between the two drain systems to prevent unpleasant pongs coming back up the rainwater gullies.

RAINWATER HARVESTING

There are now a handful of businesses in the UK selling (mostly German) gear with which you can filter, collect and pump rainwater around the house for flushing loos. More information can be found on this in the chapter on Green issues.

ROUTES

This is the other major decision to be made when looking at drain runs. The idea is to get from the house to the final dumping point with as few bends as possible. Drains have a tendency to get blocked so access is important at all bends.

Straight 110mm plastic drain runs can be machine excavated (to average depths), laid and buried for around £40/lin m. The building inspector may allow you to have a few gentle radius bends on your drain runs, provided they don't prevent rodding – that is clearing future blockages with drain rods – but generally the accepted practice is to have access to the drains every time there is a bend. The addition of inspection chambers, gullies, rodding access, etc ('fittings') more or less

doubles the basic metre rate for drain laying to between £60 and £80/lin m – the cost of one manhole is equivalent to 10 lin m of straight drains. So the general idea is to plan your drain runs with as few bends as possible.

DRAINAGE TIPS

When drawing up working details for drains, note that the plans need drawings and specifications which should include the drain layouts, the invert levels (depths), and details of junctions, inspection chambers and access (rodding) points.

Although the trade is still split between using clay and plastic (uPVC) drainage, someone new to the game would do well to use plastic. There is little to choose between the systems on price but the plastic systems are more user-friendly. There are six major players in this field and, underground at least, there is little to choose between them on quality or price. Osma are the market leaders and their installation guide tells you much of what you need to know about laying drains. They do a free (but slow) design service but you must know your main drain invert (drain depth) levels for it to be worthwhile.

Plastic pipe is sold with heavy discounts off list price. A new house project should be able to get discounts of 30-40%. All the manufacturers produce guttering and internal waste fittings as well and, if you combine your order, you will have more muscle to negotiate better discounts.

EXCAVATION OF TRENCHES

Drain trenches are normally 450mm wide (the width of a digger's narrow bucket). 100mm drain (the standard) is going to be adequate for all situations where there are less than five loos. There is no set depth, but if you lay at less than 600mm you may have to cover the pipe run with paving slabs or some form of hard standing to prevent damage from above. If the run is deeper than 1200mm, you will start to have problems working the trenches.

The optimum fall is 1:80 which is equivalent to 250mm on a 20m run. If you have to cope with gradients much steeper than this then take specialist advice - don't assume that drains will work just because they are going downhill.

Plastic pipe should be bedded on pea shingle, which is a particularly fine grade of gravel. Allow one ton of pea shingle for every 8 lin m of drain. When calculating excavation quantities, allow for 80% of excavated material to go back into the trenches once the pipes are laid.

7
SUPERSTRUCTURE

Superstructure is a long and pretentious word and I would like to use some funky Anglo-Saxon alternative, altogether more down-to-earth. Trouble is, I don't know one. Some use the term shell – as in 'Putting up the Shell' – and perhaps this isn't bad, especially if you think of it in terms of sea shells, not egg shells. But, to confuse matters, the outer walls that make up the shell get referred to as skins or, sometimes, leaves; one suggests bodies, the other trees, neither eggs nor sea creatures. It all seems a bit of a mess; hence I'll stick with the term Superstructure.

Definition? Well you have hopefully figured it out by now – it's all the above ground bits of a house up to but excluding the finishes and the wiring and piping. Literally, the super (i.e. above) structure as opposed to the sub (i.e. below or under) structure. So in Superstructure we'll look at walls (as in inner and outer skins), external doors and windows, roofs and all the fiddly bits that hold them together. Floors? The ground floor details are in the previous chapter, the first floor and above – known as intermediate floors – are buried in this chapter. If

you buy a factory-built house, it's the superstructure that you are getting. Or at least part of the superstructure. The roof covers and the external wall finishes are conventionally left to you to sort out, along with the substructural works and the finishes.

INNER SKIN

The external house walls are conventionally made up of an inner and outer skin. The inner skin tends to be the part where the work is done: it holds up the structure and provides the support for the floors and roof. The outer skin is there to provide some weatherproofing and to look good. There are, in addition to this, internal walls which are there to divide the house into rooms. These are looked at later in the chapter. Whilst there is much in common between inner skins and internal walls, there are enough differences to make it helpful to look at them (and cost them) separately.

I'll start with a look at how blockwork homes work. This remains the No 1 housebuilding method in the UK as a whole. It's only serious rival, at least in terms of numbers built, is timber frame, and I'll therefore make this section a bit of a compare and contrast between the two methods. The other build systems are looked at in the next section, Alternative Skins.

MASONRY BUILDS

You can't really get a handle on blockwork houses without looking at the whole issue of wall cavities. Cavities enabled builders to incorporate large format concrete blocks – which became widely available in the 1930s – into house walls whilst retaining a brick skin on the outside. Prior to this, houses had been built with solid brick (occasionally stone) walls in what we would now call a single-skin arrangement but back in the day they were just plain walls.

The cavity was advertised as being an 'improvement' in house construction because it introduced a barrier across which rain supposedly couldn't jump. But rain often does find a route across cavities: they are very difficult to build well, easy to get wrong. For along with cavity walls came brick ties (to knit the inner and outer walls together), returns (for joinery to sit in) and cavity trays (to divert water trickling down the inner skin across to the outer skin). Cavities had a nasty habit of filling up with bits of crud, or snots as they are lovingly referred to, which would cling to the ties and form tracks for the water to cross the cavity. As regards protecting the house from water damage, cavity walls are only marginally better than solid walls.

In the 1980s, we started to become concerned about heat loss through walls and builders began to put insulation into the cavities. Now you might think that these two alternative uses for a cavity – i.e. to stop water going one way and heat the other – are completely at odds with one another and, essentially, you'd be dead right. Yet, bit by bit, builders are learning that insulation and cavities are not an impossible marriage and many builders are now enthusiastically stuffing their cavities with all manner of insulants without suffering horrendous damp penetration problems.

LINTELS AND WALL TIES

Cavity walls need to be knitted together. And the openings in them need to be bridged. And the bases of them need protection against rising damp. All told there are a number of things you have to think about when you build a cavity wall. The knitting together is done with wall ties, once galvanised steel, now stainless steel, placed in regular patterns, dictated by the building regs. Lintels are needed over window and door openings. These are now usually steel and they need to bear at least 150mm at either end of the openings they bridge.

You also have to consider how water will behave inside a cavity: it has a tendency to funnel across to the inner skin so you have to take great care to ensure that any water trickling down the outer face of the inner skin has to be directed outwards above openings. There are a number of companies producing cavity tray products designed to keep cavities dry, a very specialised niche within the building trade.

BLOCKS

Typically, building blocks are made of cement and various aggregates like sand and stone. In many countries blocks are manufactured with feature finishes and are used extensively, instead of bricks or stone, as external wall finishes in their own right. But in Britain this hasn't proved to be a popular technique, except where cheaper substitutes for stone are sought. So when we look at building blocks we are analysing how well they perform structurally, not how good they look.

BLOCK STRENGTH

Block strength is calculated in Newton /mm², known in the trade as 'Newtons' or just plain 'N'. Roughly speaking the more cement in the block, the higher the strength (or the more Newtons it is said to have). Most blocks qualify for the basic 3.5N strength, though some applications require 7N blocks (i.e. below ground and some floor blocks). You will find a number of 'utility blocks' on the market but their strength is not guaranteed. Having said that, there aren't many applications in housebuilding that call for extra-strength blocks.

BLOCK TYPES

There is an industry standard size of block, which is 440x215mm. This is the equivalent of six standard bricks and you need ten of these blocks to build a square metre of wall: they are conventionally bought by the square metre – a ten-pack. They are usually 100mm thick, though some of the super-lightweight varieties are thicker in order to get their insulation values up to par.

THE DENSE BLOCK

Uncomfortably heavy to lift, they are usually used below ground, often at 7N strength. Cheap – full loads cost just around £8/m².

LIGHTWEIGHT CLINKER BLOCKS

Almost half the weight of a dense block, these are often used on the inner leaf of insulated cavities and in partition walls. They provide an excellent keying surface for plasters. They are also widely used in beam-and-block flooring; they are very similarly priced to dense blocks.

AIRCRETE BLOCKS

Introduced from Scandinavia in the

INNER SKIN: Key Rates per m²

Blockwork	Materials	Accessories	Time taken in mins	Labour at £25/hr	Combined
Celcon 100mm blocks	£12	£2	35	£15	£ 29
Hemelite blocks	£12	£2	35	£15	£ 29
Thin Joint Blocks	£12	£4	25	£10	£ 26
Timber Frame					
47x90mm Frame	£5	£14	50	£21	£ 40
47x140mm Frame	£9	£14	50	£21	£ 44
47x185mm Frame	£10	£14	50	£21	£ 45

Timber frame is here costed as if it was being built on site, which it rarely is in the UK. Usually, it's built offsite in a factory where many different parts (lintels, joinery) are also assembled, making it very hard to compare directly with masonry build. As a general rule, there isn't much to choose between the systems on cost grounds.

MODEL HOUSE: Inner Skin Costs

		Materials	Labour	Total
Inner Skin Area - minus joinery openings	185 m²			
Celcon type Blocks laid in mortar	£14 m²	£ 2,600		
Inner Skin Area - measured through openings	220 m²			
Blocklaying price based on above	£15 m²		£ 3,300	
Total		**£ 2,600**	**£ 3,300**	**£ 5,900**
Switch to 140mm Timber Frame	185 m²			£ 8,100
Switch to 185mm Timber Frame	185 m²			£ 8,300
Additional Beams, Battening + Other Works	185 m²			£ 3,000

Inner Skin Area — when measuring up work, brickies tend to measure "through openings" to allow some time for fixing joinery and lintels.

Sixties, these blocks have become a huge hit in the UK market and more than 70% of new homes use them somewhere. There are three manufacturers, Celcon, Forterra's Thermalite brand and Tarmac, who bought the fourth, Durox, which is still obtainable as a separate brand. Their big plus is (or was) that they packed enough insulating properties into them to allow builders to carry on with empty cavities. Current U values are now too demanding for this solution to

be acceptable.

Brickies love aircrete blocks because they are light and easy to cut. Plasterers are not quite so fond of them: they have a reputation for movement which causes plaster to crack. This is one of the reasons for the rapid uptake of plasterboard stuck onto walls (dot and dab), taking over from the old wet plastering routines.

TRADE RATES

An all-in labour rate of between £12 and £16/m² for laying blocks is OK, depending on area. All-in rate means that your brickies would fix wall ties, cavity wall insulation, joinery, lintels, airbricks, DPCs, etc. as they go, but excludes the cost of laying an outer skin, which likely as not will be in a different material.

Using an all-in rate saves the hassle of measuring non-standard runs like chimneys. A two-and-one gang should be able to lay between 30 and 40m² of blocks in a day. Combined with the cost of blocks and mortar, it creates an inner skin walling cost of around £30/m², against which all other options have to be compared. Note that when working on measured rates, brickies conventionally treat joinery openings as if they were part of their work (which arguably they are, as they fit the joinery as they go). This makes a considerable difference to overall costs, as highlighted in the Inner Skin table.

INSULATING CAVITIES

The preferred way for the majority of English builders to knock-out the inner skin/cavity detail up till 2002 was to use an aircrete block and an empty cavity. Since then, builders have got used to adding insulation into the cavities. Builders are now faced with four basic options: fill the cavity with insulation, put insulation in the cavity but leave a gap (known as partial fill), insulate on the inside of the wall or on the outside of the outer wall.

1 CAVITY-FILL INSULATION

This is both cheap and easy to do – but you do lose your empty cavity.

Cavity batts designed to completely fill the void between the walls – known as Full Fill – are usually made out of one of the woolly insulators such as glass fibre or mineral wool; these are 'wicked' (rhymes with licked) to stay rigid and are cut to fit in around cavity ties.

An alternative would be to blow the insulation (either polystyrene beads or glass fibre) into the cavity after construction. Cavity fill is only acceptable in the more sheltered parts of the country: in the rain-swept west, you have to maintain a 50mm air gap in the cavity. In other words, you look for a partially-filled cavity solution.

2 PARTIAL-FILL

Most of the regular insulation materials are available in formats designed to partially fill the cavity. Despite making special retaining clips for wall ties, the wet Tuesday in February syndrome means that it is often difficult for brickies to maintain a partially clear cavity. They drop mortar 'snots' into it.

If you want a decent amount of insulation plus a 50mm cavity, your overall wall thickness is starting to blow up to 350mm plus, and this starts to eat a significant chunk out of your internal floor area.

3 INSULATED DRY LINING

This method involves using either plasterboard laminated to insulation and sticking the whole thing on the room side (i.e. inside) of the inner skin wall. Or, more frequently, insulation fixed to the wall with

battens onto which the plasterboard is fixed. The insulation value depends on the choice and depth of insulation. Although it gets around the problem of having to partially fill the cavity wall, it leaves a number of cold bridges between floors and where internal walls meet external walls and this makes it hard to meet the U-value ratings now required for walls. It's often used in renovations where you don't want to disturb the outer wall but it's not common in newbuild. It eats floor space.

4 EXTERNAL INSULATION

Adding insulation to the outside of the external wall is commonly done on the Continent and is used here extensively when refurbishing old buildings. But it is still somewhat unusual on new builds. Where it is used, it is normally in conjunction with some sort of rainscreen, like brick slips or terracotta panels, which incorporate insulation within the system.

THIN-JOINT BLOCKWORK

Thin-joint or glue mortars are widely used in Germany and were introduced into Britain by Durox in 1991 but their uptake hasn't been as fast as the manufacturers hoped for and their use has been limited in the housebuilding arena.

There are two key elements that make it different to conventional blockwork. Firstly, it uses a very sticky mortar, more akin to tile adhesive than a traditional sand and cement mix. This thin-layer mortar starts to set within ten minutes and this makes it possible to work with much bigger block sizes - this is the second key element and the one from which the speed advantages derive. The limit on block size is set by what a man can easily handle: in fact, in response to feedback from site, Celcon's currently preferred size – 610 x 270mm – is slightly smaller than the format they launched with. Blocklayers who have moved over to thin-layer reckon that it's around 30% quicker. Any increase in material costs is more than offset by a decrease in labour rates.

The techniques used are quite different to mortared blockwork. In many ways, it's closer to carpentry than masonry: tooling up for thin-joint blockwork also requires a bandsaw, a mortar spreader, a block rasp, a mortar whisk and a wall tie puncher – you can't use traditional wall ties. Thin-joint work also requires a very level base to work off; with just a 2mm bed between the blocks you can't make good any initial errors as you go. As with many of these new techniques, the problem for would-be adopters is that there simply aren't any (or at least many) blocklayers around who know anything about thin-joint. When faced with the thin-joint option, the knee-jerk reaction is to hoick the labour rates up through the roof when, going on the evidence, they ought actually to be lowering them.

TIMBER FRAME

Tinkering around with where you put the insulation in relation to the blockwork is all very well but there is a mainstream alternative that enables you to place the insulation inside the

Cavity Wall Insulation Techniques

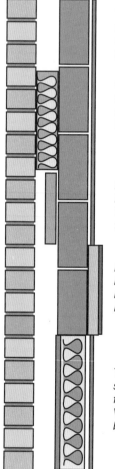

The Empty Cavity scores very badly in U value terms at around 0.6. No longer an option for today's housebuilders

Cavity Fill Insulation: usually with a mineral wool. Good insulation but no gap to stop rain penetration. OK in drier areas of the country

Partial Fill Insulation: usually with a PIR board (Kingspan or Celotex). The board has to be pinned against the inner skin.

Insulated dry lining or internal insulation. Used in conversions and renovations but rare in newbuilds because it eats up roomspace

Timber Frame: here the insulation sits within the inner skin itself, filling the voids between the studs. Variations like SIPs provide even better insulation levels.

wall, which is, in many ways, the most elegant solution. We are, of course, talking timber frame here.

Innovation flourishes here. What we once routinely referred to as timber frame is now a collection of varied offsite construction systems, and it can be difficult for selfbuilders

to navigate through the options. The strand that unites them all is that they offer factory-built superstructures and this, in turn, offers rapid and precise build times.

In North America, timber framed housing is almost always constructed on site by teams of carpenters armed

This is essentially what you get when you buy a standard UK timber frame kit home. This is the superstructure. It takes about a week to erect this on a prepared site.

with chainsaws in a process known as stickbuild. But the Europeans — starting with the Swedes in the 1920s — have always preferred the idea of pre-fabricating their timber homes and shipping them to site on the backs of lorries. Timber frame in the UK could have gone down either route but, with little native timber suitable for housebuilding and without a pool of stickbuilding carpenters, factory pre-fabrication was always favourite to win out, despite the fact that the initial boom in timber frame was largely financed by American oil money looking to house workers in the Aberdeen area in the 1960s.

However, whilst the Continentals veered towards building pre-finished, or closed-panel homes, the Brits

stuck with a more rustic, open-panel approach which simply concerned itself with getting the basic timber structure up and then fitting out all the insulation, services and plasterboard on site. The structure itself was usually built from studwork covered with OSB (Oriented Strand Board) for bracing, and one of the main advantages it held over masonry construction was that it allowed ample space for mineral wool insulation and yet still retained an empty cavity.

An alternative version of timber frame used a mixture of solid timber posts and beams and infilled with studwork, apeing the methods used by the Tudors. This style continues to thrive, having morphed into green oak building, a style almost unique to

Britain – elsewhere they use softwoods to achieve the same effect. It's never going to compete with the standard form of timber building on cost grounds – green oak superstructures are usually around 30% more than conventional timber frames – but it comes with an inbuilt sense of style and substance which people seem more than happy to pay a premium for.

The original open-panel style of timber frame is now under threat as tighter building regulations have forced a re-think. Open-panel timber frame was based on using the 38x89 CLS stud which, once braced with OSB, forms a strong box-like structure. However, an 89mm depth is no longer an adequate width for the insulation required to meet building regulations and in the past

A SIPs build in Scotland. The panels are a little different to timber frame: they consist largely of insulation encased by boards.

few years alternative approaches have come to the fore. Some stuck with the narrow studs and started adding extra layers of insulation outside the timber frame, others began using 140mm wide studwork which allowed ample space for insulation, but added significantly to costs.

SIPS

Structural Insulated Panels are a sandwich construction made up of a layer of insulation encapsulated between sheets of oriented strand board (OSB). They offer better insulation levels for a given wall thickness because they use far less timber, their strength coming instead from bonding the insulation with the OSB.

SIPS are more expensive than conventional timber frame, but not by a huge margin, and when you factor in the convenience of having the insulation already in place, the price looks more appealing. SIPS have been slowly biting into the market share of timber frame.

HYBRIDS

For many years, framed construction seemed to be turning into a battle between SIPS and conventional timber frame, but what now seems to be happening is that new hybrid forms are appearing that seem to have a foot in both camps. The hybrids seem to have bought into the idea that frames should be pre-injected with insulation, but have stuck with a framework of timber, or sometimes steel.

One such is Val-U-Therm, a system developed by Bryan Woodley and currently licensed to two UK manufacturers who target the selfbuild market, Scotframe and Flight Timber. It's a timber frame building system which uses a largely plant-based insulation foam which is factory-injected into the panels. The technology behind the injection is German, but the plant matter used in the insulation is locally sourced.

CLOSED-PANEL TIMBER FRAME

A sort of halfway house between regular timber frame, as practised in the UK, and prefabs is the closed panel systems, as used by the Germans and the Swedes. Here the wall, floor and roof sections are finished in the factory, right down to the services and decorations, and then craned into place on site. It's quicker than regular or open panel methods, which require internal finishing on site, but it only suits builders who are very organised and know exactly what they want. It has been tried once or twice in the UK but has never really caught on because the average British client wants the flexibility to change their mind every two days or so. However, whenever a German factory house builder appears on Grand Designs, the world and their aunt goes weak at the knees about how amazing it all is and just why can't we in Britain build that way as well. So much so that there are now about a dozen of these companies setting up in the UK. Amazing the methods may be, but they are not cheap. Even when sourced from Poland, the resulting houses are costing over £2,000/m² and thus they are aiming mostly at the top end of the market.

GREEN OAK/POST AND BEAM

The traditional way, that is to say Tudor way, of building large timber houses was to erect a large post and beam skeleton (usually using oak) and then to hang the house off it. Whereas modern, industrial timber frame is a fast, lightweight, cheap way of erecting walls, here we are working in an altogether different idiom. Post and beam housing has undergone a revival in recent years and it's used for both retro designs (Border Oak, Potton Heritage) and modern (Carpenter Oak). It's also essentially the form you get when you take on a timber barn conversion. It's very good for creating large open-plan spaces as you don't require structural walls. However, you do require an external weatherproof cladding.

Post and beam frames are by their very nature load-bearing but often the houses designed around them would stand on their own walls without any help at all from all that oak. Consequently, the cost of the posts and beams is almost always an extra, from the pure construction cost point of view, to the cost of building the house in a simplified, modern format. It's therefore never going to be a cheap way to build. But what's just as interesting, to my mind, is that there are a number of small developers out there who willingly pay all that extra money to get an oak framed house because they can make it back and more on the asking price.

Closed panel timber frame sees the whole wall finished in the factory, including doors and windows and inner and outer wall linings. This is a German Baufritz house being erected in Cornwall

It's the added wow factor.

CROSS LAMINATED TIMBER

Developed in Switzerland and Austria in the 1990s, CLT techniques enable us to build solid walls of softwood timber, by glueing small pieces of it together into one large panel. CLT is produced by placing these panels in layers stacked at right angles to one another and then glueing them together under high-pressure to make immensely strong panels which can be used for walls and roofs. The panels can be up to 13.5m in length and are available in 3, 5, 7 or 9 layers, varying in thickness from 57mm to 300mm.

One of the innovations used in CLT manufacture is the use of non-toxic polyurethane adhesive (solvent and formaldehyde-free) which helps boost the environmental credentials of CLT. Sustainable builders also love the fact that a timber building is actually locking up CO_2 in its structure, rather than just reducing the amount burned by incorporating energy efficiency measures.

CLT sections can also bring the beauty of timber inside the home. Here is a walling material which is good to look at in its own right, and doesn't require a sheet of plasterboard to cover it up. KLH, one of the principal producers of CLT, now grades its output in three distinct visual categories, domestic visual quality, industrial visual quality and unseen, designed to be hidden behind wall finishes. Obviously, the inclusion of CLT as an interior design element requires thoughtful design, because there will still be issues with running cables and pipes in front, but used carefully it can make a stunning feature.

In cost terms, CLT remains at the upper end of the structural element spectrum, especially so as it normally requires added layers of insulation placed outside the wall or roof in order to obtain satisfactory U values. However, CLT is not quite like other wall materials because it can also act as a beam in its own right and CLT can therefore be used over open-spans without any further support. Consequently, it has a growing fan base and there are several architectural practices which

have worked with it and know best how to use its strength and elegance. Increasingly, we are seeing it used on selfbuilds and residential schemes and it offers a unique approach to homebuilding.

PODS AND PREFABS

The past few years have seen renewed interest in prefabrication as a solution to our housing needs. Bathroom pods in particular are migrating from commercial office space into housing. They are assembled and finished in a factory and then craned into place on site, bolted into place and the plumbing is connected from the outside. Completely prefabricated dwellings are also back – steel-framed containers have been used to build hotels and MacDonalds for years and now innovative housing groups such as the Peabody Trust have started

using them as well. However, neither pods nor prefabs are likely to be of the remotest interest to self builders or small developers because, to make economic sense, you have to replicate the work many times – opinions vary as to how much many consists of but it's not less than 30 and it may be as much as 100.

Timber and steel frame homes are normally supplied in what kitchen suppliers would call a flat pack state, wall and floor units ready to be assembled on site. In contrast, pods and prefab units are supplied as ready assembled units – indeed they tend to have as much work done in the factory as possible. Transportation thus becomes the limiting factor – you can't realistically transport anything that won't fit onto the back of a lorry.

ICFs

Another technique. Another three letter acronym. Just to prove not all innovation is happening in the lightweight framing, this one uses polystyrene moulds and lots of concrete. ICF stands for Insulated Concrete Forms.

There is an umbrella group, known as the ICFA (Insulating Concrete Formwork Association), which acts as a point of reference. In 2019, it had nine members active in the UK market.

The idea behind ICFs is that you start with a delivery of hollow polystyrene blocks (or sometimes panels) which you then stack up into a house shape. You stop at each floor and get lorry loads of readymix,

Insulated Concrete Formwork (ICF) seen here at the critical readymix pour stage. Note the concrete pump at work — the tube is being inserted into the wall cavity seen top right

which you pour into the hollows in the polystyrene walls. It's a clever variation on how concrete building work is usually carried out, where you take down the formwork after the concrete has set. With ICFs, the polystyrene acts initially as formwork (or mould) for the concrete and stays in place to become the insulation for the finished house.

The polystyrene can be covered on the outside with polymer (flexible) renders; inside, however, there are many unusual techniques for fixing internal walls, frames and floor joists, which would probably completely flummox the average British builder. And whilst the idea is engagingly simple, it's not without its problems as I've seen on site when the wet concrete sometimes bursts through the side of the polystyrene blocks.

ICFs have an undoubted appeal to people wanting to take a hands-on approach to building their own walls. They don't require bricklayers and blocklayers, anybody can do it. However, there are some cost implications that have to be addressed. Even using your own sweat labour, ICFs are more expensive than blockwork or timber frame.

In their defence, the ICF suppliers point out that overall wall costs are often pretty much the same as blockwork or timber frame, at around £80/m², but that's really only true where you want to use a rendered exterior finish which can sit directly on the polystyrene wall formers.

STEEL

In some parts of the world – notably Australia – steel-framed housing is big bananas. In Britain, its heyday came and went in the 1940s in the post-war prefab boomlet. Since then, it's remained something of a curio. There are two approaches, mirroring timber frame. You can have a post and beam structure (which is what most office buildings are) or you can build lightweight wall panels (which is where most of the housebuilders' interest is). Advocates reckon it's superior to timber frame in many ways – it's lightweight, it's fast, it's accurate – but it's mostly been aimed at the mass-housing end of the spectrum.

For several years, British Steel's Surebuild was the only game in town and they regularly produced about 1,000 homes a year from an antiquated plant in South Wales. Now if you Google Surebuild, you'll only find historical references to it. British Steel were taken over by Corus, who were in turn taken over by India's Tata Steel and the housebuilding bit was put out to grass. There are often new businesses which start out to "introduce" steel frame to the UK market, but they never seem to get any traction and so this sector really remains a housing by-water, though of course it is very much No 1 in the commercial world.

OTHERS

Having been very traditional in our approach to homebuilding for decades, suddenly there has been an explosion of interest in how we might do it differently in future. All I've tried to do here is summarise some of the methods which are putting themselves across as alternatives to the mainstream. There are several more ethnic methods about which I know very little and can't really do much more than point you in the right direction.

■ Straw bale homes: a small phenomenon in North America, they have started to sprout in Britain and Ireland as well. Our best known straw bale builder is Barbara Jones who runs Straw Bales Futures (aka Amazon Nails).

■ Centre for Alternative Technology, Machynlleth, Powys. Mine of information, especially on timber and also straw bales. Wide number of residential courses on offer and good bookshop with details of all these and more.

Every other episode of 'Grand Designs' seems to feature a new take on building homes which promises to turn the construction world upside down: only I've been around long enough to know that, by and large, they don't.

PERFORMANCE STANDARDS

There is one aspect of new housebuilding trends which is worth mentioning here and that's growing interest in Performance Standards, which emphasize how well a house is built rather than just what it's built out of.

In particular I want to draw

An increasing number of selfbuilders are pushing the boat out to try new techniques and new materials. This house in Suffolk is set to be one of the first straw bale Passivhauses in the world.

But not THE first. There is already one a few miles away in Norfolk.

your attention to the Passivhaus Standard because it is making waves as the gold standard of low-energy homebuilding. There is much more on this elsewhere in the book. But the point I am labouring to make here is that you can use any kind of construction method to make a high performance home — the standards are rarely prescriptive.

Leading on from this point, you can see that what really matters more than the materials or system you choose is the quality of the building work. All these construction systems are capable of delivering fine homes, in the right hands: equally, they can all turn out to be nightmares. It's not

a question of deciding which is best: just seek out people who know what they are doing and you'll probably be fine.

OUTER SKINS

If you're reading the book conventionally (i.e. from front to back), you will have noticed that a previous section, 'Inner Skins', started with a short (very short) history lesson about the introduction of cavity walls into British housebuilding. If you weren't paying attention, the cavity splits the external walls into an inner and

outer skin. Whilst there have been numerous developments and changes in the techniques used to build the structural inner skin, the outer skin has remained largely unchanged over the years. Other than some very modern houses, which tend to swap glass or terracotta rainscreens for cavity walls, most of the materials used to clad homes haven't changed that much.

The basic choices are fairly limited. Brick – still easily No 1 in England; stone – expensive, tending to be used where local styles dictate; renders – top choice in the wetter parts; or lightweight claddings such as timber boarding or tiles – commonly used for odd decorative panels but rarely for whole houses.

There is surprisingly little difference between the prices you pay for external claddings. It's hard to build an outer skin for less than £40/m² and it's not difficult to vastly increase this figure if you specify expensive materials and finishes. Before embarking on a look at what the regular options are, a word about mixing up walling materials, something that's become very popular with developers. Mixing materials invariably creates an extra layer of complexity and therefore adds to costs. Not only are different materials and trades being brought in for relatively small amounts of work, but junction details need to be built in as well. It's difficult to be too precise about this because every situation is different but bear in mind that simplicity helps if your primary aim is to hold down costs.

SUPERSTRUCTURE

BRICK

Bricks remain the preferred material for external walls throughout England and Wales. They are reasonably cheap, they are well understood by the building trade, they can look attractive and, above all, they are durable. Not only should a brick wall not need any further care after construction, it should actually improve with age.

There are dozens of brick manufacturers and thousands of bricks to choose from. There is also a substantial business in reclaiming bricks from old buildings – though it only amounts to 1% of total brick sales, that's still 40 million bricks reclaimed each year. If you are limited by budget you will probably find your choice is rather narrow, but if you are prepared to pay more than £500 per 1,000 (that's 50p per brick) then a whole world of choice opens up.

Choosing a brick is quite an involved process and it is notoriously difficult to visualise what a brick wall will look like from a manufacturer's display board. Most British bricks are baked clay and these are the ones to go for if you are seeking out a character brick.

There are other materials, notably concrete and sandlime, that get used to make bricks but the overall effect tends to be industrial looking and, crucially, there are no great price savings to be had – unlike in the world of roof tiles and block paving where concrete is invariably cheaper than clay.

There are two technical ratings for clay bricks that you should know

about, to do with frost resistance and salt content. The frost rating is broken down into three categories being F (high), M (medium) and O (appalling), and the salt rating is split into just two categories, L (low) and N (normal). What does it matter? With frost, the problem is spalling, where the face of the brick starts crumbling away. Very soft bricks, rated O, would not be acceptable in any situation in the UK where they would be exposed to the elements – i.e. outside – but only severe frost areas (Scotland, the Welsh mountains and the English Lakes and Pennines) would require an F-rated brick. M-rated bricks are fine for almost all applications outside these areas, but note that in certain exposed spots (notably chimneys) you will be asked to add copings and overhanging courses if not using an F-rated brick.

The matter of low or normal salt content is not as important to housebuilders. In very wet areas (usually within sight of the Irish Sea) it is advisable to avoid bricks with an N rating as you may be asked to use sulphate-resisting cement. A merchant will be able to advise as to a brick's rating – but what if you're using second-hand bricks? You'll have to check your source and convince the building inspector that they are suitable for outdoor use. The building inspector will very probably have seen the brick before and will be able to assess its suitability. But do check before forking out. Take samples into the building control office if necessary.

ENGINEERING BRICKS

These are particularly hard-wearing and strong. Not only do they offer much greater structural support (and so they are a natural choice for supporting steel beams) but they are also extremely moisture-resistant. This second quality, combined with some very low prices, has seen engineering bricks being widely used as a damp-proof course (DPC). The semi-gloss finish on the bricks (which are either blood red or slate blue) can be used to good effect in creating two-tone effect brickwork both at DPC level and elsewhere on brick elevations.

SPECIALS

This is the term given to bricks that aren't a standard rectangular box shape. These get used, typically, on details like cills and brick wall cappings where you want to stop rainwater pooling. Some of the more common specials are readily available but many have to be made to order, which is a) expensive and b) time-consuming. If your chosen design incorporates specials then don't assume that they will just turn up with the rest of the bricks; you may have to wait another two months.

In response to these problems with procuring specials, there are now brick-bonding services which will cut and glue ordinary bricks into out-of-the-ordinary shapes. At between £3 and £4 per brick they are a little cheaper than unusual specials and with a turnaround of one week, rather than six, they are a whole lot quicker. It's a particularly useful service if you are using a second-hand brick from which you could never otherwise hope to obtain specials. Try Brickability.

BRICKIES' RATES

One of the key rates in building is known as the brickie's rate and it expresses how much bricklayers charge for laying 1,000 bricks. It sounds simple and it's not. For a start, it only really applies to very simple runs of stretcher brickwork, beloved by the UK's speculative developers. On such British residential sites, a two-and-one gang (that's two brickies serviced by one labourer) will lay 1,000 bricks a day – though normally they alternate between brick and blockwork. So the brickies' rate expresses how much a two-and-one gang gets paid for a day's work. The problem is that they very rarely lay this many bricks in a day. There are extra features. Work like corners and reveals and fixing joinery and insulation, not to mention fiddly details like dogs-toothing gables and soldier courses. Estimators will be tempted to measure the square meterage of brickwork and work out how many bricks that is (clue: there are 60 bricks to a square metre on single skin stretcher work). If paying brickies by the square metre, be clear whether your square metres are 'solid' (i.e. including the joinery openings in their calculations). The conventional arrangement is to measure straight through openings: there is however no additional charge for building frames into the openings.
As of 2019, our local rate was up

EXTERNAL WALL FINISHES: Costs per m²

Heavyweight claddings	Materials	Time in Mins	Labour at £25/hr	Combined
Brickwork @ £500/thousand	£ 35	85	£ 35	£ 70
Brickwork @ £1,000/thousand	£ 65	85	£ 35	£ 100
Natural stone	£ 56	180	£ 75	£ 131
Artificial stone	£ 27	120	£ 50	£ 93
Lime Render	£ 22	80	£ 33	£ 66
Monocouche Render	£ 24	120	£ 50	£ 74
Lightweight claddings				
Painted Render on mesh	£ 20	100	£ 42	£ 62
Monocouche Render on cement board	£ 23	70	£ 29	£ 52
Tile Hanging	£ 36	70	£ 29	£ 65
Terracotta Rainscreens	£ 80	60	£ 25	£ 105
Metal Claddings	£ 80	200	£ 83	£ 163
Sawn + Stained Weatherboard	£ 19	70	£ 29	£ 49
Unpainted Cedar	£ 52	50	£ 21	£ 73
Burnt Timber	£ 79	50	£ 21	£ 100

MODEL HOUSE: Brickwork costs

	Area in m²	Rate	Materials	Labour	Total
Brickwork @ £500/k	200	£ 70	£ 7,000	£ 7,000	£ 14,000

around £600 per 1,000 face bricks laid, over treble what it was in 1995. In some cheaper areas it's still down around half this at £600/k, a brickie is taking home £250 a day and the labourer £100.

BRICK FACTORS

Specialist merchants, known as factors, have developed long antennae for detecting new housebuilding activity. If you phone up a factor inquiring after bricks, the first thing you get asked is: 'Where is the site?' Why do they all want to know?

Well, brick factors get money for simply identifying (or 'covering') a new site, even if they don't get the subsequent order. So the moment

they inform the manufacturer that there is a new house going to be built in Pig Lane, they clock a commission, rising to near 20% if it turns into a sale. They also shut out competitors from this particular deal – only the initial contact gets offered the commission.

It would probably be better if you didn't know that. It's a cosy little relationship between manufacturers and merchants that reeks of rip-off Britain. But would you get your bricks cheaper if it didn't happen? Maybe.

A brick factor will wave brick panels in front of you with gusto and the bricks will not be identifiable as Ibstocks or Hansons but have names like Mellow Red or Autumn Gold – renaming the bricks makes it harder for you to get alternative quotes. Don't get me wrong: dealing with brick factors can be fun and some of them do terrific deals, but there is more than a hint of the Middle Eastern souk about the whole process. As far as I can ascertain, this rigmarole is more or less restricted to bricks, although it is rumoured to occur with up-market roof tiles and pavings.

MORTAR

You can't lay bricks without mortar and mortar actually makes up around 20% of the area of a brick wall. So what the mortar looks like is arguably as important as what the bricks look like. The current fashion is for very pale mortars, aping the lime mortars that the Victorians used. One way to get this is to use pure lime mortars instead of cement, but lime mortars are expensive and not as easy to use as cement. If you want the look but not the hassle, you can use white cement (Snowcrete) and sand mixed with plasticiser. There is a much longer section on mortars in Chapter 12.

RENDER

Rendering is the term most commonly used for an external plastered finish. It's widely used in Scotland, where it's known as harling, and in Ireland. There is a reason for this: it's better at keeping rain out than brick, and therefore the wetter the region, the more you see render being used.

Two alternative techniques are used to get a rendered finish – rendering directly on to blockwork or rendering on to metal-lathing like Riblath or Renderlath, nailed on to battens. The first would normally be used on masonry-built houses, the second on timber frame, though note that the Scottish preference is to build a masonry block wall around a timber frame superstructure and then to render (or harl) the surface of the blockwork.

Render is also widely used against insulation backgrounds, as you would expect to find with Insulated Concrete Formwork walls, or external insulation systems.

DECORATIVE RENDER

A nearly lost art, which is undergoing a revival. The finish is rather like an upmarket Artex applied to the face to enliven the appearance. In East Anglia, it is known as pargetting.

MONOCOUCHE RENDERS

Monocouche is French for single layer or bed. Conventionally, both lime and cement renders have been mixed on site with sand and applied in a series of layers or coats, never less than two and sometimes three or more. In contrast, a monocouche render is supplied in bag form ready for mixing with water: it can be applied by hand trowel or sprayed on. It's a practice which has spread here from the Continent and many of the big names in this field — Sto, Knauf Marmorit, Weber — are German in origin.

These renders use white cement and are pre-coloured so that what you are applying is as much a decorative finish as it is a weatherproofing layer. As they can be applied in one coat — typically around 15mm thick — they are a much less labour intensive process than traditional renders. The downside is of course the material cost — a 25kg bag costs anywhere between £8-£10 and only covers a square metre of wall area. This compares with a materials cost on a traditional cement render of around £2/m². But of course, the monocouche render systems claw much of this added cost back through reduced labour costs, not to mention eliminating the need for subsequent painting.

Another advantage of monocouche renders is that they have additives placed in them which make them more flexible and help to eliminate cracking. The additives vary, depending on the make-up, but they typically include acrylics, polymers and silicates, sometimes giving rise to alternative names, such as "acrylic renders."

Not all plasterers are entirely happy to apply monocouche renders in just one coat, and a site I visited recently in London has had two coats applied by hand for an overall cost of around £35/m². This compares with around £20/m² for a traditional two-coat cement render, or £30/m² for a three-coat finish.

LIME

Green builders love lime and happily apply it to all manner of unlikely surfaces such as straw bale and cob. But lime works just as well on more

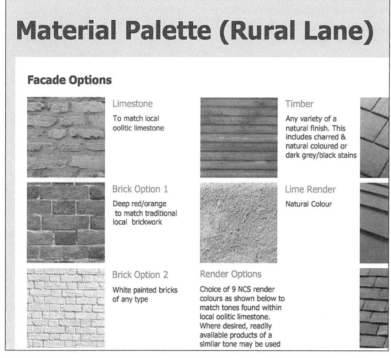

Material Palette (Rural Lane)

Facade Options

Limestone
To match local oolitic limestone

Timber
Any variety of a natural finish. This includes charred & natural coloured or dark grey/black stains

Brick Option 1
Deep red/orange to match traditional local brickwork

Lime Render
Natural Colour

Brick Option 2
White painted bricks of any type

Render Options
Choice of 9 NCS render colours as shown below to match tones found within local oolitic limestone. Where desired, readily available products of a similar tone may be used

The Graven Hill Plot Passport is a useful guide to what are the currently fashionable facades for selfbuild housing. To find more detail, visit Graven Hill> Find a Plot>select one of the larger selfbuild plots and download the Plot Passport. It also covers roofing options.

standard materials like blockwork, and it too has some advantages over cement renders. Lime is inherently more flexible than cement and you are less likely to have problems with moisture getting trapped within the wall – a noted problem when cement renders are applied to old walls. Lime also tends to look very appealing, though to keep it looking good it does require frequent coats of limewash.

Building limes are available in a variety of formats from the very traditional lime putties (which are bought wet, by the tub) through a number of distinct bagged products — hydraulic limes — which behave rather like a weak cement. They need to be mixed on site with sand, and are hand trowelled in the traditional way. Limes are a little more expensive than standard cement renders, but shouldn't really take any longer to apply.

For lovers of tradition and modern methods of construction, there are one or two lime-based monocouche renders. Look out for K-Rend (K-Lime) and Baumit.

TIMBER AND BOARDS

Plain timber boarding (sometimes known as clapboarding) has come back into fashion ever since the rise in popularity of barn conversions. There are several different styles. Roughsawn timber (featheredge) looks more rustic; planed timber (shiplap) can look a shade more sophisticated. In their raw states, they make remarkably cheap claddings, costing between £15 and £20/m² (materials only). But they drink wood stains by the gallon and, of course, they require extensive maintenance to keep looking the business. If you pay for the labour, then weatherboard is actually one of the most expensive of claddings after thirty years has elapsed.

Step forward a number of timber or near-timber solutions that don't require staining in the first place, let alone frequent re-applications. Cedar – usually Western Red Cedar – is the best-known timber promising to be fit and forget. It's five times the price of basic sawn featheredge but it lasts for 60 years. Hopefully. It's being sold on the proposition that it lasts 60 years and there are many acres of cedar cladding going up all over the place in locations that are often hard to reach so it had better last 60 years! It goes a mellow silvery-grey after a couple of years.

There are a number of mid-priced alternatives between cedar and the basic whitewood boards. Native larch is sometimes specified – it's a little cheaper than cedar. There are also some interesting heat-treated timbers coming onto the market: one is Thermowood which is a treated redwood with a 30-year lifespan. Another is Accoya, a pine which has been treated with vinegar and heat, and boasts a 50-year lifespan. And both Eternit (Weatherboard) and James Hardie (Hardiplank) produce convincing pre-painted fibre-cement boards for slightly less than genuine timber boards. Right at the bottom end of the spectrum is uPVC: sure, it doesn't rot but it doesn't really have much going for it as a cladding.

There are also a number of semi-industrial boards which can be used to clad buildings. These live really in the commercial sectors of the building trade but one or two adventurous architects sometimes specify them on housing.

Incidentally, with all external timber that requires painting or staining, it is good practice to put at least one coat of paint or stain on the boards on the ground before fixing. Timber shrinks, and if the whole board is not covered with a uniform colour you will end up with 1-2mm flesh-coloured strips wherever boards overlap.

One curio in this field which has become fashionable recently is the use of charred timber, an ancient Japanese practice involving running a blowtorch across the surface of the boarding to produce a distinctive burnt look. It is to wall claddings what Creme Brulee is to puddings. It looks great but it obviously has to be handled with care. Google Shousugiban if you want to know more. It's nearly double the price of cedar.

VERTICAL TILING

Using vertical tiling is another Victorian building feature that is coming back into fashion, particularly in SE England. Costs are very similar to plain tiles laid on roofs, although vertical hanging tends to be a little more expensive because there is more work involved in cutting corners, angles and around openings. Generally it looks best with small format plain tiles or slate and it is more important to select a good looking (i.e. expensive) tile for a wall than it is for a roof. Cedar, in the form of small tiles called shingles, also features as wall cladding.

RAINSCREENS

There is a modern variation on vertical tiling, which is known as a rainscreen. These are now commonly used in commercial developments and city centre blocks of flats and they are beginning to make their mark on modern housing designs. They can be made of a variety of materials, but many seem to use a large format terracotta tile. Look for products such as Forterra's LockClad or Wienerberger's ArGeTon.

Rainscreens are normally fixed to some steel or aluminium support rails, which replace the more traditional timber battens.

There is another variation on the rainscreen idea, which is to fit a brick-slip cladding. A brick slip is to a brick what stone cladding is to stone — i.e. a thin brick facing which can be stuck on an insulated backing. It's primarily a way of covering external insulation when applied to an external wall.

Rainscreens and brick slip claddings tend to be done on a supply and fix basis and they also tend to be expensive, but they come into their own when renovating existing walls where extra insulation is required but space is limited. They typically add only 50 or 60mm to the wall width.

There is a growing interest in using all manner of unconventional materials as rainscreens. One that catches the eye is the use of Corten rusted steel which has been around for decades but has suddenly leapt across the chasm from industrial uses into contemporary architecture and house design. This steel alloy is designed to strengthen as it rusts, by producing a thin protective film on the surface.

GLASS

Another ultra-cool design feature is to use glass as a structural material, rather than just something that sits in joinery. By combining two techniques, laminating and toughening, glass can be made thick enough and strong enough to make self-supporting wall panels and even rooflights which you can walk on.

Costing upwards of £1,000/m², structural or frameless glass is always going to be a luxury feature but its use is spreading from more mundane items like staircase balustrading to opening rooflights and frameless patio doors. Two useful contacts: Cantifix and IQ Glass.

STONE

If you live in one of the so-called stone belts you may well have to build in stone to satisfy the local planners.

Chapter 7

You may actually want to build in stone – it's usually very attractive – but it's likely to be very much more expensive than the developer's standbys: brick and render.

There are basically three approaches: you can use real stone quarried out of some hillside, you can use reconstituted stone, which is stone dust glued together with cement, or you can use stone cladding which usually gets stuck on the outside of cheaply erected blockwork.

NATURAL STONE

Building stone tends to be a very local affair. It was, after all, hewn from quarries and, in the days before cheap transportation, could only be carried the shortest of distances. Many of these old stone quarries survive and supply the demands of the local construction trade. In some areas there are thriving second-hand markets in stone walling materials, yet nowhere is natural stone a cheap material. You may be given brownie points for using natural stone in your house – more likely the local planners will insist on it – but you'll probably be adding £10,000 to the overall cost.

The cost of laying stone varies a little depending on its characteristics and whether it's coursed or not, but a good stone mason would hope to lay around 3m² a day. He would also be hoping to earn around £200 a day so you can tell what sort of price per square metre you should be looking at here.

RECONSTITUTED STONE

A cheaper alternative is to use a reconstituted stone. Bradstone is the best known and the largest producer. Although, to the practised eye, reconstituted stone will never look as good as the real thing, it will cost about half as much and, if done well, looks as good as many of the cheaper bricks.

STONE CLADDING

Stone cladding has got a reputation for being naff as hell, but this is because it's often associated with people who fix it to their brick terrace houses to 'make a statement' (such as 'I'm naff as hell'). Out of context like that it does look more than a touch ridiculous, but on a new house in a stone village chances are most casual passers-by would not even know it was stone cladding. However, artificial stone claddings are now virtually unobtainable and natural stone cladding is very expensive so if you are starting from scratch you might just as well use real stone.

One interesting option is to use reconstituted stone cladding. It sounds awful but Fernhill produce a very convincing product which is set in moulds and is so realistic that it's virtually impossible to tell from the real thing. But realism comes at a price: it costs around £35-£45/m² to buy the tiles and laying is as expensive as brickwork. It can be placed on a polystyrene backing (useful for people building with ICFs) but it's usually stuck onto an outer blockwork wall.

RUBBLE WALLS

If you know the right quarries this kind of walling material can be extremely cheap to buy, but it tends to be very time-consuming to lay.

Traditionally, rubble walling was independent of any backing materials, but now it is much cheaper to lay if it is set against a background of blockwork – which makes it a bit like very rough pebble dash. Each area of the country has its own local 'rubble' stones and seaside locations often tend to find theirs on the nearby beaches.

In East Anglia, flint is the usual material and prices vary enormously depending on how it is finished. Flint can be laid as wholestones – which gives a rough 'agricultural' look – or it can be knapped, which involves breaking the stones open to reveal a shiny black inside which is then set as the facework. You can now buy pre-finished flint blocks, which take all the hard work out of it – you just lay them like a conventional block.

PORCHES AND BAYS

Thus far I've been looking at exterior finishes but there is, of course, much more to the external design of a house than just the materials used. Features like bay windows and porches have been coming right back into fashion despite the fact that they are expensive to build. It's quite hard to separate out how much extra these features cost because they tend to get lost in the whole job costings.

A bay window, for instance, involves minor additions to almost every aspect of the construction – excavations, foundations, flooring, brickwork, joinery, roofing, guttering, carpentry and decorating (to name just nine). Individually these changes are not great but added together I estimate

SUPERSTRUCTURE

that a two-storey bay may add as much as 3% to the costs of erecting the house superstructure. For an area less than 3m² that's expensive – getting on for double the amount spent on ordinary living space.

Porches are easier to quantify, although bear in mind that the standard of construction varies enormously from something little more than a rain shelter to what amounts to a mini-extension. Being (usually) rectangular in shape, porches are not appreciably more expensive to construct than the main structure, but bear in mind that any complications that might ensue will end up taking a disproportionate amount of supervision time.

CILLS AND ARCHES

One of the classiest effects you can get on external facades is to use feature lintels above and cills below your openings. There are a number of options for doing this. The cills and lintels can be formed from special bricks or made on site with a granite and cement mixture, which is fine if they get painted afterwards. Another variation is to have reconstituted stone ones made up in a workshop: this is the most expensive option but also probably the most attractive.

Insetting joinery into the facade is not merely a decorative process. By its very nature it helps to protect windows and doors from the worst of the weather, and the building regulations acknowledge this by making recessed joinery compulsory in Scotland and in many exposed parts of the rest of the country.

DON'T RUIN IT

Having gone to all that trouble to get good-looking materials correctly proportioned, it is worth taking on board a cautionary word about the effect of those little elements, which can ruin the overall effect - like a wart on the face of a much loved friend (shouldn't that have been a carbuncle? Ed). Whether you go for period charm or ultra-modernism really makes no difference, just think about the details — remember the devil is in the detail. Here are a few style tips:
- rainwater downpipes – the fewer the better
- plastic meter boxes – hide them round the side
- security floodlighting – don't point it straight at people walking towards it
- alarm bells – potential burglars will still see them on a side wall
- satellite dishes – they can sometimes go out in the garden.

INSULATION

All materials insulate to a greater or lesser extent but only since the 1970s have we seen the widespread adoption of materials that do very little else except insulate. By and large, these materials are not prohibitively expensive and most will pay for themselves within a few years. So whilst you could design your home to avoid using insulation wherever possible, there would be very little point in doing so.

There are several materials available to insulate housing. Many are rigid, board-like. Some are woolly or even

fluffy. And some come in sheets or rolls. All have pros and cons and not all are suitable in every application; mostly they are available in a number of different formats – often in combination with other materials like chipboard and plasterboard – which makes describing them all extremely complicated.

GLASS FIBRE

Cheap, reasonably good insulator. Excellent when laid flat in lofts but when placed in walls it will sag. But help is at hand: it can be 'wicked', which stiffens it up and allows it to be placed into wall cavities without risk of sagging or, as they say in insulation speak, to 'perform well in the vertical'. Here they tend to get referred to as batts as in cavity batts or timber frame batts. Although nearly double the price of unwicked quilts, they are still good value compared to other materials.

MINERAL WOOL

In most ways it performs very similarly to glass fibre and can also be wicked to perform well in the vertical. However, mineral wool is noticeably superior to glass (and almost all other insulation materials) in terms of fire resistance. It is usually priced to compete with glass though sometimes it is 5 to 10% more. The Danish company, Rockwool, dominates production and it's often referred to by this trade name.

SHEEPS WOOL

The natural product on which both glass wool and mineral wool are

Chapter 7

based. In many ways it performs very similarly to its synthetic cousins but it's obviously much nicer to work with – the synthetic ones are notoriously itchy and unpleasant, especially glass wool. It's only really appeared as an option in the past few years and it appeals mostly to people wanting to build using natural products wherever possible. They also need deep wallets because it's rather more expensive.

EXPANDED POLYSTYRENE

Now it's on to plastics. The most familiar plastic insulation is expanded polystyrene (EPS). It gets used in buildings in two formats. The first is as a vast amorphous mass of little white beads that get blown into cavity walls from lorries. The second is in rigid boards; here two brands dominate, Jablite and Kay-cel. It performs very similarly to glass and mineral wool in terms of insulation capabilities (but not fire protection) and is similarly cheaply priced. Used widely in cavity wall construction (in both formats) and underfloor insulation (where the regs now require at least 100mm of EPS).

EXTRUDED POLYSTYRENE

This is a different version of polystyrene that is much denser and much stronger - expanded polystyrene sheets are notoriously brittle. In terms of insulation capabilities it lies midway between expanded polystyrene and the polyurethanes, but its big selling point is that it is resistant to water penetration. It's great under floors

and below ground but it's a bit pricey to use elsewhere. Businesses to check out are Dow Chemicals, who make Styrofoam, and Polyfoam.

POLYURETHANES (PIRS)

The most efficient of the mass market insulators, it is usually sold in rigid sheet format, usually foil backed. However, it is pricey even if you buy second hand, where a company called Seconds & Co is busy. The domestic market is dominated by two manufacturers, Celotex and Kingspan, though others are beginning to appear.

A big problem with polyurethane has been that its production involved the use of CFCs, now implicated in the demise of the ozone layer. This has led the manufacturers on a frantic search to find ways of making their boards with a different blowing agent, and this has produced a range of similar insulation boards made with either polyisocyanurate foam or phenolic foam. Phenolic foam (sold as Kooltherm) is actually a somewhat better insulator than standard Celotex and Kingspan, but is considerably more expensive.

Despite their cost, the plastic foam insulations are increasingly being specified because their of their superior performance as insulators which means that they are space efficient. Basically these boards are twice as good but three times the cost of the basic insulators — i.e. expanded polystyrene and the wools.

Whilst the dreadful Grenfell tower fire has brought into question their use externally, the blaze resulted from a combination of factors and plastic

insulation use was but one. On it's own, in low rise housing, it's not dangerous but it's good to be aware that it can burn. There aren't many building materials that can't.

CELLULOSE FIBRE

This is sometimes promoted as a green alternative to the other materials. For a start, it's made from recycled newspapers (so that's where they go) and it can also be used in timber frame walls without a vapour barrier, which is reckoned, by some, to be an advantage. It has one major disadvantage in that it is not available in a sheet form so it has to be blown in by specialists. Trade name Warmcel.

UNUSUAL INSULATIONS

There are numerous other materials being used as insulants, and new ones coming onto the market all the time. At the hi-tec end of things, there are vacuum-insulated panels (VIPs) which are horribly expensive, terribly thin and only last for 30 years (Nanopore or Kingspan's Optim-R). Then there are the aerogels of which Spacetherm is the best known example. It's rather brittle and dusty to use, but it has its place where you want good insulation and don't have very much space. Foamglas is another hi-tec insulant: it is made of crushed glass and carbon and is totally impervious to water, rot, vermin or any sort of damage.

Then there are various natural insulation materials. Apart from Warmcel and Sheep's Wool, look out for Hemp Insulation (Isonat),

INSULATION: Key Rates per m^2

	Underfloor	Ext Wall	Flat ceiling	Sloping roof
Approx U value needed (2013)	**0.13**	**0.18**	**0.13**	**0.13**
Rockwool	INADVISABLE	175mm Batts	340mm Roll	INADVISABLE
Cost/m^2		£10	£6	
Exp Polystyrene	200mm	INADVISABLE	INADVISABLE	INADVISABLE
Cost/m^2	£14			
Extruded Polystyrene (Styrofoam)	150mm	INADVISABLE	INADVISABLE	INADVISABLE
Cost/m^2	£21			
PIR foam boards	150mm	100mm	150mm	150mm
Cost/m^2	£20	£16	£20	£20
Blown fibre	INADVISABLE	200mm	300mm	300mm
Cost/m^2		£15	£30	£30
Sheeps Wool	INADVISABLE	150mm	300mm	300mm
Cost/m^2		£17	£24	£24

Acoustic Insulation Internal Walls & Floors

	75mm
Cost/m^2	£3

Labour rate for fixing insulation	£22 hr
Time taken to fix 1m2 (normal insulation)	10 min/m^2
Cost to fix 1m^2	£3.70
Time taken to fit superinsulation	15 min/m^2
Cost to fix 1m^2	£5.50

The total amount spent on insulation is nearly £5,400, around 2% of overall construction costs. The Ground Floor insulation is subtracted from this table because it's included in the Groundworks cost table in Chapter 6.

MODEL HOUSE: Insulation Costs

	Area	Item	Materials	Labour	Totals	Costs/m^2
Under Ground Floor	80 m^2	*125mm PIR*	£ 1,800	£ 300	**£ 2,100**	£26
NB Under Ground Floor Insulation is costed in Groundworks Table for Model House Calcs						
Ext Walls	200 m^2	175mm Dri-Therm	£ 3,000	£ 700	**£ 3,700**	£19
Ceiling Roof Insulation	80 m^2	340mm Rockwool	£ 500	£ 300	**£ 800**	£10
Acoustic Walls	60 m^2	75mm Rockwool Prorox	£ 200	£ 200	**£ 400**	£7
Acoustic Floors	75 m^2	75mm Rockwool Prorox	£ 200	£ 300	**£ 500**	£7
		Total exc Ground Floor	**£ 3,900**	**£ 1,500**	**£ 5,400**	

Hemcrete (a lime-hemp mixture), and Pavatex (wood fibre board). These materials are usually used with timber framed houses where the emphasis is on breathing walls - i.e. ones built without a conventional vapour barrier. These are usually bought via specialist suppliers: Mike Wye Associates is a useful contact as they maintain an online price list.

MULITIFOILS

The multifoils are a controversial group of insulation materials, which work on the Bacofoil-behind-the-radiator principle. That is to say they have shiny reflective barriers which bounce the heat back into the room. There are three, Actis (from France), Alreflex 2L2 (from Holland) and Airtec (British), which have some body to them and therefore tend to act like conventional insulation, though none is thicker than 25mm.

The use of multifoils is based on their manufacturers' claims that they are equivalent in insulation value to around 250mm of mineral wool, which makes them suitable for use in sloping roof spaces. This claim is, to put it mildly, controversial. When placed into a guarded hot box, the traditional method of measuring U values, multifoils only perform to the equivalent of 80mm of mineral wool. Nevertheless, multifoils have established a foothold in the insulation market, thanks to their endorsement by BM Trada, a prominent third party certifier, and whether you choose to believe the claims of their manufacturers, or not, it would be churlish of me not to mention their existence. They can be a very useful way of getting some insulation into areas like loft roofs where space is limited.

Multifoils are getting used in conjunction with other materials, such as plastic insulation boards, and the authorities are far happier to accept these combination applications.

BUYING TIPS

Generally the best place to buy insulation materials is from the insulation specialists. Sheffield Insulation (SIG) and Encon are the best-known national distributors but there are numerous local ones and a couple of online specialists. Some of the insulation installers are worth checking out for supply only. The supply and fix services offered are often a good deal; it is hard to beat them on price (or speed) except where you are not paying for site labour.

A great online resource if you want to know more is Greenspec.co.uk. It has bags of information on the different types of insulation available.

ACOUSTIC INSULATION

Generally required in timber walls and floors in new dwellings, sound absorbent insulation is a category all on its own. Usually supplied in rolls, all the major suppliers such as Rockwool and Knauf produce a denser version of their standard thermal products, and there are Sheeps Wool versions as well. The plastic insulants don't really get a look in here because it's all about density, quite the opposite to what is wanted with thermal insulation. Placing acoustic insulation into ceiling voids and internal walls is routinely done after the plumbing and wiring has been put in place, before the boarding stage, and it's a classic DIY project manager's job. It's not skilled, it's messy and it doesn't require any specialised tools. Just a good face mask, a hop up and a tape measure.

JOINERY

Joinery is the preferred architectural word for what most of us call windows and doors. The choices you make here are perhaps the most critical factor of all in determining what sort of house you build, or at least what it looks like.

Back in the day, this used to be a pretty straightforward affair. Even within the lifespan of this title, joinery options were fairly limited for all but the most upmarket homes. Things have changed. There are now far more options and styles and there is a move away from using standard fittings towards more bespoke stuff. And glazing, which used to be a matter of just sticking a pane of glass in a window, has become an area where you have to consider a range of options.

Some sites still operate using the old methods but the trend now is to get the windows and doors glazed and decorated in a distant factory, to be fitted much later in the build process. Now the brickies fit sub-frames or cavity closers around the openings, where once they put the whole window or door frame in.

BUILDING REGULATIONS

The building regulations are also driving change here. No less than six sets of regulations cover our joinery activities and you really need to be aware of the basics because if any of your choices fail to comply, you may have to replace what you've expensively installed. Let's look at them individually, based on the current regulations in England. Wales, Scotland and N Ireland have similar requirements.

FIRE (PART B)

All habitable rooms must have a means of escape other than the room door. This usually means an opening window somewhere on the ground or first floor. Higher storeys may require alternative arrangements. But it's not enough to have a window that opens. The rules state that a) the opening must be at least $0.33m^2$, b) that the opening must be 450mm high and 450mm wide and c) the opening must be within 1100mm of the floor. Technically, these are known as egress windows.

VENTILATION (PART F)

Unless you have opted for a whole house ventilation system, you have to provide ventilation in each room. This is conventionally done by fitting trickle vents in the heads of the windows. Some foreign window suppliers don't do trickle vents – they are a uniquely British solution to this problem. So you have to decide on your ventilation strategy at the outset — don't get caught out.

Some people want to opt for night latch windows which offer a slightly open but locked setting instead of trickle vents, but bear in mind that a picky building inspector may not accept this and point out that such windows are a security risk — see Part Q notes coming soon.

SAFETY GLASS (PART K)

Some doors and windows require safety glass
▨ any window less than 800mm off floor level
▨ any window less than 300mm from a door
▨ all doors and sidelights where pane width is greater than 250mm
▨ internal glazed doors with pane sizes more than 250x250mm.

What do they mean by 'safety glazing?' There are two common forms of clear, strengthened glass:
▨ toughened: baked hard to about five times the strength of float glass and, when broken, shatters into harmless lumps. Toughened glass costs about 50% more than the standard float glass.
▨ laminated: consists of two sheets of ordinary glass sandwiched around

a plastic film: when hit it breaks but doesn't collapse.

Laminated glass is conventionally 6.4mm thick and it costs around double standard float glass, considerably more than toughened glass. Consequently for these applications, toughened glass is now almost universally specified, but laminated glass is preferable if you are worried about security; it's harder to break through.

ENERGY EFFICIENCY (PART L)

Like all other elements making up the thermal envelope of the house, doors and windows have to meet defined U values, though there is a little leeway allowed here. The generally accepted standard U value for doors and windows in new homes is now 1.4, but you can have the odd solid door at a relaxed U value as high as 2.0.

This translates as double glazing on windows and composite external doors, either solid or with some double glazing. A composite door is one that is made up of insulated panels encased by another material such as steel, GRP or timber.

Your glazing performance will be assessed when the SAP calculations are carried out and the joinery you choose will have to comply and be seen to comply. Generally if it meets the 1.4 U value standard, it will comply.

There is a good case to fit joinery that beats the performance of standard double glazing — for instance triple glazing and/or solar reflective glazing — but we will look at that shortly.

ACCESS (PART M)

Part M covers the disabled access arrangements for new housing and you are required to have at least one accessible doorway where the threshold is level (defined as no obstruction greater than 15mm) and the clear-door opening of at least 775mm, which you get when you fit a door that is at least 826mm wide. There is a lot more to Part M; this bit affects your door choices only.

SECURITY (PART Q)

What was once a performance standard for doors and windows known as PAS 24, used mainly in Secured by Design schemes, became a standard building regulation in 2015 and it applies to all "easily accessible" doors and windows. Although not difficult to beat, it can catch suppliers out, especially if they are foreign and are not aware of Part Q. Look to fit "Part Q compliant" windows.

COMPLIANCE

A good designer should be aware of all these issues and should ensure that your joinery choices comply with all these regulations, but some people are not all that competent and some clients skimp on the design stages and never get around to specifying what sort of joinery they will fit until too late. Mistakes get made, and sometimes perfectly good joinery gets replaced because it falls foul of one of the Regs. Your building inspector may give you some leeway, or they may not. They will certainly be seeking some evidence that your joinery does actually comply. Sometimes this is evident from a site visit. Toughened glass is usually stamped. Door openings, window cill heights and openings are measurable on site. But security? U values? You need to ensure that your suppliers invoices or quotations reflect accurately describe what it is you have used. Expect the U values of each item to be itemised, along with evidence of Part Q compliance.

REPLACING OLD WINDOWS

There is a scheme that covers replacement windows only, governed by a body known as FENSA (England & Wales only). A glazer who is accredited by FENSA can sign off their work as being compliant with current building regs without having to trouble the local building inspector. This information may later be required when you come to sell the house so there is a semblance of a stick here to get you to comply. So look out to see if your installer is FENSA approved installer. If not, you can still go down the other route of paying for a building inspection.

One area that remains exempt from the requirements is listed buildings. English Heritage see the FENSA scheme as a uPVC window salesman's licence to rip out all that is wooden and lovely from our national treasures. The exemption may also apply to properties situated in Conservation Areas though this isn't abundantly clear. In the Conservation area I live in, people are still putting in plastic windows and no one seems to care a jot.

GLAZING

Glazing is one of the few areas of construction which has undergone significant change since I started in the building game back in 1980. Back then, double glazing was well established but it was mostly people ripping out old timber and metal windows and putting in plastic double glazed ones. As for clever glass, it came down to a choice of plain see-through or frosted (for bathrooms).

Double-glazing promised comfort and warmth. The early forms of double glazing were a significant improvement on single glazing in terms of U-Values, the common measurement of heat loss. Single glazing scores around 5 (hopeless); in contrast, a basic double glazed sealed unit scores around 3 (the lower the better). But the technology of double glazing has kept on developing and the most advanced triple-glazed systems available today have U values under 1 (better than walls were in the 1970s). That's five times less heat loss than single glazing.

FAILURES IN SEALED UNITS

In fact the building trade took a long while to come to grips with basic double glazing. There was a horribly high failure rate, usually manifesting itself in the form of misting between the panes. The gap around the so-called sealed units kept breaking down and moist external air got in, resulting in condensation between the panes.

Hundreds of thousands of double glazed units failed this way over

The trend towards factory-glazing of windows has been accompanied by the uptake of cavity closers, pictured here, which you build into the wall as it goes up. The windows and doors are clipped in later when the damage can be minimised

the years and only recently has the industry worked out how to combat the problem. By and large, factory glazing has cured these issues and now the vast majority of double glazed units are supplied in this way — i.e. ready glazed rather than site glazed.

INCREMENTAL IMPROVEMENTS

Various measures improve the efficiency of double-glazing and it's helpful to look at what they are. The simplest is to increase the distance

JOINERY COSTINGS Rules of Thumb

- The Model House has 35m^2 of joinery (inc external door openings)
- As a rule, joinery openings equate to 20% of the overall external wall area
- You can derive a m^2 rate by dividing the overall cost by the area of joinery openings
- This is helpful when comparing window prices
- Doors are more expensive than windows
- The cost/m^2 increaes as with small windows
- Unusual styles, made to measure and non-standard sizes all add to costs
- The Joinery Schedule is based on a pretty basic window!

MODEL HOUSE: Joinery Schedule

Softwood, factory glazed	Width in m	Height in m	Area in m^2	Item Cost	Fitting costs	Combined Cost
Base cost £ 270 /m^2					**£ 55 /m^2**	
Kitchen French Doors	1.8	2.1	3.8	£ 1,000	£ 310	£ 1,310
Kitchen Window	2.1	1.2	2.5	£ 700	£ 140	£ 840
Utility Door	0.9	2.1	1.9	£ 500	£ 200	£ 700
Utility Window	1.2	1.2	1.4	£ 400	£ 80	£ 480
Dining Room Window	2.1	1.2	2.5	£ 700	£ 140	£ 840
Front Door	2.0	2.1	4.2	£ 900	£ 230	£ 1,130
WC	0.5	0.7	0.3	£ 100	£ 20	£ 120
Lounge Patio Door	3.2	2.1	6.7	£ 3,300	£ 460	£ 3,760
Bed 1	1.8	2.1	3.7	£ 1,000	£ 200	£ 1,200
En suite (wet room)	1.2	1.2	1.4	£ 400	£ 80	£ 480
Bathroom	1.2	1.2	1.4	£ 400	£ 80	£ 480
Bed 2	1.5	1.2	1.8	£ 500	£ 100	£ 600
Bed 3	1.5	1.2	1.8	£ 500	£ 100	£ 600
Bed 4	1.5	1.2	1.8	£ 500	£ 100	£ 600
Grand Total			35	£ 11,000	£ 2,000	£ 13,000
Costs/m^2				£ 310		£ 370

between the panes. A 6mm gap was the old standard in the 1970s. By upping this to 16 or 20mm you reduce heat loss by nearly 25%. It's easy for the glazing manufacturers to alter the gap and there is no cost penalty here. The difficulty comes in adjusting the frames, which start to look heavy.

The next trick is to fill the air gap between panes with something other than air. The inert gas argon is the common choice (though some use krypton). Argon filling adds to the cost of the units and it results in only a marginal improvement in efficiency.

Next comes low emissivity (or low-e) glass. Low-e glass works by absorbing short wave solar heat, just like other glass, but then acting as a reflective shield to the long wave heat emanating from inside the house. In effect it introduces a layer of one-way insulation into the sealed unit.

Low-e coating is a developing technology and there are now hard coatings and soft coatings with varying emissivity levels. Soft coatings are better and, needless to say, more expensive. A hard coat will reduce the overall U-value by 25%; a soft coat by as much as 35%.

Another energy-saving technique is to use warm edge spacers around the sealed units. Traditionally, the spacers were made of aluminium which is a very good heat conductor. A classic case of cold bridging. By replacing the aluminium with something less conductive (typically plastic) you get a much more even U-value across the entire sealed unit. The smaller the units, the bigger difference warm edgings make.

Beyond this, there are adjustments you can make to the frames, which can have a major impact on heat loss. And ultimately, you can add an extra sheet of glass and move to triple glazing, which also improves efficiency by around 25%. Triple glazing is also much better for sound proofing.

Add all these 25%s here and 35%s there plus the odd 10% and you can see how a state of the art double or triple glazed unit can get a very low U-value, far in excess of what is required by the current UK regs.

The problem is that all these techniques add to costs. For instance, triple glazing is about 25% more than double glazing. In terms of value for money, none of these measures pay for themselves as the incremental heat savings are not that great. But in terms of comfort, they all make a big difference and few people who pay extra for state of the art glazing regret it.

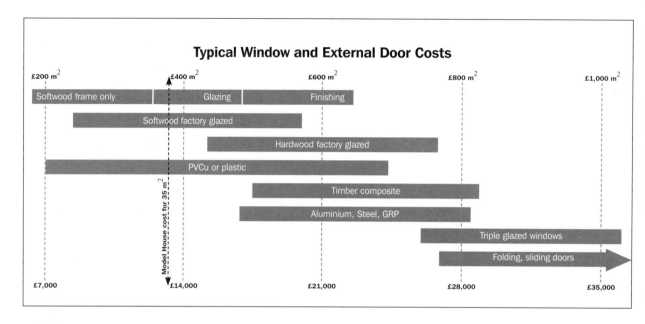

Typical Window and External Door Costs

CLEVER GLASS

There is more to glazing than energy saving and the two big glass companies, Pilkington and St Gobain, seem to be endlessly introducing new features. Check out their websites to learn more, but here are some of the interesting options available

SOLAR CONTROL

Introducing films into the glazing process enables the manufactures to do all kinds of things. Whilst low-e glass stops internal heat leaking outside, solar control glass does pretty much the opposite — it stops unwanted heat getting in. It's particularly useful in conservatories, rooflights and large expanses of south and west-facing glass (aka Big Glass), as these are the features which tend to cause overheating in summer.

The amount of solar heat coming through window is referred to as a G

factor and it's expressed as a fraction of 1 which is what you get with no glass at all. Standard double glazing lets through about 60% of solar heat, expressed as 0.6, triple glazing about 50% or 0.5 and then solar controlled films can reduce this to as little as you want, though people are advised not to go below 30% or 0.3 as although it's designed to keep out infra-red, it also loses light in the visible spectrum as well and so things start to get a little grey below 0.3.

I'm a fan of solar control glass. We installed it in our kitchen roof light and we sailed through the heat wave of 2018 with comfortable internal temperatures. The kitchen was actually cooler with the rooflights closed than it was when open to the elements. If you are wanting Big Glass in your new home, then temper it with a low G value.

The downside is that you lose

useful solar heat in the nine months of the year when you aren't too bothered about overheating. There is a balance to be struck here and there is no right answer, but a good designer and/or supplier will be able to guide you as to the best option.

ELECTROCHROMIC GLASS

The ultimate in glazing intelligence is the ability to switch the properties of glass with electricity. I first saw this in the year 2000 where it was used on the BRE's Millennium House to turn a clear window into an obscure one at the touch of a button — no more curtains or blinds!

But since then, the technology has moved on to allow you to switch between letting in lots of solar radiation in winter to keeping it out in summer. Maybe one day, all glass will be like this, but it remains an expensive luxury at present.

OBSCURE GLASS

Gone are the days of boring frosted glass. There are many decorative effects available delivering different levels of obscurity. In fact, planning conditions sometimes refer to the specific level of obscurity required in an overlooking window. Often this is "Pilkington Level 3 or similar".

Many people do not want to install obscure glazing as it seems to go against the very idea of glazing — i.e. you can look through it. But sometimes needs must. Question is, is it acceptable to use a stick-on film instead? Here is a technology that has also advanced in leaps and bounds, including the ability to electrically switch obscurity on and off. The chances are that only the most eagle-eyed building inspector would notice the difference, and in terms of the effect, the stick-on films look just as good, at least for a few years. There are lots of small suppliers out there looking for your orders.

SELF-CLEANING GLASS

Both St Gobain and Pilkington produce self-cleaning glass, which is coated with yet another film which stops droplets appearing which should stop streaking. That doesn't mean you never have to clean glass again, but it should greatly reduce the number of visits by window cleaners.

STRUCTURAL GLAZING

One of the great boom areas of building in the past decades has been the use of glass as a building element in itself, with no frame or indeed any visible means of support.

It's down to the combination of two safety techniques, toughening and lamination, which combined, sometimes in several layers, makes a material that is immensely strong and can bear significant loads.

Thus we have features like glazed safety screens for staircases and balconies, glazed walls and even the glazed floor. The prices are eye-watering, compared to conventional solutions, but the effect is often startling.

The strength of these new glazing elements has meant that there is also a trend towards using less and less frame in windows and doors, and sometimes none at all — i.e. frameless glass. Again, minimal frame styles are now commonplace (and significantly more expensive

than conventionally framed glass); frameless versions are even more expensive.

AIR TIGHTNESS

Almost as critical to the energy performance of windows and doors as their overall energy ratings, is the method used to fit them into the external walls and the draught-proofing of the opening parts when in contact with the fixed parts. Draught-proofing is now pretty well built into doors and windows but gaps around the frames, where they are built into walls, is still left very much up to the guys on site. It's not unusual to see large gaps under lintels, for instance, which would later be covered over with plasterboard: this makes a mockery of fitting high

Chapter 7

cost double glazed units.

Many suppliers are developing sub frame assembly systems, which address some of these issues. The sub frames, or cavity closers, fit into the cavity and are built-in as the wall goes up. They address the old problem of cold bridging where the internal skin was taken around a corner (known as a return) to form an opening for a window or a door, but they also act as a clip-in frame for the window to be placed directly into later without having to mess around with any screws.

In timber framed construction, the normal routine is to build a plywood boxing around the window opening with a 10mm gap all the way round, and then tape the window frame to the plywood on the inside. On the outside, the seal is usually made with expandable foam tape, known as Compriband.

CHOOSING WINDOWS

Timber or plastic? Or something else entirely? Pre-glazed or finished on site? Modern or traditional? Made-to-measure or off-the-peg? What sort of opening mechanism? There are, in truth, a lot of questions facing you when it comes to window selection. You have, in fact, a microcosm of the UK housebuilding scene right here in one product group.

There is quite a good chance that you won't have to go through all these decision processes, at least in any great detail, if you work with a designer or a package company who steer towards a window that just happens to work

with the chosen design. For instance, if you are building in the Georgian rectory style, you will almost certainly be wanting to use a Georgian sash-style window.

Windows and, to a lesser extent, doors, are absolutely critical to your overall house design and generally there is a window that works for every house design so you would be most unlikely – indeed extremely badly advised – to fit the wrong style of window into the wrong façade. Not that the typical homeowner on the typical suburban street would know this: bear witness to the dreadful mish-mash of styles and materials used in the great replacement window craze of the 1980s 1990s. But an awful lot of contemporary housing isn't tied to any style in particular and this leaves a wide range of choices available.

WINDOW OPENINGS

One of the key tricks in designing to a budget is to stick to standard industry window and door sizes. All the main manufacturers selling into this market are geared up to make thousands of standard windows and doors to fit these openings. There are cost and time penalties for varying away from these openings, so everyone sticks to these openings. What exactly are they?

The window opening heights are easy to fathom: they are in 150mm steps, which represents two bricks courses – the height options are 450, 600, 750, 900, 1050, 1200, 1350, 1500mm. The width options – 488, 630, 915, 1200, 1770mm – would at first glance seem to be selected by a random number

machine. It appears that the widths were changed in the early 1980s after a directive from Brussels indicated that the 300mm brick was about to take over Europe and that they'd better have joinery to suit. The joinery manufacturers all obliged, but bricks remain 215mm long! This is most noticeable on the 1200 wide windows, which disrupt the vertical joints on face brickwork.

The old British joinery businesses have all been taken over now but the same factories still churn out these windows by the truckload. Names to look out for are Jeld-Wen, who took over two of the big names in this business, Boulton & Paul and John Carr, Premdor (doors only) and Magnet. Of these manufacturers, Magnet are alone in maintaining a substantial branch network of depots through which they sell exclusively. All the others sell through the established builder's merchants. There are numerous others in this business like Howarth Timber who sell directly to housebuilders and the trade.

When plastic windows appeared on the scene, back in the 1970s, they were being sold almost exclusively into the replacement market and the businesses were all geared up to make one-offs. It took a long time for the uPVC manufacturers to realise that the new housebuilders only really wanted about five different window sizes and that there were economies of scale to be had here by aping the likes of Boulton & Paul. The plastic window merchants started making basic windows in the same old modular sizes and then improved on the process by introducing clip-in cavity closers which let you push a finished window into place, long after the brickies had left site. This fitting system is now available on most types of window.

COMPOSITES

There are a number of suppliers who offer timber windows capped with a durable exterior. Velux made a name for themselves producing rooflights like this and gradually the practice has spread to conventional windows as well. Andersen Windows, the American joinery giant, produce a huge range of timber doors and windows with an external uPVC coating, but the bulk of UK interest is now in Scandinavian and German origin manufacturers.

Prominent amongst these is the Velux Group (VKR Holdings) who also manufacture Velfac and Rationel, two of the most popular. Other suppliers of note include Nor Dan, Ideal Combi, Protec and Internorm. British suppliers are also now establishing themselves — look out for Allan Brothers and Kloeber. There are many smaller businesses who design and build to order. We used one, Living Wood, from Bury St Edmunds, who supplied triple glazed, Passivhaus standard timber windows and doors with a spray-painted aluminium exterior in 2018 for around £1,000/m².

COMPARING COSTS

Joinery is an expensive feature in the overall budget. It frequently makes up 10% of the final figure, and there is a large price gap between the basic stuff and the top of the range, whatever material you choose to use. If you want a shortcut price guide, look out for the cost of a unit like a 1200x1200mm window and use this to extrapolate upwards.

A basic unit in a simple configuration, say a double casement window with one opening panel, will cost around £260 fully glazed and finished. You can easily spend double or triple this amount by changing styles or materials. If you are using a joinery catalogue for pricing purposes, bear in mind that most items are normally sold at big discounts to the published prices. 30% or 35% off are often taken as read and big volumes or good haggling skills can easily increase this discount.

One of the things that throws people out is that the headline rates for timber windows from the large joinery manufacturers appears to be low, much lower than any of the finished windows. A raw timber window needs glazing, needs detailing around the openings and needs decorating as well: the combined costs of these items is more than double the cost of the raw timber window.

If you account for these extra items as the window table does, then you find that uPVC is now the cheapest way to build a window, by some margin. But uPVC itself varies enormously in quality. Top of the range products like Masterframe cost just as much as the better timber windows.

ROOFLIGHTS

A word about rooflights and, in particular, Velux windows. They are another form of composite window, being basically timber windows encased in an aluminium cladding, but they have revolutionised loft living by being simple to install, and near problem-free in operation. They cost around £500/m² including the essential roof flashings, very little more than the standard price for good quality timber or uPVC windows. Velux is not the only company making rooflights but they are the trailblazers and still enjoy by far the largest market share in this specialist market: but watch out for Fakro, a Polish company also reckoned to be very good.

GLASS CEILINGS

Developing on from sloping rooflights, we see a huge interest in glazed rooflights for flat roofs — in effect glass ceilings. Glazing developments over the past few years have brought this once exclusive technique into the ambit of selfbuilders and triple glazing has made it possible to build light into a roof without the attendant loss of heat. It's all part and parcel of the frameless glass trend and the same businesses that dominate glass walls also tend to produce glazed roofing, often combing the two to good effect. It's still eye-wateringly expensive, and if you include opening rooflights as well, the metre rates can exceed £5,000/m². But given that you get three to four times more daylight through an overhead window, it can usually be counted on to turn a dull room into an exciting one. Look out for Velux Skylights, and products by IQ Glass, Cantifix and Glazing Vision.

EXTERNAL DOORS

Many of the things that I've written about windows apply equally to external doors. Furthermore, there is a polite convention that your choice of door should not clash with your choice of window – a convention that's well worth following whatever your chosen style. As with windows, the door manufacturers tend to stick to pretty conventional ideas and all produce variations on some remarkably similar themes. One of the more daring ideas is to put a little bit of stained glass in the pocket window on some of the designs. By and large, the best that can be said about the design of these doors is that 'it blends in quite well' or 'isn't that unobtrusive?' If you want a door that makes a statement about you – and, after all, the front door is the first thing visitors come into contact with – then you'll have to look to a bespoke joiner's shop or a salvage yard. Either way expect to pay.

FRONT ENTRANCE

Most front entrance doors are now what we call composite doors, which is to say they are made up of several materials, including an insulated core which is required in order to meet the requirements for Part L, the energy efficiency regs. What you actually see fitted around the core can be timber, steel or GRP and sometimes it can be hard to tell the difference, especially if they are supplied pre-painted, already fitted into a doorset.

GLAZED DOORS

The idea of opening up a largish hole in the house facing the garden is attractive to most of us; it's a sort of poor man's conservatory. Actually, leave the poor man out of it, because big glazed doors are expensive. You have a basic choice here between sliding doors and hinged ones. Back in the day, these were routinely referred to as patio doors (1960s) or French doors (1920s). Step forward to this century and they have become sliding doors and bi-fold doors, the latter also known confusingly as folding sliding doors.

These were first introduced into the UK in the late 1980s and they mark a logical progression for large glazed openings.

The doors run in trackways located both above and below the opening, just like a sliding patio door. However, the individual doors are hinged together so that they concertina into a very small space. This means that virtually the entire door frame can be opened up, unlike patio doors where one section must remain fixed in place. This open aspect appeals to anyone who likes the idea of the house and the garden merging into one on a bright summer's day.

One thing to consider is how the doors sit when fully open, as they must extend either inwards or outwards by the width of a door leaf. The neatest arrangement is usually to have them opening inwards but to do this you ideally want to create a large return space for them to sit against, but this isn't always practicable or feasible. You also have to decide whether to split the arrangement in two so that you have doors closing each side. For easy access, many people choose to have a solitary 'traffic door' on one side, which acts like one side of a pair of French doors, allowing all the other door leaves to stack up on the other side only when the weather is suitable. An alternative is to opt for sliding doors which have no limit on them width, but do have to keep at least one leaf fixed. The ultimate in coolness here is to have a fixed sliding door which completely disappears into a wall pocket so that when fully open you see nothing at all. I hardly need to tell you that such a feature will tend to cost about the same as a small family car.

Folding sliding doors are almost invariably made to measure, so there can never be such a thing as a price list. However, generally costs start at around £800 per leaf (door) and rise to around £1400, depending on the materials used, so a seven-leaf door would cost between £6,000 and £10,000. Generally, the more leaves used, the more expensive, so sometimes you can save a little money by specifying a smaller number of wider doors (hint: aluminium door leaves can be as wide as 1200mm).

One step beyond regular framed sliding doors is the frameless glass door, either in a folding configuration or sliding. This is a more specialised area and the suppliers tend to be the structural glazers mentioned in the previous section. Check out Frameless Glass Curtains.

DOORS OR DOORSETS?

Most external doors are now sold as doorsets, that is to say the doors are already fitted into a frame, and with the door furniture already in place. Essentially this is much simpler as you just have to get the frame in place.

You can still buy individual doors and fix them into a frame, and if you do so you have to consider that the frame must match the door and that the handles, hinges and locks also match.

The problem with this approach is that since 2015 external doors have had to meet a new security standard, Part Q in England & Wales, which requires the entire door assembly (i.e. door, frame and hardware) to meet PAS 24 which is a testing regime, and it's extremely difficult to do this without buying a doorset — preferably a Part Q compliant doorset. Part Q only applies to new builds and major conversions where there is a change of use, so on extensions and renovations you won't be checked, but in new builds it forms part of the compliance routine you have to be aware of.

Part Q is quite prescriptive. For instance a letter box must be no more than 260x40mm and must be designed to hinder anyone attempting to remove keys from the inside with sticks or their hands. And a viewer must be incorporated, although a pane of glass will suffice. If you really want to fit doors in the old way, I suggest you familiarise yourself with Part Q and work back

One of the big issues with large expanses of external glazing is the risk of overheating. One way around this is to add a sunshade, or brise soleil, which is angled so that the peak summer heat is kept off the glass whilst low level winter sunshine is welcomed.

from there. For the rest of us, stick with a doorset.

UPPER FLOORS

The ground floor has been looked at in the previous chapter, Groundworks. Any floors above ground level (inc floors over basements) are referred to as intermediate floors; they act as both floors for the rooms above and ceilings for the rooms below. This makes the issues we need to look at rather different. Intermediate floors only have to be thermally insulated if they are above features like garages;

on the other hand, you have to consider sound insulation, which you don't on ground floors.

The structural elements of intermediate floors are pretty similar to ground floors. Obviously, the ground-bearing slab is not an option but otherwise you have the same choice to make between timber or concrete suspended floors. Timber floors are traditional and remain the cheapest option. The main reason for switching to something else is to get better soundproofing. In fact, timber floors don't have to perform poorly in this department but it's a widely held perception that they do.

TRADITIONAL JOISTS

The standard way to build intermediate floors in both masonry homes and timber framed ones has been to lay sawn timber joists across the floor. Span tables exist to show you just how deep your joists need to be to avoid flexing unacceptably. Once you get to a span of around five metres, you struggle to find a joist deep enough to cope, so most conventional house designs stick to spans under five metres and place load-bearing walls in the appropriate places to pick up the joists.

There are routines for dealing with openings around staircases – lots of doubling up of joists - and supporting partition walls above – more doubling up. And nowadays chippies join joists using steel hangers. There are also some elaborate rules about just where you should and shouldn't notch and drill holes through joists, rules which are routinely ignored by plumbers and electricians.

To provide stability, the joists need to be braced together: this is achieved with either diagonal struts or solid bridgings. As you can see, whilst the basic idea of laying floor joists is simplicity itself, there are a number of additional factors to consider that make it a whole lot more complex and a whole lot slower than it might be. So much so that the traditional sawn joist floor is rapidly being replaced by.…

I-BEAM FLOORS

This is an American innovation, which uses thin, lightweight timber RSJs. Like many building innovations, the I-beam has actually been around for decades. I am reliably informed that there is an estate of houses in Redditch built out of nothing but I-beams in the 1970s. Having never been to Redditch, I'll have to take it on trust. But it wasn't until the 1990s that anyone really started to push I-beams in a big way. That's when Trus Joist MacMillan started advertising them as SilentFloor.

What's the proposition? Well you pay more for an I-beam than you do for a sawn timber joist. Almost twice as much in fact on a linear metre basis. But in return you get a product that takes half the time to install, and is far easier to install services through. Instead of having to drill holes or make notches, you just tap on a preformed knock-out and you are through. And the squeaks? Well, one of the main problems with timber when used in floors is that it shrinks as it dries out. A 200mm deep timber joist may well measure just 195mm after a warm, centrally heated winter and this causes not only squeaking floors but can also lead to problems with showers and baths where mastic seals fail. An engineered I-beam cannot shrink because the web (the upright bit) is made of OSB, or some similar plywood-like board.

I-beams are also capable of spanning up to six metres, which gives them an additional edge. If you are interested in I-beams (and there are now several manufacturers), you have to order in advance, just as you would with roof trusses. They are invariably sold as an engineered solution, made up specifically for your site.

As an alternative to the solid I-beam floor joists, look out for metal web joists, the best known one being the hollow Posi-Joist. In recent years, I have come to notice far more Posi-Joists than I-Beams, though essentially they do the same thing.

JOIST HANGERS

How do you sit a timber joist on a wall? You build it in on top of your blockwork and then fill in the gaps between the joist ends with odd bits of block: what could be simpler?

Well that's how it was done for years on building sites up and down the land. But the energy wonks have cause to believe that this is very sloppy and contributes hugely to unwarranted air leaks. Not only do the brickies take very little care in filling in this void, but then the joists shrink by 5% or more, as discussed, making air leakage paths almost inevitable.

The building regs require you to pay a little more attention to this detail. They would really like joists (and I-beams) to be hung off external walls using joist hangers, but this is a fiddly detail and builders have been allowed to lay joists onto the walls, provided close attention is paid to mastic-ing around the joist ends to ensure there will be no air leakage. It's a detail that will become far more critical in the future when air tightness testing will be taken seriously. Incidentally, this is unlikely to be a problem in timber frame designs.

SOUND INSULATION

In 2003, I spent the night in a very beautiful detached new house which had cost well over £300,000 to build. Whilst the thermal U-values had been engineered down to amazingly low levels by the use of SIPS panel construction, as far as I could see – and hear – no attention at all had been paid to internal sound-proofing and I could hear all too clearly what was going on in the rest of the house during the night. God knows what they thought of my snoring! The floors were the simplest construction imaginable: hardwood planks over timber joists above a single skin of plasterboard. The walls were just as basic.

Such construction details have caused a lot of problems for a lot of people over the years. It's the simplest and the cheapest floor detail you can build and, over the past fifty years or so, it's got both simpler and cheaper to build. Manufactured boards have taken the place of denser materials and they have tended to grow less dense over time as suppliers strove to drive down costs. It all contributed to a sustained decline in soundproofing standards which many new homeowners have had cause to complain about.

Up until 2004, the building regs didn't have anything to say about this trend. They concerned themselves solely with stopping noise passing through party walls and floors between flats and terraced housing. That state of affairs changed when Part E, the bit of the regs that deals with soundproofing, was re-worked.

But it's a very basic improvement that is called for. You may want to do better. Here follows some costed suggestions; if you want to know more about what a decibel is, have a look at the section in the last chapter entitled Sound Advice.

■ **The naked floor option.** Construction - timber joists or I beams, chipboard cover, single sheet of plasterboard underneath. Cost: effectively minus zero as you aren't allowed to build like this anymore. Likely decibel reduction? Around 35 dB on the lab test scale.

■ **The English building reg requirement within the home (E2):** adds insulation in joist space and a ceiling board that is slightly heavier than we have been getting used to. British Gypsum has a product called Wallboard Ten (because it weighs 10 kg/m²) which is the building reg requirement. Cost: zero. Hoped for decibel reduction: 40dB. You can improve this rating a little by putting in more insulation into the joist space. Don't pack it tight – 80% depth is reckoned to be ideal for sound absorption.

■ **Add a carpet and underlay above**. Dramatic improvement in impact sound going down. Slight improvement in airborne sound coming up! If you really don't want carpet upstairs, add a resilient layer (an acoustic underlay) between the chipboard and the floor cover. Acoustilay and Ecoustic are two brand names costing between £10 and £20/m², depending on your spec. Reduces sound transmission by around 5dB.

■ **Use two layers of plasterboard**

or a heavier building board such as Fermacell on the ceiling. Added cost, maybe £5/m². Sound transmission reduction: 3dB.

■ **Improve this by a further 2dB** by introducing resilient bars, fixed to the underside of the joists. You fix the plasterboard to the resilient bars. These metal strips, costing just 65p/lin m, act to separate the ceiling boards from the floor joists. Isolation is one of the keys to improving sound insulation. The very best way of building isolation into a floor is to separate the ceiling joists from the floor joists, but this makes for a lot of extra work and a very deep floor void.

■ **Add a floating floor above.** There are numerous proprietary acoustic floor systems on the market: the insulation manufacturers all seem to make them, as do the plasterboard makers. They are rated either lightweight - aimed at impact noise mainly – or heavyweight. The heavyweight ones are usually made up of layers of heavy board products with names like SoundPlank. Overall, with attention to flanking sounds as well, heavy floating floors will add about 5dB to decibel reduction, cost maybe £5/m² and add 50mm to your floor depth.

PRECAST CONCRETE FLOORS

As a complete alternative, you can switch to a masonry floor system. You see an immediate substantial jump in airborne sound reduction between floors, of the order of 15dB, though impact sound reduction requires a bit more thought. However, there is also a substantial cost penalty

Chapter 7

FIRST FLOOR COSTS per m^2

	Mats	Time in mins	Labour @ £20/hr	M^2 rates
Joists	£18	45	£17	£35
I beams	£20	30	£11	£31
T&G Chipboard	£11	15	£6	£17
Weatherdeck 22mm	£17	15	£6	£22
Acoustic Quilt	£3	10	£4	£7
Acoustic Upgrades for Party Floors	£22	40	£15	£37
Beam and block (above ground floor)	£25	35	£13	£38
Hollow core	£40	30	£11	£51
Readymixed cement screed 65mm	£8	20	£7	£15
Gypsum screeds 50mm	£20 supply and fix only			£20
First Floor Options per m^2				
Timber or I beam floors to 40dB (Part E2)				£60
Timber or I beam floors to Party Floor standard				£100
Beam and Block floor with screed to 40db (Part E2)				£50
Beam and Block floor with screed to Party Floor Standard				£55
Hollow core floor with screed (all versions meet Party Floor standard)				£66

MODEL HOUSE: Floor Costs

Construction specified		Materials	Labour	Total
Timber Joists with Acoustic Insulation	m^2			
under 22mm Weatherdeck	Rates	£ 49	£ 31	£ 79
Floor Area in m^2	**80**	**£ 3,900**	**£ 2,500**	**£ 6,400**

for switching away from timber or I-beam joists.

As with ground floors, the choice is either a beam and block floor or a hollow core plank floor. The planks are better acoustically but are more expensive and are more taxing to install; they require double thickness supporting walls unless the planks span between external walls. Both masonry systems can perform well but beam and block in particular is prone to catastrophic acoustic failures. Why? Because the blocks get left out. Or taken out to make a path for plumbing or soil stacks. Whatever you make a floor out of, if you start punching holes in it, it won't work.

You also have to pay attention to how best to finish a masonry floor. Underneath, you have a problem in that you need a service void in which to run lighting cables. You can either fix battens into the floor or hang the plasterboard off special clips. Above, you have a problem with the camber on the floor beams and the manufacturers want you to lay a screed. Fine, if you want underfloor heating, but expensive if you don't.

Interestingly, the cost of installing a precast intermediate floor is not dissimilar to improving a timber floor to the standard of a precast one.

ACOUSTIC FLOORING

An innovation I first came across in 2008 is a flooring system that combines the simplicity of timber I-beams with an anhydrite screed covering, making it ideal for sound reduction and also underfloor heating. A floor which behaves like a solid concrete floor, designed to be built into a lightweight timber frame construction. Check out Screedflo dB and Lewis Decking.

PARTY FLOORS

Having gone into some detail on how to improve sound insulation levels on intermediate floors, it's worth adding that if you are involved in constructing party floors – that is floors between flats - you have to meet some very tight sound reduction standards. And you will very possibly be asked to have your floor (and party walls) tested to see if they work as designed. See the section called 'Sound Advice' in the last chapter to find out more.

Also note a couple of little points. First, carpet still works pretty well as a sound-proofer. I know it's out of fashion but a good carpet laid over a thick underlay does wonders for keeping the noise down, at least as good as many of the other more expensive solutions I have been writing about. And downlighters. Very fashionable, I know. But making holes in the ceiling is bad news noise-wise.

FLOOR FINISHES

The lowest grade of timber floor covering in widespread use, chipboard, is made out of tiny wood particles suspended in a sea of glue. It's around half the price of the much stronger plywood but is not nearly as durable. The NHBC requires that all chipboard used in new housing should be moisture resistant, but this is far from being weatherproof and it is not recommended that chipboard be built into a house before the structure is watertight – but nevertheless it regularly is.

Chipboard is now frequently laid as part of a floating floor: that is to say that it is laid – or rather wedged-in without any fixings at all – on top of polystyrene floor insulation sheets on the ground floor, or acoustic insulation sheets on intermediate floors.

Problems have been encountered with chipboard sheeting curling at the edges and with sheets getting wet and consequently expanding and cracking walls above. In theory, there is much to recommend floating chipboard floors, especially where a carpeted finish is required, and costs are no higher than the traditional cement screed topping given to ground floors. In practice it pays to use the technique with caution; lay timber battens underneath where extra support is needed such as underneath stud walls, at external doorways and at the foot of staircases.

Engineered joists like these Posi-Joists don't twist or splay or squeak and they are very easy to run services through.

INTERNAL WALLS

The traditional routine for internal partition walls is to build blockwork walls downstairs and timber studwork upstairs. Internal studwork is a little cheaper and quicker to build than blockwork. By the way, don't assume from this that timber frame houses are cheaper to build than block built ones: the external walls are slightly more expensive to build than their blockwork equivalents.

If you opt for studwork, then you have another choice to make; timber or steel? The use of lightweight steel channel is gaining momentum with the major housebuilders. When you have people who know what they are doing and a decent sized run of a few houses, then steel framed walling systems are cheaper than timber or block. GypFrame is the best known system. Increasingly, we are seeing dry lining gangs offering a steel stud wall installations service as well as plasterboarding.

Which to choose? Well the main issues to consider here are load-bearing and sound. Do you need internal load-bearing walls?

Most two storey houses with spans of more than 5 m (which is most of them) will require some way of taking the load of the first floor joists: if the span is more than 5 or 6 m, then you can't run joists (or concrete floors) across the gap without a break, and that break has to be either a load-bearing wall or a structural beam.

Now you can have internal load-bearing walls built in timber - most timber frame houses do just that - but conventionally you need to add extra support down at foundation level, usually in the form of a trench foundation. So you can see that load-bearing walls are quite a bit more expensive to build than simple partition walls.

At roof level, the issue is rarely critical because most roofs are designed to spread the load from side to side, across the wallplates, so no load gets transferred down to internal walls. This is why traditionally internal partition walls are blockwork downstairs and timber stud upstairs. We are beginning to go around in circles!

SOUND ISSUES

Builders instinctively go for blockwork if load-bearing capacity is important. The other reason why they like blockwork is of course soundproofing. Generally a block wall is pretty good at soundproofing between rooms. The current building regulations call for a minimum of 40dB sound resistance which, in truth, isn't very difficult or exacting. If you are building in timber or steel channel, you will have to add a little insulation into the void and use a slightly heavier than normal plasterboard (such as British Gypsum's Ten). To improve on this, fix double thickness boards to each face of the wall. Or switch to a much heavier building board such as Fermacell, popular in any event with selfbuilders because it's much easier to finish than plasterboard.

You can go to great lengths to soundproof your bedroom walls but bear in mind that a bedroom is only as soundproof as its weakest link and that's usually the door. Unless you go to the considerable expense of fitting an acoustic doorset, then you'd probably do well not to get too fussed about the whole process. Other design tips are to place built-in cupboards between rooms you want to isolate, and to avoid placing electrical switches and socket plates in noise-sensitive walls.

STEEL BEAMS

Every designer will tell you that you can build rooms to any size that you want – 'your imagination is the limit'

or some such nonsense. But they may not explain that once a room gets wider than the normal span for a floor joist you will run into extra costs because you have to fit a beam across the middle to split the loading. This width varies with the size and frequency of the floor joists, but once you get over 4 m, your costs start to rise substantially. Well, they do if you are working with timber joists: some of the alternative materials mentioned in the flooring section (i.e. concrete precast floors and timber I beams) are capable of much longer spans.

Steel beams themselves are not wildly expensive but fixing them is a lot of work, no matter which method you use. If they are set inside the floor void, the floor joists will all have to be hung off the steel; if the steel is put below the ceiling then it will have to be boxed in with plasterboard.

Steel also needs looking after; it needs a coat of paint and it needs protecting from the threat of fire – usually this is achieved by fixing two thicknesses of plasterboard around it, although there are fire-proofing paints that can be applied as an alternative. Despite its inherent strength, steel is actually one of the first things to give in a serious fire, so steel beams normally get extra fire protection.

Inserting a steel beam of around 5 m length is likely to add around £300 to construction costs. You will also be required to supply calculations to prove that the beam is adequate for the span: a structural engineer will need to be hired and this may well cost more than the beam itself.

Note that if you plan to fit a mechanical ventilation system in your new home, you need to ensure that there is a route through any steel beams that might effectively divide the floor void into two. A good plan will know where your duct runs will be placed and allow for a hole in a steel beam to push the ducts through.

OTHER BEAMS

Timber framers tend to use specialised beams when they want to create wider than average rooms. If you are using a post and beam system of construction such as employed by some timber frame companies like Potton Timber or Border Oak, the solution comes complete with the house as they use the massive post and beam timbers to hang the rest of the house off.

A more usual situation is to use a flitch beam, which is a piece of steel sandwiched between timbers. Flitch beams can be made up on site and are subject to the same sort of cost provisos as regular steel beams. There are various other types and styles of timber beam available; one worthy of mention is the glulam (pronounced glue-lam) beam that is made up of hundreds of small timber sections glued and laminated together. Glulam beams are rather more expensive than steel on a strength for price basis, but they look good, good enough to leave exposed even though they look a little too modern for some traditional tastes. Most specialist timber merchants will stock several sizes from around £20–£50/lin m. depending on girth.

INTERNAL WALLS Key Rates per m²

	Basic Mats	Acoustic Insulation	Accessories	Combined Materials	Time in mins (inc insulation)	Labour @ £20/hr	Combined Rates
100mm Blockwork	£12		£2	£14	35	£ 15	£ 29
90mm Timber Studwork	£6	£3	£1	£10	28	£ 12	£ 22
Steel Channel (with 15mm Soundblock)	£3	£3	£6	£12	20	£ 8	£ 20
add Acoustic Upgrades for Timber or Steel Party Walls				£8	30	£ 13	£ 21

MODEL HOUSE: Internal Wall Costs

	Area in m²	Rate	Materials	Labour	Cost
Masonry Walls	70	£ 29	£ 1,000	£ 1,100	£ 2,100
Timber Stud walls	60	£ 22	£ 600	£ 700	£ 1,300
		Total	£ 1,600	£ 1,800	£ 3,400

ROOF CARCASSING

There are two major competing techniques for building roofs. Traditionally, roof timbers were measured, cut and assembled on site – a skilled job involving complex setting-out procedures and cutting lots of obscure angles and notches. Traditional roof carpentry is an art form in itself and it has its own rich jargon involving the likes of rafters, purlins, collars and birdsmouths. However, the rise of the prefabricated roof truss is slowly but surely putting an end to all this. With trussed roofs, the brainwork is done by computer, the cutting by machine and the jargon is reduced to fink and fan, the two commonest truss designs. Erecting a series of roof trusses is generally a straightforward matter – hoist them into place, straighten them up, nail them on and add diagonal bracing.

On a simple rectangular box-shaped structure, roof trusses are about three times quicker to erect than traditional roofs and, because of the inherent strength of each individual truss, they use considerably less timber – usually about 30% less by volume.

Whereas traditional cut roofs are built from sawn carcassing, readily purchased from any builder's merchant, trussed roofing tends to get fabricated by specialists. Not that this should present a problem to builders: provided you can present a set of dimensioned plans, you will get a quote back usually within a few days. You can contact specialists or you can take your plans to any builder's merchant who will do the donkey work for you.

If you choose to build using trusses, bear in mind that prefabricated roof trusses are sensitive things and they perform well only if they are treated well:

■ care should be taken not to put any twist or undue load on to them, both whilst being handled and when being stored before erection
■ they should be stored upright on bearers (not standing on their feet)
■ they should never be altered on site. They can't be cut around chimneys and openings, so you must get the plan accurately built

Another tip is to set the truss spacings as accurately as possible using a 600mm spacing. This will pay dividends when it comes to tacking the metric length plasterboard sheets to the ceilings formed by the trusses.

So why doesn't everybody use roof trusses? Well, mostly they do but there are some situations where the traditional cut roof holds sway:

■ roof truss manufacturers sometimes get very busy and cannot deliver for several weeks
■ complicated roof shapes take longer to build whichever system you use and the difference in erection speeds – which is the trusses' big selling point – is much less marked.

Consequently, many builders specify trusses for their main roofs, but prefer to stick with the traditional methods when it comes to odd jobs like building dormer windows, porches or garages.

Chapter 7

STEEL LINTELS: key rates		
• Convention is that they need 150mm bearing at each end		
• Thus 1200mm wide window requires 1500mm lintel, or 1.!		
• These costs are averages per metre run		
Regular Type	£ 38	m
Heavy Duty	£ 49	m
Box Type (internal)	£ 17	m
Timber Frame Type	£ 14	m
Single Skin for Garage	£ 56	m
Masonry Cast Cills	£ 30	m

INTERNAL STEEL BEAMS

• Av metre run prices for shotblasted and painted channels		
Heavy duty RSJ (ie UB 203x133x30kg)	£ 47	per metre run
Lighter RSJ for short spans <4m (203x102x23kg)	£ 40	per metre run
Labour to set	£ 100	each

MODEL HOUSE: Steel and Lintel Costs

	Total Length	Materials	Labour	Total
2 Universal Beams (RSJs)	8m	£ 320	£ 200	£ 520
15 No External Lintels	25m	£ 900	n/a	£ 900
5No Internal box lintels (downstairs only)	7.2m	£ 100	n/a	£ 100
	Total	£ 1,320	£ 200	£ 1,520

ATTIC TRUSSES

There is another reason why many builders dislike the trussed roof; it effectively eliminates use of the loft space for anything other than storage. The cross-members, which make up each truss cannot easily be removed or altered and this makes it much harder and more expensive to open up the roof space at a later date.

There is, however, the possibility of using specialised attic trusses, which are designed to leave the main loft space open so that any future loft conversion can be arranged with a minimum of fuss and expense. However, whilst the speed of installation is maintained, attic trusses are between two and three times the price of regular ones and this means

that they effectively lose their cost advantage over traditionally cut roofs.

ROOM-IN-THE-ROOF DESIGNS

Where overall roof heights are restricted, it is common to build the upper storey of a house projecting partly into the roofspace. When added to an existing dwelling this is usually referred to as a loft conversion but in a new build the convention is to give the upper floor at least a metre of vertical wall before the sloping (or raked) ceiling cuts in. This type of design is sometimes known as a one-and-a-half storey house.

If you are going for a room in the roof design – and many timber frame companies specialise in this style of home – there are a number of knock-on effects which you should

be aware of. The internal sloping ceilings on these houses greatly limit what goes on underneath them; beds are usually OK, cupboards are difficult and planning a bathroom in such a space is something you should consider very carefully. You can end up with a lot of expensive dead space; you may like the idea of under-eaves cupboards or a basin in a sloping alcove, but you'll probably live to regret it and end up wishing for convenience rather than character.

When comparing floor space costs, consider space under raked ceilings to be worth considerably less than space with full-height ceilings.

The prefabricated roof truss works most effectively when you are designing roofs that sit entirely above the upstairs room space. Then the horizontal section of the trusses can sit directly onto the wallplates at the top of the surrounding walls and form the ceiling joists for the upstairs rooms. When you introduce a raked ceiling you change the truss loadings and start having to use much wider rafter sections, and if you have long sloping ceilings you will have to introduce a midway support beam known as a purlin. In effect you are back to constructing a traditional roof, so again the supposed economies of prefabricated trusses largely disappear.

However, there are roofing systems appearing now which address these problems, replacing rafters altogether with a series of insulated panels stretching from the ridge down to the eaves, with no timber cross supports. It's a variation on the theme of using attic trusses to create an open space in the roof but its selling point is that it is lightweight and quick to install. We are essentially talking about SIPS construction here (see section under Inner Skins, where it's used as load-bearing walling). There used to be specialist SIPS roofing businesses about but these days you would do best to locate a more generalist SIPS supplier/installer.

ROOF CARPENTRY COSTS per m^2

• *Roof areas measured 'in plan': that is to say, the roof pitch is ignored*

	Materials	Time in minutes	Labour @ £20/hr	Combined
Traditional or cut roof	£ 30	110	£ 40	£ 70
Fink Truss Roof	£ 25	40	£ 15	£ 40
Attic Truss Roof	£ 45	40	£ 15	£ 60
Panelised roof (simple design)	£ 50	12	£ 4	£ 54

MODEL HOUSE: Roof Carpentry Costs

• *Note these are 'in plan' measurements*

Plan Area in m^2	Rate	Materials	Labour	Total
House Roof Area (Trusses) 100	£ 40	£ 2,500	£ 1,500	£ 4,000
Total		£ 2,500	£ 1,500	£ 4,000

VAULTED CEILINGS

Some designs call for the room in the roof idea to be extended all the way up to the ridge beam at the apex of the roof. Here you have no flat ceiling area at all. This is a visually dramatic effect, often employed in barn conversions and new oak buildings where you have attractive timber rafters which are worth displaying in their own right. This is a world away from prefabricated roofing trusses, employing techniques of roof design similar to those used in mediaeval times.

ROOF WINDOWS

Once you have opted for a room in the roof design, you have to sort out how you will treat the windows for these rooms. When your natural window height coincides with a sloping ceiling you have two choices. You can 'go with the roofline' and fit a sloping rooflight window or you can 'break through the roofline' and build a dormer.

A dormer window is a fiddly construction. However it is formed, it involves building a sort of miniature

house with walls, roof and a window and then joining it seamlessly on to the main roof structure. Whilst this may appeal to the model makers amongst you, harassed builders in a hurry will not appreciate all this intricate detailing.

People buying kit homes with dormers placed on the roof might think that they are avoiding all this hassle, but they will find that finishing dormer details is still a time-consuming business. The roofers have to form valleys and often stepped lead flashings, plasterers or bricklayers have to come back to fill in tiny wall spaces on the outside, and even tacking plasterboard on the inside calls for an ability to think three dimensionally. Another pitfall associated with some dormer designs occurs when they break the eaves gutter line of the main house, which results in extra rainwater downpipes; I have seen various ways people have tried to disguise this detail but none of them look particularly convincing.

Planners permitting, you can of course forget about dormers and fit

opening roof lights. Velux is the big name in this field (though there are several others) and Velux rooflights are very quick and easy to install; on a new building an opening rooflight will cost between £250 and £500 depending on size and will add virtually nothing to labour cost – it taking no longer to install than it does to fit the roof covering over the same space. In comparison, a simple dormer is likely to cost over £2,000. It may well be that your overall desired effect demands dormer windows in your roof and, if so, so be it. Just be aware that these types of windows (like bay windows) are not only expensive in themselves but are also heavy on management time. Unless very well planned out, they are more than likely to cause snags further on down the line.

If you are converting a barn you are likely to find that the planners will not allow dormer windows and will force you to use a rooflight. In response to this, Velux have produced a range of conservation rooflights that are designed to blend in with centuries-

Roof Carpentry Jargon Buster

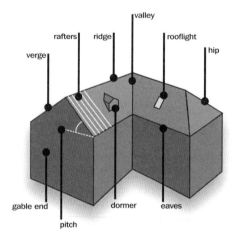

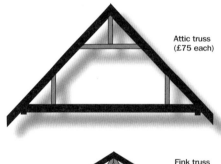

Attic truss
(£75 each)

Fink truss
(£25 each)

A medium sized 350mm light pipe will produce much more light than a 100W bulb even on a dull winter's day and will be adequate to light a room up to 15m². At around £400, they are similar in cost to rooflights but they can have advantages in certain situations - you can bend the pipes round corners if necessary.

EDGE DETAILS

One important detail to consider when thinking about roof designs is how to treat the roof edges. The ridges, hips and valleys will be sorted out by the roofing contractors, but the eaves and verge details are largely a matter of roof carpentry. Here, it makes no difference whether you've built a traditional cut roof or a trussed rafter one; you still have to sort out some sort of effective junction between the roof cover and the underlying structure.

EAVES

There are numerous variations on this theme, none of which is likely to cost less than about £20/lin m to fix (excluding decorating costs). If there is an industry standard detail it is closed or boxed eaves. The vertical section is the fascia board: the horizontal bit under it, returning to the wall, is the soffit. One of the emerging trends here is for builders to use uPVC sections. uPVC has all but taken over the guttering and downpipe market and it's a small step to switch from timber to uPVC for the supporting fascia boards as well.

An alternative is to have open eaves. These are reckoned to look less

old buildings whilst still providing ease of opening and double-glazing expected of modern roof windows. These conservation rooflights are however priced at a 30% premium to standard rooflights.

SUNPIPES

For those of you still in the dark, a sunpipe or light pipe is a highly reflective tube that allows you to pipe daylight from a roof down into the house. What you actually see is a transparent dome sitting on your roof and a translucent light diffuser – looking for all the world like an electric lampshade – fitted onto the ceiling of the room below. What you get is a credible amount of natural daylight into the darkest recesses of your home.

modern and often more attractive. Some designs dispense with fascia boards altogether and allow guttering to be strapped on to the rafter feet - this is a particularly useful technique to employ with timber barn conversions where a fascia would look out of place - but the more usual method dispenses with just the soffit boards and leaves the rafter feet exposed. An open eaves detail is a little more expensive than boxed or soffitted eaves as you still have to provide a plywood plate (albeit above the rafter feet to catch the felt) and you are left with fiddly finishing details on the exposed underside.

More expensive still is to use the Georgian-style parapet. Here you build your external walls up above the eaves line and collect the rainwater draining off the roof in a hidden lead gutter behind the parapet. This technique was once common in inner-city housing terraces and large country houses, but nowadays tends to look a little bit pretentious – unless you happen to be building a large Georgian-style house.

VERGES

Verges are only found over gable ends, so many houses without gables will have only eaves details. There are, again, two classic treatments of verge junction details. One is to lay the tiles or slates straight on to a bead of cement at the top of the supporting gable wall, the other is to oversail the wall and to finish the roof cover over a (usually timber) bargeboard. Each technique has its merits. The direct method can look horribly cheap but, equally well, is capable of being

I was a little dubious about sunpipes but my architect persuaded us to fit them over a couple of dark corners and I have been impressed by the amount and quality of light they produce. Such a simple idea — just a mirrored tube, capped top and bottom. To work well, you need to pay close attention to insulation around them.

enhanced by using some fancy dog's-tooth brickwork: the bargeboard method is rather easier to install (it too can be enlivened by adding decorative effects).

ROOF VENTILATION

It is surprising to many people that roof timbers do not need to be treated with preservatives (unless you live in a long-horn beetle area, mostly south of London) but you do need to consider moisture penetration very carefully.

For a conventional trussed roof, where the upstairs living space does not project into the roofspace, the ventilation requirements are satisfied

by the provision of a 10mm continuous air gap all the way around the eaves. You might think that this is a very straightforward matter, but there is also concern that a ventilation gap shouldn't become an open doorway to birds and insects, and therefore there has grown up a whole industry making plastic roof vents that let air in and keep bugs out. There are several different types; some are cut into the soffit boards, some are nailed on top of the fascia and some get fixed between the rafters.

RIDGE VENTILATION

When you have a room in the roof design, roof ventilation becomes a more complex problem and care has

Framed constructions designs, which includes most roofs, used to pay much attention to vapour barriers, but these days the emphasis has moved on to air barriers which are installed to a more exacting standard. The joist ends cannot pierce the barrier and the barrier joints have to be taped. The air pressure test which follows measures the success of each installation, one of the very few in situ tests which show how well constructed a house actually is.

to be taken to leave an airflow gap between the roofing felt and the insulation surrounding the living space. There is also a requirement for ventilation at the top of the roof, the ridge, and this can be expensive to achieve.

One way of achieving this is to fit a ventilated ridge, a plastic extrusion which fits under the ridge tiles: this has the advantage of being visually unobtrusive but it comes at a cost of around £20/lin m, much more than the cost of the ridge tiles themselves. Alternatively

there are several formats of ridge ventilation tiles now available: they are invariably expensive – expect to pay between £30 and £50 each – and unlike the dry ridge systems they are all too obvious from the ground.

Roof or ridge vented tiles are also useful with an internal soil pipe or an extractor fan both of which can be ducted up through the roof space. Glidevale produce the most complete catalogue of roof ventilation and also some of the best solutions for these types of problems.

If you are working with a handmade tile, Tudor Roof Tiles produce an almost-invisible venting system that uses the natural camber present on most handmade tiles to provide adequate ventilation space to take the foul air away from extractor fans and soil pipes.

UNVENTED ROOFS

If all this ventilation seems to be more trouble than it's worth, then you'll want to know about other options. In fact, if you were building a room-in-the-roof design then you would also be well advised to use an alternative because they are likely to be cheaper and easier.

If you are building a new house with a pitched roof, you will find that there simply isn't the depth of rafter to stuff insulation in and still have room for a 50mm vent gap under the roof. But just when all seems lost, Tyvek and the breathable membranes ride in to the rescue. These materials are at once waterproof and vapour permeable and their manufacturers have convinced the authorities that if you specify one of these so-called breathable membranes instead of traditional roofing felt, then you don't need to have the 50mm vent gap within the rafter space and you don't need to worry about eaves and ridge ventilation. Although they are expensive compared to roofing felt, you claw this money back by saving on other materials.

It's not quite true to say you don't need a vent gap at all because most designs call for counter battening under

Contrast these two roofs. Both are 'room in the roof' designs but the one on the right uses attic trusses, while the one on the left is built on site. They both might have used attic trusses but on the site above the builder was told there would be a delay of several weeks to get trusses on site – so he hand built it instead

the tiles or slates – this effectively gives you a vent gap on the outside of the roof, above the rafter line.

There are many variations on the unvented roof design, sometimes known as a warm roof design. It's complicated in Scotland by the requirement for roof sarking, which is a layer of solid timber boarding traditionally nailed over the rafters. However, the insulation manufacturers and the breathable membrane suppliers all have details showing ways of satisfying both the U-value requirements and moisture management – every roof design has to pass what is called a Condensation Risk Analysis.

CONDENSATION PROBLEMS

A little discussed but widespread problem concerns condensation in lofts. It's a feature of cold roofs where there is unused loftspace. The insulation gets placed at ceiling level, leaving a large mass of air inside the roof but outside the heated envelope of the building. Roofs such as these require venting at eaves level – already covered – but this isn't always enough to stop condensation.

The roof cover itself can get very, very cold, especially on clear cold nights, and the moisture in the air in the loft finds a dew point under the felt where it proceeds to drip down onto the ceiling. It seems to make no difference whether you fit felt or a breathable membrane.

The most effective solution is to build in some form of ridge venting. Combined with the eaves venting, this creates a stack effect that keeps the air flowing through the loft. Without ridge vents, the air inside the loft frequently hangs around for a long time.

Guidance on condensation in new roofs has changed in 2011 so that it's no longer adequate just to fit a breathable membrane under the roof with eaves vents. High-level or ridge venting is required as well.

ROOF COVERS

There are many different materials used to cover roofs but before we go on to examine them, consider first that most housing estates in the country have a concrete tiled roof. Why? Simply a question of cost – concrete tiles are an amazingly cheap way to provide a roof cover and, designed well, they can look effective. Sometimes but not, unfortunately, always.

The cheapest way to cover a roof is to first have a shallow pitch and secondly to cover it with a big tile. Shallow pitches give you less roof to cover and big tiles are cheap to make and cheap to lay. End of.

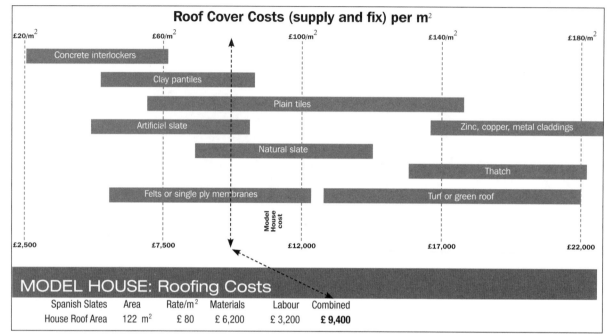

Roof Cover Costs (supply and fix) per m²

£20/m²	£60/m²	£100/m²	£140/m²	£180/m²

Concrete interlockers

Clay pantiles

Plain tiles

Artificial slate

Zinc, copper, metal claddings

Natural slate

Thatch

Felts or single ply membranes

Turf or green roof

Model House cost

£2,500	£7,500	£12,000	£17,000	£22,000

MODEL HOUSE: Roofing Costs

Spanish Slates	Area	Rate/m²	Materials	Labour	Combined
House Roof Area	122 m²	£ 80	£ 6,200	£ 3,200	**£ 9,400**

Only its not, because visually they also look pretty naff. Ok-ish on the roof of a Tesco, not so great on the roof of a house. There is a polite convention that you don't put massive tiles on top of homes.

Traditionally, the tile used on homes in most of Southern England was made of clay. Clay looks good and it weathers well in a way that concrete doesn't so a clay tile will hold its value far better, for the same reason that clay bricks will — you rarely see a concrete brick. But clay tiles are more expensive to make than concrete so clay is always seen here as an upmarket option.

The large format or interlocking tiles (so beloved of Tesco's and the other supermarkets) often measure 330x270mm, the size of six plain tiles; you don't need very many and this fact

alone makes them much quicker to lay. Large format tiles start losing their cost advantage on complex roof shapes with lots of cuts, so you tend to see them on very simple roof designs.

Small format tiles, known as plain tiles, are available from a wide range of suppliers in both concrete and clay. At the top end of the plain tile market come the handmade clay tiles: these are something else and, like handmade bricks, they tend to lend a strong vernacular flavour to any building they are put on. However, handmade clay tiles are also amazingly expensive, costing around five times as much to supply and fix as the basic concrete interlocking tile.

The roof tile market in the UK is dominated by two giants, Redland (now part of Monier) and Marley Eternit. Redland sets the standards to

which others aspire and if you want to get a better understanding of the possibilities with tile coverings, you should get hold of their Pocket Guide to Roofing; it's free, downloadable as a PDF, and it's an incredibly useful booklet which will tell you more than you will ever want to know about roof tiling. Redland tends to be more expensive than the competition (at least on single site developments) and you may find better prices if you chase Marley roofing or one of the smaller manufacturers such as Sand toft or Russell.

Most roofing contractors have cosy relationships with one particular manufacturer and you may well find that it pays you not to be too picky as to whose tile goes on your roof. Handmade tiles tend to be the province of smaller producers: if you have a deep wallet, look at Keymer and Tudor, who produce visually stunning roof tiles that are brand new yet manage to look at least 200 years old.

If you crave the look of a traditionally tiled roof but your budget doesn't stretch that far, Ibstock produce a large format concrete tile called the Gemini, which simulates the plain tile look by planting a groove down the middle of a large format tile. Slightly more expensive but arguably better looking comes Sandtoft's 20/20 and HF's Beauvoise, imported from France: both are middle format clay tiles.

SLATE

Not all tiles are manufactured. Slate became the preferred roofing choice of the Victorians when the railways provided access to the cheap Welsh slate quarries. The Welsh slate is still there in Snowdonia but it is no longer cheap; indeed it is up there with handmade tiles, zinc and thatch as one of the most expensive options for the pitched roof. In rural areas, slate is unlikely to be most people's first choice. However, planners often insist on slate roofs for the flimsiest of reasons and it is as well to be aware of that possibility.

If you want slate but are reluctant to pay the going rate for new Welsh slate, there are a number of other options. You can look to source your slate from Spain or even further afield: prices are much cheaper than Welsh slate but quality has been patchy and it's worth looking out for slate carrying a 30-year guarantee. Alternatively you can track down

a supplier of second hand slate. Prices are similar to imported slate and quality is similarly variable but, if you know what to look for, it's relatively easy to assess the quality of a recycled slate and it can make a very good buy. There are also a number of slate substitutes on the market. The cheapest are the fibre cement slates but these are liable to warp and discolour over time.

There are also a number of manufactured slate products, usually made out of reconstituted slate dust. Redland produce the best-known reconstituted slate tile called the Cambrian. It is a mid-priced alternative to the natural slates and unimpressive artificials. However, many planning officers will insist on you using natural slates, even though they couldn't tell the difference when laid on a roof.

Then again, you could stop messing around and just fit Welsh slate. The reason it's more expensive is that it's simply better than the alternatives and that's entirely down to geology. If you are looking for a reasonably local, thoroughly natural and incredibly durable roof covering, Welsh slate is the one.

STONE BELT ROOFING

Don't think that you can get away with just a stone facade if you live in an area where stone is the predominant building material. For sure, you will be required to lay a stone tile roof to match your neighbours. Local material prices vary from quarry to quarry but are invariably high. There are numerous

cheaper, artificial alternatives around that will not look in the least bit convincing but using them may save you several thousand pounds. Again you face a tricky task reconciling your budget with the demands of your local planners.

SHINGLES

Another old vernacular stand-by is the cedar shingle. A shingle is a tile fashioned out of cedar wood and is usually supplied in random widths to give a broken up effect. It is a reasonably hard wearing material – though not as good as clay, slate or concrete – and it is used just as often to do vertical wall panels as it is pitched roofing. Cedar is a naturally durable timber that doesn't require any treatment or staining, and if you covet a genuine timber house then shingles will be your chosen roofing material.

THATCH

This is really one for enthusiasts but new thatched homes are getting built in small but increasing numbers. Not only is it very expensive, but there are numerous regulations about where thatch can go on new buildings. The one that used to trip people up was a requirement for thatched roofs to be at least 12 metres from another house but if you pay close attention to the internal fire proofing arrangements, using a set of guidelines known as the Dorset model, you should find that this requirement can be relaxed. Thatch is not something that can be added as an afterthought; if you are really

Chapter 7

Coursed stone tiling: the courses get narrower as you move up the roof. An attractive vernacular feature but time consuming and therefore expensive to achieve

serious about it you must design the roof around the thatch. You are more likely to come across thatch if you are involved in renovating or converting.

METAL ROOFING

If you really want to be on trend, then metal, preferably zinc, is the material of choice. A standing seam zinc roof is a thing of beauty, especially if the detailing is crisp and sparse. Getting it right is not straightforward and metal roofers are still hard to find and can demand a very high fee for their services.

To get a handle on the way metal roofs work, you need to look at one of the websites that distributes the metals. The one I used was Metra Metals who stock copper and stainless steel as well as zinc from the two main suppliers, Rheinzink and VM Zinc. There's rather more

to it than just fixing zinc to a roof. You have to decide whether to have a warm roof or a cold roof. The purists like cold roofs and if you go this way you have to construct a ventilated cavity over the timber roof, itself an expensive and lengthy process as the zinc has to be laid on 18mm or 22mm ply. Plus all these metals (and much of the other roofing products you can get hold of) are sourced outside the UK which makes them even more expensive when our currency nosedives.

ROOF DETAILS

As most roofing is carried out by specialist contractors, usually on a supply and fix basis, there is perhaps not the need to know so much about the intricacies of roofing. However, there is a lot more to a roof than slates or tiles and even thatch or zinc. On a typical detached house

the actual roof tiles may make up no more than 50% of the overall roofing material costs. The most visible additional elements are the ridge and/ or hip tiles (usually around 20% of cost); the underlay and supporting battens are the other significant costs. Ventilation gear, which is often fitted by roofers, is another expensive item.

FELT AND BATTENS

Roofing felt is now rarely used as its been replaced by all manner of clever membranes that promise to be both waterproof and vapour permeable, and sometimes even more. But the practice of covering the roof is still routinely referred to as felting and battening and it is useful for getting a structure wind and watertight, sometimes long before the actual roof cover is applied.

On all but the largest houses, the whole process of felting and battening usually takes roofers no more than a day.

Don't make the mistake of felting and battening before choosing a roof covering: the spacing of the battens is set by the gauge of slate or tile and the gauges are very variable. Note that the Scottish practice is to build a solid timber sarking layer on top of the rafters before laying felts: this adds significantly to the roofing costs but makes a much stronger structure.

HIP TREATMENTS

The hip is the name given to an external angle in a roof – an internal angle is called a valley – and the standard way of finishing a hip is to use something very similar to a conventional ridge tile, although the hipped version is sometimes slightly differently shaped. This is a cheap and quick specification and it is really the only practical way of finishing a concrete interlocking tiled roof.

However, if you are planning on a plain tiled roof there is an alternative, which is to fix bonnets, which look very rural and vernacular. However, bonneted hips are way more expensive both in labour and materials (you'll need something like ten bonnets per linear metre as opposed to two hip tiles).

An even more expensive option, which is most often seen on slate roofs, is to cut the tiles or slates to meet exactly over the hip. This is known as a close-mitred hip and it tends to be preferred by those going for neat, unfussy solutions.

Bonnets and close-mitred hips may sound like unnecessary extravagances, but although they are way more expensive than hip tiles, the total length of hips to cover is often not that much and specifying something different here has a marked effect on kerb appeal.

VALLEYS
Another cost-sensitive area of roofing is the valley, which is formed when two rooflines meet on an internal corner. The valley is not as visually prominent as the hip and this makes it a candidate for treating as cheaply as possible. The commonest way of doing this is by fitting a purpose-made valley gutter and cutting the tiles or slates around it. Here, GRP is tending to replace lead; it's quite a bit cheaper and much quicker to lay but

labour costs are still significant.

On plain tile roofs there is the alternative of using purpose-made valley tiles. These are very similar to inverted bonnet hip tiles. Again, this is an expensive option but it is worth considering around features like dormer windows where the valleys are visible from the ground.

VERGES
The verge is the name given to the junction between a pitched roof and a gable wall. Making this detail weatherproof can be challenging.

The simplest method is to lay a mini-soffit board (known as an undercloak) on top of the brickwork (or timber bargeboard if one is specified), run the roof cover up to the edge of the undercloak and then fill the void between with cement mortar.

There are alternatives. Redland make a concrete wrap-over tile that can be used with certain tile covers and there is even a plastic verge system. However, these other methods all cost around double the cement undercloak technique and they add nothing to the look of your roof edge.

DRY TECH SYSTEMS
The parts of the roof most vulnerable to weather damage are the perimeter areas like ridges, hips and verges. The traditional way of fixing ridge, hip and verge tiles is to bed them in cement. For some time now the tile manufacturers have been trying to persuade us to use dry systems, which clip together with a series of mechanical fixings, but there is a

Hip tiles, £15/m run

Bonnets, £60/m run

Close mitred hips, £80/m run

general reluctance to take up their offers partly because of the higher prices charged for these fittings and partly because the look is even more modern and nondescript than the conventional roof. In Scotland, dry verges are the norm and housebuilders seeking a low maintenance finish are also specifying them – cement fillets on roof edges are notoriously brittle.

Chapter 7

FLAT ROOFING

With modern design in fashion, the popularity of flat roofs is waxing. New materials and techniques are arriving all the time, making this a complex area to understand, and interest in green roofs makes it more complex still.

Mastic asphalt was the first of the manufactured flat roofing materials, first used over 100 years ago. It is a two-layer system, which is hot poured over the roof area. It has many advantages over other systems because it can easily form complex shapes, although these days the roofers tend to steer you towards products like Kemperol, which is a liquid resin-based solution that is applied cold. Whilst this is an undoubted advantage, it is still not that easy to lay. It was described to me as a "combination of fleece and goop which smells quite toxic and gives you 20 minutes to get it right before it goes off."

In the 1950s, the preferred flat roofing method became felt, or built-up multilayer bitumen impregnated felt to give it its correct title . It has been used extensively on flat-roofed extensions during the past 60 years where it grew the reputation for being cheap and cheerful, and good for no more than 15 years. In truth, felt roofing is available in several different configurations, and at each price point, the performance improves so that at the top end it's as good as any of the alternatives. But increasingly builders have been switching to new materials.

At the bottom end, the preference is now for rubber roofs (EPDM). Firestone, the tyre people, are big in this market. The performance of the various rubber roofing products looks very good on paper and the price is very attractive, but they are often sold into the DIY market and many are laid with a brief reference to a YouTube video and no more. Consequently, they are often laid in a sub-optimal way which can lead to issues like ponding and bubbling. Whether Firestone like it or not, EDPM has grown a reputation as a shed roofing material.

The option that has gained the upper hand in the flat roof market are single-ply membranes, often but not always based on PVC and laid cold on a supporting fleece. Sika are big here (with two products Sarnafil and Trocal) as are Bauder and ICOpal. It is not a DIY product as the edgings are penetrations are complex and use heat guns, but the result is usually very good and often come with 25 year guarantees.

Note that if you ask a roofing contractor to quote for a flat roof, you may not get much choice as to what material you get, because they have tie-ins with manufacturers and staff tend to be trained in one system or another. Unlike roof tiles, it's not easy for the contractors to switch to alternative suppliers.

GREEN ROOFS

A popular (and expensive) variation on flat roofing is to place vegetation on the surface. As you might imagine, there is an enormous variety of possibilities here from intensive roof gardens, designed to be walked over and enjoyed as balcony areas, to extensive green roofs which just aim to provide some plant-life (often sedum) which requires little if any maintenance. You don't really want to be up there in the summer with a lawn mower.

The build-up of a green roof involves the use of single-ply membranes for waterproofing and careful attention to drainage and edging details. There is also the issue of the extra loading, which requires stronger supporting joists within in then roof structure. It's not something to fit as an afterthought.

Green roofs aren't for everyone. Ideally you need to be able to see them to enjoy the benefits and many flat roofs are barely visible. They also don't work well with rainwater harvesting, as the run-off water tends to go brown and dirty. On the other hand, green roofs are good at holding onto rainfall and some are even designed to attenuate rainfall to stop flooding. These are technically known as blue roofs.

Green roofs, when done well, are an attractive feature and certainly more interesting than a dull grey felt or membrane roof cover. Whereas most flat roofing methods can be budgeted to cost between £50 and £90/m^2, green roofs start at over £100/m^2 and head north. Whatever system you plump for, the price reflects not just the area but the complexities of the roof. Penetrations, upstands, edgings and corners all add mightily to the base price.

PV ROOFS

PV (photovoltaics) are usually thought of as a something you add to the top of a pitched roof and are considered as an item in the overall energy budget. But PV can be fitted as part of a roof cover in itself and the price has been falling dramatically over the past ten years. In 2018, the cost of a standard PV panel (1650x992mm), had fallen to under £300 and supply and fit prices were still falling. As zinc and metal roofs have been heading up in price towards £200/m², PV installed prices have been heading down towards this figure and it's entirely likely that within the next five years PV will become a competitive roofing materials in its own right. No longer will people be worried about the lack of Feed-in-Tariffs or get fraught working out payback periods. The French do a lot of integral PV roof installations and there are rubber trays (from France) available from the likes of Midsummer Wholesale which you can use to place over the roofing membranes.

A complex edge detail using the PVC single-ply membrane Trocal. These membranes, combined with metallic strips, allow you to form corners and channels which would be very much more difficult with other materials.

RAINWATER

Getting rainwater off roofs and down into the drainage systems is one of the small but very important details that can make or break the appearance of a house. Done well, with appropriate materials, it can add a little to the overall visual appeal of a house. However, done badly, it can ruin a fancy facade. The key to getting the look right is the placing of the downpipes and, as a general rule, the fewer the better.

PLASTIC

The low maintenance, low budget option is plastic (uPVC). There are around half a dozen manufacturers in the UK and they all sell through the builder's merchants. Note that there is a compatibility problem here: even though the designs are very similar, the rival manufacturers' products rarely fit each other, so don't mix and match your guttering. Generally uPVC guttering is available in four colours: black, brown, grey and white. There is also a range of sizes and styles: both half-round and square-box are common plus there are a few more ornate sections such as ogee.

When designing rainwater systems, you have to bear in mind the likely flow rates that naturally tend to vary with the area of roof being drained: if your roof areas are large you may find yourself having to fit more downpipes than you wish and one way around this is to use a larger guttering and downpipe. The manufacturers all hold data to help you specify appropriate sizes. For instance, Osma produce a StormLine gutter section, which will drain over 100m² of roof area, as opposed to the 57m² maximum specified for their

Chapter 7

You don't have to use conventional downpipe in a rainwater system. This is a chain gutter which works just by catching the falling water and directing it down to a drain below. You do need a good overhang to make this work.

There are two perceived drawbacks to using plastic guttering. One is that, as discussed, it all looks a little naff; the other is that it isn't actually any good. uPVC guttering generally, and the rubber jointing gaskets in particular, seem to break down under the effects of bright sunlight and the effective lifespan of a uPVC rainwater system is probably only about 15-20 years. Expect to start replacing bits after this time.

OTHER OPTIONS

All the other options are more expensive but all promise greater durability. The traditional British material used for guttering before the advent of plastic was cast-iron and this is still widely available in a range of period details. It is now mostly used on conservation work and listed buildings. With proper maintenance (which means repainting every five years or so), cast-iron guttering does last a long time – there are many examples of Victorian rainwater systems still in good working order.

Copper is another material, widely used on the Continent. It's very resistant to the elements and doesn't need any painting. Copper of course changes colour over time to eventually achieve a lime-green patina, which will suit some properties better than others. Copper is also used with chain pipes, an interesting technique that does away with the conventional enclosed downpipe and allows the rainwater to run down a chain to the ground - only to be recommended

standard RoundLine section. Now, this guttering is over twice the price of the RoundLine, but specifying it can sometimes actually save money by cutting down on both the number of downpipes and the length of underground drainage work.

Fixing uPVC guttering off scaffolding is at best a semi-skilled job easily mastered by a competent DIYer – the manufacturers all have concise installation guides. But note that whilst it is a relatively easy task to do from scaffolding, it can be a very dangerous and difficult thing to undertake using just a ladder. Also you need to pay attention to the brackets used to hold the gutters and downpipes in place.

There is quite a choice available, designed to cope with the whole range of materials that you may have to fix into or around. There are adjustable brackets available, which can accommodate situations where you are unable to fix into your preferred location — very useful when working with uneven surfaces that you might expect to find on barn conversions or stone buildings.

There is a current trend to install guttering and downpipes together with plastic fascias and soffits: it makes sense, as the work takes place in the same locations. There are businesses such as Floplast which produce all the necessary fittings – i.e. rainwater gear and fascias.

when you have a good overhang on your eaves.

Aluminium and plastic-coated steel are also used. Aluminium now tends to be the province of specialist suppliers who provide seamless welding. Both these systems are available in a wide range of colours and promise many years' maintenance free service.

RAINWATER HARVESTING

There is no reason to stop you putting some of this mildly acidic rainwater to good use before pouring it all away. Many people will be interested in building-in rainwater butts and these can be made much more useful and more productive if they are designed in from the beginning. For around £10, you can add a rain diverter to your downpipes, which will not only redirect your rain into a tank but is also intelligent enough to know when the tank is full and then redirect the rain back down the downpipe.

If you want to use the rainwater for domestic purposes, you are talking more serious underground storage tanks and pumps. A full rainwater harvesting system is expensive to install and needs to be maintained. There is more detail on this and on grey water recycling in Chapter 14, Green Issues.

RAINWATER AND ROOF EDGE: Key Rates

Labour	£22 hr	
Fix Fascia Boards	15	min/m
Fix Soffit Board	30	min/m
Fix Bargeboards	30	min/m
Fix Cappings	15	min/m
Fix Rainwater Goods	30	min/m
Materials		
upvc Rainwater	£15	m
Aluminium Rainwater Gear	£30	m
upvc Fascias and Soffits	£8	m
Timber Box Fascias/Soffits/Bargeboards	£6	m
Stainless steel cappings for timber	£8	m

Key Rates per Lin. M

	Mats	Time in Mins	Labour	Total
Timber Fascias & Soffits	£ 6	45	£ 17	£ 23
Timber Bargeboards	£ 6	30	£ 11	£ 17
uPVC Fascias & Soffits	£ 8	45	£ 22	£ 30
uPVC Rainwater Gear	£ 15	30	£ 11	£ 26
Metal Rainwater Gear	£ 30	30	£ 11	£ 41
Stainless steel cappings	£ 8	15	£ 6	£ 14

MODEL HOUSE: Costs for Fascias, Soffits and Rainwater Gear

	m	Rate	Materials	Labour	Combined
Fascias + Soffits	26	£ 23	£ 160	£ 440	£ 600
Bargeboards	18	£ 17	£ 100	£ 310	£ 410
Guttering & Downpipes	48	£ 26	£ 720	£ 530	£ 1,250
Rounded Total			**£ 1,000**	**£ 1,300**	**£ 2,300**

HEATING & PLUMBING

ON HEAT

Deciding on a heating system is one of the biggest bugbears facing a would-be housebuilder. And it's getting ever more complex, as the new homes we are building require less and less in the way of conventional heating. It's such a complex field and there are so many options available that it is terribly easy to get swamped by the sheer volume of information. It's all very well saying something smarmy like 'You should choose the system that suits you best' but that doesn't actually make it any easier to know what that system might be. There's nothing for it but to start at the beginning. A little background on the physics of heat will improve your understanding of all the areas discussed. Here answered for you are six questions that you'd never even think to ask.

Q1 WHAT IS HEAT?

Heat is a by-product of 'work' going on or, if you like, energy being spent. Heat is most commonly found where one substance is in the process of breaking down into its constituent parts. Our bodies (like our houses) leak heat and this leaked heat must be replaced, which we do by eating. Calories are just another measurement of energy. The colder it is outside our bodies and our houses, the more heat we leak and the more energy we have to take on board.

Q2 WHAT IS FEELING WARM?'

The rate at which we lose heat determines how hot or cold we feel. 'Feeling cold' is a signal that we are losing high and potentially dangerous amounts of heat; 'feeling warm' signals that all is OK.

Q3 WHAT DETERMINES HOW WARM WE FEEL?

- The insulating capability (U value) of our clothes (or duvets, or houses)
- The temperature of the surrounding air
- Wind speed (wind chill factor)
- Level of water vapour around
- Whether our skin is wet or dry
- How much heat is being 'given off' (radiated) by surrounding objects (including the sun).

When assessing heating systems, we use air temperature as the main indicator of background comfort but it is important to be aware that air temperature is just one of several factors at play. Anyone who has ever had a thermostatic control dial in their home will be well aware that what's warm on a dry day can be 2° or 3°C too cold on a wet or a windy day.

Q4 HOW DOES HEAT MOVE?

Heat transfers via three different methods: conduction, convection and radiation. Conduction is the passage of heat through a solid – the classic example is the poker placed in the open fire that soon gets too hot to hold. Convection is what happens to heat when it transfers into a gas (typically air) – it rises. Radiant heat is the glow you feel on your face when you are standing near a bonfire; the air temperature may be minus 10° C but you feel as warm as toast. We don't often feel conducted heat but most heating systems deliver a mixture of the other two, convection and radiation.

Convected heat (or warm air) is characterised by being very responsive – i.e. you feel warm very quickly – but it can also be rather unpleasant, drying the throat and watering the eyes – think of the fan heaters in cars. In contrast, radiant heat you hardly notice. We experience it from things like underfloor heating systems, night storage radiators and Agas. Despite their name, radiators deliver a mix of all three forms of heat. The air convects through them, they are hot to touch (conduction) and you are aware of their warmth if you sit nearby (radiation).

Q5 SO WHAT'S THE PERFECT HEATING SYSTEM?

I haven't really been much help here, have I? You just need to understand that you must make a series of compromises and your aim is to make the least bad compromise.

Q6 SO WATTS IT ALL ABOUT?

Finally a word about how we measure power output, because I know people find it confusing, not least because there are different systems of measurement in operation. By far the easiest one to plump for in the UK today is the watt (W) and its big brother the kilowatt (kW) which is 1,000 watts. These are measurements of power, rather than energy used. If you want a measurement of actual energy used, you need to express it as so much power per hour, which we routinely call the kilowatt hour or kWh.

Why the capital W in the middle of kWh? It's a strange convention to do with the watt being a unit attributed to James Watt, inventor of the steam engine. We seem to routinely refer to watts or kilowatts with a lower case w, but when it's written shorthand it becomes kWh.

To make it even more complex, there are other units used for energy measurements and one you frequently come across is the British Thermal Unit or BTU which, as you might guess is imperial. The Americans still use it. What many people don't realise is that the BTU is a measurement of energy rather than power so it's the equivalent of a kilowatt hour, not the kilowatt. If you want to know the power output of a boiler, you need to divide by hours. Thus:

$$1W = 3.41 \text{ BTU/h}$$
$$1kW = 3,410 \text{ BTU/h}$$

STANDARD HEATING

All this theory is fine but how well does a central heating system stack up? The 'wet' central heating system described below was pretty much standard in British housing between 1970 and fairly recently, both for newbuilds and refurbishments. It may now be under threat from several new fangled systems, but most people would still think of it as the norm. It remains a good place to begin.

HEAT LOSS CALCULATION

You start with a little maths. First you need to know the heating requirement for the house as a whole. The plumber or heating engineer usually carries this task out on a room-by-room basis, working on the size of the room, the number of

HEATING: Key Materials Prices

Gas Combi Boiler + Flue	£ 850
Gas System Boiler + Flue	£ 900
Oil Condensing Boiler + Flue	£ 1,500
170lt Mains Pressure Cylinder	£ 750
Primaries/Valves/Pumps	£ 500
Radiator and Pipework	£ 120
Heating Controls/wiring	£ 200
TRVs	£ 15
Room Thermostats	£ 60
Kilma UFH Electric Heat Mats	£ 20 /m^2
UFH Pipe inc Manifolds & thermostats	£ 35 /m^2
Bunded Oil Tank	£ 1,000

Plumbers rates	£ 40 /hr	Cost
Fit Boiler + Balanced Flue	12 hr	£ 480
Fit Cylinder	8 hr	£ 320
Fit Tanks in Loft	8 hr	£ 320
Run Cold to Loft	4 hr	£ 160
Connect Primary Pipework	8 hr	£ 320
Fix one radiator	1 hr	£ 40
Pipe radiator	1 hr	£ 40
Fit Whole House Heating Controls	6 hr	£ 240
Fit Individual Room Stats	2 hr	£ 80
Commission System	8 hr	£ 320
Place and Plumb-in Oil Tank	6 hr	£ 240
Lay underfloor heating/m^2	24 mins/m^2	£ 16

MODEL HOUSE Heating Costs

	Materials	Labour Hours	@ £40/hr	Combined
Gas Boiler and Flues	£ 850	12	£ 480	£ 1,300
14 Rads	£ 1,890	28	£ 1,120	£ 3,000
Mains Pressure Cylinder	£ 750	8	£ 320	£ 1,100
Controls	£ 260	6	£ 240	£ 500
Primaries (pipework)	£ 500	16	£ 640	£ 1,100
Commission System		8	£ 320	£ 300
Rounded Totals	**£ 4,300**	**78**	**£ 3,100**	**£ 7,400**

outside walls and the insulation levels of the house. The results are used to assess the size of the radiators. The boiler is then sized-up by adding together all the radiator outputs and adding 'a bit.' At least in theory.

As insulation levels have risen over the years, space heating demand has fallen, so the critical factor in deciding boiler size in new homes is now delivery of adequate quantities of hot water to the taps rather than demand from radiators. But the heat loss calcs are still useful in assessing radiator sizes (or for that matter any other type of heat delivery like underfloor heating).

BOILER

The boiler is fitted preferably against an outside wall and the exhaust gases are ducted horizontally outside, by way of a balanced flue. The boiler heats water passing through it and this water is then pumped through the primaries (large copper pipes) and thence to the cylinder and radiators. Or, if it's a combi boiler, directly around the pipes without going through a cylinder of any sort.

CYLINDER

Placed in the airing cupboard, this acts like a giant (bath-sized) kettle for heating domestic hot water (DHW). It starts to empty every time a hot tap is turned on; it is (or was) simultaneously filled from a tank of cold water in the loft space which, in turn, is filled from the water main. The cylinder is indirect which means that the water inside it never passes directly through the boiler but rather gets heated at one stage removed by the boiler water passing through copper loops inside the cylinder. In recent years, almost everyone has moved over to pressurised cylinders which don't require any loft plumbing.

RADIATORS

These are fitted and connected by two copper pipe circuits: one – the flow – takes the hot water from the boiler around the circuit, the other – the return – takes the cooler water coming out of the radiators back to the boiler. A small plastic tank (feed and expansion tank) is placed in the loft which gives the hot water in the circuit space to expand – which it does as it gets hotter. Again, the need for loft plumbing has largely been removed by the switchover to mains pressure systems, but let's not get ahead of ourselves. More on these later.

CONTROLS

The system is electrically pumped to supply even heat around the house. There is a programmer and a thermostat which turn the system on/off and also switch motorised valves so that the hot water pumped from the boiler can be switched between heating the water in the cylinder or circulating around the radiators. The radiators may also have their own thermostatic valves, or TRVs.

LABOUR CONTENT

In a new four-bedroom house, the pipework and control cabling will be 'first fixed' in three to four days; first fixing needs to take place after the structure is up but before the plastering starts. The 'second fix' (including hanging radiators) will take five to six days. Conventionally, the heating engineer also fits the sanitaryware, does the kitchen plumbing and the above ground waste runs, and all this work tends to get lumped into one quotation and carried out together.

THE FABRIC EFFECT

One of the most important things determining your choice of heating system is the energy efficiency of the structure you are trying to heat. The more clothes you wrap around the building, the less heat is required to keep it warm, so the smaller and cheaper your heating system needs to be.

At the extreme end of things – and here we are talking about the most exacting energy efficiency standards around, such as PassivHaus – you can get by without a conventional heating system because 90% of what you require comes from incidental sources; that is people, pets, appliances and lights.

But don't be sucked into thinking you can build a house without any heating. If you go away for a few days in winter, there will be no incidental heat to keep the structure warm in your absence and it really will feel cold on your return. You need to have some method in place to provide space heating, however little you use it.

WHY DO ANYTHING ELSE?

This home heating system still works pretty well for houses that are on the mains gas grid. But if you do not live or plan to build where mains gas is available, the whole issue of home heating becomes a lot more complex. Traditionally, people switched to oil but oil-fired central heating has become more expensive to run over the years and there are now green-tinged incentives to try and persuade everyone to switch to something else.

RENEWABLE HEAT INCENTIVE

This is a subsidy scheme designed to encourage low carbon heating systems, in particular heat pumps, biomass and solar thermal water heating. It operates in England, Scotland and Wales and is administered by OFGEM. It also operates (slightly differently) in N.Ireland but there it is better known as the subject of scandal.

The fine details are to be found on OFGEM's website but the first place to look for information is the excellent YouGen website (www.yougen.co.uk) which puts the latest background information out there to the public together with an overview of who is eligible and who isn't, and what the current tariffs are. The OFGEM site is where you make the application.

The subsidies as of 2019 are set to last for seven years and stand at the following amounts per kWh:

- air source heat pumps 10.5p
- ground source heat pumps 20.4p
- biomass boilers 6.7p
- solar thermal heating 20.6p

Why the difference? Why not just offer the same subsidies and let the market decide which technology is best? Here it gets quite complex because each technology is different. The installation costs are hugely different — think maybe £5,000 for solar panels and maybe £15,000 plus for a ground source heat pump — and the capabilities also vary considerably. For instance, you couldn't hope to heat a house using only solar panels.

What the subsidies are attempting to do is to cover the added costs of

Chapter 8

installing these systems instead of, typically, oil-fired boilers which tend to be what is being replaced here. But the government has chosen to make the payments spread out over seven years, rather than just making a one-off payment.

More on the logic or otherwise of these renewable technologies later. But bear in mind that you are not forbidden from using the old technologies and it's worth having an understanding of what they are.

WHICH FUEL?

MAINS GAS

Piped gas is currently available to around 85% of UK households, which includes almost all urban areas. A quick look at the comparative fuel costs table will show it's still very much the cheapest option. However, large tracts of rural Britain and Ireland are deemed too remote to justify laying gas mains and most of these areas will never have the option of a piped gas supply. Have a look at the website nongasmap.org.uk ; very helpful in this respect. Sometimes an initial enquiry will trigger the offer to extend a gas main along a side road.

Gas has other advantages. You can cook with it for starters. Gas boilers are so commonplace that the market for them is very competitive so prices for new or replacement boilers is very keen. And environmentally, it's relatively clean. Not only is the CO_2 content much lower than it is for oil or coal, it's also got less in the way of toxic particles released when burning.

LPG

Liquid Petroleum Gas is used by gasoholics who live away from the main gas grid. Its big drawbacks are that it has to be delivered by road on a tanker and it has to be stored on site in a bloody great gas tank, though these can be buried underground for a considerable extra expense. The storage tank needs to be 3m from any buildings or boundaries so there are comparatively few sites that it is suited to.

Calor Gas is the biggest supplier and they take on full responsibility for installation and maintenance of tanks. They usually charge around £300 to install a tank: this includes pipe laying to the boiler. Note that alternative suppliers such as Shell sometimes supply tanks for free but you are then bound to use them as suppliers.

Despite having a tiny fraction of the market, LPG versions of many gas boilers are available, though usually at a 10 - 15% premium. Note that LPG can also be used for cooking

OIL

The most common domestic heating oil is known correctly as 28-second burning oil, almost identical to kerosene used by commercial airliners. Like LPG, it has to be delivered to and stored on site but unlike LPG there are numerous players in this market which keeps the prices competitive — you don't have to be tied into one supplier. Indeed, every rural district has a choice of suppliers and there are

frequently buying co-operatives in place, which can slightly soften the impact of the bills. Note that there is usually a significant seasonal price fluctuation, and having a tank large enough to allow buying once a year should lower your fuel bills.

Oil-fired systems still account for around 10% of the home heating market, and were — until the advent of the Renewable Heat Incentive — much the most popular choice in rural areas where mains gas is not an option.

Oil boiler prices are 20-50% more than gas equivalents, though this is partly because they use the more efficient pressure jet burner. Oil cannot be used to cook with (unless using an oil-fired range).

Storage tanks are now all plastic and you have a choice of double or single skin. Go for double; they are much simpler, although more expensive. You can make a single skin tank into a double one if you build a masonry bund around it, but it's best avoided. At the moment you may be required to have a double skin or bunded tank if there is a danger that your heating oil would spill out into a watercourse. Single skin tanks start at around £400, double skinned ones are roughly twice the price so that a 2500lt bunded tank costs around £900. Other costs you may have to take into consideration are supporting piers, initial placement, measuring gauge, filter, fire check valve and microbore connection to boiler, in all maybe an additional £300.

Recent upgrading of the regulations means that ideally an

oil tank should be placed 1.8m from the house and 760mm from a boundary, although if you build a reasonably fireproof structure these distances can be relaxed. Oil tanks are also ugly and their careless siting can spoil an otherwise attractive elevation. They can be buried underground (like a petrol station) but the cost here soars. Camouflaging with trellis and climbers is a cheaper option and allows access for tank replacement.

SOLID FUEL/BIOMASS

This all-embracing term includes just about everything you can burn which isn't a liquid (oil) or a gas. In the 20th century, this list would have included a range of coals and coal derivatives like anthracite but hardly anyone is burning such polluting fuels anymore, at least certainly no one is installing new coal burning stoves. Today we are looking at biofuels, which refers to fuels that are derived from wood or fast growing plants. In particular, there is a growing interest in pellet fuels, which are made of wood compressed to have similar energy value to heating oil. If you plan to use wood or one of the biofuels, then it is important to build somewhere dry to store it; this takes space but can be an attractive feature in its own right.

Biomass heating systems are available as kitchen ranges, living room stoves or utility room boilers. Wood-burning stoves struggle to generate enough heat for domestic hot water and wet heating systems combined, but appliances like

FUEL COSTS 2019

	STREET COST	CONVERSION	COST /kWh	ANNUAL TARIFFS
Electricity (St Rate)	16p/unit	none	16.0 p	£ 85
Electricity (off peak)	6p/unit	none	6.0 p	£ 0
Mains Gas	5p/unit	none	4.6 p	£ 85
LPG (Calor Gas)	45p/lt	Divide by 7.6	6.6 p	£ 120
OIL (28-second)	55p/lt	Divide by 9.8	6.0 p	£ 0
Wood pellets	£300/tonne	Divide by 5300	5.6 p	£ 0
Smokeless Coal	£460/tonne	Divide by 6700	6.8 p	£ 0

ALL FIGURES INCLUDE VAT at 5%
Figures from Nottingham Energy Partnership

FUEL: Effective Costs Compared

	Fuel Cost/kWh	Appliance or Boiler efficiency	Effective Cost
ELECTRICITY			
Daytime Peak Rate	16.0 p	100%	16.0 p
Heat Pump CoP of 4	16.0 p	400%	4.0 p
Heat Pump CoP of 3	16.0 p	300%	5.3 p
Heat Pump CoP of 2	16.0 p	200%	8.0 p
MAINS GAS			
Elderly Cast Iron Boiler	4.6 p	60%	7.7 p
Condensing Boiler	4.6 p	90%	5.1 p
LPG			
Elderly Cast Iron Boiler	6.6 p	60%	11.0 p
Condensing Boiler	6.6 p	90%	7.3 p
OIL			
Elderly Cast Iron Boiler	6.0 p	70%	8.6 p
Condensing Boiler	6.0 p	90%	6.7 p
SOLID FUEL			
Wood Pellet	5.6 p	85%	6.6 p
Coal Fired Boiler	6.8 p	75%	9.1 p

ALL FIGURES INCLUDE VAT at 5%

pellet boilers are quite capable of meeting all the heat and hot water requirements of a large house. Transport costs are a big issue here because it doesn't make sense to ship wood long distances just for burning. So either buy wood locally or look at pellets, which are compressed wood. Note, there are worries about wood

and pellet prices. Generally they have tended to track oil prices, but as the renewable heat subsidies progress and huge power stations convert to biomass, as is happening at Drax, then there are fears that biomass prices will rise.

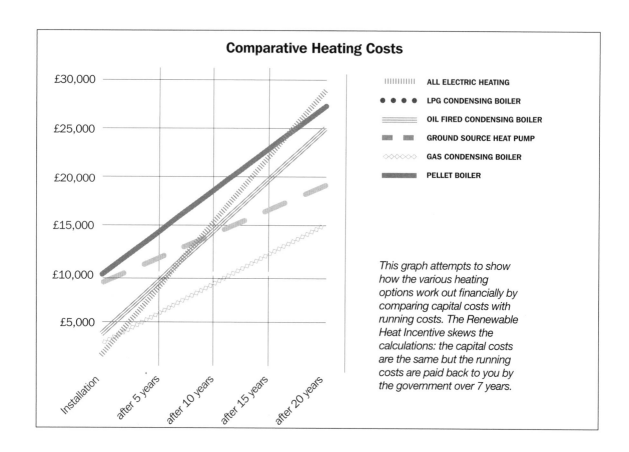

Comparative Heating Costs

£30,000

£25,000

£20,000

£15,000

£10,000

£5,000

Installation — after 5 years — after 10 years — after 15 years — after 20 years

|||||||||| ALL ELECTRIC HEATING

• • • • LPG CONDENSING BOILER

═══ OIL FIRED CONDENSING BOILER

▬ ▬ GROUND SOURCE HEAT PUMP

◇◇◇◇◇◇ GAS CONDENSING BOILER

▬▬▬ PELLET BOILER

This graph attempts to show how the various heating options work out financially by comparing capital costs with running costs. The Renewable Heat Incentive skews the calculations: the capital costs are the same but the running costs are paid back to you by the government over 7 years.

ELECTRICITY

It's not everybody's first thought for space heating and domestic hot water, but it may well be the future. This is because we are developing ways of creating electricity (windpower and PV) and ways of using it wisely (heat pumps and ventilation systems). Plus we are now developing homes (Passivhaus) which need so much less energy to keep warm that many of our long held concerns about "wasting electricity" are being challenged. But let's not jump ahead. What are the logistics of installing electricity for heating?

Installation to a new site is rarely very expensive, unless the site is extremely isolated. As it's going to be on site in any event, the only added consideration is whether you need a three-phase supply. This is only likely if you have a big house which requires a big heat pump. How much extra does a three-phase supply cost? It's hard to be even indicative here as I hear reports that vary from £300 to £15,000. It all depends on the distance travelled and access issues. Best thing is to ask for a quote from your electricity distribution company.

Heat pump suppliers have routines for getting around this issue (which are also likely to cost a little extra) so it's good to be talking to specialists at an early stage to work out what is best at your site.

SOLAR POWER SOURCES

Solar power comes in two distinct flavours, as you are doubtless aware. The main interest in the past few years has been in installing photovoltaic (PV) panels, because the electricity generated by them used to get large subsidies. No more. They were axed in 2019.

There is however an older technology, the solar thermal panel, which heats domestic hot water and this is still subsidised via the Renewable Heat Incentive.

Whilst they can be very effective, they will never do more than heat your water in the summer months, so solar hot water is only ever a partial solution. Using solar power is unlikely to save more than 10% of your overall fuel bills, whichever system you use for your main heat source.

COMPARATIVE FUEL COSTS

The accompanying table gives a reasonable indication of where we stand regarding fuel costs in 2019 You not only have to look at the actual cost per kilowatt hour of each fuel which in itself involves a little extra maths because liquid and solid fuels are not sold by the kilowatt hour, but also at the efficiency of the heating appliance you plan to use. Things get further complicated by the Renewable Heat Incentive which greatly favours low carbon heat sources for a limited time period.

ENVIRONMENTAL IMPACTS

Gas is the cleanest of the fossil fuels in that it produces very little sulphur dioxide or nitrous oxide (the acid rain gases). It's also efficient in that little is lost in transmission from source to end-user and so its combustion produces comparatively little carbon dioxide, at least compared to oil. Liquid Petroleum Gas is a more processed form and results in carbon emissions 20%

greater than mains gas.

Oil is a slightly dirtier fuel than gas (acid rain wise) and produces around 35% more CO_2 than gas.

Electricity is a form of converted energy so it is much processed before it enters the home. It is generated in a number of ways – by burning coal and gas and increasingly biofuels, by hydroelectric dams, by wind and solar power and by nuclear fission. Whatever the merits or demerits of electricity generation, much of its energy is lost in transmission along the national grid, which adds to its expense and reinforces its poor environmental rating. Despite the existence of so-called green tariffs, electricity in all forms is reckoned to produce between two and three times as much carbon dioxide per kilowatt-hour as mains gas. The exact amount depends on how much wind is blowing and how much sun is shining and how cold it is, so it varies from day to day. The plan is to reduce the so-called carbon intensity of electricity over the coming decades by switching away from fossil-fuelled sources.

As an interesting aside, in earlier editions of the Bible, I used this section to explain the basics of energy production and to show how the future was planned to be greener. In the past few years, this has all become rather controversial with lots of commentators arguing that we shouldn't be doing this, it's too expensive and that fossil fuels are just fine. I happen to be of the school that thinks they're

nuts, but everyone is entitled to their viewpoint. What they have achieved is to bring the whole topic of energy production centre stage so that now just about everyone knows about wind turbines, solar power and fracking for gas. And everyone seems to have an opinion about what we should or shouldn't be doing.

What remains more controversial, as far as I am concerned, is the green subsidies for biofuels. Biofuels release just as much CO_2 (and other pollutants) on burning as fossil fuels do but because the carbon has never been fossilized it doesn't in theory add to the CO_2 already in the atmosphere. Biofuels therefore remain part of the open carbon cycle as long as trees are planted to replace those that are burned. The reason it's contentious is that it takes around 60 years for the carbon to be recaptured by the newly planted trees and this isn't really a problem that can be left for 60 years. I think it would be far better to offer subsidies to people who build using timber, thereby using the new buildings as a carbon sink, rather than burning the biofuels.

That's a very simplified version of a very complex debate, And it won't sort your heating system out, will it?

BOILERS

Boilers are rated according to the power they can produce. Manufacturers used to work in BTU (British Thermal Units) but now everyone seems to have adopted

Chapter 8

kilowatts (kW) which are, in truth, much simpler. Just remember:
- 1kW = 3410 BTU/h.

A small application - like a one-bedroom flat – might use a 6kW boiler; a large Victorian vicarage would require something in excess of 30kW. A new four-bedroom house built to the latest thermal regulations will need – well read on, it's a bit controversial.

Conventionally, boilers are sized by totalling the radiator output (worked out from the heat calculation) and adding a bit for heating domestic hot water (DHW), and then going to the nearest size above. This is a bit hit-or-miss, to say the least.

HEAT DEMAND

The industry standard is to design heating systems capable of keeping the house around 21°C warmer than the outside temperature. Now in a new house, the amount of heat needed to keep the structure 21°C warmer than outside is surprisingly small. As a rule of thumb, you need no more than 14 watts/m^3 of living space. Take our four-bedroomed model house as an example. It has a floor area of 160m^2 which means it has a heated volume of 430m^3. The overall heating requirement is going to be around 6,000 Watts (14 x 430) or 6kW. However, any gas or oil-fired boiler fitted into this house is going to be much bigger than this because it has to heat the domestic hot water in a reasonable timespan.

A power shower will drain heat away at a rate of 1kWh every 90 seconds or so, so you would actually require a 40kW boiler to replace hot water as fast as you consume it. Now arguably the best way of counteracting this problem is to store hot water in a cylinder so that you effectively buffer the demand. This means you can afford to reduce the boiler size. Smaller boilers are not only cheaper but run more efficiently.

Most boilers now modulate the burner so that they can burn lean and green at around 6kW when they are just being called on to do the space heating, but can also ramp up the power output to 24kW or even 30kW when the hot water tank needs filling. In theory, the higher the modulation ratio, the better, but not all agree with the theory and it is not always obvious what the modulation ratio is on any given boiler. Worcester Bosch, the market leaders, certainly don't make a big thing of it. If you fit a decent sized cylinder (say 140 litres), you should be able to use a 12kW boiler and still enjoy hot baths — see later section on Recovery Rates.

BOILER HEAT EXCHANGERS

The old style gas and oil-fired boilers used cast iron heat exchangers and worked by heating up this cast-iron, which transfers the heat through to the hot water. They were characterised by being easy to install, reliable but inefficient. The cast-iron takes a comparatively long time to heat up and a correspondingly long time to cool down — hence the inefficiency of heat transfer.

Today's boilers all work rather differently. Since a change in the building regulations in 2005, they have all been condensing boilers. Why condensing? There's an interesting bit of physics to understand here. Condensing boilers have extra large heat exchangers (or, in some designs, a second one) which extract a much greater proportion of the usable energy from the fuel. 20th century boilers burned hot and quick, taking about 75% of the usable energy in the gas or oil being burned and dumped the rest out as exhaust gas via the flue at a high temperature (250°C).

There was usable heat being thrown away here but, in order to use it, the boiler had to be redesigned so that the exhaust gases spent far longer inside the chamber. In fact, the flue gets so cool that, in ideal conditions, it condenses, which in itself gives an energy boost to the process. Check out the "latent heat of condensation" on Wikipedia if you want to know more.

But condensation isn't all good news. Because it's a wet process, condensing boilers produce a significant plume of soggy exhaust gas at around 50°C to 60°C which can be a nuisance if the flue isn't well sited, and can cause some horrible staining on exterior surfaces. Condensers also produce a mildly acidic watery waste which has to be collected and piped away to a soil stack or a gulley, creating another siting issue which sometimes makes it impossible to replace an existing boiler with a condenser. The boilers themselves also have to be built with non-corrosive materials (no more cast-iron). You would think all this would combine to make condensers very expensive, but the competing boiler manufacturers have engineered their designs so well that a condensing boiler today is basically no more expensive than a conventional one was in the 1990s.

Condensing technology isn't specific to one class of boiler: they can be stand-alones, combis or system boilers, wall mounted or floor mounted, gas or oil-fired and even biomass. There are hundreds of models of condensers available: you can check out models and their efficiency ratings on www.boilers.org.uk.

BOILER TYPES

Most suppliers now split their boilers into one of three categories being
■ Heat only (or conventional)
■ System
■ Combination (or Combi).

What's the difference? The conventional boiler is the most basic and therefore the cheapest to buy. It just heats water passing through, whether it is used for space heating or domestic hot water via a cylinder. Controls, pumps, thermostats, everything else is fitted separately.

The system boiler incorporates a few bells and whistles which mean that there is less work to do elsewhere: typically a system boiler has a circulating pump and an expansion vessel within it. One

advantage of this is that you don't require any loft plumbing. System boilers are usually specified with unvented hot water cylinders.

The combi does away with the cylinder because it heats water instantly via an extra large or secondary heat exchanger. It is therefore cheaper to install than a conventional system.

Combi boilers are now well established in the UK — they account for well over 50% of all new boiler sales. Low flow rates mean they are not that wonderful for applications such as showers but they are good choices for households with erratic lifestyles, coming and going at all hours. The relatively low water content heat

Plumbing Systems Compared

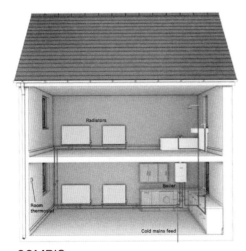

COMBIS
No water storage involved at all. The cold feeds all come off the mains. The hot water is heated instantly as it passes through the combi boiler

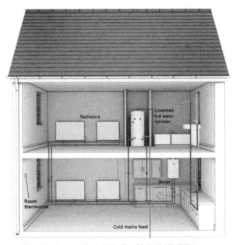

SYSTEM BOILER & CYLINDER
The hot water is stored in an unvented hot water cylinder. The radiator circuit is heated directly via the boiler.

This Grant oil-fired boiler is no thing of beauty but it can be housed outside, which is a boon for the smaller rural selfbuilds that don't have space for such a piece of kit indoors.

exchangers also mean they need rather more careful commissioning by the plumber and, even so, the heat exchangers scale up in hard water areas. Hard water scaling isn't a terminal problem — you can get the boilers de-scaled — but it won't do any harm to fit some sort of scale-inhibiting device as well.

FLUE CHOICES

Where you have a boiler, you must also have some form of exhaust pipe to get rid of the fumes. The flue, as it is known, is actually quite an expensive part of the kit and selecting the right flue is an important step. There are currently three options.

CONVENTIONAL FLUES

This is the old-fashioned, low-tech solution and involves releasing the exhaust fumes into some sort of vertical chimney. However, conventional flues require an intake of air from the outside, which must be built-in somewhere (i.e. you can't just rely on drafts). In a draft-proofed new house it really doesn't make a lot of sense, unless you have a room-sealed boiler or fire — see the section on Wood Stoves and Chimneys late in this chapter.

BALANCED FLUE

This draws fresh, combustible air in through a pipe which shares the same opening through which the exhaust fumes are expelled. Nowadays, this is the preferable option with gas and oil-fired boilers; some balanced flue versions are the same price as conventional flues

but most manufacturers add a 15-20% premium. In a new dwelling however, this is almost always going to be much cheaper than building in a conventional flue.

FAN FLUE

Popular in flats where boiler positioning is sometimes difficult. Specifying a fanned flue adds 20-30% to the cost of a conventionally flued boiler, but allows a far greater number of positioning possibilities because the fumes can be expelled at a much greater distance.

FLUE POSITIONING

There are masses of regulations about where you can and can't place boiler flue terminals in outside walls: these are set out in building regs Part J in England. For instance, they shouldn't be less than 300mm below an opening window or under the roof eaves and they shouldn't be less than 600mm from an internal or external corner. Your designer should be aware of these hurdles, but every now and then someone gets caught out and has to reposition the boiler away from its preferred spot. Generally, the regulations are not as stringent for fan flue terminals, and fitting a fanned flue boiler can sometimes be a useful (if expensive) way around an otherwise intractable siting problem.

CAST IRON KITCHEN RANGES

This is an option that appeals to many because of the intrinsic style and feel. The Aga is the best known, but it is basically just a huge cast iron cooker not a whole house-heating boiler. There are now lots of range cookers out there but what we are looking at here is a little more specialised; something that cooks and provides enough hot water for heating and the hot taps. Rayburn is undoubtedly the best known name though there are several others, The Rayburn Heatranger series is available as gas, oil, electric and solid fuel versions and can typically provide enough hot water to keep a large house warm, but is also capable of running on a summer setting that reduces output to around 1kW.

There are limitations in using ranges for all your heating requirements – no mains pressure tanks, relatively unresponsive – but the top models now have electronic time and thermostatic control and Esse even make a condensing model. No way is this a cheap option but if you have your heart set on a cast-iron cooker it is worth considering upgrading to one that does space heating and domestic hot water (DHW) as well. Having said that, the space/DHW heating capabilities come at a price (£600-£800) for which you could purchase many more efficient gas- or oil-fired boilers as well as more sophisticated controls. It is also little understood that ranges are very expensive to run, whatever the fuel. The gas-fired Rayburn uses around 30,000kWh/annum (cost £1500); this is rather more than the anticipated space heating costs for a large house and nearly twenty times the cost of conventional gas cooking.

I have also come across one or two examples of people fitting all singing and dancing cast-iron ranges into new houses only to be overwhelmed by the amount of heat they pump out. It's a problem in summer especially when it had been hoped to use the range as a cooker only and yet the cooker won't work without heating up copious amounts of hot water which has nowhere to go except around parts of the radiator system. The better insulated the house, the bigger the problem.

EMITTERS

'Emitters' is a convenient tag to use for the bits of space heating systems that deliver the heat. Go into Plumb Center and ask for an emitter and they'd most likely direct you to the local psychiatrist, but if I just call them radiators (*rads* in plumber-speak) then I am ignoring all the other weird and wonderful heat emitters that exist. More on those later. Conventional wet central heating systems use rads, so we'll start here.

RADIATORS

These are what go into most central heating systems today and most readers will be all too familiar with them. Functional rather than elegant,there are several well-known makes that tend to compete on price: e.g.Stelrad, Quinn (formerly Barlo), Myson. Plus there are specialist companies that have sprung up, such as the Radiator Company and Radiating Style. Rather like windows,

radiators come in standard shapes and sizes, typically from 300mm to 700mm high and from 500mm to 3000mm long. Most manufacturers produce three or four height options, each available in lengths which increase in 100mm steps. There are also double-panelled and finned versions that give off more heat. Roughly speaking, they produce heat in proportion to their size: the smallest (300H x 400L) will give out 0.25kW, the largest, double-panelled type (700H x 2000L) will give out around 4kW. Having carried out a heat calculation for each room, you will be faced with a choice of shapes and sizes as to how that heat load can be met and here thought can be given to radiator placing.

List prices are, as ever, indicative of where the haggling starts. Discounts off radiators can be huge (60-70% is not uncommon with some manufacturers); look to pay around £50 for each kW of output, although note that you will find that in practice most retailers still use BTU as the output unit. Remember 1kW = 3410 BTU/h. Merchants tend to have special offers going and so it pays not to be too fussy as to the make. A four-bedroomed house would use perhaps 15 rads with a total output of 15kW. Piping up the rads with 100m x 15mm copper tube, fittings, valves would cost an additional £300 in materials. Add in thermostatic radiator valves at around £10 each and a bit extra for heated towel rails and the cost sails over £1,000.

Radiators come in many different shapes and sizes. If you want something different to the bog standard pressed steel, then you can have it. But you will also pay for it. Instead of paying a meagre £50 per kW output, you will be paying out more than £100 and possibly twice as much. Zehnder is a good place to start: this Swiss radiator company doesn't do pressed steel but they do most other designs: multi-column style (similar to the old cast iron rads), low surface temperature rads (think nursing homes) and sleek die-cast aluminium designer rads in a variety of colours, plus a range of very cute towel rails. All of them well north of £100 per kW output. Another interesting company is Radiating Style who have been shaping and welding all manner of interesting objects into heat emitters since the 90s, turning radiators into fashion accessories.

Traditional cast-iron radiators are still around and available from an increasing range of suppliers. In period bathrooms and the like they are just the ticket but they do not come cheap.

SKIRTING RADIATORS

One increasingly popular alternative is to fit skirting radiators. They vary from the functional, rather institutional-looking variety to ones that look every bit as convincing as conventional skirting board.

Skirting heating delivers a more even heat than conventional radiators, and yet is just as responsive. However, costs tend to work at over £30 per linear metre and with most detached homes having well in excess of 100 linear metres of skirting, this makes skirting heating an expensive option as a whole house solution. It's probably better suited to renovations. Look out for Discrete Heat.

HEATED TOWEL RAILS

There are hundreds of designs to choose from dozens of manufacturers. Zehnder are still very much a top end option, but even Wickes sells 11 different designs, varying in price from £70 to over £500.

In fact, several radiator companies make no distinction between heated towel rails and ordinary radiators. They are, after all, just radiators that happen to be a slightly unusual shape.

Note that you often want heated towel rails on when the rest of your heating system is shut down. If this bothers you, you can opt for a dual fuel towel rail which is plumbed as a normal wet radiator on the heating system, but also has an electric heating element which cuts in when the central heating is off.

UNDERFLOOR HEATING

Available as either water-based (wet) or electric, underfloor heating (or UFH) is now widely specified in the UK selfbuild market. The electric systems are most frequently installed as mats in single rooms like bathrooms. Whole houses tend to use warm water piped systems. Overall, its market share in the UK is still small because it tends to be rather more expensive than just installing bog standard radiators. With an underfloor heating system, the floor itself becomes the emitter and, so as you don't burn your tootsies, the wet systems need to work at lower temperatures than ordinary wall rads. They are very suitable for use with condensing boilers and heat pumps, both of which work most efficiently at low temperatures. UFH is mostly laid under a cement screed, which is used as a heat reservoir (like an electric storage heater); this means that the heat is released slowly throughout the day. It is pleasantly draught-free and the heat stays close to the floor. There are now many businesses offering varying levels of service and most can be found at the selfbuild exhibitions.

Underfloor heating is not a homogeneous product: every system is different and the quotations need to be deconstructed carefully to see whether you are comparing like with like. Watch out to see if significant extras are included, such as insulation, heating controls and mesh to attach the pipe to. Note that whilst UFH does away with radiators, you still need to find somewhere to fit the manifold where the pipes emerge from the floor and connect up with the supply pipes. Manifolds are large and ugly and are best concealed in a cupboard or a utility area. In cost terms, UFH tends to work out about £1,500-£2,500 more than a standard radiator system in a largish house, pretty similar to using skirting heating or unusual radiators.

UFH UNDER TIMBER FLOORS

Whilst there is some debate about the suitability of UFH under timber floors – wood is regarded as an insulating material – virtually every supplier offers it as an option. There are several methods of installing UFH under timber floors. Some use aluminium plates to spread the heat across the floor: some require a mortar 'pug' to be built as an extra layer in the floor, some use nothing at all, the pipes being clipped to the underside of the floor after it is laid. Generally the aluminium plate system is rather more expensive than the other systems in terms of materials supplied but the mortar pug system requires a fair amount of extra building work. Some suppliers quote for installation using alternative designs: the mortar pug system usually appears to be significantly cheaper but bear in mind that it will involve other significant construction costs.

PIPE ISSUES

People naturally fear pipe failure with UFH. Suppliers go to great lengths to ensure that the pipe is up to the job, but as it is still a relatively new technique, there is some justification for at least being worried about it. Most warm water UFH is run in PEX pipe, now widely used all over Europe and reckoned to be the safe choice. An alternative is to use one of the polybutylene pipes like Hep2O. It's

There are many methods of fixing underfloor heating pipe. Left: plastic backing board used to keep everything regular. Bottom: pipe clipped to underside of timber flooring

best to specify one with an oxygen barrier as this reduces the risk of rust getting into the system.

When testing, it is now usual to put the system under air pressure rather than a water test. Accidents have happened when residual water left in the pipes after a test has later frozen.

ENERGY SAVING

Many suppliers claim that UFH is inherently energy efficient and will save you money in the long term. I have my doubts. Just because it works at low temperatures, compared to radiator-based systems, doesn't necessarily mean it will cost less to run. You are after all heating

Chapter 8

up a much larger area, using much more water. Furthermore, when placed in a cement screed, UFH is a very slow response system: it takes a long time to heat up and a long time to cool down. This in itself can waste a lot of heating because the house may be empty for long periods. Arguably, UFH is therefore best suited to lifestyles where people are around all day. Under timber floors the response times are quicker but the efficiency is reduced because of the insulating qualities of timber. Ditto when placed under thick carpets.

One common route taken by selfbuilders is to run UFH downstairs and radiators upstairs. It makes a lot of sense because a) it's a bit cheaper and b) radiators are not quite such a problem in bedrooms.

DOMESTIC HOT WATER

The traditional system, used in Britain for most of the 20th century, and outlined at the beginning of this chapter, used a copper cylinder, fed by a tank overhead or in the loft, and heated by copper tubes inside. These tubes transfer heat from the boiler primary circuit to the water in the cylinder: the domestic hot water (DHW) never passes through the boiler at all and thus this way of doing things is known as an indirect system. In the very early days, copper cylinders sat naked in airing cupboards but these days they

are all heavily insulated to keep the hot water hot for longer. They are said to be vented because they are not pressurised in any way and they have to have an expansion tank to cope with expanding hot water.

In conventional systems, there are two tanks in the loft: one (usually 227lts) feeds the cylinder, the other (usually 18lts) supplies the central heating system. Having to put a tank in the loft – avoiding this is sold as a big plus for other systems – actually costs around £250 for the water storage tank and around £100 for the feed and expansion tank (aka the Jockey Tank). I really don't think anyone plumbs a new house like this anymore.

INSTANTANEOUS HOT WATER

Small instantaneous hot water heaters are still sold but in a new house the normal way of achieving this is by fitting a Combination Boiler (or combi). So many combis are sold in the UK that they are no more expensive than system boilers, despite their capability of heating hot water for the tap as well as space heating. Because of this, combis have become the cheap and cheerful option for new central heating installations in flats and starter homes.

The main problem with combis is that the hot water flow rates achieved tend to be a bit feeble and you really begin to notice this when taking a shower. If a house has two or more bathrooms, a combi is probably best avoided.

MAINS PRESSURE HOT WATER

These systems use unvented (i.e. no loft pipework for expansion) hot water cylinders which are strong enough to withstand storing hot water under mains pressure. They answer the problem of low flow rates to showers but a cost of around £600 makes them rather more expensive than combis. To operate to full effect they need at least 2.5 bar of mains pressure and a mains flow rate of 35lts per minute.

Unfortunately, UK water companies are only obliged to provide

Chelmer's thermal stores have been at the cutting edge of this technology for many years

mains water at 1 bar pressure so many situations will not benefit at all. Phone your water company to determine your local pressure. Mains pressure hot water cylinders come with a whole raft of safety features attached and a requirement that a qualified person installs them, both requirements of the building regs.

THERMAL STORES

A variation of the unvented hot water cylinder is the thermal store. Rather than using a combi boiler to heat the water for the hot tap, the incoming cold water passes through a tank of hot water (aka the thermal store) and draws heat from this source instead. Thermal stores usually work without the need for tanks in the loft; instead they come with integral feed and expansion tanks. For a four-bedroom house, expect installation costs midway between using the standard route and using mains pressure unvented systems.

Thermal stores were first developed by British Gas in the 1980s and are produced by a number of small British manufacturers, notably Gledhill. They are particularly good when you want to combine different inputs; e.g. if you have a solar panel or a heat pump supplying hot water as well as a boiler. You can get thermal stores made to order to fit your particular application from Chelmer Heating.

SHOWER PUMPS

When all is said and done, the main reason for having mains pressure hot water is to enjoy decent showers - that's the place you really notice

the difference. If you want to stick with a gravity system but value a good shower, then you will need to fit a shower pump. There are single impeller pumps that boost the water after the mixing valve, and double impellers that boost both hot and cold before they enter the valve. There is also an increasing number of all-in-one pump and valve shower units.

Which you choose is partly dependent on the layout you have. Prices are largely dependent on the power of the pump. They can be purchased for just over £100, but a pump delivering 15lts per minute (equivalent to a reasonable mains pressure system) will cost £180 plus. Add the costs for extra wiring and fitting and you can see that a shower pump is not a very clever option in a new building, where you would be quids in by starting off with a better DHW system. Leading manufacturers: Mira, Aqualisa.

A more recent innovation for a house with a feeble water supply is the whole house shower pump which is a sensible option if you have more than one shower, as the cost is around double that of a single shower pump - look around the £350 mark. The best place to install a whole house shower pump is close by the cylinder which makes the plumbing much simpler.

BACKGROUND FACTS

■ A bath takes about 70-80lts of hot water and so water storage needs to be above this level (or instantaneous) to be adequate. Hot water cylinders

usually hold around twice this amount.

■ A typical household of four uses between 200 and 250lts of hot water a day, conventionally heated to 60°C. Officially. My experience of a household of five, including three teenagers, is that these official estimates are way out of line. The real amounts could easily be double these figures.

■ It takes 12kWh to heat 200lts of water through 50°C (the difference between the temperature of the cold water and the hot water) and the average cost of water heating (by gas or oil-fired boiler) is £250 per annum. Those are the official figures, assuming your notional family uses 5,000kWh per annum on heating DHW. I think a more realistic figure is 2,000kWh per person, which would make it around £100-120 per person in terms of cost.

■ Just under half of all water consumed in the home is heated.

SHOWERS AND FLOW RATES

A good power shower needs a flow rate of 15lts per minute. This will not be achieved by the conventional gravity-type system. A pump will be required (or else feeble showers endured).

Now our legislators take a very different view. They now regard 20lt per minute showers as an indulgence and have introduced building regs (Part G in England) to restrict shower flow rates. When you build a new house now, you have to account for all the water using appliances and demonstrate that you won't use more than 125lts of water a day for each

Evacuated tube solar panels are more expensive than flat plate collectors, but give better performance under cloudy skies

RECOVERY RATES

The time taken for cold water from the mains to get to 60°C inside the cylinder is referred to as the recovery rate. This rate is dependent on the size of the boiler or the cylinder heat exchanger – whichever is smaller. For instance, a typical cylinder for a four-bedroom house needs 8kWh of energy to heat its 140lts of water from 10°C to 60°C; an 8kW heater will accomplish this feat in one hour, whereas a 16kW heater will take just half as long.

In theory a 32kW heater would achieve the same feat in 15 minutes, but in practice this would not happen unless the boiler was also rated at 32kW, which is unlikely. Here the boiler size becomes the limiting factor in the recovery rate. Unlike boilers, cylinders are not advertised by the size of their heat exchangers; however, some manufacturers sell a 'standard' version which takes about one hour to heat up and a 'quick recovery' version which takes 20 minutes. The latter simply have larger heat exchangers.

EFFICIENCY/HEAT LOSS

All new cylinders are insulated to reduce heat loss to less than 3kWh of heat during a 24-hour period. Effectively, this heat loss can be ignored for six months of the year as it is simply transferring heat from water to space heat; during the summer you might leak something like 500kWh of heat. Many new cylinders (like the Megaflo) are encapsulated

person in the household. Whereas kitchen sinks, loos and washing machines have a marginal effect on overall volume usage, shower volumes are critical, and so the hunt is now on for low-flow power showers. Which is a contradiction in terms, but there you have it.

The word is that we should be fitting showers of no more than 6lts per minute. Whether this will really satisfy today's teenagers, I have my doubts, but I can give you some pointers.

The Nordic Eco shower is a possibility, and Hansgrohe have a 6lt shower that is said to be OK. And

Aqualisa produce some showers that have an eco setting.

The problem is that unvented hot water systems are set to deliver power showers at 15lts or 20lts per minute. In fact, this is their chief attraction. What is the point of fitting one, if you can't have a high volume shower? You might just as well fit a combi boiler where the flow rate is feeble in comparison. It is unlikely to be much better than 10lts per minute.

Bear in mind that if you are renovating, none of this water calculator malarkey applies. It only applies to new dwellings, so you can fit what you want.

by 50mm of polyurethane which reduces heat lost over a 24hr period to under 1kWh – nothing to all intents and purposes.

HOT WATER SOLAR PANELS

A 2-3m² roof mounted collector is capable of producing 3,000kWh of hot water for your cylinder during the course of a year, that's maybe equivalent to 500 five minute hot showers for free, albeit between the months of April and October. The more hot water you use, the better the payback on solar panels.

The annual savings are unlikely to be enormous but subsidies available via the Renewable Heat Incentive can make solar thermal a mildly attractive investment.

Note that to get effective use out of solar hot water panels, you need to have a large cylinder or thermal store, preferably around 50lts per person. The panels tend to produce about 3kW heat at full whack so they require four or five hours to replenish a 200lt cylinder from cold: not quick, but fine if you have adequate capacity.

The standard routine is to let the solar panels do their work during daylight hours and then top up the heat in the cylinder from your boiler during the night.

You can get more information and possible supplier details from the Solar Trade Association website. Note that if you do want to get any subsidy, you will have to ensure that both the kit and the installers are registered with the Microgeneration Certification scheme.

DEAD LEGS

The hot water piping running between the cylinder and the hot water taps is effectively an extension to the cylinder; water sitting there loses its heat very quickly.

An efficiently designed installation would have around 5lts of water sitting in the hot pipes. This may sound insignificant, but bear in mind that every time a hot tap is opened some of this water is replaced and so if every hot tap is turned on just three times a day, then 15lts of extra hot water has to be heated.

An inefficient design with much longer dead legs – i.e. bathrooms and kitchen all at opposite ends of the house - might use four or five times the length of hot water pipe. Not only does the cost of supplying hot water to the dead legs then become significant but also you start getting 20-30 second lags between opening the hot tap and getting hot water. Avoid long dead legs if possible.

There is a way around this problem which is to create a pumped hot water loop around the house so that there is always hot water at each hot tap.

However you have the added cost of installing and running a circulation pump and, to be effective, you have to insulate the hot water pipes to a high standard otherwise you will gain very little. For some, a hot water loop is just something else to go wrong at some point in the future.

HEATING CONTROLS

Before the days of central heating (around 1950), heating controls consisted of putting (or not putting) coal on the fire or, at best, an on/off switch on an electric heater. Here is an industry that has grown at a prodigious rate and there is now a bewildering range of options open to the householder. Yet the purpose of controls is quite simple:
- to increase comfort
- to decrease fuel consumption
- safety.

This section concentrates on wet heating systems; other heating systems (warm air, electric, solid fuel) tend to have slightly different control systems, although the logic behind them all remains the same.

PROGRAMMERS

Timers to the layman. These are basically the on/off switch for the whole heating system and, as such, override all the other controls (except safety features like frost thermostats). Digital display has brought big improvements to programmers and now for little more than £30 you can get separate controls for hot water heating and space heating which you can switch on and off 21 times a week.

Heating programmers have a reputation for being really fiddly to set and many people just leave them on the factory presets which rather defeats the purpose of having them in the first place. Many intrepid souls have started out to match their heating system to their lifestyle, only to give up in frustration. Plumbers just love being called back to find out why the heating isn't coming on, only to find that you've been messing around with the programmer.

Despite this, a basic electronic programmer is now considered an absolutely essential component of a central heating system. Digital displays are now almost universal, although it hasn't made them easier to use than the older ones with plastic knobs.

THERMOSTATS

Known by plumbers as just stats, these provide a secondary level of on/off switching, controlled by temperature. This means that if the air or water temperature is higher than the thermostat setting, these controls will switch the heating system off, even though the timer says 'run'.

Thermostats come in several different flavours. Room stats will cut off hot water to radiators when the set temperature is reached. Placing them requires care. Cylinder stats do much the same for the hot water cylinder. Some are integral with the cylinder, some are strapped onto the outside.

Boiler stats are usually integral with the boiler; these set the temperature of water passing through the boiler, which is the hottest part of the system.

Frost stats are a safety device which turns the heating on if there is a danger of any components freezing

– e.g. boilers in garages or other unheated spaces. It can of course take precedence over a timer which says the system should be off. Alone amongst the family of stats, the frost stat turns the system on rather than off and consequently malfunctioning frost stats can be expensive to run and difficult to pinpoint.

PROGRAMMABLE THERMOSTATS

These combine the functions of the ordinary programmer (time switching) with that of the room stat (temperature switching). They also allow you to pre-select different temperature maxima for different times of day: very clever but even less user-friendly than the ordinary electronic programmers. A potential energy saver and a potential comfort increaser and no more expensive than a programmer and room stat separately. Whereas ordinary time-only programmers can be placed anywhere that's convenient, once you introduce a thermostat you have to think very carefully about its location and which temperatures it will be measuring.

TWO-ZONE HEATING SYSTEMS

An energy saving idea which splits the space heating into two heating zones – typically upstairs/downstairs – in addition to heating the hot water. It involves using a three-zone programmer such as the Horstmann Channel Plus. Again, the benefits very much depend on lifestyle – i.e. whether you really use your house

in a predictable way. Zoning more complex than upstairs/downstairs is possible, but would probably involve longer and less efficient pipe runs which would tend to cancel out any advantage.

MOTORISED ZONE VALVES

These are what the programmer operates; they are used to switch the flow of hot water around different parts (or zones) of the system. The cheapest systems use a 3-port valve but it is better to use two 2-port valves. The simplest valves switch all water either this way or that and therefore give rise to something called hot water priority, which means that the hot water stops being pumped around the radiators when the domestic hot water is being heated in the cylinder. There are more costly valves that are capable of opening in a middle position which allows a flow of hot water both ways.

A standard set of heating controls (excluding TRVs) for a four-bedroom house would cost around £200. These controls are often sold in packages which usually include a pump, motorised valve, a programmer, a room stat and a cylinder stat. Note that wiring must be provided between all these components.

TRVS

Thermostatic radiator valves (TRVs) are apparently simple little gizmos fitted on to the bottom of radiators that can sense the air temperature and switch off supply to the radiator when satisfied. They are cheap, they increase comfort levels by stopping overheating and they reduce fuel bills. They are now fitted as standard on new radiators.

What's not to like? Well, there have been problems with the operation of TRVs. Many people do not understand the principle of thermostatic control and, when feeling cold and seeing a dial, turn the TRVs to 'Max', thinking this will make the radiators hotter. It won't. It simply turns the radiator 'On' at a lower room temperature. Radiators are either 'on' or 'off'. Furthermore, because they require manual operation, there is no way of knowing (other than learning from experience) how high to set them to achieve comfortable space heating in any given room – though note that the latest versions allow you to limit the highest/lowest settings.

Another problem with TRVs is that they are prone to sticking (usually in the off position) and many people have reported radiators not working at all at the beginning of the heating season. I know of someone who took all their TRVs off because they appeared to stop the radiators working at all. Sticking TRVs are often a symptom of having dirty water in the system: if it happens to you, you should get the system flushed and add some corrosion inhibitor.

Fitting TRVs does reduce the demand on the boiler because, although they won't turn the boiler off, every radiator that turns itself off reduces the demand on the boiler. But a better way of doing this is to have your TRVs working in conjunction with a whole house thermostat (see above) which can override the individual TRVs. This is known as having a boiler interlock. It takes a bit of getting used to, as you don't want the whole heating system to shut down when some rooms are warm and others are cold, but if it's set up right (the positioning of the whole house stat is critical), then it really does save a lot of energy by preventing the boiler from working its socks off when no heating is required.

WEATHER COMPENSATION

Perhaps the most sophisticated of all the domestic heating controls, weather compensation introduces an external thermometer which controls the output temperature of the boiler. If the external temperatures drop, the boiler output increases, and vice versa. The kit is not cheap - costing maybe an extra £150 or £200 - and the claimed-for savings are disputed by some. In theory it should make it cheaper to run boilers, especially condensing boilers which get an efficiency boost if the return temperature falls below 55°C and the boiler actually starts condensing.

HEATING CONTROLS 2.0

In 2014, a number of digital whole house heating controls became widely available. Whilst people have been beavering away at this area for years, no one had paid much attention to it until Google forked out $3billion for a company called Nest which makes a learning thermostat, a neat looking one at that. And it turns out that Nest is not alone.

All the new systems are based around replacing your existing heating controls with a new box of tricks which can be controlled by an app "from anywhere in the world" and which is either wired up to your boiler and heating system, or uses a wireless system to do the same thing. As your existing controls are already wired together, it's easy to replace them with something new without having to run extra cabling. Pricewise, the various offerings all seem to come in between £200 and £250 though note that some include installation and some don't.

British Gas Hive Active Heating is one of the simpler systems. It essentially replaces your existing heating controls with its own versions which you can then either control remotely or conventionally. In this respect, it's one of the least smart of the applications.

Nest offer a facility to switch your heating on and off automatically by linking it to your mobile, which knows where you are, a feature referred to as Occupancy Detection. Tado is a German business that does everything that Nest does without the Apple-like style, but is compatible with other manufacturers' products.

UNDERFLOOR SYSTEMS

Underfloor heating is usually controlled by wall mounted thermostat, one for each zone which roughly translates as each room (depends on your layout). If you build a really well insulated house (why wouldn't you?), you can pretty much do away with other controls as you don't really need to switch the system on and off according to the time of day, because it works by trickling heat into the floor 24/7. My experience on our 2018 selfbuild confirms this hypothesis: although there are five zones, all with their own wall mounted thermostats, the only one we ever fiddle with is the one in the main living room/ kitchen area which is usually set to 19.5°C. Occasionally, when it's wet or particularly cold, we move it up to 20°C, but mostly it's set at 19.5°C all winter long.

The only time we ever reset is when we go away for a few days, and then we put all five zones down to 15°C. Having the ability to turn this back to standard setting a day before return would be handy, but thus far we have resisted spending hundreds of pounds on a Wirsbo controller and just ask a neighbour to pop in instead.

HEAT PUMPS

Heat pumps are a hybrid heat source. They are run entirely on electricity but they capture additional energy from the external environment, most commonly heat from under the garden space (that's ground source) or from the air (air source) and, just occasionally, from ponds or streams (water source). They grab some of this low-grade heat and compress the energy into a smaller volume of water at higher temperatures inside the house.

The efficiency of a heat pump system, which is what it's all about, is measured by the coefficient of performance (CoP). This is the ratio of units of heat output for each unit of electricity used to drive the system. Typical CoPs range from 2.5 to 4. Obviously, the higher the better. A score of 1.0 would be a disaster, as that is what you get from a straightforward electric heater or immersion heater.

The critical factors determining the efficiency of the system are the performance of the heat pump itself and the input and output temperatures: the narrower the range of temperature between the source and the house, the more efficiently the system runs. However, heat pumps continue to work effectively even at sub-zero temperatures.

GROUND SOURCE HEAT PUMPS (GSHP)

One of the key advantages of using the ground as a heat collector is that the temperatures stay relatively even over the course of a year. At a one metre depth, the ground temperature in Britain fluctuates between around 5°C (in mid-winter) and 12°C (in mid-summer); as you go deeper still, the temperature fluctuations disappear altogether. Ground source heat pumps are therefore able to tap into this natural heat store even in the depths of winter and thereby maintain high CoPs throughout the year.

There are three important elements to a GSHP heating system:
1) A ground loop. This is comprised of lengths of pipe buried in the ground, either in a borehole or a horizontal trench. The pipe is filled with a mixture of water and antifreeze, which is pumped round the pipe absorbing heat from the ground (or a water source like a stream).
2) A heat pump. This has three main parts:
■ the evaporator – takes the heat from the water in the ground loop;
■ the compressor – moves the refrigerant round the heat pump and compresses the gaseous refrigerant to the temperature needed for the heat distribution circuit;
■ the condenser – gives up heat to a hot water tank that feeds the distribution system.
3) A hot water heat distribution system, no different to a conventional heating system. The house can use radiators but efficiencies are gained by switching to a low temperature underfloor heating system.

COSTS AND PAYBACK

A typical 8kW system costs £10,000-£12,000, plus to the price of the distribution system around the house, maybe another £3,000-£5,000. That's way more expensive than a gas or oil-fired boiler system, but the blow is greatly reduced by the Renewable Heat Incentive subsidy.

Does it make sense? There are, a number of variables that need to be considered, all of which impact on the payback equation.

■ Fuel costs: essentially you are comparing electricity costs with oil costs and maybe biomass as well. Mains gas is by some way the cheapest option now and you would struggle to justify a heat pump against mains gas on fuel cost savings alone. But with oil at around 50p per litre (translating at perhaps 6p per kWh after boiler inefficiencies are taken into account, then you only need a CoP on your heat pump of 2.0 to make the heat pump win this particular race.

■ Level of subsidy. In 2019 the level of subsidy offered by the Renewable Heat Incentive is reasonably attractive. If all goes to plan, the added installation costs should be covered. Paradoxically, the better the house is built, the less you will receive in subsidy because the less you will use the heat pump. New installations have to be metered, so the payments will depend on your actual usage.

■ Demand: The work you require from your heating system is a function of the size of your house, its insulation levels, its airtightness and your lifestyle. By reducing demand, you also reduce the scope for savings in running costs and hence you actually lengthen payback periods for all green technologies.

■ Actual efficiencies: A good heat pump will easily achieve its stated objective, which is usually to raise water temperatures in the house by 35°C at a CoP of 4. Many systems will do even better than this in CoP terms. But for every 1°C extra temperature lift you require, the efficiency of the heat pump drops by around 3%. The temperature

Ground-source heat pumps take up a considerable amount of space, something like the size of a tennis court for a four-bedroomed house

lift required is itself dependent on the external ground temperature, which may vary by 10°C or more, depending on ground conditions and the depth the ground loop is installed.

Which begs an important additional question. What is the achieved performance of heat pumps? In September 2010, the Energy Savings Trust released the result of a survey of 83 heat pump installations (54 ground source and 29 air source) and found very mixed results. Many were achieving the hoped-for efficiencies (CoP higher than 3.0) but an awful lot weren't and often the CoP went as low as 1.3 – remember an electric fire has a CoP of 1.0! Another data collecting survey I am aware of took place on eight separate installations in Yorkshire and again there was a wide range of outcomes with some ostensibly similar households using twice as

much power as others. The best of the Yorkshire sample achieved a CoP of 4, the worst less than 2 – only half as efficient. Two key factors which affect this seem to be the preferred space heating temperature and the demand for hot water: where both these are high, the CoP is significantly reduced.

UNDERFLOOR HEATING

Heat pumps are at their most efficient when delivering relatively low temperatures, typically around 45°C. This immediately lends itself to underfloor heating as the preferred delivery method, as this works well at these relatively low temperatures, compared with radiators.

RENEWABLE HEAT INCENTIVE 2019

Payments per kWh from April 2019 for 7 years			Monitoring	Total return over 7 yrs
Ground source heat pumps	20.87	p/kWh	To be metered	£5,000-£10,000
Air source heat pumps	10.7	p/kWh	To be metered	£2,500-£5000
Solar thermal	21.08	p/kWh	Deemed	£1,000-£2,000
Biomass	6.87	p/kWh	some checking	£2,000-£5,000
Source: Ofgem	Note the rules keep changing!			

GARDEN SPACE REQUIREMENTS

If you have a large garden, it is cheap to lay pipework in shallow trenches, excavated by digger. But if garden space is tight, there are alternatives available. You can drill a borehole, at an additional cost of around £5,000, which can accommodate all the ground source pipework, in an area as little as 2m x 2m.

GROUND CONDITIONS

Trench collectors work best with relatively wet soils, such as clay, where there is a mechanism for the heat taken from the ground to be readily replaced. In dry ground, such as sand or gravel, the ground itself can eventually freeze because the heat being taken out isn't replenished. This, of course, doesn't stop the heat pump working but low ground temperatures do reduce the efficiency. It can be that the heat transfer from dry ground falls off considerably through the winter, so the best advice is always to get some sort of ground survey undertaken.

COOLING CAPABILITIES

Some systems are capable of being run in reverse so as to provide cooling in summer. Generally this comes at a cost, not only in additional installation fees but in operating efficiency as well. A better option is to pump some of the waste cold air (the fridge in reverse) into cooling units, known as passive cooling. Whilst it's not quite as effective as reversing the whole system, it is much less energy hungry.

ADDITIONAL HEAT SOURCES

You may want to harness other power sources to boost your hot water supply. For instance, you may have a stove that can produce hot water, or you may have solar panels fitted. Most heat pumps can accommodate additional heat sources but it is important that the whole hot water supply side is designed correctly at the outset.

SWIMMING POOLS

One of the favorite applications for heat pumps is to provide heating for swimming pools. It's something ideally suited to heat pumps as they work at their best when delivering a constant trickle of heat, rather than a few short sharp bursts which typifies how oil and gas fired boilers work.

DOMESTIC HOT WATER

It's important to assess your domestic hot water needs carefully because this is an area where heat pumps are not at their best. Most heat pumps are set to deliver around 10kW maximum: this is easily enough to keep even a very large house warm throughout the coldest winter snaps. It is also quite adequate to provide stored hot water for a family. However, the recovery time taken to replace hot water is fairly lengthy in comparison with typical boilers.

The only situation where this is likely to be a problem is if you have heavy use of power showers, which drain the heat out of tanks at between 12 and 20 litres per minute, depending on how hot the water is stored. A heat pump could take an hour or so to replace the hot water, whereas a boiler, rated at 20kWh, would take half the time. If your hot water needs were more modest, then you probably would not even notice any difference.

Again, it is an issue that can be addressed at the design stage. You may be able to install booster heating elements or a secondary hot water storage tank. But the cost, as ever, is a reduced overall CoP.

NOISE AND SITING ISSUES

Heat pumps behave to all intents and purposes like refrigerators. Although clean – there are no emissions – they are probably best located in a utility room or garage rather than in living space. Most designs work with large water tanks, often around 200 or 300lts, about double the size of a larder fridge.

Adrian Thurley's Cambridgeshire house, built in 2003, is heated entirely by an Ice Energy heat pump. The heat pump is located in the basement; it's connected to two 200m long pipes that run under the front garden and it is capable of providing 18.5kW of heat, using less then a third of this amount of electricity to do so. It heats the water up to 55°C, to be stored in a large pressurised cylinder. 'It's been fascinating to see it working,' said Adrian. 'I was led to believe that it drew its heat from the ground, which remained at a constant 10°C all year around. But in fact the temperature in the garden loop has changed dramatically through the year, peaking at 21°C in summer and going as low as -1°C in winter. Yet even at -1°C, the heat pump still manages to extract 3° or 4°of heat from the pipes. For every one kilowatt of power used in running the system, we get between three and four kilowatts of heat out of it. That's the magic of heat pumps.' It cost around £10,000 to install.

There are very few house designs that couldn't incorporate a heat pump but equally its not something to fit in as an afterthought.

THREE-PHASE ELECTRICITY
Some larger units are best operated off a three-phase supply. The additional cost of three-phase is extremely variable. If it is present nearby, it can often be supplied at no extra cost, and the running costs are identical to normal single-phase supplies. But on some sites the cost of three-phase supply may be many thousands of pounds – effectively prohibitive. In such cases, it is usually possible to work around the supply restrictions.

AIR SOURCE HEAT PUMPS
Seen by some as a poor man's heat pump, the air source heat pump (ASHP) uses the same techniques to pull usable heat from the air, rather than beneath the ground. The immediate disadvantage is that the air temperature is far more variable than the ground temperature and that

An air source heat pump installed at the Milton Keynes benchmark house from Edition 9. This heat pump is being used, primarily, to heat the domestic hot water. Note that the extract from the ventilation system is located right behind the heat pump (it's that square grill in the wall) so that any residual heat being expelled from the house can be recycled through the heat pump

of hydro electricity, which is 100% renewable. The typical Swedish winter throws up temperatures of −25°C. Even at this sort of temperature, heat pumps keep Swedish homes comfortably above 20°C indoors and also supply all domestic hot water needs. Paul Wurk, a Swedish architect with close connections to the British selfbuild industry via his work with the Swedish House Company, is a keen advocate of heat pumps and finds it hard to understand why we don't use them more often in Britain. 'My 230m² house is heated entirely by electric heat pump. Although I have a wood-burning stove, I haven't used it for many years. The key to the comfort is the insulation levels we have: my 20 year-old house has 200mm of insulation in the walls and 300mm in the roof and, were I to re-build it today, I would be required to use even more. Even so, my heat pump consumes just 12,000kWh per annum and I reckon my CoP is around 3.'

the ASHP unit is likely to have to do more work, which of course makes it less efficient. However, not having to mess around with pipework under the ground makes ASHP much cheaper to install. Furthermore, advocates of ASHP are moving towards solutions that involve heating tanks of hot water to act as energy batteries for home heating, thus the ASHP doesn't have to work continuously.

There have been many problems associated with ASHP. Not least that in very cold weather, air source heat pumps either work so inefficiently that you would do better with an electric immersion heater, or they

pack up altogether. However, there are also significant developments in the technology, especially as regards water heating, and products like the Genvex Combi (£6,000 worth of whole house water heater fired by air source heat pump) keep appearing on my radar.

A SWEDISH PERSPECTIVE

Heat pumps are regarded as the standard way of heating homes in Sweden, and have been used widely for 30 years. Partly this is because Sweden has very little fossil fuel and partly because it has good supplies

BIOMASS BOILERS

Modern biomass boilers are not designed to be focal point room fires, but instead aim to replace a domestic gas or oil-fired boiler in a utility space. Many of them are also designed to automate the delivery of fuel, none more so than the wood pellet boilers which can be set up to take fuel from a hopper without human intervention.

Biomass boilers can run on

logs, but are more often set up to burn wood chips or wood pellets, which are compressed wood shavings, enabling long distance transportation as a fuel to rival oil. In contrast, log burning only really makes economic sense if the fuel is sourced very locally. Wood pellets are a common form of domestic fuel in some countries (notably Austria and Sweden) and are now becoming widely available across the UK.

Unlike stoves, boilers are designed primarily to heat water, either for space heating or domestic hot water. They are functional rather than elegant, although many models exist which blur these boundaries and would happily sit in a living room.

COSTS

Whereas you can buy wood burning stoves for between £600 and £3,000, biomass boilers tend to be very much more expensive: expect to pay anything between £4,000 and £12,000 for a top of the range, automatic feed boiler.

The Renewable Heat Incentive used to pay handsomely for installing a biomass boiler but it seems to be going out of fashion — not helped by a scandal with the N.Irish version which paid people for burning unlimited amounts of biomass in empty sheds. As of 2019, the RHI stands at 6.87p/kWh, paid out for seven years. This should amount to an overall subsidy anywhere between £2,000 and £5,000, depending on the amount burned .

SUPPLEMENTARY HEATING

The very essence of central heating is that you don't require anything else to keep you warm. Once your boiler or heat pump has fired up, every room in the house is designed to reach a comfortable temperature within an hour or two.

If you have underfloor heating, the house stays warm throughout the winter whilst you are barely aware you have a heating system at all. And yet selfbuilders still yearn for something more, something a little different, something a little bit less sterile and more social.

In short, a fire. The problem is that it's technically challenging to start introducing extra heating into a space that is already adequately heated.

What are the options?

OPEN FIRES

Open fires are particularly challenging in modern homes because in recent years there has been much greater emphasis on energy efficiency and airtightness, which makes the installation and operation of a traditional open fire problematic. There are three conflicting requirements at work here:
■ energy efficiency demands that warm air inside the house isn't allowed to seep out through unwarranted holes in the fabric (like open chimneys!)
■ ventilation requirements demand

Biomass boilers are very different to the familiar wood stoves. Rather than loading logs on manually, you burn wood pellets which can be loaded automatically. Here is an example using a hopper which you would fill daily.

that there is a constant supply level of fresh air in a house, enough to keep the air fresh but not enough to supply air to an open fire

■ an open fire requires a significant supply of air to create a draft in order to keep the fire going and draw the smoke up the chimney.

This last point is the killer. An open fire will require a permanently open vent hole of anywhere between 250x250mm up to 500x500mm, depending on the size and design of the fire. That's similar to leaving a window open throughout the winter, not a very appetising prospect when you have just paid a small fortune to insulate and double glaze your new house. This open vent can be sealed up during the airtightness test, so in theory Part L (the energy efficiency regulations) can't stop you having a permanently open vent of this size, but you will be penalised elsewhere by the SAP calculations and have to install expensive additional energy saving features to compensate. It's hard not to conclude that the days of the traditional, Victorian-style open fire are over.

But technology provides a solution — at a cost — by way of the Closed or Room-Sealed Fire. This is a hybrid design, halfway between a traditional open fire and a wood burning stove. It sits within a wall opening and looks like a traditional open fire, but the combustion takes place behind glass in a controlled environment where the air is ducted in and out without ever mixing with the air in the house. The only time the house air mixes with the combustion air is when the glass door

is opened for refuelling.

In the past, this wouldn't have been an attractive option because the glass would soon have sooted-up and the pleasure of an open-fire would have been lost behind a wall of blackened glass. But today's clean wood-burners, with their emphasis on energy efficiency, don't release any significant particulate smoke and the glass stays clear, so much so that you are barely aware that the combustion is taking place in a sealed box.

Room sealed fires, such as the M-Design range (costing around £3,300 exc VAT), burn at around 85% efficiency and come with a secondary air ducting system which allows the warm air produced by the fire to be piped around the house.

WOOD STOVES

The wood burning stove is a simpler way of achieving the same thing — having a focal point fire in a centrally heated, near airtight house. Wood burners are available in wide a range of styles and a huge price range — anything from around £300 up to nearly £10,000. Whilst the principle remains the same — i.e. to burn wood in a controlled way in a metal container — you do tend to get what you pay for and at the top end of the range, you are buying sleek modern designs with incredible burning efficiencies.

The market has also subtly changed. Burning coal has gone out of fashion in the 21st century. Everyone wants to burn wood. People are also much more interested in the efficiency of the stove which means that products like the German Xeos

stoves, boasting a 95% efficiency level are gaining traction, despite the £3,500 (exc VAT) price tag.

As with the room-sealed fires, there is an issue with air supply to wood stoves. The trend is towards room-sealed supply as well, as no one wants a permanently open vent hole in their living room. The cheaper, traditional wood stoves are designed to work in environments with free air flow and will not suit a new house built to current airtightness standards, so the air supply is a critical factor to assess, if you are considering a wood stove.

SOURCING WOOD

Wood burning is the height of selfbuild fashion at the moment, but it's not without its issues. For one thing, wood prices are increasing as rapidly as other fuels, especially now that it's being subsidised for use in power stations. In addition, the current generation of super-efficient fires and stoves depend on burning properly dried timber if they are to achieve their desired effect.

Many local timber suppliers are selling green timber which has been felled recently and has a high moisture content. Ideally this needs to be stored for 18 months or two years before it's dry enough to burn. If you haven't got time or the capacity to do this, then you should really be buying kiln-dried wood, but this is much more expensive — often double or three times the cost of a regular load.

Of course, if you have the time and space, the best thing is to create a covered wood store where you can buy two years ahead and dry your own fuel, topped off perhaps with an internal storage feature close to the fire where you can finish off the logs before you put them on the fire. A word of warning: you may be tempted to create a wood store at the front of your house — it can be a very attractive feature — but with rising wood prices this may become a target for organised theft, so it advisable to situate your wood store away from prying eyes.

HANDLING THE OUTPUT

A modern, highly-insulated home requires very little heat to keep warm and you may well find that your "little fire in the corner" ends up overwhelming you and has you rushing to open all the available windows to cool down. This is especially true if you have installed an underfloor heating system whose output cannot easily be turned down.

One possible solution is to choose a stove with a back boiler, a water-heating element, that can use excess heat to meet some of your domestic hot water demands. As a rule, back boiler stoves use far more fuel (around 75% of the output goes into heating the water) and you may not fancy having to reload so frequently.

Another option is to arrange for the heat output to be ducted around the rest of the house, either in a dedicated system or via a mechanical ventilation system. If it's the latter, make sure that the designers know what your aims are because the register next to the fire needs to be an outlet rather than an inlet.

BUYING TIPS

■ Don't oversize the stove. Stove outputs are rated in kW and, in an existing older house, 1kW will heat something like 20m³ of room space. But in a well-insulated new house, that same kW will be enough to heat up between 70 and 100m³. Bearing in mind a four bedroomed house is typically no more than 450m³: you can see that you really don't need much heat to keep it warm, especially as the chances are the house already has a central heating system in place.

■ Many selfbuilders have successfully based their entire home heating strategy on using a mechanical ventilation system with heat recovery to waft around the heat from a 3 or 4kW wood stove. I would caution against this. It's a bit hit or miss, to say the least. Ventilation systems are not heating systems and they are usually set up with the living room as an inlet, not an outlet, so the idea that heat from a stove will magically be distributed around the bedrooms is fanciful.

■ Chimney or flue? In an existing house, you may well be able to use the chimney but ensure that it's swept and free of obstructions. In a new house, you will probably want to fit a stainless steel flue, which is cheaper than a chimney.

■ Smoke Control Areas: many local authorities now have smoke control areas. Google "Smoke Control Areas" to find out if you are in one. You can still fit a wood stove in a smoke control area but it has to be a clean-burn one if you want to burn logs, or a multifuel stove on which you burn smokeless fuel. Indeed, wood burning in general has started to come in for some stick due to our increasing concerns about air pollution. The really green option now is to have no wood stove at all.

■ Check out the Log Pile website (www.nef.org.uk/logpile), an online database of stove, boiler and fuel suppliers.

ELECTRIC HEATING

Information about electric heat pumps can be gleaned in the previous section. Here I take a look at the common but non-garden variety of electric heating, the night storage heater, the convector heater, electric boilers and various forms of electric underfloor heating.

Electric heating has one or two things going for it and one very big thing going against it. That big contra-thing is the cost of electricity, by far and away our most expensive fuel source. Not surprising really, as it is still predominately made by burning fossil fuels, mostly coal and gas, and there are large inefficiencies in converting fossil fuels into electricity, not to mention piping it for thousands of miles around the country.

Against this high price, electricity suppliers have held up a trump card,

being cheap night-time tariffs. These exist because they can't turn off the nuclear power plants at night and so they have all this power pumping around the system with nowhere to go, so they sell it off cheap as electric heating. Enter the world of off-peak night-storage heating: it is the most uncontrollable, unresponsive heating system ever designed, delivering the bulk of its heat when it's hardly needed. Not to mention the fact that night-storage heaters are usually dog ugly.

To counteract these failings, the supply companies have additional tariffs with off-peak rates for three hours in the afternoon, known as Economy 10 tariffs because they give you a ten-hour split charging period. Also, they now tend to recommend electric underfloor heating topped up with ceiling heaters, which are designed to run on the new Economy 10 tariffs. These developments represent a big improvement in the outlook for electric heating: the pluses that apply to wet underfloor systems apply just as strongly to electric heating. Yet as long as oil and gas remain half the price, straightforward electric heating is unlikely to be many people's first choice.

GREEN ELECTRICITY TARIFFS

Environmentally, electricity is often thought of as a dirty fuel because its production is still mostly from fossil fuels. Can you avoid this conundrum by buying green electricity?

Whilst the supply you actually get is identical to normal electricity, the

idea is that, for a small premium, you match your usage with renewable supplies. Thus, instead of having to go to the hassle of mounting photovoltaic cells on your roof or putting a wind turbine in the garden, you can get a supply of renewable energy over the grid. On this basis, many people have opted for electric heating systems, feeling that they are not only cheap to install but cause no environmental damage whatsoever. If only. My view is that these green electricity tariffs are an illusion and they actually promote the use of all forms of electricity, whereas a more considered approach would be to reduce electricity demand wherever possible.

WARM AIR

Warm air or forced air heating systems work by blowing heated air around the house in a series of ducts. All you see of it are inlet and outlet grills, usually a pair per room. It's the most common form of heating in American homes but in Britain it's fallen right out of favour after many systems fitted in the 1960s and 1970s proved to be noisy and ineffective.

I don't think any private developers have fitted warm air heating systems into new homes since about 1985. Johnson & Starley are the only firm left producing warm air units in this country, mostly satisfying the retrofit market. They work with a conventional flued, floor-standing gas-fired boiler. The system must be installed by a registered installer and would cost around £4,000 for a four-bedroom house. This would include a gas-fired boiler and all the ducting to push the hot air around the house, but domestic hot water (DHW) would have to be supplied by other means.

Perhaps a more serious candidate for selfbuilders is the US firm Unico who are offering a forced air unit which combines heating with air conditioning. They are usually present at the major selfbuild shows and can be linked up to many different kinds of heat source, including heat pumps.

VENTILATION

Buildings need to be ventilated. Trapped water vapour in particular can be very damaging, causing condensation and encouraging mould growth and wet rot. It's a potential problem in both the external structure of a house, especially under ground floors and in roofs, - and within the enclosed living space.

The building regulations deal with the need for ventilation in both areas. Underfloor ventilation (only applicable with suspended ground floors) is by way of air bricks; roof ventilation is by eaves or soffit vents and occasionally air bricks too.

INTERNAL VENTILATION

The building regs dealing with internal ventilation (Part F in England) specify that habitable rooms must have adequate ventilation, and the default routine for this is based around opening windows, trickle vents and extractor fans.

TRICKLE VENTS

The modern British window has a slot drilled out of it at the top into which you are required to fit a trickle vent. These slimline plastic inserts have now become nearly universal on standard joinery — indeed it is a problem to find windows without them. Some manufacturers still charge extra for fitting them, some supply windows with just the slots cut out and supply the vents separately.

An awful lot of people have no idea what a trickle vent is, even less what it does, but for those in the know it is not universally loved.

COOKER HOODS

Normally fitted as standard in kitchens, although they don't have to be ducted outside – they are said to 'recirculate' if they don't. Cooker hoods are usually sold as part of a package with hobs and ovens. They start at around £50: automatic versions with humidity controlled switching are available at around £100, but the current fashion if for rather grand stainless steel ones which typically cost £300 upwards. Actually, the fashion doesn't stope there. There are all manner of expensive extractors available with costs extending well into four figures.

BATHROOM FANS

A basic, 15lts/s, fan can be controlled by a pull switch, or linked to a room light switch. Bathrooms without windows have to have models fitted with automatic overrun timers and, where ducting is required, a centrifugal fan is recommended.

Higher up the range, the fans have humidistats which can automatically switch fans between off, low and high settings dependent on humidity in the bathroom.

The typical cost of all these measures on a four-bedroomed house is around £500, though the trickle vents may not be readily costable, because they are hidden in the charge for windows

WHOLE HOUSE SYSTEMS

The building regs allow for radically different approaches to ventilation. One is to do away with trickle vents and to provide both extract and inlet ventilation via a series of ducts controlled by electric fans. A number of manufacturers produce units that will recapture some of the heat being sucked out of the house, mixing it with fresh air being brought in through the loft.

Welcome to the world of the mechanical ventilation system with heat recovery (or MVHR). The system fan usually sits in the loft or in a utility room and it draws fresh air in through a duct in the outside wall and passes it across the outgoing warm air so that the outgoing heat is transferred into the incoming cold air. It then pipes the incoming air into the 'dry' rooms (living rooms, bedrooms) and sucks internal air out of 'wet' rooms (kitchen, bathrooms).

An MVHR system will cost between £4,000 and £6,000 to install so it's not a cheap and cheerful option, and it requires a lot of design input to enable it to work effectively. It costs money to run (in truth, not

Chapter 8

Mechanical Ventilation with Heat Recovery (MVHR)

MVHR involves a lot of ducting. The inlet and extract ducts are kept separate and meet at the heat exchanger conventionally located in the roofspace. The extracts are placed in the wet rooms (kitchens, bathrooms) whilst the inlets supply the living rooms and bedrooms.

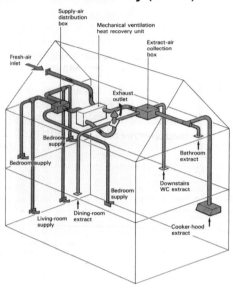

very much), it doesn't of itself save any energy and it leaves you with strange space age looking vents in your ceilings and walls. Who on earth would ft one of these?

It turns out just about everyone who is interested in energy efficient building because an MVHR system makes it possible to live in a near-sealed environment and yet still have good air quality. They are a key enabling device for Passivhaus and other low energy homes. Without such a system, all that thick insulation, air tightness tape and triple glazing would make no sense. Selfbuilders are big into MVHR, and with good reason.

There is a lot to be mastered here. Firstly, you have to design the layout when the house layout is being detailed. The key is to minimise the duct runs both in terms of length

and bends. The better systems use aluminium rigid tubes and they all have to have silencers fitted to reduce sound transfer between rooms. Cheaper systems use plastic ducting. Routinely, MVHR suppliers also design the installation as well, for which they often make a charge of several hundred pounds. Don't skimp on this: it is worth it. If you are buying a kit home or designing one from scratch, you need to make the designers aware of this at the outset because threading the ducting through floor voids and maybe through steel beams is much, much easier with a little pre-planning.

Although the actual assembly is not incredibly skilled and could be carried out by a competent DIY-er, for most people it makes sense to get a system fitted on a supply and fix basis because to work effectively,

the system needs to ne balanced as well, so that the air flow through the system is even. There also needs to be a significant airflow between rooms, so ensure that there is at least a 12mm gap under each and every bathroom or bedroom door. In order to comply with Part F of the building regulations, the finished system must be tested to show that the anticipated air flow rates at each register are close to the designed for figures, usually within ± 5%.

And having lived with a newly installed Paul Novus system, supplied by the excellent Green Building Store, I can vouch that they work. In winter, the windows stay shut and the air stays fresh. In summer, the heat exchanger gets by passed so that cool night air is drawn into the system, minimising the effects of hot nights.

MVHR systems are not to be confused with warm air heating systems. They don't actually heat anything. If an MVHR system is 90% efficient, which some of them are, this means that they retain 90% of the outgoing heat. Therefore, if it's 20°C indoors and zero (0°C) outside, the incoming air will be piped in a 18°C (i.e. 90% of the difference). Your heating system simply has to top up the air inside by 2°C to get it back to 20°C where it all started.

You can add heating elements to MVHR systems to get them to behave more like warm air heating systems, but it's not ideal as they pump the warm air into the bedrooms (where it's arguably not wanted) and draw it out of the bathrooms. Usually it's better to let the regular heat emitters (i.e. radiators, underfloor heating) get on with their job and just leave ventilation to the MVHR system.

PASSIVE STACK VENTILATION

This is another option that can be used if you are interested in whole house ventilation. Passive stack ventilation also uses ducts to extract stale air from the house but there the similarity ends. Trickle vents are fitted in all the dry rooms (i.e. living rooms, bedrooms) whilst ducts run from the wet areas (bathrooms, kitchens) up to a vented ridge tile and air pressure does the rest, drawing air in through the house and away through the roof. A whole house system (with four passive stacks) would cost around £2,000. Add a cooker hood (which is recommended) and the overall cost will be around 60% more than the standard route.

There are currently two passive stack suppliers, Passivent and Aereco and one interesting newcomer, Ventive, who appear to have invented a fully passive system that also recovers some of the waste heat. In general, Passivhaus enthusiasts tend to steer people away from this style of ventilation because it's not so reliable. Some times it works a treat, but change the wind direction and it stops working altogether.

GROUND TO AIR VENTILATION

Perhaps better known as earth pipes, these have been used in a number of countries over the years, but only very rarely in the UK. The system consists

Great care has to be taken installing MVHR systems. In order to avoid noise transmission, the ducting is routinely fitted with silencers, visible here in an open bathroom ceiling as the two rectangular boxed sections set into an otherwise circular metal array.

of a single length of pipe made of conductive antimicrobial material approximately 200mm diameter laid 1.5 or 2m below ground in a loop around the house or in the garden. One end terminates in a stainless steel tower (about 1m high) where the air is drawn in and the other links up with the supply ducting for the heat recovery unit (or vent supply fan). The costs vary depending on the size of the house: the smaller kits are priced at £2,000 and the largest at £4,000 – this is in addition to costs incurred for installing a mechanical ventilation system.

Why fit earth pipes? They have a marginal positive effect on the efficiency of mechanical ventilation

systems when running in heating mode, but they come into their own as a method of passive summer cooling, where the incoming air drawn into the system can be up to 5°C cooler than the external air temperature.

COOLING

There are home air conditioning systems available in the UK but whilst new housebuilders show increasing interest in more and more sophisticated ways of staying warm during the 25-odd week annual heating season, there is limited interest in staying cool during the 10-week high summer period.

Why? Well for a starter, it is expensive. An air conditioning system for a detached house would set you back in the region of £5,000. A one-room system would cost around £1,500. The existing models are all electrically powered and a whole house model would consume around 3-5kW of power when going at full blast — typically it would run for only 50% of the time, even on the hottest of days, providing you remember to keep the doors and windows shut. The units also tend to be noisy, though this problem can be reduced if the design of the installation is good. Like boilers, air conditioning needs to have exhaust ducting and this means that the system has to be built-in permanently and is connected to an outdoor unit.

Some of the heat recovery units and some heat pumps offer an air-cooling facility; the Villavent 4 unit provides something called comfort cooling – it will not turn the house into a fridge like the ones in American homes, but will be able to drop incoming air temperature by several degrees. And some heat pumps can run in cooling mode as well.

Generally, it is felt that cooling isn't really necessary in the UK climate if the house design is well-executed. One problem to avoid is solar over-heating in the summer months, the sort of effect that you see in conservatories. Large south-facing glazing may sound like a

wonderful idea on paper but it is likely to be quite unpleasant to live with during July and August.

HYBRID HEATING-VENTILATION SYSTEMS

Thus far I have tried to nail everything down into neat boxes. Thus we have heat pumps, cooling products, ventilation products and water heating products. But you don't have to dig very deep to see that there are degrees of overlap here and that, not surprisingly, there are new products which don't fit into these neat boxes. Let's look at ventilation systems that incorporate heat pumps and thus turn them into warm air heating systems.

Take, for instance, the Genvex Combi, an interesting piece of kit that sells for around £6,000. It's a big box which uses an air source heat pump to draw heat from the exhaust air coming from your mechanical ventilation system, and uses this to provide hot water and some warm air heating for your house.

I've seen it installed in a low energy housing development in Somerset and have to say I was quite impressed.

There are others. The PassivHaus standard – which demands whole house ventilation systems – seems to be encouraging the development of a number of compact air handling units which also provide a small element of heating using heat pump technology to achieve this. If you build a very low energy house,

like a Passive House, then you really don't require very much in the way of a conventional heating system, and these ventilation bolt-on heaters seem like a good way forward. The only proviso is that these solutions are certainly not yet mainstream and you may end up being something of a guinea-pig if you fit one.

FIRES & CHIMNEYS

Look around any 21st century housing scheme and you will see lots of clean-cut roofs, with rarely a chimney in sight. That is because chimneys are expensive to build, and stoves or fires are quite unnecessary in a modern, centrally-heated home. Penny pinching developers, quite logically, omit them. If there is a chimney, the chances are it will be a dummy made of GRC (Glassfibre Reinforced Concrete), or some other lightweight material, put there at the insistence of the local planning department.

But selfbuilders sing to a different hymn sheet and most of them long to have a focal point fire. Top of the selfbuild pops is the wood-burning stove, combining as it does elegance and efficiency.

But all wood stoves require a flue and/or a chimney. They are not quite the same thing. A chimney is a masonry structure designed to act as a flue, but you can have a flue without having to build a chimney. What are the choices?

MASONRY CHIMNEYS

Whereas a chimney was once simply constructed in brickwork as an open duct, terminating with a terracotta pot, they are now built around a core of clay or concrete flue liner. For a chimney to work well, it requires a good flow of air and the flue also needs to maintain as high a temperature as possible, so there are exacting regulations about chimney design. For instance, it's important for chimneys to be insulated as this keeps the smoke warm and lessens the chances of it condensing as tar deposits. This is particularly important with wood burning appliances, as they burn cooler than coal. Material costs for a new chimney start at around £1,000 and can spiral upwards depending on the design. However, there is generally a considerable labour element going into building a masonry chimney, and there is added complexity when wanting to place a masonry chimney within a timber-framed house.

FLUES

The budget option with a wood burning stove is to go for a pre-fabricated stainless steel flue. Whereas a gas-burning appliance can use a single-skin flue, with solid fuel you have to use an insulated twin-wall flue section in order to stop the smoke condensing inside the flue. Typical material costs for a 7m twin-wall stainless steel flue are around £1,500. Main manufacturers are Rite-Vent, Poujoulat, SFL and Selkirk.

Ceramic twin-wall flues are a more up-market option, and are 30-50% more expensive than stainless steel. Ceramic flues tend to come with a 30 year guarantee (rather than 10 years for stainless steel flues). They are recommended for heavy use, especially with biomass boilers.

Another option is to go for a pumice stone prefabricated flue: they provide a very simple way of building a long lasting, insulated masonry chimney system, at a similar cost to a twin-walled stainless steel flue. Instead of having to source components from several different suppliers, these chimney systems are supplied as kits for easy assembly. Names to look out for here are Schiedel and Anki.

Bear in mind also that masonry chimneys require foundations whereas steel and ceramic flues don't.

On the other hand, if you want a traditional pot, then you need to place it on a chimney. Flues have metal terminals instead.

RENOVATING EXISTING CHIMNEYS

Many people will want to keep an existing chimney and adapt it for use with a wood burning appliance. You need to check that the chimney is functional and adequate – a good chimney sweep should be able to help here. And it is now commonplace to install flexible flue liners, usually pushing them down the existing chimney from the top. Whilst often not essential, a flexible flue liner will help with the free flow of smoke and make for a more efficient chimney. Expect to pay upwards of £500 for

flexible flue liners plus the labour to fit.

Of course, there may be much more work you need to undertake to bring an existing chimney back into use. The brick or stone work may be weathered and need repair or repointing: the flashings may have to be replaced: the pots may need replacing as well.

PLUMBING

Conventionally, plumbers are hired to fit heating and sanitaryware; this includes all above ground waste fittings, but rarely underground drainage or rainwater goods. Traditionally, plumbers also undertook sheet-metal work on roofing, but now this tends to be carried out by roofers.

There are a couple of grey areas to be aware of. The first concerns the wiring of heating controls (which is sometimes carried out by the electrician) and the second concerns the installation of kitchen sinks and dishwashers, which is sometimes undertaken by specialist kitchen installers. Be clear, when you are hiring, who is to do what. The situation has been muddied by making most electrical work notifiable to building control, which means that many plumbers are no longer qualified to undertake things like the wiring of your central heating controls.

CHECK THE SPEC

Many contractors have only the vaguest understanding of the ins and outs of heating and plumbing

A progress shot taken on our recent selfbuild shows the inevitable march of plastic pipe for both supply and waste. Also note how crowded it is up here in Posi-Joist land.

systems and are more than happy to let their plumber design, price and install whatever system they like, and plumbers have become quite used to acting almost autonomously, as long as the kit works and the price is about right. Comparing quotations between plumbers is consequently a very difficult business because the specifications of the competing systems are almost bound to be different unless a professional has been employed to design the system beforehand, something which hardly anyone bothers with on smaller residential construction jobs.

Points to watch out for when comparing quotations are:
■ Are the design considerations identical? What temperature is each room to be heated to? How many air changes an hour have been assumed in the calculations?

■ What fuel is being specified to run the system? Have the costs of connection and storage been fully taken into account?
■ What controls are being provided?
■ How easy will it be to service the system?
■ Will pumps and cables be concealed?
■ What insulation is being provided to the hot water pipes?
■ What sort of emitters are being specified?
■ If standard panel radiators, where will they be sited?
■ Will they have TRVs fitted as standard? If so, will these be in addition to or instead of a whole-house thermostat?
■ What provision has been made for towel radiators? Heating airing cupboards?
■ What arrangements will be made

for hot water storage? What will hot water flow rates be like?
■ Where will the overflows run to?
■ What sort of guarantee is offered?

PLASTIC WASTE PIPES

Slowly but steadily, plumbing is going plastic. There are still many plumbers who wouldn't be seen dead using anything other than copper for their water feeds but you will search high and low to find one who uses anything other than plastic for waste fittings.

The whole subject of plumbing in the waste for bathrooms, loos and kitchens is surprisingly complicated and is covered at good length in the building regs (part H, if you must). The problem is that you need to stop smells getting up into the house from the drains: this is (usually) achieved by designing in water traps separating the appliances from the drains below.

There are several different trap designs around, usually named after letters of the alphabet – P and S figure prominently. Were that it was all there was to it and it would be the end of the story but unfortunately these water traps have a habit of failing, often through induced siphonage sucking the water down the pipe. What has evolved is a series of rules dictating how we should lay out our waste runs and where and when the runs should be joined together. The ones which tend to catch people out are the maximum length of basin runs – 1.7m – laid at a fall of between 18 and 22mm per metre run. It seems ridiculously precise; it's borne out of many years analysing just why basins gurgle and lose their water seals.

You can cheat: there are now non-return valves that don't require a water seal — the best known is Hepworth's ingenious HepVO valve.

The main waste runs also cause problems. The general rule is to run the appliances, such as basins, baths and showers, in small pipe sections (typically 32, 40 or 50mm) into a 110mm pipe, called a stack, which drops vertically down to the underground drain system. Stacks need to be ventilated and at least one stack on every drain run needs to be ventilated to the outside, usually done through the roof. If you have more than one stack, you can use a short version, known as a stub stack, on the subsequent stacks: these can be topped off with air admittance valves, also known as Durgos. These act in a similar fashion to the smaller HepVO valves used in small bore drain runs – letting air into the system but not letting any out.

At ground floor level, it's usual to run the waste pipes together into an external gulley and thence to the drains. The principle remains the same: to prevent smells from the drains escaping into the house. It's one part of the house fit-out which is routinely tested on completion of the job – the air test usually involves putting a bung into the drains at the highest manhole and another bung somewhere short of the air outlet and then seeing if the system between holds a given air pressure.

Indoor waste pipes have migrated across to plastic almost exclusively now but there is a choice of plastics

and a choice of working methods. The DIY route is to use a push-fit system based on either uPVC or polypropylene. Serious plumbers often prefer to use a glued system, known as solvent weld. These are typically made of ABS (acrylonitrile butadene styrene), a rather more rigid plastic. The average spend in a house on above ground waste fittings is around £300 so it's not a budget buster, whichever system you opt for.

WATER

Indoor plastic plumbing has been kicking around since the 1970s and in its time it's come in for a fair amount of stick from the professionals. It's also resulted in numerous floodings caused by duff joints or, more often, lazy installers. However, it's very easy and quick to install; it's mostly push-fit and it comes on a roll so you don't have to bother with soldering joints as you do with copper. So quick and easy that, at long last, it's really taking off in professional plumbing circles as well. Partly it's because it's used exclusively for underfloor heating (where it seems to perform fine) and partly due to new building techniques. Hepworth, the originators, have redesigned their joints to make them hopefully idiot proof and there is now competition from other big names in the field like Marley Plumbing, John Guest's Speedfit, and Polyplumb.

It's hard not to come to the conclusion that copper plumbing is on the way out, although it will continue to be used extensively for many years to come. Gas plumbing, for instance,

has to be done in copper. One area where plastic plumbing really wins out is when you are specifying I-beam floors: you can't notch I-beam floors (you can actually, but the results are disastrous) so the ability to uncoil the pipe through holes in the webbing is almost indispensable.

Chapter 9

WIRING

The wiring of new and existing homes is covered by building regs, and is a notifiable event in the life of a house, but the regulations simply insist that the wiring is done either by a competent person or to a standard that is passed as competent by a competent person. If that sounds like gobbledygook, welcome to the world of the building regs. In Scotland, electrics have always been a notifiable event, but England & Wales only fell into line in 2005 when Part P came into effect. Part P is all about notification.

The actual requirements are embedded in BS 7671, which itself is pretty much the same as the 18th edition of the IEE Wiring Regs. But what has changed is that house wiring now has to be passed by building inspectors or by qualified electricians so you need to find out if your electrician is 'Part P compliant'. If they are, they can issue you with a certificate on completion to say that the work has been carried out to the relevant standard. Very small works are exempt, but anything involving kitchens, bathrooms or externals is notifiable so, for instance, fitting a new kitchen is now likely to come under building regs.

If you are undertaking a major project, like a new house, then you will already be involved in a building regs application and you won't be required to do an additional one just because electrics are involved. Here you can simply ask your building inspector to check the wiring, along with everything else.

COSTS

The tables in this chapter show just how each element of an electrician's quotation would be made up and how this translates into a whole house quotation. Compared to most aspects of construction, electrical fittings vary enormously in quality.

For many years, the market was dominated by two British businesses, MK and Crabtree: indeed many specifiers indicate that fittings should be by either of these two firms. But there is a huge gulf between MK/Crabtree prices and some very cheap imported gear. The current TLC catalogue (www.tlc-direct.co.uk) has MK 13amp double sockets at £3.25 each; however, they also have their own brand version (Telco) at £1.50 each. There are lots of options if you want something between these two prices. And, of course, there are many, many suppliers producing all manner of fancy switches and sockets. If you are the sort that gets exercised by the differences between brushed chrome, satin chrome and polished chrome, then you can easily pay over £30 an outlet.

HOUSE WIRING
CONNECTION FEES
Electricity connection to new homes is organised by the businesses which used to be the local electricity board but are now known as Distribution Network Operators (DNOs). You can look up who operates in your area at energynetworks.org. The DNOs are free to set their own connection fees and, being monopoly suppliers of an indispensable power source, they tend to charge a lot. Even a straightforward connection is likely to cost in the region of £800.

If you are considering electric heating or an electric heat pump in your house, you may find that the DNO may offer to halve or even waive the entire connection fee as a sweetener, but more likely they will try to persuade you to have a three-phase supply which will cost 20% more. Long cable runs (say in excess of 50m) can be prohibitively expensive, costing many thousands, and should be carefully costed when assessing the plot. Each DNO has a New Supplies Department, which is where you should look for quotations; you don't need to own the plot before getting a quotation.

TEMPORARY SUPPLIES
Some builders manage without temporary electricity supplies, relying on generators and diesel-powered mixers; indeed most of the house superstructure can be easily erected without power tools. However, plumbers, electricians and second-fix carpenters are big users of power tools (albeit mostly portable ones nowadays) and you can't have your permanent supply turned on until they're finished so, for most builders, a temporary supply makes good sense.

Current regs insist that the temporary supply board is adequately housed; on most sites this means building a blockwork box with at least a paving slab roof and a lockable door. Budget a day's work and £100 materials to build an adequate shed with consumer unit and sockets on a backing board inside. Care should be given to locating the temporary supply so that long cables are not left trailing over the site where they could be run over by diggers, dumpers or lorries. Discuss your requirements with the DNO's new supplies estimator; there will be an extra charge for temporary supply but it's usually not large, provided there are no major cable detours.

METER BOXES
The industry standard is to install white plastic boxes built into the external wall. The DNOs like them because they can access the meter without entering the house; builders like them because they usually supply them free (as they do lengths of underground ducting) and they can be built into the outer skin brick wall without a lintel. The only problem is that they are ugly; ugly enough to ruin a fancy period facade. If this bothers you then either look to locate the plastic meter box where it won't detract from your kerb appeal or insist that the company supply comes into the house where it can be concealed in a cupboard.

Gas supplies have the same problem but they offer an alternative meter box concealed in the ground; however, this is felt to be unsafe for an electrical supply. Water meters are always concealed in the ground.

SMART METERS
You are not legally required to fit a smart meter when you build a new home but I think you'd be nuts not to because how else would you know that all that expensive insulation and glazing is actually working to save you energy. If you've not lived with

ELECTRICS: Key Rates

ITEM	COST
Double Socket	£ 12
Single Socket	£ 10
Fused Spur	£ 10
5-amp Socket	£ 10
Cooker Switch	£ 15
Cooker Outlet	£ 5
Shaver Point	£ 25
Immersion Point	£ 10
External Sockets	£ 30
Consumer Unit	£ 80
Residual Circuit Devices	£ 40
Each Fuse	£ 5
TV/TELECOM WIRING	
Coaxial Point	£ 10
Telephone Point	£ 10
Loft Aerial	£ 50
Door Bell	£ 30
SAFETY	
Smoke Detectors	£ 30
LIGHTING	
1-gang Switch	£ 6
2-gang Switch	£ 7
3-gang Switch	£ 8
Pull Switch	£ 6
2-way Switching	£ 5
3-way Switching	£ 10
Ceiling Light	£ 20
Fire rated LED downlights	£ 20
FANS	
Bathroom Fans	£ 50
Kitchen Fan	£ 75

Electrician's charges

LABOUR charged at	£ 40 /hr	
Sockets	50 mins	£ 33
External Sockets	100 mins	£ 67
Door Bells	120 mins	£ 80
Light Outlet	30 mins	£ 20
Each switch	30 mins	£ 20
Extenal Lights	90 mins	£ 60
extra for light fittings	45 mins	£ 30
Fans (inc kitchen extracts)	150 mins	£ 100
Smoke Detectors	60 mins	£ 40
Basic CU	60 mins	£ 40
Each circuit	10 mins	£ 7
Electric Ovens and Hobs	180 mins	£ 120

you can access it.

There have been issues with the first generation of smart meters (SMETS 1) which meant that once fitted it is very difficult to change suppliers. But in 2019 the next generation is being rolled out (SMETS 2) and these afford you the luxury of being able to switch and to keep the records from your previous supplier.

In time all meters will be smart and they will start offering varying tariffs which will enable significant energy savings both nationally and for yourself. So don't be a luddite — fit a smart meter.

CONSUMER UNITS AND RCDS

The consumer unit – what used to be known as the fuse box – is the place where the supply is split into a number of separate circuits for distribution around the house. There are conventions on how these circuits should be arranged, although the exact design will depend on each

particular layout. A 16-gang unit will suffice for all but the largest houses and it is recommended not to economise too much on this item. Miniature circuit breakers (MCBs) have now replaced the traditional fuses; instead of fusewire blowing, a little button pops out and reconnection is never more complicated than pressing the button in again.

Another development is the advent of residual circuit-breaking devices (RCDs) – now mandatory – which provide increased protection against electrocution in the event of contact with live wires. One drawback of RCDs is that they are very sensitive and can be triggered by thunderstorms or faulty equipment. This in turn may cause problems with things that must not have their power supply cut off – chiefly freezers and smoke detectors. An RCD-inspired power cut-out could have very messy consequences if it occurred during your two weeks in the Algarve, and for this reason it is recommended that freezers are run off separate circuits not protected by an RCD. The net result of all this is that you'll be spending around £100 on your consumer unit whereas in the bad old days it might have cost only £20.

SOCKETS

If you've got deep pockets, fit lots of sockets – but at £20-£25 per outlet this can rapidly become a prohibitively expensive option. If you know how you are going to arrange beds and furniture in each room you can minimise the number of sockets needed; if you want to

a smart meter before, they give you real time readings on how much electricity and gas you are using, plus daily read outs on what you've consumed. Log onto you account and you can see a detailed breakdown of what you've used every day.

This may of course be an awful bore to many (most?) of you, but it's still good to know that it's there and

MODEL HOUSE Electrical Costs

	Sockets	Lights	Switches	Data	Smoke Detectors	Fans	Shaver points	Cabling RCDs	Totals
Kitchen/Dining Area	8	12	4	2	1	1			
Utility	2	1	1			1		1	
WC		1	1			1			
Hallway	1	2	2		1				
Lounge	8	6	2	2					
Bed 1	8	4	2	2					
Ensuite		2	1			1	1		
Bathroom		2	1			1	1		
Bed 2	8	2	1						
Bed 3	8	2	1						
Bed 4/Home Office	8	2	2	2					
Landing	2	2	1		1				
External	1	4	2						
Totals	**54**	**42**	**21**	**8**	**3**	**5**	**2**		
Labour in hrs	45	53	11	7	3	13	3	20	155 hrs
Rounded Cost of labour	**£ 1,800**	**£ 2,120**	**£ 440**	**£ 280**	**£ 120**	**£ 520**	**£ 25**	**£ 800**	**£ 6,000**
Typical material costs	£ 12	£ 20	£ 7	£ 10	£ 30	£ 75	£ 25	£ 600	
Rounded Cost of materials	**£ 650**	**£ 840**	**£ 150**	**£ 80**	**£ 90**	**£ 380**	**£ 50**	**£ 600**	**£ 3,000**
				Wiring total labour and materials					**£ 9,000**

This table attempts to summarise the complexities of costing a very simple electrical installation on a new house. Selfbuilders regularly spend three or four times this when they start specifying scene lighting, whole house audio and smart home devices.

retain flexibility for each room then you'll probably need a minimum of three sockets per bedroom and four sockets in living rooms. It will cost a lot more to add sockets in the future and not having them where you want them when you've moved in is very frustrating. Also, don't think that you are saving money by fitting single sockets instead of doubles. The work involved in installing them is identical and the materials price is only pennies different. You can step-up to metallic-finished sockets for an extra £5 or £10 per outlet.

SAFETY ISSUES

Since 2005, electrical work in the home has to be either carried out or passed by a qualified electrician (Part P compliant is the thing to look out for) or passed by your building inspector. It's not made DIY installations illegal, as some claim, but it has brought in a measure of quality control that wasn't there before.

There are a number of areas where DIY housewirers – and professional electricians come to that – are prone to make untraceable errors and you would be well advised to steer clear of house wiring unless you have a thorough knowledge of the tasks in hand.

CABLES IN WALLS

Cables buried in walls must be set either vertically or horizontally from the outlets they supply. The idea is that the follow-on trades have some idea where not to drill holes. However, this requirement is frequently ignored in the rush to get jobs done and sometimes even to try and save money by using less cable. Even if you know where the cable is buried and, therefore, think it doesn't matter, don't forget that the cable will still be there long after you've moved on and some poor sucker thirty years hence could be in for a nasty surprise. Technically, you are allowed to run cables within 150mm of internal corners and wall and ceiling junctions, but this habit cannot be recommended.

EARTH BONDING

It is a requirement that exposed metalwork should be earthed to prevent it becoming 'live.' This is normally done with 10mm earthing cable (it's green and yellow). What exactly needs to be bonded?

▪ Water and gas mains as they enter the house
▪ Any exposed structural steel and oil tanks
▪ All services must be bonded together
▪ All metal in bathrooms must be bonded together.

Note that if you are plumbing with plastic pipe (such as Hep2O or Speedfit), the requirement to earth bathroom radiators and steel baths is dropped.

ELECTRIC HEATING

If you are interested in electric heating and heat pumps in particular, have a look at the relevant sections in the Heating chapter. You may have to opt for a three-phase supply.

FREQUENTLY OVERLOOKED

When designing electricity supplies to a house there are a number of points to watch out for – and easily forgotten at the first-fix, cable-burying stage. Many electricians are used to doing what they are told and no more and will be of little help in designing a better system. Here is a bulletted list of commonly forgotten wiring details:

▪ Loft lights, cupboard lights – do you want them?
▪ Separate freezer circuit – preferably not protected by RCD
▪ Separate garage supply if garage is external
▪ Outside power points, security lights, welcome lights
▪ Kitchen unit lighting – usually fixed below wall units
▪ Check the rating of your electric cooking gear – 30 amps may not be enough
▪ Wiring for electric showers and power shower pumps
▪ Wiring and installation of fans in bathrooms and kitchen, or a mechanical fan system, if required
▪ Separate circuit for immersion heater
▪ Outlets left for smoke detectors (now mandatory)
▪ Doorbell wiring
▪ Heating controls wiring: boiler, programmer, thermostats, pump and valves all need to be connected. This work is often undertaken by the plumber but the electrician must leave at least a fused spur to power the controls. If the plumber does this wiring, then a separate test certificate will be needed from him
▪ Fused spurs for waste disposal units and/or water softeners
▪ Wiring to sewage treatment plants or for any external water pumps (water features, swimming pools)
▪ Wiring for electric garage door operators: needs an accurately placed single socket, not really a problem if power is in the garage
▪ Burglar alarm first-fix
▪ Wiring for renewable energy systems, such as photovoltaics or wind turbines, both of which produce power in DC and need inverters to turn this into AC. Also meters have to be adapted if exporting the power you produce.
▪ Wiring for a car charging point, if required

LIGHTING

The best light is natural sunlight. Lux is a measurement of light density and whereas 500 lux is the generally accepted level of electric light needed for reading, bright sunshine delivers 100,000 lux and even a cloudy overcast day will produce 5,000 lux of light.

The older you get the more light you need. A 60-year-old requires ten times more light than a 10-year-old. So how do you go about providing lighting?

LEDS

There have been a lot of changes in building and services technology in the housebuilding scene since I first started writing about them in 1994. But in that time, I've never witnessed a technology that has leapt off the page and caused me to rewrite a whole section of the Bible from one edition to the next. But LEDs were that game changer. Their time has definitely come.

LED (light emitting diodes) lamps have been evolving, improving and decreasing in price fairly steadily (at around 10% per annum for over a decade) and now TLC are selling a white LED downlighter lamp for just £2.15. Admittedly mostly LED lights are still rather more expensive than this — they tended to be priced between £5 and £12 per lamp in late 2014 — but they have a performance edge on just about all other kinds of lighting ever invented. They are now brighter, they stay brighter longer, they are available in warm, cool or daylight whites, they last longer (or they should do — there are questions about just how reliable the really cheap ones are). And critically, they use a lot less energy than all the other forms of energy efficient lighting that we have come across.

They knock spots off the unpopular, mercury-laden compact flouresecents (CF). CFs had little going for them except energy efficiency and, by and large, LEDs are now far more energy efficient than CF lamps. And LEDs do downlighters just as well, if not better, than halogen. There are lots of outlets that supply them — in fact very few that don't — and if you look around you can find LED replacements for just about any bulb you might care to think of. GU10 downlighters cost around £6 each, their bayonet replacement bulbs (B22) anywhere from £7 to £14.

If you want to dim LEDs you have to buy dimmable LEDs and get a suitable dimmer switch to match the very low loads. If you swap an LED for a conventional bulb where a dimmer is present, you may end up damaging both the dimmer switch and the lamp. And if you have a low voltage halogen downlighting scheme, you need some specialist advice about replacing the existing lamps with LEDs, as the transformers may need replacing. But if you are starting from scratch, you really should not be bothering with low voltage halogen. Dimming LEDs is still a work in progress. In theory, it should all function smoothly. In practise, you sometimes get weird effects from supposedly dimmable

Lamp Efficiency					
Brightness in lumens	**220**	**440**	**700**	**900**	**1300**
Standard Tungsten Bulb	25w	40w	60w	75w	100w
Halogen	18w	28w	42w	53w	70w
CFL	6w	9w	12w	15w	20w
LED	4w	6w	10w	13w	18w

LEDs are already the most efficient light source available and are constantly improving. Currently prices are falling by nearly 10% per annum.

LEDs. However, this is a technical issue which will probably be resolved soon.

DOWNLIGHTERS

Light sources concealed in the ceiling (or wall or floor) have the big advantage of being stylistically neutral – i.e. they can blend in with any type of decor. They have the disadvantage of only being able to light a rather limited area and a large room lit entirely with downlighters can be impractical. Despite their name, downlighters do not have to point straight down: there are 'eyeball' versions which beam the light off at an angle – in effect sidelighters.

There are some very simple cheap downlighters which consist of little more than a metal ring around hole in the ceiling into which you fit the lamp. And there are some more elaborate ones which come in their own casing: these are often fire-rated. There is a good argument for always using fire-rated downlighters because they do something to cover up the hole you have made. A hole in the ceiling does little to help sound-proofing, airtightness or insulation, not to mention fire-proofing.

5-AMP PLUGS

A handy idea for living rooms where you want to have a number of sidelights is to fit a series of 5-amp lighting sockets (usually with small round-pin holes to distinguish them from 13-amp mains sockets).

These can be linked together and all switched from one point. It's convenient not only because it gives you a master switch to control all the sidelights plugged into the 5-amp sockets, but it also gives you the ability to dim. By arranging the switching next to the door, it gives you the option of doing away with central pendant lighting altogether.

If you know nothing about the art of good lighting and you are in a hurry and don't want to waste a small fortune, you won't go wrong by specifying a handful of 5-amp sockets.

You can create quite sophisticated lighting effects by using side lighting and, without spending a fortune on fittings, you can get pools of light wherever you want them whilst retaining a flexibility to change it all if you get bored and want something different. Downside is, of course, that you have to re-wire all the plugs on your sidelights.

SCENE LIGHTING

This is where lighting meets home automation. Here you programme banks of lights to come on together to create moods or scenes. It's something that is commonly seen in places like conference suites and lecture theatres but is beginning to migrate towards the home. Products such as Lutron's Homeworks works with most types of lamp and allows you to programme lighting arrangements, including dimming, so that rather than fiddling endlessly with several different switches to get the desired outcome, you can just have two or three scenes to play out as and when you want them. Not only can you switch banks of lights on and off with one button but you can also do vacation settings for security. But it comes at a frightful cost, typically around £1,500 per room and as much as £10,000 for a whole house solution.

LIGHTING AND THE BUILDING REGS

The building regs address energy efficiency in lighting and further enhancements are likely in future. They want you to fit some energy efficient lightbulbs. But where? And how many? The requirement for England & Wales is set out in the Domestic Buildings Services Compliance Guide 2013:
■ it asks for 3 in every 4 outlets to be low energy
■ it relaxes the previous requirement for the fittings to be dedicated, meaning that people will be free to

switch over to any old bulb after the building is finalled
■ the new efficiency threshold is increased to 45 lumens per circuit-watt (see Lamp Efficiency table).

Ordinary incandescent bulbs and halogen will fall foul of the regs. Fluorescent and compact fluorescent should be fine but LEDs — the coming light source — are now appearing with much higher efficiencies than we have been used to — scores of over 100 lumens per circuit watt are now commonplace, and Cree have a lamp in development that produces 250 lumens per circuit watt. Note however that not all LEDs are super energy efficient and it can be quite hard to tell what the lumens per watt rating is on individual lamps. But nevertheless, building inspectors are unlikely to get heavy handed with you if you fit LEDs.

ROOM BY ROOM
KITCHENS

Central pendant lighting is particularly inept at providing light for kitchen worksurfaces, and this is one area where task lighting is now considered essential. The conventional place for this is under the wall cupboard units, hidden from view by the decorative downstand known as the pelmet.

An alternative is to fit downlighters in the ceiling over the kitchen surfaces, but placement has to be extremely accurate and you risk getting unlit areas under the wall units. You can get downlighters that are only 20mm deep and are specifically designed to fit into a

cupboard shelf. If your kitchen design doesn't want or need pelmets under your wall cupboards and you don't want exposed lights, then this is the answer for you.

DINING TABLES

A pendant light hanging over a dining table works very well, but make sure that the lamp is well concealed by the shade or fitting. Lighting from the side is much more difficult because of the shadows cast by the diners. As an alternative to a hanging light, go for a cluster of downlighters. .

LIVING ROOMS

There are no set rules for lighting living areas. Chandeliers, spotlights, uplighters, wall lights, downlighters, table lamps, sidelights; all have a role to play and it's very much a question of taste. Most developers and selfbuilders will be planning fairly conservative interiors, particularly in their living rooms, and an awful lot of the high-tech lighting schemes would be completely inappropriate here. However, the use of concealed fittings, such as downlighters, is compatible with virtually all settings.

Lighting a room with downlighters is generally pleasing to the eye but it is expensive because of the numbers needed. Pendant fittings and wall lights may be preferred but considerable time and expense may go into selecting the right fittings for the room; downlighters actually require less thought. Another option is to go for three or four uplighters or wall lights, which will generally be enough to provide all the lighting needs (including reading) for a largish room; this presents a stylish mid-priced alternative between the expense of downlighters and the poor light quality offered by a central light. Feature mirrors need to be set where they do not directly reflect lights. A traditional effect like a mirror above an Adam style fireplace will be ruined by a chandelier directly in front of it. Picture lighting is another problem area that you can ruin if you don't get it right.

BEDROOMS

For most people, bedroom lighting will be a mixture of an ambient central pendant and table lamps for reading. Although a central pendant light source will be cheaper to install, when the cost of task lighting is included, the alternative options of uplighters or downlighters look more pocket-friendly, although you must pay attention to switching from the bed as well as by the door.

BATHROOM LIGHTING

The regulations require that bathroom light fittings should be concealed to prevent direct contact with water. Conventionally, this is done by placing a central light inside some sort of glazed casing. There are some extremely naff bathroom light fittings around and finding a good one can be difficult. An alternative approach is to use sealed downlighters.

There is in fact a raft of regulations about lighting in wet areas, covered by the IP ratings (IP here stands for Ingress Protection). Google IP

Ratings if you want to know what these are in detail, but the quick and cheerful run down is that the bathroom is split into three zones and each has to have light fittings suitable for the risk (but only if you choose to place light fittings in these zones).

■ Zone 0 is either in the bath itself or in the shower tray (why would you want a light fitting in a shower tray?) and requires top-rated fittings (scoring IP 67 or higher).

■ Zone 1 is immediately above the bath or in the shower cubicle up to a height of 2.25m above floor level. Here you require a fitting rated at IP44 or higher.

■ Zone 2 is the area around Zone 1, up to 0.6m surrounding it. This also requires an IP44 light fitting or better.

HALLWAYS/STAIRWELLS

■ Don't be tempted to hang lights where you can't change the bulb without a ladder.

■ Don't fit uplighters at the foot of stairwells where you can see the bulbs from above.

EXTERNAL LIGHTING

The bane of external lighting is the 500 watt halogen floodlight. In the last few years these have become very cheap and very common, yet their effect is blindingly unpleasant, unless well concealed. The advent of LEDs hasn't ended this practice — it's just made it more energy efficient.

Security lighting need not be unattractive. It is worth giving a

bit of thought to external lighting – unless you are building next to a well-lit road, you will find that some form of external light is essential just to negotiate the front path. By all means arrange to switch it on a timed Passive Infra Red (PIR) detector, but that doesn't mean you have to blast people in the face with over bright bulbs. PIR switches can be adjusted to trip on at different light levels and for different lengths of time – from a few seconds to several minutes.

As alternatives to in-your-face floodlights, consider wall-mounted lanterns, outdoor spotlights spiked into the ground, free standing bollards or even brick lights, which replace a standard brick in your external wall.

The energy efficiency regs also address external lighting. They demand that external lights should either be fitted with daylight detectors and timed switches or not use more than a 40W bulb. Because of the LED take-over, the regs here are looking a little dated, as a 40W LED would be the equivalent of 250W in old money.

BUILT-IN VACUUMS

Why bother to fit a built-in vacuum cleaning system? The big plus with central vacuums is that what gets sucked up stays sucked up. With a portable vacuum, efficiency depends on how well the filter works. Small particles of dust go through the filter and get re-circulated, which is why a house often smells a little bit different after vacuuming. By removing the motor to somewhere like a utility room or, better still, a garage, you are shifting all this dust out there, though it may not do much for the look of your shiny new car. And, by locating the motor out of the way, you also get another plus which is near-silent vacuuming.

The biggest minus seems to be finding somewhere to stash the pipe. The fewer inlets you have the cheaper and easier to install but the longer the pipe needs to be. Many people fit one inlet downstairs and one upstairs which means you need up to 10 m of pipe to be able to get to the far corners of the house. Coiled up this makes a considerable heap – much bigger than a portable vacuum. The solution is to build in a rack, like a hosepipe rack, somewhere handy to get to but easy to conceal. A pipe cupboard no less.

There are a number of small manufacturers working in the UK market. Most advertise heavily in the selfbuild press and can be regularly found making pitches at the selfbuild exhibitions. If you are interested, most will quote from floor plans you send them. They aim particularly at the new build market because the system is most conveniently fitted at the first-fix stage so that the ducting is easily concealed. Put another way, it's more trouble than it's worth to fit the pipes into an old house but building into a new home is relatively straightforward.

Prices for a built-in vacuum cleaner

Built-in vacuums are a niche product in the selfbuild market. They make for interesting displays at exhibitions.

system on a four-bedroom detached house are around £1,000 (excluding labour). Some businesses actually give away the wall ducting with timber frame kit homes, hoping this will create a sale later.

TELECOMS

As recently as 1995, this was a fairly short section: you stuck a phone line in, you put a couple of TV points in, an aerial in the loft, maybe a satellite dish and you were away. For many people this will still be a fine solution, but the intervening years have seen the arrival of home office working, the internet, and digital TV, and suddenly the basic house wiring doesn't look quite up to the mark anymore.

Now you have to make an educated guess as to what to put in and what to leave out, not only for your own requirements but for any possible

future buyers as well. Time to knuckle down and take a hard look at what's in and what's out in home communications.

KEY CHANGES

The twentieth century saw the near-universal adoption of three different wiring systems into the home: electricity, telephones and television, with a few homes opting for a fourth system, wiring for burglar alarms. Of these, only the first, electricity, has conventionally been cabled all over the house. Telephones initially came into the house at just one socket, more recently two or three and likewise TV outlets have been restricted to one, two or three outlets.

Whilst the electric cabling routes

around the house remain largely unchanged, the demand for more complex phone wiring and TV cabling is causing these other systems to grow and converge. Phone wiring is changing because we want more outlets and because we are using phone lines for more than just conversations. TV wiring is changing because the methods of delivering TV signals are changing. Over and beyond this, the actual cables used for phones and TVs are changing and people are starting to cable for additional reasons: things like security, audio and lighting control.

DIGITAL TV

TV signals are delivered to the home by three different methods, rooftop aerial, satellite dish and fibre optic cable. If you live in or near to a big city, you will have a choice of all three but fibre-optics are unlikely to be laid out in rural districts, so you need to find out what is available and what works well in your area.

Standard TV signals (the ones we have all grown up with since the 1950s) have conventionally been fed around the house in brown coaxial cable from the rooftop or loft aerial. The standard signal is usually adequate to service three or four TV sets – if you want more you need to add a small amplifier to the system.

Digital TV isn't so different. The signal needs to be decoded in the house, something which used to be achieved in a box of tricks called a digibox, although these days it's usually done inside a digital TV (that is a TV that has a built-in decoder). You can use just one decoder for all the TVs in the house, but if you want to watch different channels, then each TV will need its own decoder (or be a digital TV).

PHONES AND BROADBAND

Phone cabling around the house has traditionally been a simple affair. Your service provider (traditionally BT) installed a master socket and you could run a small number of extensions out from there. If you started running a business from home, you would install a second line with a fax/phone on it. It rarely got more complicated than that. Surprisingly, the broadband roll-out hasn't changed it that much. If you want to connect three computers, an X-box and a TV to the internet, you can do it all via one phone line. Broadband is now established as a medium for watching TV and video on demand, even though there are distinct signs that the infrastructure is groaning with the demand being placed on it. One of the neatest features of broadband is that you can still make and receive phone calls on the same line whilst uploading and downloading whatever from the internet, something the old dial-up connections couldn't do.

So in many ways, broadband makes life simpler for people working from home who previously would have had to install multiple phone lines.

Cable modems, an alternative way of getting broadband, are available to customers of the cable network which covers 50% of the UK population. The deals are broadly similar to other broadband offerings but link you to the fibre-optic network, run by VirginMedia, which promises much faster speeds. Open Reach is also now rolling out a fibre optic network.

WIRED OR WIRELESS?

Selfbuilders have over the past decade or so spent a great deal of money laying data cabling systems around their homes, only to find that the world seems to have migrated to wireless systems, which require nothing more than a single broadband router — usually provided free by the internet service provider – plugged into the phone line. Whereas once, we all used desktop computers (which came with all manner of wires and cables), we now seem to be using laptops, tablets and smart phones where mobility is key. Has the technology moved on to the extent that wired systems are now redundant?

WIRELESS PROS

▪ It's simple to install
▪ It's inherently flexible - you don't have to plug into a socket
▪ It's almost as quick as hard wired connection – strictly speaking not true, as wired connections are capable of much greater data transmission speeds, but the limiting factor is usually the bandwidth coming into the house, not the distribution around the house, so in reality you won't notice any difference
▪ It's more convenient with mobile devices like iPads and iPhones. In fact most of the recent phones and tablets don't have any way of connecting to cable as they are wireless by default.
▪ Far fewer cables

Chapter 9

■ It works up to 25m from the base station
■ It's easily and cheaply upgradeable

WIRELESS CONS
■ You may get wi-fi blind spots – it often doesn't work in every corner of the house: aluminium sheeting, in particular (sometimes used with plasterboard or underfloor heating), blocks wireless reception, though you can buy signal boosters to counteract this phenomenon).
■ Sometimes other devices can cause interference
■ This makes it problematic when planning ahead – how do you know whether it will work or not?
■ You still get a better, more reliable connection speed with cable.

EXTENDING WIRELESS NETWORKS
There are work-arounds for some of these problems. There are products that enable you to set up booster outlets which take the signal from the main router and relay it to parts of the home (or the garden office) where reception is difficult. Apple's Airport Express is designed to do just this, and it also enables music to be distributed wirelessly as well. The advantage of these products is that they are portable, so that you can move them around until you get the signal strength you require.

Of course, it's not either wired or wireless. There is nothing stopping you playing mix and match, so that some parts of your home network are wired whilst other parts are wireless.

The wiring closet, sometimes known as Node Zero. If you data cable a house, the aim is to bring all the cables individually back to this point so that each outlet is directly connected to the hub. Frankly, you don't really need any of this unless you are running an office.

It may be that in future selfbuilders will stop flood wiring their homes with data cabling and instead run two or three ethernet cables from the hub to strategic points around the house and then rely on wireless connection from booster stations. That is precisely what I did on my 2018 selfbuild and have no complaints.

POWERLINE NETWORKS
But there is another technology that threatens to make even this amount of data cabling redundant, because now you can transmit data through your home's electrical wiring system. Type 'Powerline' into Amazon and it'll return a dozen or so pairs of plugs at around £40, enabling you to fit these adaptors into your electrical

sockets and then connect Ethernet cabling. It saves you having to run the cabling all over the house.

Again, it's an inherently flexible system because almost every room has electrical sockets and so you can have a cabled internet connection anywhere you want. It's a particularly good solution for outbuildings and garden offices where a wireless connection might struggle. But it's still not as good as dedicated Ethernet cabling: Powerline is not nearly as quick and is prone to occasional, inexplicable cut outs.

WIRED ETHERNET
This is the 'conventional' way of doing it, even though just a few years ago it was regarded as cutting edge.

Data cabling migrated from offices where it is now as common as electric wiring. Instead of haphazardly running cables from the various input points to the various output points around the house, you designate a place in the house as a central hub (known as the wiring closet or sometimes, annoyingly, as Node Zero) and you bring all the incoming cables to this point and then distribute them around the house to wall-mounted data sockets which look very much like electric sockets.

A wiring closet doesn't have to reside in its own purpose built room – unlike the other kind of WC.

The essential element in a wiring closet is a patch panel, a wall-hung box the size of a small suitcase. The patch panel plays a similar role to an electrical fusebox in household electrical wiring where the power coming into the house is split up and sorted into different circuits. It is in here that the phone lines and TV cables are all connected. Rather than being connected up in series (or daisy chained) as many TV and phone outlets are in conventional set-ups, each outlet throughout the house is connected directly back to the patch panel. That means a double data socket will have two cables running next to each other back to the patch panel where each will terminate with its own unique number which corresponds to a number etched on the data socket.

The wiring is done with data cabling of which there are various formats like Cat 5 or Cat 6; generally the more expensive the cable, the more data it will carry. The cable itself is not expensive, typically no more than electric cable.

Similarly the patch panel and the RJ45 outlets needed to plug in your devices are commodity items.

The materials to fit out a four-bedroomed house would typically cost around £800-£1,200, depending on the number of outlets that you require. This compares very similarly with the cost of electrical wiring.

For many selfbuilders, the cabling is seen as just another DIY task to be completed along with the underfloor heating and the central vacuum system. There are now many companies offering to supply and fit structured cabling systems and prices start from about £2,000 for a basic fit out, though many of the more esoteric uses of structured cabling such as lighting control and multi-room sound systems are expensive extras costing many additional thousands.

The one major weak point with Cat 5 cabling was that it didn't deliver a very compelling TV signal. Because of this it has been conventional to run CT-100 coaxial cable as well as Cat 5 around the house and back to the patch panel.

IN SUMMARY

The question remains: if you are building a new home in the 2020s, does it make sense to fit a data cabling system to every room in the house? The short answer is no.

Mobile computing and wireless communication is taking over and few homes will have more than one desktop computer in future.

However, it may still be worth running a limited cable network to get reliable access to far-flung corners of the home. And of course, there will still be other features of the smart home (principally entertainment, audio and security systems) which are more reliable when used with cable. But then these never did use the standard data cabling systems in any event.

Whilst cable systems will continue to supply faster and more reliable data, we have grown used to the convenience of wi-fi only tablets and phones and it seems likely that wi-fi is set to sweep all before it.

10

FINISHES

Traditionally, the second-fix stage of house building begins with the internal plastering, even though these days the majority of new houses never get to see any traditional plastering. Up until this time, everything going on inside the superstructure of the house has been first-fixing — constructing walls, roofs and floors, burying pipes and cables. The key difference between the two stages is that the first-fix works will be hidden within the structure, whilst the second-fix items will be there for all to

see when the house is completed. Hence this chapter, entitled 'Finishes,' covers what some would call the second-fix.

It is also worth bearing in mind that we are entering the world of interior design. If you are selfbuilding or renovating, this is pretty much where the shopping starts and it can be both exhilarating and frustrating. Just what are you going to lay on your floor? Just how are you going to finish the walls?

You may be the sort to have very definite ideas about what you want or,

like me, you may find yourself frozen in a state of indecision. How ever much you know or find out, there will still be more that you don't know and eventually you have to plump for something otherwise the job never gets finished.

By all means start hanging out in Pinterest and find out what everyone else is doing — that's being on trend, I believe. Or even hire an interior designer if you really can't face endless trawls around websites, exhibitions, catalogues and showrooms.

WALLS & CEILINGS

Back in the 1990s, when I first started writing about selfbuild, plastering looked like it was a dying art. Everyone had started fitting plasterboard to their walls and ceilings and copying the Americans and Europeans in basically just painting over it. Besides, plasterers themselves all seemed to be wizened old men who by rights should have retired years before. They didn't have any apprentices and it was hard to see just who would apply the plaster when they finally hung up their boots.

However on my recent selfbuild, I chose to go with a wet plaster finish and had to book ahead months in advance to get some very young and capable plasterers. What has happened? Why has the worm turned.

Two reasons stand out. One is to do with the sheer beauty of a perfectly smooth finish applied to plasterboard, something which painted dry lining can never really match. The other is the new emphasis on airtight construction as a way of delivering energy efficient homes. I'm not sure my plasterers knew much about the benefits of airtight construction but in truth they didn't really need to. They simply focussed on getting that smooth, shiny surface that well-applied gypsum plaster delivers and that was precisely what I was looking for.

PLASTERING

The very term *plastering* is often misused. When we talk about

PLASTERING Key Material Costs

	Unit	Price	Divider	Metre Rate
12.5mm Plasterboard	1200x2400	£ 4.80	2.5	£ 2.00 m²
12.5mm Soundcheck Board	1200x2400	£ 8.00	2.5	£ 3.20 m²
12.5mm Fermacell Board	1200x2400	£20	2.5	£ 8.00 m²
12mm Render	m²	£1	1	£ 1.00 m²
Thistle Skim Multi Finish	25kg bag	£ 7.00	9	£ 0.80 m²
Monocouche Renders	25kg bag	£10	1	£10 m²
65mm Screed (mixed on site)	m³	£140	15	£9 m²

PLASTERERS KEY RATES per m²

	Charged Rate £22 /hr	Labour	Mats	Total
Render and Skim	30 mins	£ 11	£ 3	£ 14
Render only (Scratch Coat)	15 mins	£ 6	£ 2	£ 8
Render (Top Coat)	20 mins	£ 8	£ 2	£ 10
Tacking (Nailing) Plasterboard	35 mins	£ 13	£ 3	£ 16
Tacking Soundblock Board	40 mins	£ 15	£ 5	£ 20
Dot and Dab (Sticking) Plasterboard	20 mins	£ 8	£ 3	£ 11
Skim Finish on Plasterboard	16 mins	£ 6	£ 1	£ 7
Dry Lined Finish to Plasterboard	12 mins	£ 5	£ 1	£ 6
Fixing External Mesh for Render	12 mins	£ 5	£ 8	£ 13
Two-coat External Render	50 mins	£ 19	£ 3	£ 22
Single-coat Monocouche Render	30 mins	£ 11	£ 10	£ 21
Floor Screed, 65mm Thick	25 mins	£ 10	£ 11	£ 21
Ready-mixed Screed	20 mins	£ 8	£ 8	£ 16
Gypsum Screeds 50mm	Supply and fix only		£ 20	£ 20

MODEL HOUSE Boarding & Plastering Costs

	Area	Rate	Materials	Labour	Total
Celings (Skimmed board)	140 m²	£ 27	£ 800	£ 2,900	£ 3,700
Walls (Skimmed board)	350 m²	£ 27	£ 2,100	£ 7,400	£ 9,500
Gypsum Screed	80 m²	£ 20	£ 400		£ 1,600
		Total	£ 3,300	£ 10,300	£ 14,000

plaster, we routinely refer the pink gypsum powder which comes in bags and is spread thinly or *skimmed* across internal walls and ceilings. But plasterers do more than just skimming. They also lay the backing coats, which are usually cement-based, and many also do traditional floor screeding. And then there is the world of external renders, which have changed over the years from being a three-coat cement-based coating to all manner of fancy, through-coloured bagged products, usually hailing from Germany, which promise a lifetime of crack-free beauty. There is also a renewed interest in lime renders which had, by the 1990s, all but been abandoned in favour of gypsum-based products. I noted that

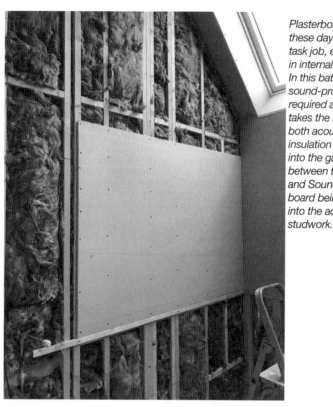

Plasterboarding these days is a multi-task job, especially in internal stud walls. In this bathroom, sound-proofing is required and this takes the form of both acoustic wool insulation stuffed into the gaps between the studs, and Soundcheck board being fitted into the adapted studwork.

whilst my old school plasterers were scornful of anything to do with lime, the current crop see lime plasters as a challenge and look forward to working with it.

Plasterers like to get their hands dirty. It is a wet trade. The ones I used to work with all seemed to come from Glasgow and spoke with such thick accents that it was often hard to make out what they were saying. Joe Quigley was the best of them and he once told me that you could write everything you needed to know about plastering on a single sheet of paper, but you could spend five years learning the trade and still not be any good.

That should be enough to let you know that if you are trying to do as much work as possible on a DIY basis, plastering is one trade you don't want to take on. You would be better advised to stick to one of the paint-only methods. There are techniques to be learned here too, but you can hope to master them relatively quickly.

BLOCKWORK WALLS

If you are plastering onto blockwork walls, then you have a choice of how to do the backing. The traditional route is to get your plasterers to apply a wet cement render, but for the past thirty years or so housebuilders

have preferred using *dot and dab* techniques to stick plasterboard onto the wall. Dot and dabbing is a skill itself, much loved by speculative housebuilders as you don't get any cracking or crazing, which sometimes afflicts cement-rendered walls. But it is lousy as an air tightness detail and, as we are now emphasising air-tightness, the attractions of dot and dab are waning.

PLASTERBOARD

If you do go for a plasterboard base, you need to look at which boards to use. The cheapest way to buy is to specify the full size boards (1.2m x 2.4m) at standard thickness (12.5mm). Use square-edged board if you are going to skim, and tapered-edge is you are painting directly (known as *taping and jointing*). However there are many instances where an improved board is either required or desirable. Plasterboards are available offering sound, fire and moisture resistance and it is likely that on a quality self-build you will be using at least one of these in large quantities.

What about fixing boards? Some plasterers offer this service, but most are so busy now that they stick to what they are best at. Unlike plastering itself, fixing plasterboard is not particularly skilled though it is often slow and intricate, especially where you have odd-shaped rooms and lots of little details to fuss over. First fix carpentry, if well planned, should provide studs and joists at spacings compatible with plasterboards, but inevitably there will be corners in every room where the spacings don't work and extra timber supports have to be inserted in order to provide a backing for the plasterboard. Internal timber walls and ceilings also require sound-proof insulation and often all this work, including the plasterboard tacking is done by the site carpentry crew rather than specialists. In fact, there is a great deal of work in turning a first-fix shell into a plaster-ready structure.

On my recently completed selfbuild, the battening out, insulating and tacking took twice as long as the actual plastering. Whilst my 500m² of plastering to ceilings and walls took just 18 days, costing £2800 including materials, the pre-plastering preparation work took 40 days and totalled £15,000. We may have put an excessive amount of timber into the supporting structures, packing out walls and ceilings where the first fix carpentry was not quite perfect, but the result is a superb finish with clean lines with very little skirting or architrave. We don't have a single plastering crack in the house.

We skim plastered in a very cold February and had hoped to start painting a couple of weeks later, but the drying out process took longer than I would have liked and I ended up hiring a dehumidifier for three weeks. At £75 a week, it is a hidden cost of plastering in winter, but a far better than holding up progress on a building site.

Watch out also for just how busy plasterers currently are. Be sure to book them well ahead if you want to stick to your timetable. Contrary to what I thought would happen 25 years ago, the trade is booming and good plasterers are hard to pin down.

NATURAL PLASTERS

There is a small but growing interest in traditional lime and clay plasters which has spread from the conservation market into new build. Clay, in particular, has a reputation for being good in wet rooms because it absorbs moisture and helps control humidity levels. Plus it looks good unpainted.

FERMACELL

Widely used in Germany, Fermacell is, in some ways, very similar to plasterboard and, in others, rather superior. It has a much higher racking strength than plasterboard and is therefore particularly useful when you want to hang radiators and bathroom furniture off timber stud walls and you don't know where the studs are. Fermacell also makes for better soundproofing. However, it is pricey in comparison with plasterboard, two to three times the price. Consequently, it is being used in the UK mostly as a backing board for kitchens and bathrooms and where soundproofing between rooms is an issue. It is usual to glue the boards together and simply paint over them for a finished surface.

Fermacell is appreciated by a breed of DIYers who don't want to be troubled with plasterers. It's fairly simple to paint it.

Other boards worth seeking out are Knauf's Aquapanel and Hardie Backerboard, cement particle boards which are completely waterproof and can therefore be specified in shower enclosures.

PAINTING & DECORATING

Of all the building trades to master, painting is by far the easiest. It thus represents a sensible way for the DIYers to add value to their project without spending an arm and a leg on professional help. As the old saw goes, if you can piss, you can paint.

By all means take it on, but there are a couple of provisos here. Firstly, although it's easy to do, it's much harder to master and you can usually readily tell whether the painting has been carried out by an expert or someone merely competent.

The second is the amount of time taken to paint the interior of a house is something to grasp before you set sail. A typical detached house — our model house for instance — has around 500m² of plastered walls and ceilings and maybe 300lin.m of skirtings, architraves, window boards, window reveals, door linings, you name it. A good painter doing three-coat work will spend between 200 hours working their way through this lot. That's about five weeks solid work for one person. If you take that on yourself, do you have five weeks spare, with nothing else to do in the interim? If you leave it to do in bits, maybe a room at a time, you risk mucking up the finishing schedule. Trying to paint a kitchen that's already in use is a mind-numbing

Chapter 10

Decorating Rates (inc Labour and Materials)

	Each coat	Cost for three coats
Emulsion to Internal Plasterwork	£ 2.40 m²	£7 m²
Lt Greene/Farrow & Ball		
Masonary Paint to External Render	£ 7.50 m²	£23 m²
Stain to External Cladding	£ 6.50 m²	£20 m²
Varnish to Hardwood Flooring	£ 6.20 m²	£19 m²
Paint One Face of a Window	£ 11.30 m²	£34 m²
Stain One Face of a Window	£ 11.50 m²	£35 m²
Paint One Face of a Door	£ 7.60 m²	£23 m²
Stain One Face of a Door	£ 7.80 m²	£23 m²
Paint Balusters and Stair Supports	£ 11.30 m²	£34 m²
Stain Balusters and Stairs	£ 11.50 m²	£35 m²
Paint Strips	£ 2.70 m run	£8 m run
Stain Strips	£ 2.80 m run	£8 m run
Wallpaper	£ 12.00 m²	

MODEL HOUSE 3 Coat Decorating Costs

	Area/Length	Rate	Materials	Labour	Total
Plasterwork White	490 m²	£7	£ 290	£ 3,230	£ 3,520
Timber lengths					
Door Linings	66 m	£8	£ 40	£ 510	£ 550
Architraves	130 m	£8	£ 70	£ 1,010	£ 1,080
Skirtings	120 m	£8	£ 70	£ 940	£ 1,010
Windowboards	20 m	£8	£ 54	£ 160	£ 214
Cupboards/Shelves	50 m	£8	£ 135	£ 390	£ 525
		Total	**£ 700**	**£ 6,200**	**£ 6,900**

experience and takes about twice as long as it does to paint a near empty room, as you are constantly moving plates and pots and pans from one place to another in order to get at ceilings.

If you have the money, I'd strongly recommend getting it done by a professional, but you can undoubtedly make the cash go further if you choose to DIY it.

INTERIOR WORK

Most interior walls are finished with emulsion paints, which are very cheap and very easy to apply, being water-based. The standard choice you need to make is between a matt finish and a silk finish. Matt finishes are characterised as being thicker (more opaque) and softer; silk finishes produce a harder, glossier look that has the added advantage of being more readily washable. There is no difference in price. Satin finishes are a halfway house between matt and silk. One tip for new housebuilders is to apply your emulsions immediately after plastering or dry-lining is finished. You can get in and have a relatively free run at bare walls without having to fiddle around with skirtings, architraves, socket boxes, switch plates and radiators.

Another tip, this one for the stylistically challenged housebuilder, is to slap magnolia on everything. White is a bit too clinical for most people's taste; in contrast magnolia has enough cream in it to soften the overall effect without making any loud statements that will clash with furnishing choices made later on. If you are in a hurry and don't want to be bothered planning colour schemes, then magnolia is the answer.

It's also a boon in homes shared with small children where walls have an endearing habit of getting drawn on. Instead of trying desperately to clean off the mess, you can just slap some more paint on it and it'll be just like new. Dull but true.

If you are so minded, you can spend an awful lot of money on posh paints like Farrow & Ball and Little Greene. Their emulsions cost around five times as much as the regular Dulux and Crown but the colours are lovely and in the great scheme of things, paint is still a pretty small beer when it comes to the overall budget. In fact, painting is one of the very few trades where the costs are more than 85% labour (mostly they are around the 50-50 mark).

WOODWORK

Interior woodwork is traditionally a three-coat gloss paint system. Back in the 1990s, woodstains seemed to be taking over from paint but now paint is back with a vengeance. There is lots of debate about whether to use a water-based paint or an oil-based one. If you've never done much painting before, the water-based ones are far easier to use, but most professional decorators still prefer the oil-based ones, as you can get a slightly better finish with them. Though dark woodstains are out of fashion, liming wood to make it lighter is very much on trend. Look out for Osmo's lovely Polyx Oil tints which isn't strictly speaking anything to do with lime but gives a very good washed effect.

The modern preference for shadow gaps and tile upstand skirtings is partly based on looks, but is also well grounded in minimising redecorating costs.

MASTICS

Mastics are something of a new feature in building, or at least the ways we use them today are new. They now tend to get applied to just about every conceivable join between materials; so wherever joinery meets brickwork or a tiled surface meets a worktop or a bathtub, there's a bead of mastic. There are mastics for sealing between plasterboard sheets and decorator's mastics for filling cracks (Painter's Mate). Just about the only thing that is common to them is that they are packaged in tubes. Where water penetration is a problem – and that includes most external applications – it is worth paying more for the silicone based ones which, whilst remaining flexible, are less likely to break down.

It is said by some that mastics are the bodger's friend and that if you build to very high standards your joints will all be tight and you shouldn't need mastics at all. While

there is some truth that good building standards are usually reflected in tight joints, mastics, particularly the silicone based ones, are now so widely used that it is inconceivable you will not have any need of them at some point. It is, however, very difficult to estimate just how much mastic you will need – that, at least, often depends on how wide your gaps are. And it is also true that mastic is a whole lot easier to apply against tightly fitting backgrounds. If you are subcontracting decorating, you should make it absolutely clear where you want mastic to be applied and which type of mastic you want to be used.

EXTERIOR WORK

You can avoid exterior decorating altogether by specifying pre-finished materials like uPVC, composites or aluminium coverings. Windows and doors are available with composite finishes and there are masonry alternatives for fascias and soffits. Renders are now available in bags which are pre-coloured. Even timber boarding is available in cementitous replica or in species like cedar that require little if any treatment. There are also an increasing number of timber options like Thermowood and Vastern's Brimstone which don't require any further treatment. Or plump for something ultra-cool like burnt timber.

Note that on my recent selfbuild, we included 45m² of Western Red Cedar, place in an unusual configuration which involved fixing the cedar planks in louvred so that it looks to all intents like a huge

venetian blind. We treated the Cedar with a fire-proofing liquid Organowood which also has the effect of pre-ageing the timber so that it looks almost instantly like it's ten years weathered.

If regular softwood timber is your thing, then you have to provide some form of protection for it if it's to be used externally. The main choice is between traditional paint and woodstains. Even though woodstains are more expensive to buy, the cost difference between the two systems is negligible because there is such a high labour content in decorating and, if anything, stains are slightly quicker to apply. What really causes decorating costs to tumble is reducing the number of coats needed to get a decent finish. Many builders do this with stains by dispensing with the third coat, which would be difficult with conventional paint, but there are now a number of one-coat paints (eg Crown Solo) that enable you to dispense with the undercoat at a price.

MASONRY PAINTS

Masonry paints, which are used to cover external render and masonry, are water-based and many will claim to last for 15 years before needing re-coating. They are easy to apply but their application should not be rushed; the underlying cement render must be allowed to dry out thoroughly. This is a drag because many builders are itching to strike the scaffolding by the time the external rendering is done and waiting for render to dry can take forever. Take the scaffolding down and it'll take you three times as long to paint the house. The moral? Only build houses with external painted panels when the sun shines. Or, better still, opt for a pre-coloured monocouche render.

ALTERNATIVE FINISHES

You are of course not restricted to painted walls and ceilings. But with plastered walls and ceiling working out at around £17/m² and painting a further £7/m², almost all these alternatives are considerably more expensive, so they tend to be used decoratively. Not in every case. Some areas require specialised wall covers such a splashbacks and shower enclosures, but even here the actual amount needed for wall protection is often far less than we choose to fit.

ARTEX

Anyone for Artex? I didn't think so. It was the go-to ceiling cover in the post war years (when it contained asbestos) but thankfully it's gone right out of fashion. Although it's much easier to apply than skimmed plaster, it is also much harder to paint which actually made it a bit of a pain in general. Housebuilders used to specify Artex on their ceilings, to help stop call-backs for cracking happening but by and large it's better to live with the cracks. Not that you should have any if you've done your board preparation well.

WALLPAPER

The fashion for all things white or off-white in new homes has not been kind to our wall paperers. It's not so very expensive but wallpaper is almost unheard of now as a whole house wall covering. It tends to be confined to children's bedrooms and even there, it's often just on one wall.

Wallpaper doesn't have to be expensive, but it's never going to be as cheap as paint so you would only sensibly use it if you are very confident that you have a statement you want to make. It works fine in many period properties, but in new homes........ I don't think so.

EXPOSED BRICKWORK

On the other hand, internally exposed brickwork can look fabulous in any sort of setting, providing the brickwork is of good quality. It's long been used around fireplaces and chimneys but the vast majority of new homes don't have such things anymore — a wood stove really isn't the same.

By all means use some panels of brickwork, or even fair-faced blockwork, but bear in mind that the larger the area you use, the more you will have to accommodate services and beams over openings. The neat way to do this is to also make these features in their own right, so that you run pipes in copper and cables in metal trunking and surface mount metallic switches.

One of the hidden joys of selfbuild is growing a familiarity with all manner of outlets you would never normally set foot in. The tile shop is a prime example. If you are happy with white metro tiles everywhere, then you'll save yourself a lot of time. But once you start exploring what's out there, it begins to eat you up.

A plug here for a fantastic tile shop in London (pictured here), Mosaic del Sur, where we ended up spending a lot of money.

TIMBER

Internal timber panelling used to be very popular in the 1970s and 1980s, and then fell right out of fashion. But unlike many building fashions from that era, timber interiors have made a comeback.

The key difference is that dark or stained timber is no longer sought after, so you won't be fitting any more stained pine matchboarding, the scourge of the 1970s bathroom along with the avocado bathroom suite. But Scandi-looking pale timbers are in and lime-washing effects are right in. Hell, people are even fitting timber panels and painting them. Check the mood boards of Pinterest for what is on trend.

In cost terms, timber panelling is intermediate in cost between painted plaster and exposed brickwork or tiling.

PLYWOOD

One wall finish I am partial to in utility rooms is plywood. OK, it tends to be dark but it's incredibly practical and it can make what might be a cold, unfriendly room somehow seem warm. The same issue you have with exposed brickwork haunts a wall surface such as plywood, but in a utility room/plant room, does it matter?

GLASS BLOCKS

One of the most intriguing trends in home interiors has been the re-emergence of glass block walls. They were widely used in the 1930s, mostly on public buildings, but then all but vanished from view. You simply didn't see them until about 20 years ago when the TV interior shows

rediscovered them and suddenly glass blocks are everywhere. Though the initial wave of enthusiasm after we re-discovered glass blocks has abated, they are still very much around and are on message. Ballpark materials costs come in at around £60/m^2.

CERAMIC WALL TILING

Tiling is not strictly speaking an alternative to plaster and paint because it is often applied on top, so 'addition' might be a better word. Its use is often entirely functional when applied as a splashback behind sinks, basins and baths, but in the Mediterranean you frequently see ceramic tiling in living rooms and bedrooms as well. In the UK wall tiling is seen in more functional terms, partly because wall tiles are so much more expensive here.

Whether you pay under £10/m^2 for some unadorned and unnamed white tiles or £80/m^2 for top of the range, hand painted tiles out of the Fired Earth catalogue, the fixing costs remain remarkably similar. The adhesives which you use to stick the tiles down with and the grouts which you spread between the tiles tend to work out together at around £6/m^2 depending on the thickness and specification. The laying costs depend on the intricacies of the task in hand, but on fairly straightforward work, it takes a tiler around one hour to fix a square metre of tiles and about 30 minutes to grout them up later. Big straight runs will be faster than this but most tiling work in kitchens and bathrooms involves a fair amount of cutting.

FLOOR FINISHES

Nowhere else in building is there such a great variety of materials at such a huge variation in price. You could carpet a four-bedroom house for less than £3,000 (inc. VAT); equally you could spend over £20,000 and not risk being accused of extravagance. If you really want floor envy, take a look at Dinesen timber floors and note how hard it is to find a price. That's because you won't be able to afford it. I'd hazard a guess that to lay Dinesen throughout the entire 160m2 model house would cost upwards of £40,000.

Enough of this. A word about the sub-floor.

FINISHED FLOOR LEVEL

Throughout the works, from foundations onwards, the key datum point is the ground floor finished floor level (FFL). Everything is built in reference to this point. However, when you come to lay a ground floor, the FFL suddenly becomes extremely critical. Not only do you want a perfectly flat floor, but you want your door thresholds to work seamlessly and you want the bottom tread of your staircase to fit snugly onto the finished floor and to be exactly the same height as all the other steps.

How do you go about working this out?

Firstly mark where the theoretical FFL actually is on your sub-floor, and work out whether your sub-floor is indeed flat. Use a laser level to mark on the walls in several places

Chapter 10

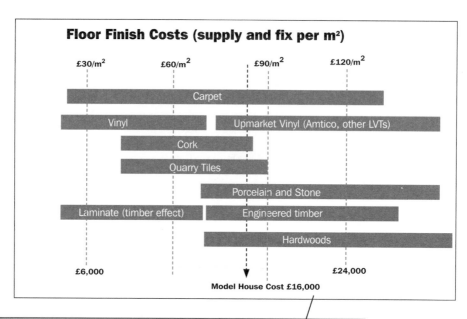

Floor Finish Costs (supply and fix per m²)

| £30/m² | £60/m² | £90/m² | £120/m² |

- Carpet
- Vinyl
- Upmarket Vinyl (Amtico, other LVTs)
- Cork
- Quarry Tiles
- Porcelain and Stone
- Laminate (timber effect)
- Engineered timber
- Hardwoods

£6,000 — Model House Cost £16,000 — £24,000

MODEL HOUSE: Floor Finishes & Wall Tiling

	Area in m²	Rate/m²	Materials	Labour	Totals
Carpet	70	£60	£3,600	£500	£4,100
Oak Flooring	60	£ 80	£3,100	£1,800	£4,900
Stone Tiling	30	£ 130	£2,200	£1,800	£4,000
Wall Tiling	40	£60	£1,200	£1,300	£2,500
		Totals	**£10,100**	**£5,400**	**£16,000**

a nominal point, conventionally 1000mm above FFL, starting from the original datum point. Then you can measure down and hopefully your subfloor level will be a little bit more than 1000mm. How much more?

It helps to select a floor finish early, or at least a floor finish depth. Floor tiles are usually either 12mm or 15mm thick (external ones are thicker), whereas timber is usually 20mm. Having said that, timber flooring is usually laid on a 3 or 5mm underlay, whereas stone/ceramic flooring needs a 10mm build up to accommodate the uncoupling mat and the adhesive. You therefore won't go far wrong if you plan for a 25mm flooring zone above your first fix floor in order to fit a floor finish. Unless of course you are going for a much thinner vinyl sheet or tile, or a carpet. Really, it pays to have at least some idea of how exactly you are going to cover your floors, even if you haven't chosen a specific finish.

UNDERFLOOR HEATING

Note that floor finishes frequently have to work with underfloor heating and here you need to be aware that stone and ceramic floors work beautifully (nothing feels quite so good as walking barefoot on a heated stone floor in the middle of winter). Thin vinyls work OK, timber floors less so as they insulate the heat within the sub-floor zone. Carpet is worst of the lot because that is like laying a coat over the floor.

It's not that underfloor heating doesn't work with sub-optimal floor finishes, it's just has to work harder to get the room above up to temperature. In other words, it is less energy-efficient and you lose one of the main attractions of underfloor heating, namely warm floors.

CARPET

Even when glued down, carpet is regarded by HMRC as a movable item and therefore subject to VAT as a furnishing – all other types of floor finish are zero-rated in the UK and therefore effectively exempt from VAT when built into a new house. Even so, carpeting still provides potentially the cheapest form of floor covering available – especially the bonded cords which also happen to be reasonably hard wearing. Beware offers of free underlay and free laying; obviously these services are not free and the charge for them is included in the price. Usually priced by the metre, carpet laying can be subject to enormous wastage because of the limited roll sizes. The DIY builder might be happier to lay carpet tiles, but if price is the only consideration, then it will still probably be cheaper to look out for the absolute basic ranges supplied and fitted by one of the carpet warehouses. Some of these carpets sell for a good deal less than a decent underlay (which can cost £3m²) so you can imagine what the quality is like.

▪ Material: Wool is the traditional and natural material for carpets; it also tends to be the most expensive. Other natural materials you can use include sisal, coir, jute and seagrass, all of which tend to give a faintly bohemian feel to your flooring

schemes. Synthetics like nylon and acrylics are now commonplace and much carpet sold these days is a cocktail of wool and synthetics – and people walking on them would not know the difference. The very cheapest material is polypropylene which looks synthetic but may be fine for your needs, especially in bedrooms.

▪ Comparing prices is difficult because a lot of carpet is not branded and as there are so many varieties on the market, very often no two outlets sell the same thing. Sticking to an established name like John Lewis will ensure that you are not ripped-off, but they are unlikely to be selling carpet below £10m².

▪ Bear in mind this rule of thumb when estimating cost: you should double the advertised price of a fitted carpet to get an idea of what it will all cost when laid on your floors. This will allow for offcuts, underlay and laying costs.

▪ Bathroom Carpeting: avoid woollen carpets in bathrooms as they will tend to go mouldy, especially if they have a hessian backing.

FLOOR TILES

There are many different materials used to tile or sheet floors and there is not space to cover them all here. In particular, there are any number of synthetic rubbery plastic type floor coverings which are generally more at home in an industrial or commercial setting than a house. Here I look at some of the more popular options.

VINYL

The very word vinyl sounds cheap but don't be misled, it's not. At the lower end of the market, brands like Polyflor advertise sheet vinyls at £15/m², but at the top end Amtico are now selling at over £100/m². The top of the range likes to be referred to as luxury vinyl tiling and has it's very own three-letter acronym — LVT flooring. A mid-priced, very popular alternative is Karndean.

The best results are to be had when the immediate sub-floor is covered either with a 5mm latex screed or thin plywood sheeting. Factor in waste, accessories and laying costs of between £20 and £30/m², and you can see the headline rate is often about half to a third of what you will end up paying.

If you are not drawn to vinyl, there are a host of other materials used. Cork was once the floor cover of choice for the Habitat generation (c 1970s-1980s), and is still around but hard to track down. Linoleum has its fans too. And there are

STONE v PORCELAIN

Somewhere in the housebuilding process you are going to cross swords with a tile retailer. Even if you don't want a stone or stone-effect tiled floor anywhere, you will still be looking out for some wall tiling for kitchens and bathrooms. Step into a tile warehouse and you will soon be overwhelmed by the choices facing you, and you will doubtless spend an inordinate amount of time thinking about tiled surfaces and wondering what your choices will say about you

Chapter 10

to everyone who comes to your home.

Perhaps the biggest thing you have to decide is whether to go for a natural stone tile or a manufactured one. If you go natural, your finishes are limited by what we can find buried in the ground, but that does encompass some very beautiful stone which will frankly be hard to fault on a appearance. It's surprising how many manufactured tiles endlessly mimic natural stone and, increasingly, timber as well. The Italian porcelain specialists have been perfecting photo-etching and some of the effects they now produce are almost indistinguishable from timber, let alone stone. The same is true of the vinyl tile producers, where they seem obsessed in getting their tiles to look like natural products.

If this is telling us anything, it's that we like natural products which makes me think that we should fit natural products and not photographs of natural products, especially where the price difference is minimal.

OK, you may make a good case for not fitting timber in a shower room and plumping for a porcelain faux-timber floor plank here instead. But elsewhere?

Having got that off my chest, there are some reasons to consider before you go natural. Natural stone cost a bit extra to lay because you have to take extra care to protect the stone if you don't want it to stain and discolour. And having laid it, it takes a bit of looking after too, especially the limestones, travertines and marbles as they react to acidic substances like standard floor

cleaners, lemon juice and vinegar, the sort of things which could easily get splashed around a kitchen floor. Darker floors, slates and granites, are not really as delicate as the limestone family but dark floors are also less in vogue.

It's not a straight choice between stone and porcelain, as it sometimes seems. There are a range of semi-handmade tiles (often referred to as Moroccan cement tiles) which are assembled using natural products set into a cement background. The beauty of the product hangs pretty much on the quality of the coloured pigments used in the manufacture, but they are usually easily distinguishable form the mass-produced alternatives.

LAYING TIPS

Laying costs for stone/ceramic floor tiles are high because it's a slow process — it really doesn't want to be rushed. The larger the tiles, the more expensive they are, but they are also quicker to lay, but aside from this there are several additional costs. It is normal now to lay a slip membrane to allow for the tiled surface to uncouple from the screed beneath, which should prevent cracking. Schluter Ditra Matting and Bal Rapid Mat are two popular options, but at £8-£12/m² they add considerably to the laying costs. And then large floors will require expansion joints as well, although these can be simply achieved by leaving a gap and filling it with the appropriately coloured mastic. Add in grouts and maybe a hired tile cutter, and the cost of all the

add-ons for floor laying will rise to around £25/m2, and that's without a £50/m2 laying cost.

DRYING TIMES

Note that floor screeds take time to dry and that you must abide by the guidelines which indicate how long a floor should be left uncovered before you lay anything on top of it. The old adage was roughly 1mm per day, so that a 75mm screed would therefore take 75 days to dry out. You won't go far wrong with this rule of thumb but in reality it depends on the external temperatures and the internal humidity. If time is of the essence, hire a dehumidifier to speed up the process once the building is wind and watertight.

POLISHED CONCRETE

One of the most fashionable floor finishes you can plump for is to lay a concrete floor slab and then "polish" the top so that it becomes a beautifully smooth surface in its own right. It's a very skilled process and definitely not one to be undertaken on a DIY basis, nor even by a groundworker who fancies having a go, because if it goes wrong (i.e. cracks), there is not much you can do about it.

When we were doing our recent selfbuild, we approached the acknowledged masters of this trade, Lazenby's, for a quotation and ended up baulking at the cost of £145/m2 or over £12,000 for our humble footprint. By the time we had finished applying the last of our limestone floor tiles (chosen because they looked like concrete, would you believe), we realised that it would actually have been a little cheaper to have gone with Lazenby's.

Just a note to say a concrete finish doesn't have to be dark. Polished concrete is available in a range of colours, including white, so that you don't have to be building a cave. The floor finish is applied a few days after the readymix pour so you are then left with a surface you have to keep clean for the rest of the build. Also perhaps worth mentioning here that finished concrete can also be used for stairs, worktops and sanitaryware. It's versatile.

One of the big pluses of a polished concrete finish is that you save on the cost of a screed, whether conventional or otherwise, because the concrete is both floor and screed. It also works really well with underfloor heating. It's got a lot going for it, but do plan well ahead. The better suppliers tend to be booked up months in advance.

TIMBER FLOORING

The rise and rise of hardwood flooring is a notable trend in contemporary home design. It was always thought of as an aspirational feature but people used to get put off by the price. It's not got any cheaper but all of a sudden people seem to be quite happily paying £40 — £80m² for hardwood floor planking and are being increasingly daring as to the choice of wood, although oak remains a perennial favourite.

The alternative option is to use an engineered timber floor which has a 4-7mm layer of hardwood stuck onto

Polished concrete floor by Lazenby's. At over £120/m², it seems expensive, but when you compare it with alternative finishes such as stone tiles, it is in fact very competitive. No wonder it's in fashion

a composite MDF backing, usually around 12mm. The thicker the timber veneer, the better quality the floor. An engineered floor is always going to be more stable because of the MDF backing which makes it more suitable for bathrooms (though arguably not as suitable as a porcelain timber-look alike floor plank for about the same price.

In timber flooring, there are an awful lot of options and a wide range of prices; oak planks can be anywhere between £20 and £80m² (not including stuff like Dinesen which is way more expensive). It's a huge price range for what you might imagine are very similar products. Of course, they're not. You really do get what you pay for here.

One of the key points to watch if you buy a solid hardwood floor is that the moisture content is right down at around 8% when you lay — this is especially important if you want to fit underfloor heating. Personally, I am a fan of the engineered timber approach as it is just more stable and

easy to lay. Floors need looking after and even occasionally sanding, which takes about 1mm off the surface, so eventually a 4mm layer of hardwood veneer will wear through, so maybe looked at in the ultra-long term, the engineered approach will not stand the test of time. But we are taking about a century here before it wears through, so I wouldn't worry about it over much.

Another approach is to use a reclaimed board or a parquet floor that has been stored undercover and is, hopefully, dimensionally stable. These vary in price from around £20m² up to £50m² and will almost certainly involve you in a lot of extra work (de-nailing, sanding, hole filling, more sanding, sealing). The huge variation in prices for reclaimed boards is of course an indication that there is a huge variation in quality as well.

Laying timber floors is generally much quicker than laying stone or ceramic tiling. The easiest and quickest method is to float the floor

Matwells can be both functional and elegant and work well with level thresholds.

on top of the sub-floor, separated by an 5mm underlay. By floating, we mean that the actual boards are neither mechanically fixed (with screws or nails) or glued down. They are simply stuck together along the tongues and grooves at each edge of the boards, then clamped tight and finally fixed in place with the skirtings around the edge. If the sub-base is sound, there should be no movement. So the secret of a good floating floor is ensuring that the subfloor is sound and level, which may involve packing it up or adding self-levelling compound to ensure it actually is. The routine is the same on both screeds and solid timber floors. Only if you are laying directly onto joists do you have to have any use any screw fixings.

MATWELLS

It's always a nice touch to see people thinking ahead and building in a sunken matwell is usually a sign that someone has been. Now that the disabled access regs require level access, usually at the main entrance door, a sunken matwell becomes even more important, as the door now opens just a few millimetres above the floor cover.

There is an industry standard matwell (which may surprise some) which is 760 x 460 x 40mm. If you stick to this you can buy galvanised steel surrounds for around £40 and these will take industry standard sized coconut matting. But you don't need to stick to the industry standard because you can create your own surround, whether in timber or tile.

Coir Mats cut to order and have a range of thicknesses so it can just slip into any spot you set for them. At £75 for over a square metre behind the front door, it works out as cheap as any of the major alternatives.

SECOND FIX CARPENTRY

We are now getting well into the finishing stages of the house and we are looking at second-fix carpentry. That's because much of this work is traditionally done by the carpenter. But also bear in mind that many of the more interesting options don't involve carpenters at all. Any one for shadow gaps? Tile upstands? Floating staircases? Glazed screens? Read on.

EDGE TRIMS

We need some way of dividing the walls from the floors and the door linings from the walls. Traditionally this is done with skirting boards (wall-floor junctions) and architraves (door surrounds). These features in themselves formed part of the great Victorian indoors which sort of echoed ancient Greek temples. There were dado rails (which are at waist height) and picture rails (for hanging pictures, stupid) not to mention glorious ceiling covings and ornate roses around a central light. The more fancy the house, the bigger and more elaborate these trim details got. There were certain standard mouldings as well: Torus, Ogee and Ovolo are three of the best known but really every joiner's shop would be knocking up their own local variations. They look great in period homes but frankly it all looks a bit dated now in a contemporary home. Plain is now king, the simpler the profile the better, making it one of the very few areas of housebuilding where things are trending towards cheaper. A round or chamfered edge, preferably made from white-painted MDF is quite the thing nowadays.

There is (or rather was) a logic behind fitting skirting boards. It is standard building practice to leave a 50mm gap between the floor and the bottom of the plaster on the wall so as not to breach the damp-proof course placed in the wall; however, damp-proofing techniques have changed and now floor membranes are lapped into wall membranes and the rising damp never (in theory) penetrates the room space at all. Today, skirting is there to fill the unsightly crack between wall and floor.

And architraves hide the gap between the door lining (timber) and the plasterwork. Whilst this can look neat when the plastering is just finished, a gap will tend to appear over time, which will tend to crack as time goes by.

Fixing times don't vary much but as regards material costs, the fancy sections are two to three times more than the utilitarian versions which are around £2/m for skirtings and architraves, whether pine or MDF. Skirtings and architraves are best nailed or screwed into the walls but, alternatively, can be stuck on with an adhesive like Gripfill or CT1, a mastic glue which can be used to bond all kinds of materials.

TILED UPSTANDS

One option when working with a stone or ceramic floor is to select a tiled upstand, using the same tiling as you have used on the floor. You need a good tile cutter but there is a good chance that you can also use up lots of offcuts here. It is undoubtedly more time consuming and therefore more expensive than using a timber or MDF skirting, on the other hand you don't have to paint it — ever. It's got a lot going for it, especially if you have chosen a nice floor tile. But it won't really do much for your door architraves.

SHADOW GAPS

The cool modern thing is to go for shadow gaps instead of skirtings and architraves. Rarely can it have been

Shadow gaps are very fashionable but very difficult to execute well. They replace traditional architraves and skirtings altogether to create a clean, modern look

so hard to do so little, because despite the fact that there's nothing there but a gap between the door lining and the plasterboard edge, they are very difficult to pull off well because you can see the gap all the way around, so it has to be done well.

To get a shadow gap, you start by fixing the door lining and then fix a plaster stop bead into the wall around it, leaving a gap between of around 10mm. Expamet make shadow gap beads, although you could elect to use a conventional stop bead. You are looking to get the surfaces of the wall and the door lining to be absolutely flush.

However, you might want to use something other than standard door linings, which are supplied with slot joints in the head section, which

will now be visible — these are designed to be covered over when the architrave is fixed. You may also find that the widths of the standard linings don't match your wall and plaster widths. Remember that planed timber is sold in nominal widths (that is before planing takes place) and the actual widths are usually 7 or 8mm less than this. So be prepared to spend a little extra on your door linings: they may have to be made up on site, or purchased as specials.

Done well, a shadow gap finish looks great. Done badly, it will look awful.

INTERNAL DOORS

Like the edge trims discussed above, the British door has its roots in

Victorian style. Panelling was the thing and decorative panelling even more so, along with ornate knobs and handles. There was good reason for this because the timber available was all planked and you had to make a large flat surface like a door in a frame — hence the panels.

20th century industrial techniques changed all that and we can now make doors out of paper-thin materials like hardboard, covering over egg-box like fillings and dressed with the thinnest possible veneers of tropical hardwood. Anyone for sapele (pronounced sa-pee-lee)? I didn't think so. Hardwood veneers have thankfully gone way out of fashion now.

The very cheapest doors you can get are around £30. They actually look fine when you've painted them but don't ever kick them. A popular variation on this theme is the embossed or moulded door; they are no stronger but they imitate the fielded panels found on timber doors and some of them imitate wood grain texture. Some superior ones use a type of fibreboard for the casing and they are strong enough to take glazing, although doors with glazing panels are much more expensive – around £70. All the major joinery manufacturers have a selection of these doors and, if you want to select a door, get hold of one of their catalogues.

Most selfbuilders will be opting for something a little beefier and probably more contemporary in style. If your budget stretches to over £200 per door, you can get some pretty good looking oak veneer doors which match most engineered timber floors and are ready finished so you don't need to decorate. Plus they are suitably heavy.

DOOR LININGS

Doors are conventionally hung in a frame called a door lining. Door linings are cheap enough but they are also very fiddly to understand. These are designed to slip into the door openings left in the blockwork or studwork, and they are routinely supplied in three pieces — two long pieces or jambs for the sides and a shorter head piece, altogether coming to 5.1m. The door lining sets also routinely come with a set of door stops which you fix to the outer linings and against which the actual door shuts. So a door lining set consists of 6 pieces of timber in all. A fire door stop is thicker than a normal door stop.

Door linings traditionally come in two different depths, designed to cope with two different wall widths. Either depth can cope with two different door sizes (762mm or 686mm). The two door lining sizes are known as 32x138mm and 32x115mm. If that's not complicated enough, these aren't the actual sizes you get because they get planed down by about 6mm. These so-called nominal sizes end up being 27.5x132mm and 27.5x109mm.

Why am I telling you this? Do you really need to know? Just possibly yes. There is a good chance that your doors won't be either 762 or 686mm wide (they are metric measurements for imperial 2'6" and 2'3"), and there is also a good chance that your walls won't end up being either 109mm wide or 132mm wide. In which case you'd better have a good carpenter onsite because you will have to adapt your door lining to suit your openings and/or your doors. In fact, it is often simpler to forget that builder's merchants even sell items called door linings and just make them yourself. But door linings are useful: don't think you can fit internal doors without door linings, whether you buy them from a merchant in pre-set sizes, or make them yourself.

FIRE DOORS

Fire doors are sometimes insisted on by building inspectors because you have to have a second means of escape from bedrooms. At first glance, you might think this condemns you to have a strange looking fire door with wired and frosted glass, but in fact the key differences are that a fire door is 44mm thick whereas a normal door is 10mm less (i.e 34mm). That gives you a much beefier door and, having discovered the difference, many people plump for a fire door even when they don't actually need one.

There is a snag to all this. If you are required to fit fire doors, you also have to fit intumescent strip around the doors so that it can form a seal should there ever be a fire. This is not something that you'd really want, unless of course a fire is in progress downstairs.

UNDERCUTS

If you are fitting mechanical ventilation with heat recovery into your home, then make sure that you leave a decent gap under each and every internal door because this becomes a critical air pathway between the incoming air (in bedrooms and living rooms) and the outgoing air (in bathrooms and kitchens). Leave at least 12mm off the bottom of the door over and above the finished floor level. This won't please the building inspector if it's a fire door, but you have two building regs (B v F) going head to head here and you can't please both sides.

DOOR FURNITURE

Door furniture is the phrase used to describe just about everything to do with doors excluding the door itself. That usually means all the bits made of metal. Door ironmongery would be much easier to understand, but the building trade likes the word furniture to be used here

The point to cotton on to here is that some door furniture is purely functional in that you don't see it or, if you do, you don't notice it; however other bits are very visual and – wait for it – tactile. Yes folks, door handles are sexy. Developers know this and consequently are prepared to spend above the bare minimum to create an impression on the would-be house purchaser.

Door handles may indeed be the only part of the house that the viewer actually touches during an inspection and female purchasers are thought to be impressed by something strong and solid which responds readily to their grasp. Or so many male housebuilders believe.

Having said that, most of the regular options are pretty limp. There are door furniture pre-packs available from builders' merchants and DIY sheds and specialists like Ironmongery Direct. They come as shrink-wrapped pre-packs at fairly reasonable prices.

These pre-packs have one big advantage going for them in that they've got all the bits you need in the pack. The alternative is to buy the bits yourself but here you risk forgetting vital bits, having to overbuy on items like screws and even buying the wrong bits – classic one here is to get the wrong-sized hinges. If your tastes veer away from these mainstream choices you'll have to brave it and go and order your very own door furniture.

If you want more unusual fittings then the DIY sheds have a surprising variety; if you want wood or ceramic knobs this is a good place to look. And Ironmongery Direct comes into its own here as it has an outstanding range.

KNOBS v HANDLES

There is one painful little trap to watch out for if you go for a door knob rather than handle. You need to fit a longer latch otherwise you will scrape your knuckles every time you open the door. For the technically challenged, the latch, in this instance, is the metal tube that fits inside the door and the hole in the latch determines exactly how far the handle or the knob sits from the edge of the door. This is known as the backset.

The standard tubular latch is around 63mm long and has a backset of just 44mm: it's designed for handles only. When fitting a knob on an internal door, fit a longer latch with a backset wide enough to get your fingers around the handle - say at least 75mm.

An external door knob will require an even longer latch – say 95mm. The pre-packed knobsets normally include 75mm latches, but if you are buying independently then watch out.

POCKET DOORS

These tend to get used where space is at a premium and where a hinged door would be inconvenient. Typically, a pocket door is specified where a tight bathroom arrangement makes it difficult to open the door inwards, or where a hinged door would impede access.

There is nothing novel about pocket doors — they were used in Victorian times — but many people are unaware of their existence. In order for them to work, you need to plan ahead and to build an encasing wall wide enough to take the door. As a standard internal door is just 34mm wide, it is not asking too much of a 100mm-wide wall to wrap itself around a door. In fact, most pocket doors are housed in steel framed kits which take the place of regular studwork.

The general increase in interest in pocket doors has seen new styles

Pocket doors tend to be fitted with pre-formed steel housings which are designed to slip into a studwork wall

emerging. You can get glazed pocket doors, and even pocket fire doors. There are several specialists offering different styles and functions: look out for Eclisse, Scrigno and PC Henderson.

Another space saving option is to have one door sliding across two openings, typically a bathroom and a cupboard. Here, you build a track across the two adjacent openings and hang a sliding door on it so that it either closes off the bathroom or the cupboard. It sounds uninviting but it can work well where privacy is only an issue on one half of the door track. It can also be much simpler to install than a complete pocket door

assembly, as the sliding track can be fitted at the door hanging stage, provided the alignments have been worked out in advance.

LOFT HATCH

Every house with an empty loft has one and they are not the most demanding of features. But take a little care in fitting a loft hatch as it is frequently a weak point in your home's battle against draughts. In terms of heat loss through the loft hatch, effective draught proofing is ten times more important than the insulation. You don't have to do anything dramatic; just make sure it sits tight. Most people now buy

proprietary loft hatches complete with a built in loft ladder.

It's worth remembering to install a permanent light in the loft just to make life easy when fixing a loft ladder. You won't regret it.

BOXING IN

Boxing in the pipes and ducts is a new facet of housebuilding that now forms a significant bit of a second-fixer's work. In the good-bad-indifferent-olde days the pipes were left naked for all to see. The stench pipe in particular was usually run down the outside of the house.

Current fashions are for internal stench pipes – concealed internal stench pipes – and this means boxing is de rigueur.

Now, depending on your disposition, this type of job can seem like an incredible almighty drag or a marvellous opportunity to show the world just how creative you can be with a bit of dead space.

Whichever camp you fall into, it helps to plan your pipe runs and attendant boxings well ahead so that the boxing can be incorporated into the overall scheme of things rather than sticking out into rooms like an ugly carbuncle.

Bathroom boxings are often tiled over, but you must allow at least some of the panelling to be removable – a trick that's accomplished with mirror screws and flexible mastic joints. If you are painting the finish, then MDF is probably the best material to use, but if you plan to stick ceramic tiles on, then a waterproof 18mm plywood would be a better choice.

Boxing is also widely used in bathrooms to create a fitted vanity unit effect. There is a range of basins (known as semi-countertop) that are designed to sit over a boxed unit, and there are also concealed cisterns which will be proud to flush behind your mini-wall. The usual choice of wall finish will be ceramic tiles but pine matchboarding is becoming fashionable once again, albeit painted not varnished.

STAIRS

Designing and installing stairs and landings is one of the less discussed aspects of housebuilding yet a staircase can make or break an interior, and getting it right it can be very challenging and sometimes extremely expensive. So what do you need to know?

There are building regulations about how you should set out a staircase so that it works safely. Too few or too many steps and it'll be difficult to climb. Handrail positions, headroom and pitch are also regulated, all with the aim of making staircases user friendly. By and large, it's worth sticking to these guidelines, although they can be relaxed in certain circumstances, such as restricted loft access.

DESIGNING THE LAYOUT

The first and most critical factor is to work out how the staircase will run. Where will it flow from and to? Will

it achieve this with a straight flight or with a turn or two? There are practical reasons for choosing a straight flight: it's usually the cheapest option and it usually makes it easier to move furniture up and down stairs. And if at any point in the future, you might want to install a stair lift, a straight flight is much the simplest option.

However, sometimes a turn will fit the available space better. If you want to create a more dramatic entrance with a full height hallway, and space is somewhat lacking, then a staircase with a half landing is a good way to achieve this. And in smaller houses where circulation space is tight, you can reduce the overall space taken up by a staircase and its top and bottom landing areas by engineering a turn or two.

There are often several options on how you can run a staircase. A good designer will work through them to see which one flows best. The polite convention is to arrange the stairs so that the base should be somewhere close to the front door of the house and that you shouldn't have to cross a room to get from the front door to the stairs. This is doubly important if there is (or maybe, at some time in the future) a third storey to the house, when the stairs have to act as a fire escape route from the loft.

TECHNICALITIES

Having established the overall staircase design (hopefully at a much earlier stage than second-fix), the next problem is to develop a technical brief for how the stairs are to be constructed.

STEP ONE is to measure the total rise, this is the measurement from finished floor below to finished floor level above.

STEP TWO is to work out the number of steps needed. Staircase builders refer to the horizontal steps as treads, and the vertical connecting parts as risers. It's usually reckoned that the best height for a riser is 200mm, so you want to be as close to this as possible — the building regulations allow you to have risers up to 220mm. Typically you get a 2600mm overall rise and this divides neatly into 13No 200mm individual steps or risers.

STEP THREE is to work out the number of treads and how they will sit. There is always one less tread than the number of risers, as the top of the stairs is designed to be level with the finished floor and you have only a connecting piece, known as a nosing.

STEP FOUR is to work out the tread width (known as the *going*), which in turn gives you the pitch of the stairs. The minimum going for a domestic staircase to comply with building regulations is 220mm and the pitch of a domestic staircase must not exceed 42°.

If you break the stairs with a landing, it's conventional to keep the same rise and going for both halves of the staircase. There is no restriction with how narrow you can go with a staircase but the width of a standard flight of stairs is 860mm, and this should be regarded as a minimum for a main staircase.

Chapter 10

WINDERS AND SPIRALS

Winders (pronounced wine-ders, not win-ders) is the name given to steps that turn corners whilst still climbing; a spiral staircase consists of nothing but winders: a more conventional arrangement uses three winder steps (usually at the top or the bottom of the flight) to navigate a 90° turn. They are space efficient: these days they are most commonly used with loft conversions, precisely because of this reason.

HEADROOM

You need a minimum of 2000mm of clear headroom above the pitch line on a domestic staircase to comply with building regulations. Having insufficient headroom can be a problem when the stairwell is located under an area of sloping roof and it's a technical detail that is often overlooked by architects and designers.

LOFT STAIRS

The regulations recognise that there are certain situations – principally loft access – where it just isn't feasible to build a standard staircase. Provided the stairs only lead up to one habitable room (plus an attached bathroom), then you are permitted to use either a loft ladder or an alternate tread staircase. The normal pitch requirements are also relaxed allowing you to fit a staircase into a much tighter space. These stairs are often marketed as space saver stairs.

TRENDS

The role of the staircase is gradually changing. In previous eras, only the grandest houses would have attempted to make a feature out of a staircase. In normal domestic architecture, the stairs fulfilled a purely functional role, and this remains true in the vast majority of developer built homes. Even twenty years ago, pretty much the only choice you had to make was whether the timber spindles on your banister were to be plain or carved. But in common with the growing interest in other interior design features, staircases have started to get modern and sexy. Instead of spending a few hundred pounds, maximum, on building a staircase, people now seem willing to fork out several thousand pounds for designer staircases, commonly using such materials as glass, concrete and steel.

OPEN RISERS

Replacing solid risers (the vertical sections of each step), with open risers is something that features high on many selfbuilders' wish lists. There is a problem here in that the building regulations don't permit any gaps in stairs wider than 100mm, in order to stop small children falling through.

The standard solution to this is to have a semi-open riser design, so that each step appears to have a little downstand underneath it, known as a riser downstand. This allows you to see through the stairs as you climb up, whilst satisfying the guarding regulation. An alternative is to have completely open risers, but to fit a horizontal bar at the mid point between the treads.

Nevertheless, you often see photographs of unguarded open riser staircases in magazines. The reason for this may be that the new staircase is a replacement of an older one, and that the work has been carried out outside building control jurisdiction. Alternatively, the guard rails have been removed after the building inspector's final visit.

FLOATING STAIRS

The ultimate in staircase chic is to go for a set of treads that appear to hang in space, connected only at one end to the wall. These are known as floating stairs and, not surprisingly, owe their existence to a fair amount of intricate steelwork hidden behind the plaster. Each one is a work of art, and the costs are to match. Expect to pay upwards of £15,000 for such a beast.

Just how you get such a staircase through the building regs beats me. And I am yet to be convinced that they will ever be child friendly. But maybe that's the point...

GLASS

Such is everyone's desire for space and light that we have witnessed a rise in demand for glass balustrading on staircases and landings. The glass has to be thick and toughened, and consequently the fixings have to be more robust and this adds to costs. If you want the cool, contemporary look of glass around your stairs, it's likely to add between £3,000 and £8,000 to the costs, depending on the scale and complexity of your design.

FUSION

Richard Burbidge introduced the

contemporary-looking Fusion stairparts range in 2000 and initially thought that they were launching a niche product, but it's turned into a big hit. The stair parts for a simple staircase with a 2m landing sells for around £550 using Fusion, around £200 more than pine, but it's much quicker to fit, 'requiring an average of just seven saw cuts as opposed to 125 when using conventional stair balustrading'. Such has been the success of Fusion that other manufacturers have now launched similar products, such as Axxys from Cheshire Mouldings.

MODULAR STAIRS

Generally made in Italy, modular stair kits offer a way of getting a contemporary design on a budget. They tend to specialise in spiral and spacesaver designs and they probably wouldn't suit a main staircase as they generally don't comply with UK building regulations but may be suitable for small loft conversions and mezzanine sleeping platforms.

STAIR LIGHTING

It's important to think about how a staircase and landings should be lit, both in terms of daylight and during hours of darkness. In some house designs, the circulation space is in semi-darkness the whole time because all the windows are placed in the living rooms, bedrooms and bathrooms. Good designers will find ways of introducing daylight: traditionally, this was achieved with a glass fanlight placed above an internal doorway which borrows light from

This open staircase meets the building regulations by adding a bar underneath each tread. The requirement is that a 100mm diameter ball should not be able to pass through the gap between the treads. This is to protect young children who might fall through.

the room behind. These days, a more common solution is to set a rooflight above the stairwell. If space is tight, an alternative option is to use a lightpipe.

The stairwell also needs to be lit electrically. The standard arrangement is to have lights both top and bottom, and for these lights to be switched from both top and bottom of the staircase, known as two-way

switching. More elaborate lighting is available; typically this will involve LEDs placed into the wall adjacent to the stairs, either on every step or, more subtly, every third step.

MATERIALS AND COMPARISON COSTS

There are two essential factors that have a bearing on costs. One is the design of the staircase, the other is the materials used to build it. Generally, the simpler the design, the cheaper the staircase. It also helps to have a standard rise between floors: if the distance between finished floors is the standard 2600mm, then you gain a small advantage in being able to order an off-the-peg staircase.

Straight flights are of course cheaper than staircases that turn, and curved staircases tend to be more expensive still.

As for materials, the cheapest stairs tend to be engineered pine and plywoods. These are best suited for fully carpeted stairs. One step up from this is parana pine, which has been the preferred timber for stair makers for many years. It is a tightly grained softwood with lots of reddy-brown colour variations and it takes a clear coat of varnish. It often gets specified with hemlock stairparts.

Hardwood staircases are more expensive still, although you can get a hardwood look for less money by specifying veneered MDFs. Hardwoods vary in price from two times the price of softwoods, to four or five times the price, depending on the choice of timber. Oak is usually the most expensive.

Other materials used include steel (popular for spirals), reconstituted stone (also popular for spirals) and glass. Pre-cast concrete is uncommon in individual houses, though it's sometimes used in basements.

Stairplan.co.uk run an amazingly helpful website with lots of guidance on choosing stairs, and they also have an online shop at www. tradestairs.com which allows you to work out prices directly. As a rule, a straightforward flight of stairs with a small, 2m landing, can be supplied for as little as £500 and fitted in a day, but if you want to use cutting edge design and unusual materials, it's not difficult to spend ten or even twenty times as much.

DRIVEWAYS & PAVINGS

Driveways are included on the list of external works that are exempt from VAT on new buildings, so there is every reason to finish the drive before occupation. Almost invariably, planning permission for new homes requires provision for off-road car parking and this means that some attention has to be paid to both where and how this is to be accommodated. So whilst a garage is arguably a luxury you could dispense with (or postpone), driveways and hardstandings must be accommodated within the initial design.

FOUNDATIONS
Whatever drive finish you decide on, the base you lay should essentially be the same: ideally 100-150mm of hardcore. A 1m³ void needs 2 tonnes of hardcore to fill it, so:
■ To lay hardcore 100mm thick, 1 tonne will cover 5m²
■ To lay hardcore 150mm thick, 1 tonne will cover 3.3m².

A superior method, particularly recommended on clay sites, is to use a Terram or Geotextile sheet underlay beneath the hardcore layer. These allow water to pass through whilst stopping mud mixing in with the hardcore overlay. Laying hardcore can be done by hand but this is backbreaking and time-consuming. The most efficient method is to use machines to spread and tamp hardcore – digger buckets are particularly effective tampers.

It is very useful to have hardcore laid as early as possible on a building job as it aids access and stops the site becoming a quagmire. However drain-laying timetables do not always allow this use of machinery and whether it is worth getting machinery in later just to lay hardcore depends on the size of the driveway.

If you dispense with or skimp on this hardcore sub-base, you will end up with a drive which will initially look good but will rapidly disintegrate. The other problem to be aware of here is rainwater drainage; on flat sites, water will tend to pool if it is not adequately planned for. To this end, it is normal to lay the drive so that rainwater collects in certain points, then drains off to a soakaway. Whilst the falls can usually be constructed when the actual driveway is being laid, the drainage obviously has to be installed before the sub-base. A minor detail? You won't think so if you overlook it.

BLOCK PAVING
Block paving is something akin to laying bricks on the ground. The blocks are a similar shape, although

usually a little thinner than a house brick, and they usually have a chamfered edge, unlike a house brick. They can be made of clay or concrete: concrete is invariably cheaper and perfectly adequate for the job, but it tends to look dull in comparison — think garage forecourts.

They are usually laid dry (without any cement) on a 50mm bed of sharp sand, and finished with jointing sand brushed over them and whacked with a compactor plate: dry laying is cheaper than wet and this makes them a cheap and attractive option for patios and paths as well as drives.

Supply and fix prices for plain block pavings tend to come in around £40m² (excluding hardcore foundation preparations), but these are at the low end of what you might expect to pay for something fancier. Kerb work obviously has a big impact on the overall costs and the value of this varies from site to site but averages about 20% of the overall costs. Fancy pavers will bump the overall price up by 50-100%.

The benchmark house in the 9th edition of Housebuilder's Bible used this contemporary arrangement for its driveway: decorative aggregate bordered by block paving. I used this as a template for costing the "Externals" on the model house.

PERMEABLE PAVINGS

In recent years, there has been a growing interest in pavings that are designed to absorb water rather than to direct it elsewhere. Welcome to the world of sustainable drainage systems (SUDS). It's actually a whole system approach to surface run-off and the pavers form only part of it: you have to use a no-fines sub-base which will hold water, and there are debates about just where

and how many geotextiles should be involved.

On small selfbuild sites, permeable paving systems are unlikely to make a huge difference to the world of storm water management (unlike a Tesco car park, for instance), but you may well be required to build a SUDS-compliant driveway as a planning condition. Usually, it's enough to direct the surface run-off to a soakaway, which can be done with drain gulleys just as easily as fancy permeable paving systems.

On the other hand, you may be attracted to a permeable paving system and there is nothing quite so eco-chic here as a grass paving. There are several systems available: these vary from block paving with spaces

which get planted out, to concrete grids with voids, to plastic cellular systems which contain gravel or grass, and even reinforced turf. It's a specialised area: the acknowledged experts here are Grasscrete.

TARMAC

Back in the world of impermeable pavings, there are other options besides block paving for driveways. Tarmac is one, although it has pretty much fallen out of fashion on the selfbuild scene. Preparation is much the same as for pavers; kerbs need to be set in concrete around the perimeter, although these are usually cheaper than the special kerbings used with block paving.

A pukka job should consist of

External Works - Key Rates

	Materials	Taken in	Labour @ £20/hr	Combined
150mm Hardcore Base	£ 11 m²	20	£ 8 m²	£ 19 m²
100mm Concrete Slab	£ 9 m²	25	£ 10 m²	£ 19 m²
2 Coat Tarmac	£ 40 m²	60	£ 22 m²	£ 62 m²
75mm Gravel	£ 7 m²	40	£ 15 m²	£ 22 m²
Decorative Aggregate	£ 15 m2	40	£ 15 m²	£ 30 m²
Paving Slabs	£ 15 m²	40	£ 15 m²	£ 30 m²
York Stone	£ 75 m²	60	£ 22 m²	£ 97 m²
Simple Kerbs	£ 8 m	50	£ 19 m	£ 27 m
Plain Block Pavings	£ 20 m²	40	£ 10 m²	£ 30 m²
Fancy Block Setts	£ 30 m²	40	£ 10 m²	£ 40 m²
Block Kerbs	£ 15 m	50	£ 19 m	£ 34 m
Pattern Imprinted Concrete	Supply and Fix only - often with a minimum charge			£ 35 m²
Resin Bonded Driveways	Supply and Fix only - often with a minimum charge			£ 30 m²
Turfing	£ 3 m²	20	£ 8 m²	£ 11 m²
Post and 3 Rail Fencing	£ 6 m	60	£ 22 m	£ 28 m
Palings	£ 8 m	60	£ 22 m	£ 30 m
Picket Fence	£ 18 m	60	£ 22 m	£ 40 m
Close Boarded Fence (1.8m h)	£ 35 m	90	£ 33 m	£ 68 m
Contemporary Slatted Fence	70 m	90	£ 33 m	£ 103 m
225mm Brick Wall (1.8m h)	£ 300 m run	360	£ 140 m	£ 440 m

MODEL HOUSE Externals

	Area/Length	Rate	Materials	Labour	Total
Base Preparation	160 m²	£ 19	£ 1,760	£ 1,280	£ 3,040
Decorative Aggregate	140 m²	£ 30	£ 2,100	£ 2,100	£ 4,200
Block Paving Setts	20 m²	£ 40	£ 600	£ 200	£ 800
Paving Slabs	15 m²	£ 30	£ 225	£ 225	£ 450
Post & Rail Fencing	30 m	£ 28	£ 180	£ 660	£ 840
Close-boarded Fencing	15 m	£ 68	£ 525	£ 495	£ 1,020
Turfing	140 m²	£ 11	£ 350	£ 1,120	£ 1,470
		Total	**£ 5,700**	**£ 6,100**	**£ 11,800**

a 80mm base course laid below a 35mm top course, known as the wearing course. A 50m² driveway with 20m kerbings should cost slightly less than a basic block paver.

Some tarmac prices appear to be far lower than this – this is the Wild West of the building trade remember – but the specification is unlikely to be the business and the finished drive may not last very long.

CONCRETE

Base preparations are again similar to pavers and tarmac; kerbs can be ignored in favour of shuttering (or road forms) for which steel formers are available to hire. The designated readymix for driveways is PAV 1 – strong and relatively expensive – and it is normally laid at 100mm depth. Reinforcement should not be necessary. Cheap and cheerless.

PATTERN IMPRINTED CONCRETE (OR PIC)

A number of specialist operators now offer patterned concrete paving where imprints of pavers are set into wet concrete to give a paved effect drive. This technique is widely used elsewhere around the world but is having difficulty catching on in the UK because of the low prices of standard concrete block paving. Having said that, you can't get concrete block paving to look like wood. If you want to see just what you can do with pattern imprinting on concrete, take the family off to Disneyworld – it's full of it.

There are some noted snags with PIC: it can crack (it shouldn't but it does), it can get slimey, it can stain, and you are stuck if you have to take the drive up for drain repairs or something like that. It's also the province of high-pressure sales teams and sometimes the prices quoted can look ridiculous. It shouldn't really cost much more than block paving.

RESIN-BONDED DRIVEWAYS

Available from specialist firms, these work by sticking small stones into a rigid sheet to give a shingle-look driveway which is as hard and durable as concrete or tarmac. Fantastic product if it's done properly but can be a disaster if not, so check the credentials of the installers. Prices tend to be similar to the Pattern

Imprinted Concrete, and minimum charges (often around £2,500) often apply.

Unlike the other alternatives to block paving, resin-bonded surfaces are very much in vogue and are used in all sorts of unlikely places like National Trust properties.

SHINGLE AND GRAVEL

This is the cheapest option and, in many rural situations, the most attractive. However, note that the better gravel driveways are actually labour intensive as they involve laying three or four layers of stones, individually rolled. Edgings need to be placed – treated timber strips are adequate – and the success of the drive overall depends on good hardcore beneath.

Top coat materials shouldn't cost much but laying costs are likely to be high, especially if there's no mechanised plant available.

Quotes to supply and lay a gravel drive often specify a simpler two layer application as this keeps the price down to around the £10m² mark (excluding foundation works). There are also a number of much more expensive decorative stone effect gravels you can use — look good, but an easy way to bump up the price.

Many selfbuilders put gravel drives in place because it's cheap and at the end of the job they are looking for ways to save money. Often they live to regret the decision, because gravel "walks" and the stones get everywhere.

Granite setts make an attractive paving but they are labour intensive to lay.

FANCY PAVING OPTIONS

There are many other materials available to lay paths and, in particular, patios. Labour costs for laying vary widely (£15-£30/ m²) depending on whether they can be laid wet or dry and whether they need pointing-up afterwards. Wet laying involves using cement (albeit usually a dryish mix) and tends to be very much more labour intensive. Some hardcore backfill is usually advisable, although when it is designed for foot traffic only, it does not need to be laid as deep as under driveways. As you might expect, natural materials like sandstone and limestone tend to be more expensive than the concrete ones, although the market has been flooded in recent years by some amazingly cheap Indian sandstones. There are numerous websites selling landscaping materials and once you start browsing you will soon get the hang of what costs what.

Chapter 10

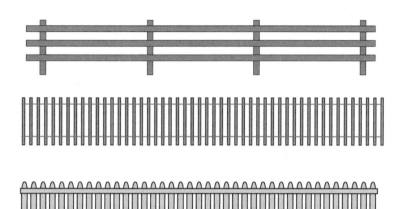

The main timber fencing options are, from the top: Post and Rail, Chestnut Palings, Picket Fencing and the Close-boarded Fence. The close-boarded fence is normally 1.8m high and thus provides an element of privacy.

Finally a plug for www.pavingexpert.com, a website maintained by paving guru Tony McCormack, where you can find out more than you possibly ever wanted to know about the black arts of paving and drainage.

SOFT LANDSCAPING

If you just want to mark a boundary and are not too bothered about privacy or security, then the cheapest permanent option is the timber post-and-rail fence. This arrangement shouldn't cost more than £12/m; it looks fine and is easily maintained. If you have longish (30m plus) lengths to erect, then the cheapest suppliers are to be found in the pages of Horse & Hound. Alternatively, a chain link fence is cheap, is more secure and should stop dogs and children straying.

Another cheapish option is 1.2m-high cleft chestnut which, being vertical, are much harder to climb over. They are easily fixed

– just whack posts in every 2m or so – but have a temporary air about them which may not appeal to all. The picket fence is similar in design but altogether more permanent in appearance and it costs around £25/m.

If you require privacy and security then you will have to go for a solid or near solid fence with a height of 1.8m (above head height). The traditional way of doing this is to erect something similar to a post-and-rail fence and then to cover it with vertically fixed, featheredge boarding. This is known as a close-boarded fence. Expect it to cost around £60/m. It is a little cheaper to use ready-made panels of the type you see in garden centres but the result is very flimsy in comparison. There are many variations on the theme of boarded fences; you can set the boards horizontally or diagonally, or alternate the boards between the inside and the outside of the fence posts (called hit and miss fencing). You can achieve quite stunning effects very simply and they don't have to be stained dark afterwards. If you want to investigate further, I recommend you get Jackson's Good Fencing Guide. They also deal with wire fencing which, I am assuming, is of lesser interest to would-be housebuilders.

BRICK WALLS
Whilst timber fencing is getting expensive at around £60/m, you are not going to get even a whiff of a brick boundary wall under £300/m and, if you use a nice brick and build

up to head-height, the cost will be around £500/m. This is a different animal altogether and ideally should be erected along with the main house so as to combine economies of scale – not to mention getting JCBs into the back garden. A 1.8m-high brick wall is actually a rather vulnerable construction, prone to blowing over in howling gales, and best practice advice now recommends that all unsupported walls over a mere 650mm high should be built two brick skins thick (225mm). In exposed locations, a 1.8m-high brick wall should be built 330mm thick. Whether your wall is free-standing or is being built as a retaining wall against some high ground, your building inspector will advise you as to the exact requirements needed. Dry stone walls are, needless to say, even more expensive, costing around £300/m for a waist-high one.

Jackson's have built a strong reputation for supplying good quality fence panels in a wide variety of styles. Their current selection includes a number of interesting contemporary styles such as louvred and hit and miss panels, which promise privacy whilst still allowing a little sunlight through.

GARDENS

Whilst we are not wishing to stray too far into the world of gardening, every selfbuild has at some point to face up to the fact that the garden needs some attention, especially if its been used as a dump for building materials and as a place to clean out cement mixers. It's not a good place to start.

You may well have to clean out the detritus you've left behind and bring in some topsoil. On some sites, the clean topsoil has to be delivered before the building work even starts because there is little of no access after the structure is up.

Really you need to hire a landscaper at this point and sort out the garden area with mini-diggers and dumpers, a sort of groundworks 2.0. It's often a surprising amount of work, and a surprising amount of money, especially if you start specifying water features, garden lighting and summerhouses.

The go-to garden cover remains the lawn which sounds cheap as turf is available at around £3/m², but if you want professionals to lay it the costs shoots up to nearer £20/m², not much different to carpet.

Bear in mind your VAT position here. Normally the provision of soft landscaping (which includes lawns) is treated as zero-rated for VAT purposes, but anything like planting trees or shrubs or hard landscaping is not, unless the planning permission specifies that it is carried out.

What about garden lighting? You can spend a lot of money on this. The HMRC advice begins to get sketchy at this point. It just states that outside lighting is an item you can claim for (i.e. get the VAT back on), and makes no mention of garden lighting. My best advice is to check for yourself either in the DIY selfbuild documentation (VAT431NB) or on VAT in construction (VAT Notice 708, section 13).

ROOM BY ROOM

KITCHENS

What prominence to give to the kitchen? It is one of the more taxing internal design decisions that you will be faced with. The two extremes to opt for are:

▨ the kitchen as utility area (hidden from view and servicing a separate dining room, aka the Downton Abbey option)

▨ the kitchen to be the main living area of the home, typically called an open-plan arrangement.

The trend is towards the open-plan kitchen; this suits the kitchen suppliers as it means a) bigger kitchens and b) consumers are more conscious of the way their kitchens are going to look. If you accept the notion that you want your kitchen to be the most important room in the house, then you are probably prepared to spend a much larger sum on making it beautiful. On the other hand, if you want to keep costs down, design your kitchen more as a utility area and have a separate dining room where you eat.

MUD ROOMS AND LARDERS

Many designs relegate the utility area to little more than a laundry room, but for some people, particularly country dwellers, a proper mud room would be far more useful; somewhere warm and light to take off wellies and wet coats, to air clothes, for dogs to sleep in. It's the natural place for a back door, but to do it properly requires a surprising amount of space. They are not called mud rooms for nothing; during the long dark winter months, just going out into the garden is a seriously mucky business and the interface between inside and outside needs thought.

The separate larder is an old idea

coming back into fashion. This can be a small room and doesn't need any daylight but to work well it needs to be easily accessed from the kitchen preparation area. In days of yore, the larder enjoyed a completely different microclimate to the kitchen - it was cool, dark and even a little damp - but this is hard to achieve in contemporary housing because of the energy efficiency demands. But even a centrally-heated larder is useful if only to store dried food and crockery: it's much cheaper than fitting it all into expensive kitchen units.

GRASPING THE KETTLE

When you've come to some conclusion about how you want your kitchen to work with the rest of the house, you can then get down to the nuts and bolts design-matters of what goes where. It is usual to start with a list of household appliances. If you have opted for a separate utility area, this will be the natural home of washing machines and tumble dryers and, possibly, freezers. The kitchen proper must have a sink, a hob, some sort of cooker and a fridge. Dishwashers are now ubiquitous and are conventionally placed close to the sink. The positioning of your appliances around the kitchen becomes the skeleton on which the kitchen furniture is hung. There are some conventional dos and don'ts to consider:

■ DO locate sinks and plumbed-in appliances where waste pipes can get to the drains. Usually this means placing them against an outside wall. If not, you have to plan your plumbing carefully.

■ DO leave worktop space either side of both the sink and the hob (or cooker top).

■ DO keep the sink, the hob and the fridge reasonably close to each other. Some kitchen planners will go on at length about the importance of the work triangle in the kitchen. Politely ignore them.

■ DON'T place a hob or a sink in a corner unless you consider an angled corner arrangement (expensive); corners tend to make poor working/ storage space.

■ DON'T place a fridge or freezer next to or under a heat source (hob, cooker, radiator).

■ DON'T forget to consider the boiler if it needs to be in the kitchen. Not only will it be hot but also there are rules concerning just where you can and can't place boiler flue terminals.

■ DON'T put wall cupboards over the sink; conventionally, sinks go under windows and for most small- or medium-sized kitchens this will always be the most practical location.

If you're a neat, logical kind of person, having got this far you should be able to draw a layout plan on some graph paper and begin to get an idea of the number of units you will need. Congratulate yourself because you're the kind of client any kitchen supplier would be pleased to have – you actually know what you want!

KITCHEN UNITS

The fitted kitchen is very much a 20th century invention. Back in the 1960s, a kitchen cabinet was thought of as something to do with Harold Wilson's unique style of government. But shortly thereafter, the fitted kitchen arrived in the home and, bit-by-bit, we have learned to spend more and more money on our kitchens. There are several procurement routes, each with its own pitfalls. Whilst the bulk of the new kitchen market now goes into replacing existing kitchens, a significant chunk gets accounted for by all the new homes built each year. And whilst a penny pinching spec housebuilder may spend as little as £3,000 on fitting a kitchen on a starter home, you only have to open a Sunday newspaper to realise that some people are happy to spend over £100,000 on a fitted (or perhaps an unfitted) kitchen. Bigger of course, better undoubtedly, but thirty times bigger or better? Undoubtedly not, but do bear in mind that a cheap kitchen probably won't last more than ten years whereas an expensive one may be good for fifty.

New fashions come but never really go, so kitchen design continually expands to incorporate new ideas whilst simultaneously recycling the old ones. The basic manufacturing process is relatively simple and cheap so that no new idea can ever be free from imitators for more than a couple of years.

The kitchen business is fully metricated and works in modular units which increase in 100mm intervals. Thus any given range of floor units or wall cupboards will be available in widths of typically 300mm, 400mm, 500mm and

600mm; 600mm is the key one, this is the building block of the fitted kitchen – appliances are conventionally made to fit into 600mm gaps. The other sizes tend to get used to fill awkward gaps between the 600mm units. By twiddling the plan about a bit, you can fill any space on any wall to the nearest 100mm – and they sell blanking-off pieces to cover any little gaps left over.

All but the most expensive kitchen unit carcasses are made from a wood pulp board like chipboard or MDF, usually covered with a melamine veneer which serves to make them both stronger and moisture resistant. The cheaper doors, which are hung over these carcasses, are made of similar materials, although here the melamine covering is usually decorated with some trim. Solid timber or plywood are more upmarket door options and there are adventurous designs using materials such as stainless steel and plastic.

FLAT PACK DIY KITCHENS
There are several ways of getting fixed up with a kitchen. About the cheapest is to go to one of the giant DIY retailers such as B&Q or IKEA and buy yourself a flat-pack. The cheaper kitchens tend to be supplied flat-packed and need assembling on site, a feat which in theory is straightforward but in practice can be damned difficult, especially when it takes you two days to realise you haven't got all the bits.

Another point well worth garnering about flat-pack kitchens is that you are buying the materials, not the fitting out. Consequently, they look much cheaper than all the other options, which come on a supply and fix basis. Now B&Q may well have a few trade cards stuck at the back of the store with names of recommended installers but tread with care here. Installing a kitchen is a complex multi-task of a job involving co-ordinating fitters, plumbers, sparkies, tilers and fitters all over again. It's not just a question of getting hold of some bloke handy with a screwdriver, he must be bloody useful with a mobile phone as well.

THE CONTINENTALS
The more innovative and interesting designs are the preserve of the up-market kitchen. The Germans were the first into this pond in the 1970s when names like Wellman, Allmilmo and Poggenpohl came to the UK. Like all things German, they have built up a reputation for superbly crafted kitchens. In terms of style however they've been left in the slow lane. The high-tech, continental look is now led by the French and, especially, the Italians – look out for Boffi's futuristic designs.

SMALLBONE, ETC
Despite exporting barely any kitchens at all (we import about 20%), the British have responded to the threat of mainly up-market invasion by inventing a whole new romantic theme – sometimes known as the English Revival style or, more often, "doing a Smallbone."

Smallbone – which started as an antiques business in Wiltshire – led the way in creating a new vernacular kitchen, which managed to strike some chord in the English middle-class psyche and led people to pay vast sums to recreate a past that never existed. Using many revived techniques and idioms (rag rolling, marbling, Welsh dressers), they created a magnificent, seductive illusion. To purchase the actual Smallbone marque is horribly expensive – the average one costs £42,000 – but the style has spawned dozens of imitators. These high prices have proved to be just perhaps a bit too high and Smallbone (and the related Mark Wilkinson Kitchens) went bust in 2009, though they continue to trade under new owners.

This school of kitchen design has grown away from providing modular boxes towards what has become known as the unfitted kitchen – an Aga here, a beech block table there, terracotta tiles on the floor, wicker baskets hanging on rails, you can almost smell the garlic and olive oil. Some of these up-market companies must be approached directly, many have just one UK outlet. The nearest thing to a directory exists in the back of 'Kitchens, Bedrooms and Bathrooms' magazine which will give you an overview of the market's top end.

KITCHEN BOUTIQUES
Another approach is to ignore the plethora of manufacturers and concentrate on your local kitchen specialists. Most small towns have at least one, and a regional

shopping centre will have several. Most will stock only three or four manufacturers' products but as manufacturers offer sometimes hundreds of options (especially door colours) this can still be quite bewildering. Typically, they will stock a mass-produced British flat-pack product that they will use to try and compete with B&Q and co, but the bulk of their showrooms are given over to displaying a more up-market continental range. They make more money on the more expensive kitchens so it is understandable that it is these that they promote.

Many people are rather reluctant to set foot inside a kitchen specialist as they think it would be a) too expensive and b) involve high-pressure selling. By and large, this is not the case; although they probably cannot compete with B&Q on kitchen unit price alone, they are usually owner-managed and tend to give a high level of personal service without resorting to any pressure tactics. Unlike the major retail outlets, prices are usually negotiable and this makes it hard to compare on a like for like basis.

Some kitchen specialists aren't simply re-sellers but actually make their own units, often with a distinctive style. If you like the house style, then they can make an excellent choice, but don't work with an outlet like this if you want something quite different to what they like to do.

On our 2018 selfbuild, we worked with just such a business, Tomas Kitchens, based in Cambridge but who work throughout the South East.

Which? magazine surveyed six flat pack kitchens and found IKEA came out tops. "The best quality units we tested," they wrote,"provided you can follow the instructions."

The personal service and the excellent quality was money well spent, as far as we were concerned, but it wasn't cheap. The cost, including appliances, was just under £30,000, making it a top end £5,000/m³ kitchen.

THE BUILDER

If you are fitting a kitchen as part of a much larger project (i.e. building a house) then it may make sense to keep the work in-house and ask your builder to fit it. That's if you are still on speaking terms by the time you have reached the kitchen fitting. There are several outlets (principally builders' merchants and joinery centres) that aim to sell mainly to builders and they have kitchen catalogues available to browse through and sometimes showrooms to visit.

Some of the major joinery firms – Howdens, Magnet – produce fitted kitchens although, stylistically, they tend to be the most conservative of all. Their catalogues are easy to get hold of and clearly priced. The builder can buy these units (and the accessories) at discounts of between 20 to 40% off list price and many will be happy to negotiate to share at least some of the discount with you – see section on the Project Management chapter, in particular find out what a PC Sum is. Even so, the prices from the volume joinery majors, even with full discount, will be slightly more than the cheapest available from the likes of B&Q; but there is one big advantage if your builder fits the units and that is that he will remain responsible for sorting out any snags. If, on the other hand, you supply your own units to your builder and, say, the hinges work loose or there are unsightly gaps here and there, then you'll have your work

Chapter 11

cut out trying to convince him it's his fault: indeed you'll have fallen into one of the contractual traps placed along the route.

COSTS

Strange as it may seem, you can quite easily compare kitchen unit costs by the cubic metre (m^3). It's actually quite helpful because it gives you a handle on both basic cost and the quantity of units.

Floor units are conventionally 900mm high (the worktop level) and 600mm deep. Above worktop wall units are 700mm high but no more than 350mm deep. Double height units are typically 2100mm high.

By way of example, the kitchen of a small one bedroom flat would consist of around $2m^3$ of units. It has maybe 10 units in all, including appliance housings. A very large detached house is likely to have around $8m^3$ upwards, say up to 40 units, probably including an island.

The model house used to compare costs in this edition has been deemed to have $5m^3$ of kitchen units (around 20 units) and is mid-priced at around £1,200/m^3. Fully finished kitchens (including appliances and worktops) are available at anywhere between £800 and £5,000/m^3. The cost gap is staggering: there is a world of difference.

SINKS

Having once been out of fashion because they were cheaply made, stainless steel is back to No 1 in the kitchen sink pop charts. Steel is actually a very good choice of material for a sink; it's strong, lightweight and easily cleaned.

The very cheapest kitchen sinks now tend to be stainless steel; single bowl/single drainers can be picked up for less than £100, a set of taps for less than £20. However, the products from the big names in kitchen sinks (Leisure, Carron, Franke, Blanco, Barazza) can be much more. Expect to pay £250 upwards plus for something as good as a Franke one-and-a-half bowl sink.

SYNTHETICS AND CERAMICS

In the 1990s, a whole bunch of composite materials were used to make sinks but they have pretty much gone out of fashion now. As with bathrooms, where everything is now white, kitchen sinks have reverted to either stainless steel or white ceramics, or the sink-cum-worktop effect you can get with Corian (see below).

The old fashioned butler's sink tends to look a wow in the kitchen showroom, particularly when it is inset in a hardwood surround with drainage grooves. It's not changed from the original Victorian design (i.e. a large white rectangular box) and this adds an air of authenticity to it which nothing else in a modern kitchen can touch, not even an Aga (which hails from the 1930s). Consequently, it's become an item in all Smallbone-inspired kitchens and its very size and weight stand as statements of contempt for the standard mass-produced fitted kitchen. Butler's sinks, such as the Armitage Shanks Belfast, cost between £110 and £150 depending on size. Taps and waste are extra: these sinks are most definitely not sold in packs.

TAPS

Depending on your bowl arrangements, a moveable tap is a very handy thing to have and one on a hose is even more useful. The longer the hose, the better as far as I am concerned. Separate taps and simple mixers cost next to nothing, but a fabulous Hansgrohe pull out spout stainless steel kitchen tap can cost £600 or more.

BOILING WATER TAPS

We seem to have come up with an entirely new kitchen gadget in recent years, the boiling water tap which basically replaces a £25 kettle with a £500 instant hot water tap. For a few quid more, you can add an ice-cool tap as well. It's the sort of thing which we, as well trained consumers, will tend to lust after, and doubtless once experienced will never be able to live without. But as someone whose only ever come across them in showhouses, I think I can make do with a kettle. Lots of people now making them, Screwfix are selling them. Make sure your chosen sink has the tappings to take one.

WASTE DISPOSAL UNITS

Almost universally fitted in America, waste disposal units are still something or a rarity in the UK. They sit under the kitchen sink and are electrically powered to spin at very high speed and macerate food waste so that it can pass down an ordinary 32mm kitchen sink waste pipe and out into the sewer system. The best known name is InSinkErator, costing between £200 and £400 depending on the model and the power.

If you are a successful composter, then you will eschew such a hi-tech, low sense way of getting rid of tea bags, coffee grounds and food waste. But they do overcome the issue people have with smelly bins in smart kitchens.

KITCHEN WORKTOPS

The worktop is the name given to the main shelf in a kitchen where all the action happens – the food preparation, the cooking and the cleaning. Everything else is just storage. Getting the worktop right is a crucial part of kitchen design and, although it may not be the first thing you think about when selecting a kitchen, it will be the single most important element in your kitchen. The standard width for worktops is 600mm, which is sufficient for most kitchen configurations. Peninsulas, islands and breakfast bars may all require wider surfaces; there are a few extra-wide sizes available with two good edges, designed for these types of applications.

Buying worktops is not straightforward because they tend to need a little configuration in order to fit a kitchen. Typically a hole will be cut for a kitchen sink and a joint will

have to be made where two sheets meet. And there will be edge details and a splashback to think about too. So here the headline rate is only the beginning of the journey.

But, as ever, the headline rate is the place we all start. The bottom end of the market is dominated by laminate boards, usually with a post-formed or rounded edge. These used to be what everyone fitted back in the days when fitted kitchens were a new idea. You can buy a 3m long laminate worktop for under £50, so here the main cost is the hole cutting and jointing.

Other materials are available. Laminated hardwoods were fashionable in the 1980s but proved to not keep too well. Granite and other stone tops were in vogue in the 1990s but they tend to be a bit dark. These days the vogue surfaces are composite materials like Corian or manufactured stone products known as Quartz, which of course cost about ten times more than the old plastic-based laminates.

Corian in particular is unusual in that it can be formed into sink-shapes so that you can appear to have a seamless kitchen sink which looks and feels exactly like the rest of the worktop. Corian however is not quite as durable as the quartz worktops and materials like Dekton are now appearing which you can put a hot pan on and not cause any markings. All these options (except the basic laminate worktops) can be machined to give you drainage grooves next to the sink if you wish. There are numerous worktop specialists around who take on this type of job and if

you hire a kitchen fitter they will probably use such a specialist to fit the worktop. A fitted worktop in a material like Corian or Dekton will cost upwards of £750 per linear metre (based on a 600mm wide worktop, the standard width). Islands and peninsulas will of course cost even more.

KITCHEN APPLIANCES

All prices quoted in this section will include VAT. Trade prices invariably exclude it whilst retail outlets invariably include it. Whichever way, new housebuilders in the UK cannot reclaim VAT on kitchen cookers or appliances with the sole exception of cooker hoods, which are regarded as a ventilation item.

COOKING

The standard practice today is to buy a built-in oven with a separate hob and a hood, often sold together as a package. Every supplier offers a choice of gas or electricity for your hob without any effect on price, but a gas oven is more expensive than an electric one. The budget developers' packages are priced at around £300.

Appliances are mostly made to modular sizes so that they slip easily into any kitchen unit assembly although there is no compulsion to source your appliances from the same place as your units. Neither of course is there any compulsion to stick to the same brand of appliances throughout the kitchen, though for convenience many people do.

Chapter 11

STAND ALONE/SLOT-IN COOKERS

Go into Currys, and you will still find a range of very 1950s-style gas and electric stoves. I don't think very many go into new homes (unless you are specifically going for that 50s retro-look) but they are very cheap. However, 21st century housebuilders all go for fitted ovens and hobs. The question is which oven, hob and hood? In recent years the choice has multiplied alarmingly making this once simple task extremely taxing.

OVENS

At the basic end you get a single electric oven with a timer clock and two or three functions. That is enough for 90% of us. It'll cook a Christmas dinner, what more can you ask? Well, a lot. What's happened with ovens mimics what's happened with computers. They have grown more functions and controls. Take a top of the range Miele single oven. It comes with ten functions. It also has ThermoClean plus pyrolytic cleaning with Air Clean catalyser. Don't yer luv this stuff? You need to go on a course just to see how it works and, not surprisingly, Miele, along with a handful of other manufacturers, run cookery demonstration courses.

SPECIALIST OVENS

The relentless rise of the microwave has seen it elevated from being a countertop accessory to being a built-in second oven in its own right. Most people find it far more useful and flexible than having a double oven. Despite being limited in their uses,

microwaves are excellent in a number of areas (eg boiling vegetables, reheating, defrosting) where conventional cooking is cumbersome. They are quick, clean and energy efficient.

As an alternative to fitting a separate microwave unit, most manufacturers now make multi-function or combi ovens that include a microwave function. You can use these as either conventional only, microwave only or both functions at once which allows you to halve the cooking time for something like a chicken or roast potatoes but still get an element of crispy browning. However operating them in combined mode is quite complicated – it requires a whole new set of cooking skills.

Steam ovens sell themselves as healthy alternatives to microwaves. They tend to be quite small, not much bigger than a microwave, and they work by boiling water and blasting steam into the cooking chamber (some of them do this under pressure). Like microwaves, they are surprisingly versatile and can do much of the cooking undertaken on a hob as well as useful little jobs like defrosting and sterilising bottles. Again, it's a whole different approach to cooking that has to be learned afresh. Steam ovens are still quite a specialised item and they are not cheap, prices starting from about £600 from de Dietrich or Miele.

HOBS

Where they have a choice, most people go for a gas hob. Gas is fast,

responsive and cheap to use: its drawbacks are that they are hard to clean and they have a dislike of pans boiling over. If mains gas is unobtainable, then consider having bottled gas just for the hob. Gas cooking has another big, often unspoken plus going for it in that it continues to work in power cuts, something many rural areas still suffer from frequently.

Whilst electric hobs have been seen as the poor relation, there are a number of developments that make them more interesting. First the ceramic hob came along which was easier to clean, if nothing else, but they perform only slightly better than conventional electric plates. They do, however, make a pleasing orange glow.

More recently we have seen induction hobs that work via a magnetic field rather than an element. When magnetic pans are placed on the surface, a field is created which produces heat. The field is only generated where the pan touches so induction cooking is efficient and extremely quick – faster even than gas. Induction hobs are also horribly expensive – expect to pay around £500 for one of these beauties. And buy new cookware – it has to be magnetic.

The more up-market suppliers can also fit you out with specialist hoblets where you can mix and match your cooking surfaces and include griddles and fryers as well as the more usual plates. Most manufacturers also give you the option of having extended hobs if you find the standard 600mm width a bit limiting.

Be aware that the standard electrical supply for electric cooking in the kitchen is a 30amp cable. This is only capable of supplying 7.5kW of power (you need 4 amps for each kW). Double ovens will use as much as 6kW with everything on and an induction hob or a five or six plate ceramic hob can take as much as 8kW with every ring in action. You can elect to either uprate your supply to 45amp or run separate circuits for the oven and the hob.

COOKER HOODS

Cooker hoods now seem to come in about five flavours. The standard version is a rectangular box which sits between 650 and 750mm above the hob: you get a three speed fan and a light (actually very useful) but they are cheap and usually noisy.

Then there is an 'integrated' variety which gets concealed in an overhead wall cupboard and is activated by pulling the top-hung cupboard door open. Next, a slimline or telescopic version which is typically no more than 25mm deep and these are turned on just by a gentle tug towards you; the fan itself sits in a dummy cupboard above.

The traditional up-market option is to go for a canopy cooker hood which acts more like a conventional chimney: usually finished in stainless steel, look to pay north of £350 for this type, though much cheaper ones can be found on eBay and the like. But you can easily track down canopies costing over a grand.

About the most upmarket option is to go for a worktop ventilation unit, otherwise known as a downdraft hood, which is designed for cooking on an island unit. It sits in a slot behind the hob on and emerges up from the worktop at the touch of a button. Costs typically more than £2,000, and some complex sub-floor venting is required to get them to work

Should you have your kitchen extractor venting to the outside or simple re-circulating the extracted air back into the kitchen having passed through a grease filter and a charcoal filter? The plain extractors are simpler and cheaper but they simply throw the air out of the house: it needs venting which may not always be easy (especially on an island) and may require ducting which is awkward. The re-circulators don't work quite so well and require occasional filter changes, but will work fine if you don't live on fry-ups.

In fact, most of the time, kitchen extractors do remarkably little and people often cook on hobs forgetting to turn on the extractor and it doesn't make much difference to the air quality.

If you are going for a low-energy house, you will already have plans for a whole house ventilation system and here the system kitchen extract is routinely fitted with a grease filter in any event. The manufacturers all tend to steer you away from using whole house ventilation as a kitchen cooker extract because the thought of clogging up a ventilation system with grease if just too horrible, but if you never fry anything what exactly is the problem?

One to ponder. I'm one of a growing number of people who live in a new home without a kitchen extract at all and are happy to take a chance using the whole house ventilation system plus the occasional open window to do the work. Thus far, so good, but it's early days....

WHICH MAKE?

There is an awful lot of snobbery about kitchen appliances. Classy kitchens need white goods with German (or at least German sounding) names like AEG, Bosch, Siemens or Miele (it's pronounced like Sheila). Very classy kitchens need classy German makes like Gaggenau. British manufacturers like Hotpoint, Tricity Bendix, Creda have reputations based on price rather than quality, as have Philips Whirlpool and most of the Italian manufacturers with the exception of Smeg (yes, they are Italian) who have levered themselves up to Premiership status. The very cheapest appliances often come with little-known brand names and obscure East European origins.

Getting confused? It gets worse. White goods branding is an extremely complicated area. There is much cross-manufacturing of parts and 'country of origin' labelling should more correctly read 'country of final assembly'. As an example, most European cooker hoods are made in Italy and perform to much the same (rather noisy) standard whether they are branded Candy, Neff or Creda. Much of the upmarket German kit is actually assembled in Turkey or Portugal.

Chapter 11

No wonder purchasers often subcontract the decision making as well as the installation. Broadly speaking, if you want to create an impression then the brand names have to be German. The very best cookers tend to be German, but don't assume that a German brand name is necessarily a sign of quality. Also, if you want anything unusual like a built-in griddle you will need to seek out the high quality brand names. However, if low price is your main concern, then you should check out Currys' own brands or alternatively specialists selling to developers – Arrow, Allied, or BCG.

AGAS

The Aga remains the item for the complete country kitchen. Despite their exorbitant cost (new price anywhere between £6,500 and £15,000 plus the need for adequate foundations, suitable chimney arrangements and fitting costs) and their exorbitant running costs (around 50 litres of oil or 275kWh of electricity a week – you work it out), otherwise rational people still salivate at the thought of having an Aga in the kitchen. They can't do chips, they can't grill and boiling a kettle takes forever but, to quote the sales blurb: 'An Aga transforms even the most functional kitchen into a warm and welcoming gathering place for all the family. It becomes the heart and hub of your home.'
The fact that this description is often spot on usually says more about the state of the rest of the house than any unique attributes of the

Aga. Any large radiant heat source will be immensely attractive on a bitingly cold day and it's this aspect of the Aga – over half a tonne of hot cast-iron – which fuels its seemingly unending popularity. A large storage heater would fulfil the same function at a fraction of the cost but, I'm afraid, it would completely lack the necessary style.

If you are contemplating an Aga for your home, you must plan for it from the ground upwards. Though not designed as water boilers, for an extra £300 you can go for an Aga with a boiler capable of heating not less than 400 litres of water a day (ie enough for about eight people) and – provided yours is a new house qualifying for VAT zero-rating – you can reclaim VAT on the purchase which instantly saves around £500. HMRC is usually happy to accept this distinction and it cannot insist that the boiler is ever connected to your hot water cylinder. Agas come in gas-fired, oil-fired, solid fuel and electric (Economy 7) versions, and it has recently unveiled a biofuel-enabled range.

There are a number of cast iron stove makers besides Aga and they are usually quite a bit cheaper. Many of them incorporate boilers so that you can use them as both cookers and house heaters but although this sounds economical, it can be a mixed blessing when it's your only heat source – it's not so much a case of being warm in winter as boiling in the summer.

No way can you reconcile having an Aga with hopes of building an

eco house. I am sorry. Much as you might hope to just slip one in as a sop to the wife (that's the usual story), such is the energy consumption of these behemoths that it just can't be done. If you want to see a splendid example of a company trying to defend the indefensible, have a look at Aga's Green Issues web page. 'It's built from recycled materials,' they trill. 'It'll last much longer than an ordinary cooker.' 'It'll store energy from renewable power sources.'" 'Some of our Agas will be biofuel enabled.' Yes, yes. All true and all utterly irrelevant. Denial is a thing of wonder.

RANGES

There are alternatives between the splendour of the Aga and the industry standard 'tin boxes' which are sold as part of a fitted kitchen. When the first edition of this book came out in 1995, hobby cookers were unheard of. Now every kitchen showroom has them on display at prices starting at around £600. They are now referred to as range cookers and they are about half as wide again as the industry standard 600mm so you get six rings instead of four. You can get them dual fuel so that you get an electric oven and a gas hob: indeed this is the most popular option.

WHITE GOODS

DISHWASHERS

If you want a dishwasher, the big decision facing you is whether to go free-standing or integrated. If you are buying a fitted kitchen you will come under a little pressure to go for an integrated one which will slip behind a kitchen-unit door so that you wouldn't know there was a dishwasher there at all.

Now, despite the integrated ones having less in the way of metal casing, they invariably cost more. Sometimes it can be hard to compare because the models are not directly equivalent. Take a good, solid German make like Miele: their basic free-standing dishwasher is available for around £550 but if you want it integrated it costs £200 more.

If you succumb to the allure of an integrated dishwasher, you have a further choice to make; to hide the entire machine behind your chosen kitchen unit door – that's known as fully integrated – or to let the control panel peep out at you in a way referred to as semi-integrated by some and as drawer line by others.

If you find the distinction between fully and semi-integrated dishwashers all a bit too precious, then save yourself a couple of hundred quid and bung in a free-standing one. And avoid stainless steel fronts and save yourself another couple of hundred quid.

Stainless steel looks good, photographs well but as anyone who has lived with one will tell you, they don't half show the fingermarks. If you want the stainless steel look to stay looking clean, then you actually need aluminium, which is even more expensive.

LAUNDRY

You can get integrated washing

Much as I don't get Agas, even I have to admit that they do sit well in a country kitchen.

machines and tumble dryers but generally these items get placed in a separate utility room and they are therefore normally purchased as free-standing items. Hotpoint and Bosch are the biggest name in washing machines. Their basic stand-alone models start at around £250-£300 but as you add features the price increases.

TUMBLE DRYERS

You'd think choosing a tumble dryer would be simple but, of course, it ain't. There are a number of factors to consider, most importantly whether to go for a vented one or a condenser. Or splash out on a heat pump one?

The difference? The vented ones are the simplest and cheapest. They work by throwing the warm, moist air out of the house via a 100mm flexi-duct. This isn't very green as you

are just throwing heat away from an expensively built energy efficient home.

The condensers have to do more work and therefore use more energy: they also cost between 50 and 80% more than the simpler vented ones. As its name suggests, condensing tumble dryers produce a lot of water which either has to be manually emptied from an in-built bucket or plumbed into the waste pipes.

A new development is the heat pump tumble dryer: many of the regular manufacturers have introduced them. They are very expensive, upwards of £500 to buy, but they offer much lower running costs because of the heat pump technology. They work as condensers so need plumbing into the waste pipes, but they use much less power. In fact, they are rather slower than conventional tumble dryers and this can be a good thing because they are less likely to shrink clothes.

Whilst we are on the subject of clothes drying, don't forget the traditional methods — washing lines in the garden and hanging rails in the utility room. Both useful, even with a tumble dryer, but both need planning ahead to get full value from them.

COLD STORAGE

There are numerous options of above- and below-freezing point storage and there are also numerous arrangements for their housing. You have the same decisions you get with cookers – whether to integrate or go free-standing. Free-standing is invariably cheaper. Or was until the arrival on our shores of the giant American fridges which you haven't a hope of integrating into any MDF kitchen unit. Now a whole raft of new names (to us) like Admiral, Amana and Maytag are selling enormous fridge freezers with ice dispensers and are getting to over £2,000 for some models. Quite a change from a Whirlpool under-the-counter-job for £150.

And Smeg has appeared with some curved edge 1950s style fridges in a range of pastel colours, looking fabulous and definitely not for concealing, especially with a £1,000 price tag. Ice dispensers anyone? Don't forget they need a water supply.

All attempts to add value to what are essentially nothing more than cold cupboards. Again, if you are trying to save a little money, consider building an old fashioned larder, located off the kitchen, where you can store even more than you would get in a 26.7ft3 Maytag Sovereign. I figure even a small larder will be five times the volume – but where would you put the ice dispenser?

KITCHEN WASTE

Regular bin collections have become more sporadic and we are now expected to sort our waste in-house. This represents a challenge for kitchen designers because it effectively means we have to have two or three different bins in each kitchen. Or at least have a plan for dealing with all the waste.

Much of this isn't terribly difficult to achieve. You just need a few extra bins. If you are really bothered, you can build these into your kitchen cabinets but this is expensive. The cheaper options are to use good looking bins in the kitchen – currently Brabantia are the best established name with their stainless steel offerings – or get a load of plastic boxes and put them in the utility room or the garage. The trouble with putting bins out of the kitchen is that the act of throwing stuff in bins gets problematic and is therefore prone to high failure levels.

Compost bins are something else. I have lived with compost bins most of my life and, whilst the theory is all fine and dandy, the practice is anything but. Firstly, if they aren't emptied frequently, ideally daily, then they get smelly and fly-blown. Secondly the compost heap itself needs a lot of attention if it is to work as advertised. Otherwise it too becomes smelly and fly-blown and acts as a magnet to the local rat population. And unless it gets turned over every now and then, it doesn't even make useful compost.

One step is to keep chickens which will dispose of most of your vegetable spoil but then chickens need even more work than a compost heap. Another is to turn in the opposite direction and get a waste-disposal unit, as discussed in the previous section (see under Sinks).

Whatever route you choose, don't be fobbed off with a kitchen design based around a mini-swing bin of 20lt or less. Even the greenest households need a waste bin that will hold a 50lt bin liner. If storing great quantities of waste is a problem you can't see an easy way around, consider a rubbish compactor that reduces the volume four or five times. They are an expensive option, costing around £700 and taking up as much space as a large bin!

BATHROOMS

The bathroom is a multi-trade zone. Do not be fooled into thinking that bathrooms are all about plumbing-in sanitaryware: that's just the beginning. Ventilation, wall tiling, mirrors, accessories, obscured glazing, enclosed light fittings, pull switches, underfloor heating mats, towel rails (heated or otherwise) and specialised floor coverings all combine to make bathroom fitting a complex and elaborate process – and one that is easy to neglect in the hurry to finish a house.

Bathrooms are also expensive. Bear in mind that it's not the size of the bathroom but the fittings in it. Big bathrooms are becoming very popular; many people want to fit cupboards and furniture in them and the en-suite bathroom, in particular, seems to be getting bigger and bigger, eating chunks out of its attached bedroom. But there is no need to follow these American-led trends slavishly. Our Continental cousins still prefer family bathrooms and, although the word en-suite would seem to be French, you won't find many in France.

BATHROOM SUITES

Budget bathrooms are most usually sold as three-piece suites. Normally a bathroom suite includes:
- Bath, bath taps, plug
- Bath panels (to conceal the fact that the bath is plastic)
- Basin and supporting pedestal
- Basin taps and plug
- WC, cistern, seat, handle.

If you don't buy a suite, you'll have to remember to get all these items separately – items like cistern levers are easily overlooked. If you want to opt for a separate shower instead of a bath you may be able to find a two-piece 'cloakroom suite' (be warned: cloakroom basins are often minute).

A very basic bathroom suite will cost £300 upwards. Most bathroom outlets have a range of four or five suites going up in price to around £400; after that, you get into more up-market designs where all items come priced individually.

Prices tend to get softer as they get higher and trade discounts of 'no more than 10%' on budget lines suddenly rise to 30% or more when your spend rises above £1,000.

TAPS

To date, baths and basins have been available with all manner of tap arrangements. The old British standard of hot tap on the left and cold tap on the right has gradually been superseded by various mixer taps which are often extremely unintuitive.

In 2010, the regulations were amended so that, in future, all bath taps will have to be thermostatically controlled. This is to prevent around 20 deaths and 600 serious scaldings that occur every year because of hot water, in bath, in particular. The problem is that hot water is routinely stored at 60°C and this is about 18°C hotter than you want a bath or a shower. Thermostatic taps premix the hot and cold water and include temperature limiters to stop water going above a pre-set temperature.

The ultimate in safety and convenience is to fit an electronic bath filler tap which presets both temperature and bath depth. Crosswater and Aqualisa make them and the overall cost is little different to conventional taps.

ACCESSORIES

Most suites offer a wide range of matching accessories (shelves, soap holders, loo roll holders, toothbrush holders, toilet brush holders, towel rails) at prices well over the odds for what you would pay in a DIY shed. Even on a fairly basic suite, you could easily spend over £100 on buying matching fittings, adding another 20% to your suite price. If you want a bidet, expect this to add around 30% to the basic three-piece suite price.

STYLES

You can have any colour you want as long as its white. Just where this craze for white bathrooms arrived from, I am not sure, but it upsets me just a little, because I come from a generation which regarded coloured suites as being mildly sophisticated and now everyone just laughs at us. I can remember in earlier editions of this book giving advice on how to colour co-ordinate your sanitaryware with your tiling scheme. No more. That would look far too dated, far worse than not having the latest regs at my fingertips. But it seems so illogical. How come you can still get coloured wall tiles? Or are they all going to be nothing but white soon?

There are still defined groups of bathroom suite styles but whereas it was once a straight toss-up between trad and modern, now it's a little harder to define. Check out bathstore.com, Wolseley's consumer-facing spin out, and see if you can work out which is which. Actually bathstore.com isn't a bad place to start, even though it sometimes gets horrendous reviews from customers: I find its showrooms are well laid out, and its prices are certainly keen.

SHOWERS

Showers are popular both as attachments to bath taps (known as shower mixers) and in their own right in stand-alone shower cubicles. Apart from style – and there are showers to fit every style – there are two things to look out for: thermostatic control and adequate flow rate.

THERMOSTATIC CONTROL

Thermostatic control automatically adjusts the balance of hot and cold water flowing through the shower head as other taps in the house turn on and off. It is expensive, usually adding around £70 to the cost of a shower. A cheaper alternative is to have a shower with a high-temperature limiter that will avoid scalding but may still leave you drenched in cold water when a hot tap opens somewhere else.

ELECTRONIC SWITCHING

Rather than faffing about with taps,

adjusting flow rates and temperature settings, you can fit a digital shower and just programme this stuff in. And you can, of course, arrange two-way switching so that you don't even have to be in the shower to turn it on. Aqualisa's Quartz shower (which does all this) has proved to be a big hit, despite it's £400-odd price tag. The switches, which you have to press quite hard, give you visual feedback to tell you when the shower is up to temperature so there is no more dipping in and out of the shower to test whether it's just right. It also works with baths too – you can enjoy a Digital Bath, which tickles me somehow.

SHOWER POWER

There are many routes to getting a good pressure through your shower head. The most effective is to install a mains pressure hot water system or a thermal store (see section on Domestic Hot Water). The least effective is to install an electric shower or a combination boiler, both of which heat water instantaneously and therefore suffer from low flow rates. In between these extremes come a whole gamut of power showers which aim to add whoosh to feeble pressure from tanks in the loft. There are single impeller pumps, which boost the water after the mixing valve, and double impellers, which boost both hot and cold before they enter the valve. Which you choose is partly dependent on the layout you have and prices are largely dependent on the power of the pump. They can be purchased for just over £100, but a pump delivering 30lts per

minute (equivalent to a good mains pressure system) will cost £180plus. Leading manufacturers: Mira, Aqualisa.

If you want a power shower in a new house, you would be well advised to avoid all these products and go for a mains pressure or near mains pressure hot water system. Having taken us decades to accept mains pressure hot water systems in the UK – they weren't admitted until 1987 – they have now pretty much swept the field in new housing: the days of water tanks up in the loft appear are gone.

Against this are building regulations which seek to limit the flow of water through showers — see the upcoming section called the Water Calculator. You don't actually need a shower to deliver 30lts/minute. Half that much is still a pretty good shower and you can get a perfectly adequate shower from as little as 8lts/minute. Possible low flow showers which you might want to check out include the Nordic Eco shower and Hansgrohe's 6lt shower. Wolseley Sustainable Building Center promotes Mira's Eco handset which, it says, gives a good 6lt shower.

SHOWER ENCLOSURES

Acrylic trays can be had for under £50 but they are not recommended because of problems with leaking caused by the trays flexing. The most popular option is the ceramic stone trays: Matki's are good. For a little more, you can buy them with an under-tile upstand that will minimise any possibility of leakage.

The standard size is 760mm square (which suits the standard pivot doors). There is a small cost penalty if you want a larger tray, however note that some people find the standard 760x760mm size uncomfortably mean.

As for doors, many arrangements no longer require doors. It rather depends how much space you have. Conventional showers still require some sort of door. Pricewise there is little to choose between a free-standing shower enclosure or one built into an alcove – the cost of a tiled wall being similar to the cost of a glazed side panel. The alcove option usually looks the most professional; you finish the opening with either a pivot or a bi-fold door Matching side panels tend to be 60-80% of the door price. If your shower is incorporated with your bath, then you have a choice of a simple shower curtain hung from a rail or a glazed shower screen.

A good wet room will be designed so that it can be easily accessed by a wheelchair user, but doesn't splash everything in site. A simple glazed screen usually suffices.

WET ROOMS

What price open showers running into a floor drain? It's a detail regularly seen on the Continent and has been widely specified in this country in special needs bathrooms. You dispense with the conventional shower tray and your enclosure need only be a shower curtain, though a screen looks much better.

The usual routine with wet rooms is to buy a kit which comes with a pre-formed tray with a fall built in and a hole for the drain. Some also come with shower screens. There are various sticky tapes which combined with cementitous goop give you waterproof walls and upstands. Having fitted it all, you can then tile over it to get the desired wet room look.

You don't have to enclose the shower at all as the tray is designed to drain away any water falling on the floor, but open showers are not without their issues. Like it or not, you end up with a wet floor after using the shower and subsequent bathroom users don't really appreciate wet floors, especially if they are wearing shoes or socks.

AVOIDING LEAKY SHOWERS

In theory, this is no problem; in practice, tiled shower cubicles often ship water where they shouldn't and tiled floors will tend to fare even worse. It really is worth paying a lot of attention to the construction of shower enclosures generally because their failure is one of the commonest faults in new buildings. Don't skimp on the linings – use a waterproof plywood or a waterproof board like Knauf's Aquapanel or Hardie Backerboard rather than regular plasterboard – and use the best adhesive you can afford to fix ceramic tiles with.

Chapter 11

The key failure point, however, is the joint between the walls and the floor (or more likely tray) and with most designs you are dependent on a bead of silicone mastic to stop water finding a route through the defence. Your silicone sealant will stand a much better chance of success if the joint is tight and even, something that usually depends on how good your carpentry is. But failures can also occur in the tile grouting and around the shower fitting itself.

THE WATER CALCULATOR

In 2010, a new building regulation was introduced (in England only) which for the first time set out to limit the amount of water we use in our new homes. When building a new home (and only when building a new home) Part G requires us to put all our water-using devices through a Water Efficiency Calculator which assesses how much water we will use on a daily basis. The hurdle rate has been set at a notional 125lts per person per day and the combined effect of our choices should not be greater than this.

Now this doesn't actually mean we have to use this much water, but it sort of imagines that if Mr and Mrs Average were to live in the house, this is what they would use. By and large, it's not that difficult to meet the hurdle rate if you pay attention to your bath size and, in particular, your shower flow rate.

It might have been easier if they had just said that, in future, baths can only be of a certain size (say max 200lts) or showers should be restricted to 12lts per minute. But they have chosen a more complex route whereby you have to fill in your projected water use into the water calculator (basically a horrible looking spreadsheet) and left it for you to justify your choices of taps, loos and showers.

You can find versions of the Water Calculator online as well as lots of useful advice on how to fill it in.

■ Showers: You need to find showers that have a flow rate below 12lts per minute, preferably even 10lts per minute. This isn't very much flow, in the great scheme of things, as most power showers like to deliver well over 20lts per minute.

■ Baths: Specify a bath less than 175lts capacity if possible.

■ Toilets: All new ones are now dual flush and have a maximum flush of 6lts or less, so these are generally fine.

■ Taps: You are looking for taps with a flow rate of 6lts or less; it can be hard to find any information on tap flow rates at all. This may change as Part G begins to bite over the coming years.

■ Washing machines have a default score of 8.17lts per kg dryload. You may find better, but it's not going to make a lot of difference.

■ Dishwashers have a default score of 1.25lts per place setting. Again, it doesn't make a big difference if you beat this.

■ Waste disposal units. They don't like these – they all score 3lts per person per day.

Your building inspector will request sight of your water calculations in order to pass the new house, but it is doubtful whether they will check its veracity. For one thing, it can be hard to find out what the flow rate on individual taps and showers actually is as the manufacturers don't always publish this information, or they say it depends on the overall water pressure, which is not in your control. But you should pay attention to it and someone in your team needs to check that it's at least been filled in.

BEDROOMS

For developers, bedroom space is cheap space. All that really has to be provided is enough room to fit a bed and an item of furniture plus enough space to manoeuvre about between them – the technical term for this is swinging a cat.

DESIGN CONSIDERATIONS

You can of course give far more consideration to the whole issue. It's worth visualising the layout of the bedroom furniture so as to work out where to place radiators and power sockets. Also it's a nice touch to arrange light switching so that it can be reached easily from the bed. On the other hand, if you want to maintain maximum flexibility, then fit power sockets on every wall so you can accommodate various layouts. In reality there may only be one sensible place where a bed can go, but there may be other considerations. What is appropriate as a nursery for a toddler is unlikely to suit a teenager and you should consider how the uses a bedroom gets put to will change over the years. Don't always assume that a bedroom will remain a bedroom.

SIZE

It is conventional to rank bedrooms by size. Now, you might think that in a four-bedroom house you would provide a double bedroom for mum and dad (or whoever tickles your fancy) plus three smaller but similar sized rooms for the children. But no; the British way of doing it is to build bedrooms in ever decreasing sizes.

It's also the British way of doing things to rank – and price – houses according to the number of bedrooms they have. Almost all developers switch to four bedrooms when the overall floor size creeps over 110m². When you are working with relatively tight floor areas, which goes for 90% of UK housebuilding, squeezing an extra bedroom in is a seen as a vital sales booster, even if the resulting bedrooms are horribly cramped.

A space-saving idea is the bed that folds up into a wall, also known as a Hideaway Bed. As our homes are tending to get smaller, this design is migrating from caravans and mobile homes into the study-bedroom. Also useful in spare rooms with multiple uses.

WARDROBES

Not usually included by developers and not usually included in any summary of building costs, the wardrobe is, nevertheless, a near essential item in any bedroom. There are basically three approaches to creating bedroom storage space:
- Use free-standing furniture: it costs but you can take it with you
- Use specialist bedroom fittings
- Make your own.

The last method has one major advantage in that it is regarded

as zero-rated for VAT purposes. Typically you would design your bedroom wall partitions with various strategically placed kinks into which you slip a hanging rail and a few open shelves and then hang a door or two in front. It's probably the cheapest option for new housebuilders as the cupboards can be created as you go rather than being added on afterwards.

Building your own wardrobes may sound straightforward but it's time

consuming and therefore expensive. The average house needs rather more wardrobe/cupboard space than it needs kitchen unit space and the cost is pretty similar, whether you build it in or buy it as furniture. As a rule, every adult needs about 2.5m³ of storage space and children not much less. At the budget end of things you can supply this space at around £1,000/m³ and at the top end anything upwards of £3,000/m³.

Chapter 11

THE HOME OFFICE

Pick up any paper or magazine and you're likely to find articles about working from home, as if it had just been discovered as the panacea of all modern ills. This is completely daft. Working from home is what most of us always did, long before they invented factories and offices, and there are still loads of trades and businesses which have always worked from home. What is new is that there is a whole host of office workers, who would previously have commuted some distance to work, now padding a few feet down the passageway. Journalists in particular are able to work from home which is, just possibly, why you read so much about it in the newspapers and magazines. But my farming friends just scratch their heads and wonder what everyone is talking about.

What's the upshot of all this? Well, what most people think when they think of working from home is that they need an office, or at least some office space. The physical requirements for all this are remarkably small, usually satisfied by a few shelves and a working space serviced by a couple of power outlets, a telephone socket and a broadband router. There really isn't much designing to be done, you just take over the box bedroom and have done with it. Even if you are inclined towards the hi-tech office with PCs, printers, scanners, copiers, routers and the like, you still don't really need anything more in the way of infrastructure – although extra power points and phone sockets would certainly come in handy.

PLANNING ISSUES

However, for many others, working from home will need considerably more thought. You may require meeting space or consultation rooms which are best kept quite separate from the rest of the household in order to maintain a professional atmosphere: sometimes this can be quite neatly achieved with an additional ground floor room which has its own external entrance.

On the other hand, you may need workshop space which will create dust or noise or smell and which is ideally situated in a separate building. These are specialised concerns and really no one is going to understand them better than yourself, so it is pointless me wittering on. What I should point out though is that the more specialised and separate your workspace becomes, the more problems you are likely to encounter at the planning stage.

These problems are likely to hinge on whether you can extend the terms of the planning permission to include non-residential uses. Solo home office working is frankly not going to be an issue but anything that a) makes a lot of noise or smell or b) attracts a lot of visitors is not going to be passed through on the nod; in fact, it's probably unlikely to get passed at all if the area is zoned purely residential. However the buzz word of contemporary planning, sustainability, is on your side here. For decades the planning system has worked to separate the residential zones from the industrial zones on the premise that the two don't mix well, but as much of our working activities have become cleaner and quieter, the wisdom of this zoning has been called into question. Now the boot seems to be on the other foot because the car – more particularly the car journey – has become the bête noire of planning departments. Anything that can be done to reduce the number of car journeys is said to be sustainable, which is planning speak for a good thing.

LIVE-WORK UNITS

Most spec housing continues to be built without dedicated office space although this changes as you move up market. In London and some other metro areas, you occasionally come across live/work units that are designed to appeal to singletons. You might be tempted to use this home working scenario to gain a little planning leverage – reducing car journeys, etc – but do bear in mind that there are potential tax traps.

The house may be deemed to be partially commercial space which will mean that part of it becomes exempt from your principle private residence tax shelter and that you may be assessed for commercial rates.

GARAGES

Before you commit yourself to spending good money on garage space consider for a moment whether it is really necessary. Although current fashions in house styles tend towards the traditional, there is absolutely nothing traditional about a garage. Its nearest equivalent in pre-20th century housing is the stable or, perhaps, the cowshed; but the housing of cars is an altogether different affair. Furthermore, whilst thirty or forty years ago it was a good idea to keep vehicles undercover to facilitate winter starts and to stop rust, cars these days are made to very much higher standards and it is really not necessary to keep them undercover.

Nowadays, security is often cited as a reason for building garages – but does this really justify spending as much on a garage as it costs to buy a small car? And for many practised car thieves, a locked garage doesn't really represent much of an obstacle in any event, especially as people tend to be much less security conscious on outbuildings.

Of course, garages have many other uses besides providing undercover car parking, as is shown by the numbers of people who have them but never park their cars inside them. Solid fuel, tools, lawnmowers, gardening equipment, bicycles, golf clubs, baby buggies, deep freezes, paddling pools, paint, you name it, it gets stored out there, and very useful it is too. But if you are designing a house from scratch, you may come to the conclusion that what you need is a larger utility room or a basement, not a garage.

Garages are obviously valued by a great number of people otherwise speculative developments wouldn't include them as a matter of course, but don't just fall into the trap of assuming that a house must have a garage because it's not a proper house without one. Having said all that, you still want a garage. Next question is...

WHEN TO BUILD IT?

You can, of course, decide to leave the construction of a garage until an unspecified later date, provided that it's not integral to the house. If it is included on your planning permission drawings, the right to build it cannot be taken away once you have started the main house. NB This ruling goes for conservatories, swimming pools and any other fancy accoutrements that you aspire to but can't afford. Therefore just drawing the plans might represent a good compromise solution for those who don't really need a garage but worry that the house might be difficult to sell without one. Against this, you should be aware that any building work that takes place after you move into a house will not be exempt from VAT, so it will cost you 20% more to construct. Also, it is worth pointing out that many people find it very useful to build the garage before the rest of the house as it provides a useful and secure store-cum-site hut whilst the main construction forges ahead. Indeed, with a bit of adaptation, you could just about live in a garage for a few months – certainly not much worse than the average caravan.

SITING

By and large, house designers do not like garages. They are difficult. On most sites, access demands that they are located somewhere prominent near the frontage and yet, by their very nature, they are more akin to outbuildings and sheds. Now, polite architectural convention dictates that you don't put a humble shed in the front garden and so you are left with the problem of having to make the garage look good without costing too much.

One way around this conundrum is to have an integral garage, one that is built into or at least attached to the main house. The points for this are:
■ It makes for a more effective utility room-type garage, if that's what you have in mind
■ You can use it to house boilers and freezers
■ The arrangement fits better on narrow fronted sites (under 12m wide).

Against this, it doesn't usually do much for the look of a house. Most garage doors are better suited to largely unseen parts of your estate – i.e. they are naff – and placing one prominently in your front elevation can be very ugly. The problem of the garage door is particularly acute when you are building in a traditional style. One way of alleviating it is to have an 'L' shaped house and to tuck the garage into the bit of the L that projects forward towards the road. This softens the impact of the integral garage on the all important kerb appeal.

Given a site without space constraints, most builders will plump for a detached garage. The main attraction of this arrangement is that it maintains the integrity of the house design but, even so, the siting of the garage can still overwhelm this. Ideally, it will be well away to one side but most plots these days are not large enough to make this a viable option and so very often the house is half-hidden by the detached garage in front of it. Effectively, this means that the garage plays a crucial role in people's initial views of a house, and developers have responded to this by spending more and more money on external appearance, commonly including fancy roofing effects not seen on the main house.

BUILDING COSTS

Many of the costs of building a garage – whether integral or detached – are no different from the costs of building the main house. Garages do not have to meet the standard building regulations as regards insulation and damp penetration and this allows them to be constructed with thinner, single-skin walls. However, groundwork costs and roofing costs are basically identical, and despite the fact that garages are rarely fitted out with all the paraphernalia of a finished house, the construction costs of a garage are still as much as 60% of those of a finished house when compared on a floor area basis.

CAR PORTS

One alternative approach is just to build a lean-to car port or undercover car parking bay. You need some form of hard standing for the car and then the rest is up to you. The finished result could be anything from a flimsy timber construction which might look better as a garden pergola to a fully-fledged garage without a door.

PREFABRICATED

There are several small manufacturers who produce prefabricated garages at prices way below standard construction costs. But what you are buying is probably little different in quality to a garden shed. That may be exactly what you are looking for of course. They are very utilitarian and would probably be best sited away from the main house.

UNDERGROUND

An underground garage is unlikely to be a cost-effective option unless space is at a premium. Access ramps (budget £8,000) and potential drainage problems make the totally underground garage an expensive luxury. However, the economics look far friendlier when sorting out sloping ground.

There are instances where burying car parking below ground can actually free up ground elsewhere for more cost-effective uses (like building extra houses), but this is unlikely to be relevant to many single housebuilders.

GARAGE DOORS

For many designers, the problem with garages begins and ends with the garage door. Until the 1970s garage doors were strictly functional and utilitarian, often made of steel with no attempts at embellishment. Since then, a large number of imitation traditional door styles have sprung up, aping the move back to other traditional forms. The trouble is, that whilst a window or a front door can be made in styles copied from old doors, there are no old garage doors to copy from. Hence a mock Georgian or mock Tudor garage door looks more than faintly ridiculous. Double doors, over 4 m wide, look particularly strange and attempts to mould classical patterns on them merely emphasise how strange and out of place they look.

If there is a traditional British garage door it is the side opening style that you see on houses built in the 1920s and 1930s, made from solid timbers and lit by small square frosted-glass panels, sometimes called a Pattern 301 door.

Garage doors are large and therefore tend to get pricey. It's a specialist business and your best bet is to Google 'Garage Doors' and seek quotations from there. Steel is much the cheapest material but also the least attractive. Timber and GRP are around twice the price. GRP doors are usually produced to look like timber – in fact they can look incredibly realistic. They can also be stained; their main advantage over timber is that they are (hopefully) maintenance-free, yet many people will prefer to stick with timber. If you don't like any of the commercially available doors yet still crave the convenience of an up-and-over door, then check out Hormann's sub-frames that you can fill in with your own designs at your leisure. They are called Open-for-Infill doors.

OPENING MECHANISMS

As already stated, most garage doors these days open vertically. But it's not quite that simple. There is vertical and vertical. The simplest type of opening is the canopy or up-and-over door; when open, about a third of the door protrudes outside the frame, forming a canopy. They are usually hand operated and canopy double doors are something you could live without as they can get very heavy and awkward to lift.

As its name suggests, the fully retractable door glides all the way back into the garage on a set of tracks. These are much more suitable for double doors and for remote operators.

The North Americans like to fit sectional garage doors. These split into, typically, four panels which slide up a set of vertical tracks and then, one panel at a time, turn through 90 degrees and end up under the garage roof. The advantage of this is that the door doesn't protrude when opening so that you can park hard up to both the inside and outside face and still open the door.

Finally, there are various makes of Roller Doors around which perform in much the same way as sectional doors. However instead of turning

through 90°, these doors roll up like a carpet. They look like steel shutters, which is what they are, and so kerb appeal is limited.

HOW WIDE?

The traditional width for a single garage door in the UK has been 7 ft (2134mm). It's mean. There are an awful lot of cars around that will struggle to get through such a gap, particularly so if the entry angle isn't dead straight. If you have the room, go for doors that are 7 ft 6 in wide (2286mm). If space is very tight, you can usually gain a crucial few inches by locating the supporting frame behind the walls rather than between them. Height is also an issue. Some big cars won't fit under a 7 ft doorway.

If you are planning a double garage, you have the choice of a double door or two singles. Two single doors usually work out cheaper; although you have to build a dividing pillar, the cost of this is offset by the extra cost of a 4.5 m lintel to cross the gap above a double door opening. Opening double doors by hand can also be quite a hassle, particularly if the spring mechanism works out of adjustment. On the other hand, if you plan to use an electric door operator you save yourself the cost of installing a second one.

REMOTE CONTROL OPERATORS

An increasingly popular item which allows you to open and close your garage door automatically from both a switch inside the garage and a remote

control unit which you can keep inside the car. They are not cheap – coming in at around £400 which includes a remote control device (or two if you are lucky) – but they do make a lot of sense when you consider the hassle involved in opening garage doors manually. All the garage door suppliers sell these and they come in varying levels of sophistication. Hormann and Bosch market multi-function ones that can switch on welcome lights and open entrance gates as well. However, even the most basic ones come with timed welcome lights that come on whenever the door is opened: this is very useful.

Electric operators also come in different flavours. Most work with a geared chain but there are some (Hormann's SupraMatic) that work on a Kevlar belt which promise virtually silent opening. They tend not to work on the basic canopy up-and-over doors although Cardale's Autoglide is an exception: in fact it can be retrofitted onto existing doors. If you are going to spend £12,000 plus on a garage, then it's probably worthwhile spending the extra on an operator so that you actually get to use the garage for its intended purpose.

ADDING SPACE

For every new house built in Britain, there are something like three or four homes extended and/or improved. The exact figure can only be guessed at but it's a huge industry in the UK, more so than in other countries. Why?

In most other countries, the rate of new housebuilding per head of population is way higher than it is in the UK. And the ones we do build are depressingly small – our average house size is just 75m², the smallest in the EU.

Consequentially, the home improvement market in the UK is enormous, far bigger relative to the overall population than anywhere else in the world. This chapter looks at the options facing you if you are out to extend rather than to build from scratch. Many of the techniques are no different, but the ways of going about things are.

Here, ranked in cost order, with the cheapest first, is a summary of ways you can gain extra living space.

- 1. Convert existing floor space into habitable space, such as a garage conversion
- 2. Convert existing loft space
- 3. Build an outhouse in the garden
- 4. Extend the existing structure
- 5. Excavate a basement

Is it possible to put sensible prices onto these? Let's ignore the fitting out costs. Not that these aren't considerable, it's just that they shouldn't vary an awful lot whichever method you use to gain space, i.e. a kitchen or an office fit-out shouldn't be that different in cost wherever you choose to put it.

I would have said that there is a range of costs between £400/m² for upgrading existing space to meet building regs standards for habitable rooms and £5,000/m² for creating new cellar space under an existing house. The bulk of this sort of work clusters around the lower end of these two extremes. Anticipate simple loft conversions to cost around £500/m², extensions from £500 and £800/m². And once again, don't forget I am ignoring fit out costs which can sometimes double the basic build cost. What I am trying to say, politely, is that there is a huge range of costs likely to be encountered in this sort of work and it's possibly not that helpful to attempt to boil it all down to "£xx/m²."

DESIGN

Many of the important things that are to be said about design have already been said. But there are one or two salient points to be boned up on when you are just mapping out small pieces of a house or an outbuilding.

How much individual design, let alone flair, is required to turn an idea and some money into a usable structure is dependent almost wholly on what you are trying to achieve. The projects covered by this chapter include many where the design comes with the product: I am thinking here of garden sheds, stables and sometimes conservatories. At the other end of the scale are projects every bit as complicated as a new house where a good design is required to gain planning permission and to add value to the works. And, in between, will be many projects like simple loft conversions and extensions, where the constraints of the site are such that what design is required is needed simply to facilitate

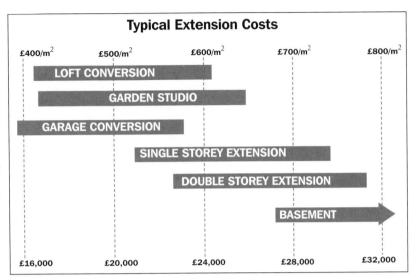

Shell-build costs for an area of 40m². Fit-out can easily double the finished cost

the building work. In other words, it may not be much more than a glorified shopping list.

Which probably isn't much help to you. You instinctively know this stuff already. What isn't always clear is when to go straight to a builder and when to go to a designer for some interpretation of your requirements and some professional help in turning them into a building contract. Where do you draw the line?

For what it's worth, I reckon that a requirement for planning permission also acts as some sort of litmus test here. By and large, it's the larger jobs that require planning permission. And, by and large, it's the larger jobs that require a little bit more from the design department. For a start, your work is unlikely to gain planning permission without some form of technical drawings and so there is a natural reason to hire a designer.

Having done that, it's a much smaller step to using this same person to put together tender documents for builders to quote from.

The main alternative option is to work with a builder from the off, to create a design and build contract, where the builder also becomes responsible for undertaking the design and maybe sorting out planning permission for you. It can work well even on relatively large and complex jobs: it really does come down a lot to personalities and capabilities.

PLANNING AND RED TAPE

Whereas a new house always requires planning permission, a large amount of remodelling in an existing house doesn't, which is good news for remodellers. The bad news is that it's often far from clear just what you can and can't do without going cap

Chapter 12

in hand to the local planners. First, I'll try and give some guidance on just what you might expect to be able to do without planning permission and then I'll discuss what to do if your proposed work does require permission.

PERMITTED DEVELOPMENT RIGHTS

The basis of our planning regime is the Town & Country Planning Act, which came into effect in 1948, part of the post-war Old Labour 'rebuilding Britain' package that also saw the introduction of the NHS and the nationalisation of much of our industrial backbone. Before that, you didn't have to apply to anyone for permission to build, or so rumour has it.

This 1948 date has become a cut-off point. Whatever had been done to your house before 1948 was said to be 'existing': whatever has been done to it since is said to be 'extending'. It's a long time ago now and the chances are that the house you live in was built long after 1948 but nevertheless it's still a point in time worth being aware of.

The Town & Country Planning Act sought to control what and where we could build. Its intention wasn't to prevent development, merely to enhance it and to ensure it took place in everybody's interest. So that the local planning department didn't grind to a halt – that took another 50 years – the Act incorporated a provision that allowed you to extend your home up to a certain amount without having to

trouble the planners. This provision has come to be known as our Permitted Development Rights, PD Rights for short. It applies to houses at their built-shape in 1948 and it applies to houses constructed since 1948, although there are one or two exceptions. It wouldn't be planning if there weren't one or two exceptions.

To make things even more complicated, the system of PD rights that existed merrily since 1948 was rewritten in 2008, so that several of the old conventions, which everybody in planning was familiar with, were obliterated and replaced with even more complex rules. This is particularly true of extensions and outbuildings where the rules have undergone some subtle changes.

And then the Coalition Chancellor, George Osborne, sought to relax the rules in 2012 for a period of three years in order to try and stimulate growth. Since then there have been further moves to loosen PD Rights so as to make office space and barns easier to convert to residential.

And of course, this being the United Kingdom, you can count on the fact that Wales, Scotland and Ireland all have their own versions of permitted development rights. Broadly speaking, they are very similar, but they are different enough to make things very awkward for books trying to explain what is what.

The good news, as far as I am concerned, is that the internet is now a repository of knowledge on these matters and that rather than me trying to point out what you can and can't do, I will simply point you to the

relevant web page.

The advice must always be to run your project past the planners. They should be able to give you a clear indication about whether planning permission is required. In fact, you can apply for a Lawful Development Certificate to make it clear to all and sundry that what you are about to undertake doesn't require planning permission. The current fees for minor planning applications are £172, so even if you do have to apply it's not a ruinous amount although it may well take months to sort through.

PLANNING PORTAL

In England and Wales: www. planningportal.gov.uk > Go to General Public Area, then household planning rules. Visit the interactive houses so you can figure out just what you can and can't do without planning permission.

Remember, you may have already used up some of your PD rights if the house has been extended after 1948. For the other territories in the UK, start by Googling the name of the country followed by Permitted Development Rights. That short cuts you to the relevant pages with the most up to date rules.

PD TIPS

If planning permission for what you want to do is at all contentious, you can occasionally get cute with your PD rights and use them to try and run rings around the planners.
▪ If you apply for planning permission to extend above and

beyond what the PD Rights give you, you don't get to keep the unused PD Rights to use elsewhere.

But just suppose you want to extend in two directions, say sideways and backwards. Assume that your PD Rights are still intact but that the additional size of both extensions exceeds the permitted limits. Decide which of the two extensions is the more controversial and apply for planning permission to build the other bit. If this is granted, you can then use your virgin PD Rights to build the controversial bit first without compromising your already granted planning permission.

■ You can reclaim your PD Rights by demolishing something built after 1948. Say you have a particularly naff attached garage put up in the 1960s without planning permission. If the extension you would like to build takes you over the amended PD Rights limits, because the garage eats up most of the allowed volume, you can reclaim the rights by taking down the garage.

■ PD Rights are also useful when negotiating a replacement dwelling. Often local councils have guidelines restricting the size of the new dwelling, relating to the size of the existing. Galling when you have a tiny bungalow on an acre plot. If the old bungalow had never used up its PD Rights, be sure to include them in your calculations.

PARTY WALL ACT
More information on the workings of the Party Wall Act is included in the main section on Planning, earlier

in the book. It affects all properties in England & Wales but is only likely to have any bearing on your project if you have close neighbours, as you would expect to find if you live in a semi or a terraced house, or an apartment. Do be aware that it comes into effect if you are planning to build off a neighbours wall, as well you might when undertaking a loft conversion, and that it also kicks in if you excavate new foundations, deeper than your neighbour's, within 3m of your neighbour's foundations.

This might easily be the case with an extension, especially if the neighbour's property is over 100 years old, before the time that excavations were dug deep.

There is a good explanatory booklet downloadable from the building regs website, which will tell you more than you would ever really want to know. Note that this really should be sorted out two months before the building work starts: otherwise you are courting delay.

BUILDING REGS
In April 2010, I received the following email:

Dear Mr Brinkley,

I have just read your latest book on house building as we are having a kitchen extension done. I am a little disappointed in your lack of information about Building Control. The book makes little mention of Building Control other than the costs. I spoke to East Cambs Building Control yesterday and they told me that there are statutory visits that they must make when a house/extension is being built. I have just printed them

off. Should you not at least include a paragraph on these inspections, when they have to start, what they include and the end inspection which, I believe, is a sign off of the building? I can't find mention of these statutory visits, and if I was doing a DIY job and didn't have all the inspections and the sign off at the end surely the whole job could go seriously awry?

Also, given the proliferation of 'cowboy' builders wouldn't the building control officer pick up that a job wasn't being done properly before too much work had gone ahead?

We managed to build a boarding cattery in Cambridgeshire without consulting Building Control (through ignorance, no one told us we should be using them) and almost didn't get a regularisation certificate as one of the buildings was, in theory, too close to a farmers barn. Hence how I know about building control. So if I were using your book as my 'bible' I am not sure I would know that I had to use Building Control, and at what stages.

Yours

Carole Cooke

I thought the best thing was to include the text in full, as I couldn't make the point any better. In my defence, I touch on building control in much more detail in the chapter on Project Management, forgetting that many people would be dipping into this chapter alone because they are only doing an extension or something similar. So if that means you, then heed this warning now and bear in mind that Chapters 4 and 5 are just as much for you as this one.

But, to re-iterate Carole Cooke's

point, if you are carrying out substantial building works, you need to get the building inspectors on board although they no longer have to be local council building inspectors – you can use other approved inspectors, if you can find them.

It's true that there are some minor works that don't require inspection, but generally, the larger the job, the more chance there is of building regs being required: extensions and loft conversions always require building control approval. On renovation and alteration work, the picture isn't as clear although the tentacles of building control have a habit of spreading wider and wider.

For instance, the introduction of Part P in England & Wales in 2004 brought almost all electrical work within building control for the first time, even when it is carried out in structures like conservatories and outbuildings which are normally building control exempt. And changes to Part L, the energy efficiency regs, have brought replacement windows and replacement boilers within building control.

The trend is clear. The government doesn't want to hire thousands more building inspectors to cover all these extra items: it wants the tradesmen carrying them out to be competent and certified, and for them to sign off their work and for you, the homeowner, to keep the guarantee for when you come to sell the house.

Generally, you are required to apply for building regulations for the following works:

An application needs to be submitted when you intend to:
- Erect a building such as a new dwelling
- Extend an existing building.
- Make structural alterations to a building, such as removing a load-bearing wall or a chimney stack, or forming an opening in a structural or fire-protecting wall
- Underpin all or part of a building
- Convert a loft into living space
- Install services and fittings such as replacement glazing, central heating systems, boilers, flues, laying new drains or altering electrics. (Some of these may be controlled under competent persons schemes)
- Change the use of a building such as converting it into a house or flats or to make more than one dwelling.
- Erect a large conservatory, one with a floor area greater than 30m^2. A conservatory less than 30m^2 is exempt provided at least 75% of the roof and 50% of the walls are of translucent material and it is thermally separated from the dwelling by walls, windows and doors with U-values and draught stripping provision at least as good as elsewhere in the dwelling.
- Carry out work to the thermal elements of a house such as re-plastering, replacing a roof, or undertaking external rendering or cladding.
- Make alterations or extensions to commercial premises, schools, hospitals.
- Carry out work to improve access or provide facilities for disabled people.

You can find an up-to-date explanatory booklet from the building regs website. This tends to reside under the planning services part of your local authority website.

EXTENSIONS

Building an extension is like building a mini-house and essentially the very same processes have to be gone through. In some ways, extensions are actually harder than houses to build because there is always the matter of tying onto the existing structure, which frequently creates little teething problems.

BUILDING REGS

The building regs are essentially no different for extensions than for whole houses but in one or two instances they are made a lot simpler because it is inappropriate to use them for only part of the house. In particular:

PART M – THE DISABLED ACCESS REGS

These are designed to be applied to new houses and the essential aspects of Part M, being level thresholds, maximum and minimum socket heights, wider doors and a downstairs WC, don't make any sense when applied to just the extension of an existing house. The one aspect of Part M which may be applied to an extension is if you are somehow contriving to make matters worse for disabled visitors. Thus if your access was level and you were about to make it stepped, or you were to remove a downstairs WC.

If your house was built after 1999, then it should already be Part M compliant – you will be able to tell from the socket heights. If it is, then any additional work on the house will be expected to also be Part M compliant.

PART L – THE ENERGY EFFICIENCY REGS

The regs apply to extensions and to some renovation work but in a much-simplified format. Gone is the requirement for whole house SAP calculations and pressure testing. Instead, you can just design your walls, floors and roofs to meet certain U values, in the traditional method.

Note that boiler replacement and window replacement, two common restoration tasks, are required to meet Part L standards. Your boiler will have to be a condensing one and your replacement windows will have to be FENSA approved to show that they comply with the maximum U values.

ACCESS

Access for building work is likely to be much more restricted than it is for a new build. This is one of the factors that often makes extensions much more expensive to build on a per square metre basis. Specifically, you are often unable to get large plant around the back of an existing house and you therefore find that in consequence foundations may have to be hand dug and materials may well have to be purchased in small loads and barrowed or handballed around the building.

You may also have problems with scaffolding, especially if you are building on the boundary. Your neighbours may or may not take kindly to your building work but even if they do, it can be difficult to even locate scaffolding sometimes.

As a rule of thumb, difficult access may well add up to 20% to building work costs. Extensions can be built from inside if external scaffolding can't be provided, but this is slow and tedious and will add to costs as well. Generally it is worth pointing out to your neighbours, that a brick wall looks far better when it is built from the correct side!

OPENING UP WALLS

The typical extension job requires that you break a hole into the existing structure and use this to form the access to the extension. If it's a two-storey extension, then the hole will open both storeys of the house.

Knocking down walls is an art in itself and most builders are very familiar with such a task. The key point to understand is that the structure which depended on the walls you are about to knock down has to be supported both during the demolition and building work and permanently thereafter.

The standard procedure is to support the floor joists, if they run into the soon-to-be-demolished wall, so a beam, usually steel, gets inserted to provide permanent support. If you are just having a door between the extension and the existing, then there is unlikely to be any problem but for any opening over 2m wide, you need to be sure that the loadings are correct. Your building inspector will advise and is likely to require you to hire a structural engineer to prove the beam size.

The new structure will have to be tied into the existing. If the structure is brick or block, then this can be done carefully by toothing out the existing and building into the gaps, or you can cheat and use stainless steel profiles which you just screw into the existing.

Some people are snobby about profiles and suggest that the traditional and therefore better method is always to tooth into the existing brickwork. But the existing brickwork isn't always as good as you might hope for and sometimes the existing brick courses are unequal, which makes tying in a minor nightmare.

FLASHINGS AND WATERPROOFINGS

Obviously where the roof of the extension abuts the existing, you have to make some provision for rainfall to be collected and channelled away. However, if the wall you are abutting is a cavity wall, you have an additional and extremely fiddly piece of work to undertake, namely the insertion of cavity trays.

FLOORS

The section on floors covers the actual floor construction options. But extensions have one extra problem up their sleeves, which is the matching up of floors between the old and new. Normally, it's just a question of planning ahead carefully and deciding what level the finished floor should be and sort of working backwards from there. Just occasionally you will find that the existing floor is not level and you get left with an awkward decision about how best to get the two floors to match up.

MOVING DRAINS

One frequent problem which arises when working on extensions is drains. Normally drains exit the house as quickly as possible, typically at the back of the house or into a side passage. But in many older properties, especially in terraces, the drains are shared with a number of other houses. You can in fact build over domestic drains: the standard routine is to bridge the existing drains when you place the foundations so as to ensure that the drains are not damaged. If there is a manhole or inspection chamber under the floor of your proposed extension, you have a problem but it's rarely insurmountable. You may be able to cover it over and to replace it with a new one outside the extension. You may even be able to keep it there and to have it accessed through the floor, although this is far from ideal. It's a principle of good drain design that you don't want to have to access drains from indoors!

Finally, you may be able to re-route the existing drains around the outside of the extension. There are problems if the drain runs along one of your foundation trenches, but there are often solutions. The one situation that can cause major difficulties is if there is a mains sewer running close to your house: the regs regarding mains sewers are much tighter.

ADDITIONAL HEATING

The extension will require heating in one form or another. Just how this can best be achieved depends largely on what heating you already have in the existing and whether it is man enough to carry the extra load imposed by the additional space. Really only a survey of the existing arrangements will reveal this and it's pretty pointless to speculate about that here. But note that if the boiler is old and requires replacing, the latest regulations require that you use an energy-efficient condensing boiler in its place.

Condensing boilers themselves require a drain off point to collect the condensate. This isn't always possible in conventional boiler locations and you may be able to argue for a dispensation to use a non-condensing boiler instead.

However you do it, the chances are that the work will involve some disruption to the existing house.

EXTENDING ELECTRICS

The issues with extending electrics are similar in many ways to extending the heating and maybe plumbing. The newer the house is, the less likely it will be to require a complete rewire, but there is a chance that the installation you already have in place will not be adequate to handle the extra load imposed on it by the new extension, especially if the extension houses power hungry appliances like cookers and hobs.

Again the most useful thing to do here is to get the existing installation surveyed prior to work starting out on the extension.

Note that electrical work is now covered by the building regulations and has to be certified by an approved installer, although if the electrical work forms part of a much bigger job, like an extension, you don't have to make a separate application. Indeed, you can ask your building inspector to include the inspection of the electrics as part of their service.

ENERGY EFFICIENCY MEASURES

During the last three consultations over energy efficiency regulations, there has been a proposal put forward to insist that anyone doing work on their home which required building regs approval should be required to spend an additional amount, possibly as much as 10% of the overall budget, on improving energy efficiency in the existing structure. Typically, the householder would have been required to:
- undertake cavity wall insulation
- replace the old boiler with something more efficient
- add extra loft insulation
- add draft proofing to windows and doors

There is logic in this proposal. All the energy efficiency regulations that have been introduced since 1976 have been aimed at new build or extensions to existing builds. The situation has now come to pass that new builds are reasonably low in energy demands and it has become increasingly difficult to introduce cost-effective ways of improving matters still further. However, older housing stock remains largely untouched by the energy efficiency drives and it's an anomaly that is beginning to irk our energy-saving boffins.

However, to date this proposal had been edited out by various housing ministers, and most recently by the then Prime Minister, David Cameron, who called such a proposal "bonkers" in April 2012. Since when there has been a deafening silence on the matter.

By and large the building regs have been very careful not to interfere with existing structures and having flirted with this idea they decided that this was not perhaps the best time to start. But the 'consequential improvements' debate hasn't gone away and one or two local authorities have started introducing something similar via their planning departments, so you may yet be faced with demands to undertake works you hadn't originally envisaged.

The author in a fink truss loft assessing the head height. Barely enough. This loft remains unconverted to this day.

LOFT CONVERSIONS

The loft conversion is a thoroughly modern phenomenon. A generation ago, nobody thought to extend their living space into the roof. People who wanted more space generally moved house. Their lofts sat gathering dust, holding old photograph albums and abandoned suitcases. But as land values have risen across the country, so the pressure on space has increased. And, as moving on to a larger house has become more and more expensive, people's attention has turned to making the most of what they already have. Increasingly, that has meant utilising the dead space in the roof.

It's little wonder that the past thirty years has witnessed an explosion in the number of loft conversions being carried out in the UK. However, it's important to bear in mind that the loft conversion is not always the best or most appropriate solution. This is especially true with single-storey dwellings that appeal largely to older people who value not having to negotiate stairs. The stairs are a limiting factor, which means that lofts are generally not best suited for dayrooms and kitchens. In contrast, they are excellent for extra bedroom space or quieter hobby rooms or home offices.

INITIAL ASSESSMENT

All loft conversions start with an initial assessment. The first thing to look out for is the head room. You need to be able to stand up in the middle of the existing loft and ideally you should be struggling to touch the ridge plate running along the top of the roof. The things which determine the space you have in a loft are the span between the eaves and the pitch or slope of the roof. Most detached and semi-detached homes have a wide enough span and, if the slope or pitch is more than 35°, then you should have enough volume to make a decent-sized room. It's something you can tell easily enough just by getting up into the loft space. You need to be looking for a minimum distance of 2.3m between the underside of the ridge and the ceiling below.

If you haven't got this space in your loft, you can't have a useful loft conversion without some alterations to your roof shape, which will obviously be much more expensive.

The next step is to have a look at the shape of the roof. Generally, the simpler the roof-shape, the better. What loft converters love above all else is a straightforward pitched roof with gable walls at either end. These allow you to easily transfer all the roof loadings onto beams stretching between the gable ends.

A hipped roof presents problems but not insurmountable ones. Similarly with roofs which form an L-shape. If the upper floor of your house is built partly into the roof (the so-called one and a half storey house is a case in point) then a loft conversions is likely to be a non-starter as there is rarely enough headroom left above the ceiling to make any usable loft space.

The presence of a chimney may present problems, depending largely where it's located. Anything central is likely to be difficult: it's hardly worth generalising about this because it's likely to be obvious from a cursory inspection whether the chimney is an obstruction or not.

If it is, and you no longer use the chimney, it is usually quite acceptable to take it down during the course of the works, although planners and listed building officers might just have a different opinion.

ROOF STRUCTURE

Another important factor to consider is how the roof is built. There are two main methods of building roofs. The traditional method was prevalent on all roofs until the 1960s and is the easiest to convert. It involves carpenters cutting the roof timbers on site – it is sometimes referred to as a cut roof – and fixing the timbers one-by-one to make up the roof structure.

This method was to a large extent replaced by a system of engineered roof trusses, developed in America, which swept through the housebuilding industry in the 1960s because they were quicker and cheaper to erect.

A trussed roof arrives on site on the back of a lorry in large triangular sections. These are hauled up onto the roof and nailed in place side-by-side. It's very much quicker than doing a cut roof and also much less skilful. Because their strength is derived from the fact that the sections are already triangulated, you can use much smaller pieces of timber to make a truss roof. Once you know what you are looking for, it's easy to tell a trussed roof from a traditional one. Look out for thin sections of planed wood, typically no more than 75mm or 3 inches deep. There will be a number of these small timbers running from the top of the truss to the bottom and joined onto the outer timbers by tell-tale rectangular metal plates, easily visible from the side.

In contrast, a traditional or cut roof uses larger sections of sawn (not planed) timber (often 50x150mm) and these are cut on site and usually

nailed together. They frequently have supporting beams called purlins located midway under each rafter, running along the length of the roof. Unlike traditional cut roofs where the individual timber rafters are load bearing, the roof truss derives its strength from the combination of all the small pieces of timber working together as one. Altering a truss roof is possible but is a much more involved process than adapting a traditional roof although recently there has been a lot of interest in this field and a number of specialist firms are offering trussed roof conversions at prices not substantially more than traditional cut roof conversions.

In more recent years, truss designs have grown more complex and you can now have a house built with attic trusses which are designed specifically to leave usable space in the loft but you are very unlikely to have attic trusses in your home without knowing about it – it's a major selling point.

STAIRS

If you have established that your loft can be converted, the major internal design issue is access. One of the largest areas of extra expense when considering loft living is the fitting of a staircase. In three storey designs, because of fire regulations, you ideally want to position the top staircase close to the lower one and this can rather limit your room layouts. When converting loft space in an existing house, the normal staircase regulations are relaxed somewhat to allow for various space saving designs such as the alternate tread staircase which work with a much steeper pitch than regular stairs. However, where you have the space available, a traditional staircase is the preferred option – it's both cheaper and far more practical. It is not always an easy matter to design a traditional staircase under a sloping roof – you may well find that the top of the staircase ends up slap in the centre of your loft living space, which may make the subsequent room division tricky. Each case needs to be examined on its merits but, as with so many other issues with house design, the more space you have at your disposal, the greater are the number of workable solutions.

Occasionally, you will be faced with a situation where the disruption caused by fitting a second staircase is so great that it outweighs the benefit from converting the loft. If you feel this to be a significant stumbling block, you would be well advised to hire a professional designer to look at the problem because there are often many ways of fitting staircases that are not at all obvious. An experienced professional may be able to see solutions which evade you. It is often surprising just how many variations you can work into a small floor plan.

There are many other issues to be resolved but generally they are of a relatively minor nature. If you have the headroom and you can fit a staircase, then the two biggest obstacles to converting your loft are out of the way.

PLANNING PERMISSION

The guidelines about what can and can't be done without planning permission have already been dealt with earlier in the chapter in the section on Design. It's all a question of whether or not you have used your PD Rights. Currently, the planning fee for all domestic alterations, including loft conversions, is £172 in England. Don't press ahead with a loft conversion if you are in any doubt about whether you need planning permission. You will undoubtedly be asked about this if and when you come to sell the house and it may prove very costly to obtain it retrospectively. It costs nothing to check with your local planning department and, if you are in any doubt about whether you need permission or not, it is the obvious first port of call.

BUILDING REGULATIONS

Whilst the planning angle is fairly straightforward, the building regulations covering loft conversions are something of a minefield. Some simpler storage-only loft conversions are undertaken without any reference to building regulations but if you intend to use the new rooms as habitable space you should ensure that the work is carried out in accordance with the regs.

If you are altering the timbers in a roof space, you need to be satisfied that the new design will be strong enough to bear the new loads. Usually your existing ceiling joists will not be strong enough to act as floor joists for the loft conversion

and there are various ways of beefing them up. The normal method is to leave the existing joists in place – so as to cause minimum disruption to the ceiling below – and place larger joists by their side in order to take the added weight of the new floor. The roof carpentry will also have to be carefully designed to ensure that it stays in place whilst the structural alterations are undertaken and is then adequate for the open roof space you need. This may require the insertion of steel beams to support the new loadings. Alternatively support can sometimes be provided by knee walls, tying the rafters to the new floor joists. The important points to bear in mind are that the new structure must be strong enough to bear the weight of the new loads and also be rigid enough to stop the roof shape deflecting. The building inspector will want to see that some calculations have been carried out to ensure that these aims have been met.

INSULATION

Another area that causes considerable headaches for loft builders is rearranging the insulation so that it follows the roofline, rather than just being laid along the ceiling joists. The required U value (as of 2015) has fallen to 0.15 which translates as a minimum 200mm of foam insulation such as the type made by Celotex and Kingspan. There are more options if you chose to re-roof at the same time as this allows you to use a breathable felt which gives you a little extra room for insulation – you can avoid the requirement to maintain a 50mm ventilation gap on the immediate underside of the roof. But generally it is felt that whereas once you could get away with just placing insulation between the rafters, now you have to combine this approach with extra layers of insulation on the underside (room side) of the rafters. This has the advantage of providing better insulation – the cold bridge caused by the rafters themselves is eliminated – but there is some resulting height loss in the room; this may be critical in smaller lofts and is something to consider carefully. You also now need to plan for that 50mm ventilation gap to be left to the underside of the rafters in order to get adequate insulation in.

One popular method of insulation is to use a multifoil type insulation such as Actis Tri-Iso Super 10 combined with a high efficiency foam. The acceptability of these multifoils is still a matter of contention. A few private building inspectors are happy with them, but the great majority aren't. However, as they are only 25mm thick they do make it very easy to insulate a loft with a restricted head height.

The definitive word on whether multifoils really work is still awaited but the weight of evidence so far makes it look like the more extravagant claims of their manufacturers are just that — i.e. extravagant claims – but there is clearly a place for multifoils when used in conjunction with more conventional insulation.

However you design the insulation,

in almost every conceivable case, it will now protrude beneath the rafter line and consequently there will be some lofts where this loss of height is critical, surely an unintended side effect of the new regulations.

FIRE SAFETY
But perhaps the biggest hurdle faced by loft converters is meeting the onerous fire safety regulations. When you create habitable space more than 4.5m above ground level, you must allow for the fact that people will not be able to climb out of a window to escape a fire below. You have to provide at least one window that you can escape from via a fireman's ladder – known as an egress window – but in addition to this, you need to provide a fire-proofed route from the loft down to the front door. Half-hour fire-proofing is not particularly difficult to achieve but it will require additional work to be carried out on the doorways leading onto your escape route – typically the bedroom doors opening onto a landing. These doors will have to be treated (either with fire resistant paint or some fireproof board) and they were once required to have self-closing mechanisms as well. The requirement for fitting these was relaxed (in England) in 2007 because so many people disabled them once the building inspector had finaled the loft conversion.

You may face additional problems if your existing stairwell exits into a living room or kitchen, rather than an enclosed hallway. This sort of arrangement is not acceptable and you might have to build an enclosure

around the staircase or find another route down to the ground (such as an external fire escape).

SERVICES AND FINISHES
More often than not, there will be water storage tanks in the existing loft that will have to be moved or replaced. Normally these are located in the middle of the loft and sometimes there is enough room to relocate them to the eaves or against an end wall. However if you plan to have plumbing in the loft space, either a wet radiator or perhaps a bathroom, you have to raise the tanks above the level of the outlets which may involve putting the tanks on raised platforms.

As an alternative, you can switch to a more modern pressurised plumbing system which doesn't require separate tanks: a pressurised cylinder can be located anywhere in the house and can supply central heating as well as hot water. The downside on switching to a pressurised system is the cost: the cylinders alone cost around £600 and the additional plumbing needed to install one can be complex.

HEATING
With such high levels of insulation now required the additional heat required to keep the new loft space warm is minimal and it will almost always be possible to add a small radiator or two without having to upgrade the existing boiler. Alternatively you can fit underfloor heating – either warm water or electric – or small electric storage heaters or convector heaters.

Electric heating systems are invariably cheap to install but expensive to run, but you are likely to find that the heat loss is so small that they may only ever be needed as a back-up heating system on the coldest nights: most of the loft's heating needs will be met from background sources such as electric lights, sunshine and heat rising up from the house below.

ELECTRICS AND LIGHTING

Electrical alterations can usually be fairly easily accommodated, provided the new loads are generally limited to lights and a few sockets. One feature that may cause problems is the use of recessed downlighters. Whilst this may seem an ideal way to provide light when ceiling height is restricted, the physical breaching of the vapour barrier conventionally placed behind the plasterboard ceiling is likely to cause condensation problems in the roof space behind the fitting. It is generally best to try and separate the internal air from that within the roof construction, wherever possible. Therefore spotlights and wall lights are a better solution for lofts. If you must go for recessed downlighters, make sure they are good ones – look for fireproof ones, or acoustically rated ones.

Wall and floor finishes for lofts are not otherwise affected though because you are working with a timber framed backing it makes good sense to stick with relatively lightweight coverings, such as plasterboard or timber boarding.

SOUNDPROOFING

Soundproofing may be an issue you wish to consider, particularly if there are bedrooms below. There are some very expensive floor/ceiling solutions on the market that may be quite impractical for your loft unless you have a great deal of headroom available. These solutions usually work by adding cushioning layers between the floor joists and the floor covering and, additionally, fixing a false ceiling underneath the existing one. In practice, in domestic situations, you would be far better advised to use a thick carpet as your floor covering in the loft space.

BUILD ROUTE

Few people would feel competent to undertake a complete loft conversion without some professional help. But whether you go with a full-blown architect service or stick with a competent builder is a matter of debate. There are lots of builders specialising in loft conversions — they now have their own section in Yellow Pages, quite distinct from ordinary builders – and for straightforward conversions where there is often not a great deal of intricate design involved a good builder should be fine.

The scale of the works may be quite small compared to building a house or even a large extension, but the placing of staircases and the rearranging of the roof structure, especially when dormer windows are involved, is never easy and it's not unknown for a set of expensively drawn plans to have to be reworked by the builders on site. On the other hand, a good designer with a feel for the job can produce an elegant solution in the tiniest of spaces, a skill not to be sniffed at. As ever in these instances, if you have someone recommended to you, whether architect, designer or builder, you would probably do well to seek them out.

Loft conversions are usually tackled from the outside via scaffolding. Not only does this make it easier and cleaner to get materials up into the loft but it means that the messy process of breaking through into the existing living space can be left towards the end of the job when the staircase comes to be fitted. The complexity of the job often depends on whether the windows are roof-lights (which run along the pitch of the roof) or dormers (which stick out from the roof). Dormers are time consuming to construct and expensive to build in comparison but in certain roofs they may add significantly to the overall roof-space. Many lofts are designed with full width dormers on one side and this is a good way to get extra space.

BUDGETING

One way to budget for loft conversions is to take the foot print area of the loft (ie the ceiling area of the storey below) and use this as a multiplier to get a budget figure. Very simple lofts with roof-lights and an easily fitted staircase tend to cost around £400/m² (making a minimum cost on a terraced house of £16,000).

This figure can double as the shape

of the loft becomes more complex: full width dormers, balconies, hipped roofs, plus expensive fittings such as bathrooms will all tend to push the unit area cost up beyond £500/ m². So a largish loft conversion in a detached 1930s house could easily cost upwards of £25,000, still cheaper than an extension.

CONSERVATORIES

The conservatory industry exists in its own little bubble. It's obviously related to mainstream building, to home improvements and the world of extensions, but it is the province of specialists who, by and large, don't do much else. There are enormous numbers of new conservatories built in the UK each year — at its peak it was well over 200,000 and even today it's still going to be an impressively high number.

The question is why? There are one or two things that conservatories have going for them which can make them a very cheap way of gaining extra space. One is that they very rarely require planning permission. Another is that they very rarely require building regulations. Thus the two big administrative heavyweights designed to send us bonkers are, at a stroke, banished from the world of conservatories.

You can just go and order one and you don't have to bother with red tape. Of course, Britain being what it is today, there are numerous exceptions to these rules. 'Very rarely' doesn't mean 'never'. Sir Cliff Richard, no less, was ordered to pull down a conservatory he built in Virginia Water because his Permitted Development Rights had been removed without his knowledge.

In fact the Permitted Development Rights routines used to control regular extensions apply to conservatories in exactly the same way. That is to say that you probably won't need permission unless you have already built a substantial extension or maybe a large loft conversion. The situation with building regs is rather more complex. Most conservatories don't need to trouble the building control department but there are some aspects of conservatory building which will come into the building regs ambit, forming a nice grey area (shall I? shan't I?). To avoid having to apply for building regs:
- the floor area must be less than 30m² (though it's only 8m² in Scotland)
- the conservatory must not form part of the 'heated envelope' of the house – ie there must be separating doors
- the roof is at least 75% glass or polycarb sheeting
- the walls are at least 50% glass or polycarb sheeting
- the conservatory must all be at least 1m from the garden boundary
- it must be at ground level.

Now that does cover the great bulk of bolt-on conservatories, but it might not cover yours. But even if your planned conservatory falls outside building regs, you are still required to comply with the safety glazing directives (in Part K of the building regs) and also if you have any electrics installed, it becomes a notifiable event, if not carried out by a competent electrician who can sign it all off against his insurance. There is also a potentially nasty little problem to do with conservatories being located under means-of-escape or egress windows, which some local authorities seem to be more concerned about than others. This is a complicated area because first-floor windows have only had to be egress windows since 2002, so it cannot logically be applied to the 95% of the UK housing stock that was never built with egress windows. It is the sort of grey area where you might want to think about installing mains-operated smoke detectors in the house, which is in fact the single most effective fire safety measure you can make to an existing dwelling.

There is no requirement for conservatories to be double-glazed. However, if you want to make the conservatory a 'walk-through' feature with no dividing doors, then the price you have to pay is that the conservatory will be assessed as part of the normal living space and it will have to meet exacting energy efficiency standards, which will certainly include double glazing.

So much for red tape. The bigger question is, why bother to fit a conservatory at all? If you like gardening, why not build a greenhouse? If you like light, why not build an extension with lots of glazing? If you like sunbathing, why not buy a timeshare in Tenerife? Or a sunlamp? Why are there so many conservatories added onto existing homes each year? Could it be that, for most people, it's seen as a cheap way of getting an extension? Yes, I think it just might.

For whilst there are the odd aspirational companies around like Amdega who sell a very up-market product (probably referred to as an orangery) at prices way in excess of normal extensions, the great bulk of the conservatory market is made up of the sort of thing you can pick up at Wickes for around £3,000. It'll be built-up off a brick plinth, itself built-up off pretty minimal foundations, and it'll be stuck onto the back of the house with a few screws and the roof will have a stuck-on flashing connecting it to the main house. If it leaks, it's really not a disaster, and if there is a little subsidence, then that won't really matter that much either. In fact, this sort of conservatory is a throw back to how we used to build in days of yore, and how they build shanty towns today in Brazil. Bash it up – it'll do.

Now it's easy to be sniffy about this sort of building, but it does have a place. If you haven't got a lot of dosh and your house is just too cramped, then a bolt-on uPVC conservatory may be just brilliant for you, especially as you don't have to be bothered with the boys from the council crawling all over your house.

Conservatories don't have to be "bolted on." But too often they are. To my mind, this one serves as a prime example of how not to do it.

You know it's never going to feature on Grand Designs, so what?

THE UP-MARKET OPTIONS

There is a yawning gulf between these bolt-on plastic extensions (95% of the market) and the beautiful one-off designs you see in the magazine adverts. There is a surprising correlation with the kitchen market where you can easily put in a fitted kitchen into a modest house for under £5,000, but the top of the range can cost more than ten or twenty times as much.

For a start, if the conservatory design tips into the zone where you have to have building control involved – and it will if it is large or there is no thermal break between the house and the conservatory – then the full weight of the energy efficiency regs comes into effect.

This loosely means that glazing to have a maximum U value of 1.8, which translates as argon-filled, low-e coatings and large air gaps.

The cost of the glazing jumps from around £25/m² up to over £80/m², which makes it more expensive than conventional walling or roofing materials. Having spent all this money, you then have to think about having a very cold space in winter (do you provide heating?) and a very hot space in summer (blinds? ventilation?).

You can, of course, choose to not use your conservatory when it's either too hot or too cold or too dark, but that's an awful lot of times for a room that's so expensive to build, and it makes little sense when you consider the size of the initial investment.

Chapter 12

An existing garden shed in Cambridge was converted into a home office by insulating, double glazing and running an electric cable down the length of the garden

GARDEN WORKSPACES

The growing trend for home working combined with the relaxed planning rules has led to a mushrooming demand for garden workspaces. Many people will be upgrading existing structures for a few thousand pounds but others will be looking to build new structures. These can vary from the utilitarian through to individually designed, hand crafted architectural gems. Prefabricated offices are becoming increasingly popular, mirroring the growth in the kit homes market. Most modules use some form of timber framing and this can vary from traditional log cabins through to the hi-tech insulated panel systems. They have the advantage of you having both a design and a price on the table so you can window shop the various systems before committing to spending any money.

If you do decide to build a garden structure, make sure that it is adequate for the job in hand. In particular, if you wish to work in there during winter and you use sensitive equipment like computers, the structure will need to be both secure and warm.

Garden offices are easily and often broken into and if you plan to leave expensive equipment in there think carefully about how it can best be protected. A good 5-lever lock is essential and also think about using laminated glass in the windows as this will deter casual thieves.

Adding an alarm is probably over the top but a passive infra-red switched external light will be a boon both for you on those dark winter evenings and for deterring unwanted visitors. Alternatively, use a passive motion detector set to alert you in the house.

If you plan to use a computer, opt for a laptop which you can take into the house at night. If you go away on holiday, bring the most valuable items from the garden room back into the house and leave the windows uncovered so that ne'r-do wells can see that there is nothing inside worth nicking.

You will probably want some form of heating to make the room pleasant to work in. You will also want to keep the night time temperature above 12°C inside if you want to prevent condensation and mould growth. Assuming that you aren't able to add onto the hot water system in the main house, your options as regards heating are rather limited to electricity which is always expensive to run. And of course the key to doing this at a reasonable cost is to insulate the office really well: I would take the insulation standards used for new housing and apply them to the office.

Night storage heaters are a good method of supplying heat to garden rooms. They are cheap to run, if you use an Economy 7 tariff, they are good at combating condensation damage and they provide the best of their output during the daytime when the room is probably most likely to be being used. However, they do have their drawbacks, principally that they are very inflexible: you can't turn them up if there is a sudden cold snap and you really need to leave them on all winter whether you are using the room or not.

Other options include electric underfloor mat heating, convector heaters and fan heaters. None of these has the thermal mass advantages of storage heaters (I am assuming here that the structure is likely to be lightweight) and they are likely to leave you with a very cold office overnight, which will be bad news on the condensation front. Either that or you leave background heating on all night during the winter, which I wouldn't recommend.

If you do install electric heating, you will need to lay a on a supply, usually via a buried armoured cable between the house and the garden structure you are building. The load will be determined by what you are proposing, and it's likely that the heating load will be the significant feature. Although a structure up to 30m² in your garden isn't covered by regular building control, note that laying on an electrical supply is a different matter and this work would have to comply with Part P in England & Wales. This means broadly speaking that the work would have to be undertaken by a suitably qualified electrician.

The planning rules are surprisingly relaxed about what they will allow you to put up in your back garden.

Well, relaxed for Britain! Provided the structure isn't too high (i.e. it's single storey), you can cover a large area with buildings. Rules for conservation areas are of course much stricter and Scotland and Ireland have different legislation as well. The best advice is always to check with your local planning department.

BASEMENTS

One of the most significant recent changes in the selfbuild market has been the rise and rise in the popularity of the basement. It's gone from being an expensive problem waiting to trap the unwary, into something approaching a must-have item, an aspirational choice to rank alongside the hardwood floor, the underfloor heating system and the kitchen range. Suddenly the basement is a selfbuild fashion item. What's going on?

A little history is in order. There have been periods in our history when basement building has been common place: you only have to visit many of the 18th and 19th century inner city areas of our major cities to see plenty of examples of homes built with basements or cellars, as they were called in those days. However with the coming of the railways and the opening up of the suburbs and the countryside to housebuilding, building land became cheap and plentiful and the basement fell from fashion.

In other countries the basement has prospered. In the USA and

Canada, many new homes are regularly constructed with basements. In some areas, such as the mid-west Tornado alley, they are built as storm shelters as much as anything. But other parts of North America just value the amenity benefits of a basement, a room which is usually used as a utility and storage area. Germany is another country with a strong basement culture: here at least part of the reason is that the planning regime is very strict about house sizes and ridge heights but discounts basement space from the overall living area and so immediately there is a strong incentive for Germany's huge number of selfbuilders to start off by building down. Whilst the number of basements being built in the UK is measured in hundreds per year, in Germany the figure is in tens of thousands. Not surprisingly, the Germans have the developed a number of advanced techniques for building basements some of which are now beginning to appear in the UK.

The renaissance of the British basement seems to be coming about partly through high land prices (which make it worthwhile spending extra money on construction) and partly through the advantages of basements becoming more widely known. Selfbuilders in particular want larger than average homes and planning constraints often prevent them from building out sideways, so the German idea of building down starts making a lot of sense. What every new home in Britain has had for the past 40 years is a garage yet we increasingly use garages for storage and park cars outside. The penny has dropped for many selfbuilders who realise that the typical family home is built with far too little space and adding a basement is an entirely sensible response to this issue.

The waterproofing element is the key issue in basement design. The structural matters relating to the foundations and the strength of the retaining walls are rarely anything out of the ordinary for experienced engineers and ground-workers. However the requirement to build a waterproof tank – a reverse swimming pool as it's sometimes called – calls for careful design and painstaking installation. In certain conditions, high water tables will exert considerable hydrostatic pressure on the basement walls and any weakness in the tanking details will soon be exposed.

Just how you go about waterproofing the basement depends on a number of factors. These are detailed in a publication called the *Approved Document: Basement for Dwellings* that defines four grades of waterproofing. Which grade you go for depends on how you plan to use the space, whether it is acceptable to be musky and occasionally damp or whether it needs to be as dry and airy as above ground living areas. What measures are necessary to achieve your chosen grade depend on a close analysis of the ground conditions you are faced with. However they broadly fall into three categories which Basements for Dwellings defines as Types A, B and C.

Type A waterproofing is often thought of as being the simplest and cheapest to undertake. This involves adding a waterproof membrane around the basement, which is usually applied externally but can also be sandwiched inside the walls. Typically this would involve some form of membrane laid under the floor and sealed to a tanking layer or sheet running up the basement walls. It is commonplace as well to build in some french drains at the external base of the walls to aid the removal of groundwater. If the basement is on a sloping site, these drains can be directed around the basement and on down the hill, but on a flat site the collected water would have to be pumped away at some point.

Whereas a Type A basement wall can be built out of blockwork, a Type B basement has to be built from a water-resistant concrete because the walls themselves become the main barrier to water penetration. Actually many basement builders choose to combine Types A and B so that there are effectively two water barriers, the reinforced concrete walls and the external tanking. Type C basements are most frequently seen in retrofit basements, dug out from under an existing house. Here, any water penetrating the external walls is channelled away to a sump where it is later pumped off site.

There are several other design considerations to take on board if you are considering a basement. For habitable rooms (usually defined as either bedrooms or living rooms but,

interestingly, not kitchens) then you must have more than one fire exit route from the basement. This is easily accommodated on a sloping site but will require an escape window or a door on a fully below ground basement.

Ventilation is another key issue; basements have a reputation for being dank and mouldy; this is due as much to poor ventilation as it is to damp penetration. The solution is to install a background ventilation system which removes the stale air — this is particularly important when building a Type C basement which allows water to penetrate the external walls.

ESTIMATING THE COST

One of the major factors holding back the construction of basements is the presumption that they are very expensive to build. Evidence from recent basement studies suggest that basement building costs are little different to above ground costs although the finished costs are usually very dependent on just what the basement area is used for and how it is finished. Recent British experience suggests that our new build basements are costing between £500 and £800/m², not dissimilar to building on the equivalent extra space as an extension or as a detached garage block.

On the one hand a basement involves specific costs not found in above ground construction such as reinforcement in the walls, floor rafts and waterproofing: on the other hand there are a number of obvious savings such as not having to build an external skin and not having to build a roof.

PLANNING PERMISSION

Many people wrongly assume that because a basement is barely visible it won't need planning permission. This is not the case. Neither is obtaining planning permission a routine matter. Attitudes to basements appear to vary considerably in different planning authorities.

At one extreme, Surrey selfbuilder Richard Evans commented to me: 'I was told any 'underfloor' habitable space would be deducted from my above floor plans and that if I went ahead after planning was agreed they would slap an enforcement notice on me'.

Contrast this with Richard Owen's experiences building a basement in Gwent. 'You could put six cars or a light industrial unit in the basement space we are building. The planners didn't even blink. The only concerns the planners raised were that the patio doors became French Windows and that they reserved the right to approve the colour of the balustrading. I have to say that I was surprised and amazed.'

Several selfbuilders have been stymied in their attempts to add a basement to their house plans. No planning department seems to regard this as a minor amendment – all want an entirely new submission that not only involves much extra cost but also a potential delay of months. The crucial point of dispute seems to be how the local authority regards the extra space added by the basement.

Many authorities have guidelines about just what size of house should be permitted on each individual plot and the addition of a basement may be enough to break these space guidelines. It's a strange and, to many, an intrusive aspect of our planning system that gives local authorities such arbitrary powers but it is remains a fact of life that, at the present time, some planning departments are not basement friendly. Indications are however that this attitude is rapidly changing as everybody begins to appreciate the need to use our available building land more effectively.

Another aspect worth bearing in mind is the use to which the basement will be put. Planners are less happy with additional bedrooms or living space, seeing this as unjustifiable over development. But uses such as utility areas, garages, hobby rooms, gyms and swimming pools are harder to argue against as these could alternatively be placed in independent buildings in the garden, often without the need for any planning permission.

RETROFIT BASEMENTS

Most basements are constructed under new housing. Yet in London, land prices are so high and loft conversions so widespread, a number of companies have sprung up offering to build a basement under your existing house. They are known as retrofit basements and they are not for the faint-hearted: it's very much an extension of last resort, expensive and difficult to achieve. And whilst £200,000-plus for a basement under a terraced house may sound like an awful lot of money, when the housing is worth two or three million, the stamp duty and estate agent's fees combined mean that it can cost almost as much to move somewhere new. The London Borough of Kensington & Chelsea is where it is mostly happening and in 2013 there were no less than 450 retrofit basements built there, some of them ginormous, creating so-called iceberg homes with swimming pools and gymnasiums located far below ground level. In late 2014, the council there approved new rules restricting these beasts to one storey deep and no more than 50% of the garden area.

It's such a specialised area that it would be pointless to go into the subject here in any depth. The businesses that have got into this market tended to have started life doing underpinning; there is in fact a great deal of similarity between the two techniques. One of the advantages of this is that the bulk of the work can be carried out without breaking through into the existing house: the external walls are underpinned and then the ground is excavated. Most homes with a suspended ground floor are technically able to have retrofit basements, but cost-wise, it really only makes sense in the most expensive areas where land prices are at a premium.

SHOPPING

If you love shopping, it's a given that you'll love housebuilding. One of the secret joys of building homes is that you can indulge yourself on the greatest shopping trip of your life. But successful housebuilders are always canny shoppers, not spendthrifts, and there are a few basic lessons to be learned before you launch into it. Firstly, do not simply get carried away and choose items way beyond your budget. Secondly, know where to look. And thirdly, know how to shop, how to strike a bargain. It's well worth studying the buying process. This is the logic of this chapter. It doesn't cover everything, but it does cover important areas that have been otherwise ignored up to this point.

TAKING OFF QUANTITIES

A bill of quantities is a fancy, construction professional's term for a shopping list. Making a comprehensive one is fundamental to controlling costs and is one of the major benefits to derive from having a properly designed, properly specified job. Many times in the past I have measured off plan to estimate a cost and then gone and measured again on site to order materials. I must also admit to having measured three or even four times when the bit of wood I write the measurements on gets nailed into some studwork or gets painted over. If I had taken the advice that I'm offering now I'd be a little bit richer and a little bit fatter.

Now, serious construction professionals will engage the services of a quantity surveyor (known on site as 'the QS') to work out what is needed. However, QSs don't come cheap and many small builders work on their own rules of thumb for estimating the right quantities. These are not usually as accurate as a QS would get them but they are much better than nothing.

If you are a selfbuilder or a rookie builder, I'd strongly advise you use a QS to price up your project at an early stage, preferably before planning permission goes in, because it's a lot cheaper and quicker to make the changes on paper (if you need to) before you have a full planning permission. If the project is unusual, the QS bill is likely to be in four figures, but I still think this is worth it.

FREE TAKE-OFFS

However you may decide that your project is straightforward and you want to develop your own bill of quantities. Many builder's merchants offer a free or at least cheap take-off service, ideally suited to the needs of rookie builders. Or check out one of the very cheap internet estimating services, like Estimators Online – around £150 for a house, £90 for an extension.

Much of the repetitive grind of measuring and recording is carried out by computer and, provided the job is relatively straightforward, they are pretty accurate. The closer you stick to industry standard solutions, the better the outcome and they are quite capable of generating accurate results from a basic set of plans and elevations.

TRADITIONAL ROUTE

Let's compare it with the traditional way of doing a take-off. Traditional here means that your source document is a written schedule of works (often known as the spec), not the plans. You use the plans to calculate the areas and volumes but you work methodically down the written list so as not to miss anything out. To give you a flavour of what I'm on about, here is a clause taken from a house built in 2005.

■ External (house) walls of 275mm 3.5N clinker blockwork cavity work incorporating 100 mm Rockwool or similar full fill cavity insulation and 200 mm s/s butterfly brick ties at max 900 mm horizontal and 450 mm vertically and at every block course adjacent to openings. Additional 105 mm skin of face brickwork (bricks to client's choice) forming plinth wall and tied to blockwork with s/s butterfly ties as described above. Plinth wall extends 10 courses above DPC.

Hardly a riveting read, but it's clear enough. The job of the QS is, if you like, to rewrite this specification with the quantities added in so that it might read:

■ 158m² double skin external (house) walls of 275mm 3.5N clinker blockwork cavity work incorporating 145/m² x 100 mm Rockwool or similar full fill cavity insulation and 580No. 200 mm s/s butterfly brick ties at max 900 mm horizontally and 450 mm vertically and at every block course adjacent to openings. Additional 55m² x 105 mm skin of face brickwork (bricks to client's choice) forming plinth wall and tied to blockwork with 130No. s/s butterfly ties as described above. Plinth wall extends 10 courses above DPC.

You don't need any specialised equipment. All you need are your finished plans, a decent ruler, a calculator and a pencil and paper (rubber would be handy). And bags of common sense. If you've got a computer and you know your way around a spreadsheet you'll save yourself a bit of work, but not that much.

MEASUREMENTS TO TAKE

Take your measurements from your detailed plans (which are now conventionally drawn in metric scale which makes scaling up a damn sight easier). If the distance you want is referred to on the drawings then use it, otherwise you must measure off plan in millimetres and scale up to get actual sizes; thus, if drawings are 1:50, then you multiply your measurement by 50 to get the actual measurement.

Many of the dimensions you need will be written in on the plan so you won't need to measure. Where an area is needed you multiply the two sides together, but when this area is not a simple rectangle you must split the overall area into a number of smaller rectangular boxes and add these together. Remember that the area of a triangle equals half base x height.

For all but the very largest houses all this measuring should take about four to six hours. Complicated building details like split levels, curved work, dormer windows or raked ceilings make the measuring much more complex too and it is well worth double-checking as a mistake here will have costly ramifications on down the line. Oh, and don't forget to write the answers down where you won't lose them.

I also find it incredibly handy to make little notes next to the calculations, which remind me what assumptions I have made when doing the calculations. Typically these read as 'have assumed no skirtings in conservatory' or 'have allowed for three courses of face brickwork below DPC.' It's a good idea to decide whether your derived quantities are 'as measured' or whether you have added an allowance for waste. It really doesn't matter which method you employ but you must be consistent otherwise you will end up adding 15% to the quantities several times over and you will over-order by miles.

The further your house gets away from the good old box-shape, the more complicated it gets to measure out and, if a feature like a bay window or a fancy chimney is difficult to quantify, then you can bet that it will also be difficult to build.

WORKING THROUGH THE SPEC
You work methodically through the spec quantifying everything that is quantifiable. Have a look at the Model House Quantities table in Chapter 1 to give you a flavour of it. You then have to sweep through the whole thing a second time to generate a shopping list; some of the things you have quantified will have to be amalgamated with other sections, others will have to be broken down still further.

Blockwork is a good example. It usually appears in several different places, such as external walls, garage walls, some internal walls, around chimneys and sometimes in the floor (as in beam and block flooring). Presuming that they are all the same species of block (unlikely), add them all together to get an overall total for blockwork. And then consider that blockwork includes not just the blocks themselves, but the sand and cement making up the mortar, not to mention the labour to lay them with. These totals have to be extracted from the blockwork total and added to the brickwork total which, to add to the confusion, will have different square metre labour rates and uses different volumes of mortar.

WRITTEN SPECIFICATIONS
Well, that's the traditional route. It's time consuming but it works. If you plan to do your own project management it may even be worth going through this exercise to familiarise yourself with the job in hand. However, many housebuilders never bother with anything so elaborate as a written specification of works but just make do with plans on a couple of A1 sheets. This is fine if you know what you are doing, but using a set of plans without a written spec can be a bit like trying to cook a new dish for which you have a list of the ingredients but no instructions on how they go together. Arguably it doesn't matter which order you measure quantities in but the danger is that if you don't work methodically through a list, you will miss whole chunks out. If you have skimped on this stage of the design process, then this is where your chickens come home to roost.

APPLYING MEASUREMENTS
From all these measurements plus various details drawn in on the plans you should be able to construct a reasonably accurate bill of quantities. You may not actually want to make up a shopping list for paint at the planning stage, but the point is that by having taken all these measurements you shouldn't have to keep taking them throughout the job. You have the figures. From these figures plus a little close scrutiny of your house plans you can work out quantities for:
- Excavation
- Concrete (approximate)
- Flooring materials
- Walling materials
- Roofing materials
- Insulation
- Plasterboarding and plastering
- Decorating materials
- Skirting and architrave
- Scaffolding
- Guttering and downpipes
- Whole house heat-loss calculations.

Joinery is treated rather differently.

If you've got a pukka written spec, there will be a joinery schedule attached that will list all the opening sizes and the window and door styles which will fit in the openings. I find it helpful to start with the joinery: I work out the overall areas and use this sum to subtract from wall areas. The joinery schedule can also be used to calculate approximate quantities for glazing, lengths for lintels and cavity breaks and a subsidiary schedule for door furniture.

AVERAGE PRICES

The rates I quote throughout the book are all rates current for building work in southern England in 2018, especially around my home town of Cambridge. The key rate is £22 per hour, equivalent to around £180 per day, £900 a week, or just over £40,000 per annum, typical wage for good tradesmen. Your area may (almost certainly will) have different prices in operation by the time you start building, but bear in mind that Cambridgeshire is quite a bit above the national average on building costs.

Early editions of this book (it first appeared in 1994) were able to neatly summarise both material and labour costs right across mainland Britain – only Ireland diverged significantly. But since then, labour rates in boom areas seem to be up by 50 to 100% whilst slack areas are little changed from the 1990s. London in particular is very expensive but there are other parts of the country

where labour can be just as pricey. My prices are intended only as a guideline by which you can compare your own quotations, so bear in mind that the indicative labour rates here may have to be adjusted up or down considerably depending on where you are building.

ALLOWING FOR WASTAGE

If you manage to work out the theoretical quantities of just about everything you need, you are still faced with the problem of knowing how much extra to order to cover wastage.

Wastage is a wonderfully vague term that covers just about any and every mishap that can occur on a building site from defective materials being delivered to perfectly adequate materials apparently walking off site.

There's really no way of knowing in advance what your wastage rate will be, but experience suggests that you'd be wise to over-order by between 8 and 10% on heavyside materials like bricks, blocks, sand and cement and also plastering materials.

You should be able to work out timber quantities exactly, but here you will probably be blighted by timber quality not being what you require and again you would do well to add extra lengths to your totals.

Buying more than you actually need is, of course, expensive but so are the frequent shopping trips that happen when you buy too little.

ENTERING THE BAZAAR

The British consumer is used to being able to see what something costs. Visit any high street or supermarket and the price you pay will be clearly labelled on the goods or, at least, on the shelf underneath. Haggling over the price is something that you might do on holiday in Morocco or Turkey but it's thought not to be part of the British way of life.

This is far from the truth. Step off the high street and into the world of commerce (or house buying or even car purchase) and we Brits are out there haggling with the best of them. Generally speaking, when there are three or more zeros on the end of the price tag, the gloves come off and any pretence at civilised shopping goes out of the window. Anyone responsible for purchasing building materials would do well to bear this in mind because a well-organised buyer can achieve savings of 20% or more over the unprepared novice.

It helps to be an established builder. To have a proven trading record stretching back over some years and, better still, to have had a record as a prompt payer will stand anyone in good stead with their suppliers. But, these days, merchants are keen to attract any custom (except the doubtful payers) and if you can establish your credit worthiness and the fact that you might be a substantial customer, if only temporarily, then you will have a strong bargaining chip. Also bear in mind the proliferation of internet-based merchants which makes price comparison and checking a whole lot easier.

INSIDE A BUILDER'S MERCHANT

Like any business, builder's merchants and all the related building trade suppliers are buying in goods and selling them on at a mark-up. The services that a merchant provides for this mark-up are:

- accessibility
- delivery (usually free)
- advice.

After a round of take-overs and mergers, there are only three national chains left. Jewson is the largest: it took over Harcros in 1997 and Grahams in 1999, and was itself taken over by the French conglomerate St. Gobain in 2000. Travis Perkins (which swallowed Keyline in 1999 and Wickes in 2005) is No 2 and Builder Center (part of the giant Wolseley group) comes in a distant third. In addition there are around thirty regional operations (typically with five to ten outlets) and still a fair number of small independents, one- or two-branch outfits which may well turn over less than £1 million per annum.

There are also many specialist trade outlets dealing with plumbing, electrics, roofing, joinery, ironmongery and glass. Whether they are any good or not depends an awful lot on the quality of the staff working in any particular branch and, especially, the branch manager. Needless to say, the smaller operations tend to give a more personalised service but can't always match the prices offered by the large chains.

A general merchant will hope – indeed need – to make an average mark-up in excess of 50% to stay in business. Thus, if they purchase some paint for, say, £100 then they will need to sell it for £150. An awful lot of their business is conducted with preferred clients at mark-ups much lower than this 50% and so to balance this out they must sell a great deal at mark-ups of 70, 80 or even 100%. So, one of the keys to getting good prices from a builder's merchant is to become known as a preferred client. Step one is to open an account.

To set up an account with a builder's merchant, you would normally be asked for a bank reference and two trade references. The bank reference shouldn't be a problem (depending on your relationship with your bank, of course) but trade references could prove difficult if you've never had a trading account. Instead, write a letter of introduction saying who you are and what your project is. This will carry far more clout if you include a copy of the plans, which they may well offer to quote on.

If you've never had a trading account (and if you are not in business on your own account there is no particular reason to have had one), they operate under a very simple code. When you pick goods up or have them delivered you get a dispatch or delivery note. The tax invoice arrives a few days later by post or, increasingly, by email (this is the one you must keep for VAT records) and every month you are sent a statement of account which summarises all the invoices you have run up on your account in the previous calendar month. Normal terms are that you must pay off the outstanding balance on your account at the end of each subsequent month, so if you spent £500 on account with Jewsons during April, you would be required to give them a cheque for £500 at the end of May. In effect you get between 30 and 60 days' credit depending on whether your purchase happened at the beginning of the month or the end of the month.

Sometimes postponing a purchase by a day or two – so as to avoid the month end – can get you an extra 30 days' credit. Builders merchants know all about these tricks and they consistently get more sales in the first week of a month than they do in the last week.

Don't just open an account and start purchasing materials as and when you need them – you'll pay top whack this way. If you've got the whole job priced up you know that you will have some serious prices back because they suspect you will have got prices from the competition. You may well be able to improve on these quoted prices.

A question you occasionally get asked over the phone by a builder's merchant is 'Is this a job you are actually doing?' Probably sounds rather silly but they are sounding you out: if you're just estimating you get one price, if you are buying you get a better price. They quite expect you to go the rounds of local suppliers and they want to have a bit of fat they can lose on the next call.

This practice of haggling over prices is common to almost all areas of building supplies except the DIY sheds (Homebase, B&Q, etc.). It's partly volume driven (that is, if you buy 150 sheets of plasterboard you'll get a better rate than if you buy just one), but it also has much to do with the cosy understanding that exists between builders and their suppliers, which goes to make builders' rates look cheaper than they actually are – or to put it another way, to discourage the DIY enthusiast from getting out of bed.

The levels of discount vary from product to product and just to make it complicated some merchants operate two, three or even four levels of discount off the retail price. Some products are sold with a list price from which you have to negotiate the biggest discount you can get; other products have no list prices and the prices paid for them just come down to negotiation. Purchasing well is an art. Get too pushy and the merchants will get annoyed and shut up shop. Too relaxed and they'll squeeze whatever extra they can get out of you.

Now, once upon a time, what I have just written would have practically barred me from ever setting foot in a builder's merchant again. But slowly the worm is turning and the trade merchants are far more aware of a) the competition from the DIY sheds and b) the growth of the selfbuild market. Most merchants I

Endless shopping may sound like fun, but sifting through trays of cupboard handles at B&Q, looking for the perfect ones, begins to make Sudoku look exciting.

talk to are only too willing to supply one-off builders at somewhere near their best prices. They have had too many cosy relationships with 'trusted trade customers' turn horribly sour and now the order of the day is to do any business which pays.

One further point. Don't assume that your work is done after you have agreed some good prices. You have to check that you are invoiced correctly: builder's merchants, large and small, have an annoying little habit of ignoring agreed prices and invoicing you at top whack. Keep your quotes somewhere handy and cross check against them when the invoices arrive. To hazard a guess, I would reckon that 10% of invoices from builder's merchants come with prices higher than agreed – never lower!

BUYING DIRECT

This whole question of who supplies whom is still a pretty murky area. Most manufacturers take the view that they should support the established distribution channels (i.e. the general merchants) and consequently you will have to shop there for the product. For instance, you can't buy plastic drain ware direct even if you are Barratt Homes. On the other hand, there are manufacturers like Ryton's (who produce roof ventilation) who readily sell via mail order to all comers but who, consequently, tend to get blackballed by builder's merchants so that their product is little known.

As a general rule, manufacturers do not deal direct with end users except where they set up their

Chapter 13

Toolstation tends to open branches within eyesight of Screwfix. Whether this makes Screwfix happy is doubtful, but it keeps prices keen and it's convenient for us shoppers

own distribution channels, such as Magnet. To make the whole picture thoroughly confusing, you will find that some distributors (notably Jewsons) will have own brand items on sale, which suggests that they are manufacturers. Just like Sainsburys are farmers. But this doesn't mean you are buying direct. What really matters is not which brand or where you bought it from but was it cheap and was it any good?

THE DIY SHEDS

One of the reasons for the success of the edge of town DIY sheds is

the perceived unfriendliness of the builder's merchant to non-trade customers. The Saturday afternoon patio-building brigade have long felt that they have been treated as second-class customers at trade outlets and, what is worse, have been forced to pay over the odds for this dubious privilege. How much more convivial to shop at a place where the prices are actually displayed, even if they aren't particularly cheap, and where the staff probably know even less than you do.

As a rule the DIY sheds are not very competitive on heavyside, bulky

materials but tend to be pretty good on the finishes, provided you are not looking for anything fancy.

One exception is Wickes, whose prices are keen right across the board. Wickes is a hybrid between a builder's merchant and a DIY shed; the prices are close to (and sometimes better than) a regular builder's merchant's trade prices but they are also on full display – a big advantage to rookie builders. Wickes have been taken over by Travis Perkins but they continue to run quite separately to the main chain. Don't pull up to a Wickes branch and expect to put things on your Travis Perkins account. Wickes is a cash business, just like B&Q.

Screwfix is another outlet to be aware of – you can hardly ignore it anymore, it's everywhere. It started life as a mail-order ironmongery specialist founded by Mark Goddard-Watts. It grew and it grew and in 1999 it was bought out by the Kingfisher Group, owners of B&Q. Since then, it has expanded both its remit and its way of selling, so that they now have 300+ trade counters dotted around the country. Although it's not the place to buy heavyside materials, it's prices for everything else are always keen and it's range is surprisingly large. If it fits in a van, it'll be there.

Four years after selling Screwfix, Goddard-Watts started out all over again and beget Toolstation, which has a natty habit of opening its branches next door to Screwfix. Toolstation tends to stock a little less than Screwfix but tends to be a little cheaper. Goddard-Watts then sold Toolstation too, this time to Travis Perkins (who already owned Wickes). Having two rivals trading side-by-side certainly keeps the prices keen, but behind all these brands are a decreasing number of mega-businesses.

SPECIALISTS

The general builder's merchant is to the building trade what a convenience store is to the high street shopper. You can get just about anything you want there and the prices are reasonable. However, for the serious shopper, intent on sniffing out bargains, there are any number of specialist suppliers who can usually undercut the general merchants in their own areas. The trouble is they take some hunting out, and often they don't want to be bothered by small fry, one-off housebuilders, let alone amateurs. You could spend an awful lot of time tracking down specialist suppliers and not save more than a few hundred quid overall, and it may well be that you decide the convenience (and often helpfulness) of a local builder's merchant is worth hanging on to.

However, I would not be doing my duty if I weren't to make you aware of how the professionals do it. Where do they go shopping? Anyone with a broadband connection (does anyone not have one now?) will probably head straight for Google and start their enquiries there. In the old days, you would have started by opening the Yellow Pages: the principle is the same, only the technology has changed.

The general builder's merchants do still get a look in. They are particularly strong when it comes to supplying cement, drains, timber, plastering materials and joinery, but they tend to be out-priced by specialists in most other areas. However, do bear in mind that whilst the general merchants are to some extent geared to Wallies asking stupid questions, the specialists usually expect you to know what you are talking about. Ask a steel stockholder what you should use to reinforce your garage floor and you'll probably get told some crap mother-in-law joke.

If you want to look for specialists, here are some leads to search on:

- Sand and aggregates: buy direct straight from quarries or via specialist hauliers..
- Cement, lime: general merchants are usually the best place to buy unless you want one of the speciality limes in which case you want either a local producer or an eco-merchant.
- Bricks, blocks, pavings: besides the general merchants, there are a number of specialist brick wholesalers (or factors) who specialise in supplying full loads direct to site. Look out for Brickability, particularly good for sourcing facing bricks.
- Building stone: either direct from quarries or via brick or stone merchants.
- Readymix concrete: buy direct from Readymix outfits.
- Drainage: general merchants do well, although there are some specialists who are worth checking out. John Davidson Pipes (now JDP)

are good for Osma and Burdens are good all round groundworks suppliers.

- Joinery: mass-produced joinery is usually best sought out via the general merchants. Magnet Joinery, which is characterised by being 'good value', is alone amongst the major producers in being only available from its own depots, which run a sketchy delivery service.
- Timber and timber boards: general merchants tend to do well here although some are conspicuously better than others. There are some specialist timber merchants and these are the places to look for unusual species. We like Vincent Timber, based in Birmingham.
- Roof trusses: many timber merchants run up roof trusses as a sideline and this is a good line of approach. There are specialists although they are few and far between.
- Insulation: there are many specialist suppliers in this field and they usually undercut the general merchants. Sheffield and Encon are big names here.
- Roofing: another area where specialists reign supreme as both suppliers and subcontractors.
- Guttering: buy from general merchants unless you want something better than the industry standard uPVC fittings.
- Lintels: again buy from general merchants.
- Steel beams, reinforcing: usually the steel stockholders offer the best value.
- Glass: these days normally bought

with doors or windows, so specialist glass suppliers don't interact with builders. But if it's architectural or structural glass you are after, then specialists rule the roost. Good contacts here are Cantifix, IQ Glass and Glazing Vision.

■ Plumbing: plumbers buy from specialist plumber's merchants. Every town has a selection of specialists but also look online.

■ Electrics: similar story as plumbing supplies.

■ Kitchens: as the section on kitchens, hopefully, makes clear, your kitchen could come from any one of a huge number of sources: joinery shops, general merchants, kitchen specialists, you name it. There are also worktop specialists, appliance wholesalers and more than 1,000 kitchen unit manufacturers, many supplying direct to the public.

■ Plastering: general merchants pick up the great bulk of sales to plasterers. Floor screeding is increasingly done by specialists, as are one coat renders.

■ Paints, stains: Decorators' Merchants are in every town but for many a DIY shed will be just as cheap and more convenient.

■ Ironmongery: there are specialist stockists offering wholesale prices but a one-off housebuilder is still going to do better by buying the right amounts rather than chasing extra keen prices. General merchants discount heavily on bulk orders and do well here, but Screwfix and Toolstation pick up lots of orders as well. Ironmongery Direct have a smaller range but are better at it.

■ Ceramic tiles: Again, you are never far from a tile outlet and online sales are significant too.

For items like central vacuum cleaners, underfloor heating and heat recovery units, where there may well be no local agents, the obvious place to start looking is online, but also check out the selfbuild shows where you get to meet the people behind the products, which may or may not be a comfort.

ONLINE

The internet is an incredible source of materials and a great place for smaller suppliers to access the national market, rather than staying local. You'd struggle to build a whole house from online suppliers, but when it comes to finishing materials, it's often hard to beat.

There are downsides. One is that you frequently get hit by high delivery charges, something the local suppliers tend not to do. Sometimes there are also minimum order quantities which can be very awkward if you are only building one house. And of course incorrect orders or damaged goods are not so easy to deal with when the conversation takes place via email.

Having said that, on my recent selfbuild I used around 40 different online suppliers — everything from window film to door mats — and all but one came up trumps. I was impressed by how little grief we had.

SALVAGE

One other important area I've not touched on is the salvage yard. Time was when salvage yards were a source of cheap building materials, but there has been a flight to quality in this market and these days you are much more likely to be sniffing around expensive architectural gems which you probably won't be able to afford.

If you are seriously into using salvaged building materials, you would do well to identify as early as possible what exactly it is you are going to get because incorporating changes to materials specification during construction can be very costly.

There are hundreds of reclaimed building materials yards all over the country, varying in size from a couple of sheds in a back garden to multi-acre sites better equipped than the average builder's merchant. If you want to look further afield than your hood, search on Salvoweb who keep a good database of material recyclers all over the UK.

TRUCKING

Moving materials around the country is expensive. A lorry with an off-loading crane (usually a HIAB, pronounced high-ab) and driver will cost around £250-£400 to make a trip of more than half a day – although this will be less with an ordinary flat-back truck without a crane. This sum will be the same whatever the load and so from the buyer's point of view it makes good sense to get as near to a full load as possible. The best economies come when ordering 20 tonnes, which is usually a full payload.

What's in a Full Load? A 20-tonne lorry can shift:

■ about 8,000 standard bricks

■ or 7,200 block pavers (144m²)

- or 1,440 dense blocks (144m²)
- or 2,400 clinker blocks (240m²).

Aerated blocks (like Thermalite or Celcon) are so light that the capacity constraint on haulage tends to be volume rather than weight. 20 tonnes of super-lightweight blocks would be about 6,000 blocks, which would be 36 double packs.

There are no industry standards as to how masonry materials should be packed, although there is a tendency to use shrink-wrapped plastic (which keeps watertight) and to pack in weights and quantities that fit on to a pallet. A forklift can handle more than two tonnes and a common pack size is around one tonne (which allows two packs to be lifted at once). When ordering direct loads, you'll have to accept the nearest pack size quantity so if, for instance, you wanted 8,000 bricks and your selected brick is packed in 410s (as many are), you would have to settle for either 19 packs (19 x 410 = 7,790) or 20 packs (20 x 410 = 8,200).

Packs will either come palletted or with fork holes for forklift off-loading. The chances are a fully laden 20-tonner will not be able to get off the road, so hire of a rough-terrain forklift may be the best solution for unloading. A rough-terrain forklift and driver should be available at around £150 for a half day and is usually money well spent if the site is big enough to warrant one. Bricks and blocks can (sometimes) be set around site, making labouring much quicker and easier. A JCB with forks can be used as an alternative to a rough-terrain forklift.

PLASTERBOARD

The plasterboard manufacturers all pack in the same sizes. Better prices are usually negotiable on full packs. A 22-tonne direct load would be enough for three or four large timber frame houses – probably a bit too much for your average individual builder – however, by buying in full pack sizes you should be able to make savings.
- 1200 x 2400 x 9.5 mm plasterboard comes in packs of 80 (1.76 tonnes)
- 1200 x 2400 x 12.5 mm plasterboard comes in packs of 60 (1.66 tonnes).

TIMBER

Timber has to be purchased in 20m³ lots to take advantage of bulk discounts. 20m³ is an awful lot of timber. Furthermore, studwork, which is perhaps the commonest size of timber used in timber frame buildings, has to be ordered in 40m³ lots. The average timber frame house uses around 1,000m of studwork – a paltry 5m³! Full loads of timber can undercut merchants' best prices by as much as 30%, but you have to have some site going to justify such orders. By and large, you'd do better to try and concentrate on buying good rather than cheap timber.

PALLETS

Builder's merchants once routinely charged a £15 deposit on pallets used to supplied heavy goods to site. A pile of pallets would soon mount up and

you were faced with the unenviable task of returning them to base in order to get the deposit back. And to reclaim the deposit, you needed to have your invoices sorted out to show that you had actually had said pallets from said supplier. It was a hassle but it was one of the few green aspects of buying building materials.

But note how I am writing in the past tense here. On my recent selfbuild, only one supplier, Travis Perkins, charged a pallet deposit and that only seemed to be occasionally. The practice has all but died. Instead we ended up putting twenty or more pallets into a skip and had to pay for their collection. At least they will have been recycled by the skip operator (at least I hope they were).

CONCRETE

One person working with an electric or diesel mixer will mix 1m³ of concrete in about an hour. That's fine for odd bits and pieces but hopeless for major projects like foundations. As a rule, readymix will be cheaper when more than 2.5m³ is needed. Readymix loads are always going to be preferable where consistent concrete strength is important. Really, for anything other than laying the odd patio, it has to be site-delivered readymix concrete every time.

STRENGTHS

Traditionally the design strengths of concrete have been expressed in ratios of volumes cement:sand:gravel (as in 1:3:6). However, things are stirring

Concrete pumps greatly reduce the amount of labour required to pour readymix

When you add water to readymix, you weaken it. It often leaves the readymix yard in a perfect condition and is watered on site, making a joke of its original spec. Watered concrete is the biggest single cause of concrete failure.

If you take any of this on board you will already be ahead of the game. My friendly local readymix supplier, Allen Newport, told me: "99 people out of a 100 who phone up here haven't got a clue what type of concrete they want. Even with the professionals, it's only about 50% who know what they need."

CONCRETE PUMPS

To hire a concrete pump, allow around £200-£250 per session. They pump a full load (6m³) in 20 minutes, about three times quicker than three men barrowing might do. Concrete pumps make financial sense on jobs with more than 30m³ of concrete to be poured but there are other reasons for using them, notably when speed is important or access is difficult. If using a pump be sure to let the readymix supplier know, because the mix design is wetter and the through-put of lorries is much faster than on a normal job. It's also a little more expensive.

STEEL

Steel can be used in a wide variety of applications in new housebuilding and there are moves afoot to introduce steel framing as an alternative to timber framing. However, most housebuilders use it sparingly, preferring to use the

in the sleepy world of concrete and there are now at least three other labelling systems in operation. If you are mixing concrete on site, the old ratio system, as described, is fine and is actually very useful as you can use it to gauge how many shovels need to go into the mixer, although note that it is usually most convenient to have a sand and gravel mixture delivered to site – ask for 'all-in ballast'. If, however, you phone up for a readymix delivery you may do well just to explain what it is you want the concrete for and let them work out which mix it is you need. If you have employed a structural engineer to design your foundations, then the concrete mix should be in their instructions.

Foundation mixes: 1:3:6 is traditional for on-site batched concrete. In readymix terms, this is now known as a GEN 1 mix.

Floor slab mix: 1:2:4 is the traditional volume way of looking at it – it's a bit stronger than the foundation mix. The readymix equivalent is usually referred to as a GEN 3. If you are screeding over your slab, you may be able to use a GEN 1 instead of a GEN 3. Basically, the lower the GEN number, the cheaper the mix. GEN 3 and GEN 4 are about 5 to 10% more expensive than GEN 1. There are lots of other more specialised mixes around. Reinforced work requires reinforced mixes, designated RC. Driveways and paths have their own mix known as PAV 1. If in doubt, ask the readymix rep.

traditional materials brick, concrete and timber wherever possible. Steel is the No 1 choice for standard fixings like nails and screws but elsewhere its use is restricted to a few specialised areas.

REINFORCING

The commonest form of steel reinforcing used in housebuilding is A142 anti-crack mesh, which is often set in concrete floor slabs to add strength. Note that you'll need bolt croppers on site in order to cut it. It is usual (though by no means universal) to lay this in garage floor slabs. It needs to be located towards the bottom of the concrete layer in order to do its work properly. There are many other forms of steel reinforcing used in concrete but you are unlikely to come across them in housebuilding unless you have to lay specialised foundations.

LINTELS

Even though reinforced concrete is much cheaper, for many years now steel has been the preferred material for bridging the openings in outer walls made by doorways and windows. The problem with concrete is that, in insulated new houses, it remains a large cold bridge through the wall, which is bad news thermally and attracts condensation. Also, when viewed from outside, concrete lintels look crude and cheap. In contrast, steel can be insulated and the outer leaf support is hidden seamlessly over the top of the window or door. The market was dominated by two Welsh

Even in timber frame houses, steel usually plays a part somewhere. You would be very unlikely to buy the steel separately as it comes with the rest of the superstructure.

steel businesses, Catnic and IG, and designers still routinely specify their products. But Catnic is now part of Tata Steel and IG was taken over by Irish competitor Keystone, so the way is open for alternative suppliers. The most commonly used IG lintel is the L1/S, very suitable for bridging openings in cavity work with cavities up to 100 mm. There is a heavy duty version, known as the L1/HD. They are made in lengths from 600 mm to 4800 mm and they increase in 150 mm increments. The minimum end bearings must be 150 mm so that an opening of 900 would need to be bridged by a lintel of 900 + 150 + 150 = 1200 mm.

In contrast, concrete lintels still

tend to be the preferred choice to bridge internal doorways in masonry work only. Here the lintel is completely covered and the heat loss/condensation issue is irrelevant. The steel lintel manufacturers do produce an internal door lintel but it is not widely used. Timber framers tend to use timber lintels, but note that where a brick skin is specified for the external wall, there are special steel lintels designed to do the job of just supporting the outer skin.

CAVITY WALL TIES

Where the facing material is brick, block or stone you need approx 3.5 wall ties/m^2. If the inner skin of the cavity is timber frame rather than blockwork, the wall ties are a different shape and you need slightly more (about 4/m²). Since 2004, you have had to use stainless steel wall ties rather than the cheaper galvanised.

Wall ties are seen as a significant cold bridge and moves are now afoot not to use steel. The Passivhaus builders seem to be using the Teplo Wall Tie from Magmatech, made of basalt fibre and therefore not a cold bridge.

MORTARS

The standard building cement, packed in 25kg bags, is known as OPC, which stands for Ordinary Portland Cement, and sometimes this is referred to as Portland Cement. The cement (and concrete) market is dominated by a small number of firms, once all British, now all foreign owned. RMC is now Cemex (from Mexico), Blue Circle is now Lafarge Holcim (French Swiss), both ARC and Castle Cement are now Heidelberg (Germany). It being a mature industry, you'll find that there is remarkably little variation in cement prices – although cynics may have an alternative explanation for this. By all means shop around – 2019 prices are hovering around £200 per tonne (£4.60 per 25kg bag) – but note that it is worth sticking with the same manufacturer once you've made your decision; cement colours vary and you can ruin face brickwork

with a nasty change in mortar colours. A detached four-bedroomed house, built of brick and block, will require something like 6 tonnes of cement (excluding concrete) so, with a total value of under £1,200, cement purchase is never going to be a bank-breaker.

MIX DESIGNS

How strong do you want it? Strong mixes (one part cement to three parts sand, henceforth 1:3) are used where the mortar must stand on its own (a floor screed) or is likely to get very wet (underground work); for brick and blockwork and for wall renders, it is important not to get an over-strong mix and also to get some plasticity into the mix.

This is usually accomplished by using additives (such as Femi or Cementone) or by substituting lime for some cement. Given the choice, many bricklayers like to work with hydrated lime in the mortar but it's not universally admired; it's bulky and easily wasted and transporting split bags is a pain. Also mixing has to be carried out more accurately as the addition of a third ingredient adds to the likelihood of changes in mortar colour.

MASONRY CEMENTS

There are several other options available, all designed to make on-site gauging a little easier and a little more accurate. Masonry cements add fillers to the mix which take the place of plasticisers and can be used in all the major cement applications (concrete, brick mortars, renders and screeds) and will go fatty enough

in a mixer to be used without any additional additives. One brickie I know is very uncomplimentary about them, to the extent that if I were to print his comments, all you would see would be a whole bunch of asterisks. Look for names like Mastercrete and Multi-cem.

Another option is to use a pre-mixed mortar (i.e. even the sand is mixed in for you) – RMC (OK, Cemex) can supply these either in skips or tipped off lorries or in small bags.

LIME

There is no compulsion to use cement for the construction of new buildings and there are many restoration projects where it would be advisable to avoid it altogether. The use of cement in housebuilding did not become widespread until the 1920s. Before that, people used lime-only mortars which never set as hard as cement, and one of the big advantages of lime mortars is that the mortar can be cleaned from the brick, making it possible for some bricks to be reused in other buildings. In contrast, most cement mortars cannot be removed from bricks and cement-bedded bricks are good for nothing more than hardcore. Another advantage is that lime mortars remain slightly plastic and this provides a certain amount of flexibility to walls, which helps to withstand subsidence and cracking.

However, it's not that simple just to switch to lime as a replacement for cement. The really traditional limes, sold in liquid 'putty' format in tubs, are around six times as expensive as

Mortar Mix Chart

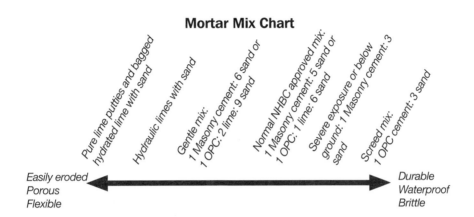

Pure lime putties and bagged hydrated lime with sand	Hydraulic limes with sand	Gentle mix: 1 Masonry cement: 6 sand or 1 OPC: 2 lime: 9 sand	Normal NHBC approved mix: 1 Masonry cement: 5 sand or 1 OPC: 1 lime: 6 sand	Severe exposure or below ground: 1 Masonry cement: 3 sand	Screed mix: 1 OPC cement: 3 sand

Easily eroded
Porous
Flexible

Durable
Waterproof
Brittle

Mortar Table 1 - Key Costs

Cement (OPC)	£ 4.65 25kg bag	£ 0.19 kg
White Cement (OPC)	£ 11.50 25kg bag	£ 0.46 kg
Hydrated Lime	£ 9.40 25kg bag	£ 0.38 kg
Hydraulic Lime	£ 11.00 25kg bag	£ 0.44 kg
Lime Putty	£ 10.00 per 20 lts	£ 0.50 lt
Sand	£ 35.00 per tonne	£ 0.035 kg
Plasticiser	£ 1.00 per lt	£ 1.00 lt

MODEL HOUSE Mortar Costs

	Area in m²	m³ per m³	Total
Brickwork	200	6.7	£ 108	£ 720
Blockwork (plasticer mix)	255	3.2	£ 108	£ 340
65mm Screed	80	5.3	£ 142	£ 760
Rounded Total for All Mortar			**£ 1,820**

Mortar Table 2 - What's in a m³ of Mortar

		SAND			CEMENT			LIME			PLASTICISER	
	Cost per m³	Lts	tonnes	Cost	Lts	Kg	Cost	Lts	Kg	Cost	Lts	Cost
Screed Mix (1:3)	£ 142	1000	1.6	£ 56	330	462	£ 86					
Masonry cement mix (1:5)	£ 108	1000	1.6	£ 56	200	280	£ 52					
Plasticiser mix (1:6)	£ 103	1000	1.6	£ 56	175	245	£ 46				1.2	£ 1
Snowcrete mix (1:6)	£ 170	1000	1.6	£ 56	175	245	£ 113				1.2	£ 1
OPC/Lime mix (1:1:6)	£ 141	1000	1.6	£ 56	175	245	£ 46	175	105	£ 39		
Hydrated Lime Mix (1:3)	£ 130	1000	1.6	£ 56				330	198	£ 74		
Hydraulic Lime Mix (1:3)	£ 140	1000	1.6	£ 56				330	198	£ 87		
Lime Putty mix (1:3)	£ 200	1000	1.6	£ 56				330		£ 165		

Mortar Table 3 - How far does a m³ of mortar get you?

	m³ of mortar lays			m³ mortar/m²	lts mortar/m²	Typical Cost/m²
Bricks, single skin work, with frogs up, 10mm bed	1800 No	or	30 m²	0.03	33	£3.60
Bricks, single skin, frogs down or no frogs, 10mm bed	2800 No	or	47 m²	0.02	21	£2.32
100mm Blockwork, single skin, 10mm beds	800 No	or	80 m²	0.01	13	£1.35
12mm Render			80 m²	0.01	13	£1.35
50mm Screed			20 m²	0.05	50	£7.10
65mm Screed			15 m²	0.07	67	£9.50

OPC cement and cannot readily be used below temperatures of 10°C: use that on your external brickwork and you'll be hanging around forever waiting for the stuff to set. Alternatively, there are different types of bagged lime available which you can use as an alternative to putty. Hydrated lime is essentially dried lime putty and readily available from builder's merchants but lacks strength without a little cement to bind it, whilst hydraulic limes can be used instead of cement and having once been difficult to obtain is now also widely available from builder's merchants.

Hydraulic lime mixed with a sharp sand gives a lovely natural colour to a mortar which goes down well with conservation officers, but it can be very slow to lay and bricklayers will probably not love you for specifying it.

If you want the lime look without the lime hassle, then you can cheat and use white cement, sold as Snowcrete. It's over twice the price of OPC but still a little cheaper than using lime.

TIMBER

You rarely see the price of timber advertised and you rarely see it on display in timber yards. This is because there is a wide range of prices charged for timber. The regular trade prices are usually around 33% less than those charged to casual in-off-the-street customers and large orders will get another 5 to 10% off the regular trade prices. The way to get good prices is invariably to send your (hopefully) large order in for quotation at least two weeks before you require it. By all means include second-fix items like skirting boards which you may not need for several months; it makes you look more like a serious customer.

CARCASSING

Most construction grade timber is spruce, usually referred to as carcassing, whitewood or deal — presumably because it's a good deal. It is relatively cheap and easy to work but it suffers from being one of the least durable timbers available. Of more interest to the builder is the strength of any particular piece of timber and there are several grading systems run by the timber trade for assessing this. The commonest form of grading at present is to see timber labelled as SC3 or SC4. SC4 timber is the stronger and the advantage of paying the 5% more for SC4 timber is that you are allowed to use them over longer spans. For instance the longest distance you can bridge with a 50x175 mm section of timber is 3170 mm in SC3, but this length rises to 3380 mm in SC4. SC3 and SC4 are British Standards and moves are afoot to replace them with Euro gradings, C16 and C24 respectively.

KILN-DRIED TIMBER

In 1995, it became compulsory to use low moisture timber in all internal structural applications – which means joists, studwork walls and roofs. Low moisture is defined as having a moisture content below 20% and in effect this means using kiln-dried timber.

The advantage of kiln dried timber is that it is dimensionally stable – it will not twist or warp as cheaper timber will, especially if it's been treated – and that it is regularised, which means that it has all been milled to an accuracy of 1 mm. It is thus very much quicker and easier to put up accurate studwork and to fix flooring joists; non-regularised timber can sometimes vary in depth by 5 mm or more and this is very noticeable when flooring is being laid over it.

Having said that, there is a lot of supposedly regularised timber around which varies by plus or minus 5mm, sometimes even more, so the term is regularly abused. And in truth, 20% moisture content is still much higher than the final settlement level reached in a centrally heated house (about 8%), so shrinkage still takes place. But kiln-dried timber is still a step in the right direction.

TIMBER TREATMENT

Spruce is not classified as a durable timber and this means that it is liable to rot if exposed to continuous damp. This has led to the increasingly widespread use of timber preservatives to add durability. These preservatives can be applied by brush on site but more normally the timbers are immersed in a vacuum-pressure tank, which leads to them being referred to as having been 'vacuum treated'. There are two rival systems in regular use in the UK, Tanalising and Protimising. There is little to choose between them in price – they add around 10% to the cost of the raw timber – but they do perform rather differently.

Tanalising is a water-based treatment which tends to dye the wood a light green colour although there is now a brown-dye version as well (useful if you plan to use brown or black stains). Protimising is spirit-based and usually leaves the wood uncoloured, although sometimes a red dye is added. You can usually tell if timber has been Protimised from the pungent, petrol-like smell. Generally tanalising is preferred in applications where there is contact with the ground, like fencing, and protimising is preferred for structural timber (and joinery) because it is less likely to cause the timber to twist. Tanalising used to use arsenic as one of its ingredients; it has been reformulated to avoid this particular gremlin and is sometimes referred to by a different name, such as AC500. However, it will take a good few years before British builders get around to calling it anything other than tanalising

JOINERY GRADE REDWOOD

The other commonly used wood in UK housebuilding is pine, or redwood as it is known. This is a denser and slightly more durable timber than spruce, and it is commonly used to manufacture windows and internal applications like skirting boards, floorboards and matchboard walling. It is more easily worked than spruce and it is most frequently seen in timber yards with a planed finish, usually referred to as Planed All Round (PAR) or Planed Square Edge (PSE). Scandinavia is the major supplier of redwoods.

You can use cheaper whitewoods for internal applications but they suffer from having what are called dead knots, which tend to work loose and fall out with time. Your mice may appreciate the odd dead knot in your skirting board but you will probably prefer to have timber with live knots that move with the timber as it expands and contracts.

SPECIALIST SOFTWOODS

There are a number of more specialised softwoods:

■ Douglas Fir is particularly resinous and durable and it performs as well as many hardwoods. It is a favourite in high specification windows although one problem is that it doesn't hold paint well: wood stains are the solution.

■ Hemlock is another North American speciality softwood that is mostly used in door construction.

■ Cedar is particularly durable and really doesn't require any sort of on site treatment at all. However, its use is limited, tending to be restricted to external claddings such as garage doors, and roofing, and increasingly, weatherboarded exteriors.

■ Parana Pine. This is a lovely looking South American timber, popular in several internal applications such as window boards and staircases. It is anything but durable and is very prone to buckling.

HARDWOODS

Generally, hardwoods are not an alternative to softwoods. Rather, they tend to get used in particular applications like flooring and kitchen worksurfaces where softwoods are not commonly used. Joinery is the obvious exception to this rule: see the section 'Joinery' in the Superstructure Chapter 7, where the pros and cons are examined. Also check the chapter, 'Green Issues', for the low down on tropical hardwoods.

14

GREEN ISSUES

Most of the interest in this field – and indeed, most of this chapter – is to do with saving energy. Our fascination with this topic really began during the 1974 oil crisis when people assumed – incorrectly – that we were facing a permanent fuel shortage and consequentially rocketing fuel prices. However, in more recent times, concern has grown that the ambient temperature of the entire planet Earth is increasing rather rapidly, a phenomenon known to us all now as global warming or climate change. Despite many people claiming that this could be a natural phenomenon,

a very large finger of suspicion is pointing at us and, in particular, our dirty habit of burning masses and masses of fossil fuels and thereby releasing carbon dioxide (CO_2) into the atmosphere.

Reckoning that it is probably better to be safe than sorry, many governments have been signing accords to reduce levels of carbon emissions although, as environmentalists point out, not by very much and sometimes by nothing at all. And then there's Trump...

As private households contribute about a third of our national CO_2

emissions, the effect of these undertakings has for many years been trickling down to the Building Regulations in the hope that stricter codes for new building will bring about some reduction in our energy consumption. Hence many of the changes to the building regs are to do directly with reducing CO_2 emissions.

Energy saving is, however, not the be-all and end-all of environmental concerns and I'll start the chapter by taking a look at some of the other issues, including an assessment of how much energy is used in actually constructing a new house.

CONSTRUCTION AUDIT

This book may be green-tinged but it is not what anyone would call an eco-handbook. If you want to know more about green options then there are dozens of other titles available and I can especially recommend *The Whole House Book* by Pat Borer and Cindy Harris, which gives a good overview of the many different ways there are to build and Tim Pullen's *Sustainable Building Bible* which covers the materials and technology in greater depth than I have here.

Whatever your personal views on green issues, what can't be denied is that the green perspective has caused mainstream housebuilding to examine just what it does, and to look at ways it could be improved.

For most of the 20th century housebuilding in Britain was driven by the desire to make houses cheaper and easier to construct. Now the agenda is subtly shifting so that at last we are beginning to worry about what it is that we are building. Is it any good? How much damage does it cause in order to get built? How long will it last? Can it be safely disposed of when we've finished with it? In a word, sustainability. How does a typical new house stack up?

TRADE BALANCE

Materials going into a masonry-built detached house, such as our

MODEL HOUSE Construction Audit

Material Quantities and Embodied CO2 Used to Construct Benchmark House

MATERIAL	MATERIAL QUANTITY	DENSITY MULTIPLIER	WEIGHT (in tonnes)	Kg CO2e/kg	Embodied CO2 (in tonnes)
Concrete	25 m³	2.3	60	0.10	6.0
Bricks	12000 No	0.003	36	0.23	8.3
Aerated Blocks	255 m²	0.1	26	0.30	7.7
Concrete Floor Beams	95 m²	0.15	10	0.10	1.0
Sand	15 t		15	0.01	0.1
Cement	5 t		5	0.73	3.7
Natural Slate	122 m²	0.05	6	0.06	0.4
Concrete Paving	35 m²	0.15	5	0.10	0.5
Hardcore and Gravel	50 m³	1.6	80	0.01	0.4
Timber	12 m³	0.5	6	0.30	1.8
Chipboard/Plywood	5 m³	0.5	2.5	0.40	1.0
Plasterboard	500 m²	0.01	5	0.38	1.9
Acoustic Insulation	10 m³	0.04	0.4	1.40	0.6
Foam Insulation	36 m³	0.05	2	3.50	7.0
Steel	1 t		1	1.50	1.5
Double Glazing	35 m²	0.03	1.1	0.80	0.9
Plastic/uPVC	0.25 t		0.25	2.70	0.7
Sanitaryware	0.4 t		0.4	1.50	0.6
Others Materials	1 t		1	1.00	1.0
TOTAL			**260**	**0**	**45**

COMPARISONS		kWh/annum	Tonnes CO2	
Annual energy use	A: Benchmark House Built to 2013 standards	14,000	3.1	20% elec: 80% gas
	B: Same House Built to Passivhaus standards	8,000	2.0	30% elec;70% gas
	C: Same House Built to 1975 standards	24,000	5.3	10% elec: 90% gas
	Family Car Doing 12,000mls/annum		3.5	
	Family of 4 flying to Spain and back		2.0	
	16 PV panels saving 1 tonne CO2 per annum		3.6	

Upgrading a new build to Passivhaus standard saves just over a tonne of CO2 per annum, at an additional load of around 4-5 tonnes embodied CO2 (mostly insulation and triple glazing).

Switching away from masonry construction and plastic insulation towards timber and other natural materials has the potential to halve embodied CO2.

But in the long run energy efficiency still trumps embodied energy as a way of reducing CO2 usage. As long as the house survives longer than 25 years.....

PV panels have a 3 - 4 year energy payback.

model house in Chapter 2, would weigh around 260 tonnes, the vast majority of which will have been produced within 200 miles of the house. Timber (6 tonnes) is the only significant import by weight, although copper (used extensively in plumbing and wiring) and kitchen appliances are also imported. Traditional housebuilding remains an overwhelmingly British business. It is low-tech and uses a lot of very bulky materials that are costly to transport. Even where foreign companies achieve market penetration in Britain, production is usually UK based.

As a rule, Britain runs a trade deficit in building materials. We are net exporters of steel, wallpapers, paints, sanitaryware and even a few bricks (mostly to Japan), whilst timber accounts for around 90% of our net imports, with heating and plumbing gear being the only other significant contributor on this side of the account. Take away timber from the equation and everything else pretty much balances out.

EMBODIED ENERGY

Energy use involved in building any house can be divided into three areas: material production, transport and construction. Broadly speaking, the less a material is processed, the less energy it takes to produce, and the less distance a material travels the less energy is used in getting it there. On-site construction energy use is remarkably low, unless heating and lighting are employed, and even this is unlikely to make a huge difference. The Construction Audit

table summarises the energy used in constructing the model house and it is based on the following figures, taken from Craig Jones's ICE (Inventory or Carbon & Energy) project.

Natural materials take the least energy to produce. Sand, stone, and gravel come into this group: energy used in production is typically under 100kWh/tonne.

Cement is a relatively high energy consumer but it is never used on its own. Cement-based products like concrete and render are surprisingly low on energy use because they have a high proportion of natural sand or stone mixed in with the cement. Concrete products consume around 300 – 500 kWh/tonne.

In contrast, clay-baked products like bricks and clay roof tiles use around three to five times as much energy in production, 1500–2000kWh/tonne. They have to be fired at very high temperatures and this is the main reasons they are more expensive than concrete imitations.

Aerated concrete blocks (i.e. Celcon, Thermalite) use much more energy to produce than standard concrete products, between two and three times as much. But because they are pumped full of air, they are much lighter and so a tonne of these blocks goes a lot further – two to three times further, neatly cancelling out the difference in energy consumed in manufacture.

Timber is an interesting case. The ICE project reckons on a figure of around 2000kWh/tonne. Part of this is explained by the energy costs in

transportation and in kiln-drying, but it's also partly explained by the carbon present in the timber itself. Many sources regard this as sequestered or captured carbon and go as far as claiming that timber as a product is therefore carbon positive. ICE takes a different view and suggests that it ignores the fact that eventually this carbon will be released into the atmosphere. Furthermore, they take a view that on a global scale timber is still being used faster than its being replaced, so that it's just plain wrong to count it as a renewable material.

You can see that this embodied energy stuff is not straightforward. Not straightforward at all. Timber products like chipboard, OSB and plywood score even worse than sawn timber. However, bear in mind that timber is relatively lightweight so a tonne goes a long way.

Other typical scores include:
- Plasterboard, around 800kWh/tonne
- Glass: uses 5,000 kWh/tonne
- Steel: uses around 7,000 kWh/tonne
- Copper, brass, zinc: use between 10,000 and 15,000kWh/tonne
- Aluminium: uses 40,000 kWh/tonne
- Plastic (including uPVC): uses 20,000 kWh/tonne – but a tonne goes a long way.

A word about these figures. I have used the kWh/tonne figures unchanged since the first edition of the book back in 1995. In this edition, I have, in addition, converted the kWhs to tonnes CO_2 released, which is arguably the whole point of this embodied energy exercise. However, the conversion rate is also a matter of guesswork as we really have little idea just how the goods were actually made. I have assumed that all the fired products (i.e. cement, bricks, glass, steel) will have been cooked with gas. It's probably safe to assume they didn't use a microwave. My big point is, however, all these figures should be treated with caution. Although this is The Housebuilder's Bible, they are not gospel!

COMPARISONS

The table breaks down the embodied energy that went into the model house, which I calculate at around 180,000 kWh, equivalent to 36 tonnes of CO_2. This sounds like a lot but let's put the figure in context. 36 tonnes of CO_2 equates to around ten years motoring in a family car, or flying the family to Australia and back three times.

More pertinently, the UK releases around 10 tonnes of CO_2 per head per annum, and the model house, with three residents, will be expected to release about four tonnes. In it's older, pre-insulated state, this four tonnes would be as much as 15 tonnes so a new house is saving a lot of CO_2 compared to the older housing stock.

Were it to be a replacement dwelling, it would claw back the 36 tonnes of CO_2 released by building it within four years. But of course, it's not a replacement dwelling so even though it is relatively energy efficient, its very existence is still adding to the overall national carbon emissions.

Bear in mind, finally, that when we hear talk about our housing stock producing 30% of our national CO_2 emissions, it's not actually our housing stock but the people who live in our housing stock. Left to its own devices – i.e. empty – our housing stock doesn't produce anything.

ENVIRONMENTAL AUDIT
EXTRACTION OF AGGREGATES

Around 90% by weight of the model house is composed of sands and gravels and clays, much of it bound together with cement. With 180,000 new houses being built in the UK each year, something like three cubic miles of materials are being extracted annually to meet this demand.

That's an awful lot of holes in the ground and it's one area where new house building is particularly greedy. Quarries pose no long-term health risks and, arguably, the scars of quarrying are actually healed remarkably quickly. However, that doesn't make quarries attractive to nearby residents and new quarrying proposals are always hotly disputed.

TIMBER

The weight of timber used to construct houses is minute in comparison with masonry/concrete products. The model house uses about 12m³ (6 tonnes) of wood and wood-based products. Were it a timber-frame build, this figure would probably double. On the face of it, building with timber would seem to be very desirable but there are a few snags:

■ Logging often has more in common with mineral extraction than agriculture; even so-called sustainable sources are often permanently damaged after the virgin crop is removed to be replaced by monotonous, species-thin plantations.
■ Almost all structural timber has to be imported into Britain, making it the one major building component not to be sourced in the UK.

TROPICAL HARDWOODS

The problem with using tropical hardwoods is to do with the way in which they are harvested (or plundered) with acres of virgin rainforest being destroyed often to fell just one particularly nice mahogany tree. By and large this land is then cleared and used for rather poor cattle grazing. This sort of wanton destruction is going on all over the tropics and, in truth, is as much to do with burgeoning population growth as it is with extracting hardwoods, but there is no doubt that the hardwood trade plays a significant part.

However, the environmental problems resulting from using these hardwoods in new housebuilding should not be exaggerated: their use is rare precisely because of their expense. Brazilian mahogany is specified as standard as a cill detail on timber door frames but otherwise you have to go looking for materials – chiefly joinery – made out of tropical hardwoods. Another area where you may stumble across them is as constituents of better-grade plywoods (Far Eastern) and blockboards, but these are more commonly used for shelving than construction; MDF can be used as a cheaper substitute.

HEALTH RISKS
FORMALDEHYDE

This glue is used to bind timber panel products, chiefly chipboards, MDF and plywoods. Some people are known to react badly to the fumes that are released very slowly over a period of months after manufacture, a process known as off-gassing. However, adverse reactions are rare and exact causes are difficult to pinpoint. Almost all volatile organic compounds (VOCs) have come under suspicion – including carpets and clothes – and it remains a complex and poorly understood area. You can, of course, build and furnish a house from entirely natural materials but it is an expensive option and it's still not guaranteed to avoid VOCs.

SOLVENTS

Solvents are used in oil-based paints, stains and varnishes, as well as adhesives and mastics. Many people actually like the smell of solvents but long-term exposure to them has been linked with brain damage. Occasional users probably need not be alarmed, but be aware that solvents are likely to be far more damaging to young children than to adults; if youngsters (and pregnant women) are present then you would do well to consider using water-based paints and stains indoors.

WOOD PRESERVATIVES

One normally associates timber treatment with remedial work carried out on old houses, but a great deal of new timber gets pre-treated with either water-based tanalith or solvent-based protim. The tanalising treatments used to be based on the copper-chrome-arsenic compounds (CCAs) whilst the spirit-based systems use a cocktail of chemical nasties such as lindane, pentachlorophenol (PCPs) and tri-butyl-tin-oxide (TBTOs). Neither is particularly pleasant and the tanaliths have been reformulated to be less toxic to us. They serve a dual purpose: one is to reduce risk of fungal infestations such as dry rot, the other is to reduce risk of insect attack such as woodworm and death watch beetle. The idea is that treated timber will taste so foul that insects and fungus will steer well clear: the danger is that these chemicals won't do us much good either.

External joinery is pre-treated as a matter of course and NHBC regulations require that timber in exposed walls is treated. There is a potential long term hazard, although this is rather along the lines of the formaldehyde and VOC threat – i.e. no one can say what it is – but there is also a more immediate danger to site carpenters who inevitably come into physical contact with treated timbers. Wearing gloves is not really an option for a chippie: the best precaution is to ensure that the timber is dried properly before it is worked; sometimes it arrives on site still dripping with the chemical preservatives, having just come out of the vacuum tank.

Some commentators maintain that if the design detailing is good then the timber does not need preserving, but preservation is now an industry standard. Note that timber frame kit houses tend to come with pre-treated timber specified everywhere, whether it's actually needed or not.

ASBESTOS

Asbestos was widely used in the UK building industry through most of the last century. It was only during the 1980s that it started to become blacklisted and it was still being used, mixed with cement, through till 1999. The danger from asbestos relates to breathing in the dust. In its solid format, it doesn't represent a threat (unless you start bashing it about, thus releasing the dust).

It was used in all kinds of places: Artex (which was 2% asbestos until 1984), asbestos-cement roofing sheets, inside airing cupboards and around stoves and boilers, pipe lagging, ironing boards, night storage radiators, fire doors, artificial slates, wall boards. One of the most dangerous formats was a fire-proof board called Astbestolux, later replaced by an asbestos-free version called Supalux. There is a lot of asbestos about and if you get involved with demolition or renovation of an old building, you need to know how to handle the risk.

There are some fairly exacting requirements in place for commercial enterprises, including builders and demolition contractors. Every commercial building is now meant to have an Asbestos Register detailing if and where asbestos is located. But the situation with private householders is still largely unregulated, which means that if you have asbestos in your house you can more or less dispose of it as you wish. Except you can't just take it to any old tip, but to one designated to take hazardous waste.

My local council, South Cambs, offers sealable sacks to householders in which to place their own asbestos remains and there is one tip in the county you can take it all to, for which there is no additional charge. I guess they have to consider the alternative: fly tipping.

MDF

The problems related to formaldehyde have already been touched on and are not unique to MDF. However MDF is the board that gets worked most and it tends to produce the finest dust which sails through the average dust mask as if it's not there. This combination is reckoned (by some) to make MDF a hazard on a par with asbestos and moves are afoot to produce a similar board made with safer resins. Passive consumers of MDF products are unlikely to be at risk but you should look out if you work with a lot of MDF dust.

CEMENT

Human skin does not react well with wet cement and concrete mixes; there is no instant sign that burning is taking place and many people assume that it is therefore harmless. It's not; prolonged exposure will cause very nasty burns. Bear in mind, that much the same thing happens with lime as well.

GLASS FIBRE

Glass fibre insulation, together with the closely related mineral wool, are unpleasantly itchy on skin, and eyes like it even less. Thought by some to be similar to asbestos in effect, others claim that the fibres are generally too large to cause lethal irritation. Whoever proves to be correct, it makes sense not to be macho about it. Wear gloves and a mask when insulating. Or use sheep's wool, if you can afford it.

UPVC

The use of uPVC has been growing steadily in housebuilding. You will find it in plastic guttering and drainage pipes, in electric cable and, of course, uPVC windows and doors. However there is a vociferous campaign (led in this country by Greenpeace) against the use of uPVC, principally on the grounds that its production is a dirty, polluting business leading to the release of dioxins and the dumping of chlorine. What is not clear is whether uPVC manufacture is any worse than the rest of the chemicals/plastics industry.

THE ENERGY EFFICIENCY REGS

The building regulations regarding energy efficiency in the home have grown progressively more complex over the years. In England & Wales building regs are broken up into Parts that are lettered from A through to R (with the odd confusing letter like I and O missed out). Part L is the one that deals with energy efficiency and Part L is now a complex beast which has been through many changes. Part L used to have a table in it that told you what U values you needed to meet, and it was a fairly simple calculation to get from that to a particular depth of insulation. No more.

In its sixth iteration, the 2006 version, it moved everything across to a whole house heat calculation approach and asked for the sum of the heat loss for the whole house to be no more than a certain figure, known as the Dwelling Emission Rate. Technically, this is a superior method of going about things because it allows you to trade off one poorly performing element against a better one somewhere else in the design. But from the point of view of simple comprehension, it is a disaster because no one really knows how to meet the regs anymore, and they have to hire expensive consultants to work it out.

In 2010, Part L included for the first time a Fabric Energy Efficiency Standard (or FEES) as an approach to meeting the regs. This is very similar to miles per litre or gallon on a car and for the first time gives some indication of how much fuel a home is likely to burn. The idea was that a very exacting standard would be imposed by the time the 2016 version of Part L came into effect.

2016 was critical because this was the point when we were meant to be building nothing but zero-carbon homes. But since the zero-carbon house was first mentioned back in

2006, the exact definition of what it meant was the subject to hot debate.

The Labour government flunked it and left office in 2010 without ever having resolved this issue. The Coalition never really got to grips with it and for five years it stayed on the back burner. But when the Tories were unexpectedly re-elected in 2015 without the LibDems to keep them in check, they dropped the zero-carbon proposals like a hot brick.

Out went many of the renewable energy subsidies, the Code for Sustainable Homes (of which the zero carbon home target was the clowning glory) and any aim to further tighten the energy efficiency regs. Part L was last tightened in 2013 and that looks like it will be where it will stay, especially as Brexit now looms large on the horizon. Not that Part L had an awful lot to do with Europe (building regs are still steadfastly national), but I suspect our government will have its focus on other matters for the next few years.

The real deal, in terms of energy efficiency, is being left to a German performance standard known as Passivhaus. More on this later.

So what's in Part L, the 2013 version? It's split into four sub-parts, known as L1A, L1B, L2A and L2B. The L1s deal with housing, the L2s with everything else. The 1s deal with new builds and the 2s deal with renovations and conversions. You can download them for free at the Planning Portal website (Celtic territories have their own websites too).

So L1A (new homes) basically requires that any new house you

build is 6% more energy efficient than the version you would have built before 2013. It leaves it up to you how to do that, but your design has to be measured against a document known as SAP (Standard Assessment Procedure) which indicated the likely energy loss from all manner of details.

Once upon a time, you could go through this exercise with a pencil, filling in values into boxes, but now it's all done by spreadsheet. Every aspect of the build, from the shape and dimensions, through the orientation and the shading, to the way its actually built and heated, gets fed into the spreadsheet, and the answer has to be below 'x' to get a pass. If your answer doesn't meet the target, then you have to go back and redesign the house until it does. You get penalised if you plan to burn anything other than mains gas or biomass, and therefore have to make the structure even more energy efficient. And there is still a table with limits on your design standards:

- The roof must have a U value of 0.2 or less
- The walls must have a U value of 0.3 or less
- The floor must have a U value of 0.25 or less
- Any party wall must have a U value of 0.2 or less
- Windows, roof lights and doors must have a U value of 2.0 or less
- Air permeability must be 10 air changes an hour under pressure or better

Now these are not the standards. If you were to build to these levels, you wouldn't meet Part L 2013. You have to be better, but exactly how much

better is difficult to tell. Gone are the days when we could safely say 'stuff 80mm on mineral wool in the wall cavity and you'll be fine'. But when all is said and done, there will end up being standard solutions – probably about 150mm of mineral wool insulation in the walls.

L1B is a bit different. As it deals with how you insulate an existing structure, you can't really go around doing whole house heat loss calcs. So it's rather more like the older versions of Part L in this respect. In fact, lurking inside Part L1B is the table that tells you what U values you should be using, the one that is so annoyingly hidden from view in Part L1A. It goes like this:

- Walls – U value 0.18
- Roofs – 0.13
- Floors – 0.13
- Windows – 1.4
- Solid doors – 1.0
- Air tightness – 5 air changes per hour

There was once a move to introduce consequential improvements for home extenders, so that you would be forced to spend additional money on upgrading the energy performance of the rest of the house, but this has never been implemented, due to fear of negative 'Daily Mail' type publicity.

PERFORMANCE METRICS

A word about how these energy efficiency standards are measured. Back in the old days (before 2006), we were used to talking about walls with such and such a U value. Generally, the lower the U value, the more energy efficient the house was likely to be, as the way to lower the U value is to stuff insulation everywhere.

But whereas U values can be a good indicator of how individual elements, like walls, behave, they don't tell you an awful lot about whether the whole house is energy efficient or not. So the move is now underway to describe the energy efficiency levels in terms of how many kilowatt hours a year (expressed as kWh/m²/annum) it takes to keep a house warm and comfortable.

These metrics are known as Fabric Energy Efficiency Standards or FEES. At the moment, it is reckoned that the 2013 building regs will come out at around 60kWh/m²/annum: the PassivHaus standard looks to score no more than 15kWh/m²/annum.

UNDERSTANDING U VALUES

You can't really get to grips with the concepts behind energy efficiency in buildings without having an understanding of what a U value is. So now is a good place to digress into the world of building science and to try and establish just what a U value might be.

Like most of the other values in our society, U values are declining; however, in this case, declining values are broadly welcomed. You see, a U value is a measure of heat loss and a material with a low U value loses less heat than one with a high U value. In many ways, that's all you need to know. However, a U value is not like a

moral value which you either have or haven't got; it's actually a scientifically derived measurement and knowing your U values will help you make a whole lot more sense of your decisions about how to build and heat your house.

A U value is a measurement of the heat flow (measured in watts) through a square metre (m²) of a building element for every 1°C temperature difference between the inside and the outside. That reads like the horrible sort of definition you had to learn for science A-levels, which is why you never did one. It's actually got three different bits to it and in an algebra lesson they'd call them a, b, and c and make it even more unintelligible. However the point that it's trying to make is dead simple: some things are better at retaining heat than others. It's something you know instinctively without ever having to ascribe a value to it – after all you know just how many clothes you need to wear to feel comfortable. The U value is just some poor sod's attempt at quantifying this fact.

In fact the U value of just about everything you could ever think of using to construct a house has been worked out under laboratory conditions. What they do is establish how quickly heat leaks out of any given material – the boffins call this thermal conductivity. The answer is expressed as a value, known as the lambda value, which is in fact the same as the U value for a one metre thick slab of this material. The better the insulator, the lower the heat leakage rate.

Our best insulators, things like polyurethane foams, have a lambda value of 0.025watts whilst a poor insulator like granite has a value of 2.9watts. From which you can deduce that polyurethane is around 100 times better than granite as an insulator or, put another way, a 1mm strip of polyurethane would keep you as warm as a 100mm wide granite block.

The final U value of a material is found by dividing the lambda value of the material by its actual width in metres. Thus 50mm (or 0.05m) of polyurethane foam (lambda value 0.025 remember) has a U value of 0.025 ÷ 0.05 = 0.5.

Now that's all fine and dandy but there is a mathematical problem to be faced here. A wall is conventionally made up of maybe four or five different elements. Each one has its own U value and each contributes in some way to the insulating capabilities of that wall. In order to work out the cumulative U value of the wall you need some method of combining these values. You can't just add the U values together or subtract them from one another; you get a nonsensical answer. The trick is done by switching U values into R values, resistance values. R values are a mirror image of U values – the higher they go, the more they resist the passage of heat.

To switch between U values and R values you always divide the number you are working with into 1. So a U value of 0.5 is an R value of 2.0 (i.e. 1 ÷ 0.5 = 2). And an R value of 4 is the same as a U value of 0.25 (i.e.

R Values for Common Building Materials

	THERMAL CONDUCTIVITY	DEPTH IN mm	R VALUE
INSULATION			
Mineral Wool Loose Quilt	0.04	100	2.50
	0.04	150	3.75
Cavity Batts	0.038	200	5.26
	0.038	100	2.63
Timber Frame Batts	0.038	150	3.95
Expanded Polystyrene	0.038	140	3.68
	0.04	100	2.50
Extruded Polystyrene	0.04	200	5.00
	0.03	80	2.67
Polyurethane or PIRs	0.03	150	5.00
	0.025	80	3.20
OTHER MATERIALS			
Softwood	0.13	25	0.19
	0.13	50	0.38
Hardwood	0.18	25	0.14
	0.18	50	0.28
Plywood/Chipboard	0.13	9	0.07
	0.13	18	0.14
	0.13	22	0.17
Plasterboard	0.25	9.5	0.04
	0.25	12.5	0.05
add for Foil Backing			0.20
uPVC	0.4	2	0.01
Clay Brick	0.77	102	0.13
Clinker Blocks	0.57	100	0.18
Aerated (Celcon)	0.18	100	0.56
Concrete Blocks	1.9	100	0.05
Granite	2.9	100	0.03
Limestone	1.7	100	0.06
Sandstone	2.3	100	0.04
Clay Tile	1.0	10	0.01
Concrete Tile	1.5	12	0.01
50mm Screed	0.4	50	0.13
65mm Screed	0.4	65	0.16
100mm Concrete Slab	1.3	100	0.08
150mm Concrete Slab	1.3	150	0.12
Render	0.57	12	0.02
Finish Plasters	0.57	3	0.01
AIR GAPS			
Cavity 25mm plus			0.20
10mm or less			0.10
Ventilated Loft Space			0.20

R Values into U Values

Element	R Value
External Surface Resistance	0.06
Brickwork	0.12
150mm Cavity Insulation	3.66
100mm Blockwork	0.30
Plaster	0.12
Internal Surface Resistance	0.12
Combined Total of R Values	**4.38**
U value = 1/R value	**U Value**
U Value of Wall	**0.23**

$1 \div 4 = 0.25$). Unlike U values, you can add R values together and get a coherent answer. When you've added all the R values together to give you a cumulative R value figure, you can then convert this total back to U values. It's not that difficult.

Interestingly, the Americans prefer to work everything in R values and you rarely see them refer to U values. Note, however, that if you get hold of some US building literature and you think their R values look amazingly high, it's not because they only build eco-cabins but because they use imperial measurements. A metric R value is worth 5.68 imperial ones. R values are arguably a simpler concept than U values – the higher the better – but U values are more useful because you can use them for whole house heat calculations.

COMMENTARY

The R value table covers most of the regular building elements that you might meet in constructing a new house. You can use it to roughly work out your own construction's U values by adding all the R values together

and dividing 1 by the result.

I have used the most regular thicknesses, but if you are not using one of these, remember that R values can be scaled up or down directly in proportion to the thickness of the material so that you can readily calculate your own. And also bear in mind that in more complex layers, such as a timber stud wall where the voids are filled with insulation, you have to work out the average R value based on the proportions of the area that are timber and insulation – typically 20% is timber and 80% is insulation.

Eagle-eyed readers will be asking 'Where's the glass?' Glass is a special case; when it's sunny, it gains heat. Windows tend to get attributed U values depending on the performance of the overall glass and frame combo; they also get marked up or down depending on the orientation.

GROUND FLOORS

U values for ground floors are also a special case and the process for calculating them is a little different, partly because heat has a reluctance to travel in a downwards direction. More importantly, the cold bridging effect around the edges of the floors is pronounced and so a key calculation is concerned not only with the R values of all the bits of the floor but in establishing a ratio of the edge or perimeter of the floor with the area of the floor. You measure the length of the perimeter walls (heated area only) in metres and divide the result by the area of the floor (heated area only) in square metres. It makes no difference

Ground Floor R values

EDGE: AREA RATIO	R VALUE	U VALUE
0.2	2.8	0.36
0.3	2.0	0.5
0.4	1.6	0.6
0.5	1.4	0.7
0.6	1.2	0.8
0.7	1.1	0.9
0.8	1.0	1.0

if your ground floor is suspended or ground bearing, timber or concrete. On the model house the calculation looks like this:

■ Perimeter walls of house are 40m long; ground floor (heated area only) is 80m². Calculation is 40÷80 = 0.50.

This ratio has to be looked up on a table from which the R value and the U value can be read off - remember the U value = 1 ÷ R value. Deconstruct the table and you can see that the bigger and squarer the building, the less heat it loses through the ground floor.

HEAT CALCS AND ENERGY RATINGS

So if we are required to undertake a heat loss calculation by the building regs, let's look at what this involves. I have run some simplified heat calculations through the spreadsheet showing how it's all done. The measurements are taken for one of my old benchmark houses but the U values and the ventilation rates are adjusted with

some licence. I then compare the building standards.

The 1975 house reflects how we built homes then, with little or no insulation. As you might suspect, it leaks heat.

The 2013 house is built to the standards in place in England and Wales at the time of going to press (2019).

The Eco House or Passivhaus standard is an example of an ultra-low energy dwelling which requires very little heating. The principles are always the same. Increase the insulation levels to such a degree that lightbulbs, appliances and body heat (the so-called incidentals) cover the vast bulk of the heat loss for the house, right down to your designed-for minimum external temperature.

The calculations work as follows:

■ 1. You start with measuring the areas of the different parts of the house fabric - i.e. walls, roof, floors, joinery. NB The walls and roof figure should exclude the area taken up by the joinery.

■ 2. You then attribute a U value to each of these areas.

■ 3. You multiply each area by its U value. The result is the specific heat loss (SHL) for each area.

■ 4. You add a bit on to account for thermal bridging – that is unanticipated losses through bits of the structure which are not quite so well insulated as you might hope: for instance, through wall ties, lintels, junctions, meter boxes.

■ 5. You then work out the specific heat loss for the ventilation. To do

this you need to know the volume of the heated air space in the house in cubic metres. And you need to factor in the number of air changes per hour. This used to be very hit and miss affair but the last (2013) changes to the building regs bring air tightness to the fore and require you to undertake an airtightness test, even though the standard required is not very exacting.

If you are building a new home you could probably hazard a guess that you would get to around the half air change per hour mark. Multiply the air changes per hour by the volume and you get the volume of new air passing through the house every hour. Multiply this figure by 0.33 Watts, the specific heat of air (or the heat required to lift 1m³ of air through 1°C) and you have a specific heat figure for your ventilation requirements.

■ 6. You then add all these figures together to give you a specific heat loss for the whole house. This is the amount of heat, in watts, that it takes to lift the entire house through 1°C. This is the critical figure in the calculations, known as the specific heat loss. It's sort of a sum of all the U values. The lower the specific heat loss, the better insulated the structure is.

As it's a measurement in watts, you can easily apply a multiplier to it to find out how much heat you need to keep the house warm on the coldest day.

Normally we work to a design temperature of -1°C in England and Wales and -4°C in Scotland.

MODEL HOUSE Specific Heat Loss

Elements	Area		U VALUE	Build Standard 1975	2013	Passivhaus
A: UPSTAIRS FLAT CEILINGS	80	m²				
1975 - little or no insulation		x	0.8	64 w		
2013 standards 180mm Pu		x	0.18		14 w	
Passivhaus		x	0.12			10 w
B: EXTERNAL WALLS	200	m²				
1975 - no insulation		x	1.5	300 w		
2013 standards		x	0.22		44 w	
Passivhaus		x	0.12			24 w
C: WINDOWS & DOORS	35	m²				
Single Glazing		x	5.0	175 w		
Double Glazing to 2013 standards		x	1.4		49 w	
Passivhaus		x	0.8			28 w
D: FLOOR	80	m²				
No Insulation		x	0.7	58 w		
2013 standards		x	0.18		14 w	
Passivhaus		x	0.15			12 w
E: Add allowance for THERMAL BRIDGING				99 w	99 w	49 w
F: VENTILATION	430	m³				
Specific Heat of Air	0.33	w/m³				
Heat required for 1 air change/hr	142	w				
1 air change/hr(1975)			1.0	142 w		
2013 standard (0.6 air changes/hr)			0.6		85 w	
Passivhaus (with MVHR)			0.2			21 w
WHOLE HOUSE HEAT LOSS						
Specific Heat Loss	A+B+C+D+E+F			840 w	310 w	140 w
Heat load required for 20°C uplift	SHL x 20 ÷1000			17 kW	6 kW	3 kW
20° uplift/m³	Heat load ÷ volume			39 w	14 w	7 w

ENERGY RATINGS

Energy ratings take the heat loss calcs one stage further and attempt to speculate about how much energy you will actually burn in your home each year. A full-blown energy rating on a house is a complex beast involving many different interlinked calculations. The standard one used by the powers that be is the SAP Rating. Its full title is the Government's Standard Assessment Procedure for Energy Rating Dwellings, and it's forever being tweaked here and there as new products come on to the market. From these figures it's possible to make a stab at your probable energy usage per annum expressed in units of energy, financial cost and CO_2 emissions.

It's very easy to pull holes in energy ratings, if you want to. Much of it is incredibly detailed to an altogether anal degree. Yet other bits use broad-brush assumptions that can only ever approximate real energy use. For instance, hot water use is estimated to rise in proportion to the house floor area. Anyone can see that it's actually more likely to be affected by the number of people living in the house but a dumb spreadsheet can't speculate about that, can it? So in order to be able to compare one house with another, floor area is used a lot. Yet energy ratings are a useful exercise if only to help us understand just how houses work and how they do and do not burn energy.

Rather than go through the SAP calculations step-by-step, I have built a very dumbed down version in the table 'Model House: Energy

Although you are under no obligation to stick to them, the industry standards for desired temperature in each room are as follows:

- Living rooms/kitchen   21°C
- Bedrooms   18°C
- Hall/stairs   16°C
- Bathrooms   22°C

To make the calculations a bit simpler, you can even out all these temperatures to get an average temperature of around 18°C, maybe 19°C if you're a bit of a wuss. In order to keep our homes say 18°C warmer than the minimum design temperatures you would multiply the SHL by 19°C in England & Wales and 22°C in Scotland. The results are always surprisingly small. Try and persuade your plumber that you only need a 5kW boiler in your five bedroom house!

MODEL HOUSE: Energy Ratings

			1975 House	2013 House	Passivhaus
A	Specific Heat Loss (1°C temp diff)	kw	0.84 kW	0.31 kW	0.14 kW
B	Incidentals Heat Gains(body heat, electrics)	kW	1 kW	1 kW	1 kW
C	Incidentals ÷ SHL	B÷A	1.2 °C	3.2 °C	7.1 °C
D	Base Temperature for heating		19.0 °C	19.0 °C	19.0 °C
E	Required uplift after Incidentals	D-C	17.8 °C	15.8 °C	11.9 °C
D	Degree days of heating (look-up in tables)		2,500 dd	1,560 dd	600 dd
G	Annual space heating demand	Fx24xA	50,000 kWh	12,000 kWh	2,000 kWh
	Add for Domestic Hot water				
Ha	say 4 people at 1500kWh ea/annum		6,000 kWh	6,000 kWh	6,000 kWh
Hb	Passivhaus uses solar panels (50% off)				-3,000 kWh
H	Net use for DHW	Ha-Hb	6,000 kWh	6,000 kWh	3,000 kWh
I	Combined total for space heating and DHW	G+H	56,000 kWh	18,000 kWh	5,000 kWh
Gas					
J	Allowance for boiler efficiency		68%	90%	90%
K	kWh actually consumed	I÷J	82,400 kWh	20,000 kWh	5,600 kWh
L	Unit cost of gas/kWh (in pence)	4.0 p			
M	Annual cost (exc standing orders)		£ 3,296	£ 800	£ 224
N	Carbon emissions for gas	0.2 kg/kWh			
P	Carbon emissions in tonne/annum		16.5 t	4 t	1.12 t
Q	Carbon emmissions (kg/m²)	160	103	25	7
Oil					
J	Allowance for boiler efficiency		70%	90%	90%
K	kWh actually consumed	I÷J	80,000 kWh	20,000 kWh	6,000 kWh
L	Unit cost of oil/kWh (in pence)	4.6 p			
M	Annual cost (exc standing orders)		£ 3,680	£ 920	£ 276
N	Carbon emissions for oil	0.3 kg/kWh			
P	Carbon emissions in tonne/annum		24.0 t	6.0 t	1.8 t
Q	Carbon emmissions (kg/m²)	160	150	38	11
Dirty Electricity					
J	Allowance for efficiency		100%	100%	100%
K	kWh actually consumed	I÷J	56,000 kWh	18,000 kWh	5,000 kWh
L	Unit cost of electricity/kWh (in pence)	15 p			
M	Annual cost (exc standing orders)		£ 8,400	£ 2,700	£ 750
N	Carbon emissions for elelctricity	0.52 kg/kWh			
P	Carbon emissions in kg/annum		29.1 t	9.4 t	2.6 t
Q	Carbon emmissions (kg/m²)	160	182	59	16
Electric Ground Source Heat Pump					
J	Efficiency (assumes CoP of 3.0)		300%	300%	300%
K	kWh actually consumed	I÷J	18,667 kWh	£ 6,000 kWh	£ 1,667 kWh
L	Unit cost of electricity/kWh (in pence)	15 p			
M	Annual cost (exc standing orders)		£ 2,800	£ 900	£ 250
N	Carbon emissions for electricity	0.52 kg/kWh			
P	Carbon emissions in kg/annum		9.7 t	3.1 t	0.9 t
Q	Carbon emmissions (kg/m²)	160	61	20	5

Ratings' which shows the basics. The big variables are the Specific Heat Loss (worked out for three different standards in the other table), the fuel used and the boiler efficiencies. Common sense really.

Here are a few notes on the table to help make sense of it.

■ A: Specific Heat Loss (SHL). This is calculated in the table 'Model House: Specific Heat Loss.' It is the basis of the energy rating. Normally it's expressed in watts but here I've divided the watts by 1,000 to express it kilowatts because it makes better sense later on in the table.

■ B: Incidentals. This is the heat that you pump inadvertently into the house by way of lights, appliances, solar gains from sunshine, all those standby lights on computers and TVs and, of course, body heat. A person at rest gives off just over 100 Watts, whilst moderate physical exercise gives off around 400 Watts. In all, incidentals probably contribute between 2,000W (2kW) and 3,000W (3kW) to a typical household. Like much in the world of energy rating, incidentals are very variable and so a vague approximate figure is used. Gains from the residents themselves are ignored.

■ C: Incidentals divided by the Specific Heat Loss. Why? The SHL represents the rate of heat loss from the house for every 1°C temperature difference between inside and outside. If you wish to keep the inside of the house

Degree Days

Base Temp in °C	Degree days	
1	0	
2	60	
3	120	
4	185	
5	265	
6	360	
7	480	
8	620	
9	775	Eco House (Norfolk)
10	950	
11	1140	2013 house (Cornwall)
12	1345	2013 house (Norfolk)
13	1560	
14	1780	20013 house (Caithness)
15	2015	
16	2250	1975 house (Norfolk)
17	2490	
18	2730	
19	2970	
20	3210	

your overall heating requirement. So this figure tells you how much of your heating load will be accounted for by your incidentals. And the answer can be expressed in degrees Celsius because each SHL unit is 1°C. Neat, isn't it?

■ D: Degree days, which are an indicator of how much heat we need to get us through a winter heating season. Every day it goes below an agreed temperature (15°C) counts towards the annual total, and the lower it gets, the more it counts. For instance, if it gets down to zero, then that day would clock up a degree day score of 15, because it was 15°C below the trigger. Total it up for the whole year and you get an annual

degree days total. In Britain it varies from 1,800 DD at Land's End to 3,000 at John O'Groats. The figure of 2,500 DD is taken here, just above average. It's the figure embedded within the SAP calculations – a sort of national average.

■ E: Reduction due to incidentals. Now here's a tweak and a half. Read this one carefully. If your incidentals can be expressed in degrees of heating (see above), then it follows that they can be subtracted from the number of degree days you need to cover. In effect, they lower your 15°C base temperature. Each degree less heat required because of your incidentals amounts to roughly 200 degree days less over a year - in fact the relationship isn't directly proportional but this is a dumbed-down table – what did you expect?

■ G: Having done this calculation, you can then have a healthy stab at how much heat you will actually need in your home to keep it warm throughout the heating season. You take the adjusted degree days, you multiply by 24 because there are 24 hours in every day and then you multiply this by your SHL figure. Voila. You have an answer in kilowatt hours (kWh) used per annum.

What is fascinating here is to momentarily reflect on the role of incidental heating in all this. Although the actual amount of incidental heat doesn't alter a great deal between the three different houses I have examined, the reduction in degree days rises dramatically as you increase the insulation levels, thereby reducing the

SHL. In the extremely well insulated Eco House, you need just over 1kW of incidental heat to cover the anticipated heating requirements for the whole house whereas in the 1975 house the same amount of incidental heat is (I can't resist it) virtually incidental.

Back to the task in hand.

■ H: Domestic Hot Water (DHW) requirements. As already discussed, this part of the calculation is largely guesswork. But 4,000kWh is enough for 180lt of hot water every day of the year, about 2.5 bath fulls. That's probably what four people would use. I have given the Eco House some credit (2,000 kWh) for having half their hot water being supplied by solar panels.

■ I: Combine space heating and DHW and you have an estimate of annual energy demand (in kWh).

■ J and K: Boiler efficiency. Now boilers are not a 100% efficient. They have been getting more efficient and the latest, state of the art, condensing boilers have broken through the 90% efficiency barrier, but you still need to factor the boiler efficiency into the calculations. I have included a separate calculation for electric heat pumps which I have assumed work at 300% efficiency, which is what a CoP of 3.0 look like when expressed as an efficiency ratio.

■ L and M: Fuel costs. Now we have a figure for consumption, we can calculate a fuel cost.

■ N to Q: Carbon emissions. Each fuel has a carbon emission factor. From this you can readily work out the total CO_2 release for each house type, by fuel type. And divide by the floor area to get a kg of CO_2/m^2, which is how the Dwelling Emission Rate (DER) is worked out. The SAP worksheets have used several targets over the years. Originally, the final sum was known as a SAP rating and this was based on likely fuel costs. Then came the Carbon Index in 2002, which has now been abandoned: just as well because no one understood it. Now it's down to CO_2 emissions per m^2 of internal floor area, similar to the Passivhaus standard although the current regs are of course nothing like so exacting.

LIGHTWEIGHT v HEAVYWEIGHT CONSTRUCTION

Is timber frame more energy efficient than masonry build? It's a selfbuild perennial, this one, and there really isn't a simple answer to it.

The one big plus that timber frame has going for it is that it is largely hollow and this provides lots of space in which to stuff insulation. In contrast, masonry is invariably solid, which means that the insulation has to be placed either inside, outside or, more commonly, within the cavity between the two skins. Whilst this isn't necessarily a problem, it means that masonry walls tend to be a little thicker overall, and this is generally regarded as a bad thing because thick walls eat floorspace.

However, even this point is contentious because it is possible, by judicious substitution of one insulating material for another, to build brick and block walls no thicker than 375mm that are

well able to satisfy the insulation standards of 2013. With the timber frame industry now switching over from 90mm to 140mm wall studs, this is only about 25mm more than a timber frame wall with a brick facing skin. Timber frame can get external wall thicknesses down below 250mm overall but only by switching to a lightweight cladding such as weatherboarding or render.

But this is an argument about wall thicknesses, not energy efficiency. Insulation levels are critically important when it comes to determining energy efficiency but they are not the be all and end all. As our insulation standards have risen over the years, it has become apparent that other factors play a crucial role as well. And because insulation thickness is subject to the laws of diminishing returns, these other factors have become more significant as we have now moved to a world where the building regulations demand that all new buildings are well insulated, at least by historical standards.

AIR TIGHTNESS

One factor that has leapt to the forefront is air tightness. The British have never been overly concerned about air tightness. In Canada and Sweden this issue is taken very seriously but then they regularly get winter temperatures of minus 25°C and consequently unwanted drafts are a matter of life and death. In contrast, we have grown up in a culture where it remains commonplace to sleep with the windows open, throughout

the depths of winter. Trying to impose Scandinavian levels of air tightness on us is seen as somehow alien and just possibly unhealthy. But from an energy saving point of view, airtightness is critical because an extra 50mm of insulation in the walls and the roof is utterly pointless if the occupants subsequently leave the windows open. There is little the legislators can do about this but they can insist that buildings are constructed in such a way that they don't inadvertently leak. To this end, in 2006 the energy efficiency regs introduced an airtightness test for new houses. The required standard is not very onerous: in fact, it would have to be a very poorly built house to fail the test, but it was a marker for the future, and it may be made more stringent as time moves on.

So how do the two building systems compare on air tightness? Generally speaking, it's not the walling systems that are the issue with air tightness. Rather, it's the insertions that puncture them and the junctions that enclose them. We are talking about ill-fitting windows, doors, meter boxes and loft hatches and poorly detailed eaves. Paradoxically, one of the most significant causes of air leakage is the connection between timber and masonry elements. Not only do they have differing rates of thermal expansion but timber tends to shrink significantly as it dries out to the background moisture levels in the building as a whole. This means that gaps can appear around joists built into masonry walls and at

This is the blower door test in operation. The front door is removed and this temporary fan door is set in its place. The house is then pressurised and you can then measure how much air is required to meet the pressure standard. It's one of the very few tests you can carry out on an as built house to see if it performs as designed.

wallplate level under roofs. A house built entirely of timber or entirely of masonry wouldn't suffer air leakage in this way but such houses are extremely rare: in reality our timber frame homes tend to use a lot of masonry and our masonry homes use a lot of timber.

THERMAL MASS

The other energy saving issue bubbling away in the background surrounds the concept of thermal mass. Put quite simply, thermal mass is the capacity of a material to store heat. Heavy materials, like concrete, brick and cement screeds, will store a lot of heat – typically around 60kWh/m³ – whilst lightweight materials, like timber frame walls covered in plasterboard, store as little as 2kWh/m³. Masonry homes have high thermal mass and because of this they take much more energy to warm up from cold. But having warmed up, they have become like giant night storage heaters and will keep warm much longer than a lightweight house because of all this extra heat stored within the walls and floors.

Now if a house is kept at a constant background temperature throughout the winter, it shouldn't really make any difference to energy consumption whether it is a high or low thermal mass. Once the heavy masonry house has achieved equilibrium, which may involve storing as much as 500kWh of heat within the structure, it motors along all winter, evening out the warm and cold periods. But high thermal mass houses have a trick up their sleeve here in that, if the interrelationship of the glazing and the high thermal mass elements is correct, they can absorb significant amounts of free radiant heat from the sun during the daytime. This is the effect known as passive solar heating.

How much heat can be absorbed this way? In some climates where there is an abundance of clear sunny days in winter, passive solar design can provide the bulk of a house's heating load. Unfortunately, the British Isles rarely enjoy such weather and so passive solar heating is realistically only ever going to contribute a small proportion of what is required to keep warm.

But it's a plus for the masonry house builders. And in the see-saw arguments that rage over which system is better, the masonry boys are quick to crow about this benefit.

But there is a downside to high thermal mass homes as well, which they are much less likely to acknowledge. This concerns the lifestyles of the occupants or, to put it another way, how a house is driven. High thermal mass homes work best when the building is constantly occupied, as there is always someone there to enjoy the heat radiating from the walls and floors. But a typical DINKY (Double Income No Kids) household may spend less than a third of their waking hours in their home and for them all this thermal mass is largely wasted, keeping an empty house warm. For them, the extra heat required to get the house warm in the evenings will more than cancel out any free heat gained from passive solar. And if you go away for a week's winter break and turn the heating off, the stored heat in the walls and floors will leak away and you will have to replace all 500kWh on your return. The heavier the house, the longer it takes to return to a comfortable temperature.

You can build a low energy structure using either masonry or framed building methods. And I don't think one system is inherently more energy efficient than the other. If anything, heavy structures have an edge when the buildings are occupied during the daytime. Lightweight structures will do slightly better when occupation is intermittent. And the average house? Probably somewhere between the two!

One of the advantages of selfbuilding from new is that you can build-in items like solar PV. Redland PV tiles are integrated within the Stonewold roof cover, a much better look than bolted-on roof panels.

RENEWABLE TECHNOLOGIES

I can't have a chapter on green issues without mentioning renewable energy. But renewable energy isn't central to the issue of green building, despite what you might think, so I am not going to labour the topic too much.

Besides, it's a topic which has become as much about harvesting subsidies as it has about the technologies themselves, and the decision about what if anything to specify on your build is now largely down to how much money is on offer. Which I don't like. For one thing, I end up having to write about the subsidies in more detail that the technology, and the capricious government has, in any event, a nasty habit of changing the subsidies at a whim, so that anything I write is almost bound to be out of date before this edition leaves the shelves.

The Seventh edition had the Clear Skies grants. This was replaced in the Eighth edition by the Low Carbon Buildings Programme grants (with different versions for Scotland and N Ireland). That went as well. The Ninth edition had to take on board the Feed-In Tariff and the Renewable Heat Incentive. Now the Feed-in-Tariff has been axed (as of April 2019) and, at time of writing, it's not clear whether it will be replaced by anything at all. On the other hand, the Renewable Heat Incentive is still going strong. Who knows how long that will last. It's been a sorry story.

RENEWABLE HEAT INCENTIVE

The Renewable Heat Incentive (the RHI) sets out to do make no and low-carbon heating more attractive. The technologies subsidised are biomass heating, heat pumps and solar hot water. Arguably, it's of more interest to selfbuilders because it concerns heating systems, which aren't optional. Without subsidy, these heating methods are at best

Chapter 14

The Solar PV Home

	Power rating	Annual output
Power rating of 1 PV Panel	280w	270 kWh
Power rating of 16 PV Panels	4500w	4320 kWh

ANNUAL electrcity demand for efficient appliances	Demand	No of panels required
LED lighting scheme (80 lamps for 1500hrs)	1000kWh	4
Dishwasher	500kWh	2
Washing Machine	400kWh	2
Tumble Dryer	250kWh	2
Electric Cooking	1200kWh	5
TVs/computers/chargers	500kWh	2
Hot water demand for two people	3000kWh	12
Space heating demand for Passivhaus via GS Heat Pump	1000kWh	4
Overall electricity demand for eco home	**10,000kWh**	**33**

Full charge on an expensive Tesla	100kWh does 335ml	
Annual demand for a Tesla (12,000mls) 35 full charges	3500kWh	14
Full charge on a Renault Zoe	40kWh does 300mls	
Annual demand for a Renault Zoe (12,000mls) 40 full charges	1600kWh	6

People get very excited about the possibilities of producing enough onsite electricity to power their homes. It's a sexy idea, in a way much of the rest of green building isn't. But is it wishful thinking? How much power can we produce? How can we store it? And how much do we need?

As far as production is concerned, there is really only one game in town now and that is solar photovoltaics, or PV. Other contenders such as windpower and combined heat and power have fallen by the wayside in the domestic arena. PV achieved an enormous boost when it attracted government subsidy (the Feed in Tariff) during the 2010s, but that is now a thing of the past.

But such has been the global success of PV that the installation costs of a rooftop system have fallen to such an extent that it's now not far from being competitive with other roof covers, so new builders can consider it as an alternative to zinc or Welsh slate. A roof-integrated 16 panel, 4.5kW solar array would cover 24m² of roof and would hopefully cost around £5,000-£6,000. If you can get a quote for integrated rooftop PV for under £200/m² whilst you are recovering a roof, or building from scratch, then it's looking attractive in its own right.

But how much solar PV do you need to run a house? That all depends on the house and what you might want from it. The accompanying table gives you a good idea of what common appliances use. Some of them work well with PV as they can be used in the daytime, but most demand comes at night when PV isn't available and you would have to use a battery back-up. Here it starts to get murky.

The Tesla Powerwall is the most advanced domestic battery. It costs over £5,000 and lasts maybe ten years, so it's more expensive than a standard-sized PV system. Fully charged it holds 13kWh: that sort of matches the anticipated daily output from a 16-20 panel array. You could run the lights and the appliances in a house on this, but it wouldn't be enough to run a heat pump for heat and hot water and neither would it be enough to charge a small electric car, like a Leaf or a Zoe. For that you would need far more panels than you could fit on your roof plus another couple of batteries.

In short, PV without subsidy is marginally attractive to homeowners, but the typical rooftop set-up will only ever deliver around a quarter of your energy demands in the UK.

marginal choices; none of them have a sensible payback against mains gas condensing boilers, but they all start to look more interesting when compared to the more expensive oil-boiler systems that you would have to chose if you live off the mains gas grid.

The technologies covered by the RHI are all dealt with in Chapter 8, Plumbing & Heating, and so I won't touch on them any further in this section.

PHOTOVOLTAICS OR PV

PV arrays convert sunlight into electricity. They normally sit on the roof, although they can be mounted in arrays on the ground or built into wall claddings.

A PV cell consists of two layers of a semi-conductor, invariably silicon, and when exposed to sunlight, electrons start flowing between the layers creating a small electrical current. The current is direct and has to be converted to AC for normal domestic use, which includes exporting to the grid. This is done with a bit of kit called an inverter.

The reliability of PV cells is good as there are no moving parts. However it is reckoned that the potential to produce electricity will decline over time and cautious observers reckon that they may need replacing after just 20 years if they are to continue to perform adequately.

The PV market was expanding quite rapidly thanks in good part to the success of the Feed in Tariff. Now that that's gone, the hopes are that the industry can prosper due

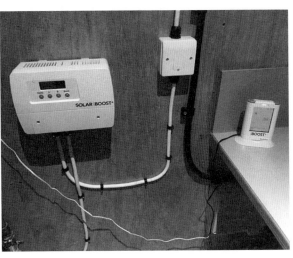

The Solar iBoost is a diverter. It switches any unwanted electrical current from your PV panels away from the grid and into your domestic hot water tank. It has the potential to make solar thermal a redundant technology as it does the same job (heats hot water) without any additional rooftop panels.

to the falling cost of the PV panels themselves. The panels themselves (conventionally around 1.0m x 1.6m) have been falling in cost and are now available for under £250 each. Although the panels themselves are the largest cost, there are not the only ones and a fully installed system still costs about £4,000 and up, depending on the ease of the work and the size of the installation. A single panel is usually rated at around 250watts — that's the theoretical maximum power it can produce on a cold, sunny day — and the annual output from one of these is around 200-300kWh, depending partly on where you live — southern Britain gets rather more sunshine than Scotland.

WIND TURBINES

We are all familiar with the huge windfarms, which cause so much controversy around the countryside.

The domestic wind turbine is the junior relation, which sits in your garden or, more likely, your paddock. It is connected to a generator which produces direct electricity but at a price now more expensive than solar PV. Like PV cells, domestic wind turbines have an anticipated lifespan of around 20 years.

They may be of interest to people living in remote areas where the wind blows and neighbour are few, but the normal domestic market has moved on.

COMBINED HEAT & POWER

At a community level, combined heat and power plants (CHP)make sense. In Denmark, spiritual home of CHP, around 50% of all homes have a piped hot water supply from a district grid, and small grid systems are now being built into innovative estates in the UK.

But at a domestic level? What you have in effect is a very expensive

A homemade heating coil rigged up to a mechanical ventilation heat recovery system to boost warm air supply to a low energy house. MVHR doesn't qualify for any grant aid, which paradoxically encourages innovation like this.

boiler that produces some electricity as well as your satisfying your heating and hot water demand. British Gas tried and failed with their Whispergen, Baxi tried with their Ecogen, but even with a hefty subsidy the uptake was minimal. Now the Feed in Tariff has gone, don't expect to hear much more from this sector.

HYDROELECTRICITY

Water mills, by any other name. This is of course another very well established technology – hydroelectric damns and electricity generation have been around since Victorian times. It's also very green in that it's all powered by gravity.

However its use in the domestic sphere is limited by the requirements for falling water on site, not something widely seen in many new estates although it may well suit some remote off-grid sites. If you have a site that's suitable for hydropower, there are a number of commercial businesses which can build and install plant for you and the costs per peak kW are reckoned to be as little as £500. Check out www.british-hydro. org.

APPLIANCES

Are there even such things as green appliances? Just possibly not.

However, every new home ends up being stuffed with appliances so, if you have the money, it is worth buying kit that is at the efficient end of the spectrum.

Problem is that all modern kits claims to be energy-efficient and many of them also claim to save water as well. For most selfbuilders, these issues are of minor issues, ranked behind price and usability. Who buys a TV based on its energy performance? How do you even find out what the energy performance is?

Being told it has an A rating isn't even that helpful as over the years everything has migrated to A ratings and the ratings agencies have moved onto A+ and A++ and even A+++.

Take tumble dryers. Here's a bit of kit that a lot of people do without, as all it actually does is dry your clothes and a washing line or a clothes horse will do just as well. However, for many people a tumble dryer is near essential as they don't have a garden or any space for a clothes horse. Turns out tumble dryers come in different flavours at different price points.

The cheapest and simplest is the vented tumble dryer which throws the moist air out the back into a flexible duct and there out into the big outdoors. Then comes the condensing tumble dryer which draws out the moisture and drops it into a tank or down the waste pipes. The heat generated inside the tumble dryer stays in the room. At the top of the range comes a heat-pump tumble dryer which is the more expensive because it has an energy-efficient heat pump instead of just an electric heater. Each machine on the market, and there are many, comes with a product data sheets which allows you to look at the energy performance. Thanks to AO (Appliances Online) for the info trawl here:

▪ £169 4kg Indesit vented dryer uses 330kWh/annum
▪ £199 9kg air vented Candy uses 630kWh/annum
▪ £200 8kg Candy condensing dryer uses 561kWh/annum
▪ £500 9kg Beco heat pump dryer uses around 176kWh/annum

Whilst you can see that in general the more you pay, the less energy you consume, it is also dependent on the drum size and a smaller drum will call for less heat. On the other hand, a tumble dryer with a large drum (i.e. 9kg) will dry the same load better and with fewer creases and may thereby save on your ironing. And guess how much power an iron uses?

It's complicated. I wouldn't blame you if you just tuned out and bought the best you could afford. Nobody wants an energy inefficient tumble dryer, but in reality it's just one of a number of factors people use to decide on what to buy.

If price is no object, you can of course really get into it and spend over £1400 on a Miele heat pump tumble dryer which is not only very energy efficient but is wi-fi connected so you can control it from your smart phone (really?) and has a steam cycle to reduce creasing, not to mention two fragrance capsules you can set to make your laundry smell just so. You may not be saving the planet, but at least you will leave it smelling nice.

Energy use for household appliances

Appliance	rating in watts	Hrs used per annum	kwh used per annum	Mains gas 4.6	LPG 6.6	Electricty 16.0
				Annual running costs		
Hobs	2000	200	400	£ 18	£ 26	£ 64
Oven	2000	300	600	£ 28	£ 40	£ 96
Microwave	2000	100	200			£ 32
Dishwasher	1200	400	480			£ 77
Washing Machine	1200	350	420			£ 67
Tumble Dryer	1000	300	300	£ 14	£ 20	£ 48
Small fridge (120lt)	25	8760	220			£ 35
Fridge/freezer	50	8760	440			£ 70
Kettle	3000	100	300			£ 48
Iron	2000	50	100			£ 16
TV	100	1500	150			£ 24
Computers	150	1500	230			£ 37
Stand-by equipment/chargers	10	8760	90			£ 14
Heavy use GLS lightbulb	60	1500	90			£ 14
Heavy use LED lamp	8	1500	10			£ 2
Typical LED lighting scheme 80 lamps			1000			£ 160

Fuel costs in pence per kWh

SAVING WATER

Although most UK property is still charged for water and sewage by a rating system, newly constructed housing in England & Wales is invariably metered (not so in Scotland and N. Ireland). Living with a metered water supply is a novel experience for many of us and it takes some getting used to. If you are connecting your drains into the main drains as well as tapping into the local water supplies, your bills will be broken down into four sections:
▪ Standing charge for water supply
▪ Volume charge for water supply
▪ Standing charge for sewage disposal

▪ Volume charge for sewage disposal.
Properties that dispose of waste by other means (usually onsite treatment tanks) will have other costs to pay instead of sewage charges – see section on Drains, Chapter 6, 'Groundworks'.

METERING: HOW IT WORKS

Only the water supply is metered. The volume of discharge you pour back down the drains is worked out from the amounts of water you consume: some companies reckon it to be 100%, some 95% and some 90%. If yours works on a 95% figure then, if you were to consume 100m³ of water, you would be charged for 95m³ of sewage.

Water Bills in England & Wales

ANNUAL CHARGES/ m³			WATER	SEWAGE	COMBINED
	Average Standing Charges		£35	£50	£85
	Average Volume Charges		£ 1.50	£ 1.80	£ 3.30
WATER USED BY 4-PERSON HOUSEHOLD			**ANNUAL VOLUME CHARGES**		
ACTIVITY	**Litres/day**	**As %**	**WATER**	**SEWAGE**	**COMBINED**
Drinking/Cooking	20	3%	£ 11	£ 13	£24
Baths/Showers	300	44%	£ 164	£ 197	£361
Flushing Loos	150	22%	£ 82	£ 99	£181
Washing Machine	70	10%	£ 38	£ 46	£84
Dishwasher	35	5%	£ 19	£ 23	£42
Others	100	15%	£ 55	£ 66	£121
TOTAL	**675**	**100%**	**£ 370**	**£ 443**	**£813**
STANDING CHARGES + VOLUME CHARGES			**£405**	**£493**	**£898**
VARIATIONS					
	4-person household, Highest charging area (South West)				£820
	4 -person household, Lowest charging area (Northumbria)				£478
	Average for 3-person household				£690
	Average for 2-person household				£490
	Average for 1-person household				£290

A four-person household will typically use and discharge 185m³ water/annum (equivalent to 2300 baths, that's just over six baths a day). This 185m³ figure is very much an average and a new house with lots of thirsty appliances like dishwashers and power showers, not to mention children, could easily use 50% more. When I was living in a house with three teenage sons, we used as much as 365m³/annum. The main culprit, I believe, was my teenagers love of power showers lasting ten minutes at a time, consuming around 20lt/minute, maybe 400lt/day or 150m³/annum. I don't think our family was that unusual and I suspect that the quoted average figures probably underestimate a typical user. Heavy users with swimming pools, water features and garden sprinklers and the like would propel your annual usage way over even these suspect usage figures.

COMPARISONS

The charges for average water usage are larger than the anticipated heating bills for a new home. Assuming an average of 250m³/annum is consumed by our notional four-person household, the average bill, including standing charges, will be over £650/annum.

What immediately stands out about these figures is how little water actually passes into our bodies (3%) compared to how much is consumed largely to keep us and our homes clean and hygienic. Part of the justification for higher water prices is the cost of maintaining drinking water standards but, on reflection, it seems extraordinary that we should go to such trouble to purify our water supplies in order to pour 97% back down the drains. In theory, at least, there is ample scope to use non-potable water (ie non-drinking), and ample savings to be made by avoiding relatively expensive metered supplies.

USE LESS

Before delving into esoteric water-saving schemes, there are a number of common sense ways that water consumption can be reduced without making you smell:

■ Don't stand under the shower for ten minutes every day

■ Check out lo-flow shower heads. 8lts/minute is fine. You really don't need upwards of 15lts/min.

■ Fit the smallest WC cisterns possible – the industry standard is now down to 6lt/ flush, thanks to a recent change in the water bylaws, but you may be able to source even smaller cisterns. Dual flush at 4lt/6lt are widely available

■ Buy A+ rated appliances. A water-efficient washing machine will use around half as much as an older model. Same goes for dishwashers

■ Don't run washing machines and dishwashers unless they are full

■ Look to fit water efficient taps to basins and kitchen sinks

■ Don't water lawns; water plants in

the evening to avoid evaporation
▥ Use water butts (although
attractive ones are hard to find)
▥ Don't build a swimming pool.

PART G

The building regulations now make
water efficiency mandatory – in
England the relevant section is Part
G. This requires us to undertake a
water calculation when designing
the house to show that our overall
consumption shouldn't average more
than 125lt/day, a feat achieved largely
through specifying small baths and/or
low-flow showers. There is more on
Part G and the water calculator in the
Bathrooms section in Chapter 11.

WATER SAVING

Water-saving schemes are sommat
else. They can be divided into two
areas: rainwater collection which
replaces water you'd normally buy
through your water meter, and grey
water collection which recycles some
of the water you have already used.

RAINWATER HARVESTING

Even in dry lowland England
(average rainfall equals 750mm/
annum) a four-bedroom house plus
detached garage will get around 60-
75m³ of rain falling on to it during
the course of a year. That sounds like
a lot but it's probably only around
what one person consumes in a year,
or enough for a household of four or
five to flush the loos. The calculation
is as follows: take your average annual
rainfall in metres and multiply it by
your catchment area in square metres.
So if you have a 100m² roof and

0.75m of rainfall per annum (that's
30 inches) then you might hope
to collect 75m³ of water. Actually,
rather less, because inevitably a
significant amount gets spilled or
lost via evaporation. In wetter areas
to the north and west this figure
could easily double as rainfall levels
are so much higher. The potential is
there; the problem is that rainfall is
not only unpredictable but sporadic
whereas household usage is basically
quite constant. You need to build a
reservoir capable of holding enough
rainwater to supply basic household
needs, which is exactly what your
own water company does on a much
larger scale. Starting your very own
water supply business may be an
appealing prospect for some but it is
likely to prove expensive to build and
time-consuming to run. The bigger
your reservoir, the more effective your
own supplies will be in replacing
your metered supply, but the more

problems you are likely to have with
construction and maintenance.

Rainwater harvesting has become
quite trendy in no time at all and a
surprising number of selfbuilt homes
are fitting tanks, filters and pumps so
that they can reuse at least some of
their free rainfall in a similar fashion.
Prices quoted are between £2,000 and
£4,000: for this you get underground
storage tanks (either plastic or
concrete), filters to take out most of
the leaves and twigs and a pump to
lift the water back up to the house.
Most people use it just for flushing
loos, installing a second plumbing
system supplying the cisterns from the
storage tanks, but there is no reason
you can't supply the bulk of your taps
with rainwater. You can rig it up so
that the storage tanks never empty
– the mains water cuts in when the
level falls too low. More sophisticated
arrangements allow rainwater to
be used as drinking water, but this

*Rainwater harvesting
tanks are usually buried
underground but if
you have space and
don't mind the slightly
agricultural feel, you
can save money by
housing them in the
garden.*

requires on site treatment which is a more complex affair.

Whether it is really worth doing from an economic perspective is debatable. It only makes sense if you have a water meter, for a start. Even then, a 1,000lt of water, which is by definition a cubic metre, is currently charged at anywhere between 80p and £1.20, depending on your water company, so your maximum saving is unlikely to be more than about £80 a year.

GREY WATER

Grey water is the term given to waste water which is reusable, notably the waste from baths, showers and wash basins. There is potential to recycle this water in the garden and especially for flushing loos. Because the waste from baths and washing is much more regular than rainfall, the storage facilities do not have to be nearly as large to be effective. A large bath-sized tank will be enough to flush ten loos and should get refilled most days.

As with rainwater harvesting, there has been a flicker of interest in grey water recycling and there are now proprietary systems available using pumps and a small holding tank that can be placed in the loft. The grey water has to be treated with cleaning agents and passed through a carbon filter so it's not for the faint hearted, especially as the resulting water is not always as clear as we have come to expect.

BOREHOLES

There is another way of avoiding water company charges – and infrastructure charges – and that is to sink your own borehole and draw your own water supply up from under the ground. It's where most of the water comes from in SE England and in many other areas besides and, whereas your local water company has a monopoly on piped supplies, there is nothing to stop you tapping into the enormous natural groundwater reservoir directly. That's an oversimplification; there is the small matter of installation costs that can vary from £2,000 to £20,000, depending on such matters as the depth of the borehole and the water pressure. You will also need a licence from the Environment Agency.

For most people, that makes it an extremely expensive way of going about getting water and sends them straight back into the arms of their local water company.

If you are one of the small number who plan to draw their own water supply from under the ground, then you will be responsible for your water quality. That's not to say that you won't have to submit your water for analysis to the local Environmental Health Inspector: indeed most councils will be around testing you every couple of years or so. Simple bacteria tests tend to be done in local hospitals and cost around £30; however tests for pollution are more expensive – I was quoted £100 for a nitrate test. The Environmental Health Inspector has the power to condemn your supply but this rarely happens because almost everything can be filtered out – at a cost. My local inspector reckoned that ground water pollution was something of an overstated problem and that when he did come across it, it was very often the house itself that was the cause of the pollution; he advised not to use ground water supplies in conjunction with a septic tank. Obvious really.

PAYING FOR LEAKS

Whilst the problem of a dripping tap is well known (and costly for metered households), it pails into insignificance compared to the potential nightmare of an underground leak. You, the householder, are responsible for all water consumption downstream from the water meter – which is conventionally located outside, close to the plot boundary. Spring a leak underground between the meter and your internal stop tap and you may know nothing about it until a massive water bill arrives on your doormat (as much as six months later); if you are lucky, the water company will let you off paying the sewage charge, but even so a bad leak might lose as much as 20m^3 of water a day which would cost £1,500 by the time you get your water bill. Be warned that sloppy installation (and loose connections) of metered mains supplies can be very expensive.

WATER TREATMENT

There are two very distinct processes here. You soften (or condition) water in an attempt to prolong the life of your domestic appliances, whereas you filter water in an attempt to prolong your own life. Both techniques are surrounded by a veil of mystery and intrigue which is hard to penetrate, and the whole subject is so rife with claim and counterclaim that it makes the job of the humble commentator akin to negotiating a minefield.

SOFTENING

If you live in a soft water area (which includes most of Britain above a line drawn between the Humber and the Severn) then this section is one to miss. If in doubt, phone your water company to get figures on local conditions.

Even if you live in a hard water area there is no need to panic. Households have been known to function quite adequately for years without so much as a hint of any water softeners about. However, many sane people swear by water softeners and insist that they produce tangible benefits – even if it's only to reduce the amount of soap powder they use in their washing machines

TRADITIONAL SOFTENERS

For between £600 and £1,000 you get a big box into which you add salt – you need around three 25kg bags of salt per person per annum, so this alone will cost you £15 each every year.

As these boxes actually chemically change the water supply, their output should not be drunk or cooked with. Design your plumbing so that the kitchen tap, at least, comes direct from the mains.

Softeners work by separating out

the hard bits in the water, exchanging them for softer sodium bits. The box needs an electrical supply and a drain-off point. It also needs, ideally, to be located somewhere close to the rising main so that it's relatively easy to plumb in. 'Under the utility sink' is an obvious place but, be warned, most water softeners require a fair bit of space around and above them in order to be got at for maintenance and weekly salt refills. You may have to adjust your utility worktop to suit.

The long-term benefits include reduced water heating bills and savings on soap powders (combined unlikely to be worth more than about £25/annum).

Evidence that water softeners increase the lifespan of hot water appliances is – careful now – inconclusive but almost everyone who has one reckons they do make the water feel softer and the laundry appears cleaner.

In 2005, I installed a water softener, never having had one before: I actually didn't like the 'feel' of the water as much as genuine soft water, but one place where the chemically softened water was really appreciated was in the bathrooms where limescale became a thing of the past, making cleaning a doddle. If you plan to install glazed shower screens in a hard water area, then you will really appreciate a water softener.

PHOSPHATE CONDITIONERS

These are a sort of junior version of the big water softeners. They are designed to stop hot water appliances from scaling up and they are usually

sold in conjunction with combination boilers and/or mains pressure hot water cylinders. You will see them in plumber's merchants – look for names like Combimate and Combicare.

They work by adding phosphate solution to the incoming water, which inhibits scale formation – they don't 'soften' the water as such but they are reckoned to prolong the life of water-heating equipment in hard water areas.

They cost around £80 and they don't need power or drainage facilities but the phosphate cartridges need replacing every year (cost £15 a time). Again the treated water is not ideal for drinking but these conditioners are normally only fitted to water heating devices.

INHIBITORS

Unlike the two preceding methods, which are chemical treatments, inhibitors act by passing a magnetic or an electrical charge through the water which – it is claimed – prevents the hard bits in the water from sticking to the pipes. They are relatively cheap (£30-£60), easy to install and need no maintenance., and they don't affect the quality of the drinking water. Some need electrical power, most operate without. But do they work?

You may figure they are so cheap that there is nothing to lose in trying and you may well be right. But how will you know that your investment does the biz? Another thing to ponder on during those long dark nights.

In 2018, I was persuaded to fit yet another type of device, an Aquabion,

Chapter 14

which though small in size was also rather expensive. I don't begin to understand how it works, but it appears to do something. It doesn't exactly prevent limescale but it does make it easy to remove what limescale forms. After trialling it for a year, I have still to decide whether it was worthwhile. That's perhaps the nature of inhibitors.

FILTERING

In the last few years, there has been an enormous growth of interest in the subject of tap water quality.

Whereas the Victorians basked in the glory of the technical achievement of providing clean drinking water to all homes, we have now become blasé about this and tend to worry that much of this water runs through lead pipes and, in any event, doesn't taste very good. Added to which there are fears (in lowland England at least) that we are now getting nitrate and pesticide residues in our tap water.

There is a huge choice of water filters available, ranging from the free standing plastic jug affairs which can be picked up in Boots for a few quid to expensive, in-line purifiers.

There are no British Standards for water purifiers ('tap water's just fine, old boy') and there is little concrete evidence on the effectiveness of the various methods. There is also concern that many filters may themselves be health hazards, providing spawning grounds for bacteria.

Nevertheless, interest in water filters continues to grow and one of the more innovative companies

working in this field is Culligans who supply the whole range of water treatment gizmos from softeners and scale reducers to filters and ultra-violet disinfection units.

If you remain unconvinced but would still like a source of filtered water, you could do worse than snap up a Brita Filter kettle for about £40.

CODE FOR SUSTAINABLE HOMES

In December 2006, the then Labour government created the Code for Sustainable Homes. And in 2015, the Conservative government abolished it. I could just leave it at that, but in its time it had enormous influence over the way we build homes.

The Code didn't arrive out of the blue. It built on something similar called Eco Homes which, like the Code, came out of the resources of the Building Research Establishment in Watford. These are essentially checklists with which to measure just how eco your eco house actually is. Points were awarded for all kinds of green features, and although energy saving grabbed the headlines, there was also water saving to be done, recycling and various other good design features.

Planners started insisting on its use for all manner of new housing developments, including selfbuilds, and because of this it started running into heavy opposition from the influential housebuilder's lobby.,

which is more than probably why it got jettisoned once the Tories had themselves jettisoned the troublesome LibDems in 2015.

The Code was split into six levels, each one greener than the one below. Code Level 6 was the ultimate in eco homes and included the zero carbon house, which only ever got built as a demonstration level. Parts of the Code survive within the building regulations. The energy efficiency regs, Part L, 2013 version, are roughly equivalent to Code Level 4 and buried within Part G is a water calculator which determines how big a bath you can have and how much water can flow through your taps. Only the water calculator never got to a level where it would begin to become challenging for installers or homeowners.

The fate of the Code also demonstrates just how fragile government initiatives are. Virtually the whole building industry was gearing up for the implementation of Code Level 6 in 2016 and was busy re-inventing itself for a green, sustainable future. But at the stroke of a pen, the whole edifice was consigned to history.

What happens next depends on how Brexit plays out and at time of writing it looks most unclear. But the government needs to come up with some solution to climate change and just leaving everything to the building regulations seems a little arbitrary.

In the absence of any government initiatives on how we might build more sustainably, the way has been left open for alternative standards

318 13th EDITION • **HOUSEBUILDER'S BIBLE**

to act as beacons, and none more so that the internationally recognised Passivhaus standard.

PASSIVHAUS

Many forward thinking builders are starting to concentrate on the Passivhaus standard as a viable alternative to this Code for Sustainable Homes. Passivhaus is an demanding technical standard which more or less guarantees not only very low energy consumption but very high building standards. It just concentrates on energy use and comfort. If people want to add water efficiency measures or renewable energy devices, that is up to them, but it's not part of the classic Passivhaus standard.

The three pillars of Passivhaus are demanding insulation levels, close attention to the details of achieving airtightness and a reliance on mechanical ventilation with heat recovery. A Passivhaus is characterised by almost always having triple glazing and very little in the way of space heating. They aim to be warm and comfortable all year around with an absolute minimum of space heating required. However there is no insistence on any of the other ecological measures which make up the Code for Sustainable Homes, though recently the Passivhaus Institute has introduced new standards which incorporate renewable technologies as well.

You might think that Passivhaus is a national standard, perhaps a

Passivhaus Standard	
Maximum annial space heating requirement	15kWh/m^2/annum
Maximim annual energy budget	120kWh/m^2/annum
Maximim heating load	10 watts/m^2
Maximum U value for roof and walls	0.15
Maximum U value for windows and doors	0.8
Minimum efficiency of heat recovery systems	90%
Maximimum air changes per hour (tested by blower door)	0.6@50 Pascals

The Passivhaus standard is far more exacting than our building regulations. Whereas our current FEES standard for space heating is around 60kWh/m^2/annum, the Passivhaus standard sits at just 15kWh/m^2/annum

German version of the Code for Sustainable Homes. But in fact the Passivhaus Institute is a private organisation based in Darmstadt in Germany. For a house to qualify as a certified Passivhaus, the builder must not only meet the required standards, but also undergo a degree of inspection and auditing some way in advance of what happens with our common or garden building regulations. This auditing comes at a cost, but is seen as an essential part of the process.

The Denby Dale Passivhaus was built in 2010, one of the first to be built in the UK. Although Passivhaus is sometimes criticised for encouraging "the box format", this design shows that boxes don't have to be boring

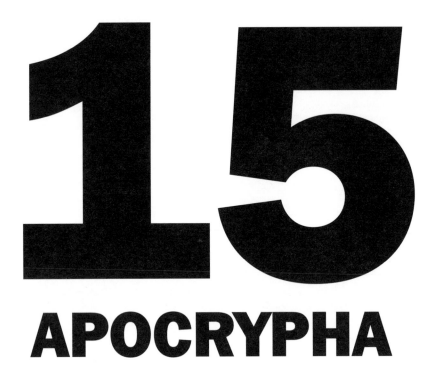

APOCRYPHA

The original Apocrypha were written at the same time as the Holy Bible but were felt by the editors to be not quite up to the mark, so they published them separately. This Bible's Apocrypha is a little different because it's just a late chapter which consists of a few odds and ends that simply don't fit into the rest of the book.

Analysing housebuilding as an activity is a bit like trying to figure out where every strand of spaghetti begins and ends. Some are easy to spot, some take some figuring out and some you just can't do, no matter

what. So these are the bits to go into the Aprocrypha. All essential stuff of course, but it just doesn't fit neatly into the jigsaw.

BEWARE BUILDING COSTS

You may have a very good idea of what you can afford but, unless you are an experienced developer, you are unlikely to have much idea of how much and what sort of house that money will build.

You can quickly unearth data

online (search on Jewson Build Cost Calculator) and it will give you an "average" build cost for a given square meterage. The results are remarkably low. Persimmon maybe able to build at these prices, but I very much doubt a selfbuilder will either be able to match these rates, or indeed even want to match them

But ballpark figures stick in the mind, and it's very easy to get attached to them early on in a project. What I want to look at here is not so much how much you may or may not spend on a project, but just what exactly is meant by the "/m²" bit.

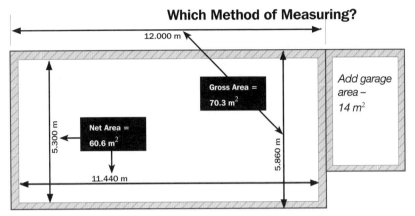

Which Method of Measuring?

12.000 m

Gross Area = 70.3 m^2

Net Area = 60.6 m^2

5.300 m

11.440 m

5.860 m

Add garage area – 14 m^2

External walls here are 280mm thick, usually 12-15% of the gross floor area

One bungalow, three different methods of measuring it.

The net area – I think this is the correct one – shows a floor area of 60.6m^2.

The gross area adds the external walls and comes out at 70.3m^2.

Whilst the third way adds the 14m^2 attached garage, making the floor area total nearly 40% more than the net area.

What exactly defines a build cost?

There is no British Standard and there isn't really such a thing as an industry standard either. Neither is there complete agreement on just how floor areas of houses should be measured. Different businesses use different methods and this makes a minefield out of the task of comparing costs and setting budgets.

MEASURING FLOOR AREAS

The most widely used floor area measurement in Britain is the one which refers to the internal floor area of the house. It expressly excludes the area of the external walls, although (largely for convenience when carrying out the measurements) the area taken up by the internal partition walls is included. This measurement is also known as the net floor area.

GROSS v NET

There is another floor area

measurement commonly in use, the gross floor area, which includes the area of the external walls. The effect of including the external wall areas in the calculation is to increase the apparent size of the building by up to 15% as external walls are, these days, usually constructed at thicknesses of 300mm – 400mm. On the Continent, it's the gross floor area that people usually refer to and many of the kit home suppliers use gross floor areas in their sales literature without being explicit about the fact and there is often no way of telling which area they are talking about other than by measuring it up yourself with a ruler. Using a gross floor area will appear to reduce unit area costs by 15%.

GARAGES

Garages should not be regarded as living space, even when they are integral to the rest of the house.

Again, there is no check other than you and your ruler and you need to be very careful when evaluating sales literature of kit home suppliers to see that any integral garage is not included in the overall floor area. In contrast, detached garages are unlikely to be included as part of the floor area of a house in such literature, but here the trick is to exclude their building costs from any overall budget calculations. As a garage will typically cost anything upwards of £10,000 to build, either its inclusion in floor areas or its exclusion from building costs will have a dramatic (and wholly misleading) effect on apparent unit area cost.

Added to possible confusion over net and gross floor areas, the lack of a consistent benchmark for measuring floor areas means that a four-bedroom house with an integral garage could be given as 150m^2 by one method and as much as 200m^2 by another.

Chapter 15

GREY AREAS

There are a number of other features worth examining. When you get into the swing of measuring house sizes off plan, you will undoubtedly come across features which are not clear cut. Again there are no hard and fast rules but I would suggest the following assumptions are fair.

■ Cupboard space: storage space such as under-eaves cupboards which are common when your upper storey is built into the roofspace, should be excluded from internal floor area. However, built-in full height wardrobes should be included as normal living space.

■ Utility Areas: normally these would be included as part of the living space. Sometimes it is hard to judge where a utility/storage area ends and a garage begins; if you're in this position don't worry too much because at least you understand what the issues are.

■ Internal Walls: conventionally, these are measured straight through and they are included as part of the internal area.

■ Stairwells: normally measured straight through on both floors and therefore included as internal floor area as if it was regular circulation space. The exception comes when you have a large open plan arrangement, not often seen in new houses but common in barn conversions where large openings have to be preserved. How do you decide when your ordinary stairwell becomes extraordinary? The rule is that if the upper floor opening is restricted to just the functioning stairwell,

then measure straight through on both floors; if the open area extends beyond the immediate staircase, then you must exclude the entire stairwell area from the upper floor area.

BUILDING COSTS

So much for defining the internal floor area. The 'building costs' are even harder to define. There is no official standard but there is a sort of British way of defining building costs. Making long lists and producing definitions is all very well, but what I am trying to get at is that building costs are really just a subgroup of development costs and that to concentrate on building costs to the exclusion of other costs is potentially disastrous. Like building costs, development costs can vary enormously and in this respect there is no greater variant than the price paid for your building plot. Some building plots are far more expensive to develop than others; problems can arise with bad ground, slopes, difficult service connections, difficult access, trees, legal covenants, intransigent planners – you name it! Now, the art of property developing is to be able to predict these problems and to negotiate a price on the land that reflects the cost of getting around them.

And you also have to consider what a building cost leaves out at the other end of the process, namely the finishing details. Normally floor finishes are included, but not always. Landscaping? Driveways? Window dressings? Wardrobes and cupboards? Bathroom storage? All

usually ignored from a building costs perspective, but all costs you will have to face when it comes to turning a house into a home.

Of course, you can reduce costs by undertaking some of the work yourself. But all of this will pale into insignificance if you fail to budget the project correctly in the first place; to achieve significant savings, you need to buy and develop your plot appropriately, be very organised and able to stick tightly to a budget.

My advice is to hire a quantity surveyor once the initial plans are in place, especially if you are proposing to build something a little unusual. The online services will be fine if the house is very conventional, but not if you want to try something a bit different. Spend the money to see if you plans are buildable at your budget and, if they are not, change the plans before you put them in for planning permission. The later you make changes, the more it will cost.

ACCESSIBILITY

Provision for disabled access in housing became part of the building regulations in 1999 – in England it's all in Part M. Part M was greeted with enthusiasm by disability campaigners but has had a lukewarm reaction from both the housebuilders and the general public who felt that it was political correctness run riot. Personally, I'm torn between the extremes.

The little Tory in me reacts negatively to having meddlesome legislation shoved across my soon-to-be-levelled doorstep; then a few days later I find myself talking with a builder whose wife is confined to a wheelchair and, as he describes the struggles they both have in coping with her disability, I suddenly chide myself for being so mean-spirited and wish that the regulations went much further than they do.

Although Part M is phrased in such a way as to make you think they are designed solely for wheelchair users, the groups who benefit from the regulations are far reaching, including the blind and partially sighted and families with pre-school children.

Part of the problem is that there are actually very few severely long-term disabled people around, so making every new house conform to a rigid set of standards in order to meet their requirements seems both expensive and illogical. Perhaps. Perhaps not. It actually costs very little extra to build a Part M compliant house – in contrast it's always frighteningly expensive to retrofit such measures into an existing house. We are building homes that may well have a life expectancy stretching well into the 22nd century and during this lifespan there is every chance that several occupants will come to appreciate some aspect of Part M.

WHAT'S IN PART M?
▣ To comply with Part M every house has to have one level threshold — ideally, but not necessarily, the front door.

▣ This doorway should have a minimum clearance of 775mm between frame and opened door, which translates as having to use an 838mm door.
▣ A level threshold is defined as one which has a bump of no more than 15mm under the door.
▣ This entrance should be easily approachable from the outside. In practise this means there should be no steps and no incline of more than 1:20.
▣ Every home must have a downstairs toilet. This room doesn't have to be big enough to accommodate a wheelchair. It's just the door has to be wide enough to get a wheelchair through (838mm again).
▣ Ground floor corridors and doorways must be wide enough to allow wheelchair users easy access. There is a trade-off here; wider corridors can have narrower doors but the rule of thumb that seems to have developed is to have all ground floor doors 838mm wide and to have corridors at least 1050mm wide.
▣ Power sockets and switches must be placed no lower than 450mm and no higher than 1200mm above finished floor level throughout the house.

LEVEL THRESHOLDS
The standard (pre-1999) British front door involved stepping up from the ground into the house – indeed the internal floor level is typically 150mm – that's two brick courses – higher than the external ground level. Like many standards, this front step had never been a regulation but

was simply a detail that had evolved, primarily as a way of keeping water from flowing in under the door. The level threshold requires the doorstep to be re-engineered and to have a level or ramped access as well.

Traditionally front doors open inwards and traditionally floor covers have not been an issue because of the step. But level thresholds force you to consider carefully how you will finish the floor internally. Consider it carefully. A sunken matwell covering then area where the door opens seems to be a good solution for many.

LIFETIME HOMES
From the point of view of the disabled, Part M is very tame. It concentrates on making new homes 'visitable' but it does little to make them more 'usable.' The future would seem to lie with a more advanced version of what is already in Part M, known as the Lifetime Homes standard, developed by the Joseph Rowntree Foundation in 1991. In 2016, Part M was expanded to include many of the Lifetime Home provisions, but on the understanding that they would only apply to homes specifically designed for people with impaired mobility.

What would turn a Part M compliant home into a Lifetime Home? It's a set of 16 features intended to make homes readily adaptable for disabled users.
▣ 1 Car parking space should be easily capable of enlargement to attain a width of 3300mm.
▣ 2 The distance from the car parking space to the home should be kept to

Level threshold with matwell. It looks very simple here and it's not that difficult, but care has to be taken to ensure that rainwater drains away from the doorway

a minimum and should be level or gently sloping.

■ 3 The approach to all entrances should be level or gently sloping.

■ 4 All entrances should be illuminated and the main entrance should be level and covered.

■ 5 Communal stairs should provide easy access and where levels are reached by lift, the lift should be fully wheelchair accessible.

■ 6 Doorways and hallways have to be at least 750mm wide, or at least 900mm wide when the approach is head-on.

■ 7 Dining and living areas should have space for turning a wheelchair and there should be adequate circulation space for wheelchair users.

■ 8 The living space should be at the level of the entrance.

■ 9 If homes have two or more storeys, there should be space at entrance level which could be used as a convenient bed space.

■ 10 There should be a WC at the entrance level of the property and, in larger properties, there should be drainage provision enabling a shower to be fitted in the future.

■ 11 The design of the property should provide for a reasonable route for a potential hoist from a main bedroom to the bathroom.

■ 12 The design of the property should incorporate a provision for a future stair lift and a suitably identified space for a through-the-floor lift from the ground to the first floor.

■ 13 Walls in the bathrooms and toilets should be capable of taking adaptations such as handrails.

■ 14 The bathroom should be designed to incorporate ease of access to essential amenities such as the bath, basin and WC.

■ 15 Living room window cills should be no more than 800mm from the floor and be easy to open.

■ 16 Switches, sockets, ventilation and service controls should be situated between 450mm and 1200mm from the floor.

Whilst many people bridle at the thought of being told how their house should be designed, most of these steps are easily incorporated into a new house and cost either very little or nothing at all. They really only become difficult to incorporate in smaller homes where some of the space requirements become hard to meet, in particular the requirement for a downstairs bathroom to be capable of adaptation for wheelchair users, plus the requirement for a shower drain in the downstairs bathroom.

SECURITY

Just as disabled access arrangements have been subsumed into our building regulations (via Part M), improved security standards have also become standard regulations as well. Part Q, as it is known, came into effect in 2015 and, as with all the building regs, is available for free download. At just ten pages, it's an amazingly short document, and it largely consists of guidance on windows and external doors and the ironmongery that should be fitted to them to make them Part Q compliant. A secure doorset and window should meet a well established British Standard, PAS 24, which formed the backbone of a once aspirational building standard known as Secured by Design. PAS 24 is a test involving using jemmies and crowbars to try and break through doors and windows and a Pass now means that your chosen door/window fits the bill. Just as Lifetime Homes gave birth to Part M, Secured by Design became Part Q.

In order to meet Part Q, you simply have to ensure that your external joinery is Part Q compliant.

There is more to Secured by Design than simply having good doors and windows. It was a project started by the police in 1989 in response to crappy new building standards where it was possible to break into a house simply by taking out a double glazed sealed unit, held in by no more than a few screws. It includes advice on estate layouts and the like, but this is unlikely to be of much interest to selfbuilders. However, they do publish a useful guide, updated every two or three years, which is available for free — search on Secured by Design>Design Guides. There is a lot of useful background information here on what makes a secure house and even a secure garden. Much of it is common sense but it's still very handy to have it summarised in one place.

PREVENTING BREAK INS.

Whilst Part Q compliant windows and doors make it harder for a burglar to gain entry, they won't stop someone really determined to get in, especially if the doors or windows are left open. The rear of the house is the preferred area of entry for burglars. This is largely because the back of the house is almost always more private and is often screened from neighbours. A burglary often starts with a casual casing of the front of the house; if it looks as though there is no one at home, the second stage will be to go round the back and take a closer look. Only when they're convinced the coast is clear will the break-in proceed. If access to the back of the house is impeded, then the would-be burglar may abort the job at this early stage in the hope of there being easier pickings further up the road.

A 2m fence and a stout gate, even without a bolt, will provide a considerable measure of defence against unwanted prowling. A tip from my 2010 Milton Keynes benchmark house is to use a 2m fence but to have the top 300mm made up of a see-through trellis which is just as difficult to get over but allows you to see who is walking along behind it. Back gardens can be protected, to a lesser extent, by walling or hedging them in. Plan in any obstructions that will at least slow down the progress of a potential burglar.

BURGLAR ALARMS

There is a huge variety of different alarm systems out there and it's not easy deciding what to fit, if anything at all. A wired system is particularly well suited to new housing as the wiring can be concealed during first-fix stage. Installation quotes for a four-bedroom house are likely to vary from £500 for a basic system based on a mixture of internal infrared detectors and contact points to over £1,000 for external vibration detectors which are triggered by interference with doors and windows.

Should you not want to go to the expense of installing an alarm, as an alternative, the wiring can be first-fixed in a day for between £100 and £200, so that the intruder detectors can be fitted at a later date without disruption to the decorations. Burglar alarms are eligible for zero-rating of VAT when building a new home.

Fixing a burglar alarm should not be beyond the capabilities of a competent DIYer and there are a number of systems designed for just this. DIY alarms usually consist of a control panel, the detectors and an external siren. The wired systems are the most reliable and are probably best suited to new builds. However, wireless alarms have their advocates and are easily fitted as an afterthought. The standard wireless systems still need mains connections for both the control panel and the siren but the latest generation work entirely on radio signalling: the siren and the control panels are solar powered and you activate the alarm by using a remote control.

Chapter 15

More features tend to add to the cost but it is still possible to get a well-featured wireless system for under £200. Zones are the areas covered by individual detectors and most burglar alarms allow you to arm or disarm any of your zones individually. This is useful if you have pets or if you want only the downstairs armed when you are upstairs at night. Better systems have a capability of checking that all component parts are working – a feature sometimes referred to as a 24 hour zone.

MOVEMENT SENSORS

Alarm systems don't have to just concern themselves with making loud noises or sending messages off to police stations. You can also rig up detector beams running across the front and the back of your house which set off a buzzer inside when they are crossed.

They vary in sophistication from simple passive infrared beams like the ones used to trip lights, to multi-height beams running between two concealed posts which aim to be cat and fox proof. The well designed systems will give you fairly reliable intruder alerts: a poor system, tripping out every time a bird flies by, will just make you paranoid.

SECURITY LIGHTING

Passive Infrared (PIR) detectors, similar to the ones used on internal movement sensors in burglar alarms, are also used on external lighting. These can be very useful around dark entrances although the halogen bulbs (sometimes 500W) can be so bright that you dazzle passers-by and tend to make them think you live in a high-security prison. There are some very cheap versions on the market (at around £10-£15) which are best avoided; at around £30 you start to get ones where it is possible to change the bulb. Better forms of external lighting exist that can be wired to PIR switches, as well as manual override switches, which give pleasant external illumination as well as some form of security .

There are also a number of products that can be used to give the effect of occupation when the house is empty. For around £20, you can buy a gizmo which fits in between a lightbulb and its lamp holder that acts as a light-sensitive switch, useful for simulating occupation when you are away.

SAFES

Home safes are available from £150 for a wall fitting one and from £200 for one bolted to the floor. Placing a safe in an existing house can be awkward but in a new house it's a doddle – if you've planned ahead for it.

VIDEO DOOR BELLS

There are various video doorbells — the best known is the Amazon-owned Ring — you can fit which give you the ability to interview the caller without having to open the door. They sell themselves on being able to talk to delivery drivers when you are far, far away, provided you have a good wi-fi or 4G connection. My experience of Ring (based on 9 months usage at time of writing) is that they are anything but convenient. By the time the remote connection is up and running, the driver has long since given up and moved onto the next drop. The times it does get through, we end up having this strained conversation which neither of us can understand. Maybe it's the solution to a problem we don't really have.

CCTV

I also have recent experience of external CCTV, mounted on a neighbour's gable end wall, watching over our urban construction site which was guarded by nothing more elaborate than standard security fencing (aka Heras). During the groundworks stage, we had a break-in from under the Heras fencing. The guy took some hand tools from back of the site and a lawn mower from the neighbour's shed. I spent around two hours looking through the recordings and finally tracked the event down to 6am in broad daylight, with our burglar wearing a hi-viz jacket, pretending to be a building worker on an early call. He even said hello to one of the other neighbours, who didn't suspect a thing. He was on site for 40 minutes, checking things out and helping himself to stuff like nails and hammers — there wasn't much else there — total value about £45 quid.

I sent the tape to the police who were delighted to have such evidence. They put some stills on their Facebook Crimestoppers page and our man was shopped within half an hour (apparently by an old girlfriend).

This open and shut case took about ten months to wind its way to court and of course it turned out he'd been doing this sort of stuff for years and then selling the loot at car boot sales. His house was stuffed with incriminating evidence, including stolen car number plates. He pleaded guilty, got a suspended sentence and had to wear a tag for a year. End of. No fine, not even community service. Neither we nor the neighbour saw a bean in compensation.

In theory, CCTV acts as a fantastic deterrent, especially during the oh-so-vulnerable construction phase. But when you see how the law deals with such cases, you wonder why you bother.

On the other hand, how do you deal with persistent petty thieves like this? I feel this is perhaps another book altogether.

FIRE SAFETY

In June 2017, Grenfell Tower went up in flames, killing 72 people in the process. Part B of the building regulations, which deals with fire, went from being an obscure reference work to front page news overnight.

Everyone wanted to know how it had happened and what exactly went wrong. Were the building regs stuck to or ignored? Or were the regs themselves inadequate? What should we do to stop it happening again?

There is an interminable enquiry underway which may or may not

report back whilst this edition is still in circulation, but the finger of suspicion pointed at certain aspects of the tower refurbishment which had happened a year or two before the fire. In particular, the plastic-based insulation which had been employed to make the tower more energy efficient and therefore more comfortable to live in had caught fire big time and had melted in the extreme heat, causing the fire to spread quickly and giving off toxic fumes in the process.

None of this is particularly relevant to the world of low rise detached housing. The main reason so many died at Grenfell was because of the height of the tower which exacerbated the chimney-updraft effect of the flames and also made it impossible to reach the residents from ladders. What hasty changes that have been made to Part B as yet only concern buildings higher than 18m.

You might think that the Grenfell after effect has caused people to give plastic-based insulation a wide berth, but that's not really happened, as you can't really build a house without using some inflammable materials and there is no particular reason to think that plastic insulation is going to be either the cause of a blaze or will make a fire much worse.

The possible exception to this is in timber-framed housing during the construction phase when there are usually a few weeks when the insulation (conventionally plastic) is placed in situ but not covered over by plasterboard on the inside. During the past ten or fifteen years there have

been a number of timber framed flats which have been arsoned at this stage, but I've never heard of it affecting a selfbuild.

You can switch to mineral wool insulation but, although it won't catch fire, it has its own issues. For a start, it's not as energy efficient so you need more of it, which means wider walls and ceilings, which eats up valuable internal space. Then it has a habit of slumping in situ which means its as built performance rarely matches the designed for standard. And it's also harder to get a tight fit which means there tend to be rather more cold bridges in a mineral wool structure. There are reasons why plastic foam insulation has become so popular.

There are other alternatives, including a range of natural insulations like hempcrete and wood wool. Problem here is that organic materials also tend to be flammable and many of them have binders added to them which make them more flammable. Given a high enough temperature, almost everything burns and the issue becomes somewhat academic.

The plastics themselves vary in their fire performance. The cheapest and worst is expanded polystyrene which we are all pretty familiar with. It starts to melt at 100°C and ignites at around 360°C. Phenolic foam (marketed largely as Kingspan Kooltherm) is the best (ignition point about 550°C) but also the most expensive.

Getting to the bottom of this story is still some way off and in time I have no doubt that Part B will be re-written with much sensible advice about how we should be constructing our buildings. Until then, I wouldn't over worry about your build choices in a low rise house.

WHAT THE REGS REQUIRE

The purpose of the fire safety regulations is, in any event, not to stop buildings burning down but rather to allow the occupants time enough to escape from them if a fire starts.

The main danger in house fires occurs when soft furnishings catch fire, and the smoke quickly engulfs the occupants. Whilst there has been a steady introduction of non-flammable materials into the home furnishing market, the biggest step forward in the world of fire safety came in 1992 when smoke detectors became mandatory. Since then, all new homes have been required to have smoke detectors not just fitted but mains-operated with a battery backup as a fail safe.

Smoke detectors cost around £30 and should be wired in in all new homes. Electricians are all au fait with what's required. The regs are that there should be smoke alarms on each storey and that they shouldn't be further than 3m from any bedroom door, so that some larger designs will require two or more on the upstairs landing.

What the regs don't go into is the different types of smoke detector you can choose. The cheapest and commonest are the ionisation detectors which are very sensitive to small particles of smoke produced by flaming fires, such as chip pans, and will detect this type of fire before the smoke gets too thick. But you can also specify optical ones which are more effective at detecting larger particles of smoke produced by slow-burning fires, such as smouldering foam-filled upholstery and overheated PVC wiring. Optical detectors are more prone to going off in error; either the mirror gets dirty or thunderflies get in.

A third and possibly more useful type is the heat sensor which gets triggered when temps reach around 55°C. These are placed in the kitchen but not too near the cooker. Whatever you choose, they have to be interconnected so that when one is triggered, they all go into action. Some smoke alarms have additional capabilities, such as emergency lights and silence buttons to override false alarms.

Other safety features you might choose to look at are the provision of fire blankets in the kitchen and extinguishers in garages and near open fires. Your best bet is to stick with local firms which offer maintenance.

INNER ROOMS

If your house design is such that you have to pass through another room to get to an external door, then you are deemed to have created an inner room and an inner room is required to have a secondary means of escape. Just what is meant by passing through another room is open to interpretation but generally speaking if your staircase takes you into an open plan kitchen and/or living room, then you can expect to have your upstairs bedrooms deemed to be inner rooms.

This means in effect that you not only have to have an egress window (you do anyway), but that it has to lead to a potential escape route if there was to be a fire down stairs. On two story houses, this escape route can simply be down to the ground below, but on three storey homes it gets more complicated because the fall is too great. Note that inner rooms can appear on the ground floor in some open-plan configurations, so ensure that you always have an egress window in every bedroom.

THREE STOREY HOMES

There is a critical safety level, defined as having a floor 4.5m above ground level, when it becomes necessary to beef up your escape procedures. One of the principal requirements relates to how your main staircase runs through the house. Ideally, the staircase should lead directly to the front entrance door within an enclosed hallway: what is frowned upon are open-plan arrangements, particularly when the staircase exits via the kitchen (reckoned to be the highest risk area).

You also need to consider how to protect the stairwell from encroaching fire. You have to make the entire stairwell what is called a fully protected enclosure; this means that the walls around the landing and stairwell must be rated at 30 minutes fire resistance and the doors opening onto the landing must be rated at 20 minutes. You also need to consider the floor construction which also needs to meet the 30 minute fire rating.

If you are undertaking a new build or a major renovation, it's not difficult to meet these standards; in fact in terms of walls and floors it's quite difficult not to meet them. The only place where you are likely to come unstuck is on the doors that need to be uprated to fire door standard.

SPRINKLERS

In 2014, Wales broke ranks with the rest of the UK by introducing a requirement for sprinklers in all new homes. Thus far, no one else has followed suit. Whilst sprinklers are proven to reduce serious burns and other injuries, and to decrease fire damage generally, their mandatory imposition is not without its critics because — at between £3,000 and £5,000 — they are an expensive way of addressing a very small problem. New housing generally is much safer than old housing and many feel that resources would be better spent elsewhere.

Fire sprinklers are only activated when the temperature in the room in which a fire is burning exceeds the preset temperature of the sprinkler head — nominally 68°C. Sprinklers operate as individual heat sensors, meaning that water is only released in the area where there is a fire. They are not activated by smoke. Sprinklers typically deliver 60lts/minute (compared to 1000lts/min from a fire hose): systems are usually plumbed with copper pipe or rigid cPCV pipe,

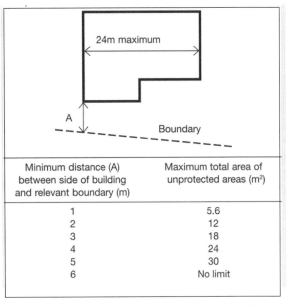

Part B, the Fire Regs, is full of virtually incomprehensible diagrams like this one. Someone, somewhere, has calculated the risk of fire on a boundary wall where the material used is deemed to be unprotected.

24m maximum

A

Boundary

Minimum distance (A) between side of building and relevant boundary (m)	Maximum total area of unprotected areas (m²)
1	5.6
2	12
3	18
4	24
5	30
6	No limit

teed off the rising main. Ideally they require a 32mm cold feed into house as the systems need a good flow. Sprinklers can be a God send in certain situations (it's that open plan, again) when other options for meeting Part B cannot be satisfied. But otherwise, it tends to be a very Welsh problem.

If you decide to install a sprinkler system at home, do ensure that the company you choose is working to the industry standard (BS9251) and is preferably FIRAS accredited. A useful starting point of contact is the Fire Sprinkler Association www.firesprinklers.info.

NEIGHBOURING BUILDINGS

Part B is full of hard to interpret diagrams and there is one to do with using combustible materials like timber on an external wall when it

is close to a boundary and might, therefore, be a pathway for a fire to spread from another building, even if that building has yet to be built. You can use combustible claddings on or near to boundaries, but you are restricted as to how much, depending on the distance involved. It covers most single dwellings, less than 24m in length and not more than three storeys high.

A similar reg also relates to windows on a boundary. There are size limits to boundary windows which are referred to here as Unprotected Areas. This is an area where adding sprinklers to your home helps because this enables you to relax the unprotected area rules. No one said it would be easy.

FIRE ENGINE ACCESS

There are regs too about access tracks for fire engines which can sometimes

Chapter 15

throw a spanner in the works, especially on isolated rural sites. The driveway needs to be at least 3.7m wide, and capable of taking 12.5 tonnes. There must be a passing point every 20m and a turning point on drives over 20m long. The fire engine needs water and you may even have to fit a fire hydrant outside the house to fulfil this demand. Negotiations with the building inspector and the planning authority are likely to tease out these issues at an early stage, but be aware they may cause issues. Once again, specifying sprinklers in the house should relax some of these requirements.

SOUND ADVICE

This section of the Apocrypha looks at the background behind sound reduction measures for builders. Guidance on how to achieve better soundproofing is to be found lodged in two earlier sections on internal walls and internal floors, both back in Chapter 7. But do try to wade through this section before you decide what to do about your walls and floors; I think it will be worth it, if only to learn what the hell a decibel is.

ACOUSTICS FOR BEGINNERS

Sound is a form of energy. It moves in waves through the air and it can be absorbed and transmitted through solids as well. The human ear is adept at picking up sound in a range of frequencies and at different volumes. There are more qualities to sound

than just frequency and volume but we'll concern ourselves with just these two, as it's their interplay that makes much of the debate about soundproofing so intriguing.

Frequencies are measured in hertz (Hz) and kilohertz (kHz): these correspond to the wavelengths that various sounds travel at. Low frequency sound has a very long wavelength; high frequency sound consists, conversely, of energy moving at very short wavelengths. Humans tend to hear sounds between 50 Hz and 15,000 Hz (15 kHz); this upper limit reduces with age.

Sound energy is measured in decibels, routinely written down as dB. The decibel scale is non-linear: it doubles every 3dB. However, what we perceive as sound is a little different: humans perceive a doubling or halving of volume roughly every 10dB. Thus a 60dB noise would sound, subjectively, twice as loud as a 50dB one, which, in turn, sounds roughly twice as loud as a 40dB one.

Whilst the ability to hear sounds is regarded as one of life's more pleasurable experiences, we also worry inordinately about hearing noises we don't want to hear. Noise is defined as unwanted sound. As regards building design, our concerns are usually to minimise sound transfer through walls and floors.

Sound energy transfers through buildings in three different ways. The easiest to understand is airborne sound. This is how sound gets to us when we speak to one another. If there is a wall between us when we speak, then some of the airborne

sound gets absorbed by the wall and the amount of sound absorbed by the wall is said to be so many decibels of sound reduction. Thus, if a wall is said to have an airborne sound reduction level of 40dB, it means that, should a 60dB conversation be taking place on the other side of it, you would only hear about 20dBs on your side.

But sound is capable of travelling through solids as well. In certain instances, walls and, in particular, floors have a nasty habit of not absorbing sound at all but instead acting as a conduit for sounds. Impact sounds, as we call them, are usually mechanical in origin: tapping, hammering, drumming or just walking across floors with hard heels. The actual volume of the sound may not be that high but a floor without adequate impact sound insulation can be very annoying.

The third method of noise transfer is called flanking sound. It occurs when airborne or impact sounds get to you via an indirect route. Consider a wall between two adjacent rooms. Now suppose that you soundproofed this wall so well that no noise was capable of travelling through it. You would still be able to hear noise in the other room because sounds can travel via other routes. Maybe via the corridor shared by the doorways of these two rooms, or via their windows, or transmitted through the ceiling overhead. These are flanking sounds.

Another way of looking at flanking sound is that is represents the difference between the sound reduction performance of an element (i.e. a wall or a floor) tested in a laboratory and the as-built situation. There is a close parallel here with what happens with thermal insulation when the designed-for U value of an element is compromised by cold bridging.

It wasn't until I spent an afternoon witnessing an acoustic test that I really began to understand the difference between the different sorts of sound transfer. Paul Goring, once NHBC's head of acoustics, was testing a floor between two flats in a newly built nurses' hostel and it took him a good couple of hours to do it. On floors, it is routine to test for both airborne sound and impact sound and the procedure for testing them is a little different and worth describing.

To measure airborne sound transmission through a floor, he placed a multidirectional loudspeaker in the upper room and set it to pump out 100db of noise: 'pink noise' it is referred to as, a horrible cocktail of every audible frequency you can think of. At 100db you really don't want to be in that room for a moment longer than you have to be: even with ear defenders on, it's physically unpleasant.

The measuring equipment was in the room below. Airborne sound insulation is measured by taking the difference between the output from the pink noise and the sound in the receiving room. Your decibel rating for the floor in question is the difference between the two measurements. Straightforward enough. The airborne tests consist of five different samples from around the receiving room, each taken from two different locations for the pink noise box in the room above.

Impact noise is measured in a different way. The noise is made by a series of hammers inside a wooden box, resembling a mechanical drum machine, which you sit on the floor above and then let rip. Impact noise is conventionally measured directly: you don't subtract the noise made in one room from the noise received in another: you just make a British Standard sort of impacty-noise from the drum machine and measure how much gets through the floor. Impact noise is only ever considered on floors.

So there is an important distinction here. When you see decibel-rating tables, the airborne decibel ratings are for sound reduction capabilities. Therefore the higher the decibel rating on airborne sound reduction, the better: a 50dB-rated floor is much better than a 45dB-rated one. But for impact sound ratings, the reverse is true. The rating just tells you how much sound got through the floor: the lower the figure here, the better.

Flanking sound isn't measured directly, but it contributes to the overall scores and makes significant differences to the scores between lab tests and field tests. You don't experience flanking sound as something different to airborne sound or impact sound but when there is a lot of noise being made, you can sometimes be aware of it. In my case, I was able to actually feel the walls vibrating when the pink noise machine was on. This was flanking sound in action.

MEASURING UP

The equipment that measures sound – or noise, as it would be referred to in this instance – is expensive and sophisticated. Paul Goring used a Danish system costing around £15,000. It measures sound at 16 different frequencies and gives 16 different readings that have to be interpreted and analysed. This is where things start to get very complicated. Legislators want a yes or no answer to the question, 'Does this floor or wall meet a defined sound reduction standard?' The regs invariably hone in on a pass rate expressed in decibels but the data comes in measured over 16 different frequencies, some of which may look OK and others not.

What has evolved over the years is a number of calculations that offer a 'best fit' answer to the riddle of how much noise is being made at any one time. None of them are perfect and there are big debates about which measuring systems should be used. Normally, this really wouldn't be of concern to anyone outside the cosy world of acoustics but during 2003 this debate took centre stage in the formulation of the latest set of building regulations, because the different ways of sampling decibels give some widely different results.

There are four main methods of measuring sound reduction used in Britain. If proof were needed that acousticians do not come from this planet, these different methods are referred to by a complex sequence of letters and punctuation marks, some italicised, some suffixed. When they

Chapter 15

speak English, these labels roll off their tongues in capitals and don't sound so weird, so I will be anglicising them, if only to help my typesetter.

The simplest rating, written as Rw and referred to by all as 'RW', is derived from laboratory measurements of airborne noise. It's a useful tool for considering the best performance you can get out of a particular construction detail but it doesn't look at the likely performance of a wall or floor in a building: flanking noises are ignored. By way of example, the simplest (and cheapest) timber joist floor with 18mm chipboard over it and 12.5mm of plasterboard nailed under it, will have an RW sound reduction rating of around 35-38dB.

The next sound reduction rating, written as DnT,w (known as 'DNTW') is worked out from the measured airborne sound reduction through a wall or floor element on site, rather than in a lab. Not surprisingly, the DNTW ratings tend to be lower than the Rw ratings, usually by around 5dB. That's the flanking sound effect. DNTW ruled the roost as far as the building regs went until the 2003 changes. But because of various bits of research undertaken in recent years, it was felt simple DNTW didn't adequately reflect the types of noise that are currently being made through our party walls and floors so a variation, giving far more emphasis to low frequency sounds, has been unveiled, known as the Ctr or CTR bias.

Ctr is additional to, not a replacement for, DNTW so that the post 2003 regs require you to provide 45dB of airborne sound reduction (DnT,w + Ctr). It's complicated, but not that complicated, and if you look at it long enough you can begin to see the funny side. The point about DNTW plus Ctr measurements is that it creates a higher standard to meet because low frequencies are harder to block. However, the Ctr effect is not uniform: on some structures, it may make the figure just 2 or 3dB lower; on others it may be as much as 10 or 15dB lower. Our basic timber floor is particularly badly affected by Ctr bias: its sound reduction rating, depending on the low frequency performance, can fall to around 20dB.

There is a fourth measuring scale used solely for impact sound. It's written L'nT,w: gets called LNTW. Impact sound is only measured on floors and, as already discussed, is measured directly rather than being subtracted from a source sound, so the lower the dB rating, the less noise gets through the floor.

In summary, let's take our very basic floor and see how it stacks up on the different scales. It's a timber-joisted floor with just a chipboard cover and plasterboard nailed to it underneath. It scores:

- 38db on the RW airborne scale
- 33db on the DNTW airborne scale, (roughly −5dB difference between lab and field)
- 20dB on the DNTW plus CTR airborne scale (Ctr of, say, -13dB)
- 70dB on the LNTW impact scale

None of these are any good at all! To find out how to improve them, check the Sound sections on Upper Floors and Internal Walls in back in Chapter 7.

MINISTRY OF SOUND

You can, hopefully, see that sound reduction levels expressed in simple decibels don't actually mean very much unless you know which scale they are referring to. The switch to the added Ctr measurements has divided the acoustics community; although everybody agrees that bass sounds are more prevalent, not everyone agrees that this new measurement system is the best way of approaching it.

When the building regs were revamped in 2003, the actual sound reduction levels demanded by the regulations appeared to get less but this was because of the new method of measuring them. However, the changes are not uniform and there are some constructions that would have failed the old regs that now pass the new ones, so the improvement in standards is neither consistent nor universal.

However, it was another aspect of the changes in regulations which took centre stage in 2003. That was the insistence that not only should party walls and floors be built to the new standards but that they should be tested on site to show that they had in fact achieved these standards.

But when the powers-that-be first ran their suggestions past the housebuilders, pandemonium broke out. Not only was acoustic testing reckoned to cost around £600 per test, but also rectifying failures in already completed schemes would be a nightmare. Years of acoustic testing had shown that there is often a large gap between the designed-for sound reduction and that actually achieved. The acousticians felt strongly that it wasn't enough simply to tighten the old standards: to improve matters significantly, you had to test, which, coincidentally, was jolly good news for acousticians.

Well a fudge was worked out. After much badgering and a very rushed research programme, the government accepted a Super Level sound proofing standard, to be known henceforth as the Robust Standard Details or RSDs. This sets an airborne soundproofing target a full 5dB better than that required just to meet the regs for new party walls and floors but – crucially – doesn't call for any testing.

So what emerged when the regs were set in stone were four different levels of soundproofing:

■ Level 1: 40dB (Rw scale) airborne sound reduction. Applies to internal walls and floors within individual homes. No testing required.

■ Level 2: 43dB (DNTw + Ctr scale) airborne sound reduction plus (floors only) 64dB (LNTw scale) maximum impact noise. Applies to party walls and floors between flats and attached houses when they have undergone renovation. Requires testing.

■ Level 3: 45dB (DNTw + CTR scale) airborne sound reduction plus (floors only) 62dB (LNTw scale) maximum impact noise. Applies to party walls and floors between flats and attached houses if they are newbuild. Requires testing.

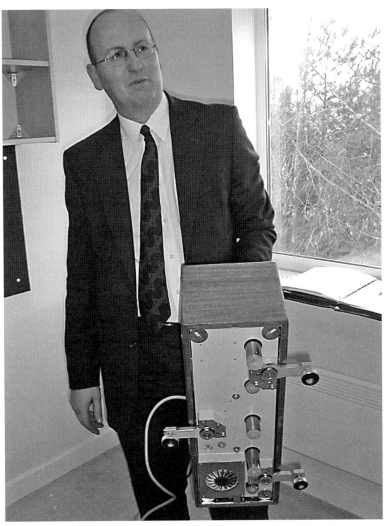

Acoustician Paul Goring pictured here with an impact sound testing device

■ Level 4: 50dB (DNTw + CTR scale) airborne sound reduction plus (floors only) 57dB (LNTw scale) maximum impact noise. A series of approved robust standard details (known as RSDs) that can be used by new builders (only) who wish to avoid the expense of testing.

Now currently these details are available to download for free — search on Robust Standard Details>Patterns. Take a brief look and you can see that the measures required are very thorough and rather complicated.

What is worth pointing out is

Chapter 15

that there is a big jump between Level 1 (detached homes) and Level 2 (everything with a party wall or floor). It may look like a mere 5dB difference but notice that the scales are different and 40dB on the Rw scale is probably only about 30dB on the more exacting DNTw + CTR scale. So there is lots of room to improve the very basic standard found in Part E2 of the regs, which applies to individual homes.

Incidentally, if you are worried about sound proofing internally, you should probably raise the issue with your designer at an early stage. Having just completed a timber frame/SIPS hybrid house, which meets the standard sound proofing routine (i.e. Level1), I don't have a problem with sound transfer. But then we are old and it's a quiet home with no teenagers.

BARN CONVERSIONS

The world of converting redundant buildings is a little different to new housebuilding. You have to be prepared to have rules imposed on you which you might think are unreasonable and unfair.

The very fact that we are allowed to convert redundant buildings rather than just pulling them down demonstrates that we are engaging with the British obsession of preserving the past, and the planners have a number of ways of making sure that certain rules are adhered to in exchange for the right to create a

home in a place you otherwise would not be able to.

Chief amongst these is the idea that what you build should continue to look like what was there before. And not in any way look like a conventional house. This goes for conversions of nearly all redundant buildings with some degree of historic interest; chapels, schools and pubs to name but three. But the bulk of single home conversions are going on in rural barns as these are by far the commonest rural structure up for conversion.

THE RULES

▪ reuse existing doorways, even if they were designed for carts
▪ don't block up existing openings
▪ no masonry chimneys – stainless steel flues acceptable only if kept away from the ridge
▪ as few new windows as possible – and any new windows should be as plain as possible
▪ no changes to the roof. Certainly no dormers and preferably no rooflights. If rooflights, preferably on the side no one sees
▪ repair the original material wherever possible.
▪ if it simply has to be replaced, use something similar. If it's timber, it must be timber that matches the old style.

What a lot of barn designers end up doing is building in a large glazed screen area where once stood the main barn door. This is often inset into the structure – this borrows a little extra light for the rooms opening off the hallway behind the glazed screen. No matter that what you end up with

doesn't look a bit like a farm building, but it does make a very attractive structure. In fact the barn conversion, particularly the timber barn conversion, has attained iconic status as a fashion item in its own right. Whilst the history of the original barns has been documented by the likes of RW Brunskill, the history of barn conversions has yet to be written.

Barns tend to come in two distinct flavours, timber and stone. Timber predominates in the south and east where they tended to be built for threshing and storing corn. Stone barns are more common in the north and the west – the Scots refer to them as steadings – where they were most often used as cattle sheds. As cattle don't like going up stairs, the stone barns tend to be single storey, the timber ones are routinely two storey or, more accurately, high enough to accommodate a second storey. There are of course masses of exceptions to this rule of thumb and there are also masses of sheds and barns built of other interesting materials like cob and clay lump.

After a penal brick tax was removed in 1857, a lot of brick barns were built which are also now ripe for conversion. I have even seen steel framed agricultural buildings (you can hardly call them barns) dating from the 1950s getting the modern barn conversion treatment, complete with stained weatherboard exterior.

PLANNING CHANGES

In 2014, the government made a change to the planning legislation designed to make barn conversion (in England only) a whole lot easier. Before then, there had been numerous hoops to have to jump through to win permission to convert agricultural buildings to residential use. For instance, you had to carry out an economic assessment that proved there was no longer any commercial use for the building.

The 2014 changes have put a very different complexion on things and more or less given the right for farmers to convert redundant buildings without even applying for planning permission under an extension of the Permitted Development scheme normally used for household extensions. Buildings up to 450m² in size can be converted into a maximum of three dwellings per holding. That at least was the headline.

But of course it wouldn't be planning if it didn't have a few exceptions and it turns out there are so many exceptions that it's not altogether clear that it has made that much difference. For instance, national parks and areas of outstanding natural beauty will not enjoy the new permitted development rights. Nor will barns which form part of a listed farmhouse complex. And stable blocks won't be included. And councils are still able to block development if they feel that the highway impacts are detrimental, or they don't like the look of it, or they simply don't like it. So despite officially no longer requiring planning permission, it seems that councils are still able to turn down a barn conversion if they so wish.

The planners "Barn from Hell." Almost everything that could upset a conservation officer is included in this design.

TIMBER BARNS

One of the advantages of the old system was that it invariably required a detailed survey before an application could proceed. It's still a great idea although and the earlier it is done the better, preferably before any sale is made.

Start with the foundations. Rarely will any of these buildings have what we now consider to be foundations in any shape or form. Stone or brick plinth walls just tended to spread a little below ground; there were never any attempts to dig down a metre or so on to good bearing ground. However these barns have stood the test of time so the principle to be observed is that, if you don't change any of the loadings, there really

shouldn't be any need to alter what exists. Given that the alternative is underpinning and that underpinning is very expensive then it's well worth avoiding new foundations if possible. So if you wish to build in an upper storey, you have to find a way of keeping the added load of this new floor off the existing walls.

The solution lies in building a platform inside the barn; this can be achieved with stud walls underneath or, more commonly, using a series of beefy posts which themselves get bedded on concrete pads.

Then consider the ground floor. The condition of these varies from compacted earth through to level concrete in good condition. Concrete sounds like an advantage but bear in mind that in order to meet the latest U value requirement for floors you will almost certainly have to put insulation on top of it and consequently you may be losing significant height; sometimes it is better to dig out an existing floor and put in a new one.

There are two additional points to consider here. You don't want to go down so deep that you expose the base of the walls otherwise you will suddenly find yourself in an underpinning situation – a couple of exploratory test digs should reveal how far down your walls go under the ground.

On the other hand, if you are planning on building an upper deck, you may find that you have to negotiate a tie beam, tying the roof trusses together. Ideally you want your finished ground floor level to be at least 4.5m below any tie beams otherwise you will have to go on hands and knees to get under the tie beams when you want to go to the bathroom.

Incidentally, there is no minimum height for rooms or doorways encoded in our building regs, but realistically you need 2.1m clearance on doors to make them comfortable to pass through. If you haven't got a reasonable clearance there may be ways around the problem by gaining access to the different bays from half landings or maybe installing a second staircase.

It is perfectly acceptable to jack a timber structure up when carrying out restoration work. Expected even. The procedure is to strip away everything that you don't intend to keep. Often this means reducing the barn to nothing more than a timber skeleton. You then build an internal scaffold cage and then place pins under the header plates at the top of the walls which take the weight of the roof. The whole structure then gets lifted gently off the supporting walls at the bottom and this then allows you to get to work restoring these walls and go about replacing the sole plates at the base of the

Converting timber barns is far from straightforward. Here is a before and halfway-through shot of a very dilapidated Cambridgeshire barn getting a makeover

timber structure which are usually the timbers which have the worst signs of rot.

If all the bottom joints between the sole plate and the wall studs have rotted, it is standard practice to cut the wall studs shorter and fix a new sole plate in a slightly higher position than the old one.

You will then have to add a couple of courses of brick or stone onto the plinth wall underneath to make up the difference. At this point you would be expected to let the structure down again to sit on the repaired plinth.

From here on in, the timber barn conversion becomes a new build. The walls will normally get covered in plywood or something similar and you need to add insulation to the structure – in this respect a converted barn must perform to the same standards as a new house. In timber barns, most people want to see as much as possible of the original timbers and therefore the tendency is to find insulation systems that wrap around the exterior.

STONE BARNS

Stone barns pose rather different problems. There will certainly be no jacking up of the structure, rather there may have to be a painstaking repair of what is there. And the requirement for good insulation levels means that one face, usually the inside, will have to be covered over. You may need to underpin, especially where new openings are formed and the wall loadings are altered – it very much depends on the ground conditions beneath.

An additional problem is to make the structure watertight, something which it was probably never designed to be in the first place. A typical stone barn consists of two skins of sorted stone separated by a rubble filled cavity. The existing walls will often be as much as 450mm thick so, on most barns, it's quite impractical to build another skin on the inside. So you have to work with what is there. It's difficult to install an effective damp proof course and it can be difficult to stop rain penetration through the walls as well, so often the emphasis is on creating structures which can breathe (i.e. where building moisture can evaporate).

The planners are unlikely to accept a waterproof render being applied to the outside face, the best you can realistically hope to do is to point up the gaps between the stones. And accept, perhaps, that you are not living in a new build and that you may have to put up with the odd damp patch from time to time.

COST

Barn conversions cost rather more than new housing on a square metre basis. On a like-for-like basis, the unit area rate works out at between 30% and 50% more than new builds. An upper deck will be slightly cheaper to construct on a square metre basis making two floor barns cheaper than single storey ones. But the saving is not that great.

Stone barns will tend to be a little more expensive because stone is always time consuming and therefore expensive to work with. Modern (brick) barns will be cheaper because the structure is usually in better condition. The more exceptional the barn, the more it is likely to cost to convert.

Most barns are not listed unless they happen to be in the grounds (or the curtilage, in planning speak) of a listed farm in which case there may well be extra features to consider (such as thatch). Generally speaking, most barn conversions are undertaken by selfbuilders. Spec builders tend to shy away from them because they don't like the unpredictability – although one or two plucky ones will go as far as importing barns from France in order to get the right feel in a property.

SNAGGING

One of the many things that bedevils building work is quality. If you buy a new car or a computer, you can usually sort out any quality issues at time of purchase or shortly afterwards, under guarantee. But with building work, it's not quite so easy because for starters it's often quite hard to tell when a building job has finished and even then there are often tell-tale snags which crop up at any point. Doors which fitted fine initially start binding (sticking), stairs develop a squeak, gaps open up, and things that looked good at first turn out to be not so good when you live with them for a while.

With the best will in the world, a good builder is still going to leave behind them a long list of items to be rectified, which is why building contracts have developed over the years to include a retention clause, withholding some money for six months after completion. This call-back work is all part and parcel of building work and is sometimes referred to as third fixing. More often, it just gets called snagging.

DEFECTS

The bulk of snags tend to be little jobs that have just been overlooked and are fairly easily remedied. The usual way of dealing with this is to make a snags list and to work through it item by item. Snags list have an annoying habit of growing, as you spot more and more items yet to be completed. But eventually the snags list is finished and you reach a stage where things start to go wrong and it becomes a repairs list.

But sometimes there are issues which are not readily resolved. There are sometimes more profound defects which will require time and money to fix and then it can become difficult because you have to decide who is going to pay for it. This of course all depends on the contract you have been working with. If you have hired a builder to do everything at a fixed price, then the buck stops with the builder. If you've been acting as a project manager, things are murky because it may not be clear who is to blame for the issue, or if it was a subcontractor on a day rate, they may well, all of a sudden, be rather hard to contact.

And there is the thorny problem that something that might annoy the

fuck out of you, simply makes other people question your sanity.

Defects, supposed or otherwise, are a particular problem for professional homebuilders because they are in the business of selling 'the perfect home' and common sense tells us that they are not really in the position to deliver snag-free houses. The best builders manage the buyer's expectations and ensure that any follow-on snags are dealt with promptly but nevertheless the whole subject causes loads of grief for both new home buyers and their builders. A lot of this flack gets directed at the warranty providers, such as the NHBC, and even though their warranties specifically exclude minor snagging, it still takes a lot of their time and also causes a lot of bad publicity.

CONSISTENT APPROACHES

In an attempt to manage this process more systematically, the NHBC produce a document called a Consistent Approach to Finishes which sets about trying to define acceptable standards for new housebuilding. It's become so important to them that it is now incorporated into their general building standards and has a chapter all to itself. As of 2019, the guidance has grown 24 pages in length. The NHBC, despite being viewed by many as an exclusive builder's club, makes its technical standards free to view and you can find them by searching on NHBC standards and then looking up Chapter 9.

If you are project managing, you can also use this guide to look at the

work of your subcontractors.

There is enough information here for you to act as your own building surveyor, but you are most unlikely to access it unless you have reason to doubt what is going on on your project. But use it with care. As the NHBC's guide states: 'This guide is not intended to deal with every situation that may arise and discretion should be exercised in its application in specific circumstances'.

What they are getting at here is that their Consistent Approach to Finishes is not so much a checklist but a tentative rule book on what is or isn't acceptable in terms of finish standards.

GLAZING DEFECTS

Take the thorny issue of damaged glazing. Current practice is to install glazed joinery early on in the build program in order to make the site wind and watertight, not to mention secure. The downside of this is that it increases the risk of the glass being damaged whilst the scaffolding is still up and there is building work going on all around. But just what constitutes damage? And who is to say whether blemishes are acceptable or not.

The 2019 NHBC standards suggest the following.

■ Glass should be free of unwanted defects. So far so good, no one would argue with that. But how do you define defect?

■ next the ground rules for the checking procedure. Glass should be checked in daylight, from within the room and from a minimum distance of 2m (3m for toughened, laminated or coated glass). From these distances, you should not be able to see:

- bubbles or blisters
- hairlines or blobs
- fine scratches not more than 25mm long
- minute particles
- and that all of the above should not be within 6mm of the edge of the pane.

Don't get me wrong. It's a laudable idea to introduce some objective criteria by which to judge whether defects are real or imagined, but this guidance is about as clear as the offside rule in football. And why the dispensation if the defect is within 6mm of the edge?

Furthermore, I have seen damaged sealed units — triple glazed ones, no less — where the defect was a strange discolouration that made the units look stripey. Clearly visible in daylight, but not covered by the NHBC defects list. How do you account for defects that are real enough but not on the defects list? Hopefully with diplomacy and tact.

WHAT'S IN A TON?

Conventionally when the word is written Ton it refers to an imperial ton. When it's written Tonne, it's a metric ton(ne). The old imperial ton was 20 cwt (hundredweight): the metric tonne is 1,000 kilogrammes. The imperial ton is all of 1.6% heavier than the metric tonne and therefore, to all intents and purposes you can ignore the difference.

Not so the differences between cubic metres and tonnes. Now quarries or merchants can sell by using either method. In fact many suppliers use both – volume up to 10m³ and tonnes above that level. The conversion on sand is 1m³ equals 1.6 tonnes but be warned that sand is much heavier when wet and so you'll be getting up to 20% less if you are buying by weight in wet weather. However, at £6-£10/ for 10 tonne loads, it's cheap enough to not worry unduly over. Other important volume to weight conversions are noted in the Material Densities section of the adjacent table.

Note the critical one is water, which is used to define the relationships between metres, litres and tonnes. Materials with a density greater than 1 are heavier than water and will sink, whilst materials with a density less than 1 will float. Try dropping a Celcon aerated block in a bath full of water: it will amaze the kids, if nothing else.

Crucial Measurements

Weight

1lb =	0.454kg	
1kg =	2.2lbs	
1 imperial ton =	1016kg =	1.016 tonnes

Length

1 millimetre (mm) =	0.039 inches	
1 metre (m) =	39.4 inches =	1.094 yards
1 inch =	25.5mm	
1 foot =	305mm	
1 yard =	914mm =	0.914m

Area

1 sq. metre (m²) =	10.76 sq.ft (ft²)	
1 ft² =	0.93m²	
1 hectare =	10,000m² =	2.47 acres
1 acre =	4047m² =	0.4 hectare
Area of triangle =	half base x height	

Volume

1 UK gallon =	4.5 litres	
1 cubic metre (m³) =	1000 litres =	220 gallons
1 m³ of water =	1 tonne	

Heat

1 kiloWatt (kW) =	3410 British Thermal Units
1 kilowatt hour (kWh) =	1 kW burned for one hour
1 joule =	1 watt burned for a second
1 gigajoule (GJ) =	278kWh
Specific Heat of Air =	0.33watts/m³/1°C

Material Densities

1m³ water @ 4°C =	1 tonne (by definition!)
1m³ of dry sand =	1.6 tonnes (+20% wet)
1m³ of aggregate =	1.8 tonnes
1m³ of cement =	1.4 tonnes
1m³ hydrated lime =	0.6 tonnes
1m³ concrete =	2 tonnes
1m³ clinker blocks =	1.6 tonnes
1m³ bricks =	1.2 to 1.6 tonnes
1m³ aerated blocks =	0.6 tonnes
1m³ softwood =	0.45 tonnes
1m³ hardwood =	0.65 tonnes

For more conversions, check out www.simetric.co.uk

INDEX

A

Accelerator Mortgage 61, 63
Accessibility 322
Actis 135, 270
Aga 176, 248
Aggregates 285
  297
Air Source Heat Pumps 189
Air tightness 141, 307
Appliances 181, 91, 199, 245
Approved Documents 51
Architects 53, 70
  certificates 88
Architectural technologists 54
Architrave 226
Asbestos 96, 298
Attic trusses 152
Auctions 29

B

Barn conversions 334
Basements 275
bathroom 206
Bathroom lighting 209
Bathrooms 217, 232, 251
Bay windows 132
Beam and Block 101
Beams 101
Bedrooms 254
Bi-fold doors 144
Bill of Quantities 278
Biomass 171
Biomass boilers 190
Blockwork 117
Boilers 173
Boiling water taps 244
Book-keeping 88
Boreholes 186, 316

Boundary disputes 31
Brick 126, 199
  Boundary walls 238
  buying 285
Brick factors 128
Bricklaying rates 128
Brick slips 131
Brinkley's Slope Law 104
British Thermal Units 167
Broadband 211
  connections 108
builders
  working with 5
  work with 5
Builders
  profit margin 66
  selecting 72
Builder's merchants 282
building contracts 5
Building Contracts 76
Building control
  fees 51
Building costs
  model house 16
Building Costs 320
Building plots 27
Building regulations
  Joinery 136
Building Regulations 50, 87
  disabled access 264
  energy efficiency 265, 299
  inspections 263
  lighting 208
Building Research Establishment
  98
Building surveyors 54
Burglar alarms 325

C

CAD packages 55
Capital Gains Tax 93
Caravans 65
Carbon emissions 306
Carpentry
  second fix 226
Carpet 223
Cashflow 65
Cavity
  insulation methods 119
CCTV 326
CDM regs 84
Cedar 130
  shingles 131
Ceilings 153
Cellulose fibre 134
Cement 299
Chimneys 199
Chipboard 149
Circulation space 61
Clapboarding 130
Clayboard 106
Clay Plasters 217
Climate Change 294
Code for Sustainable Homes 318
Combined Heat & Power 311
Community Infrastructure Levy
  12
Competitive tendering 70
Computer Aided design 55
Concrete 287
Condensation 157
Conservation officers 47
Conservatories 272
Consumer unit 110
Consumer Units 204
Contaminated Land 35
Cookers
  hoods 247
Corten steel 131
Covenants 31